CW00688799

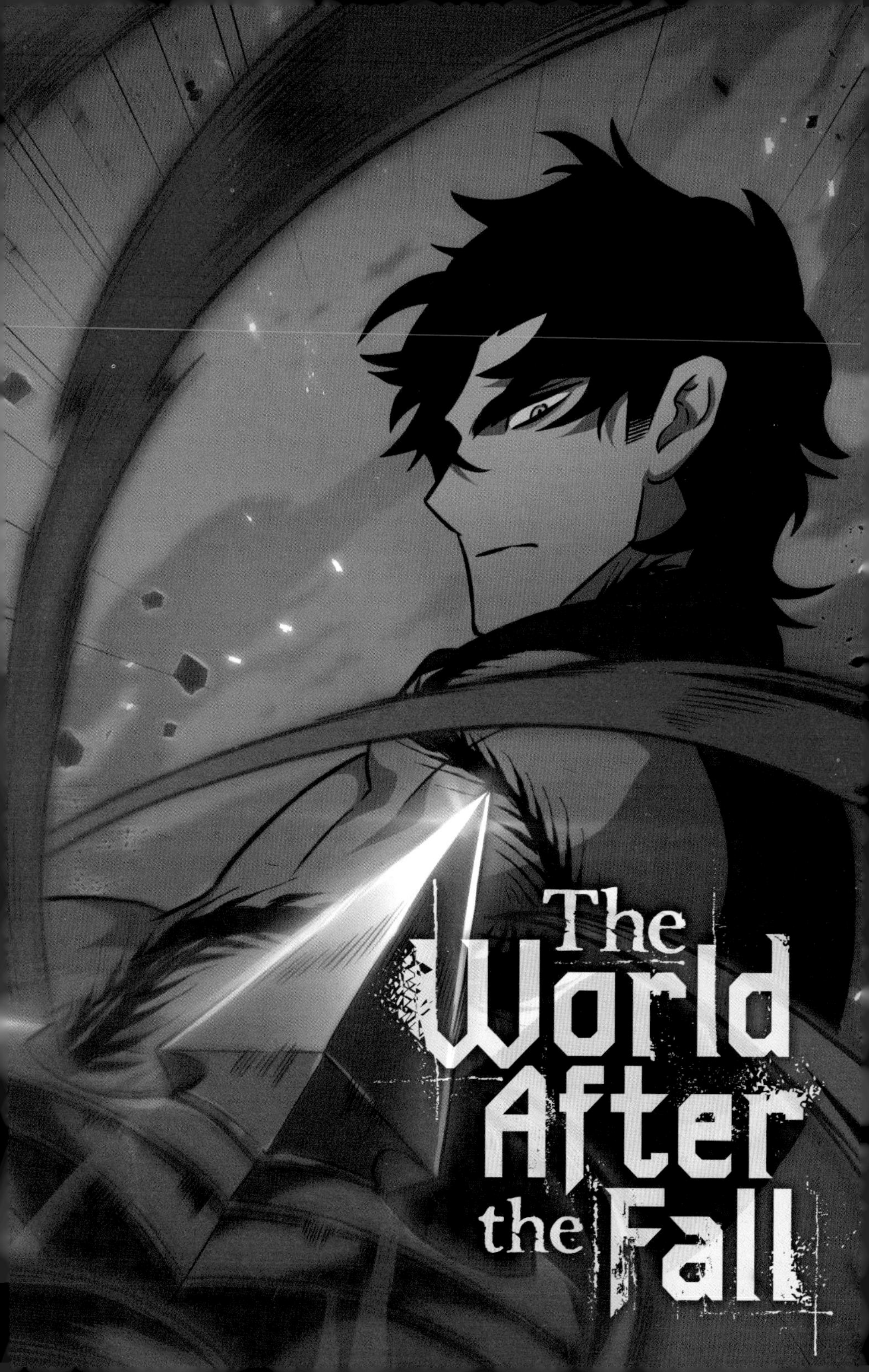
The World After the Fall

The World After the Fall

TABLE OF CONTENTS

The World After the Fall

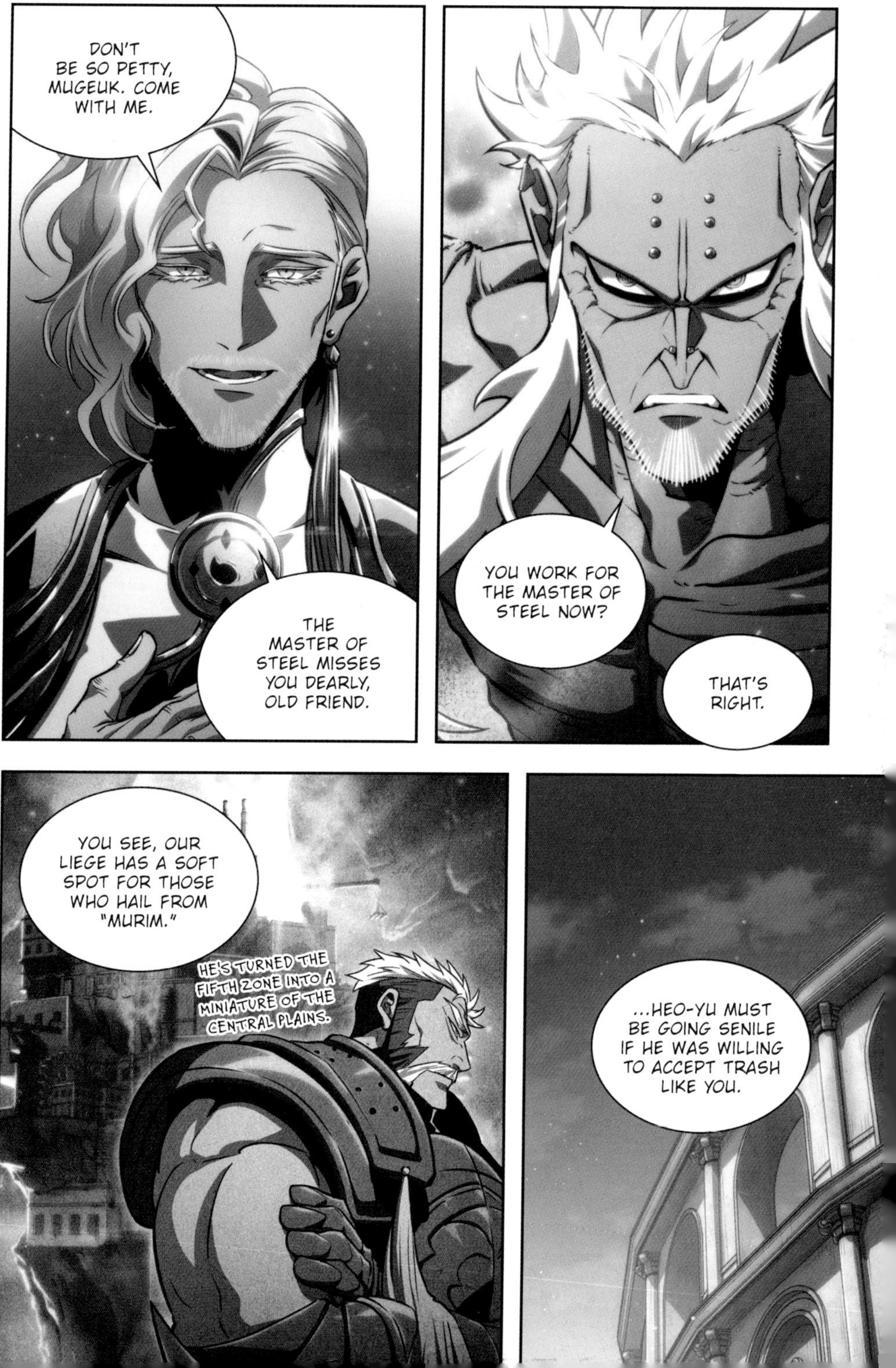
DON'T BE SO PETTY, MUGEUK. COME WITH ME.
THE MASTER OF STEEL MISSES YOU DEARLY, OLD FRIEND.
YOU WORK FOR THE MASTER OF STEEL NOW?
THAT'S RIGHT.
YOU SEE, OUR LIEGE HAS A SOFT SPOT FOR THOSE WHO HAIL FROM "MURIM."
HE'S TURNED THE FIFTH ZONE INTO A MINIATURE OF THE CENTRAL PLAINS.
...HEO-YU MUST BE GOING SENILE IF HE WAS WILLING TO ACCEPT TRASH LIKE YOU.

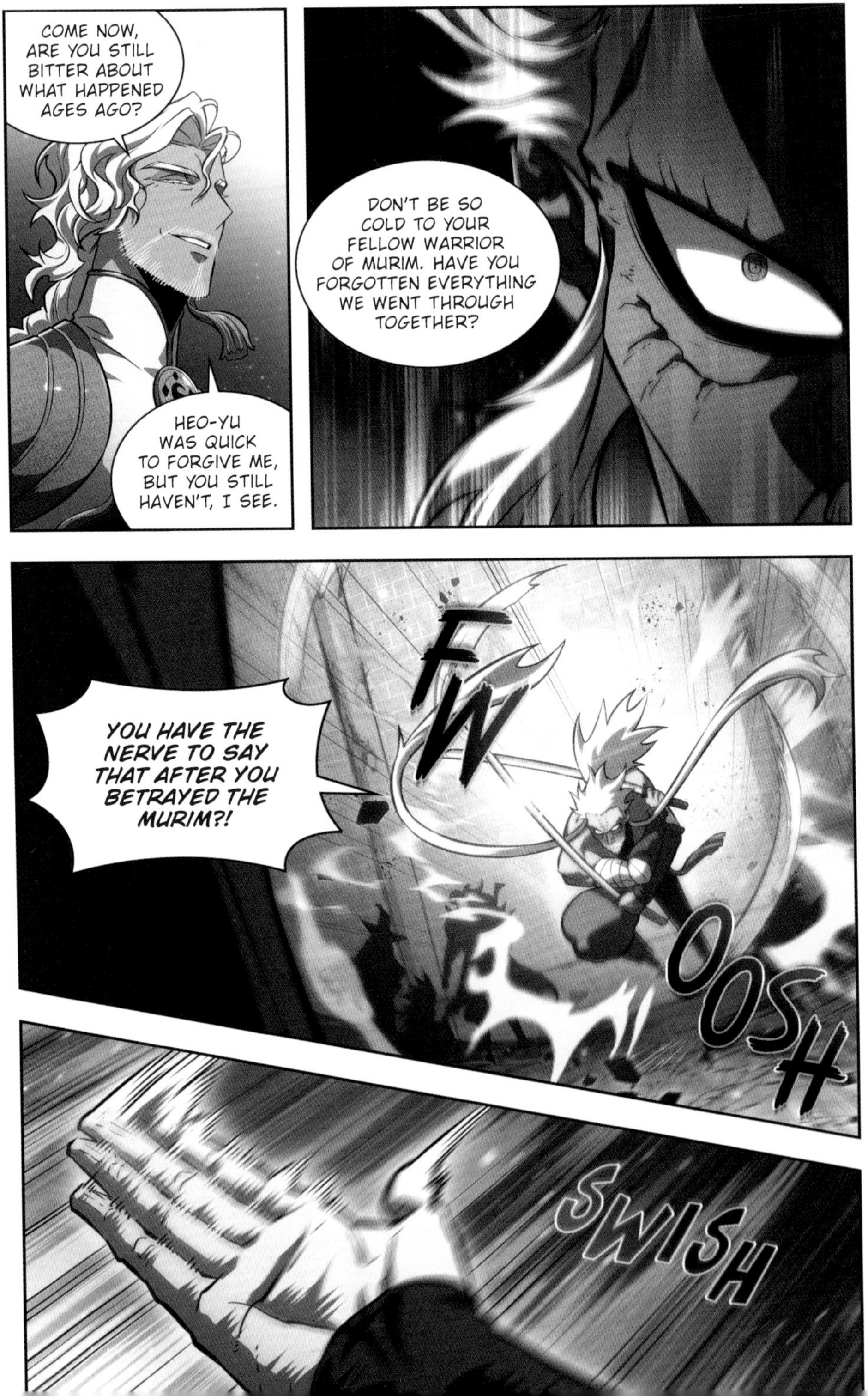
COME NOW, ARE YOU STILL BITTER ABOUT WHAT HAPPENED AGES AGO?
HEO-YU WAS QUICK TO FORGIVE ME, BUT YOU STILL HAVEN'T, I SEE.
DON'T BE SO COLD TO YOUR FELLOW WARRIOR OF MURIM. HAVE YOU FORGOTTEN EVERYTHING WE WENT THROUGH TOGETHER?
YOU HAVE THE NERVE TO SAY THAT AFTER YOU BETRAYED THE MURIM?!
FWOOSH
SWISH

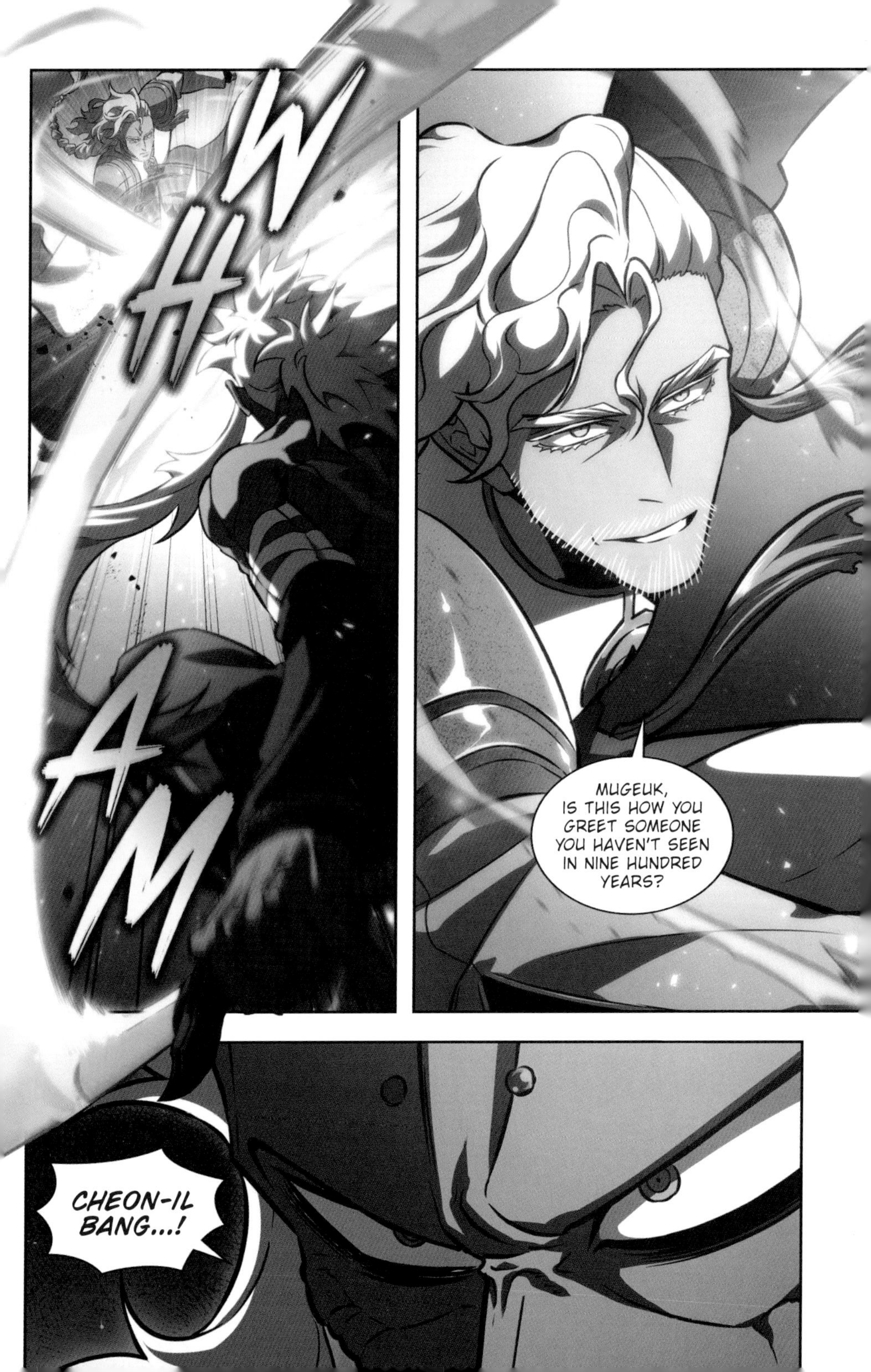
WHAM
MUGEUK, IS THIS HOW YOU GREET SOMEONE YOU HAVEN'T SEEN IN NINE HUNDRED YEARS?
CHEON-IL BANG...!

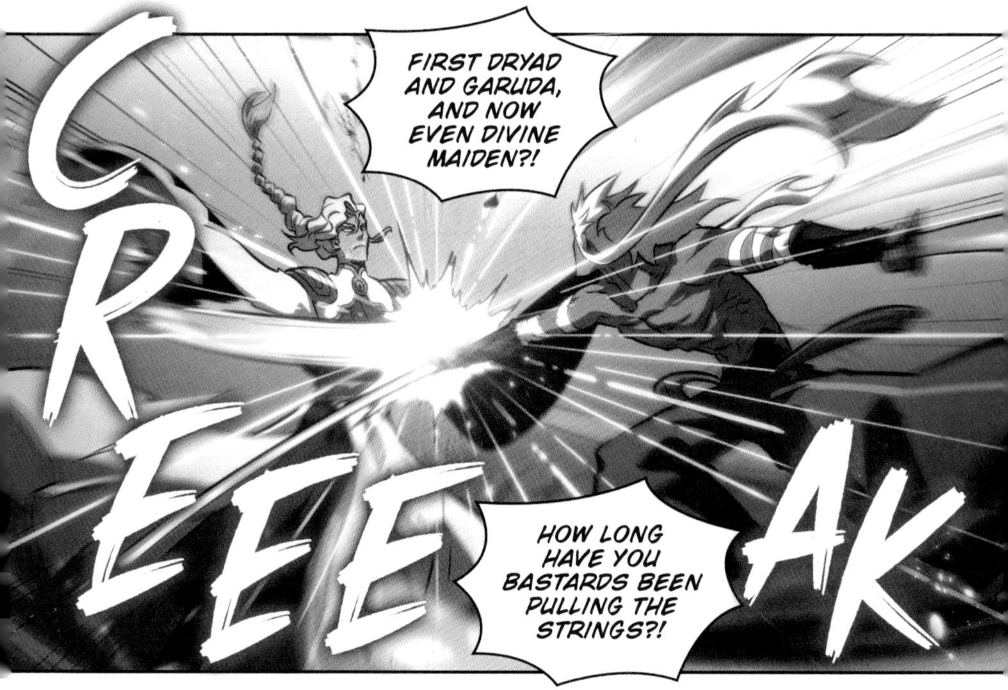
CREEEEAK
FIRST DRYAD AND GARUDA, AND NOW EVEN DIVINE MAIDEN?!
HOW LONG HAVE YOU BASTARDS BEEN PULLING THE STRINGS?!

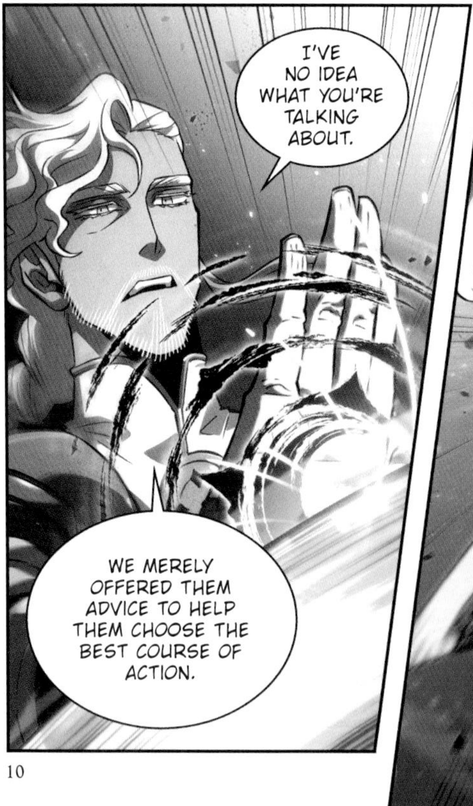
I'VE NO IDEA WHAT YOU'RE TALKING ABOUT.
WE MERELY OFFERED THEM ADVICE TO HELP THEM CHOOSE THE BEST COURSE OF ACTION.

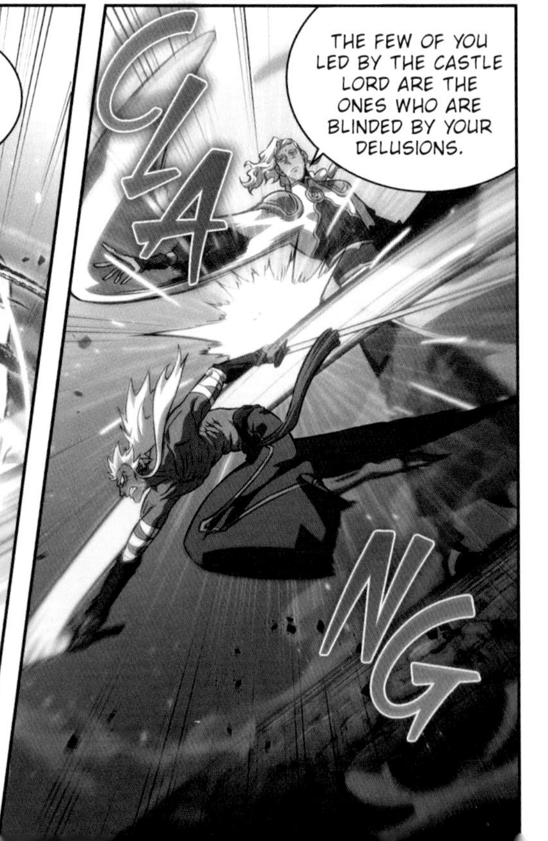
THE FEW OF YOU LED BY THE CASTLE LORD ARE THE ONES WHO ARE BLINDED BY YOUR DELUSIONS.
CLANG

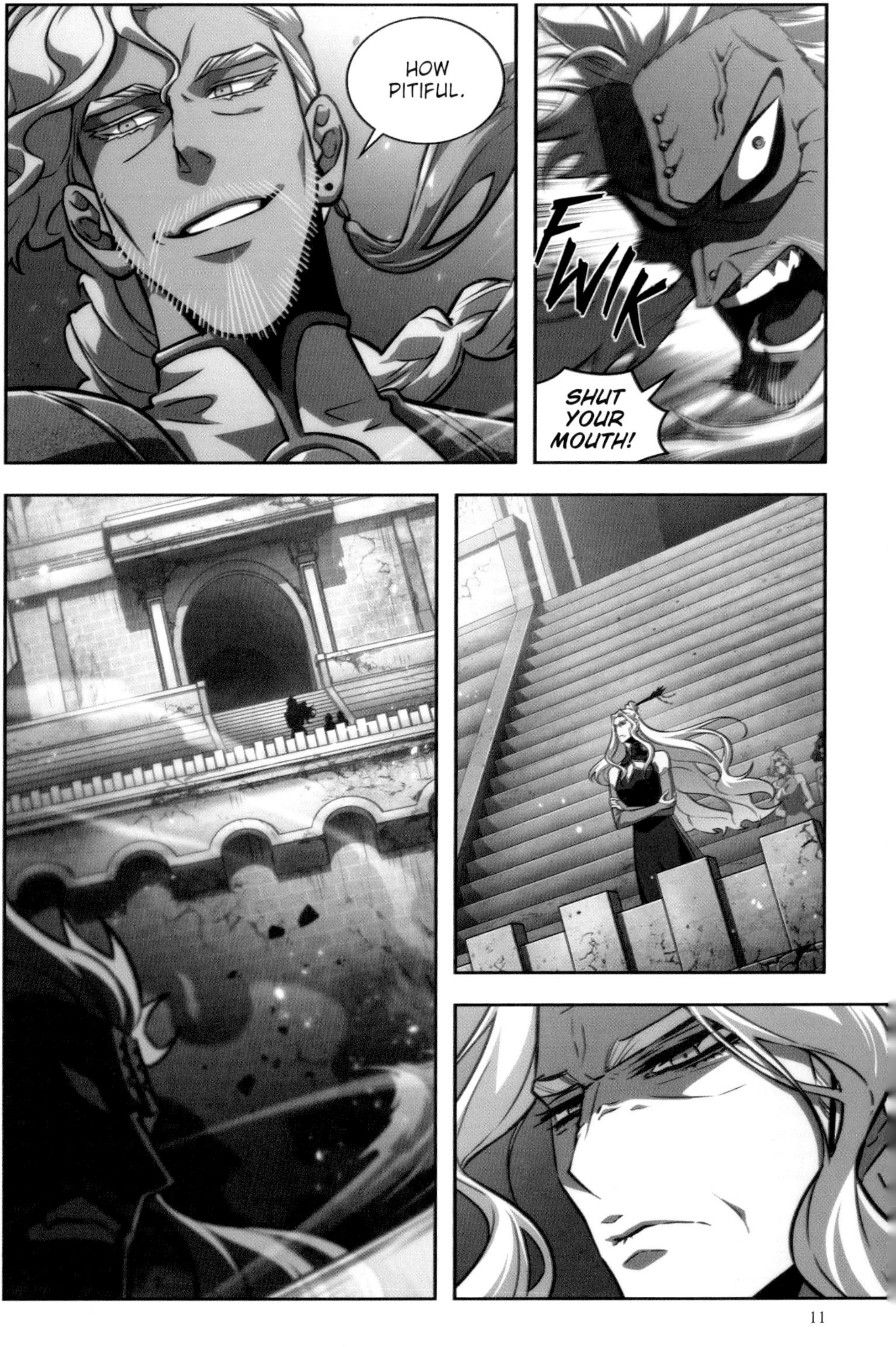
HOW PITIFUL.
FWIK
SHUT YOUR MOUTH!

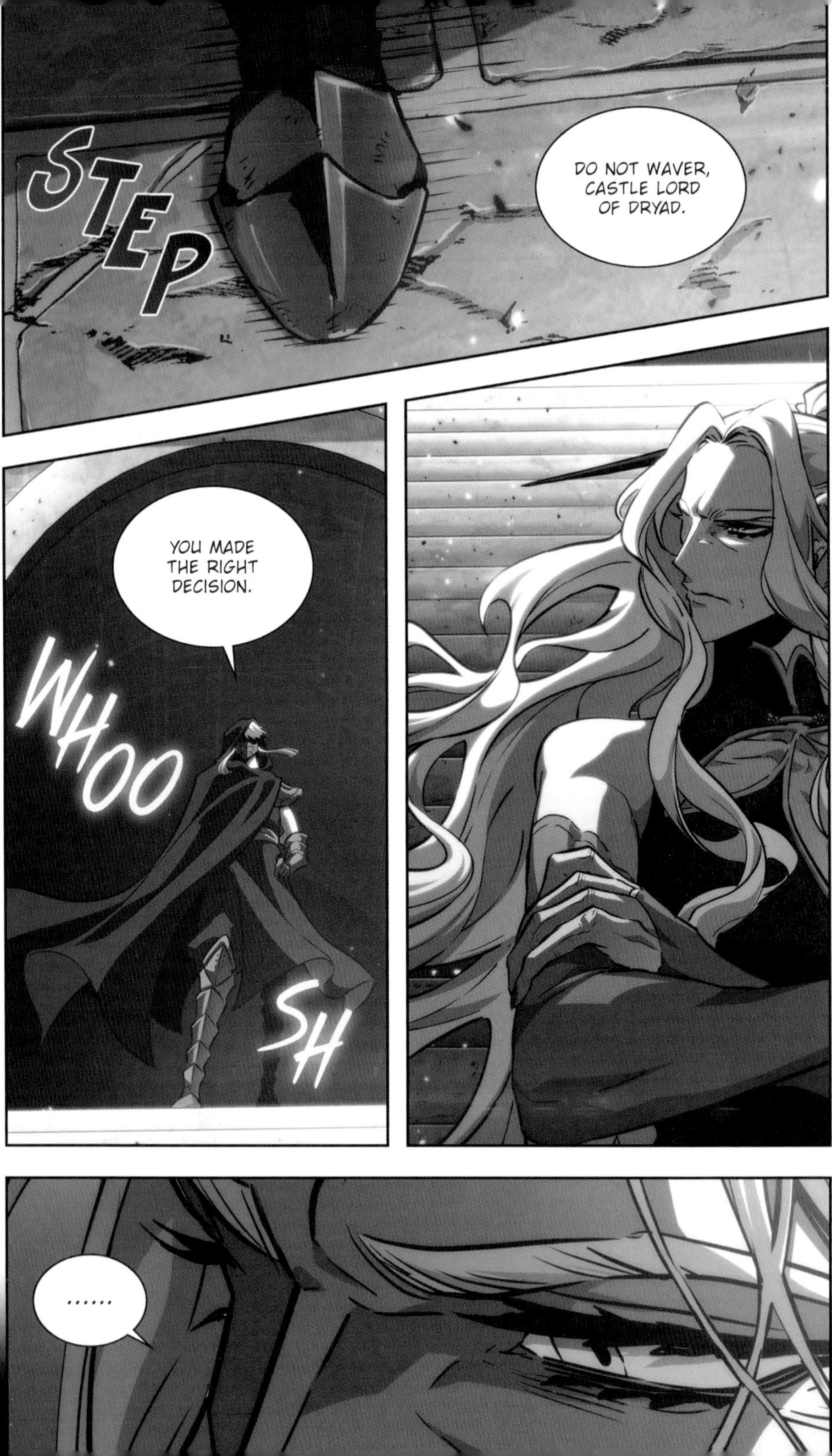
STEP
DO NOT WAVER, CASTLE LORD OF DRYAD.
YOU MADE THE RIGHT DECISION.
WHOOSH
......

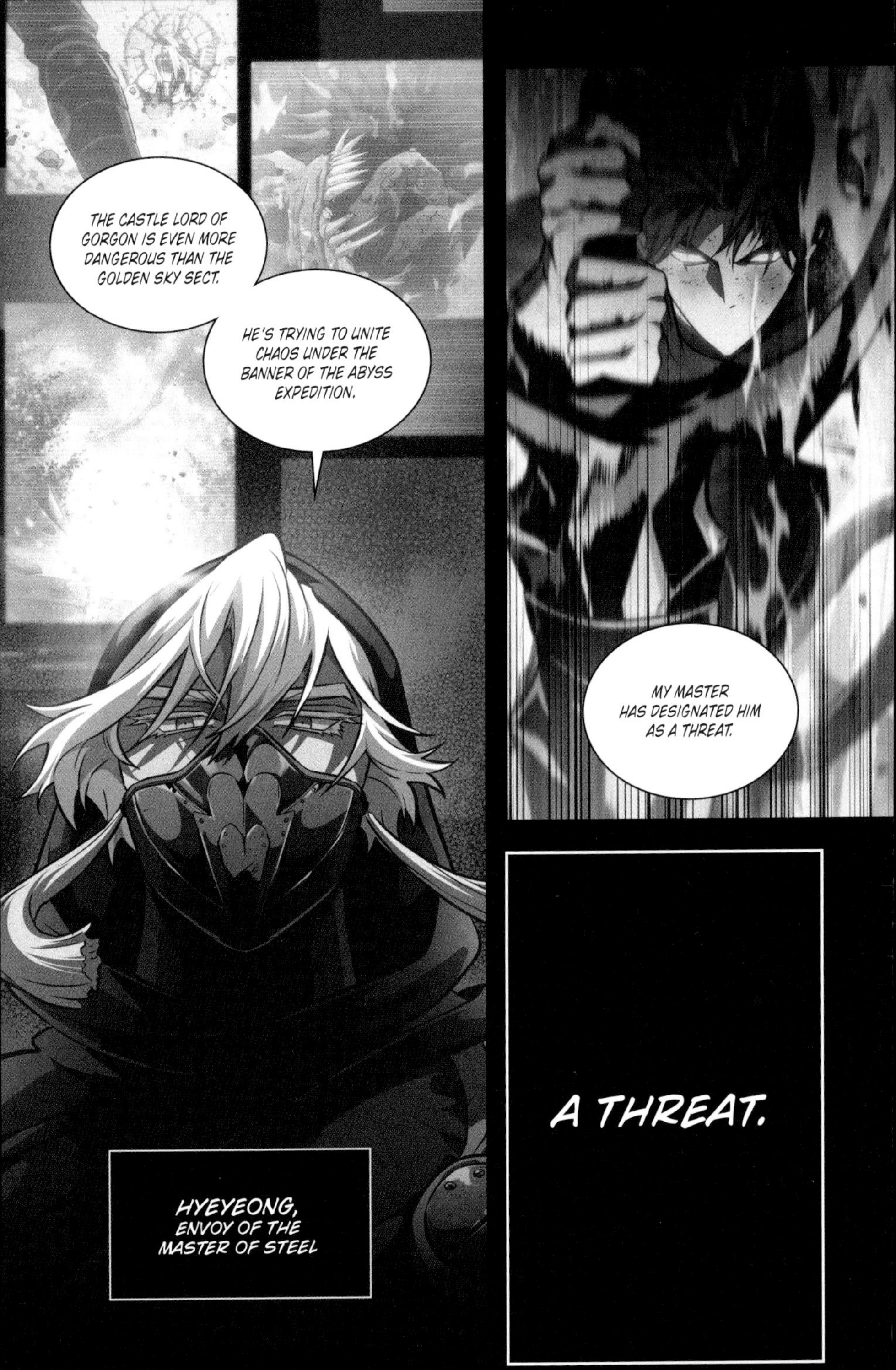
THE CASTLE LORD OF GORGON IS EVEN MORE DANGEROUS THAN THE GOLDEN SKY SECT.
HE'S TRYING TO UNITE CHAOS UNDER THE BANNER OF THE ABYSS EXPEDITION.
HYEYEONG, ENVOY OF THE MASTER OF STEEL
MY MASTER HAS DESIGNATED HIM AS A THREAT.
A THREAT.

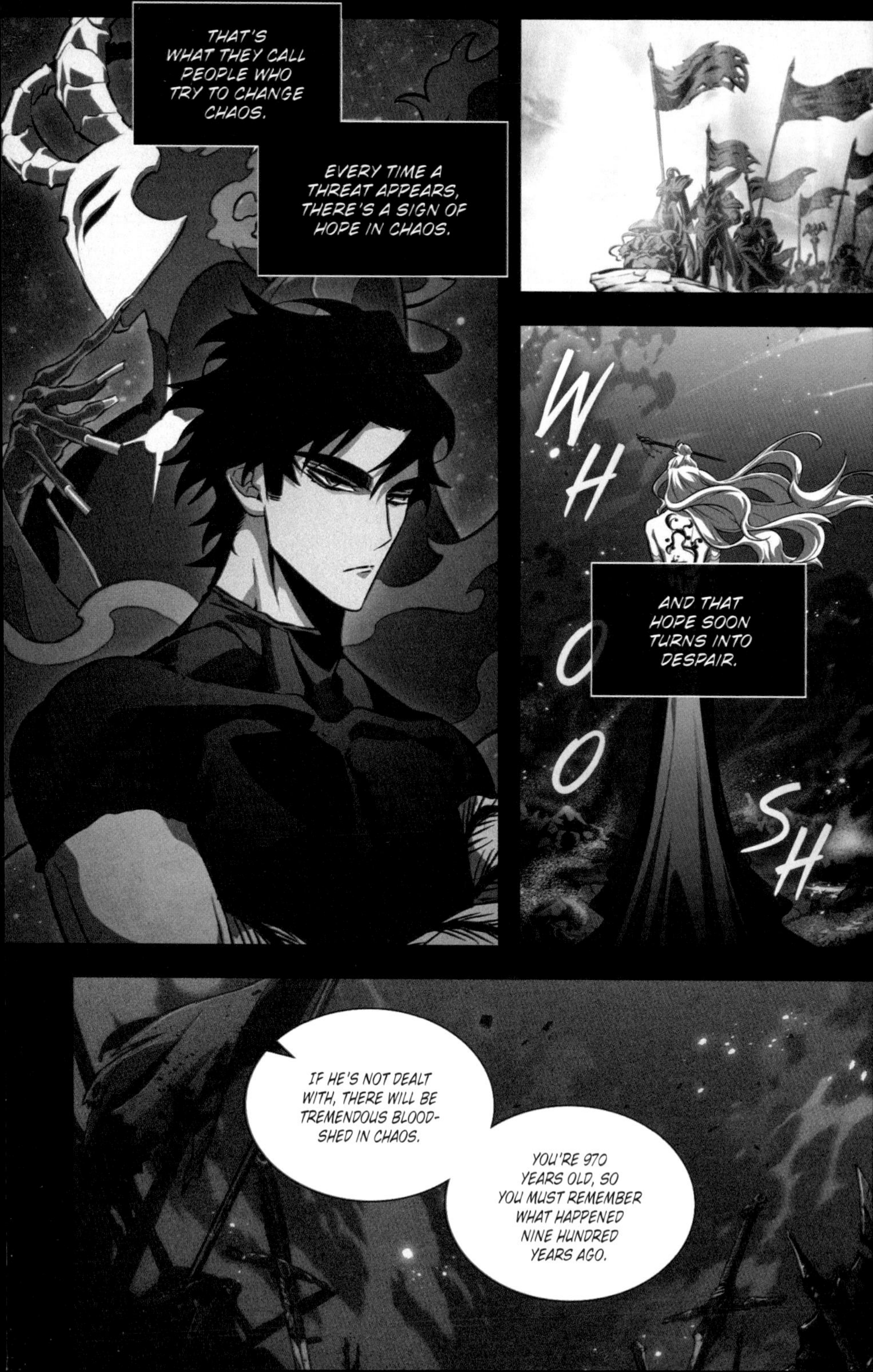
THAT'S WHAT THEY CALL PEOPLE WHO TRY TO CHANGE CHAOS.
EVERY TIME A THREAT APPEARS, THERE'S A SIGN OF HOPE IN CHAOS.
WHOOOSH
AND THAT HOPE SOON TURNS INTO DESPAIR.
IF HE'S NOT DEALT WITH, THERE WILL BE TREMENDOUS BLOOD-SHED IN CHAOS.
YOU'RE 970 YEARS OLD, SO YOU MUST REMEMBER WHAT HAPPENED NINE HUNDRED YEARS AGO.

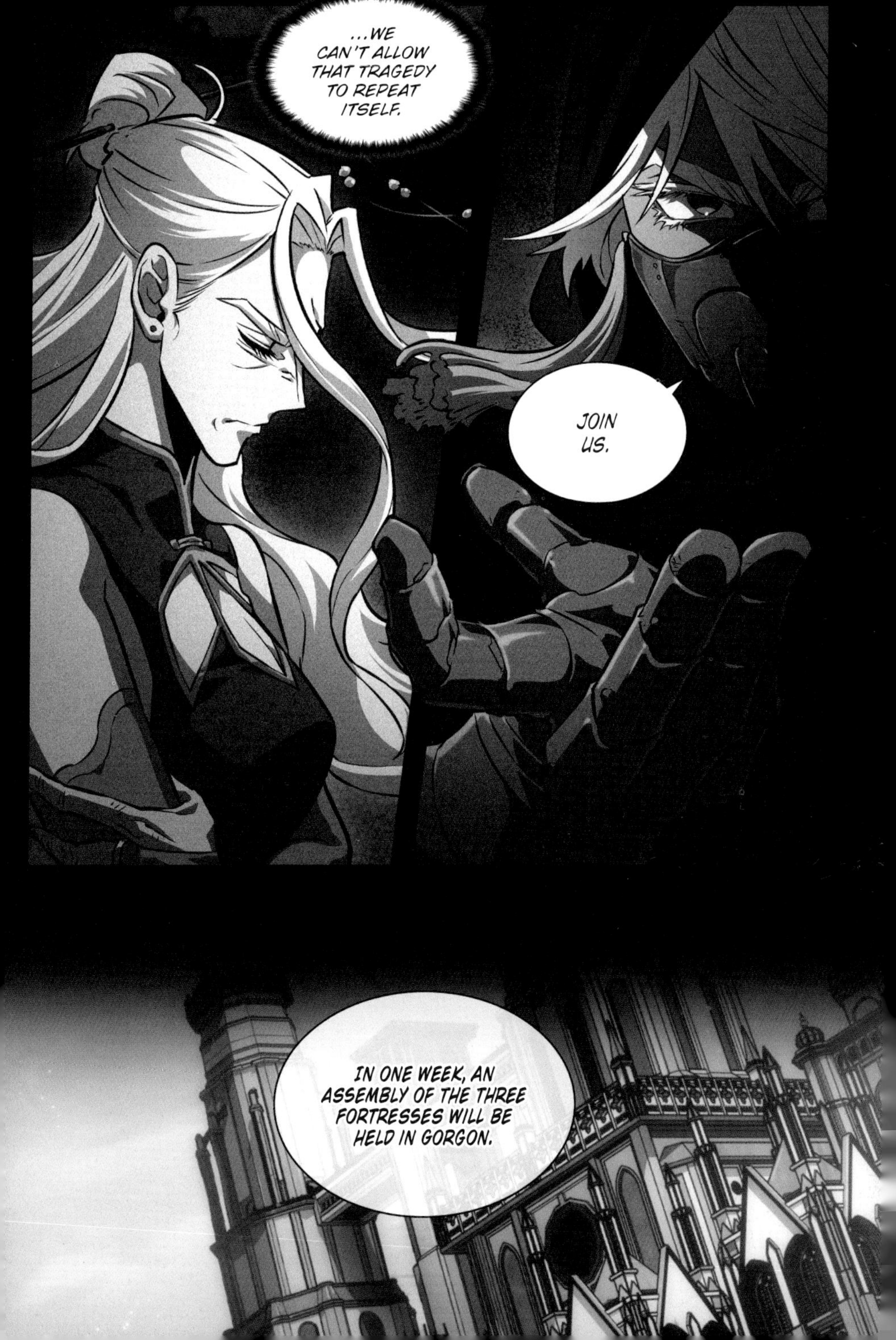
...WE CAN'T ALLOW THAT TRAGEDY TO REPEAT ITSELF.
JOIN US.
IN ONE WEEK, AN ASSEMBLY OF THE THREE FORTRESSES WILL BE HELD IN GORGON.

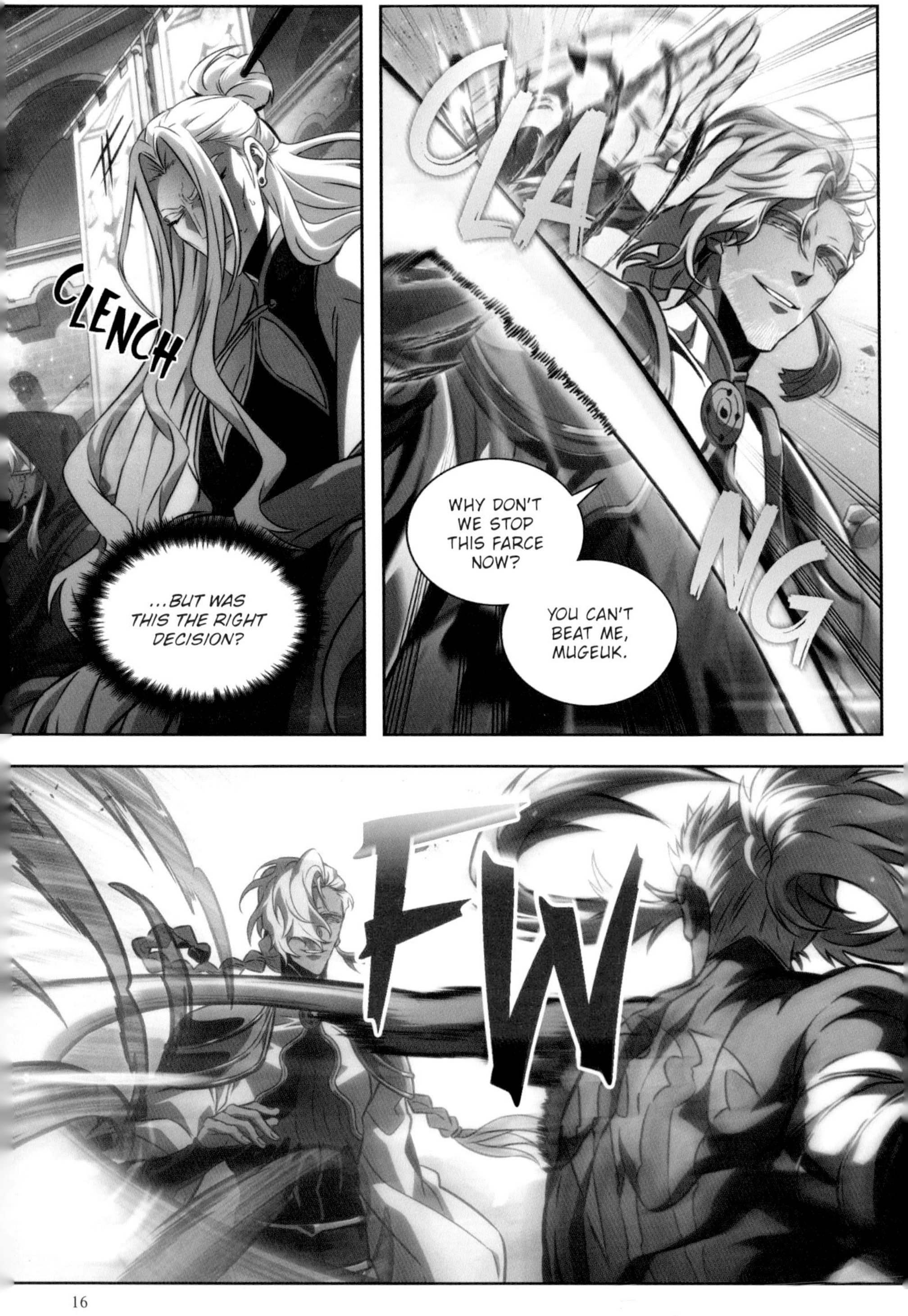
CLENCH
...BUT WAS THIS THE RIGHT DECISION?
CLANG
WHY DON'T WE STOP THIS FARCE NOW?
YOU CAN'T BEAT ME, MUGEUK.
FW

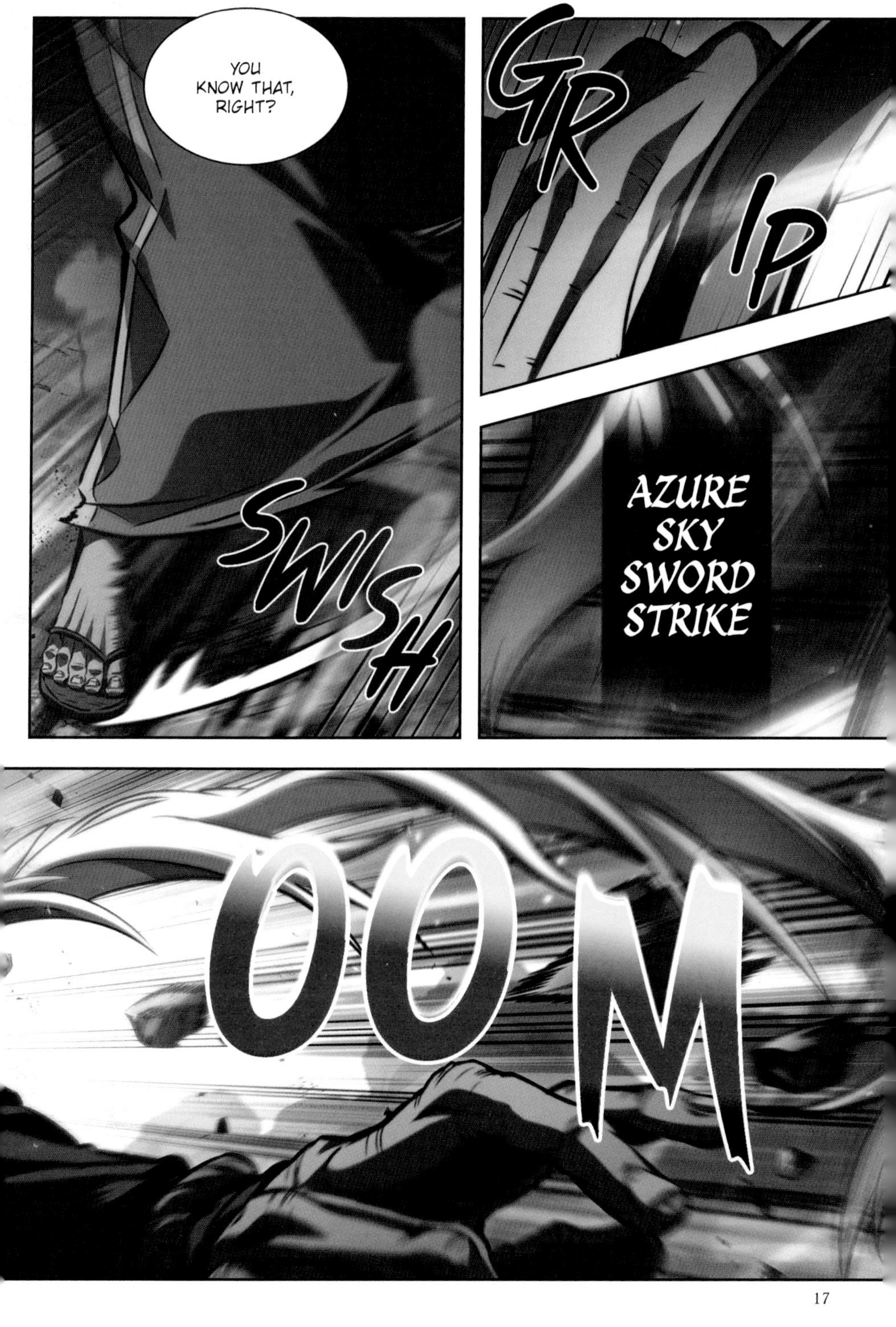
YOU KNOW THAT, RIGHT?
SWISH
GRIP
AZURE SKY SWORD STRIKE
OOM

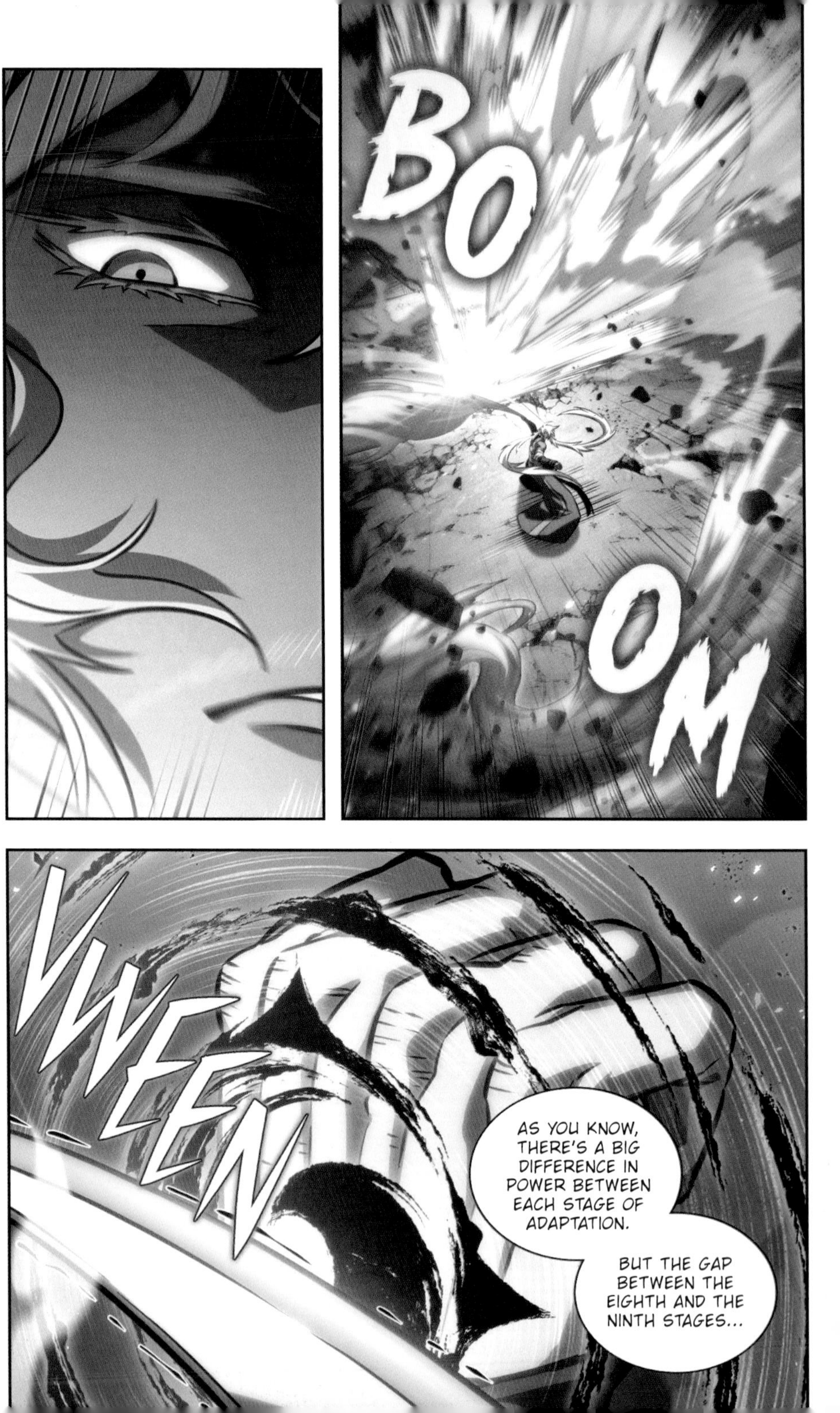
BOOM
VWEEN
AS YOU KNOW, THERE'S A BIG DIFFERENCE IN POWER BETWEEN EACH STAGE OF ADAPTATION.
BUT THE GAP BETWEEN THE EIGHTH AND THE NINTH STAGES...

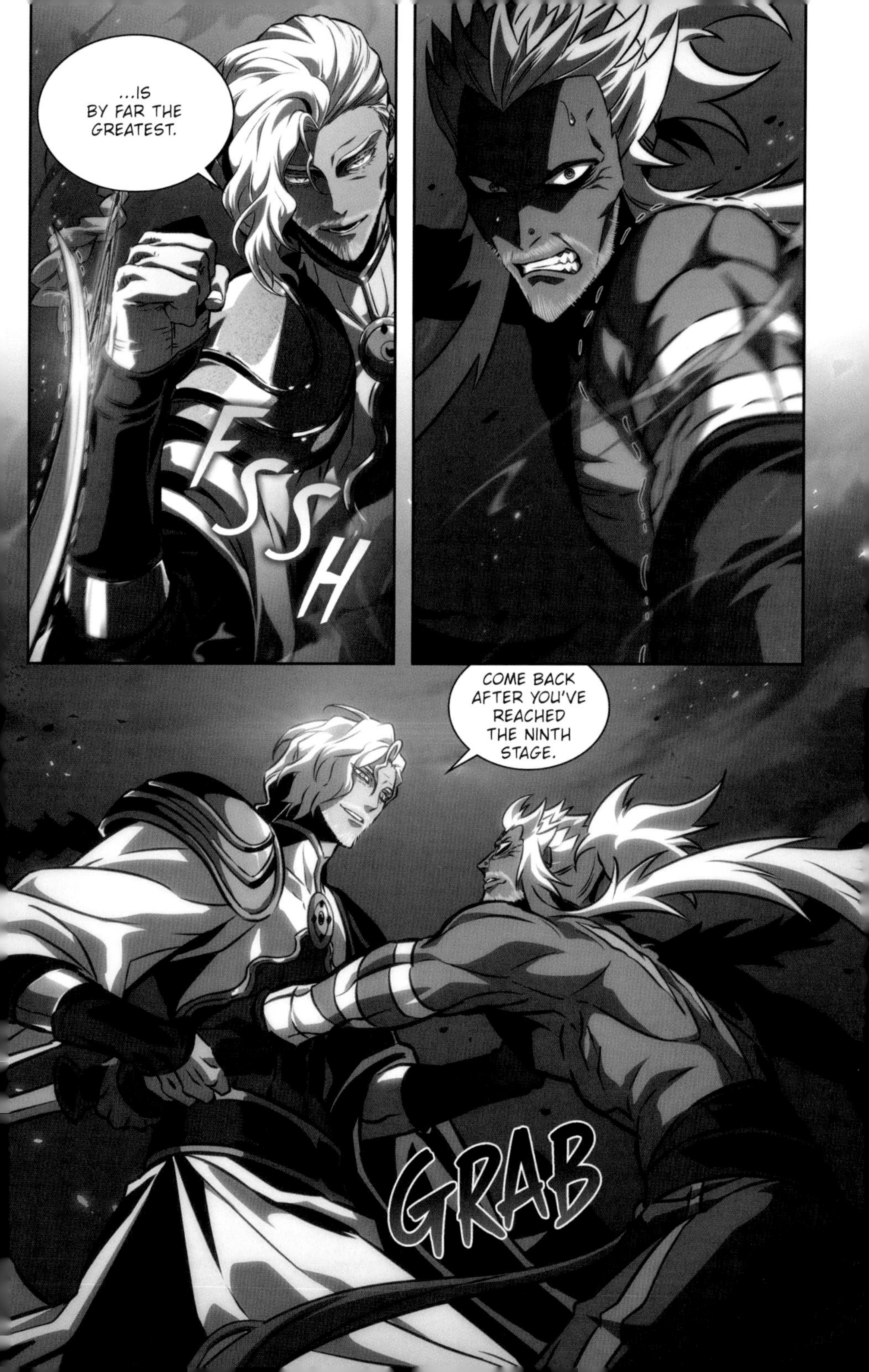
...IS BY FAR THE GREATEST.
FSSH
COME BACK AFTER YOU'VE REACHED THE NINTH STAGE.
GRAB

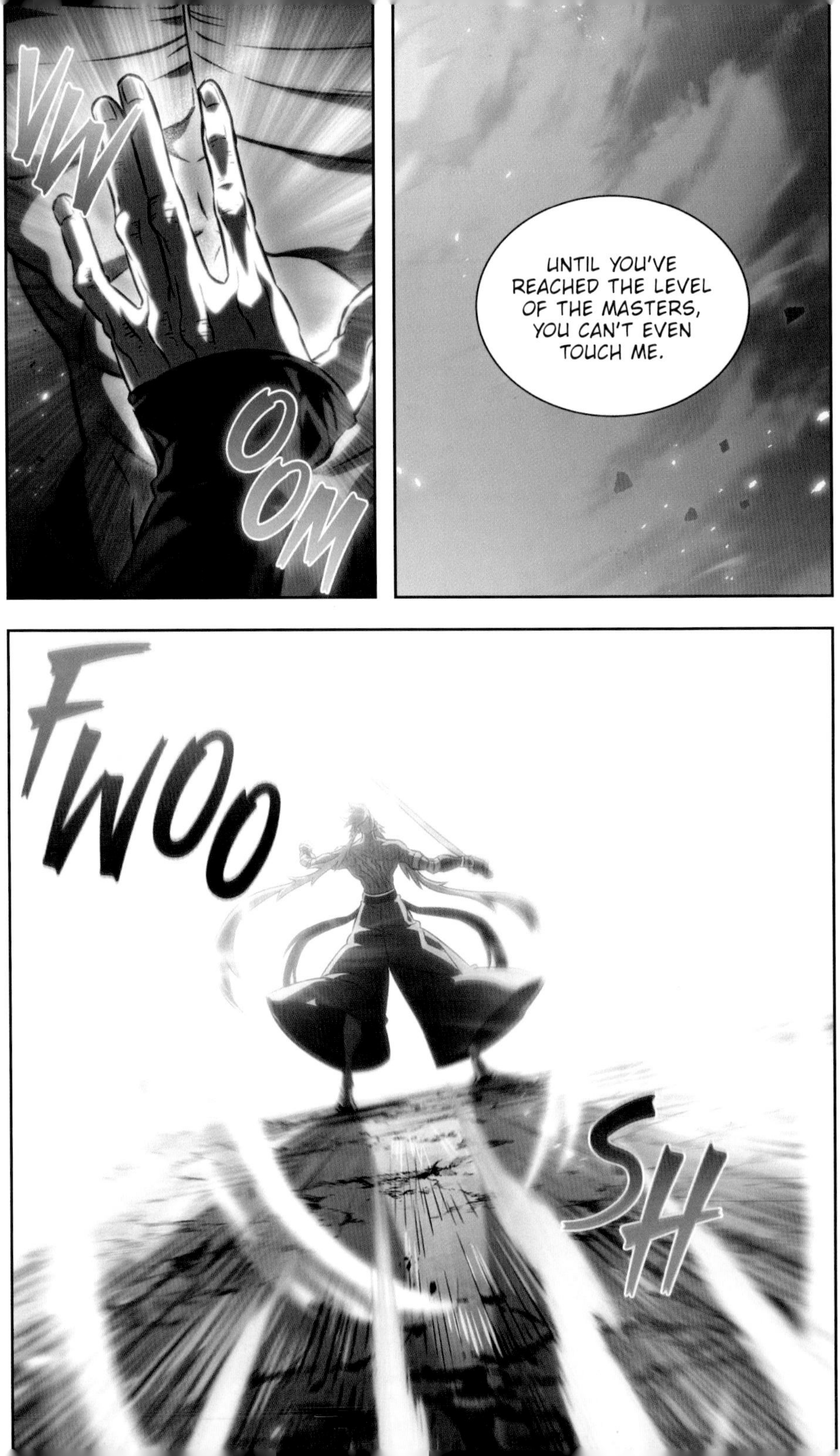
VWOOM
UNTIL YOU'VE REACHED THE LEVEL OF THE MASTERS, YOU CAN'T EVEN TOUCH ME.
FWOOSH

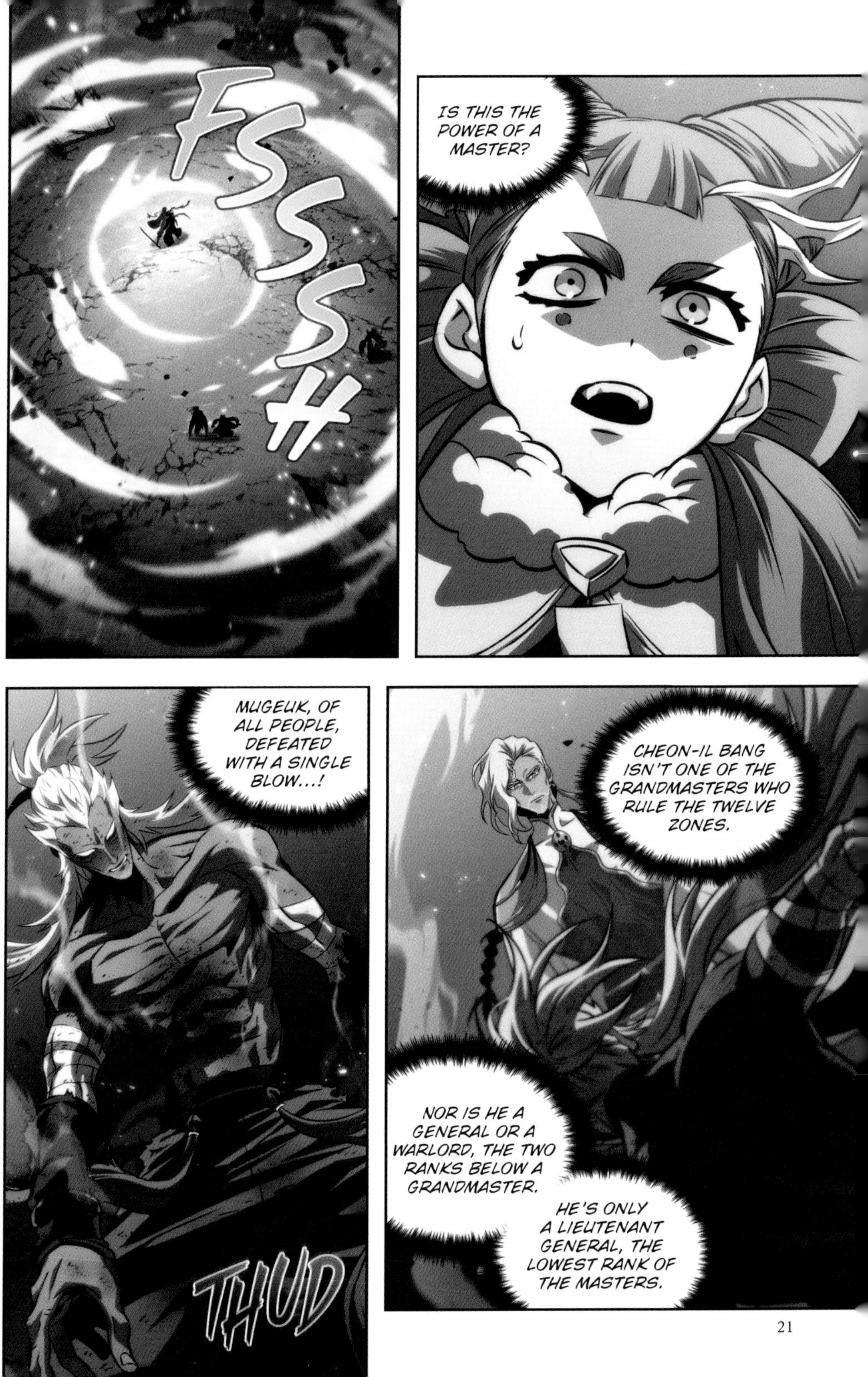
FSSSH
IS THIS THE POWER OF A MASTER?
MUGEUK, OF ALL PEOPLE, DEFEATED WITH A SINGLE BLOW...!
THUD
CHEON-IL BANG ISN'T ONE OF THE GRANDMASTERS WHO RULE THE TWELVE ZONES.
NOR IS HE A GENERAL OR A WARLORD, THE TWO RANKS BELOW A GRANDMASTER.
HE'S ONLY A LIEUTENANT GENERAL, THE LOWEST RANK OF THE MASTERS.

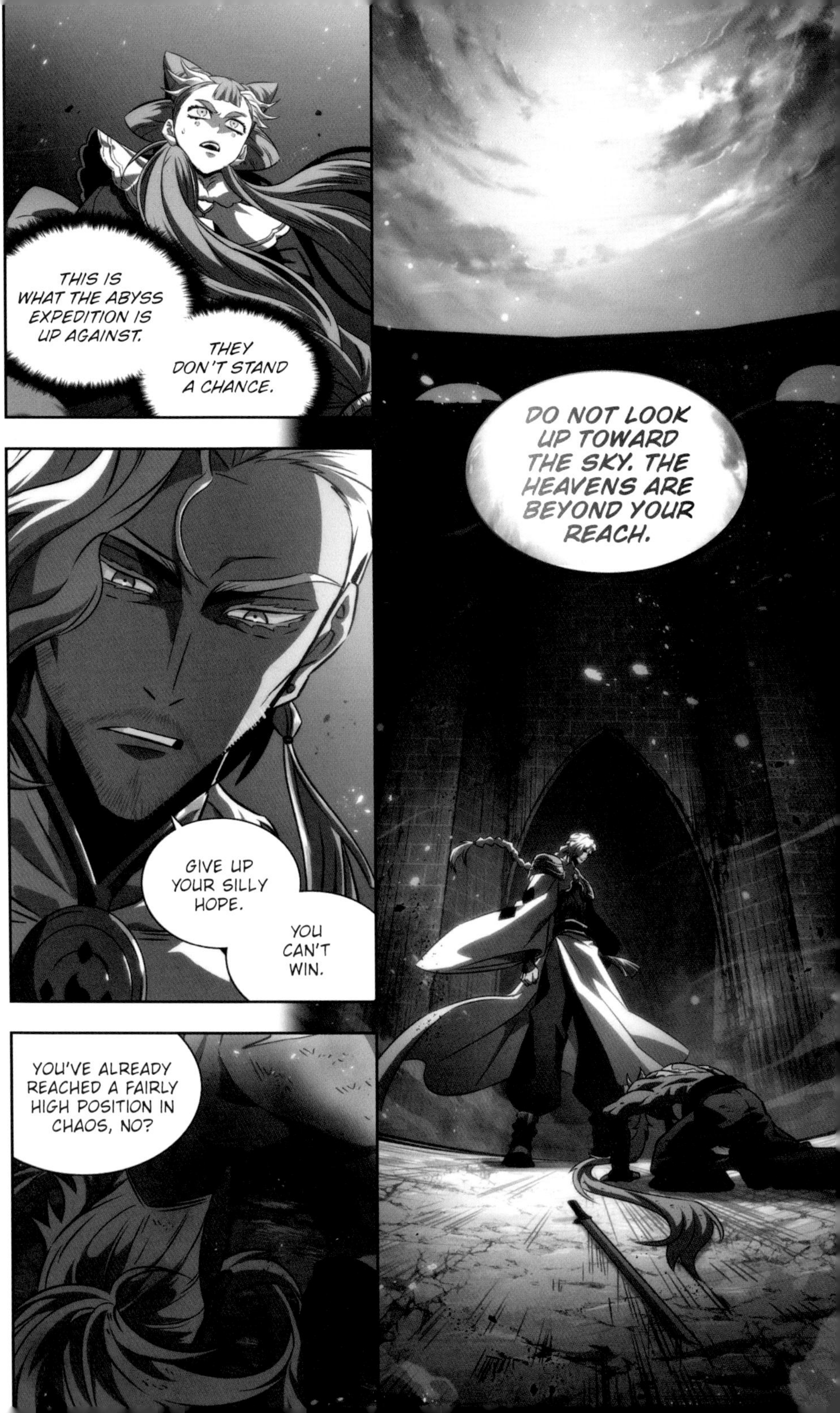
THIS IS WHAT THE ABYSS EXPEDITION IS UP AGAINST.
THEY DON'T STAND A CHANCE.
DO NOT LOOK UP TOWARD THE SKY. THE HEAVENS ARE BEYOND YOUR REACH.
GIVE UP YOUR SILLY HOPE.
YOU CAN'T WIN.
YOU'VE ALREADY REACHED A FAIRLY HIGH POSITION IN CHAOS, NO?

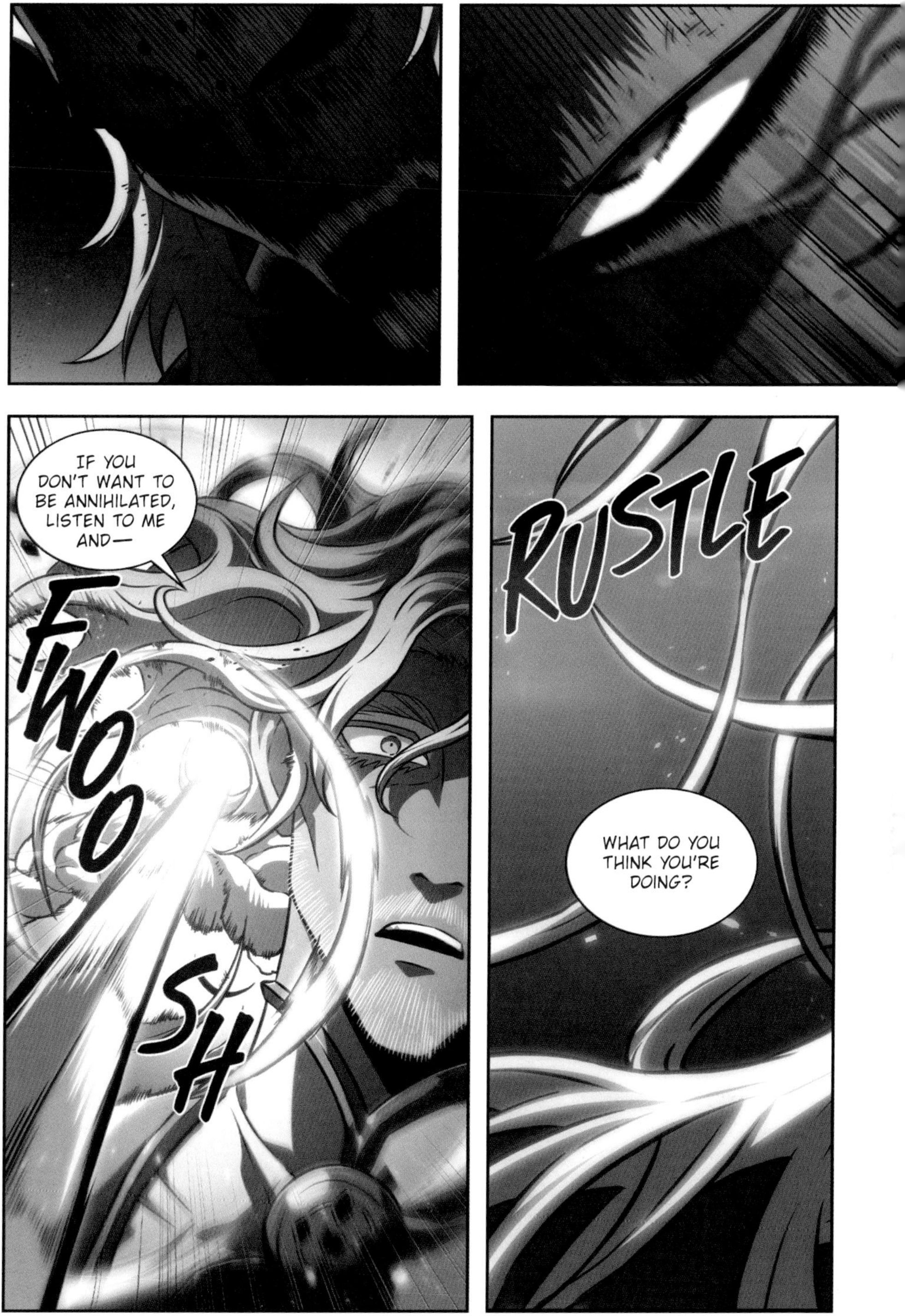
IF YOU DON'T WANT TO BE ANNIHILATED, LISTEN TO ME AND—
FWOOSH
RUSTLE
WHAT DO YOU THINK YOU'RE DOING?

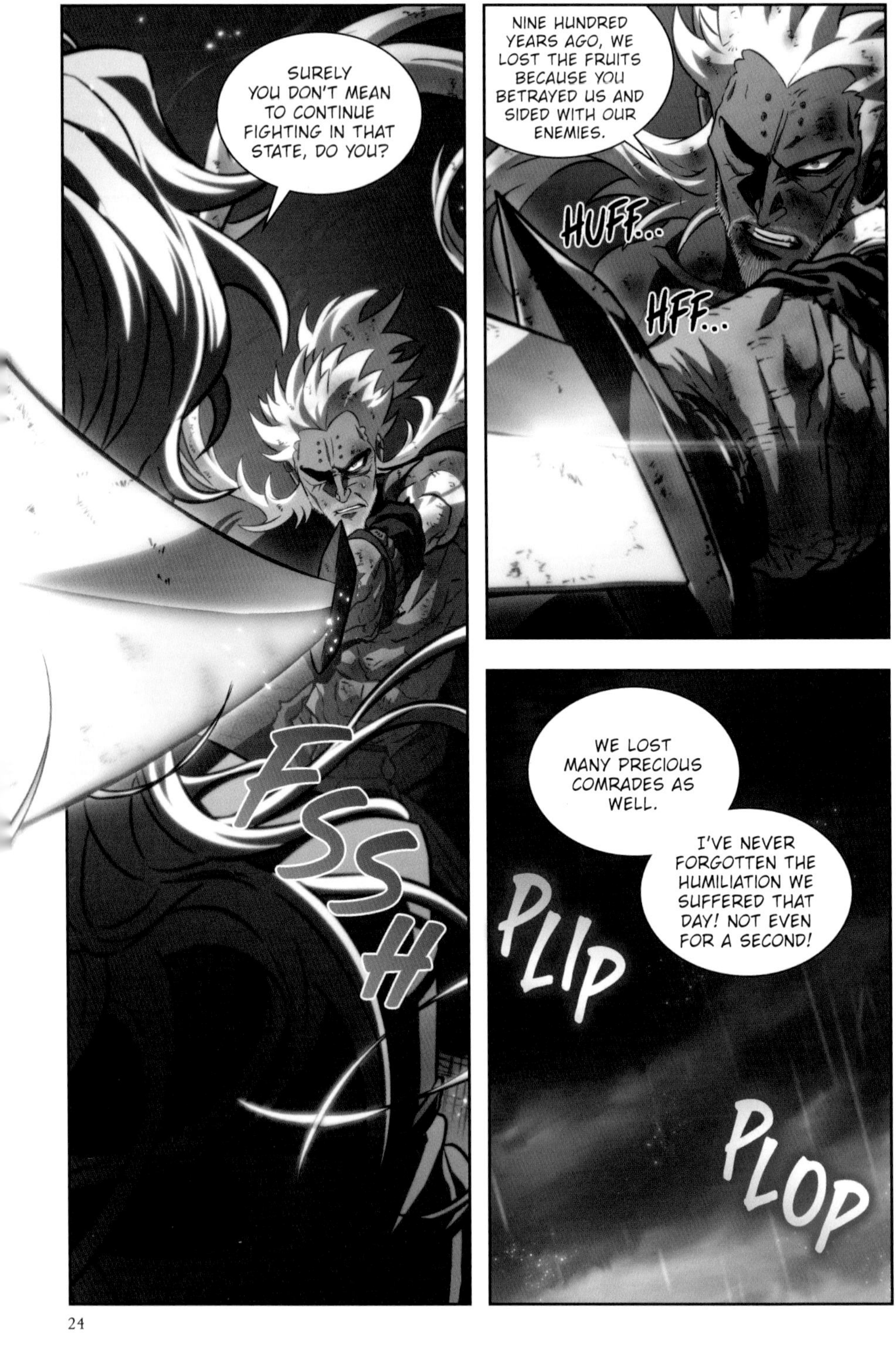
SURELY YOU DON'T MEAN TO CONTINUE FIGHTING IN THAT STATE, DO YOU?
FSSH
NINE HUNDRED YEARS AGO, WE LOST THE FRUITS BECAUSE YOU BETRAYED US AND SIDED WITH OUR ENEMIES.
HUFF...
HFF...
WE LOST MANY PRECIOUS COMRADES AS WELL.
I'VE NEVER FORGOTTEN THE HUMILIATION WE SUFFERED THAT DAY! NOT EVEN FOR A SECOND!
PLIP
PLOP

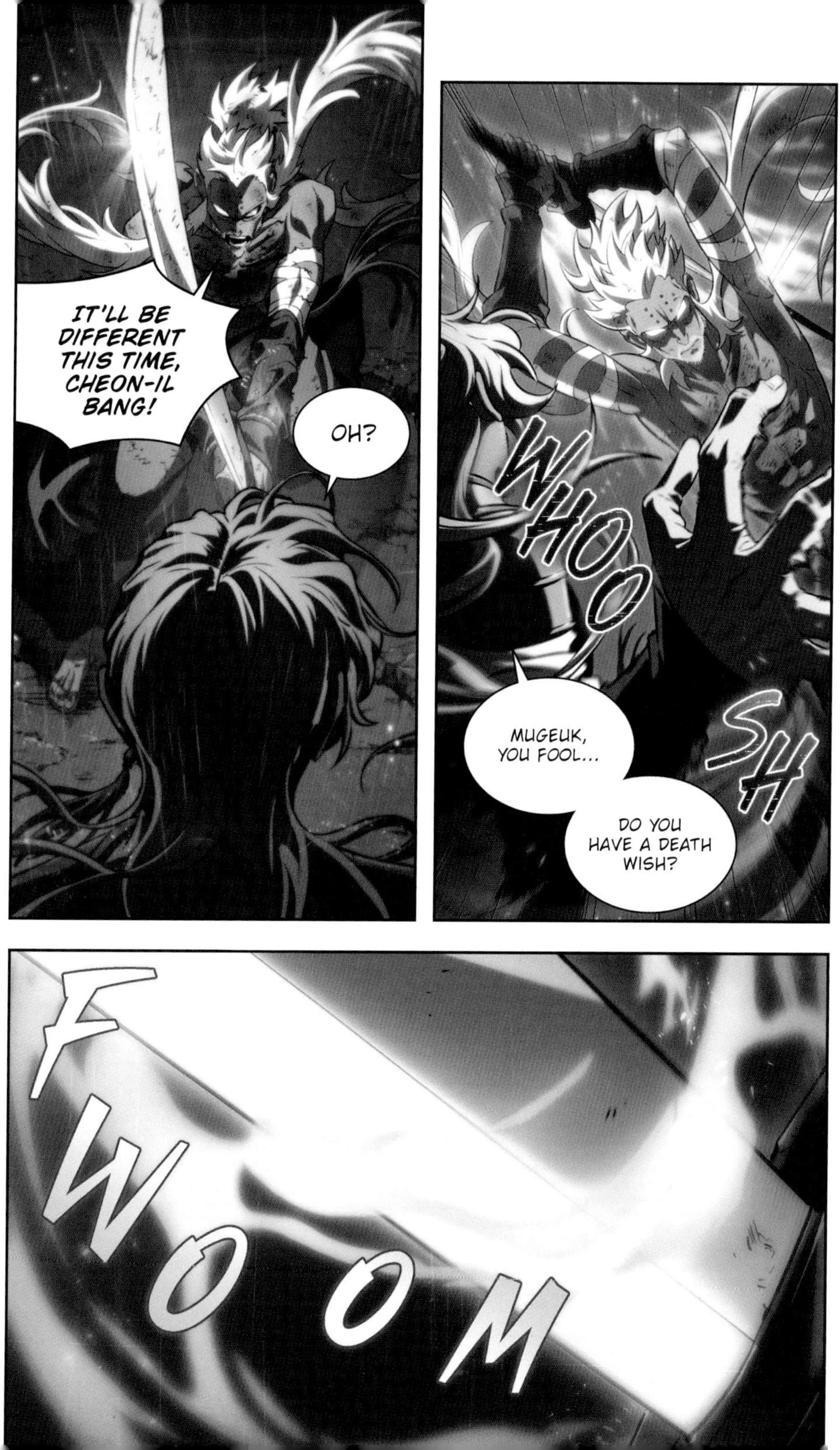
IT'LL BE DIFFERENT THIS TIME, CHEON-IL BANG!
OH?
WHOO
MUGEUK, YOU FOOL...
DO YOU HAVE A DEATH WISH?
SH
FWOOM

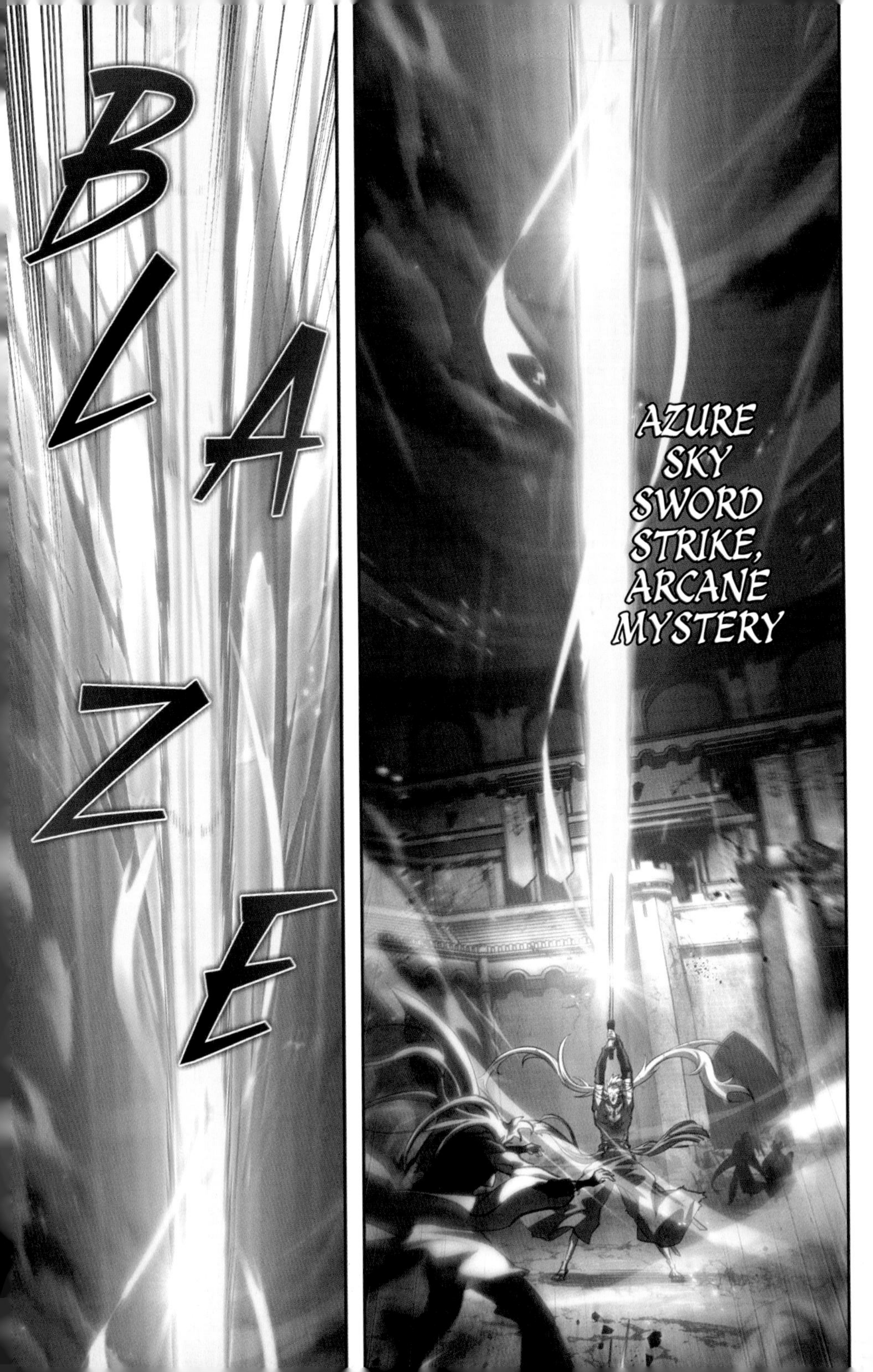
BLAZE
AZURE SKY SWORD STRIKE, ARCANE MYSTERY

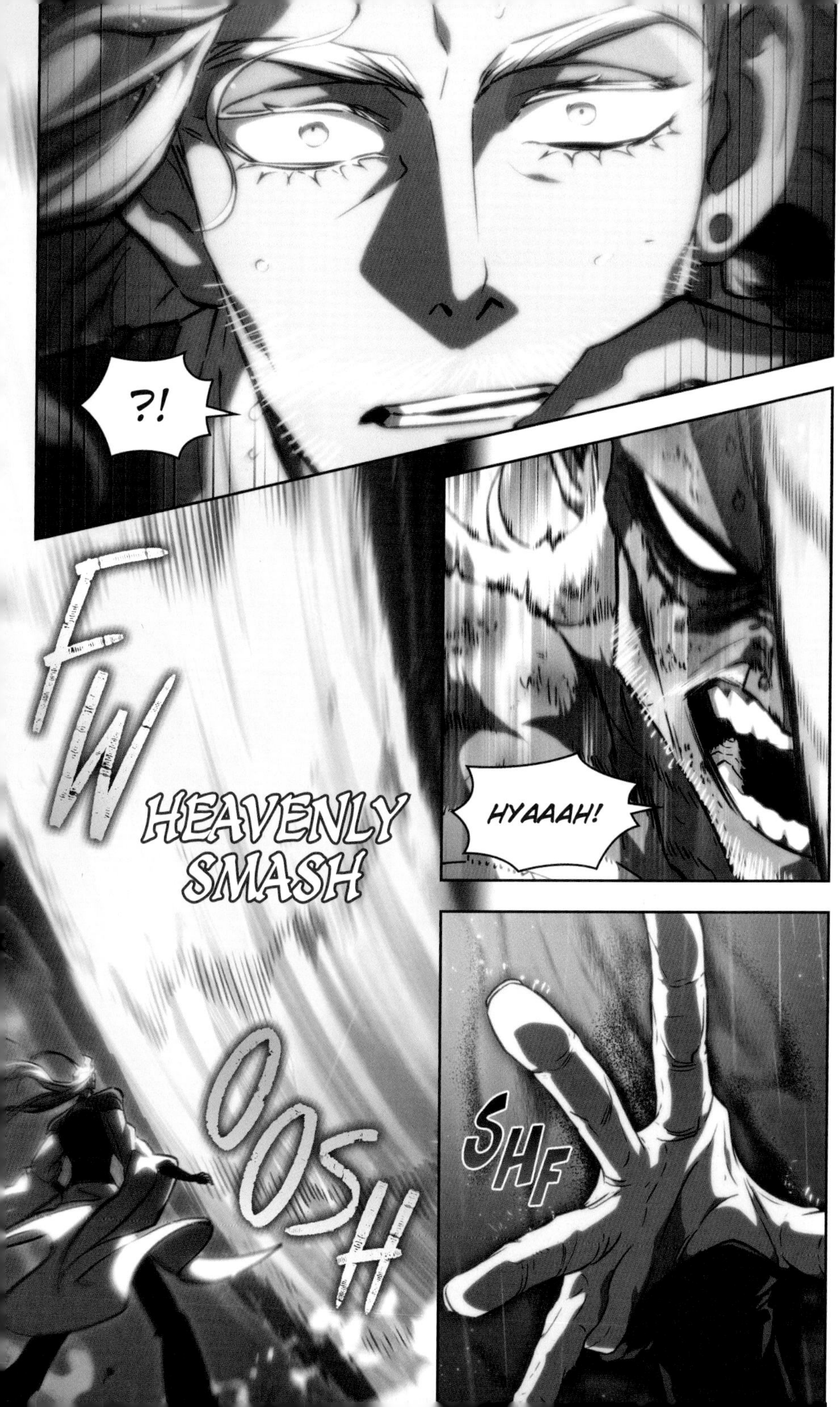
?!
FW
HEAVENLY SMASH
HYAAAH!
OOSH
SHF

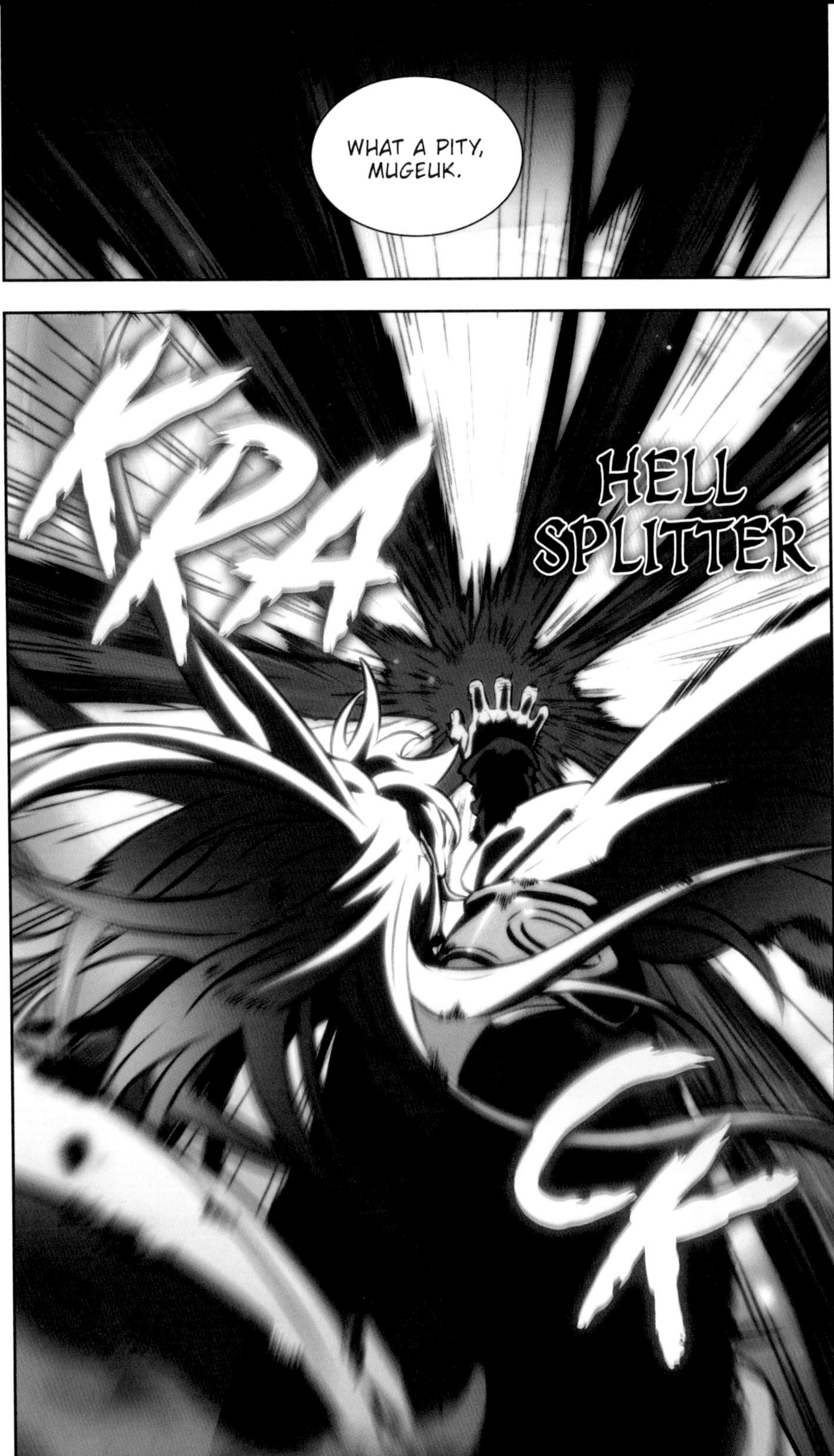
WHAT A PITY, MUGEUK.
KRA
HELL SPLITTER
CK

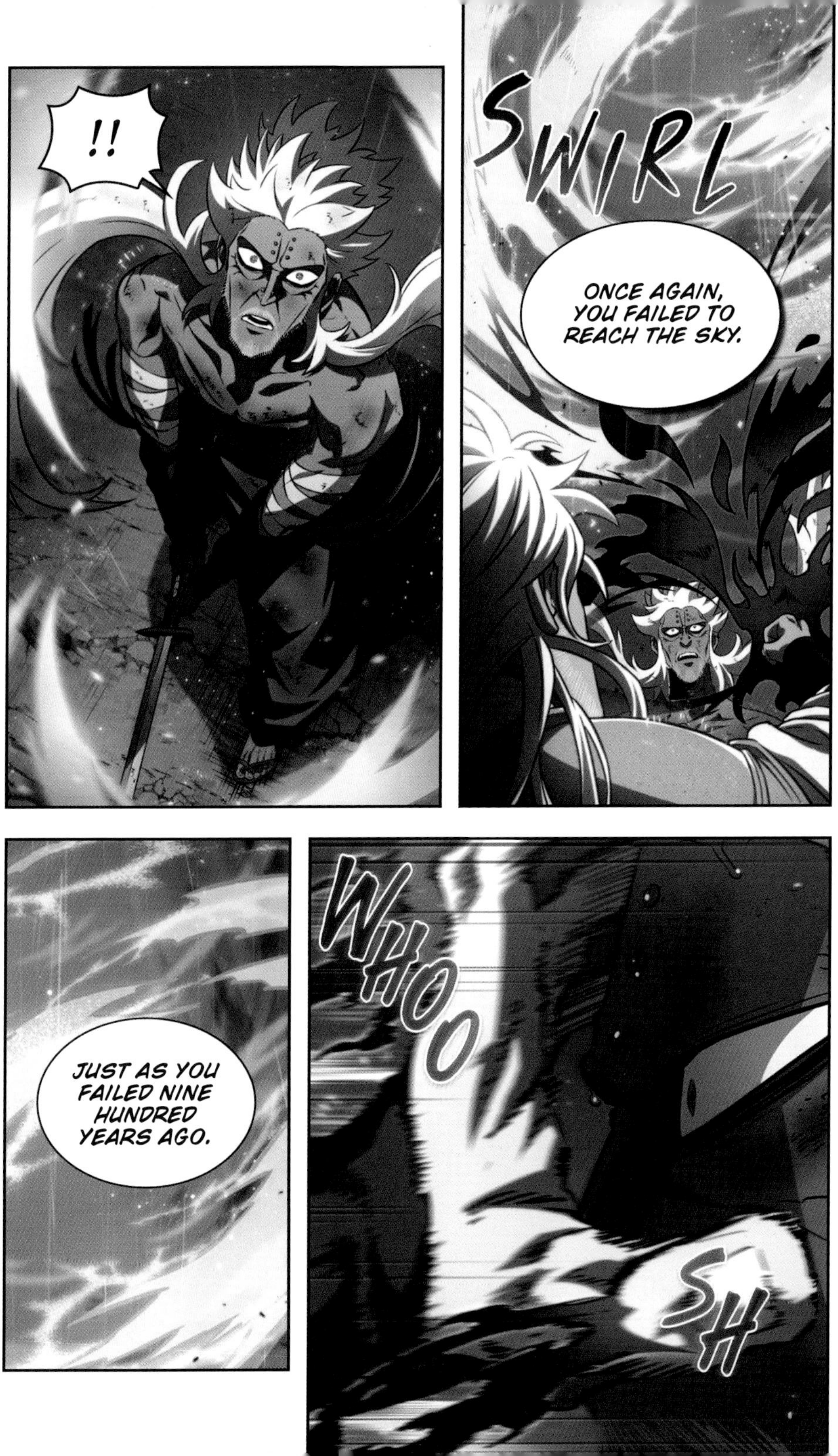
!!
SWIRL
ONCE AGAIN, YOU FAILED TO REACH THE SKY.
JUST AS YOU FAILED NINE HUNDRED YEARS AGO.
WHOOSH

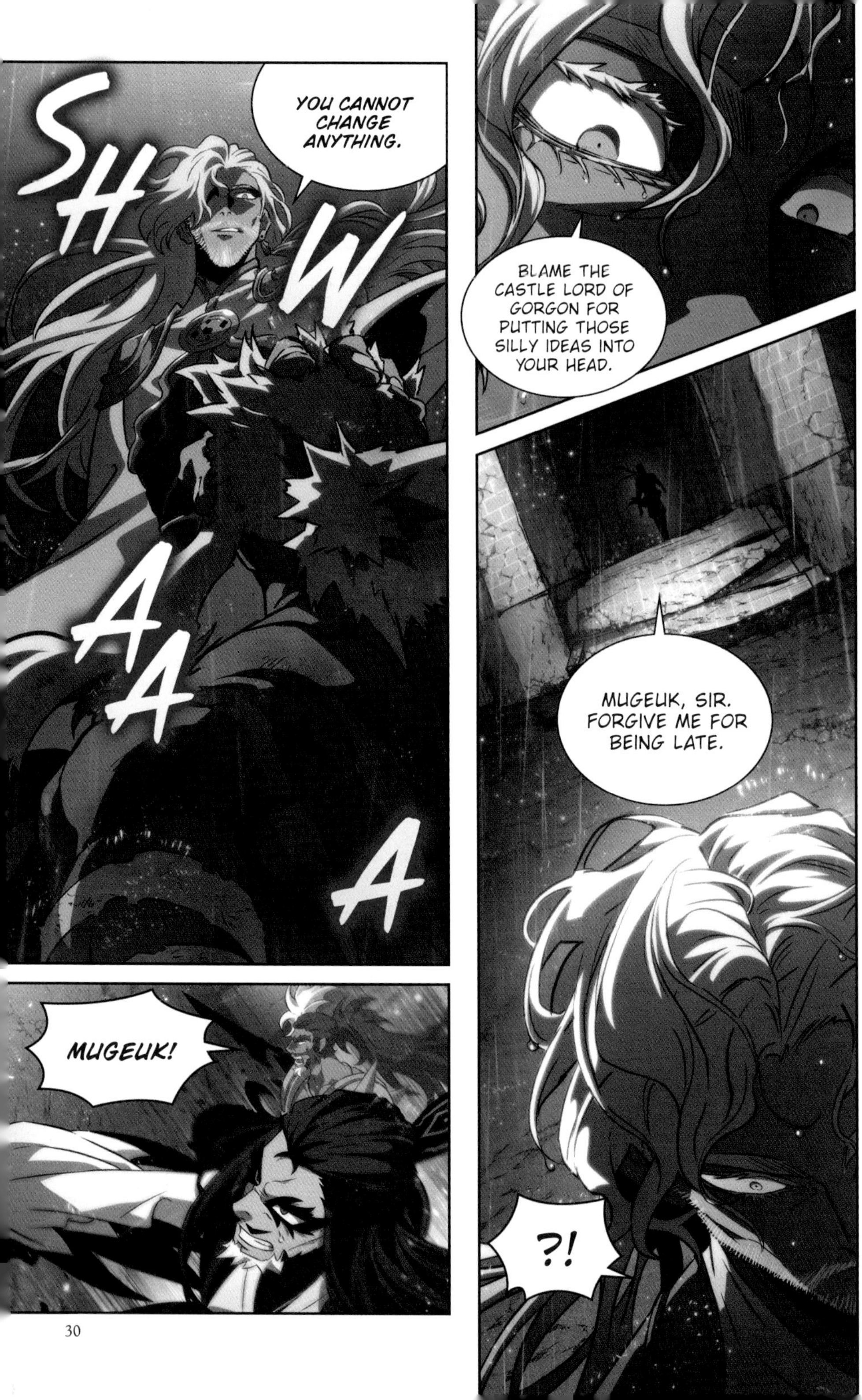
YOU CANNOT CHANGE ANYTHING.
SHWAAAA
MUGEUK!
BLAME THE CASTLE LORD OF GORGON FOR PUTTING THOSE SILLY IDEAS INTO YOUR HEAD.
MUGEUK, SIR. FORGIVE ME FOR BEING LATE.
?!

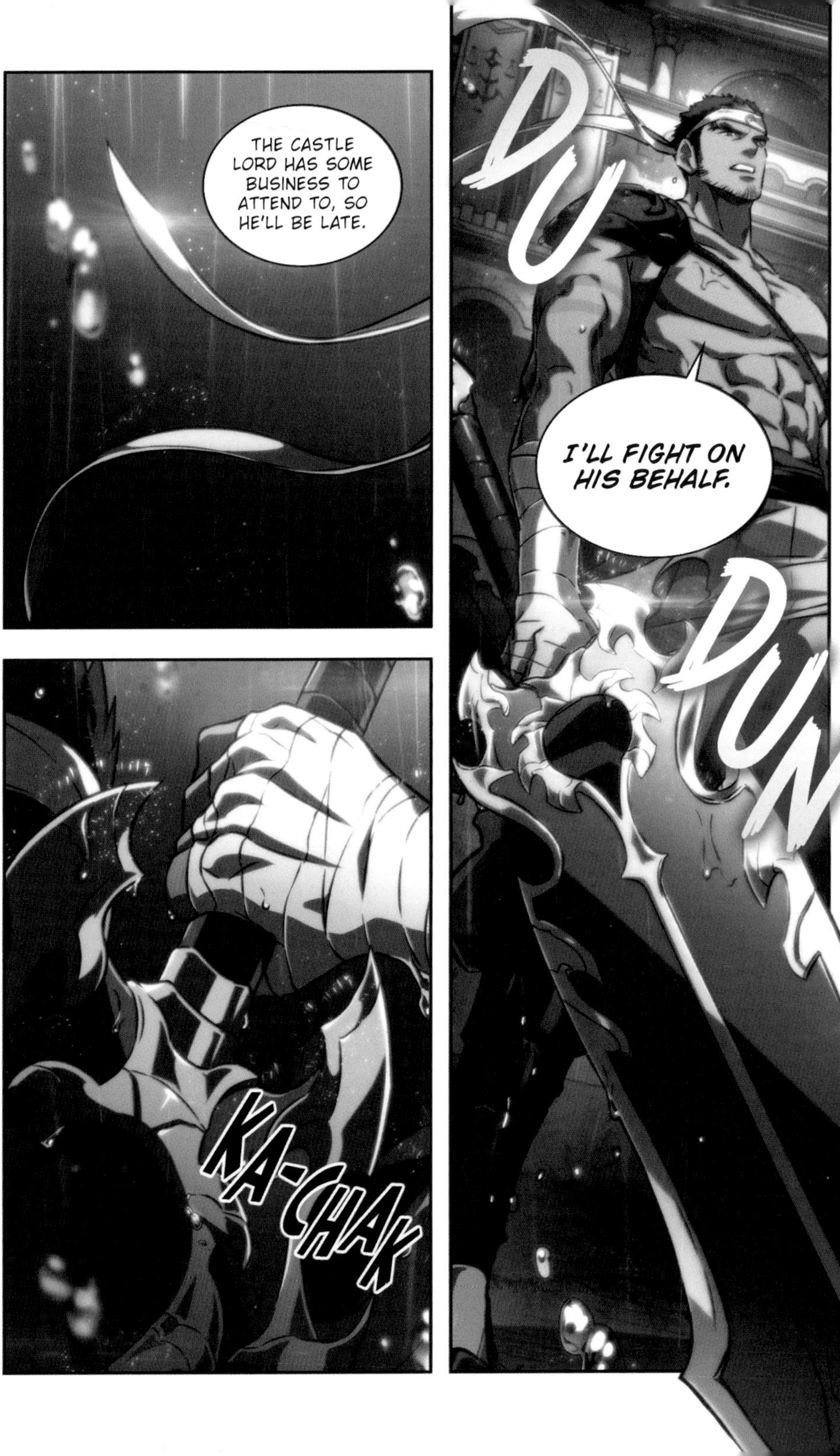
THE CASTLE LORD HAS SOME BUSINESS TO ATTEND TO, SO HE'LL BE LATE.
KA-CHAK
DU
I'LL FIGHT ON HIS BEHALF.
DUN

The World After the Fall

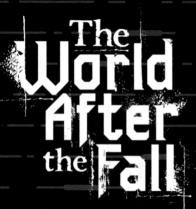

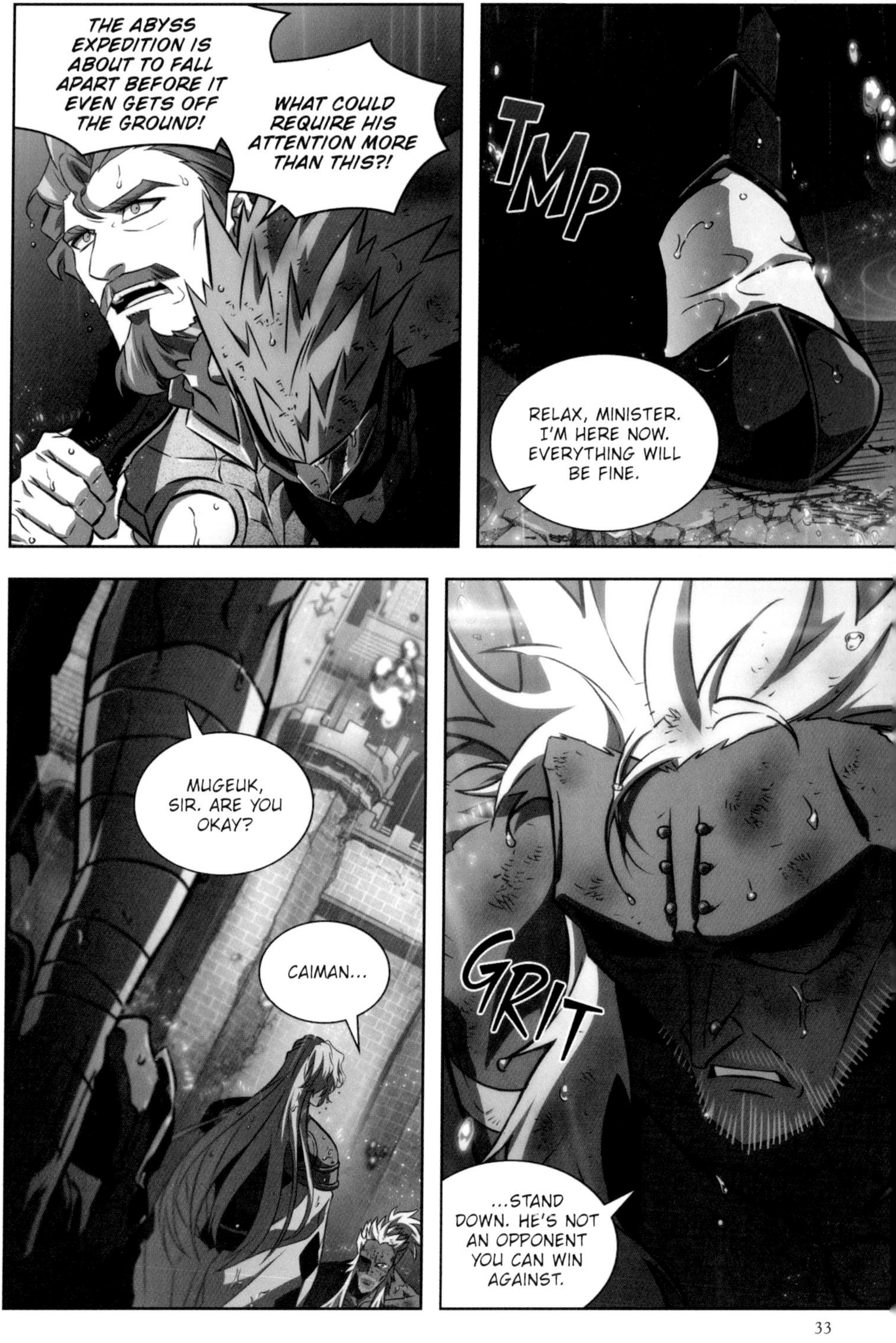
THE ABYSS EXPEDITION IS ABOUT TO FALL APART BEFORE IT EVEN GETS OFF THE GROUND!
WHAT COULD REQUIRE HIS ATTENTION MORE THAN THIS?!
TMP
RELAX, MINISTER. I'M HERE NOW. EVERYTHING WILL BE FINE.
MUGEUK, SIR. ARE YOU OKAY?
CAIMAN...
GRIT
...STAND DOWN. HE'S NOT AN OPPONENT YOU CAN WIN AGAINST.

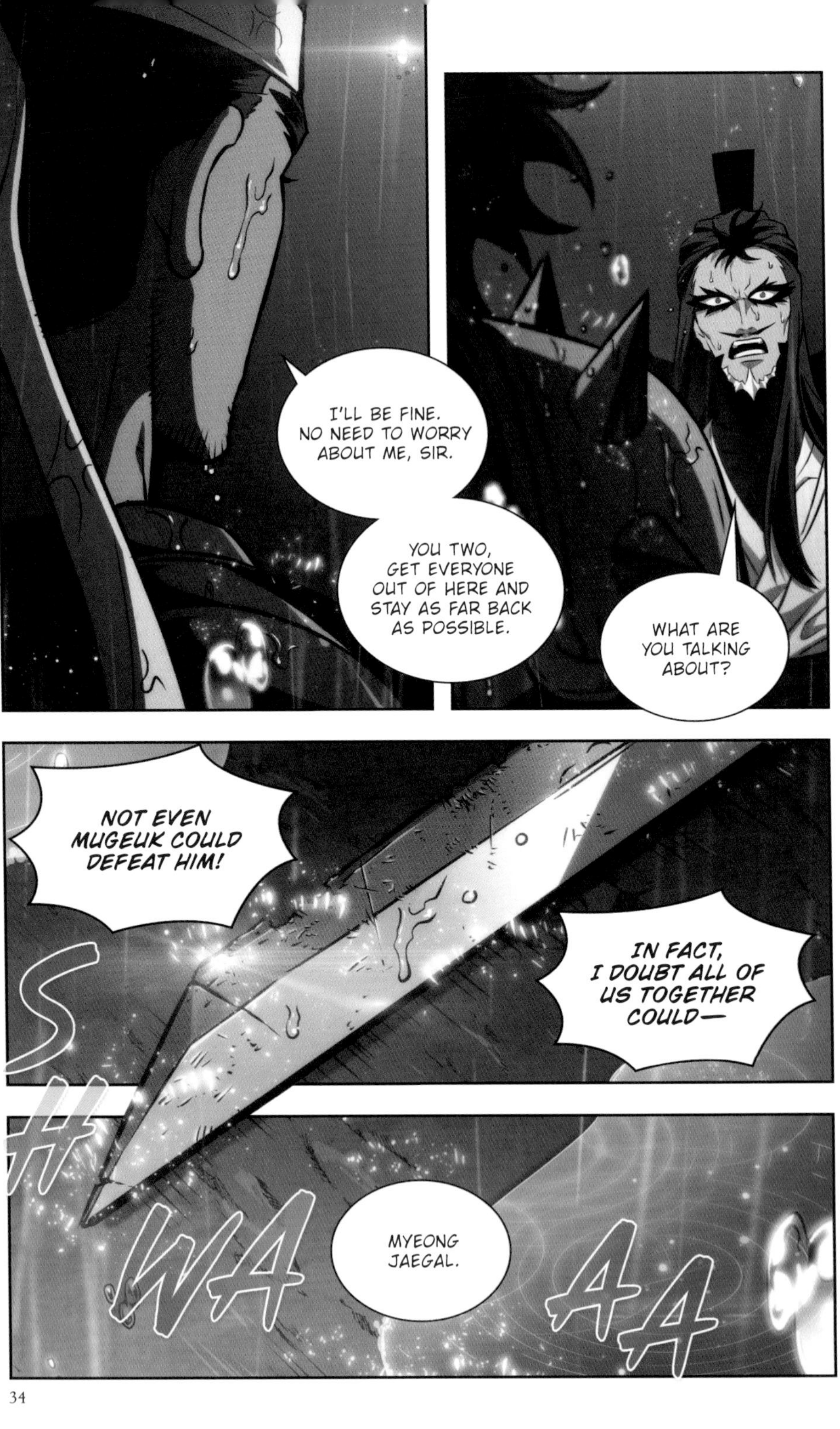
I'LL BE FINE. NO NEED TO WORRY ABOUT ME, SIR.
YOU TWO, GET EVERYONE OUT OF HERE AND STAY AS FAR BACK AS POSSIBLE.
WHAT ARE YOU TALKING ABOUT?
NOT EVEN MUGEUK COULD DEFEAT HIM!
IN FACT, I DOUBT ALL OF US TOGETHER COULD—
SHWAAA
MYEONG JAEGAL.

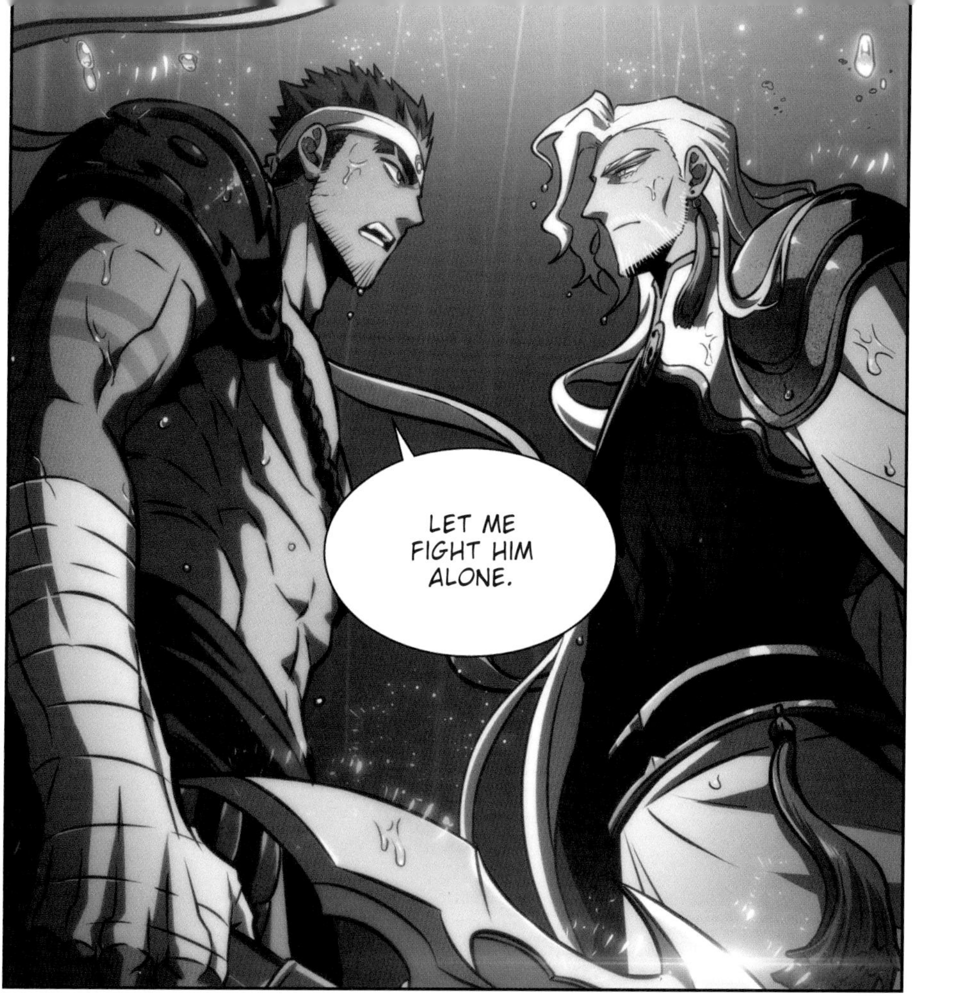
LET ME FIGHT HIM ALONE.

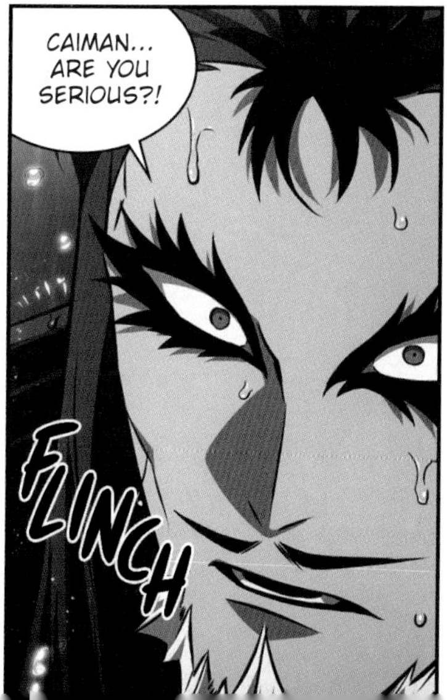
CAIMAN... ARE YOU SERIOUS?!
FLINCH

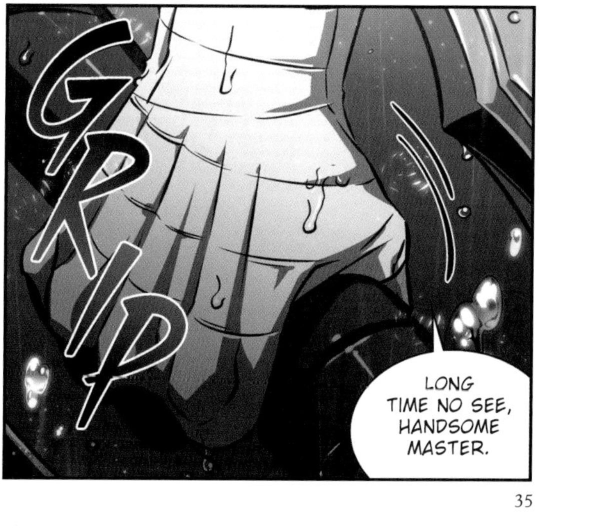
GRIP
LONG TIME NO SEE, HANDSOME MASTER.

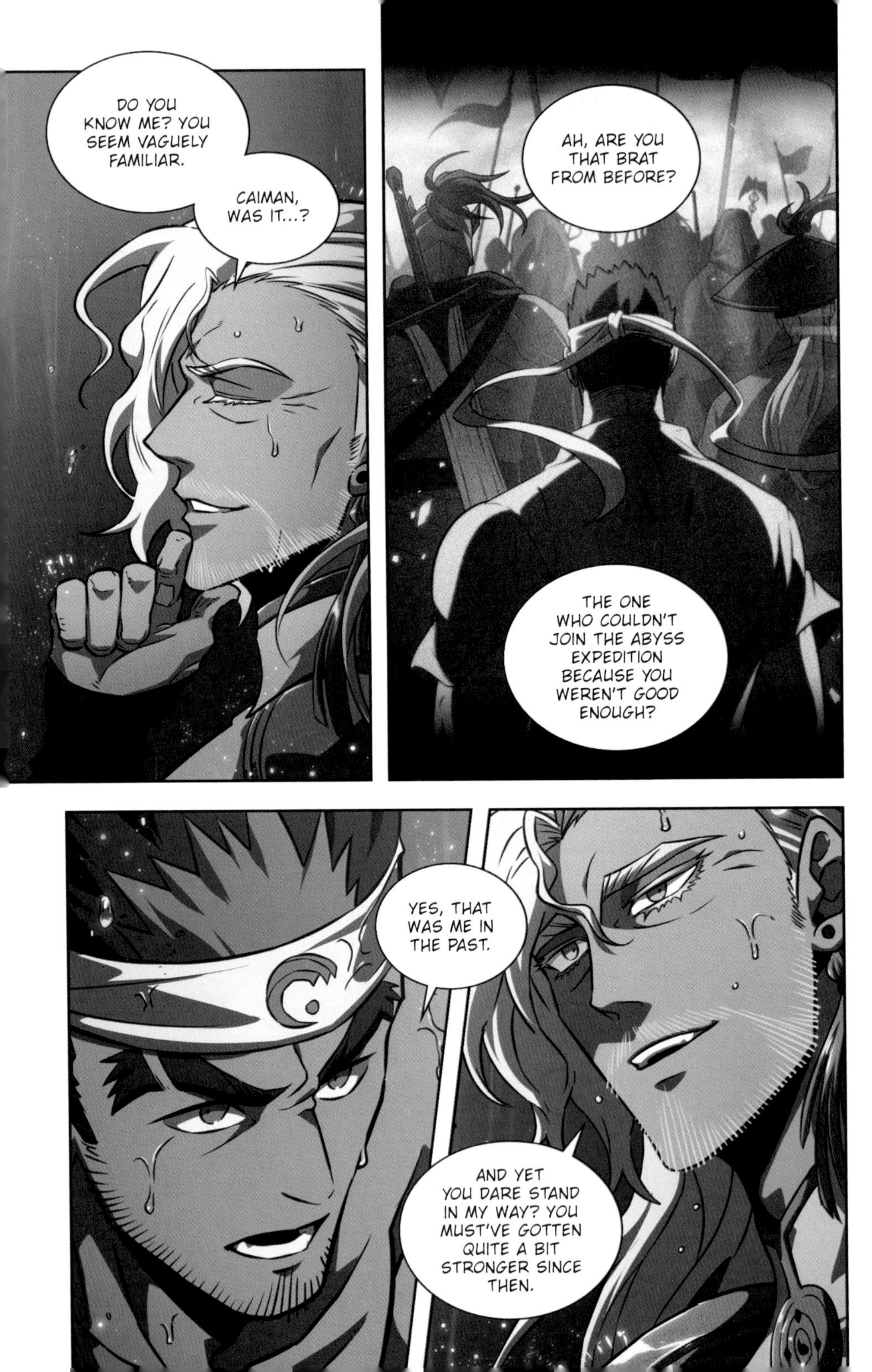
DO YOU KNOW ME? YOU SEEM VAGUELY FAMILIAR.
CAIMAN, WAS IT...?
AH, ARE YOU THAT BRAT FROM BEFORE?
THE ONE WHO COULDN'T JOIN THE ABYSS EXPEDITION BECAUSE YOU WEREN'T GOOD ENOUGH?
YES, THAT WAS ME IN THE PAST.
AND YET YOU DARE STAND IN MY WAY? YOU MUST'VE GOTTEN QUITE A BIT STRONGER SINCE THEN.

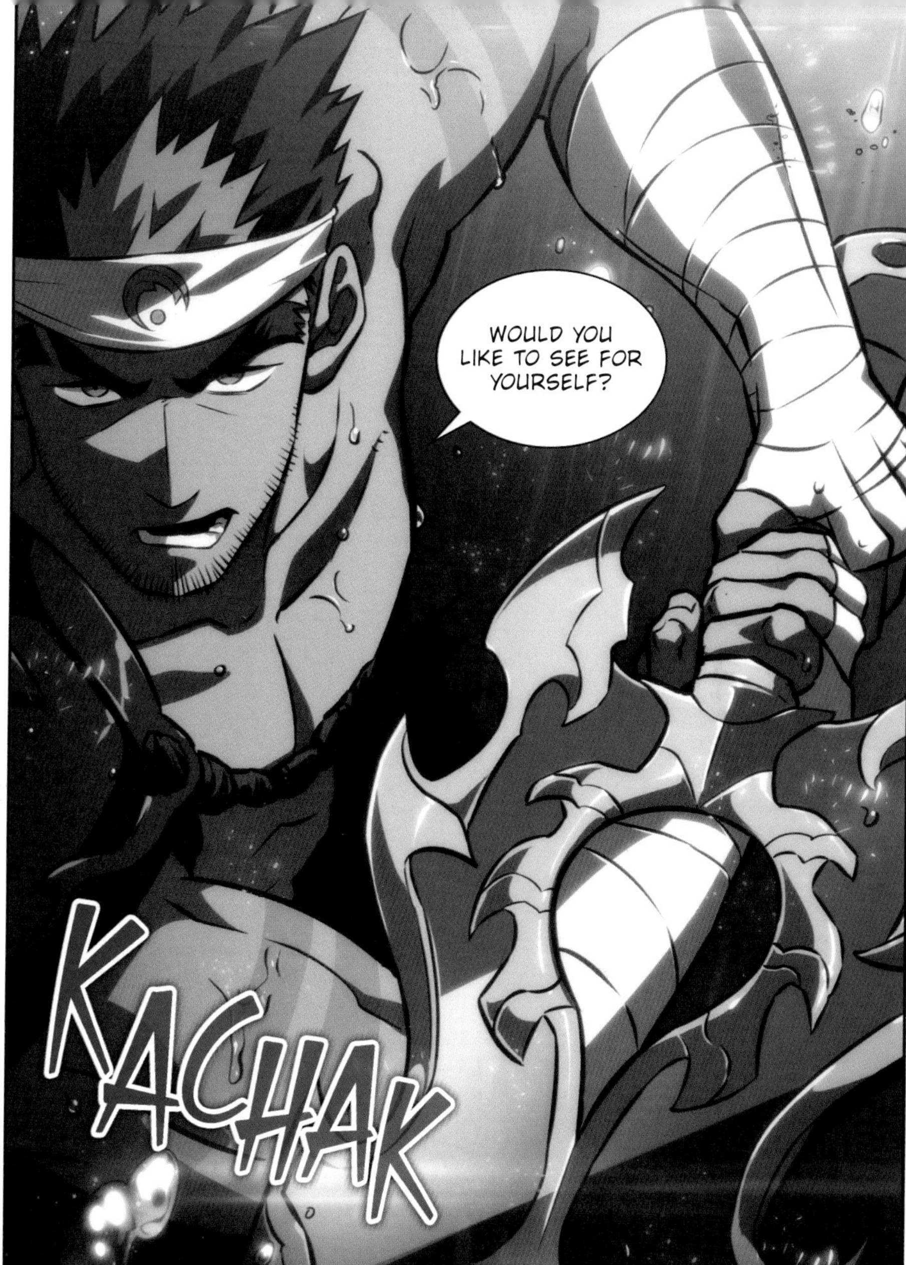
WOULD YOU LIKE TO SEE FOR YOURSELF?
KACHAK

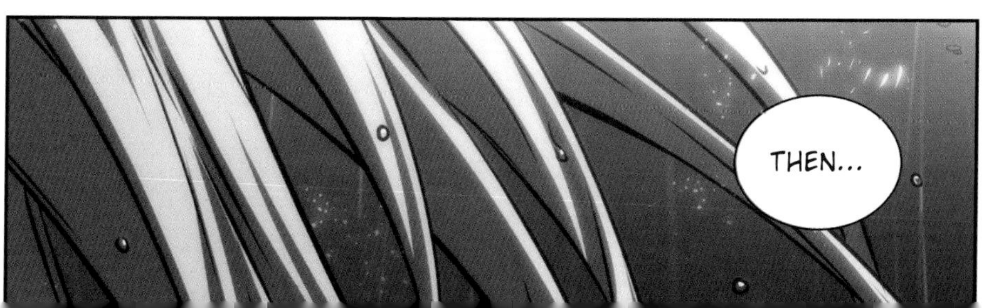
THEN...

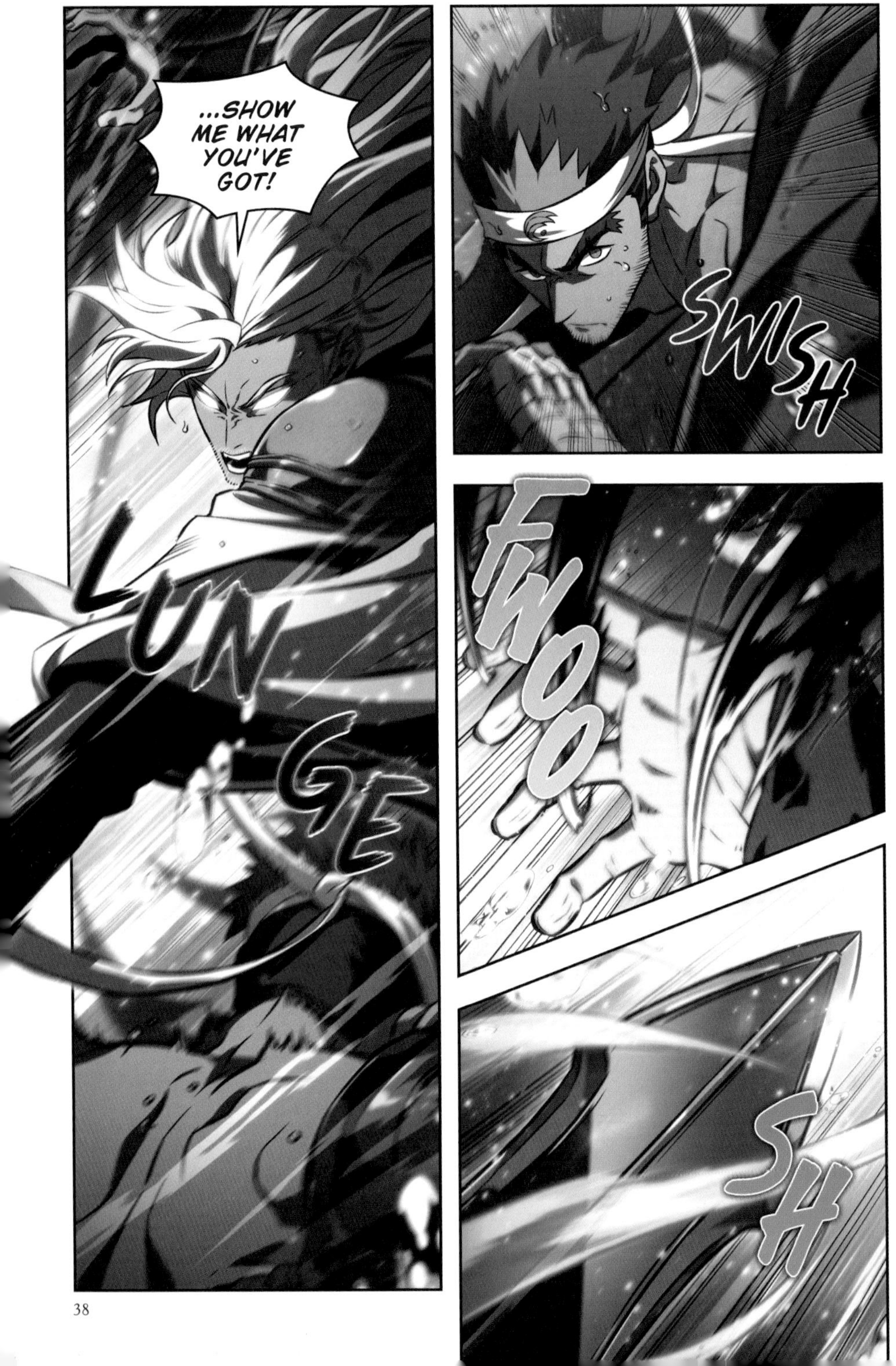

...SHOW ME WHAT YOU'VE GOT!
LUNGE
SWISH
FWOO
SH

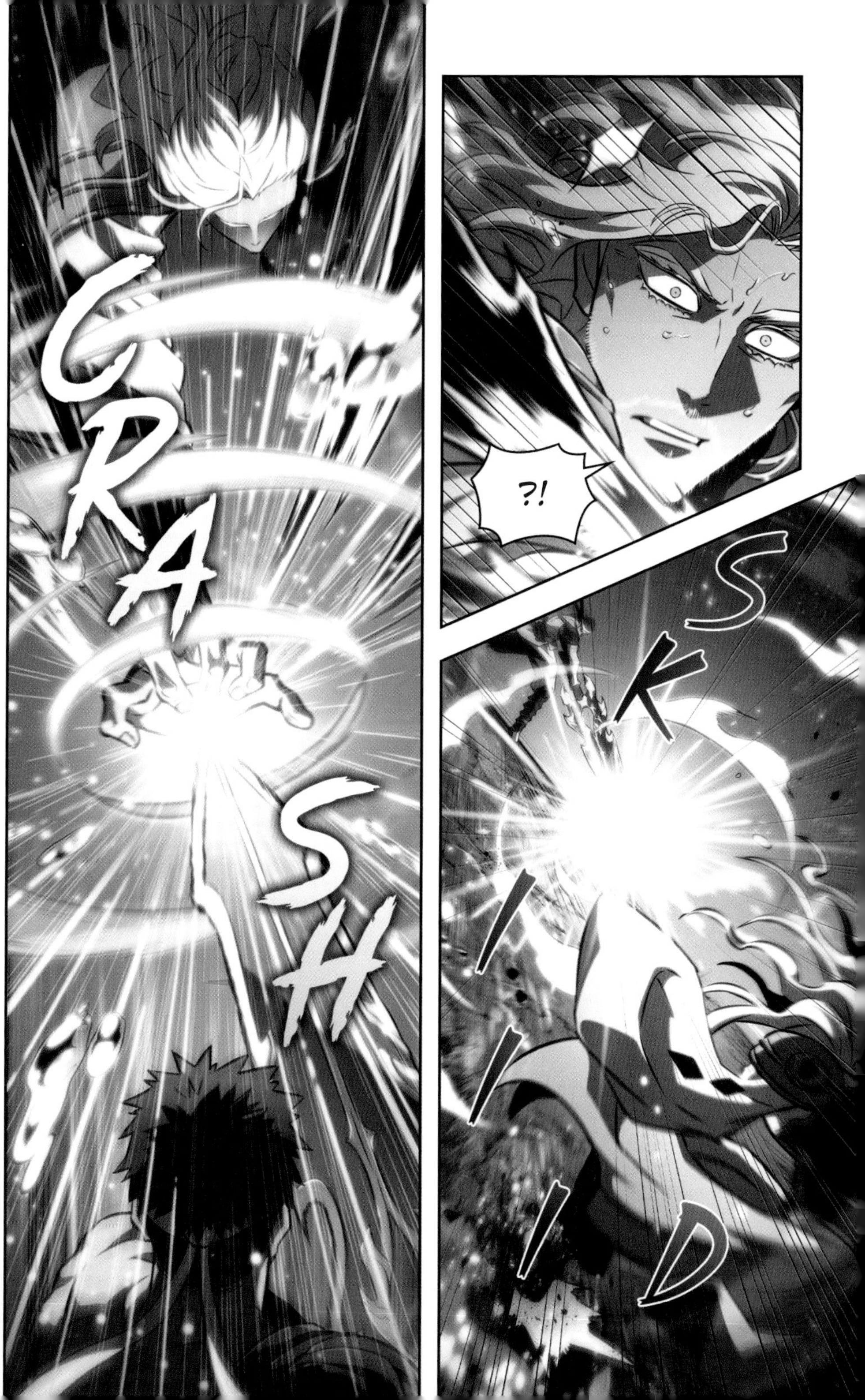
CRASH
?!
SKIIID

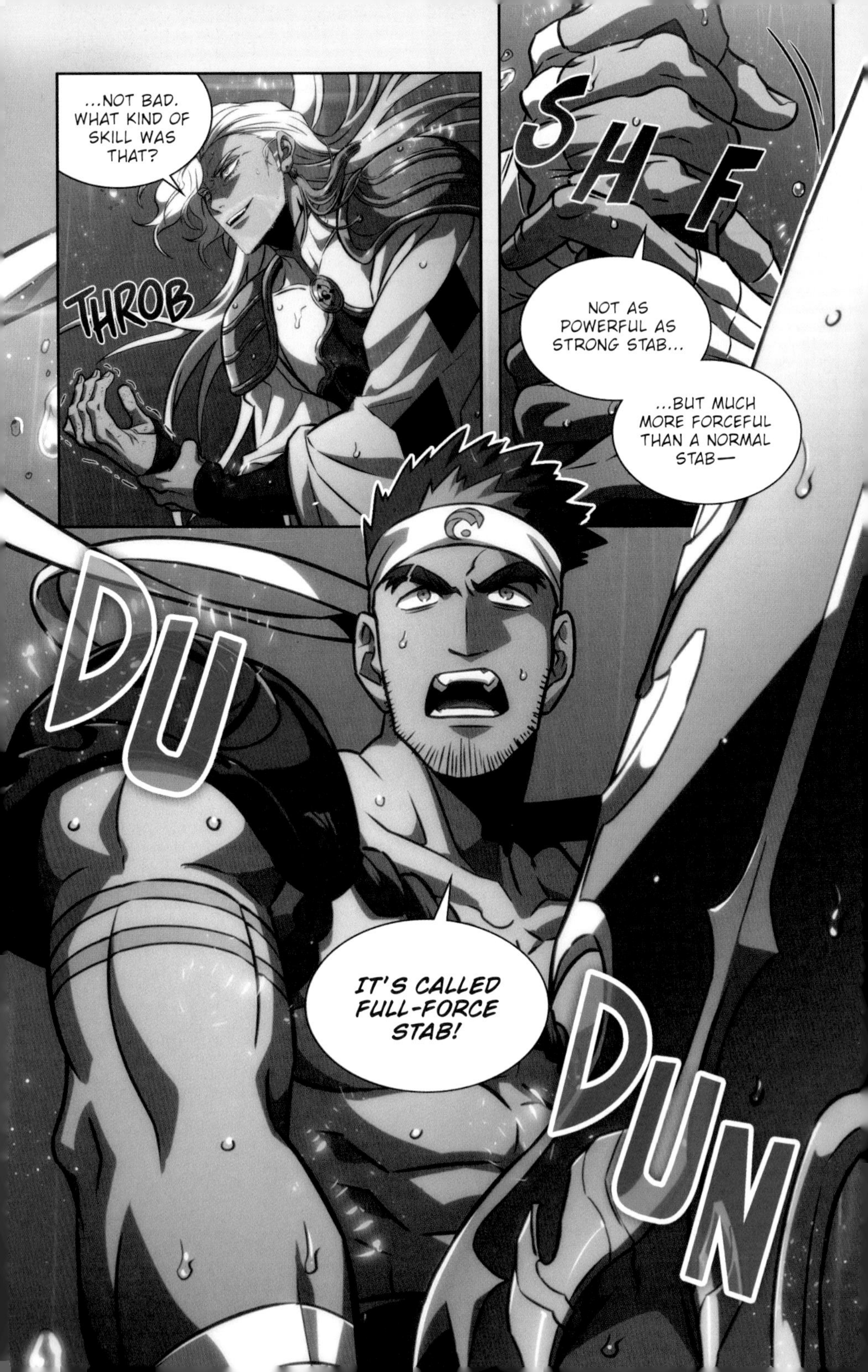
...NOT BAD. WHAT KIND OF SKILL WAS THAT?
THROB
SHF
NOT AS POWERFUL AS STRONG STAB...
...BUT MUCH MORE FORCEFUL THAN A NORMAL STAB—
DU
IT'S CALLED FULL-FORCE STAB!
DUN

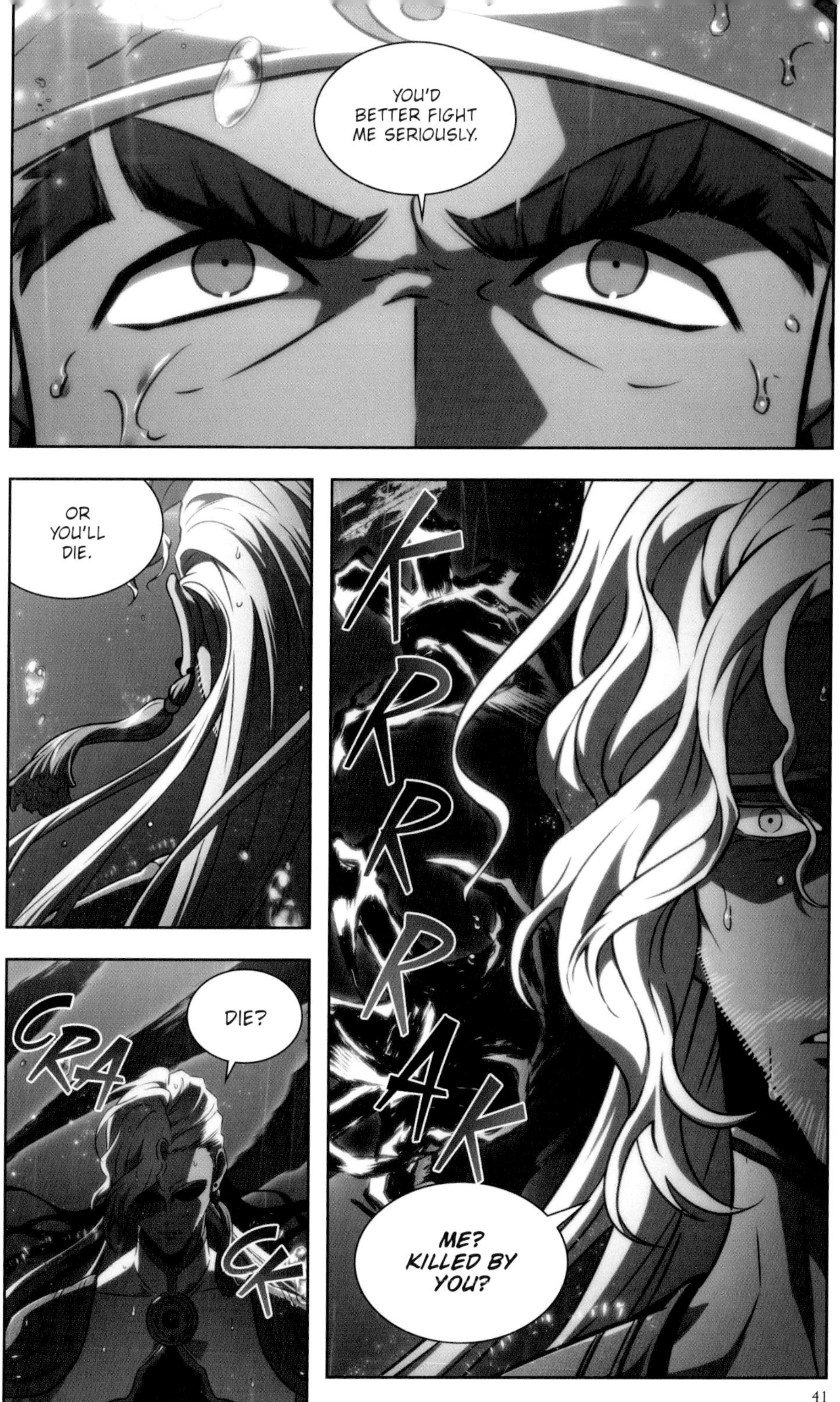
YOU'D BETTER FIGHT ME SERIOUSLY.
OR YOU'LL DIE.
KRRRRAK
CRA
DIE?
CK
ME? KILLED BY YOU?

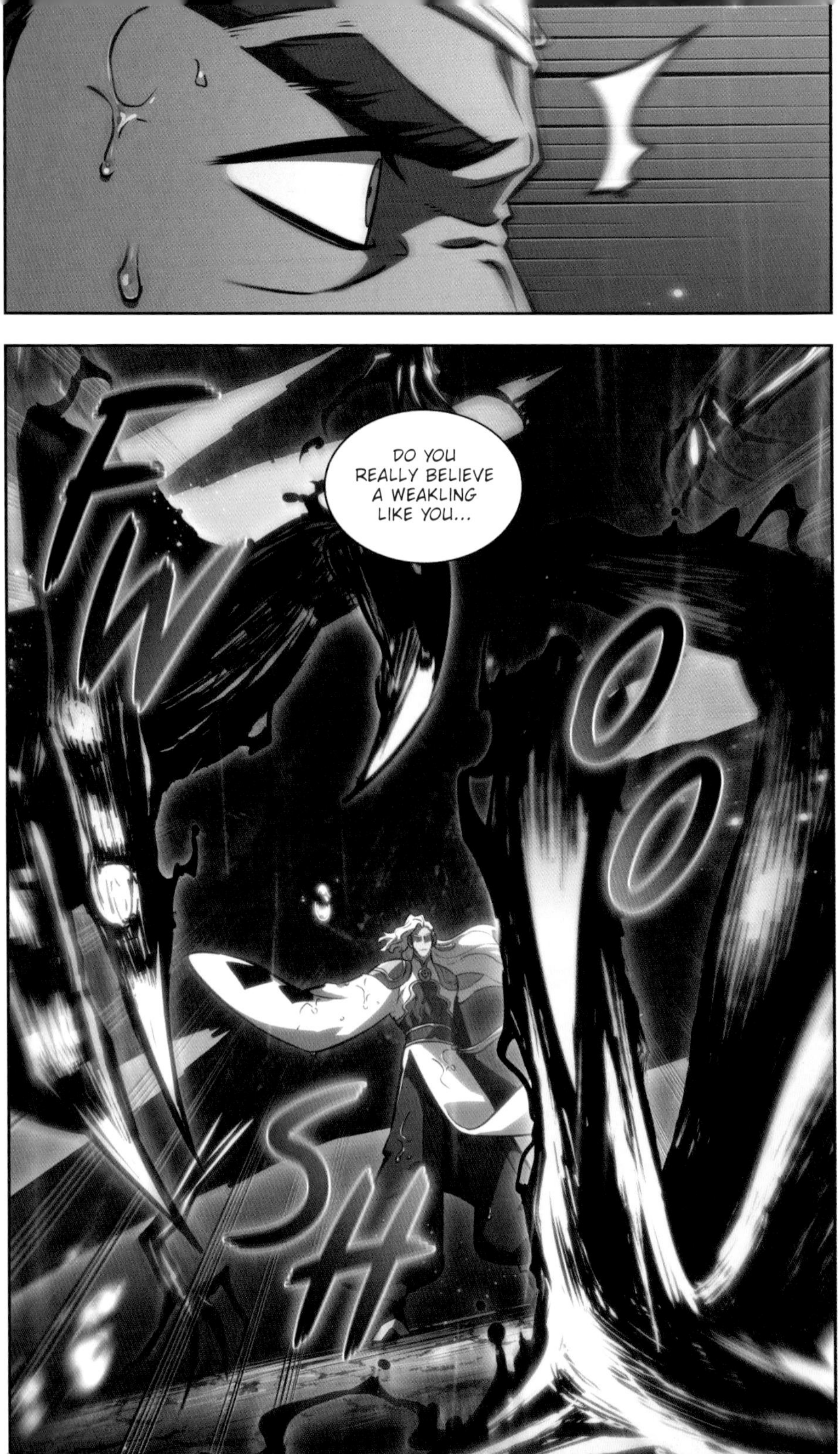
DO YOU REALLY BELIEVE A WEAKLING LIKE YOU...
FWOOOSH

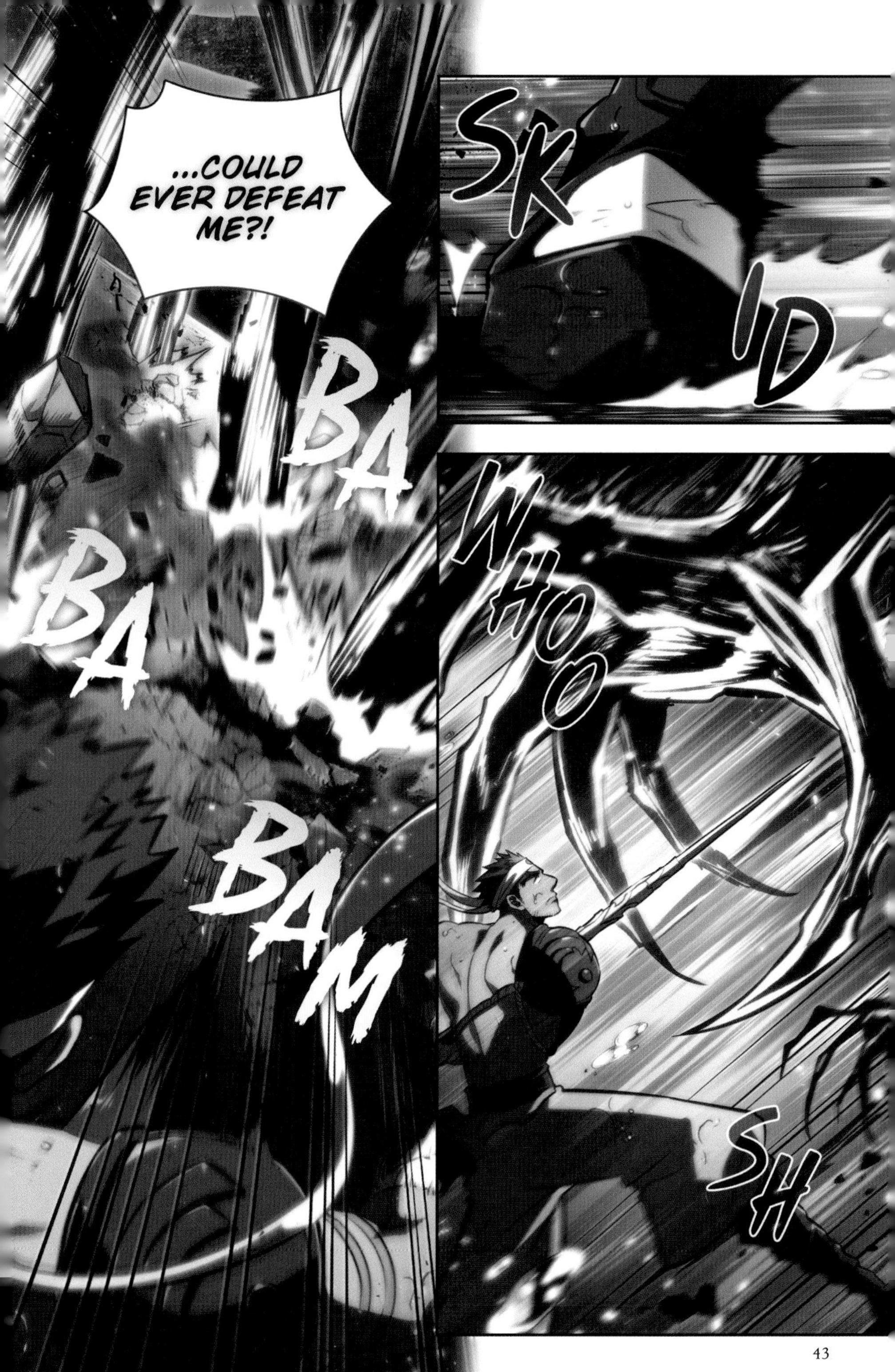
...COULD EVER DEFEAT ME?!
BA
BA
BAM
SKID
WHOO
SH

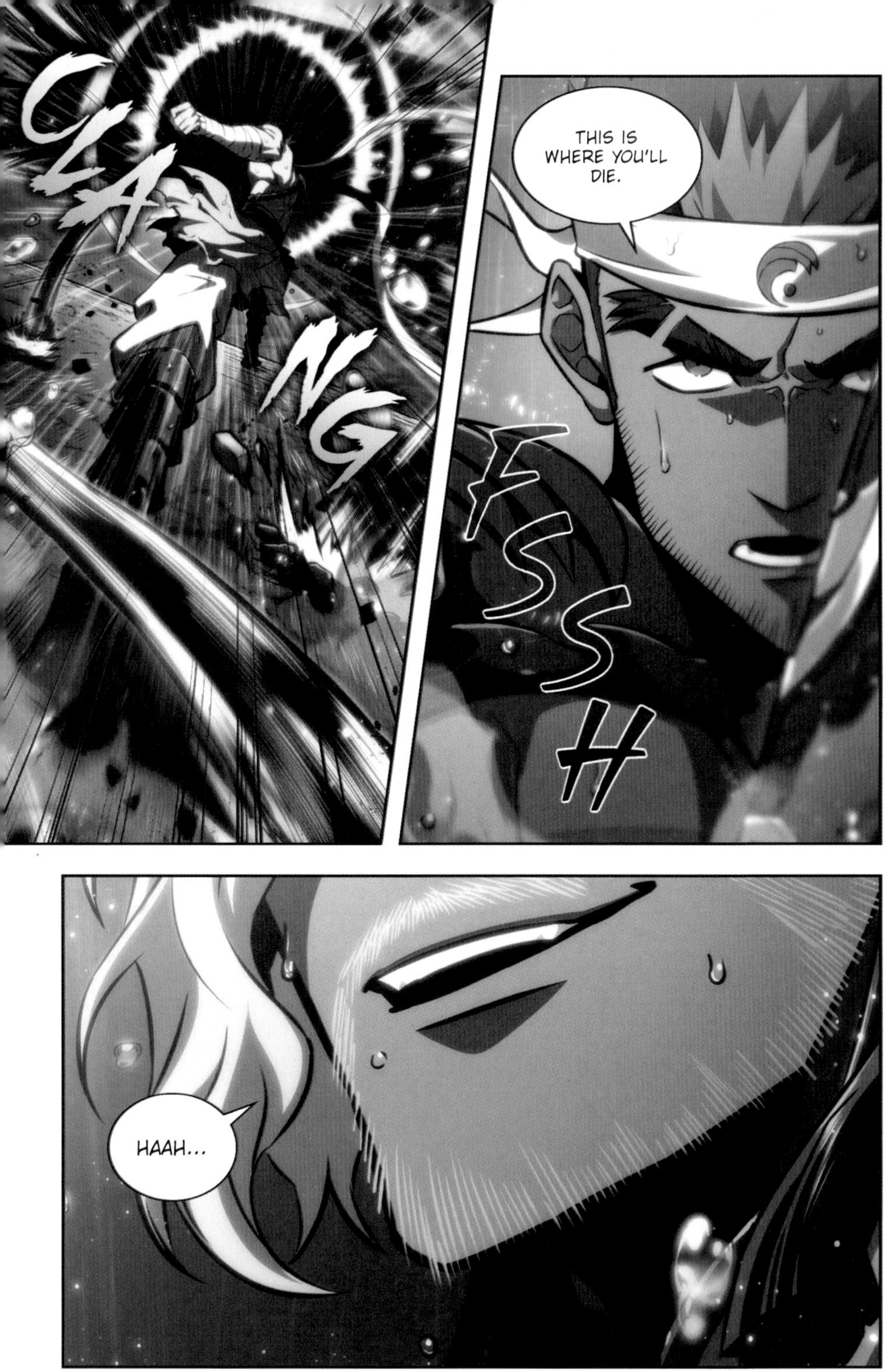
CLANG
THIS IS WHERE YOU'LL DIE.
FSSSH
HAAH...

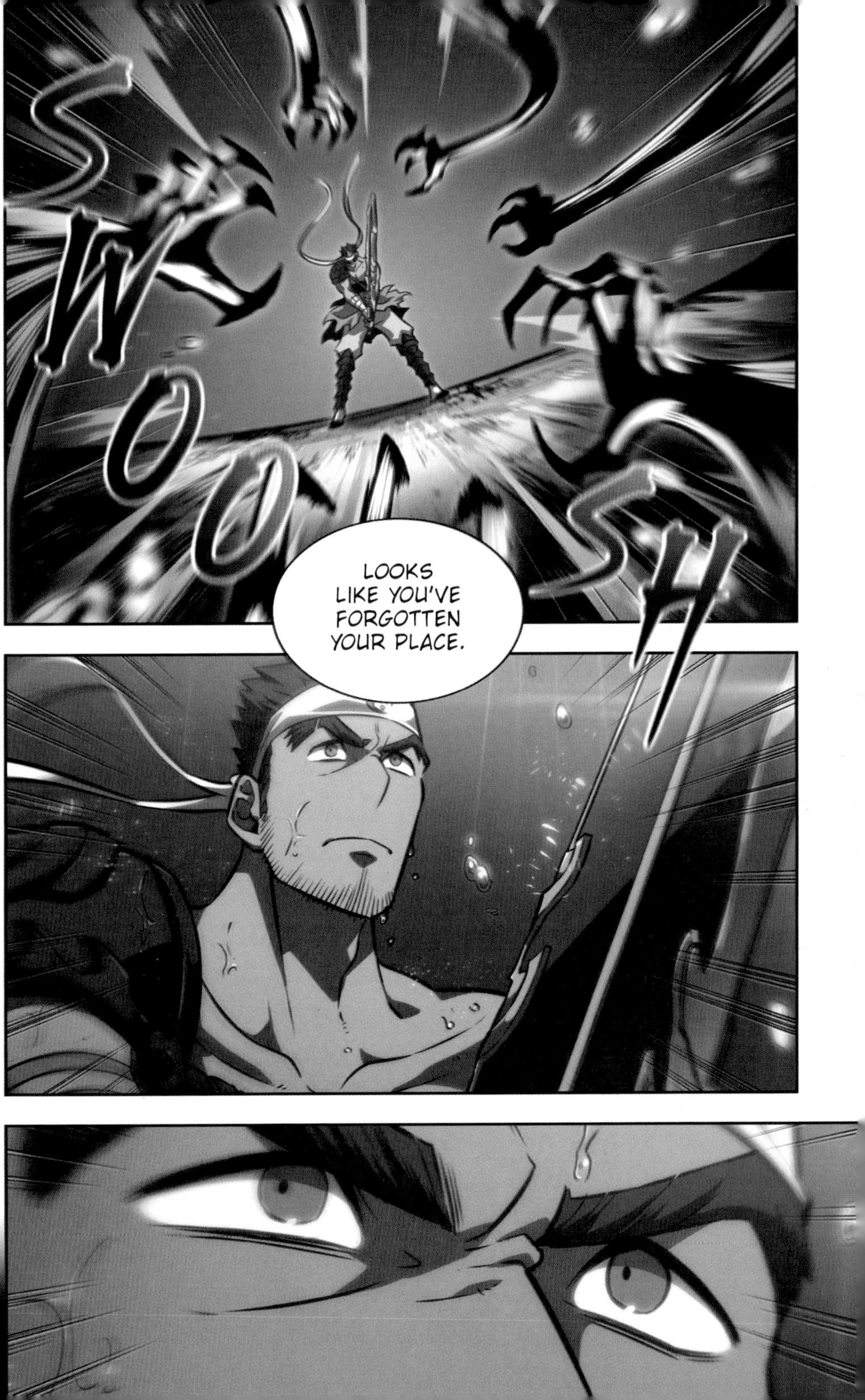
SWOOOSH
LOOKS LIKE YOU'VE FORGOTTEN YOUR PLACE.

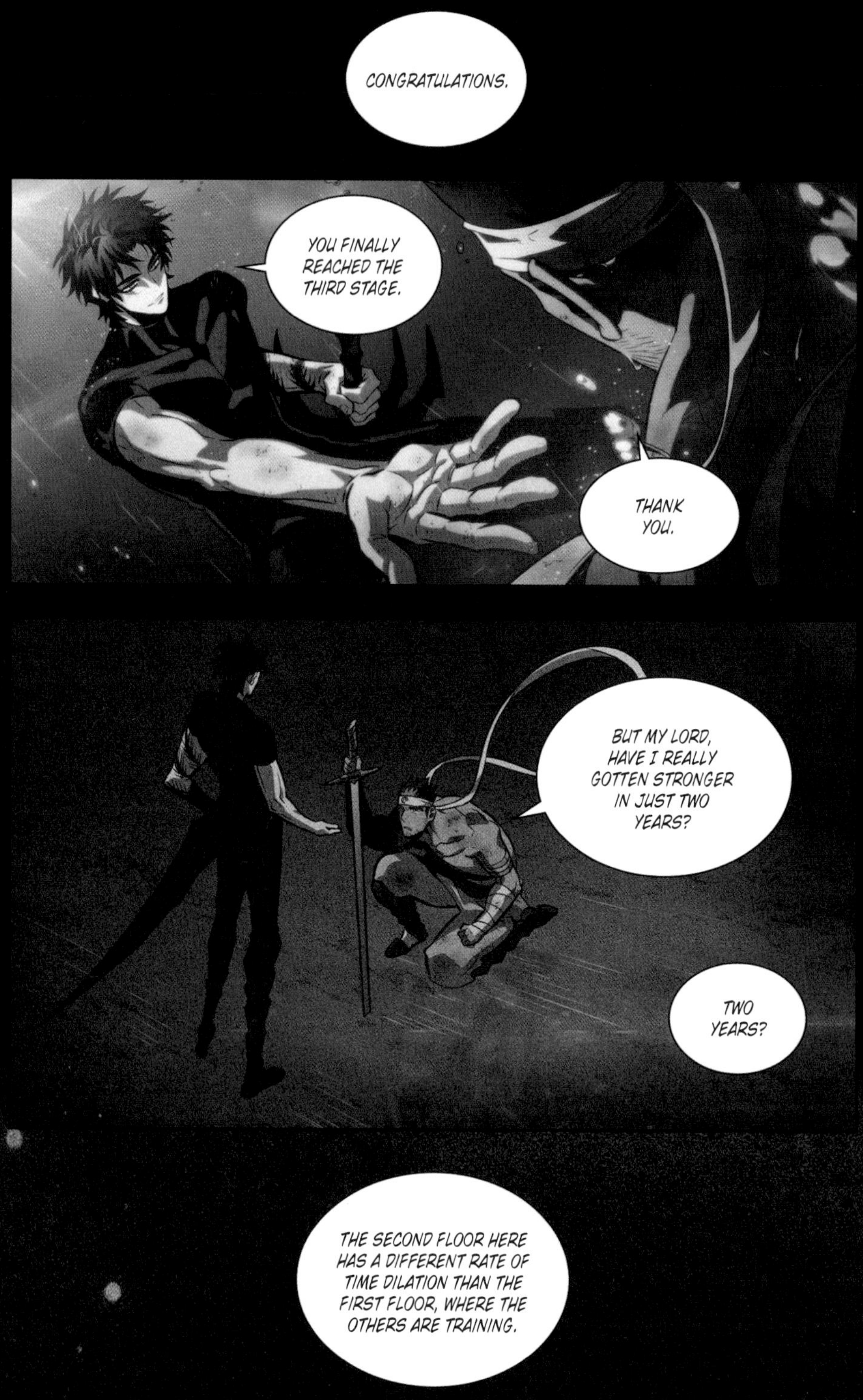
CONGRATULATIONS.
YOU FINALLY REACHED THE THIRD STAGE.
THANK YOU.
BUT MY LORD, HAVE I REALLY GOTTEN STRONGER IN JUST TWO YEARS?
TWO YEARS?
THE SECOND FLOOR HERE HAS A DIFFERENT RATE OF TIME DILATION THAN THE FIRST FLOOR, WHERE THE OTHERS ARE TRAINING.

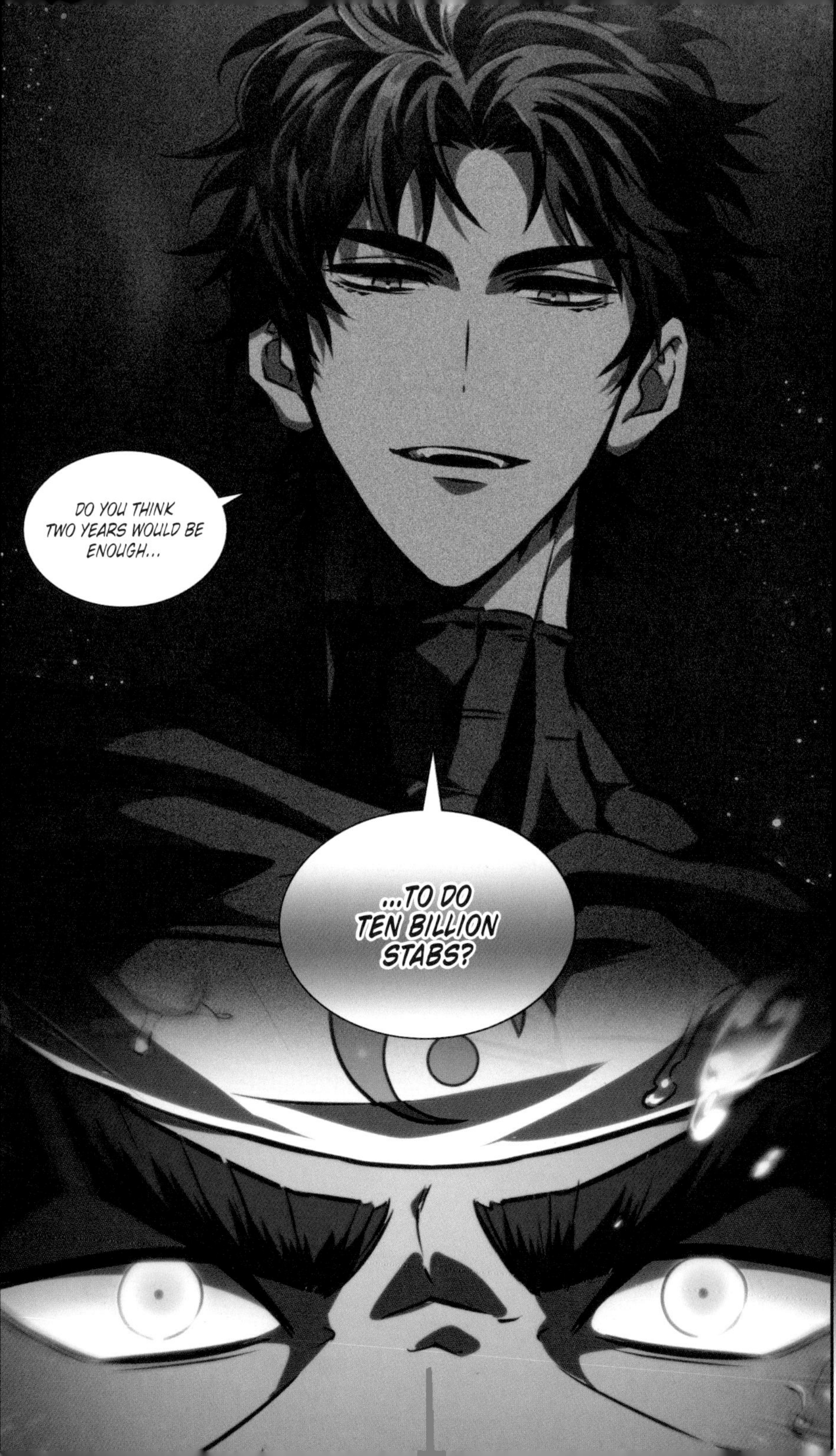
DO YOU THINK TWO YEARS WOULD BE ENOUGH...
...TO DO TEN BILLION STABS?

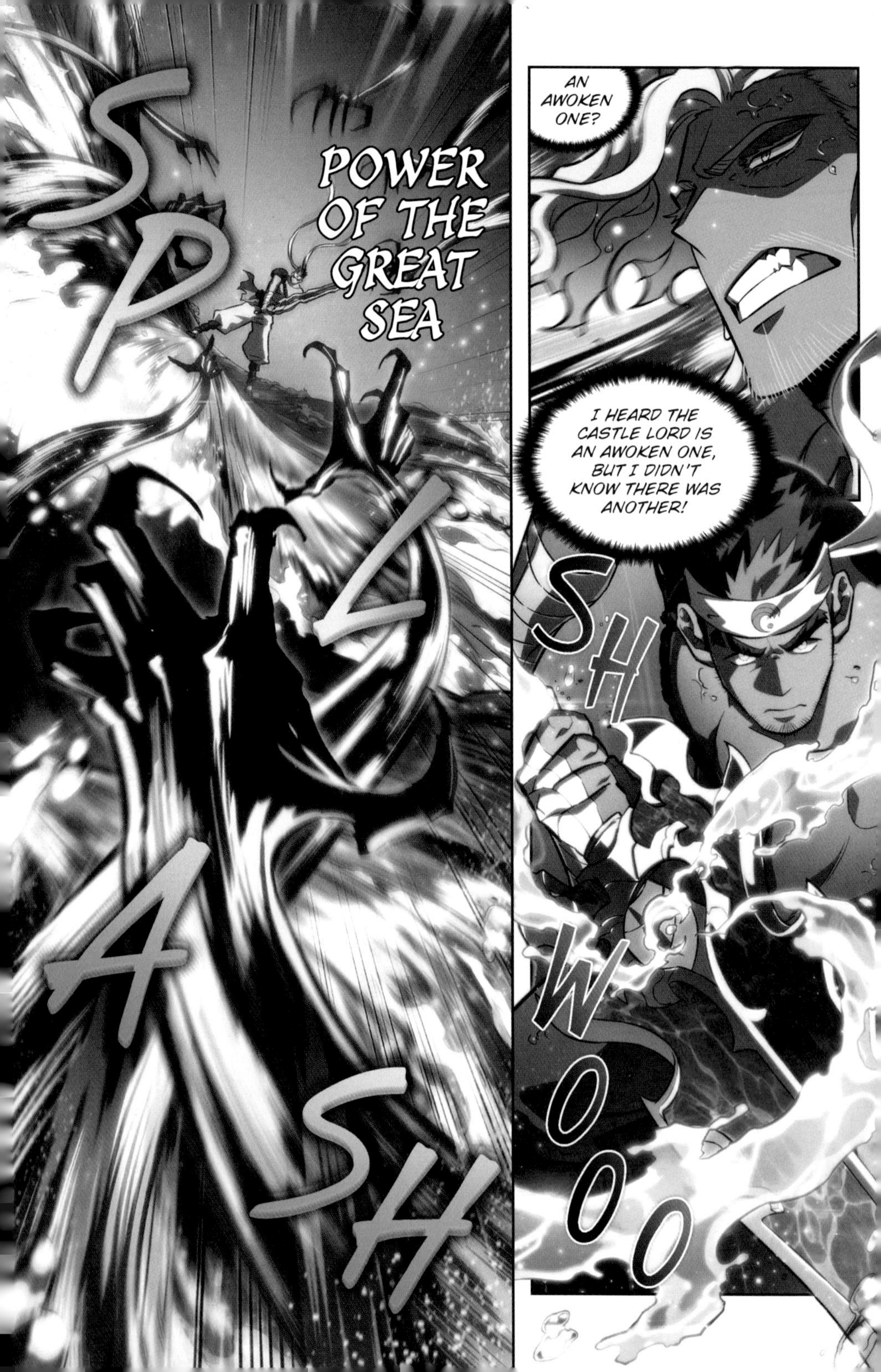
SPLASH
POWER OF THE GREAT SEA
AN AWOKEN ONE?
I HEARD THE CASTLE LORD IS AN AWOKEN ONE, BUT I DIDN'T KNOW THERE WAS ANOTHER!
SHWOOO

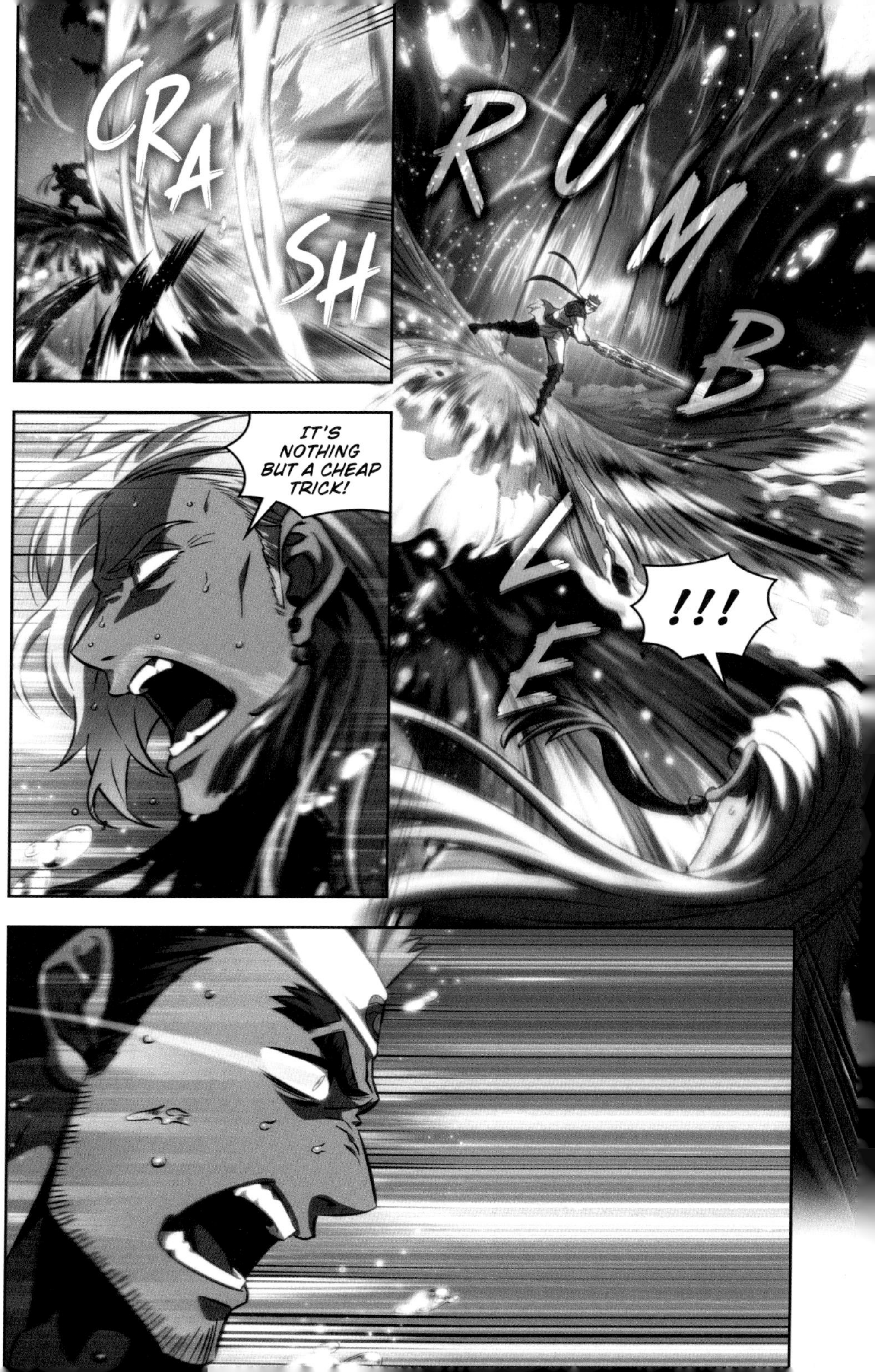
CRASH
RUMBLE
IT'S NOTHING BUT A CHEAP TRICK!
!!!

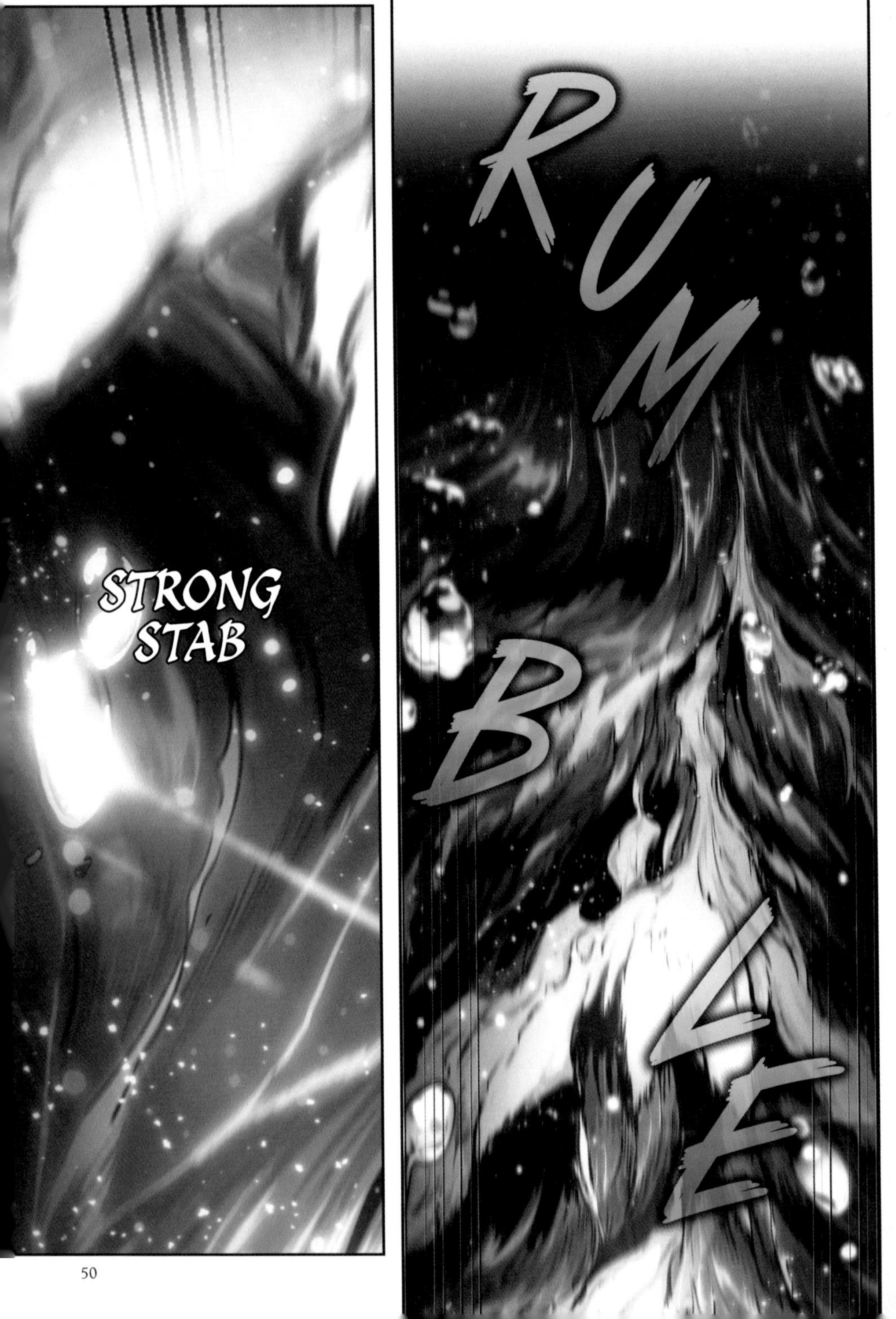
STRONG STAB
RUMBLE

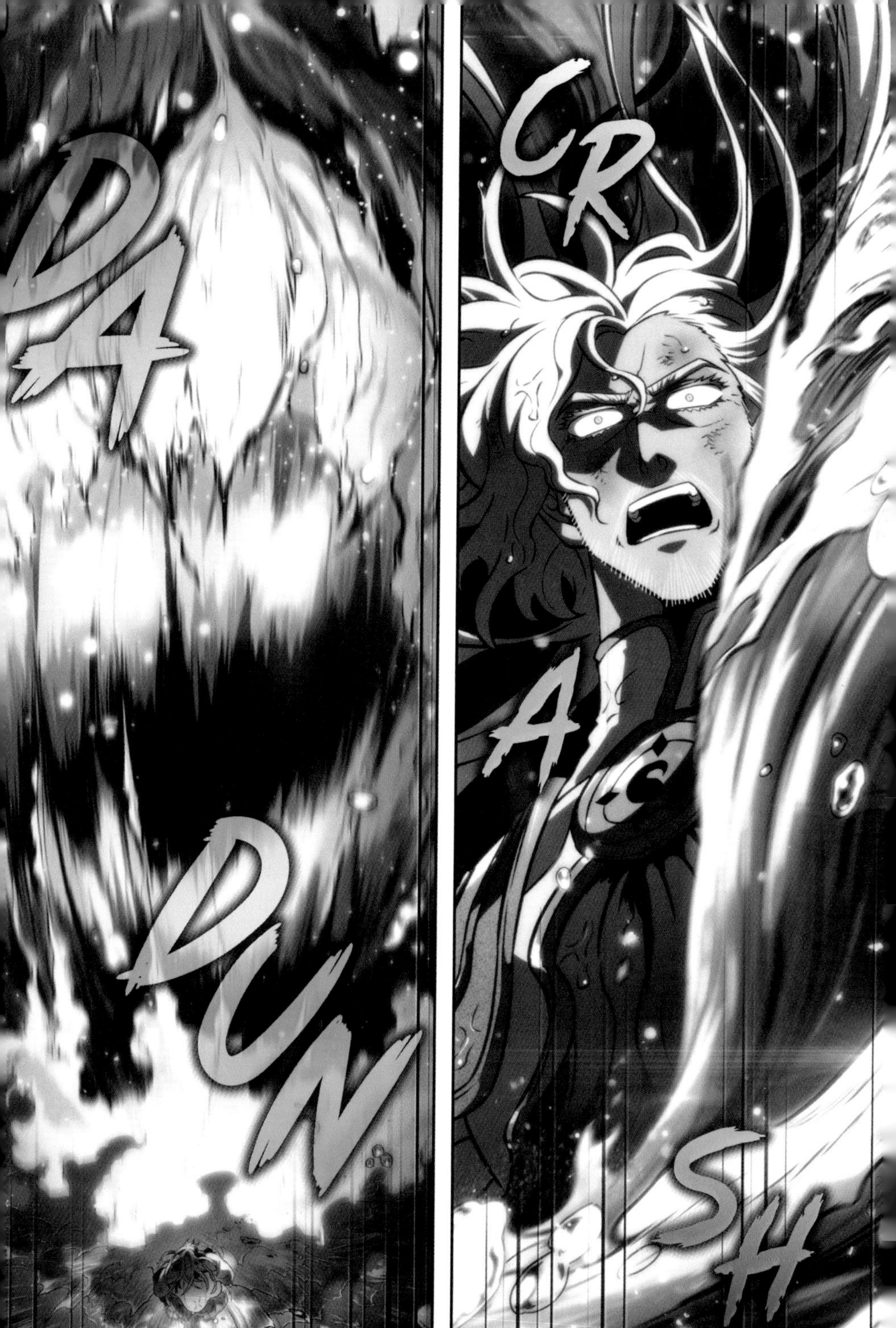
CRASH
DA DUN

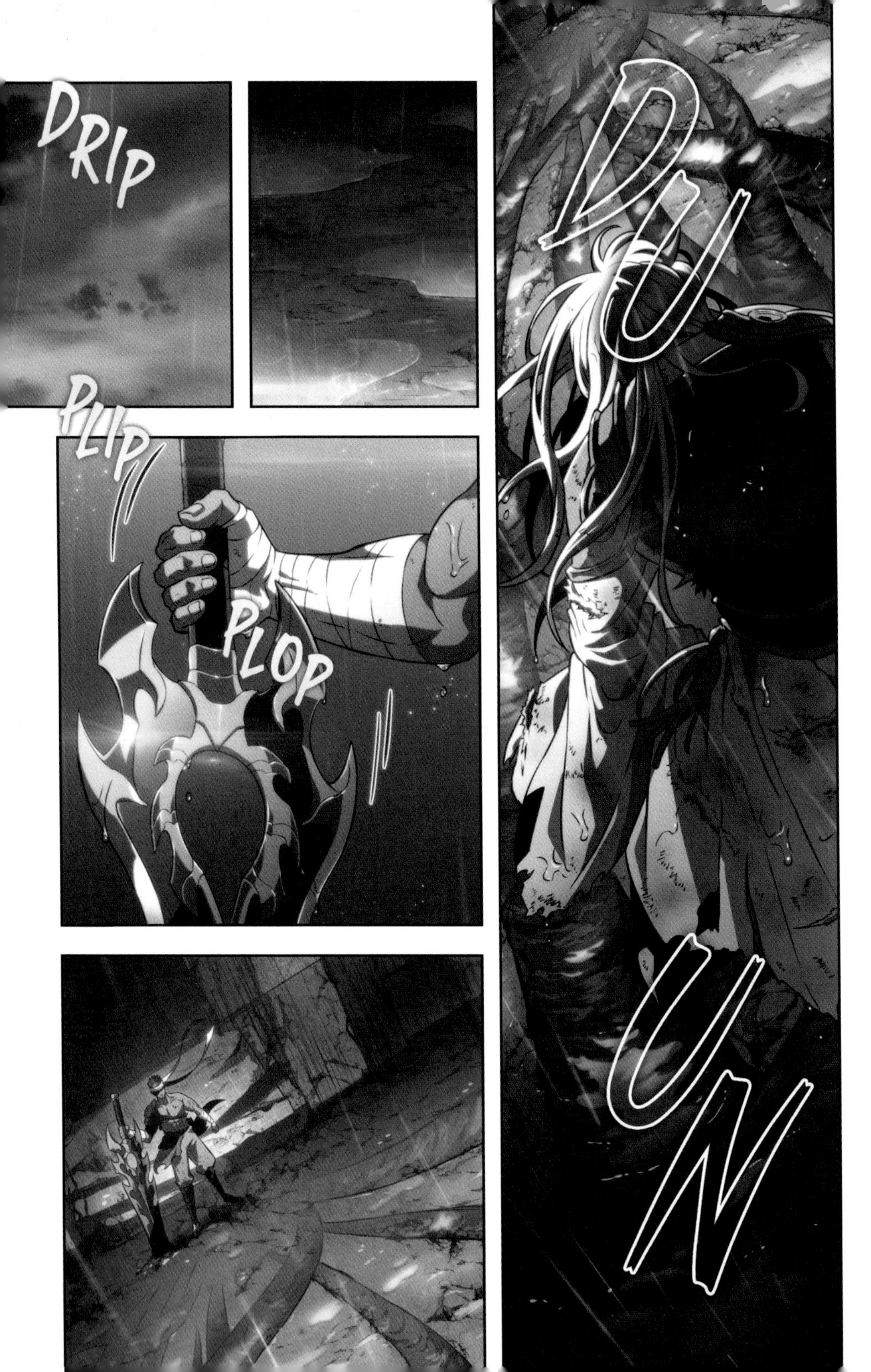
DRIP
PLIP
PLOP
DUUUN

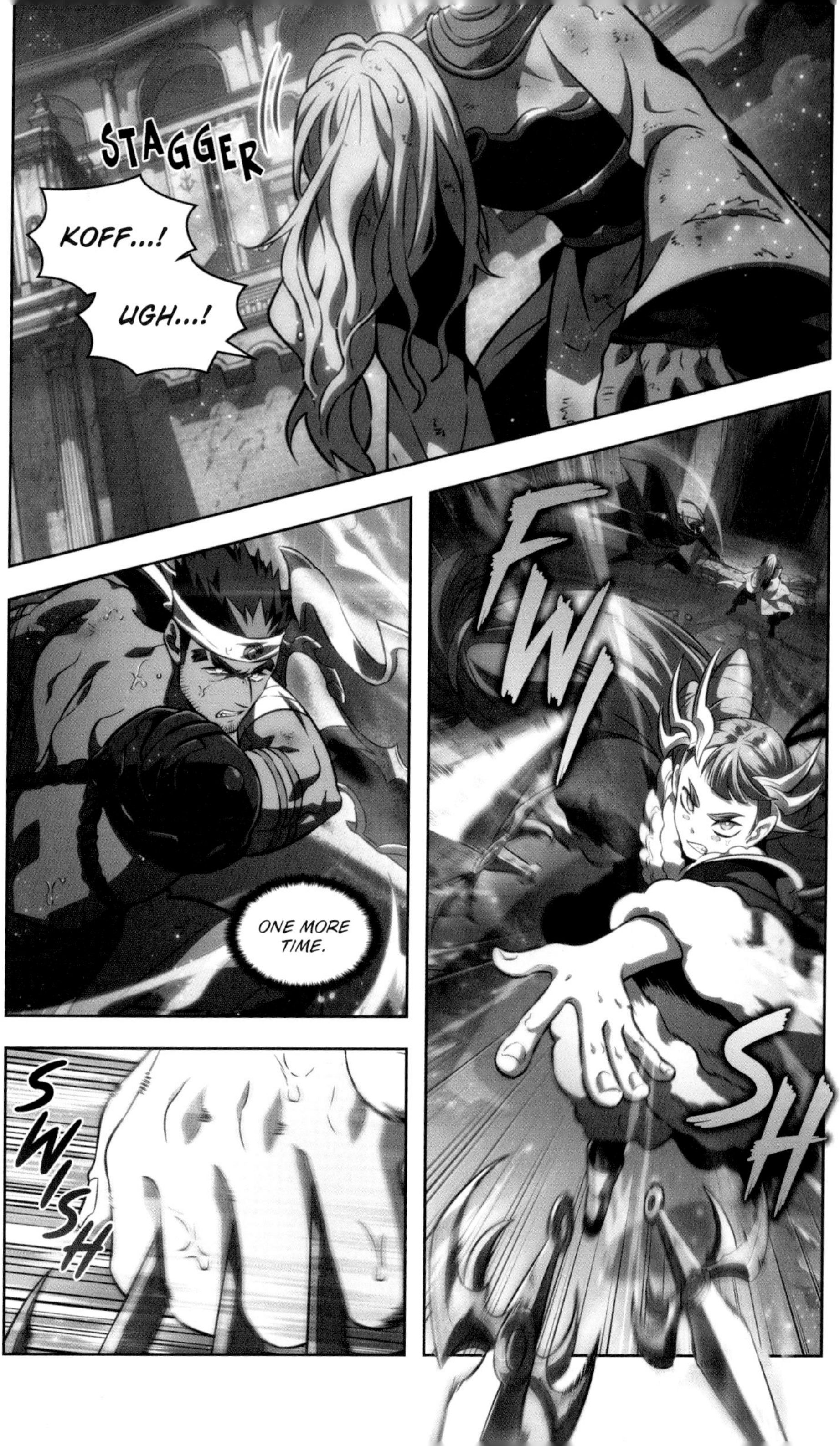
STAGGER
KOFF...!
UGH...!
FWI
ONE MORE TIME.
SH
SWISH

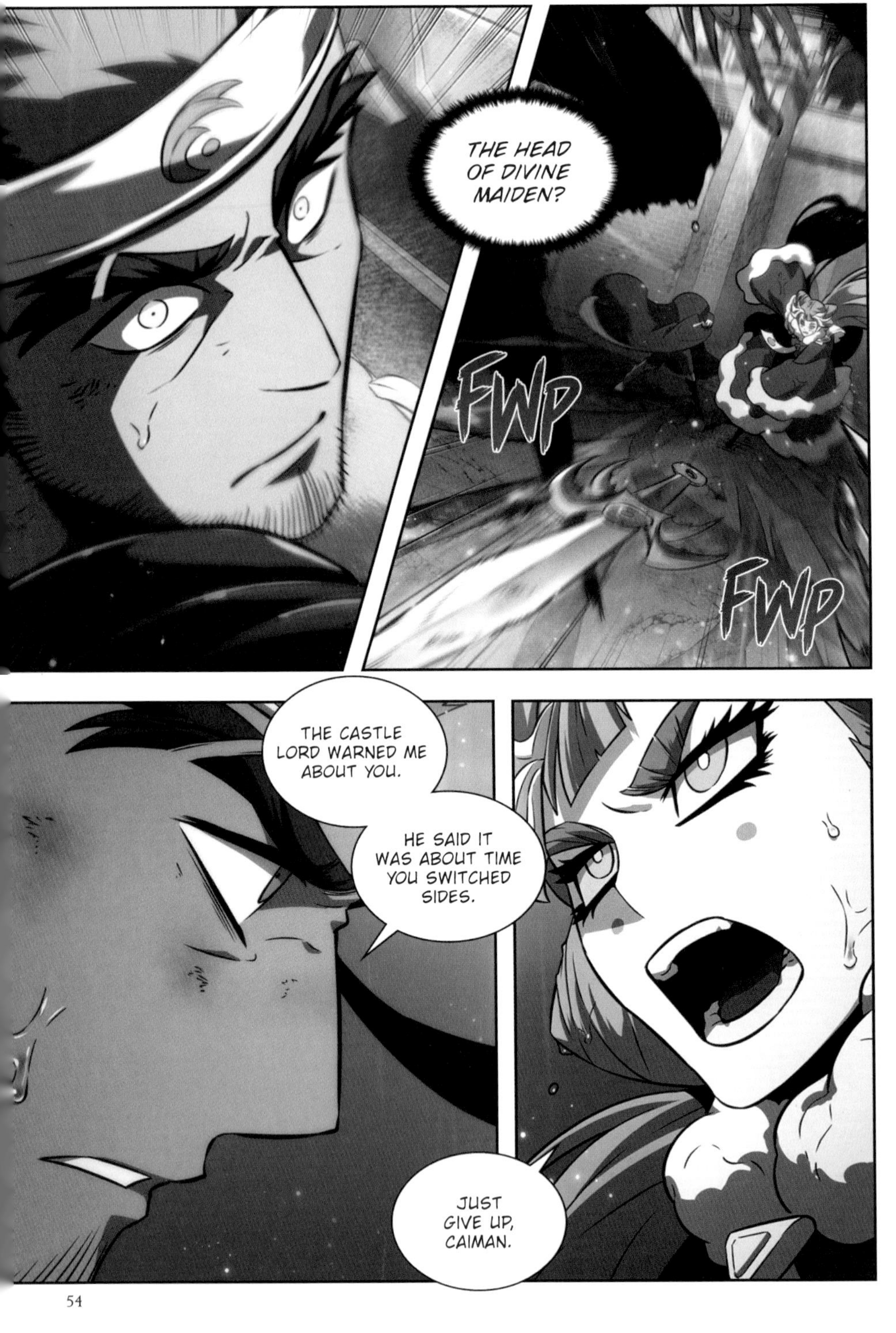
THE HEAD OF DIVINE MAIDEN?
FWP
FWP
THE CASTLE LORD WARNED ME ABOUT YOU.
HE SAID IT WAS ABOUT TIME YOU SWITCHED SIDES.
JUST GIVE UP, CAIMAN.

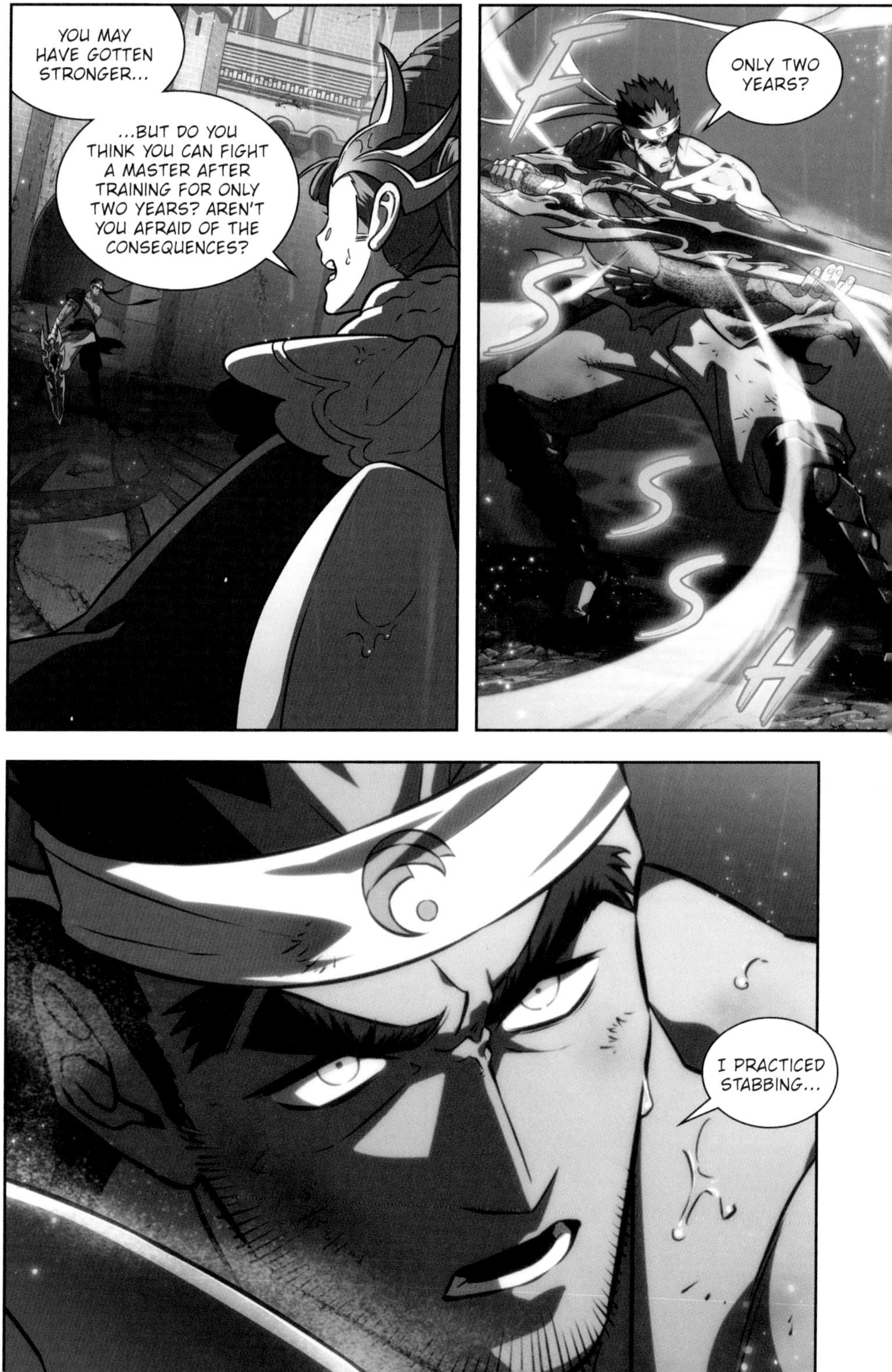

YOU MAY HAVE GOTTEN STRONGER...
...BUT DO YOU THINK YOU CAN FIGHT A MASTER AFTER TRAINING FOR ONLY TWO YEARS? AREN'T YOU AFRAID OF THE CONSEQUENCES?
ONLY TWO YEARS?
FSSSH
I PRACTICED STABBING...

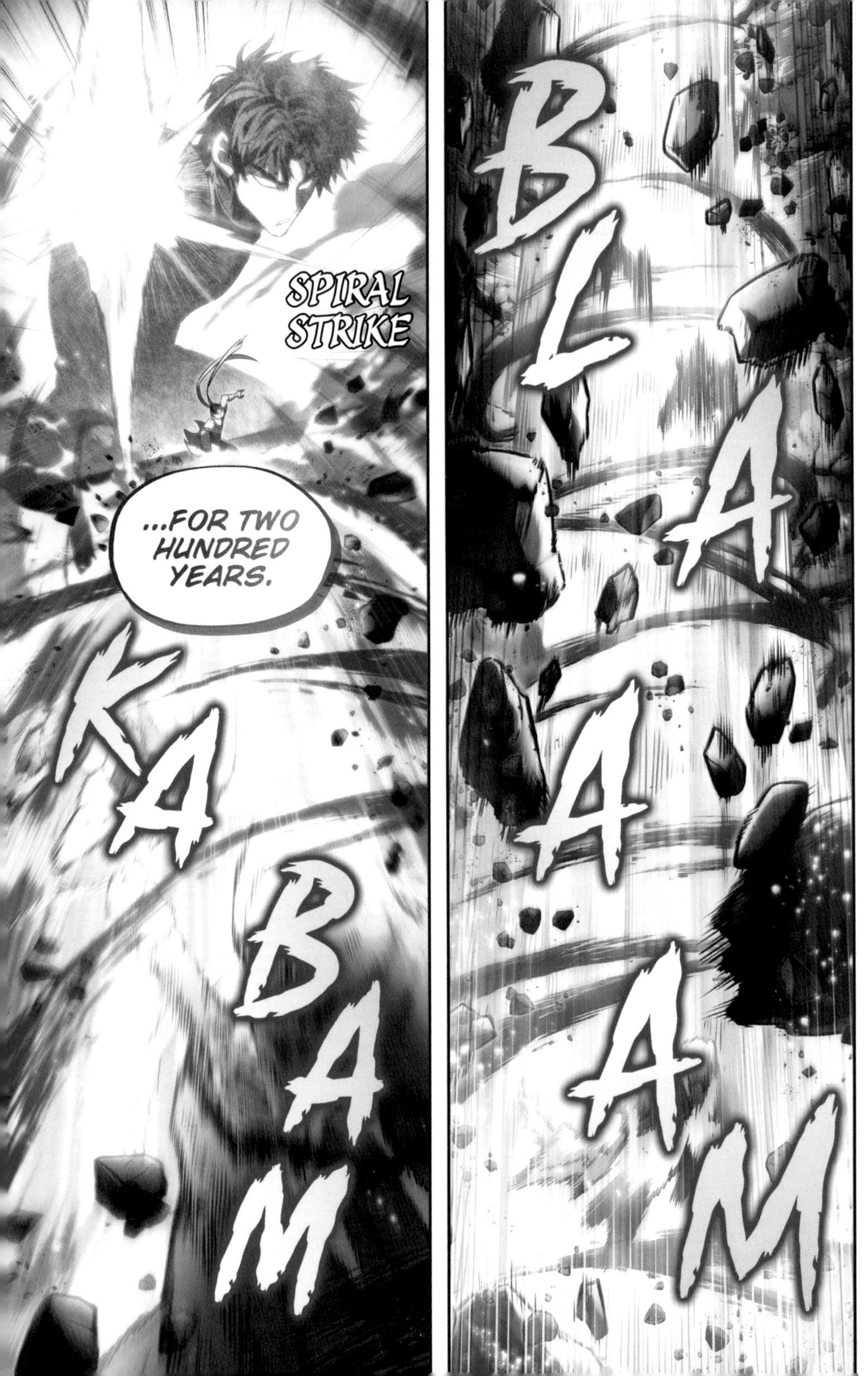
BLAAAM
SPIRAL STRIKE
...FOR TWO HUNDRED YEARS.
KABAM

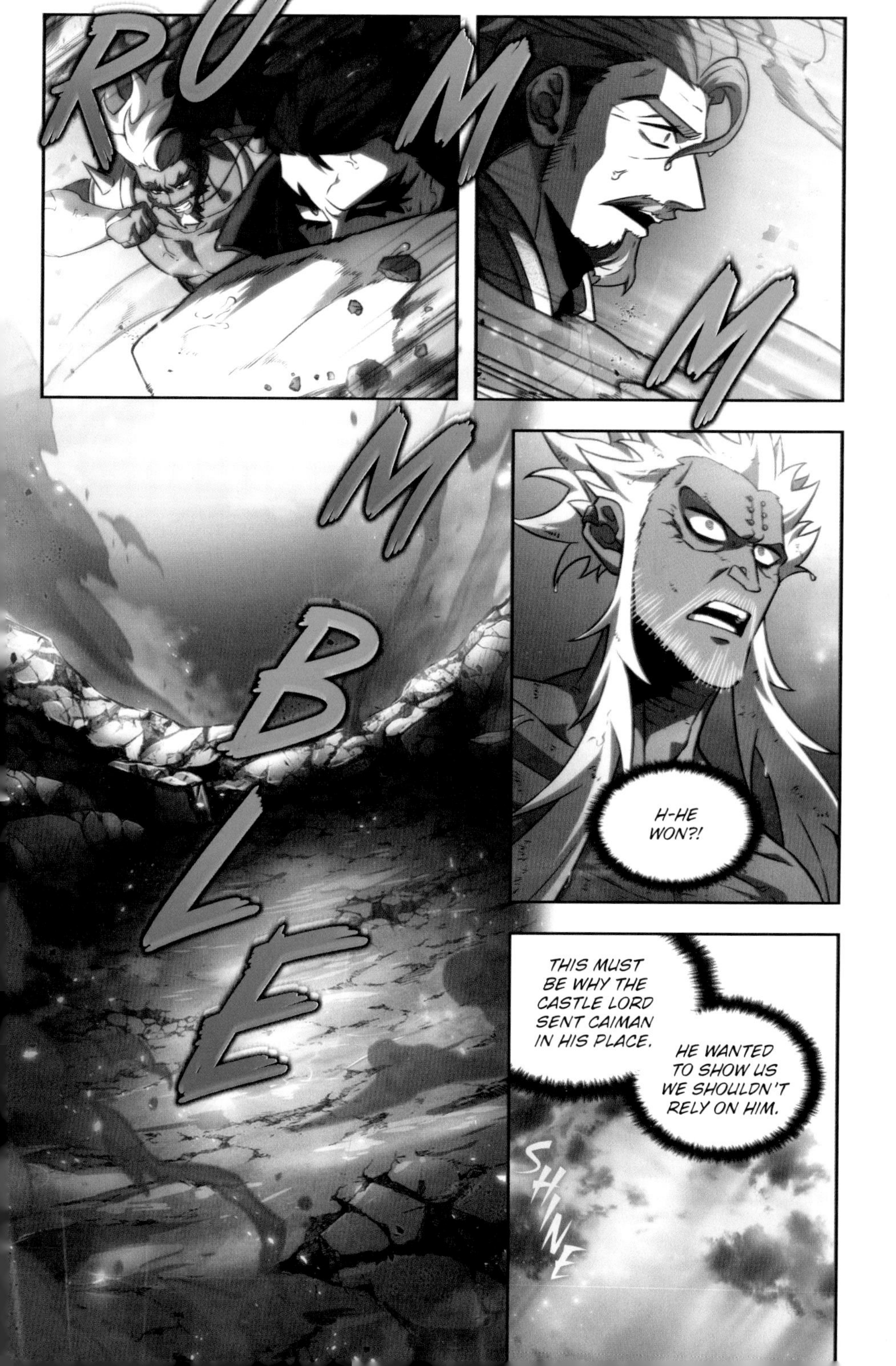
RUMMMBLE
H-HE WON?!
THIS MUST BE WHY THE CASTLE LORD SENT CAIMAN IN HIS PLACE.
HE WANTED TO SHOW US WE SHOULDN'T RELY ON HIM.
SHINE

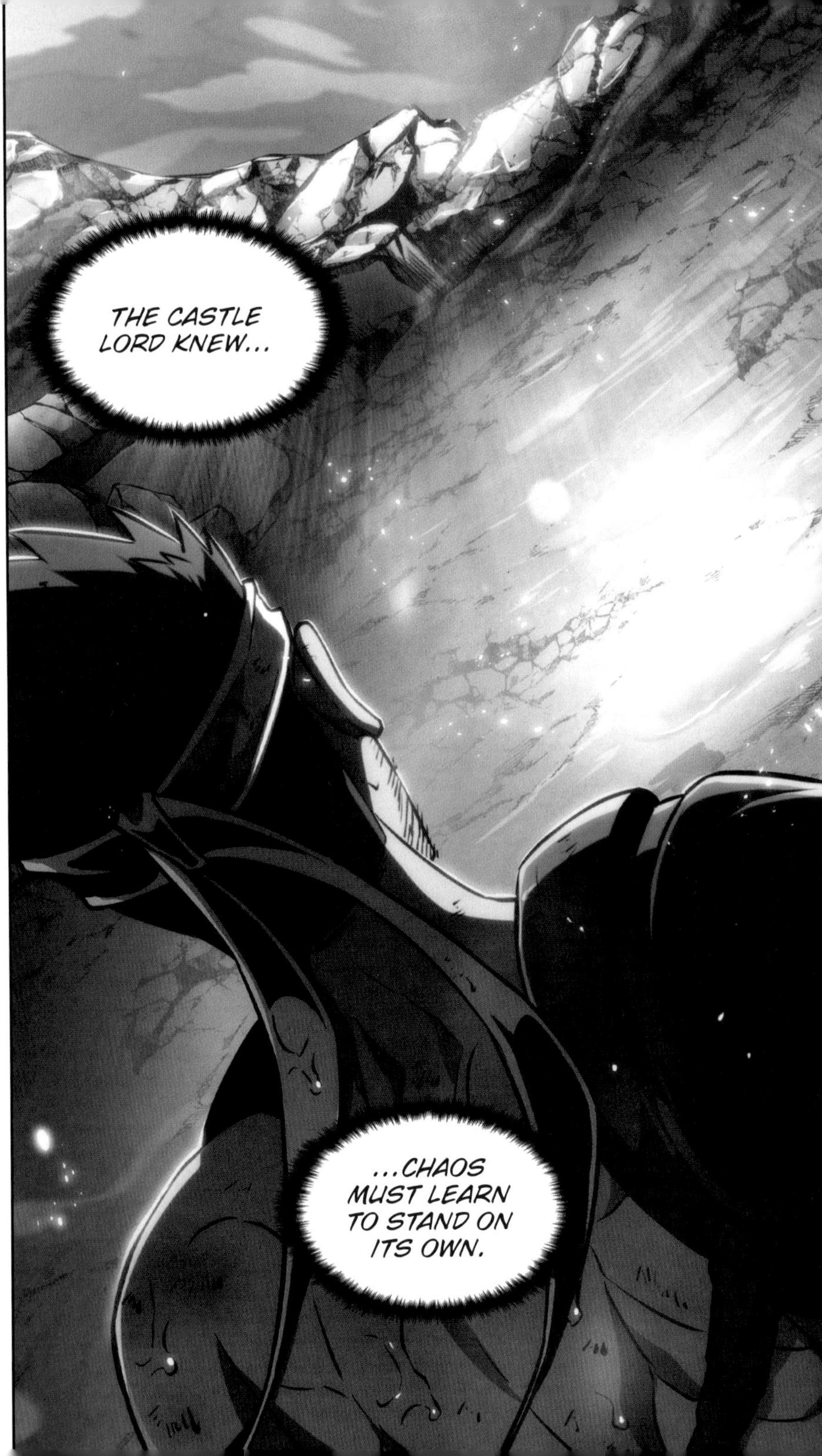
THE CASTLE LORD KNEW...
...CHAOS MUST LEARN TO STAND ON ITS OWN.

The World After the Fall

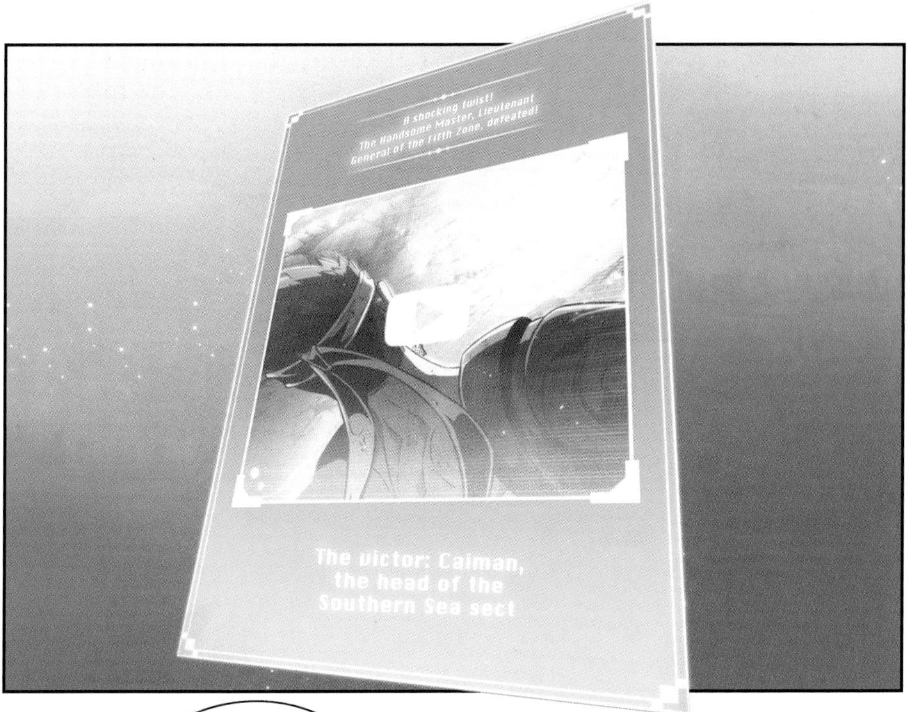
A shocking twist!
The Handsome Master, Lieutenant General of the Fifth Zone, defeated!
The victor: Caiman, the head of the Southern Sea sect

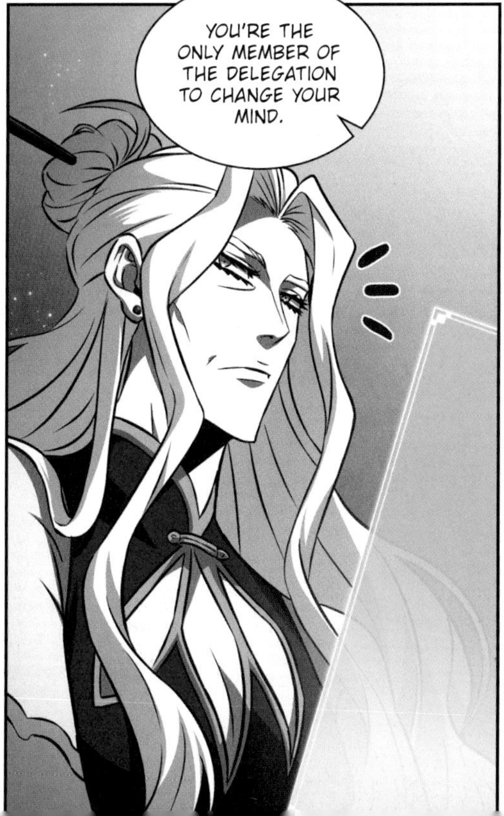
YOU'RE THE ONLY MEMBER OF THE DELEGATION TO CHANGE YOUR MIND.

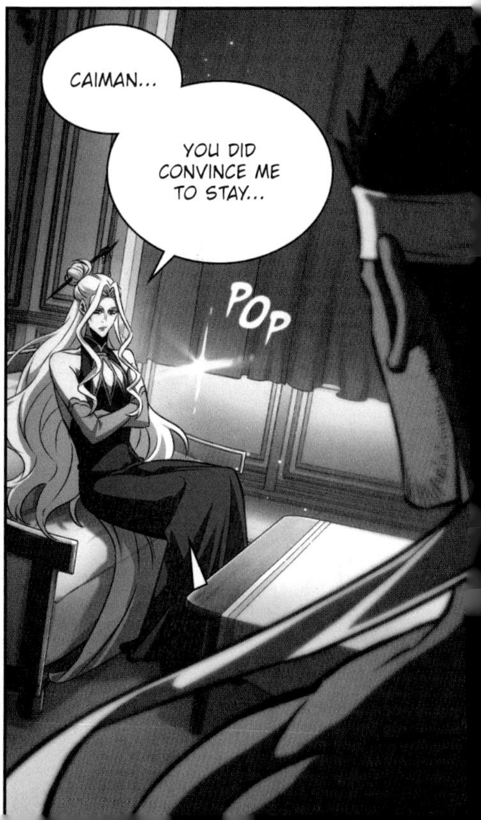
CAIMAN...
YOU DID CONVINCE ME TO STAY...
POP

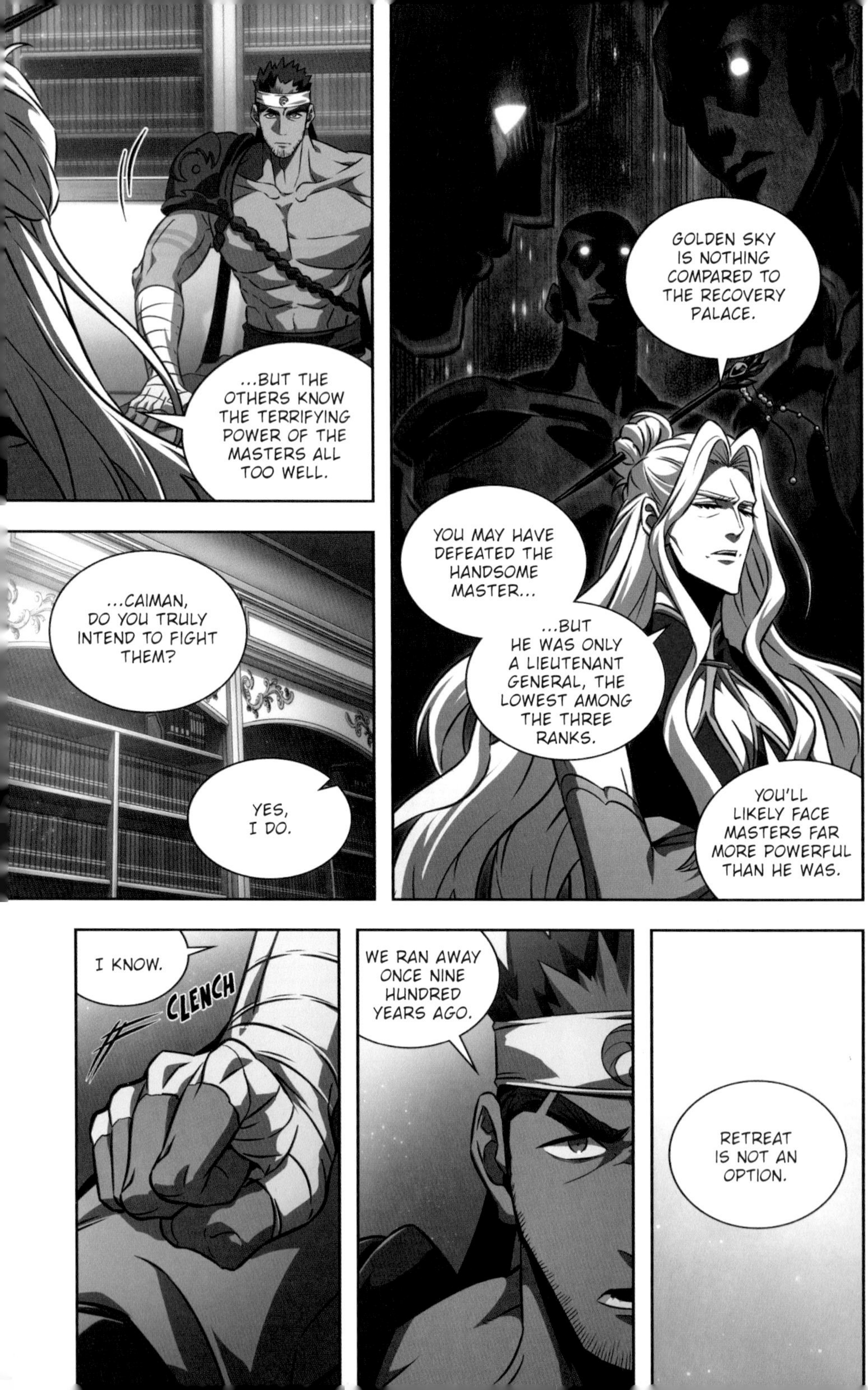
...BUT THE OTHERS KNOW THE TERRIFYING POWER OF THE MASTERS ALL TOO WELL.
GOLDEN SKY IS NOTHING COMPARED TO THE RECOVERY PALACE.
...CAIMAN, DO YOU TRULY INTEND TO FIGHT THEM?
YES, I DO.
YOU MAY HAVE DEFEATED THE HANDSOME MASTER...
...BUT HE WAS ONLY A LIEUTENANT GENERAL, THE LOWEST AMONG THE THREE RANKS.
YOU'LL LIKELY FACE MASTERS FAR MORE POWERFUL THAN HE WAS.
I KNOW.
CLENCH
WE RAN AWAY ONCE NINE HUNDRED YEARS AGO.
RETREAT IS NOT AN OPTION.

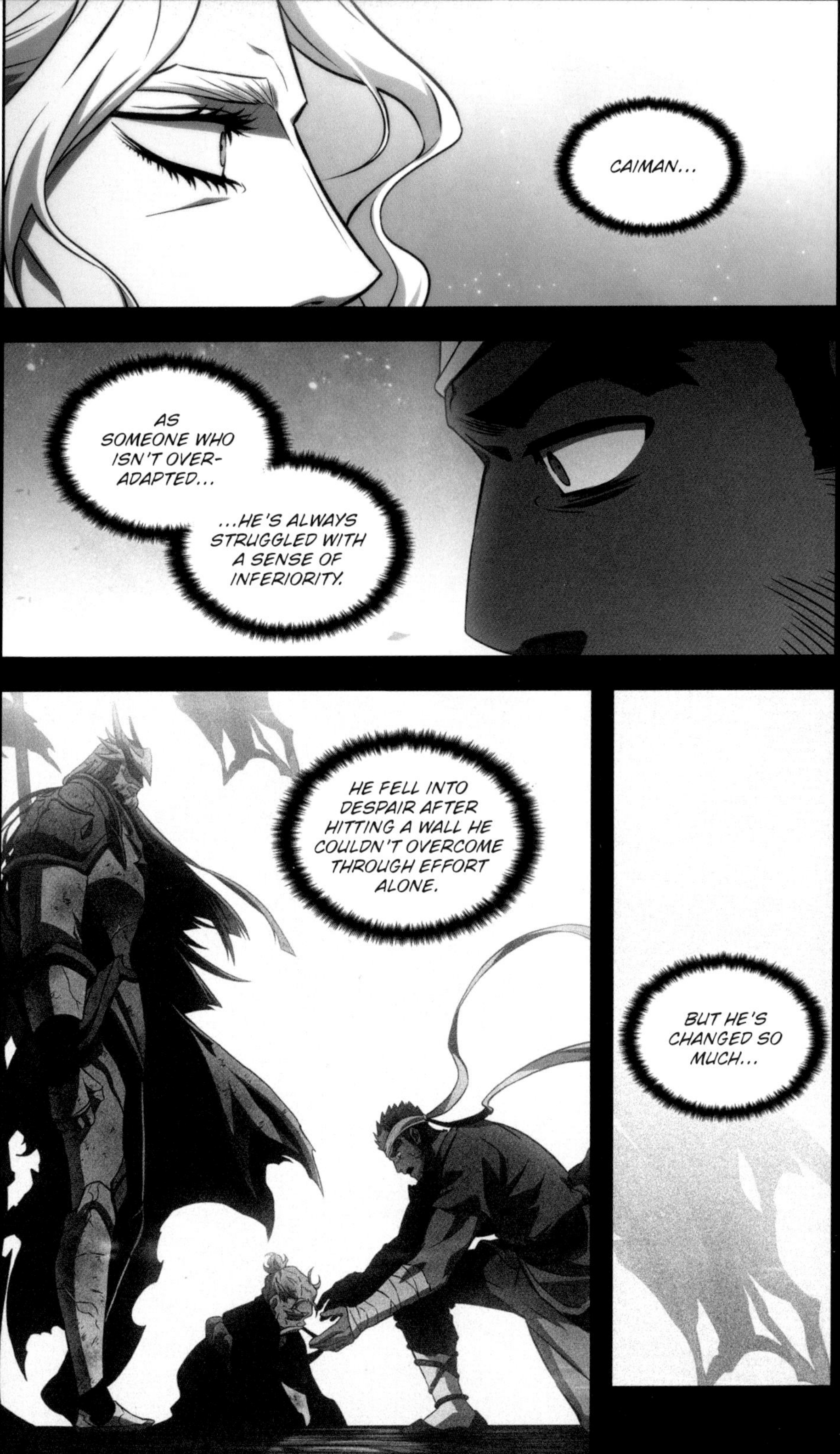
CAIMAN...
AS SOMEONE WHO ISN'T OVER-ADAPTED...
...HE'S ALWAYS STRUGGLED WITH A SENSE OF INFERIORITY.
HE FELL INTO DESPAIR AFTER HITTING A WALL HE COULDN'T OVERCOME THROUGH EFFORT ALONE.
BUT HE'S CHANGED SO MUCH...

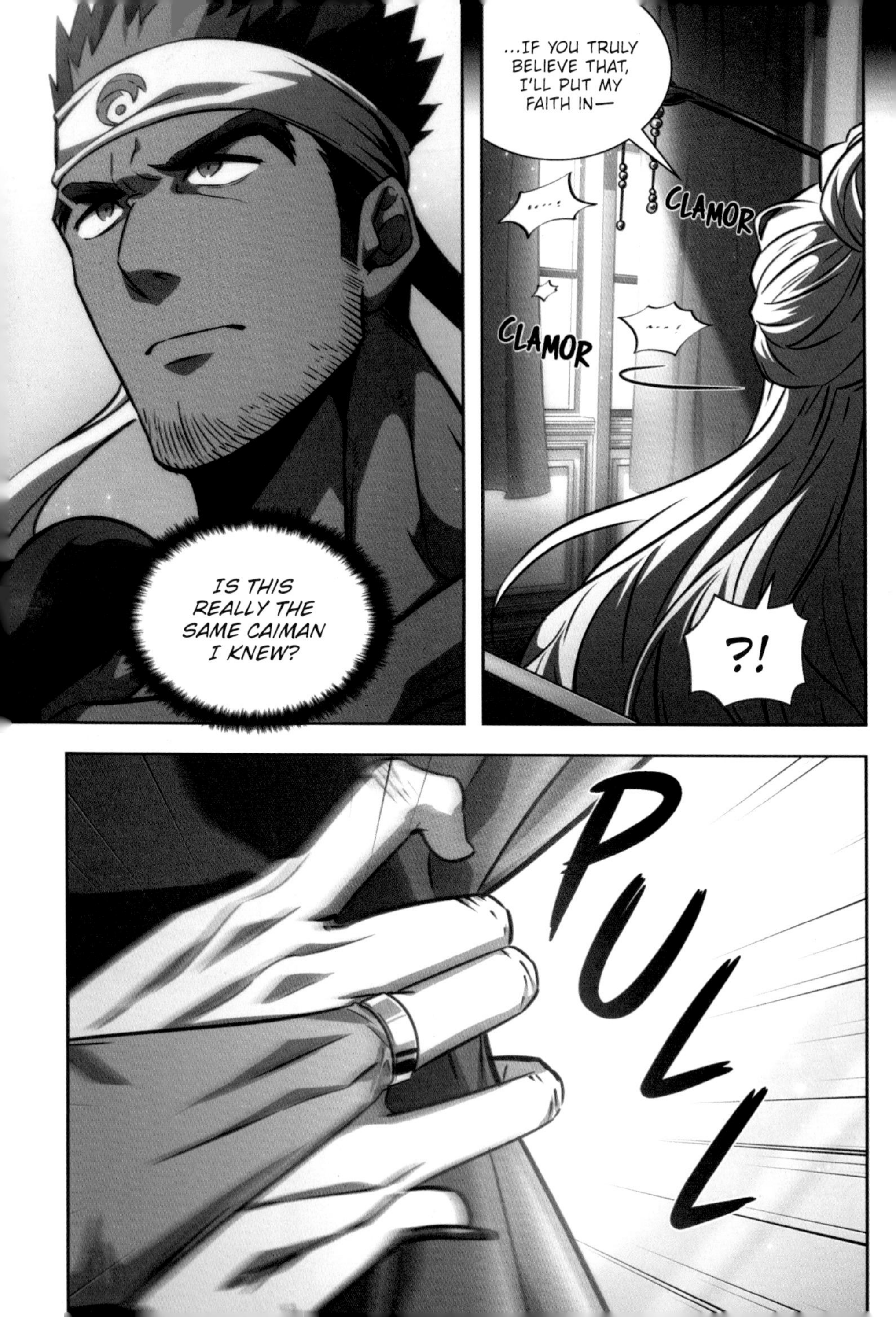
IS THIS REALLY THE SAME CAIMAN I KNEW?
...IF YOU TRULY BELIEVE THAT, I'LL PUT MY FAITH IN—
CLAMOR
CLAMOR
?!
PULL

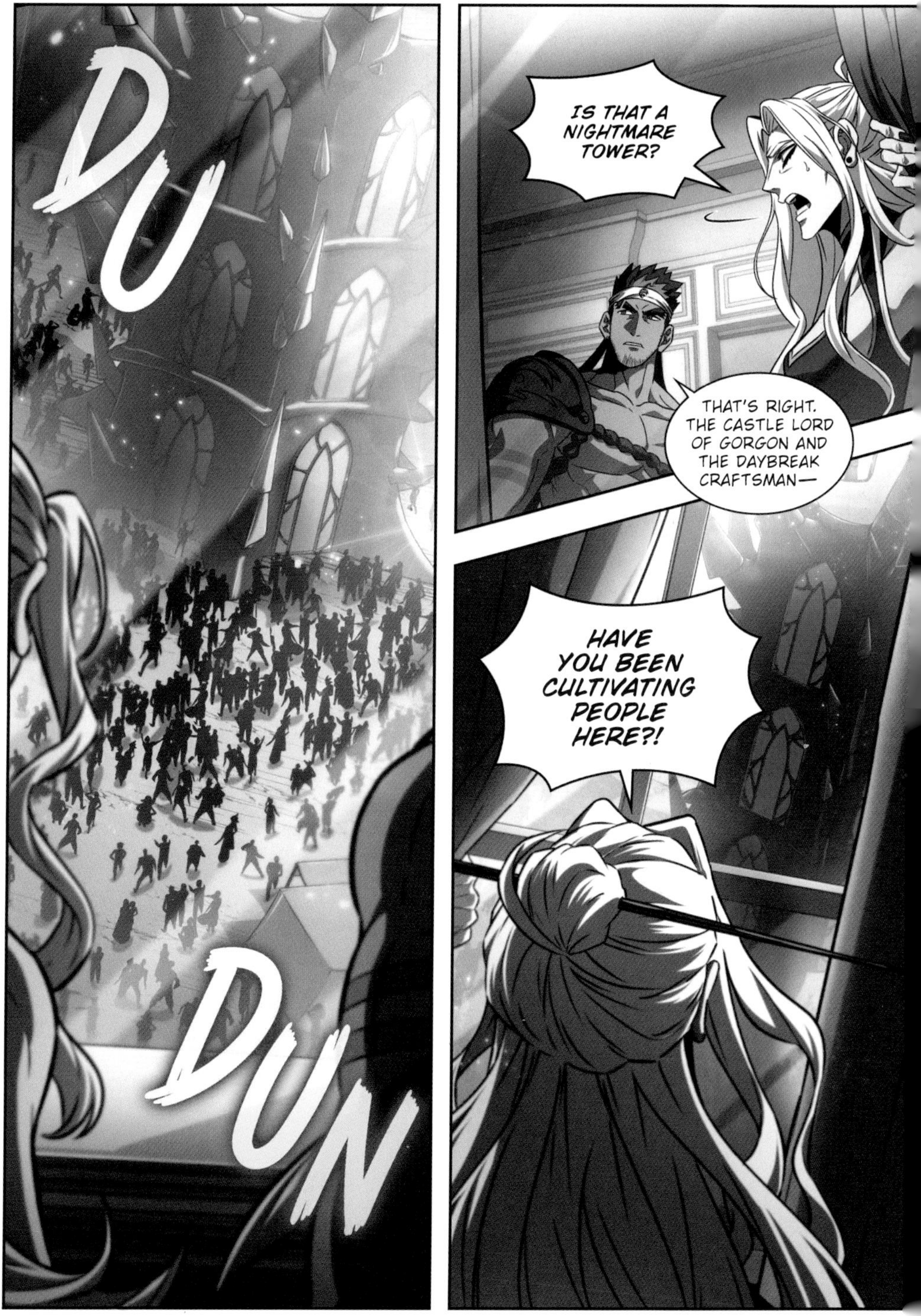
DU
DUN
IS THAT A NIGHTMARE TOWER?
THAT'S RIGHT. THE CASTLE LORD OF GORGON AND THE DAYBREAK CRAFTSMAN—
HAVE YOU BEEN CULTIVATING PEOPLE HERE?!

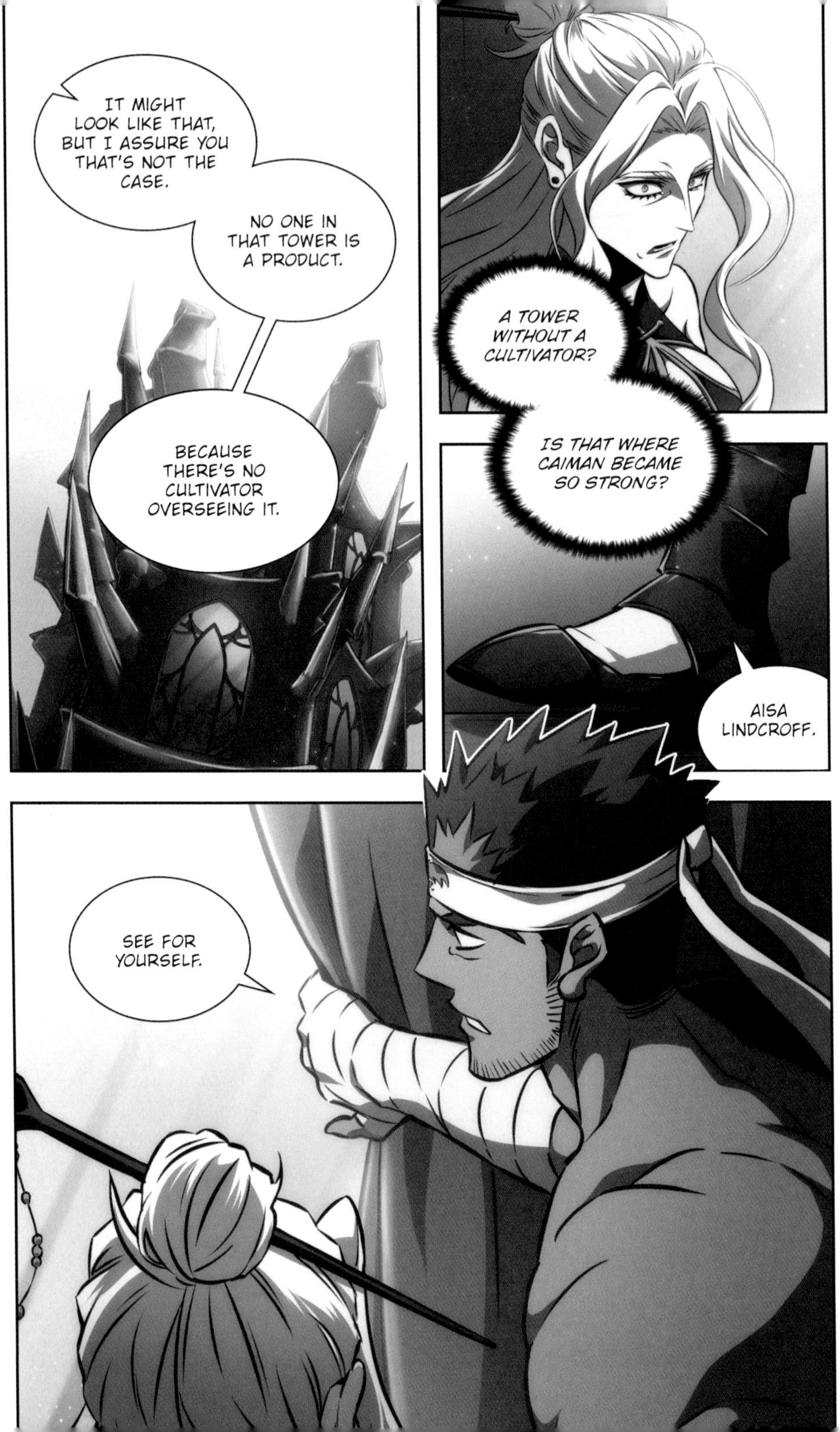
IT MIGHT LOOK LIKE THAT, BUT I ASSURE YOU THAT'S NOT THE CASE.
NO ONE IN THAT TOWER IS A PRODUCT.
BECAUSE THERE'S NO CULTIVATOR OVERSEEING IT.
A TOWER WITHOUT A CULTIVATOR?
IS THAT WHERE CAIMAN BECAME SO STRONG?
AISA LINDCROFF.
SEE FOR YOURSELF.

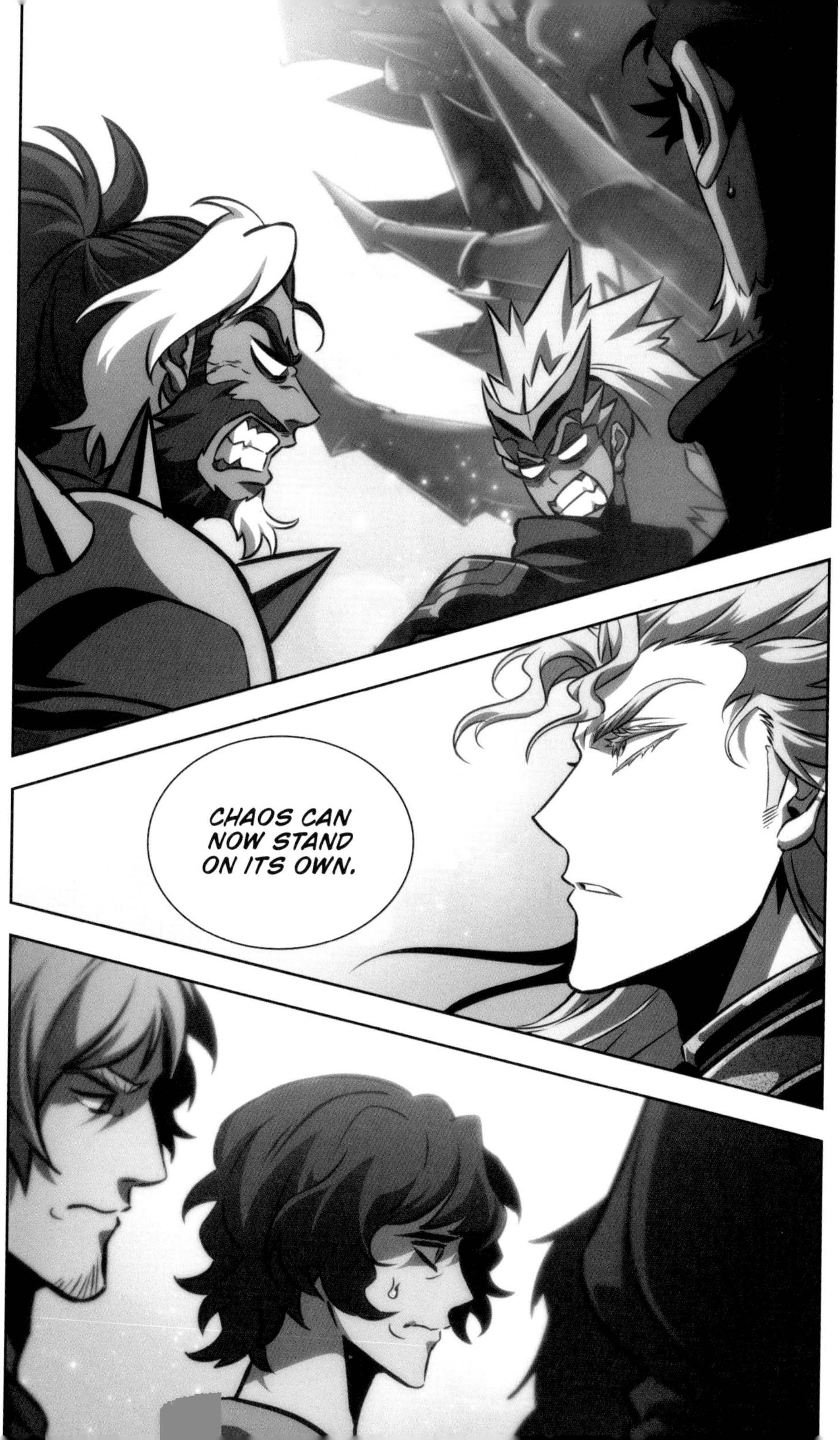
CHAOS CAN NOW STAND ON ITS OWN.

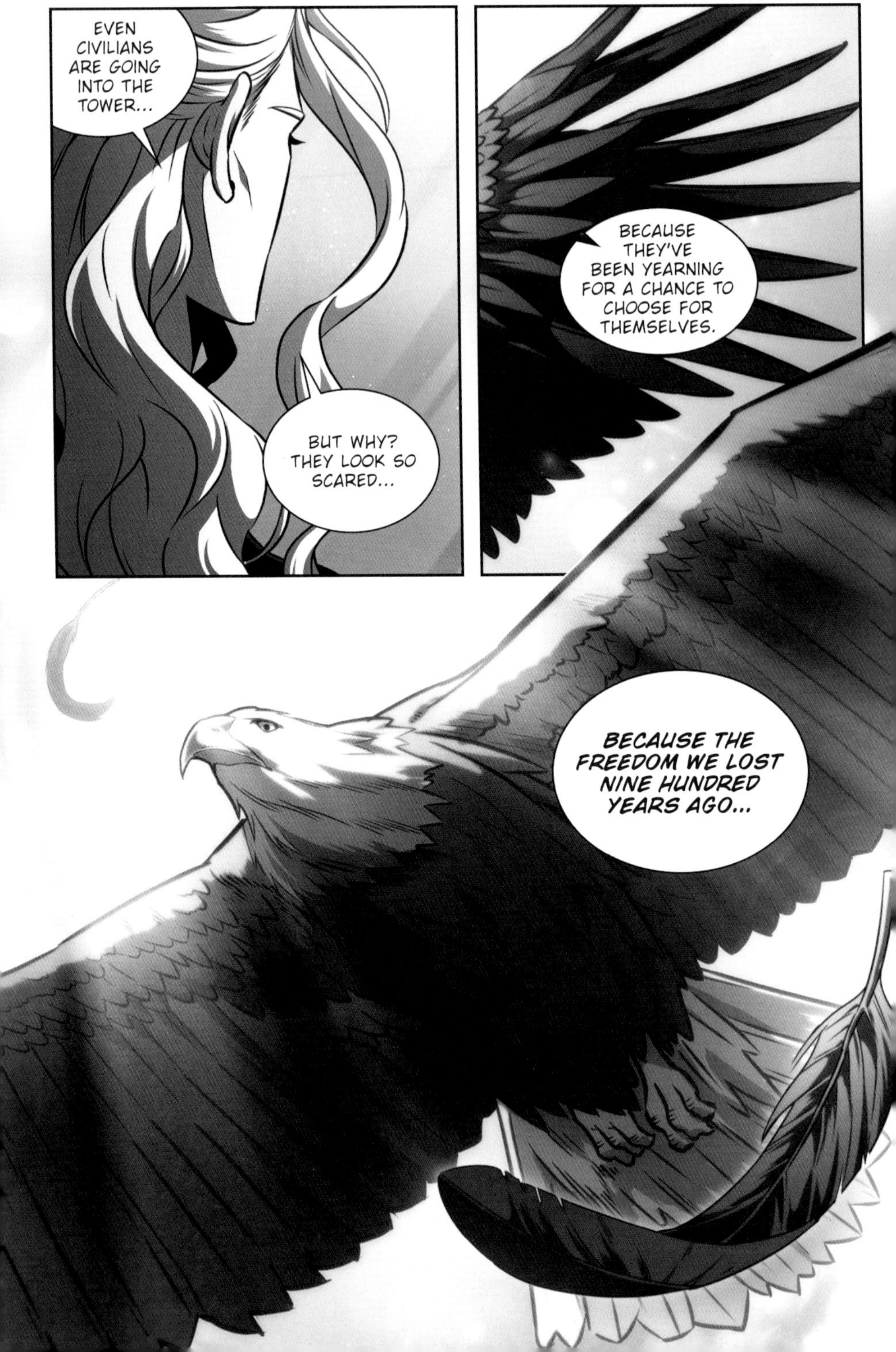
EVEN CIVILIANS ARE GOING INTO THE TOWER...
BECAUSE THEY'VE BEEN YEARNING FOR A CHANCE TO CHOOSE FOR THEMSELVES.
BUT WHY? THEY LOOK SO SCARED...
BECAUSE THE FREEDOM WE LOST NINE HUNDRED YEARS AGO...

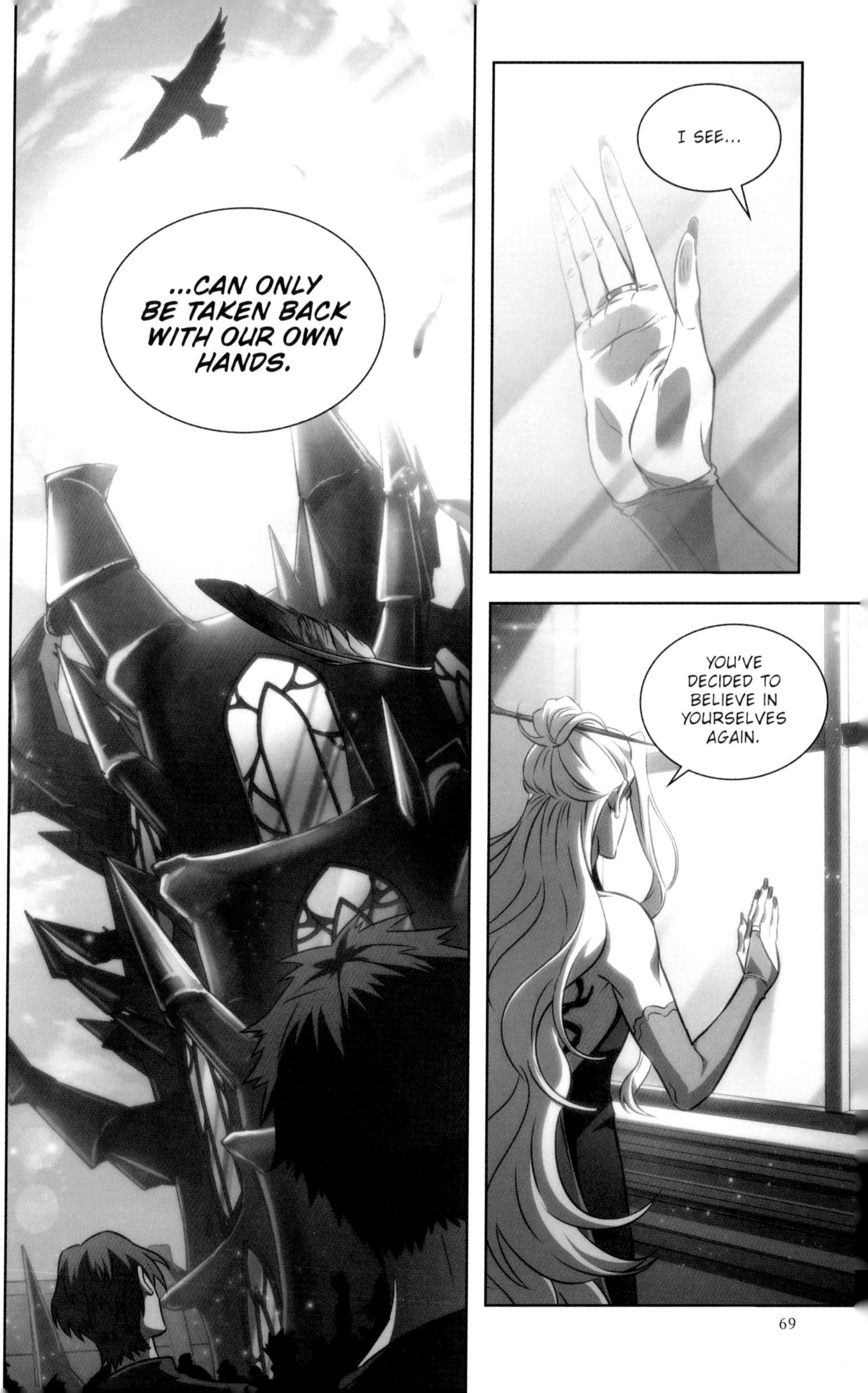
...CAN ONLY BE TAKEN BACK WITH OUR OWN HANDS.
I SEE...
YOU'VE DECIDED TO BELIEVE IN YOURSELVES AGAIN.

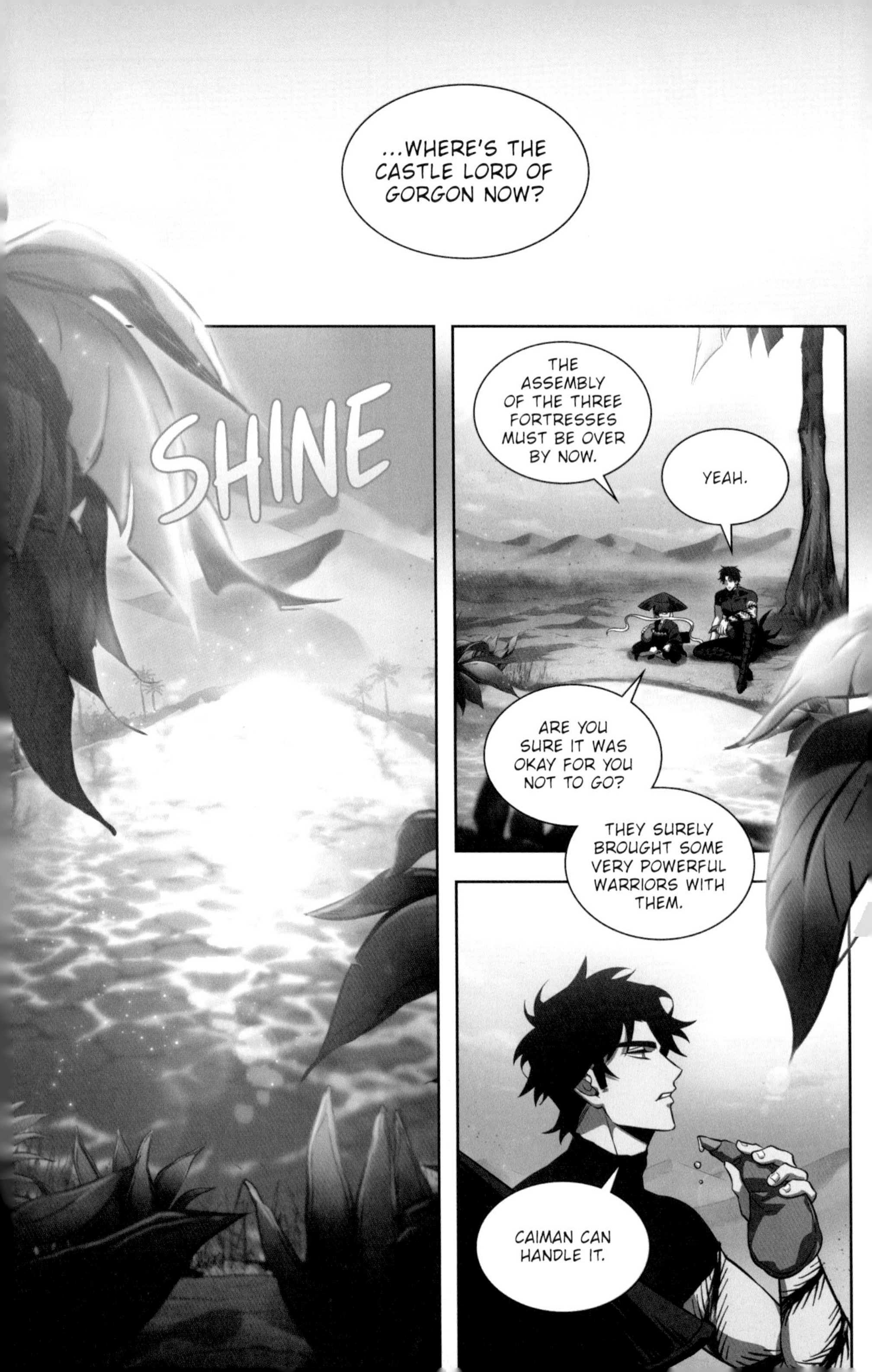
...WHERE'S THE CASTLE LORD OF GORGON NOW?
SHINE
THE ASSEMBLY OF THE THREE FORTRESSES MUST BE OVER BY NOW.
YEAH.
ARE YOU SURE IT WAS OKAY FOR YOU NOT TO GO?
THEY SURELY BROUGHT SOME VERY POWERFUL WARRIORS WITH THEM.
CAIMAN CAN HANDLE IT.

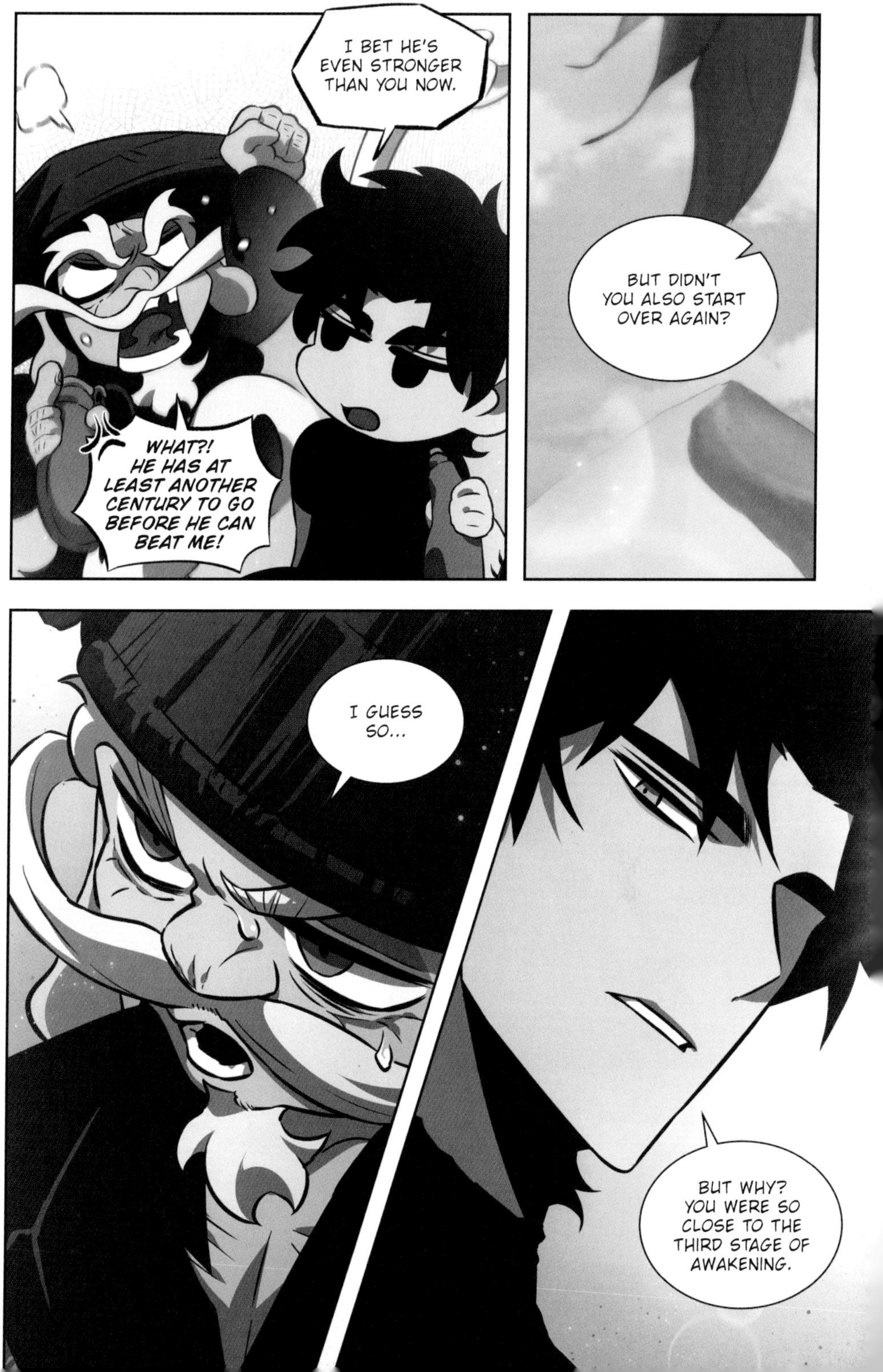

I BET HE'S EVEN STRONGER THAN YOU NOW.
WHAT?! HE HAS AT LEAST ANOTHER CENTURY TO GO BEFORE HE CAN BEAT ME!
BUT DIDN'T YOU ALSO START OVER AGAIN?
I GUESS SO...
BUT WHY? YOU WERE SO CLOSE TO THE THIRD STAGE OF AWAKENING.

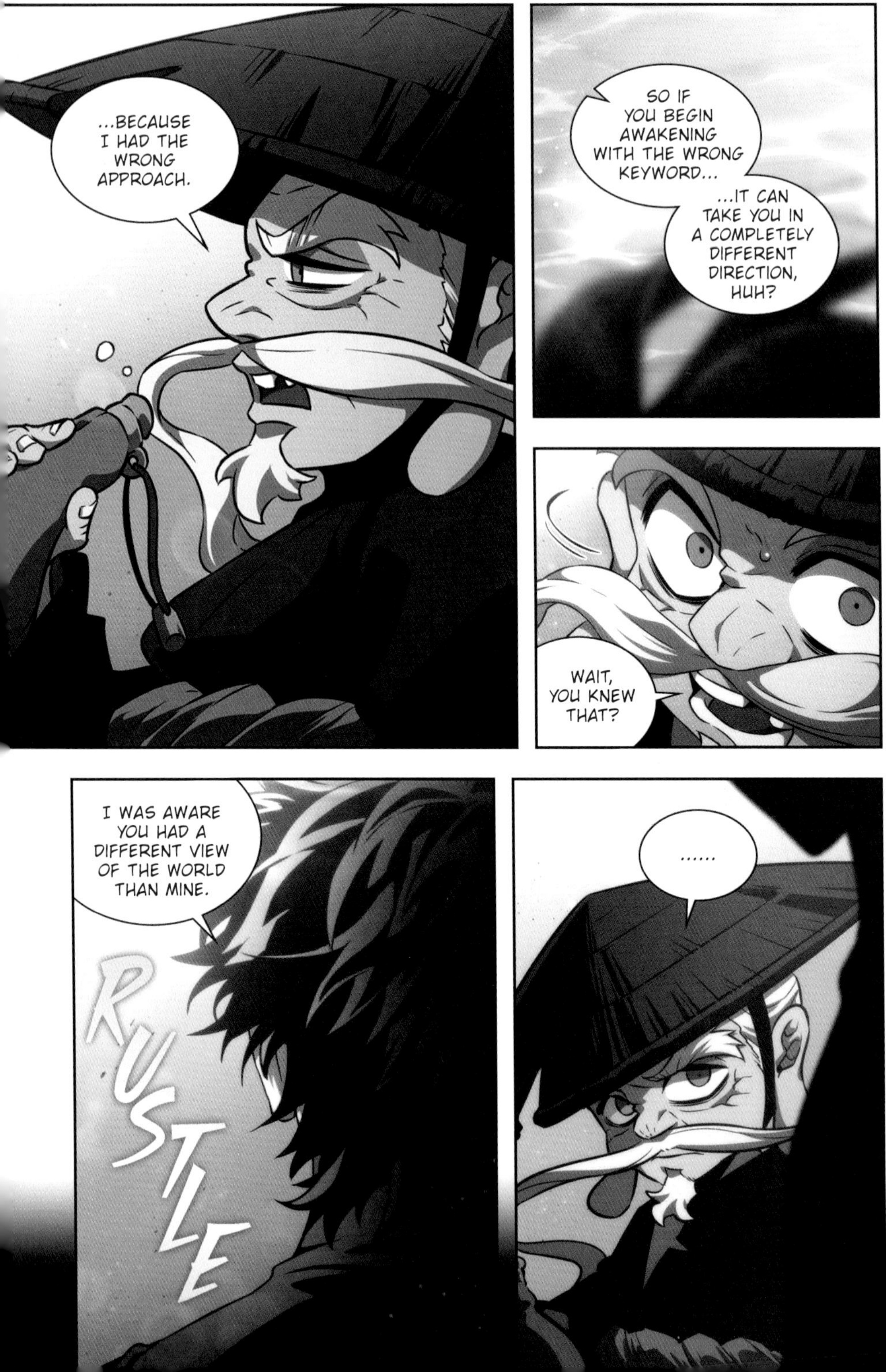
...BECAUSE I HAD THE WRONG APPROACH.
SO IF YOU BEGIN AWAKENING WITH THE WRONG KEYWORD...
...IT CAN TAKE YOU IN A COMPLETELY DIFFERENT DIRECTION, HUH?
WAIT, YOU KNEW THAT?
I WAS AWARE YOU HAD A DIFFERENT VIEW OF THE WORLD THAN MINE.
RUSTLE
......

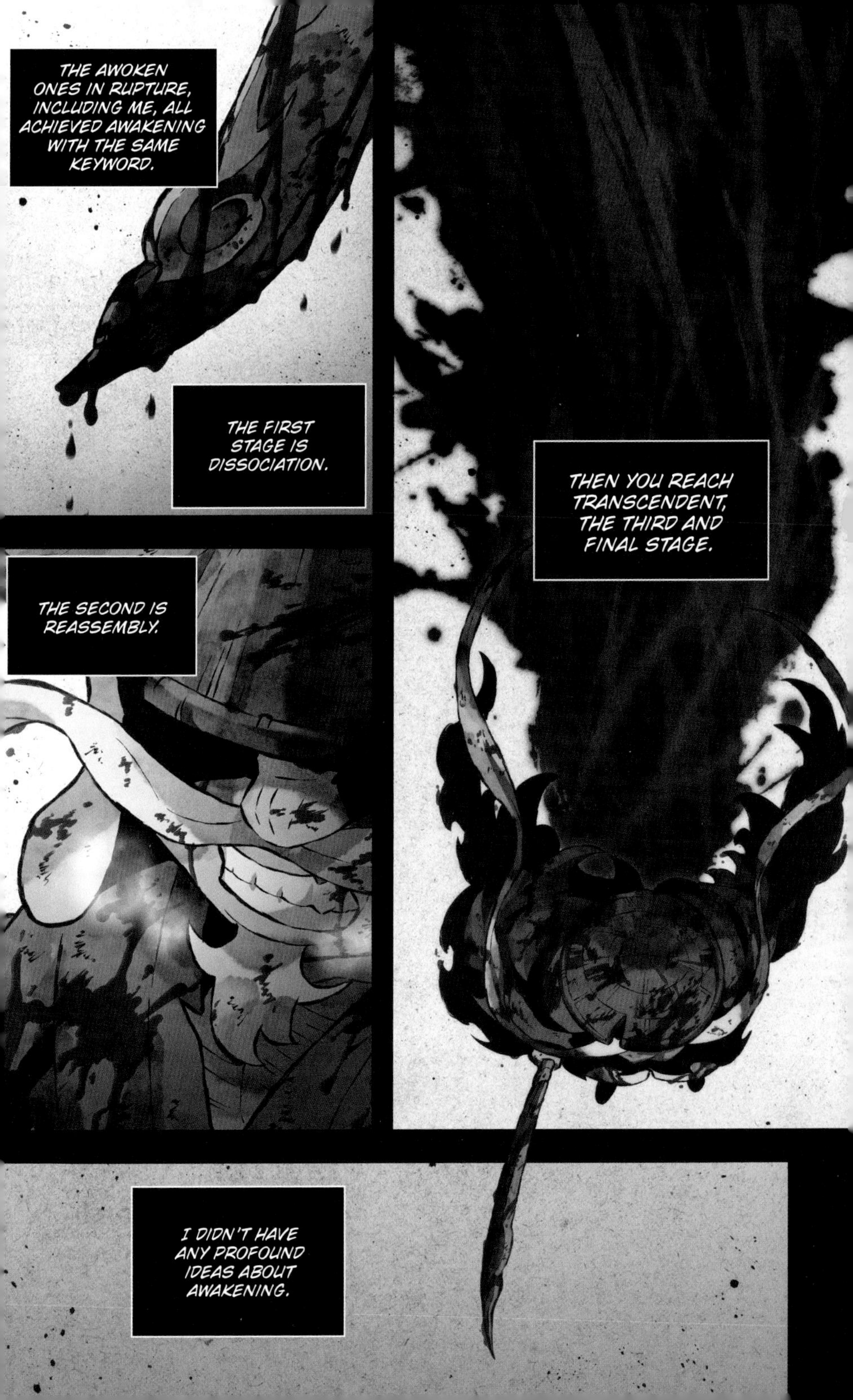
THE AWOKEN ONES IN RUPTURE, INCLUDING ME, ALL ACHIEVED AWAKENING WITH THE SAME KEYWORD.
THE FIRST STAGE IS DISSOCIATION.
THE SECOND IS REASSEMBLY.
THEN YOU REACH TRANSCENDENT, THE THIRD AND FINAL STAGE.
I DIDN'T HAVE ANY PROFOUND IDEAS ABOUT AWAKENING.

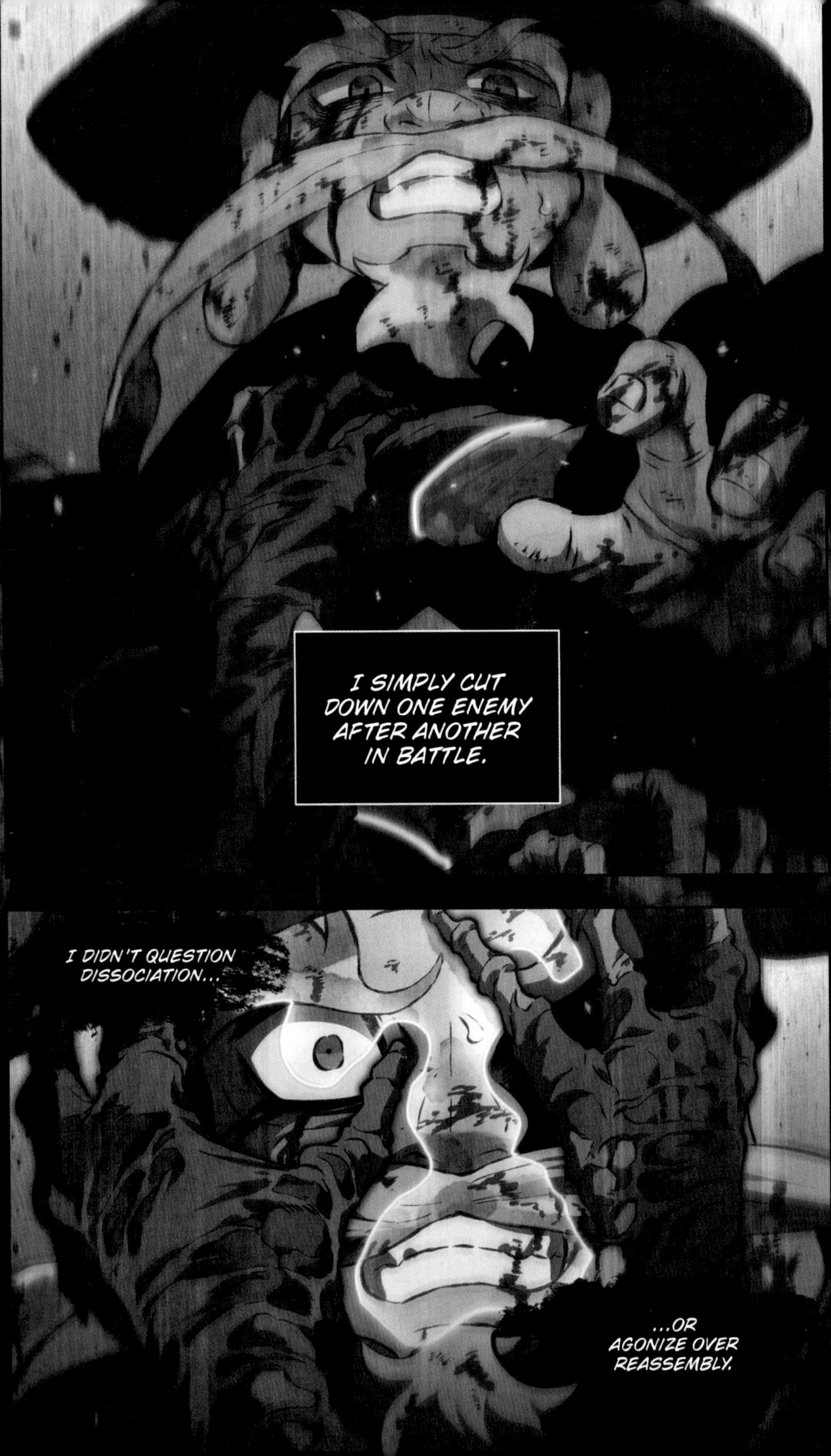
I SIMPLY CUT DOWN ONE ENEMY AFTER ANOTHER IN BATTLE.
I DIDN'T QUESTION DISSOCIATION...
...OR AGONIZE OVER REASSEMBLY.

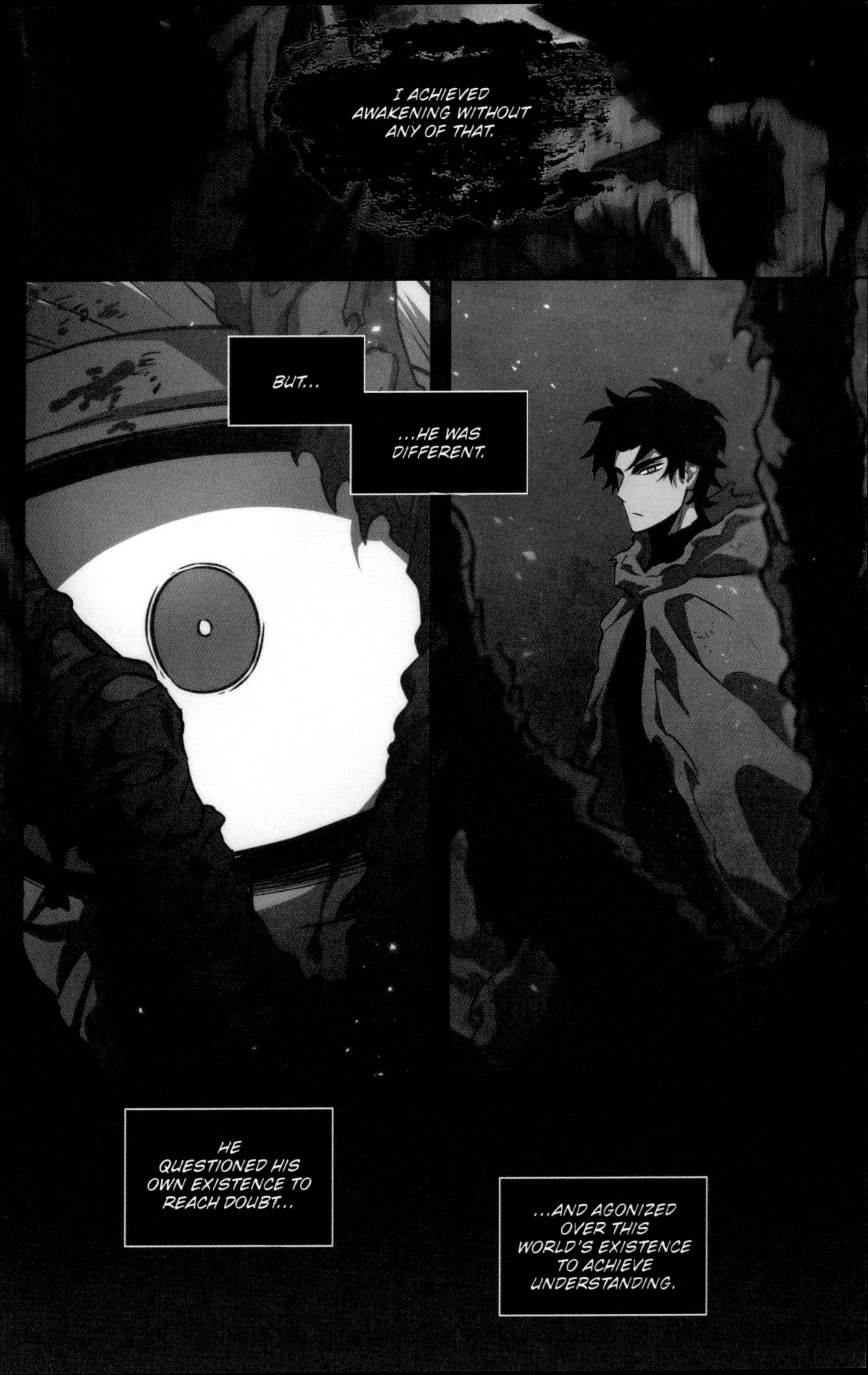
I ACHIEVED AWAKENING WITHOUT ANY OF THAT.
BUT...
...HE WAS DIFFERENT.
HE QUESTIONED HIS OWN EXISTENCE TO REACH DOUBT...
...AND AGONIZED OVER THIS WORLD'S EXISTENCE TO ACHIEVE UNDERSTANDING.

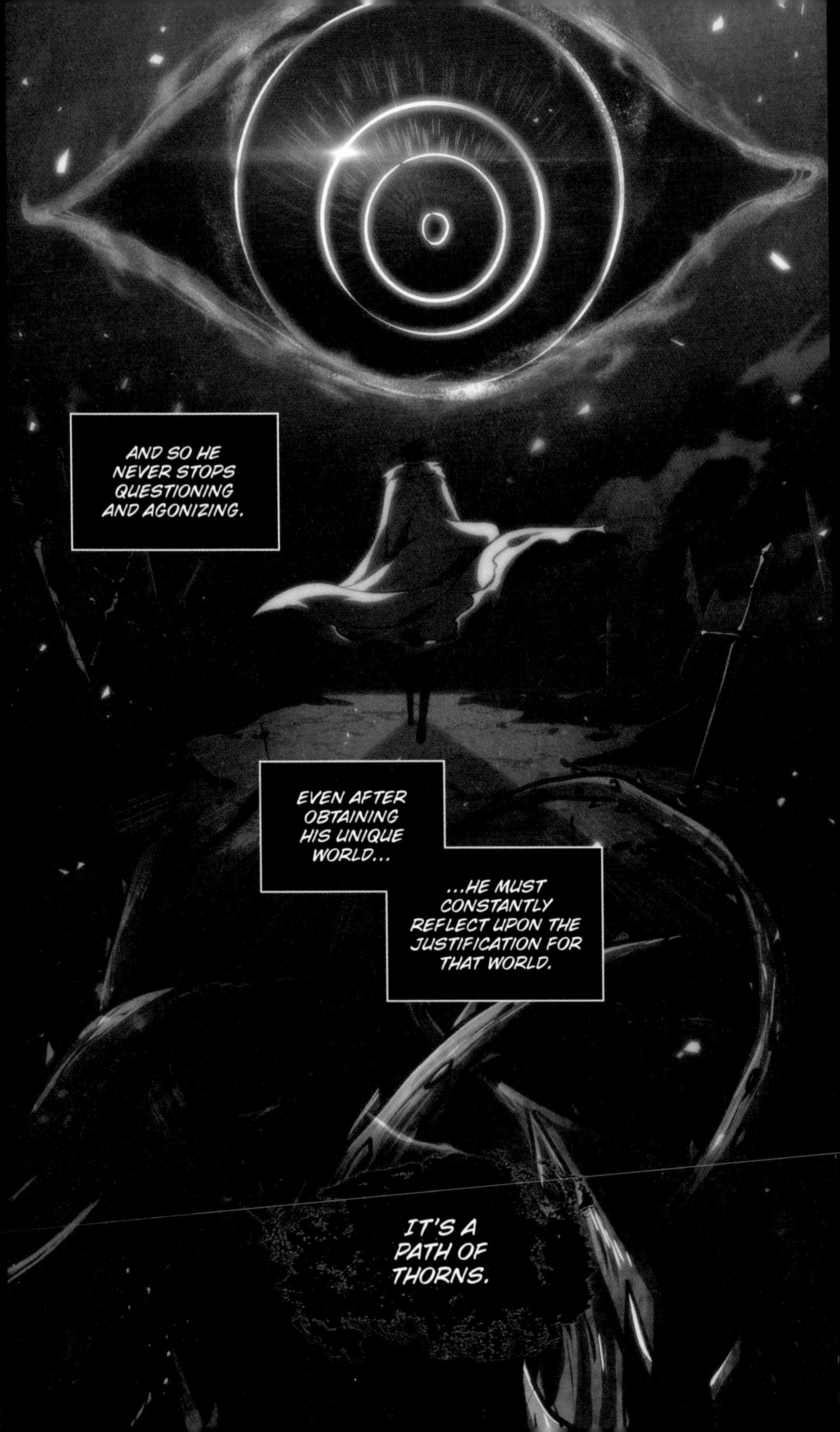
AND SO HE NEVER STOPS QUESTIONING AND AGONIZING.
EVEN AFTER OBTAINING HIS UNIQUE WORLD...
...HE MUST CONSTANTLY REFLECT UPON THE JUSTIFICATION FOR THAT WORLD.
IT'S A PATH OF THORNS.

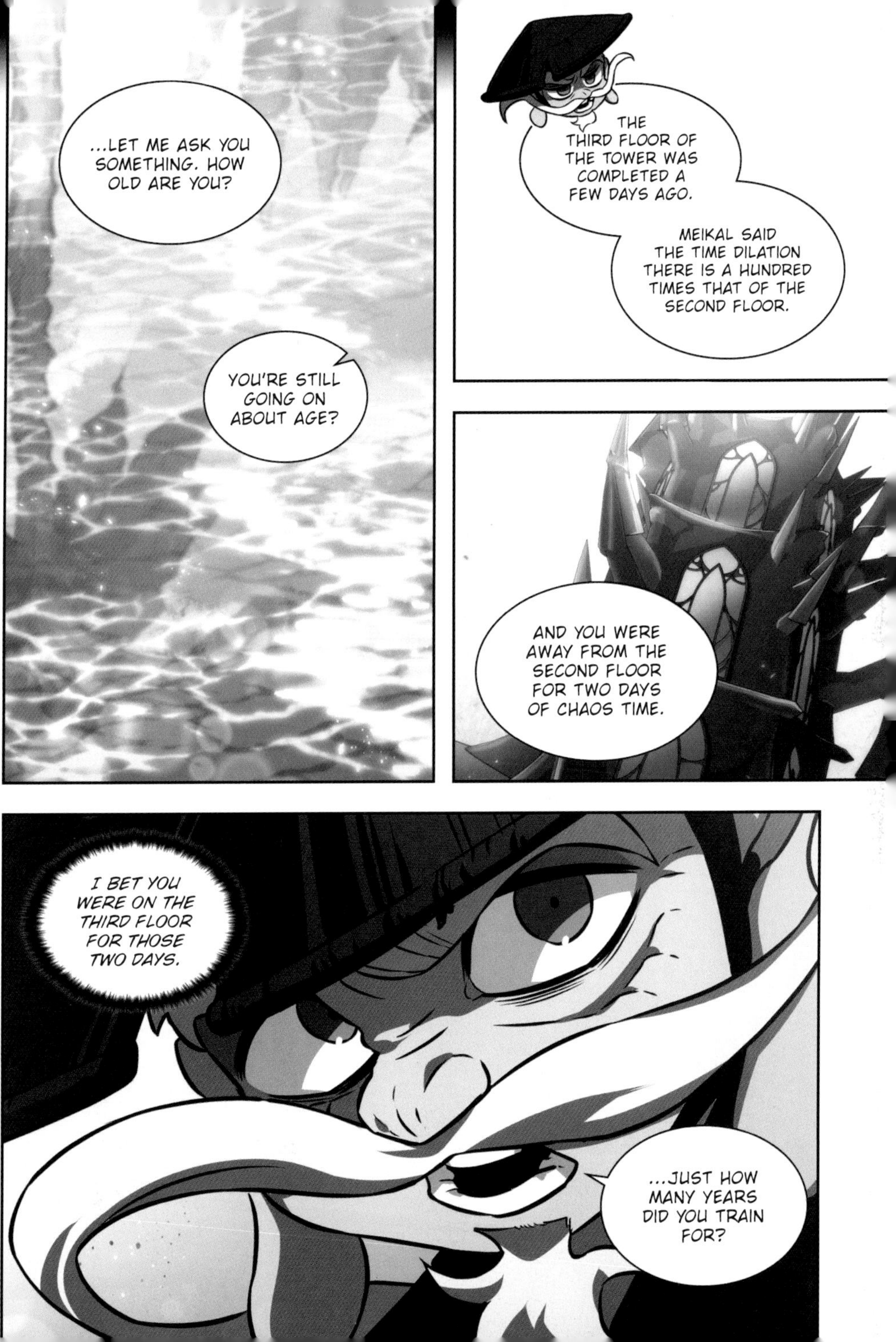
...LET ME ASK YOU SOMETHING. HOW OLD ARE YOU?
YOU'RE STILL GOING ON ABOUT AGE?
THE THIRD FLOOR OF THE TOWER WAS COMPLETED A FEW DAYS AGO.
MEIKAL SAID THE TIME DILATION THERE IS A HUNDRED TIMES THAT OF THE SECOND FLOOR.
AND YOU WERE AWAY FROM THE SECOND FLOOR FOR TWO DAYS OF CHAOS TIME.
I BET YOU WERE ON THE THIRD FLOOR FOR THOSE TWO DAYS.
...JUST HOW MANY YEARS DID YOU TRAIN FOR?

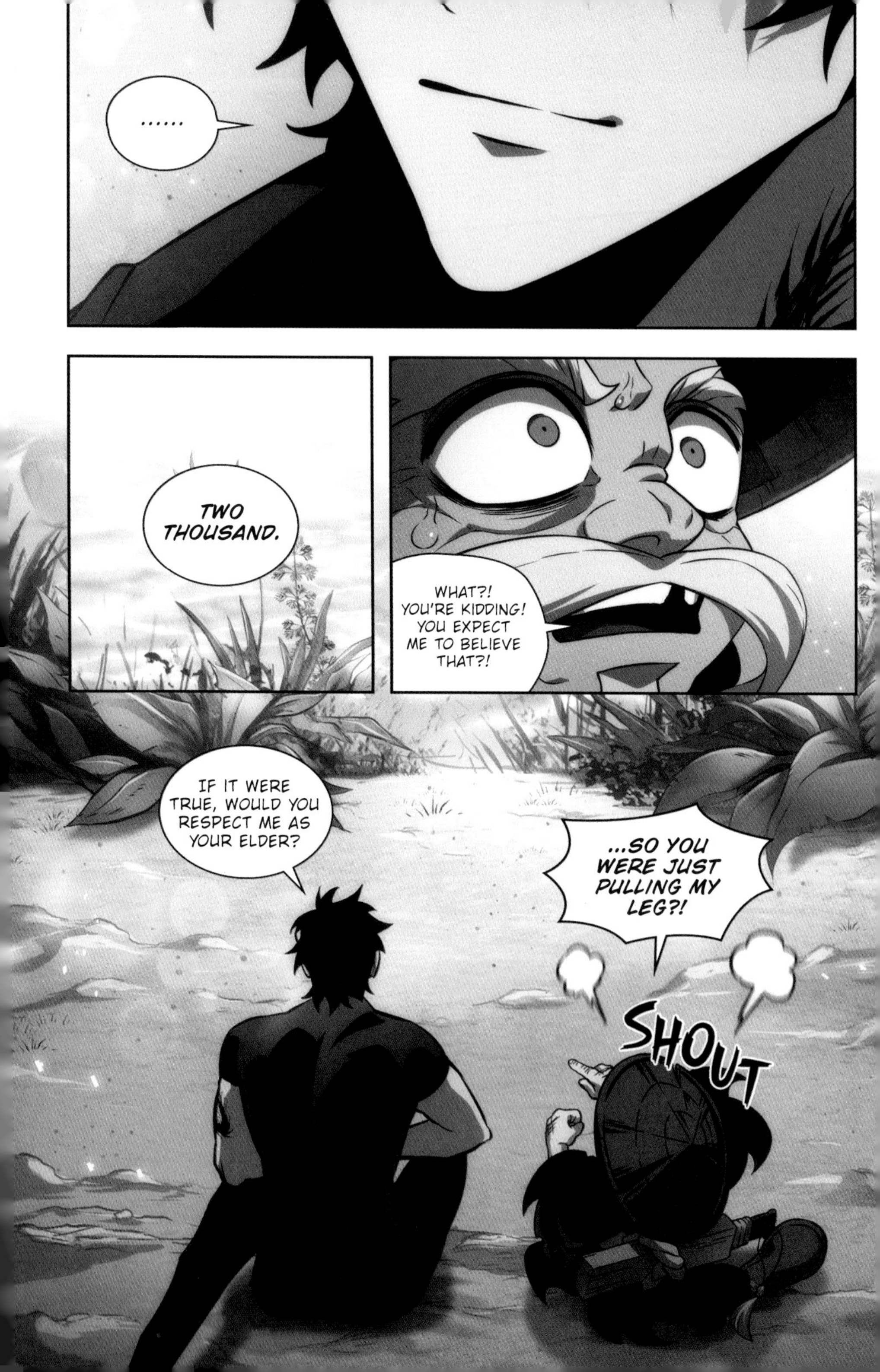
......
TWO THOUSAND.
WHAT?! YOU'RE KIDDING! YOU EXPECT ME TO BELIEVE THAT?!
IF IT WERE TRUE, WOULD YOU RESPECT ME AS YOUR ELDER?
...SO YOU WERE JUST PULLING MY LEG?!
SHOUT

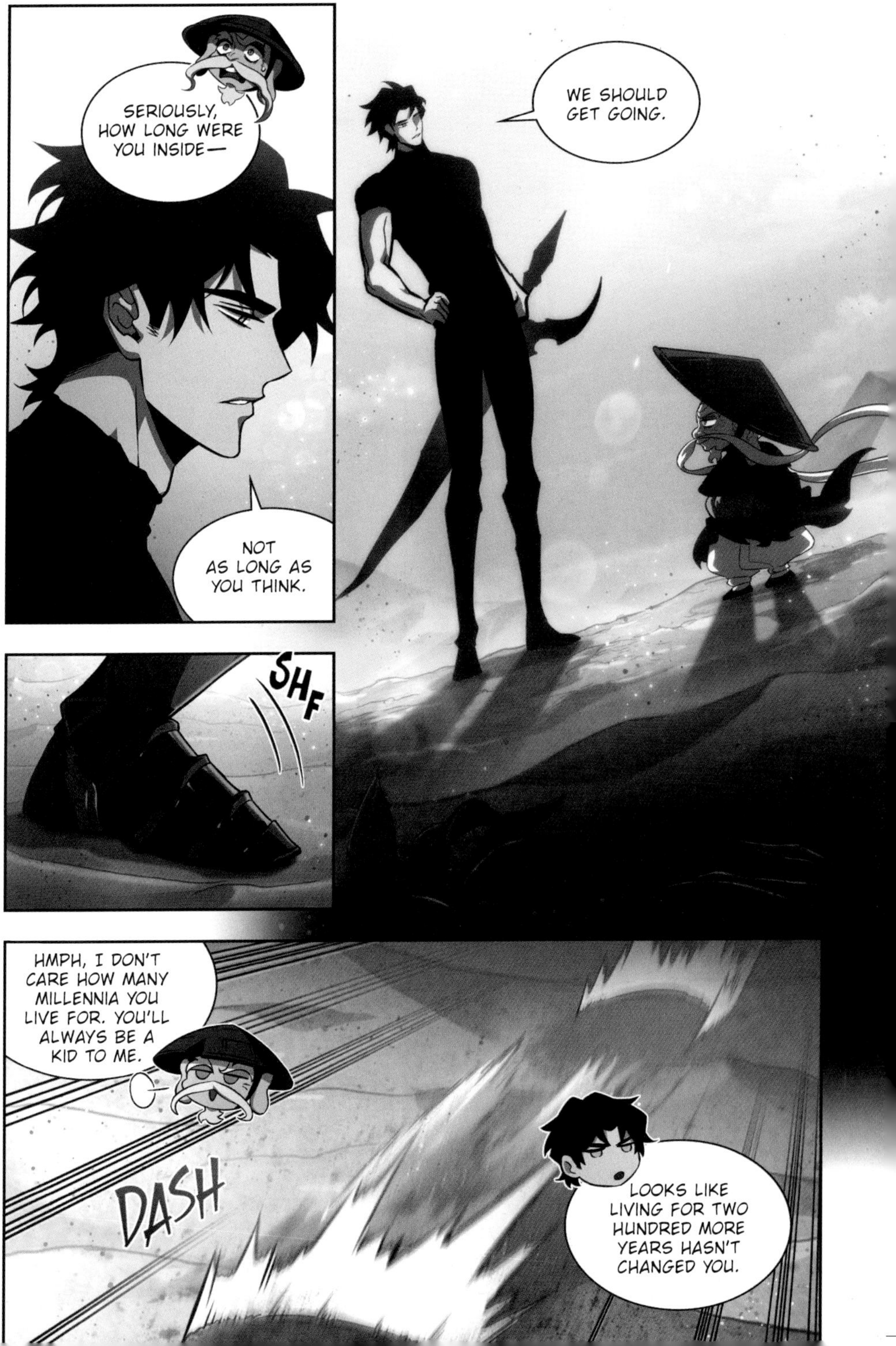
SERIOUSLY, HOW LONG WERE YOU INSIDE—
NOT AS LONG AS YOU THINK.
WE SHOULD GET GOING.
SHF
HMPH, I DON'T CARE HOW MANY MILLENNIA YOU LIVE FOR. YOU'LL ALWAYS BE A KID TO ME.
DASH
LOOKS LIKE LIVING FOR TWO HUNDRED MORE YEARS HASN'T CHANGED YOU.

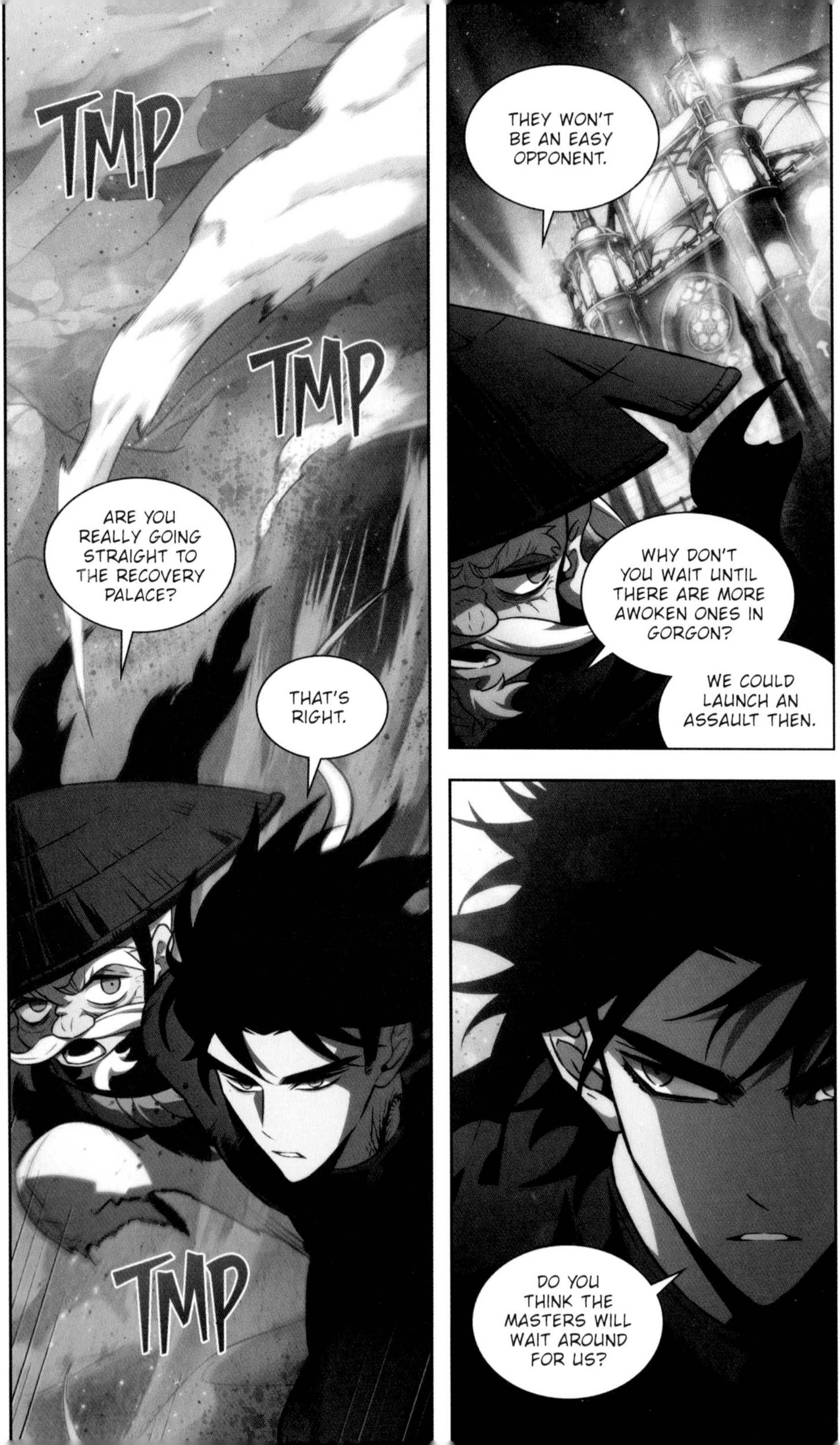
TMP
TMP
ARE YOU REALLY GOING STRAIGHT TO THE RECOVERY PALACE?
THAT'S RIGHT.
TMP
THEY WON'T BE AN EASY OPPONENT.
WHY DON'T YOU WAIT UNTIL THERE ARE MORE AWOKEN ONES IN GORGON?
WE COULD LAUNCH AN ASSAULT THEN.
DO YOU THINK THE MASTERS WILL WAIT AROUND FOR US?

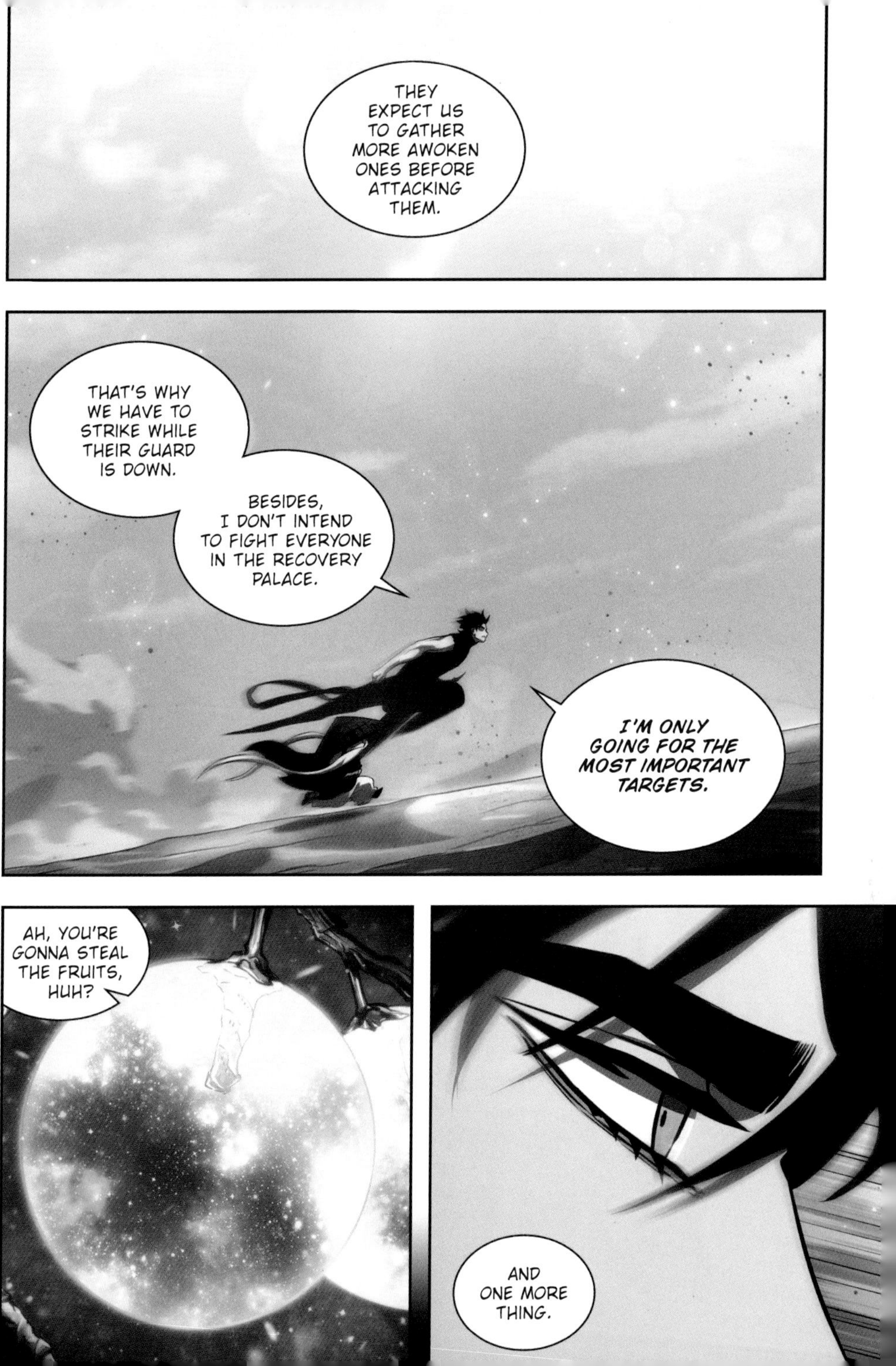
THEY EXPECT US TO GATHER MORE AWOKEN ONES BEFORE ATTACKING THEM.
THAT'S WHY WE HAVE TO STRIKE WHILE THEIR GUARD IS DOWN.
BESIDES, I DON'T INTEND TO FIGHT EVERYONE IN THE RECOVERY PALACE.
I'M ONLY GOING FOR THE MOST IMPORTANT TARGETS.
AH, YOU'RE GONNA STEAL THE FRUITS, HUH?
AND ONE MORE THING.

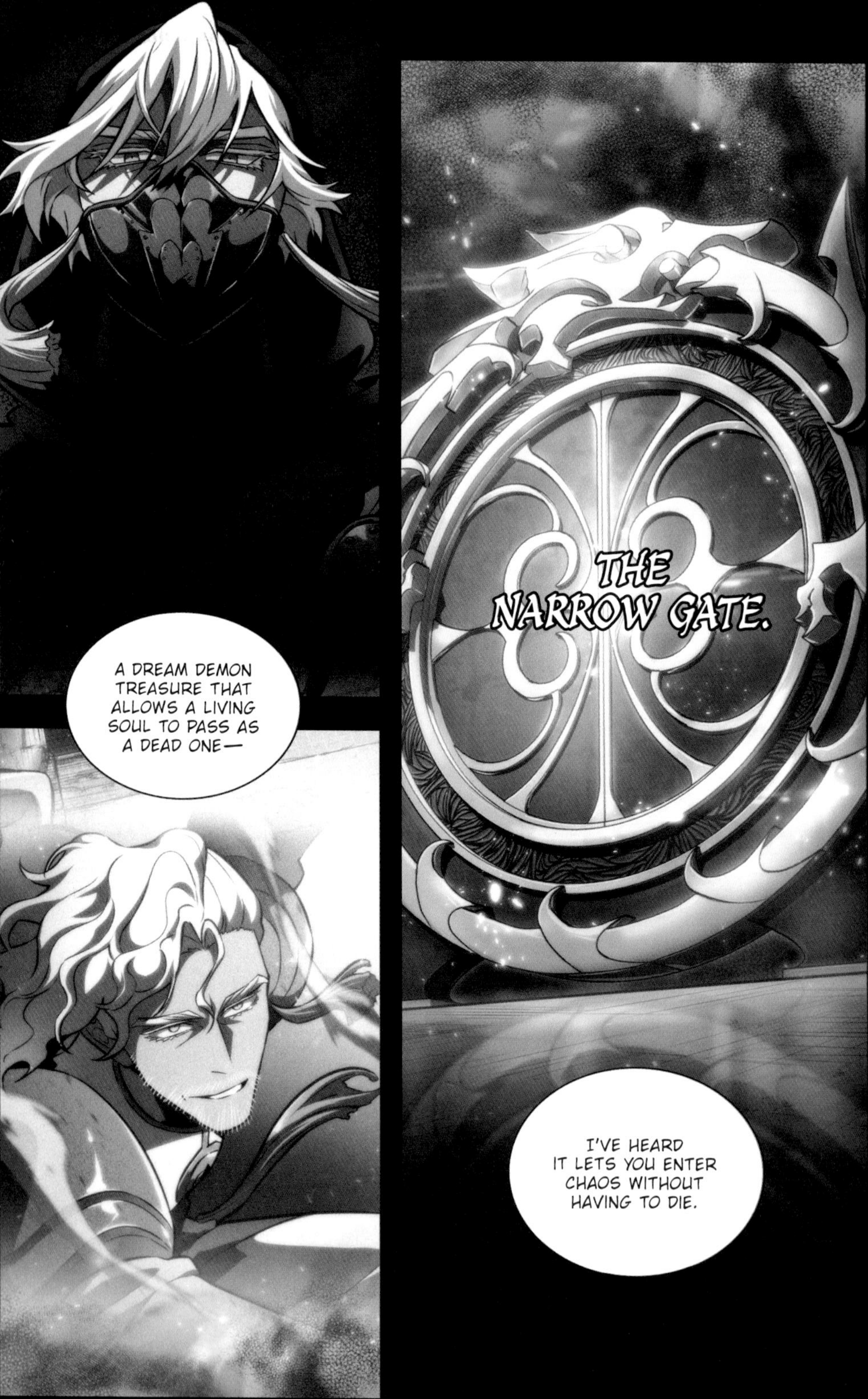
A DREAM DEMON TREASURE THAT ALLOWS A LIVING SOUL TO PASS AS A DEAD ONE—
THE NARROW GATE.
I'VE HEARD IT LETS YOU ENTER CHAOS WITHOUT HAVING TO DIE.

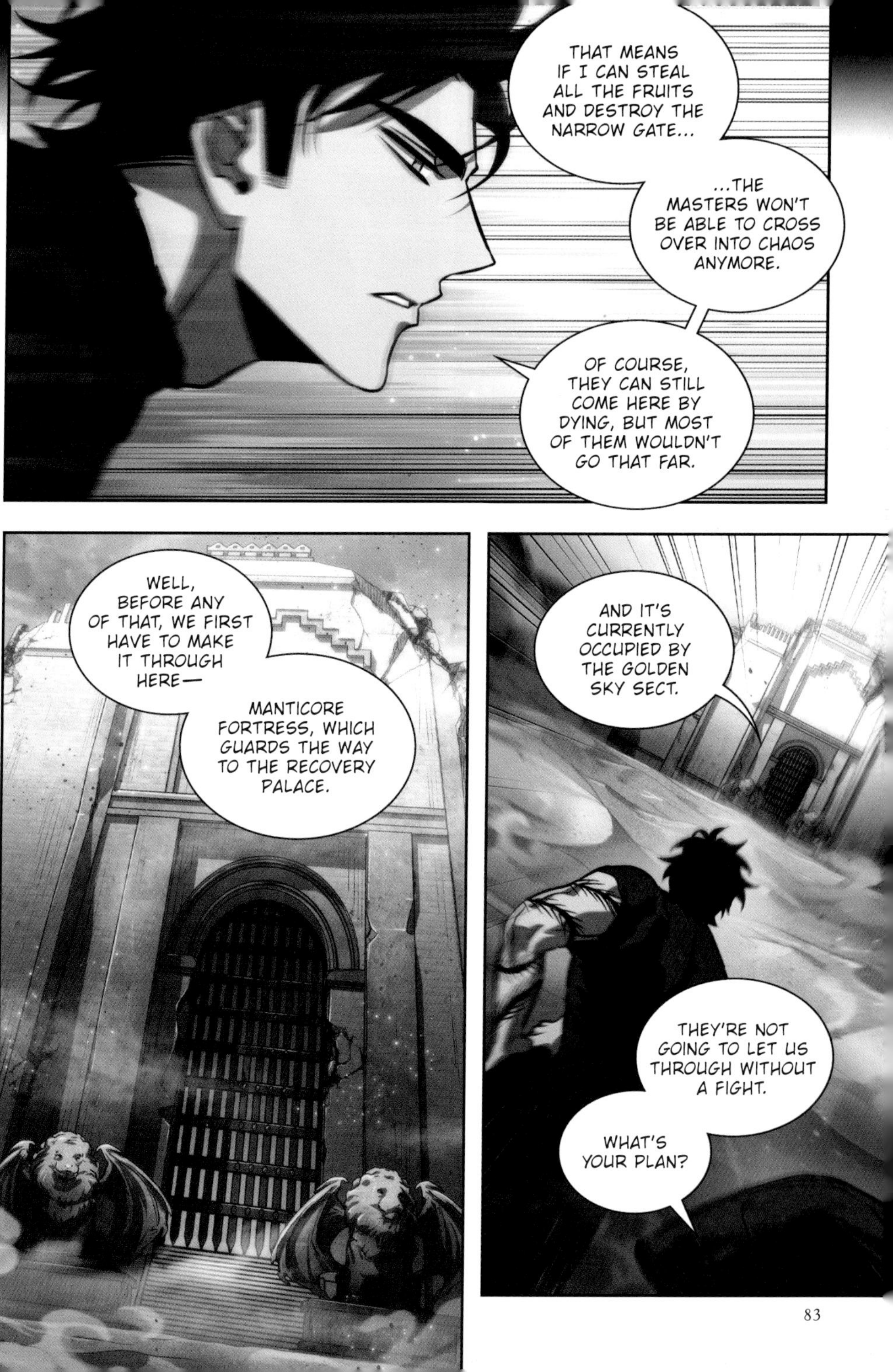
THAT MEANS IF I CAN STEAL ALL THE FRUITS AND DESTROY THE NARROW GATE...
...THE MASTERS WON'T BE ABLE TO CROSS OVER INTO CHAOS ANYMORE.
OF COURSE, THEY CAN STILL COME HERE BY DYING, BUT MOST OF THEM WOULDN'T GO THAT FAR.
WELL, BEFORE ANY OF THAT, WE FIRST HAVE TO MAKE IT THROUGH HERE—
MANTICORE FORTRESS, WHICH GUARDS THE WAY TO THE RECOVERY PALACE.
AND IT'S CURRENTLY OCCUPIED BY THE GOLDEN SKY SECT.
THEY'RE NOT GOING TO LET US THROUGH WITHOUT A FIGHT.
WHAT'S YOUR PLAN?

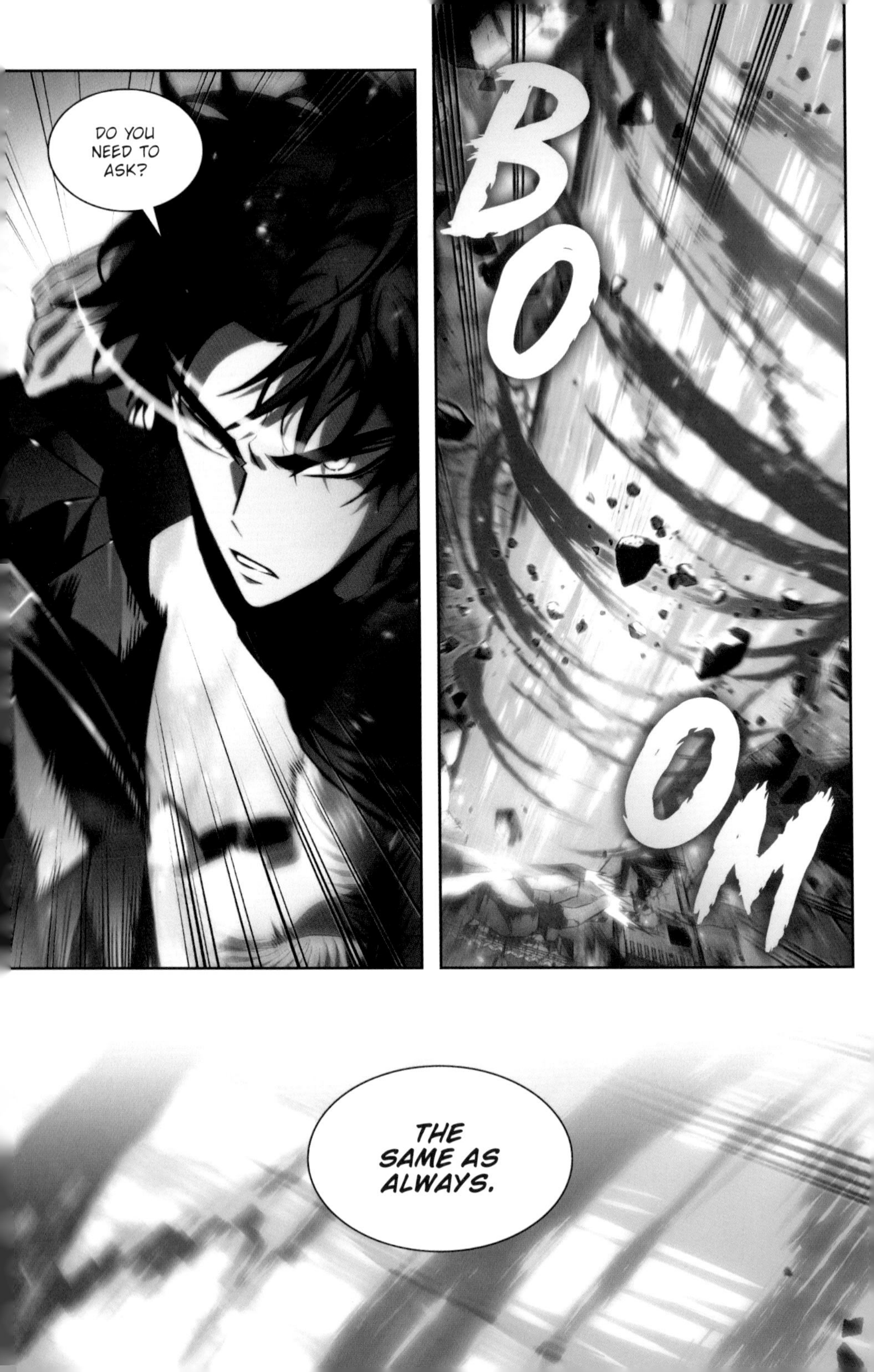
DO YOU NEED TO ASK?
BOOOM
THE SAME AS ALWAYS.

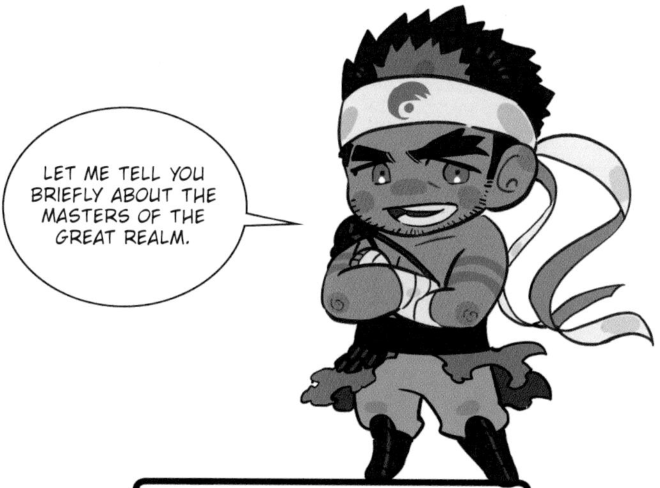
LET ME TELL YOU BRIEFLY ABOUT THE MASTERS OF THE GREAT REALM.

MASTERS OF THE GREAT REALM

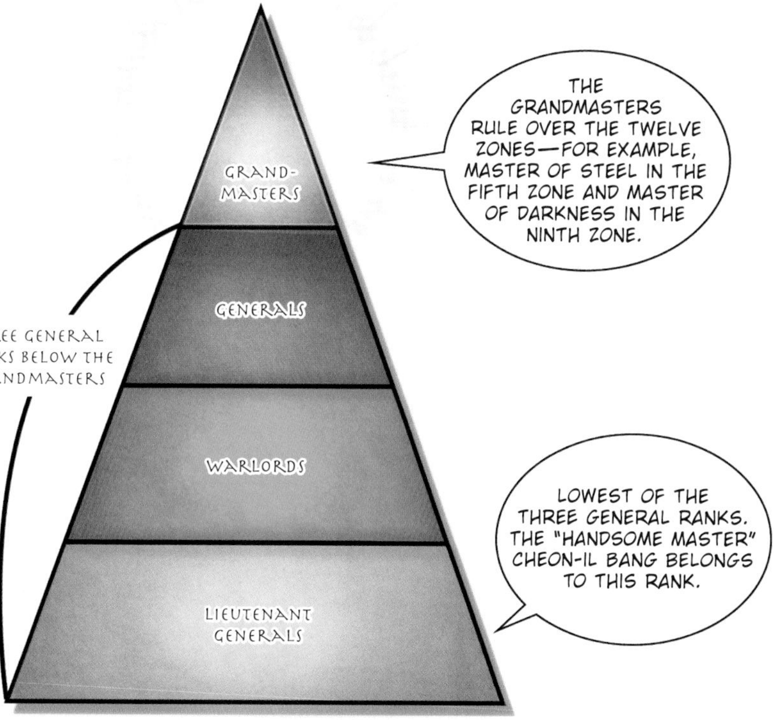
GRAND-MASTERS
GENERALS
WARLORDS
LIEUTENANT GENERALS
THREE GENERAL RANKS BELOW THE GRANDMASTERS
THE GRANDMASTERS RULE OVER THE TWELVE ZONES—FOR EXAMPLE, MASTER OF STEEL IN THE FIFTH ZONE AND MASTER OF DARKNESS IN THE NINTH ZONE.
LOWEST OF THE THREE GENERAL RANKS. THE "HANDSOME MASTER" CHEON-IL BANG BELONGS TO THIS RANK.

The World After the Fall

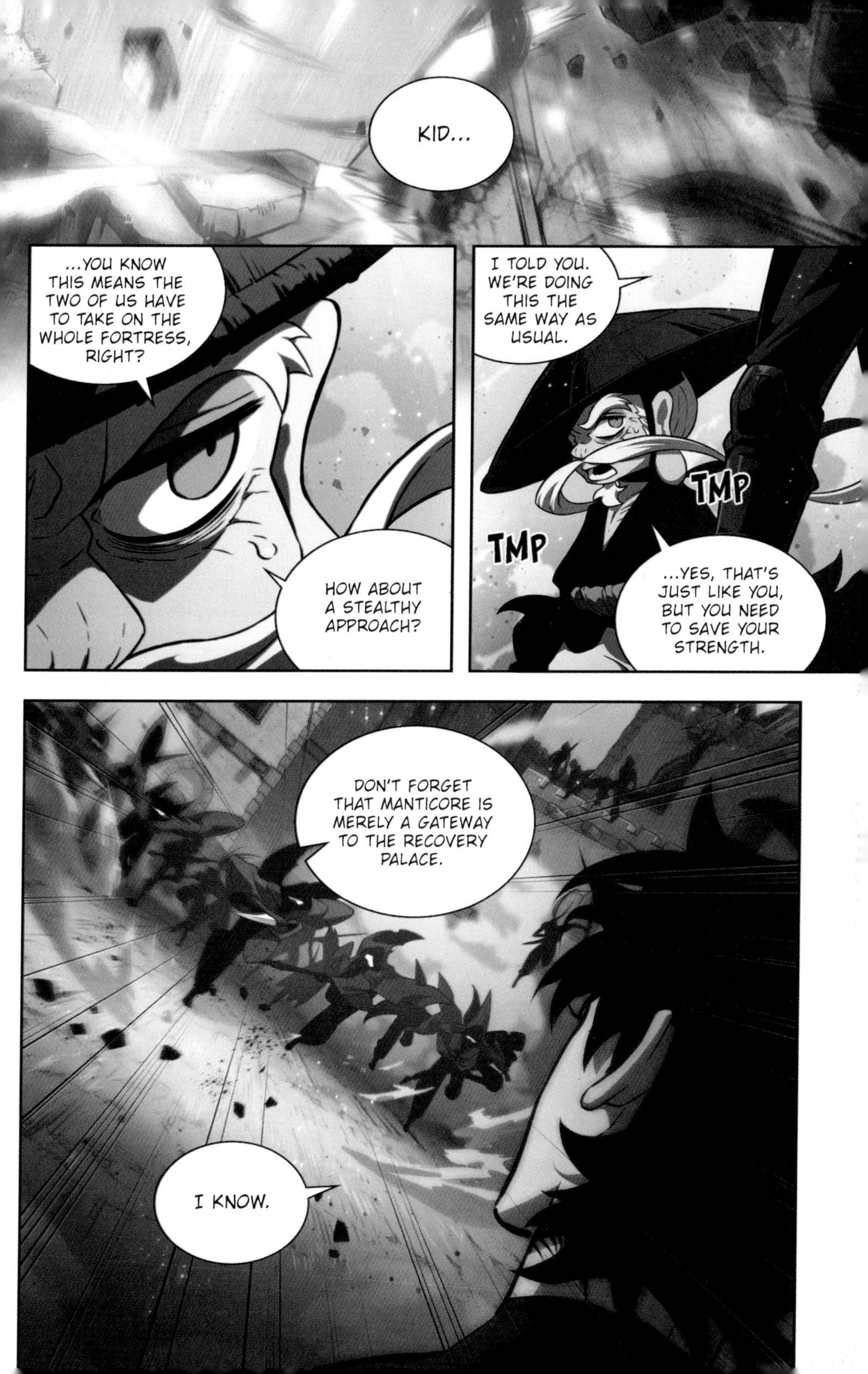
KID...
...YOU KNOW THIS MEANS THE TWO OF US HAVE TO TAKE ON THE WHOLE FORTRESS, RIGHT?
HOW ABOUT A STEALTHY APPROACH?
I TOLD YOU. WE'RE DOING THIS THE SAME WAY AS USUAL.
TMP
TMP
...YES, THAT'S JUST LIKE YOU, BUT YOU NEED TO SAVE YOUR STRENGTH.
DON'T FORGET THAT MANTICORE IS MERELY A GATEWAY TO THE RECOVERY PALACE.
I KNOW.

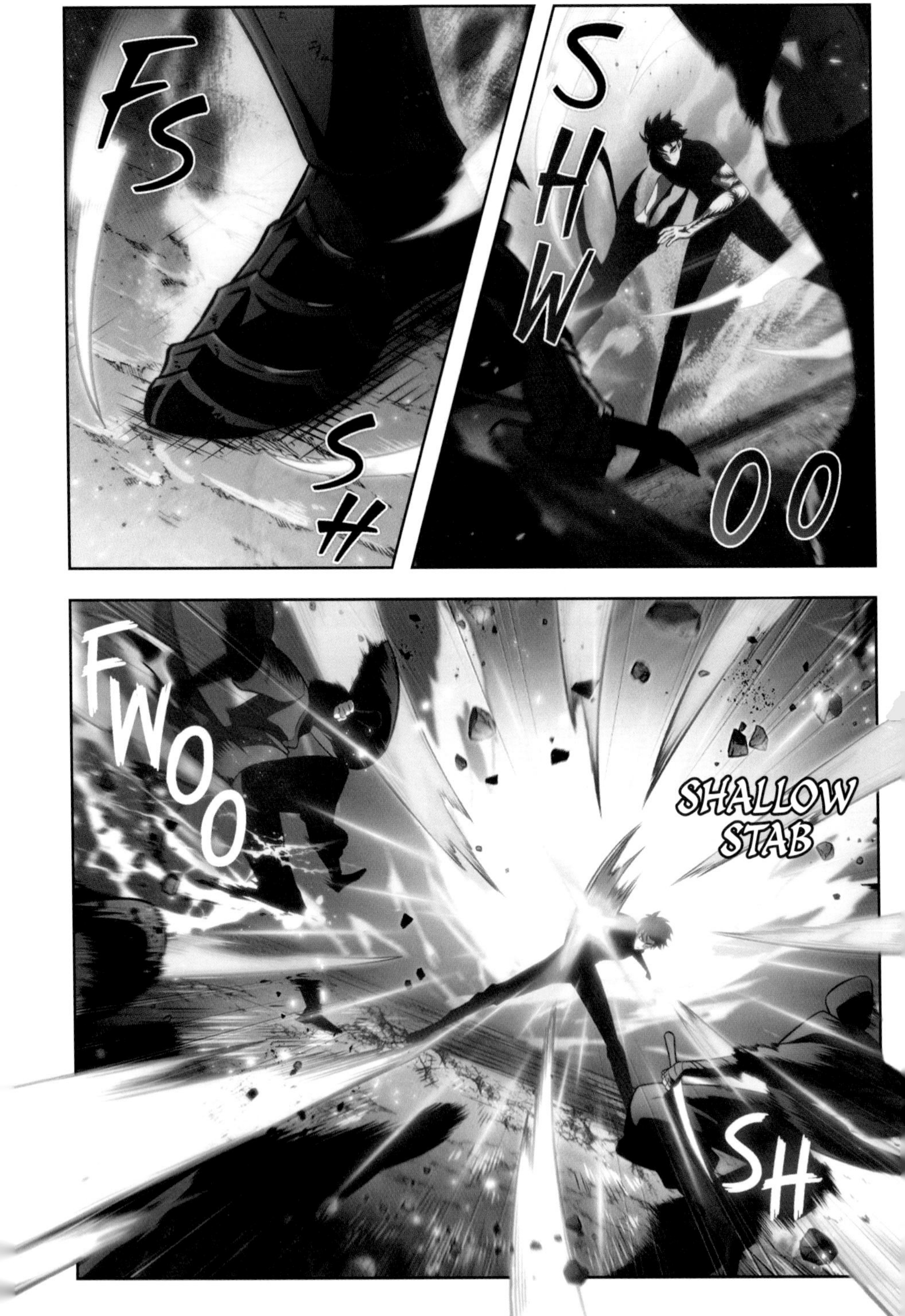
SHWOO
FSSH
SHALLOW STAB
FWOO
SH

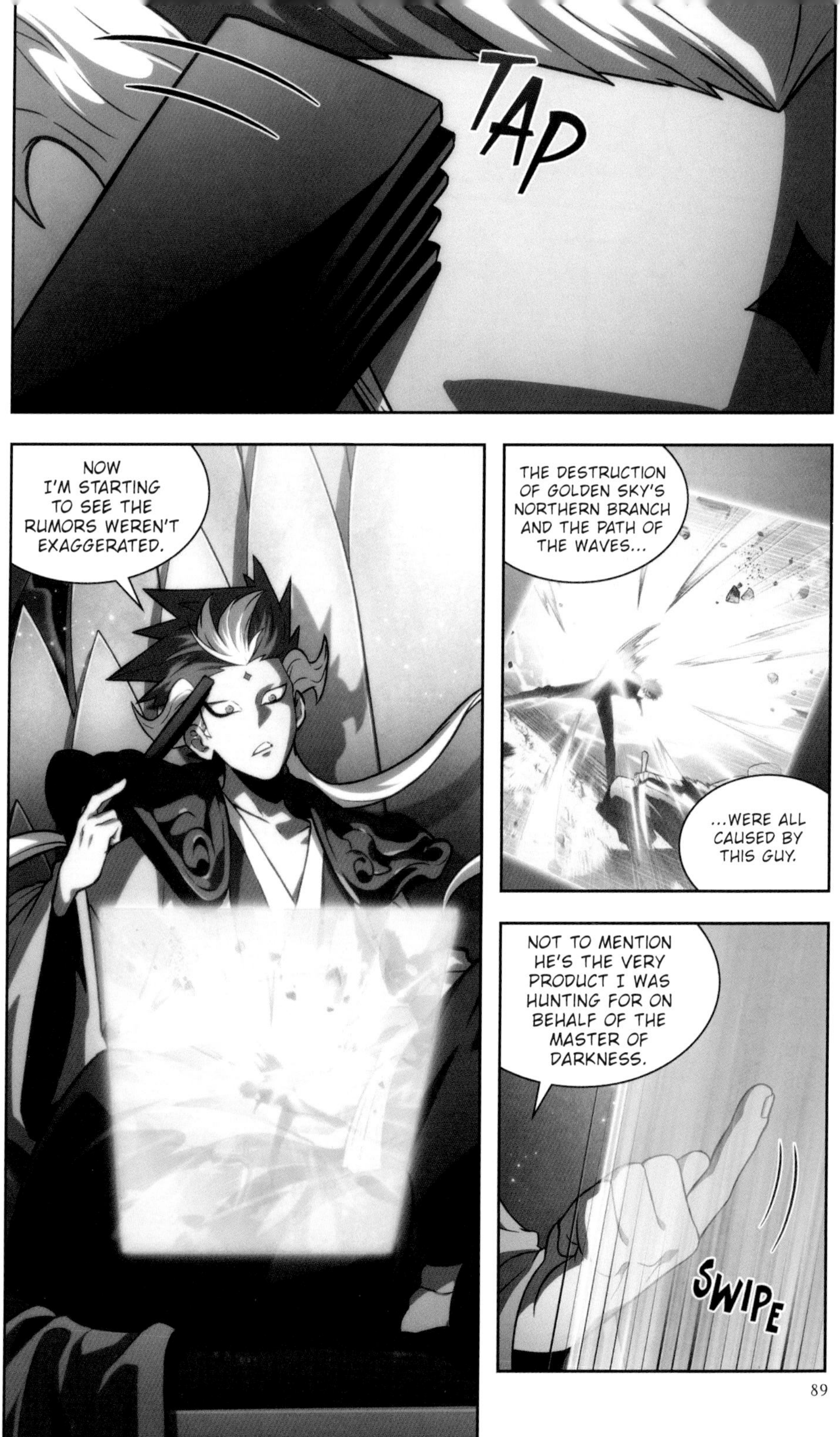
TAP
NOW I'M STARTING TO SEE THE RUMORS WEREN'T EXAGGERATED.
THE DESTRUCTION OF GOLDEN SKY'S NORTHERN BRANCH AND THE PATH OF THE WAVES...
...WERE ALL CAUSED BY THIS GUY.
NOT TO MENTION HE'S THE VERY PRODUCT I WAS HUNTING FOR ON BEHALF OF THE MASTER OF DARKNESS.
SWIPE

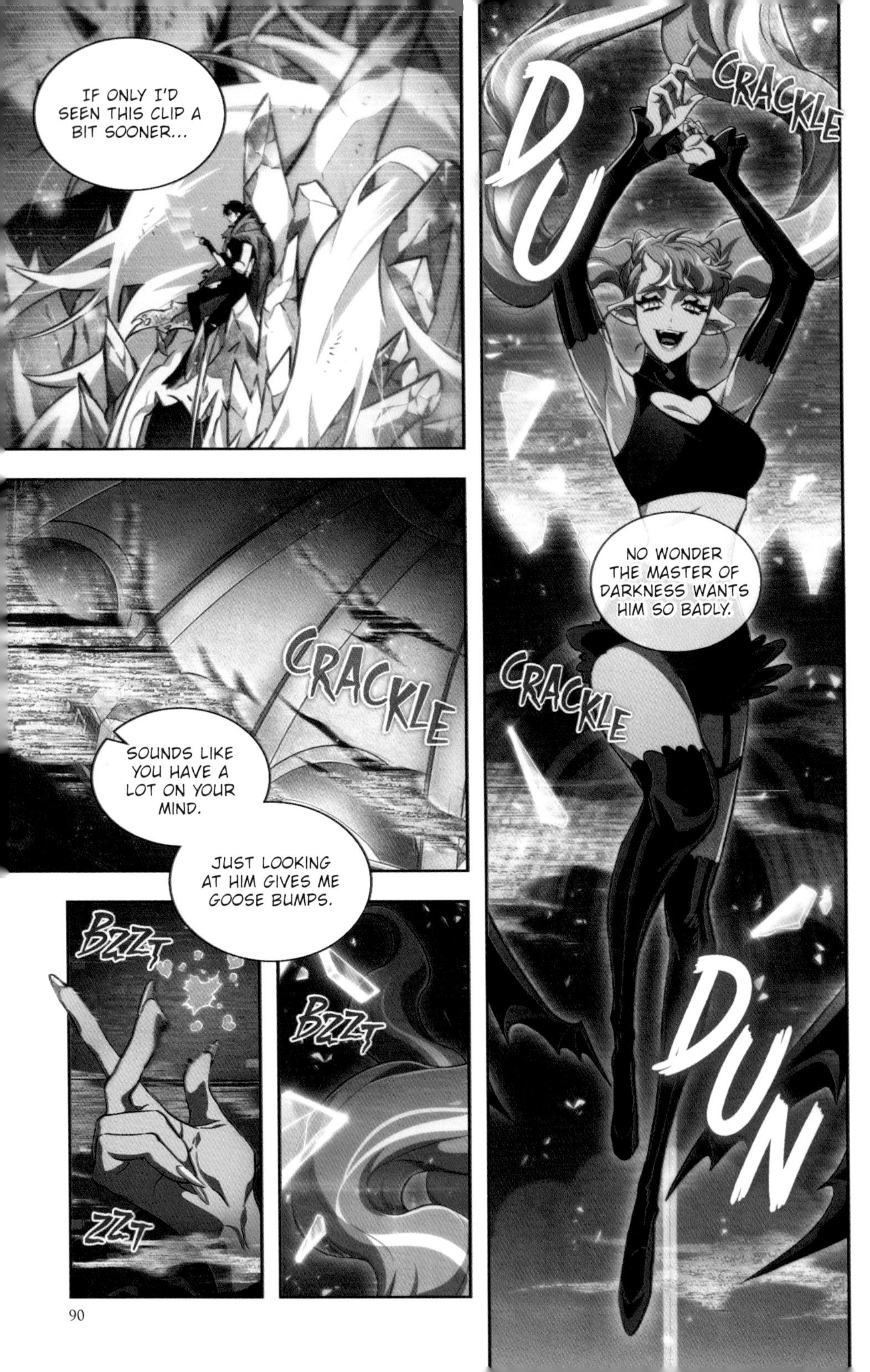
IF ONLY I'D SEEN THIS CLIP A BIT SOONER...
CRACKLE
SOUNDS LIKE YOU HAVE A LOT ON YOUR MIND.
JUST LOOKING AT HIM GIVES ME GOOSE BUMPS.
BZZT
BZZT
ZZT
DU
CRACKLE
NO WONDER THE MASTER OF DARKNESS WANTS HIM SO BADLY.
CRACKLE
DUN

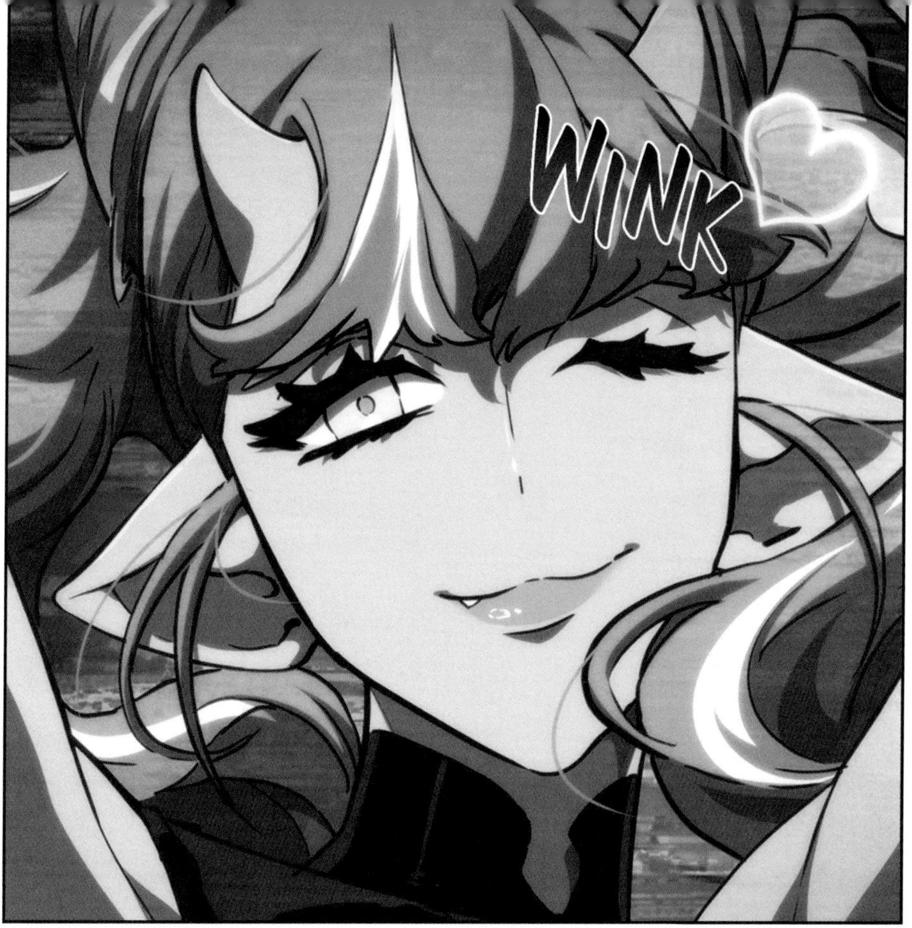
WINK

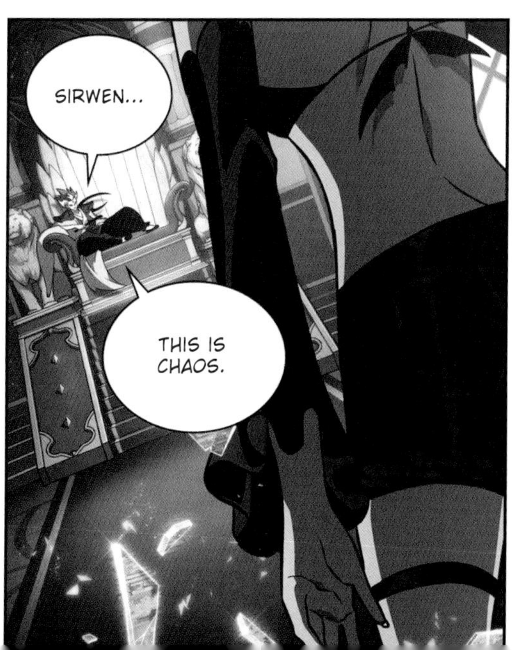
SIRWEN...
THIS IS CHAOS.

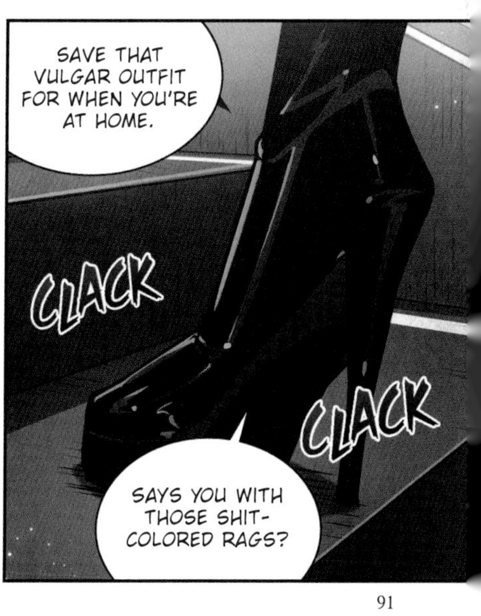
SAVE THAT VULGAR OUTFIT FOR WHEN YOU'RE AT HOME.
CLACK
CLACK
SAYS YOU WITH THOSE SHIT-COLORED RAGS?

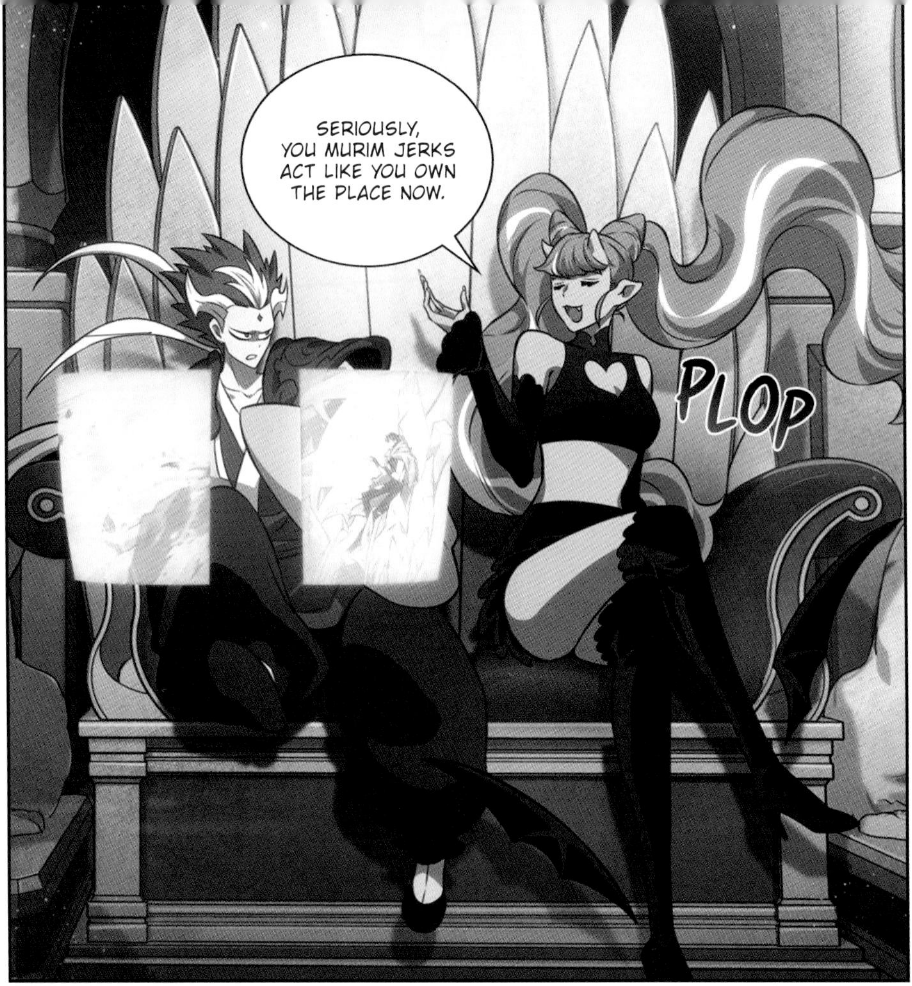
SERIOUSLY, YOU MURIM JERKS ACT LIKE YOU OWN THE PLACE NOW.
PLOP

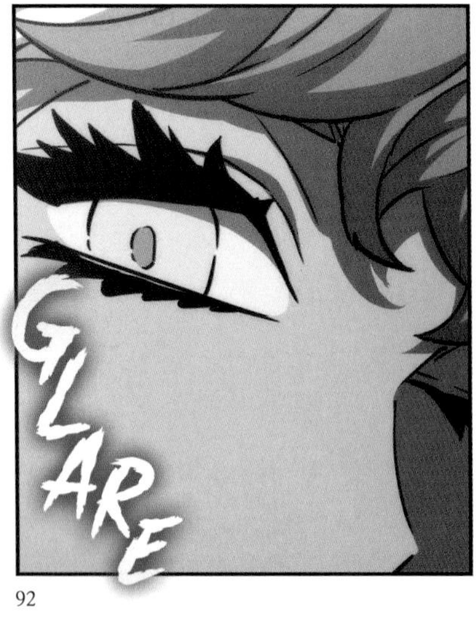
GLARE

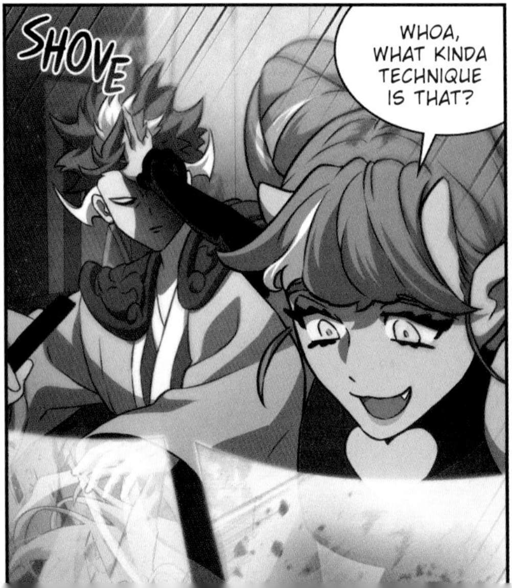
SHOVE
WHOA, WHAT KINDA TECHNIQUE IS THAT?

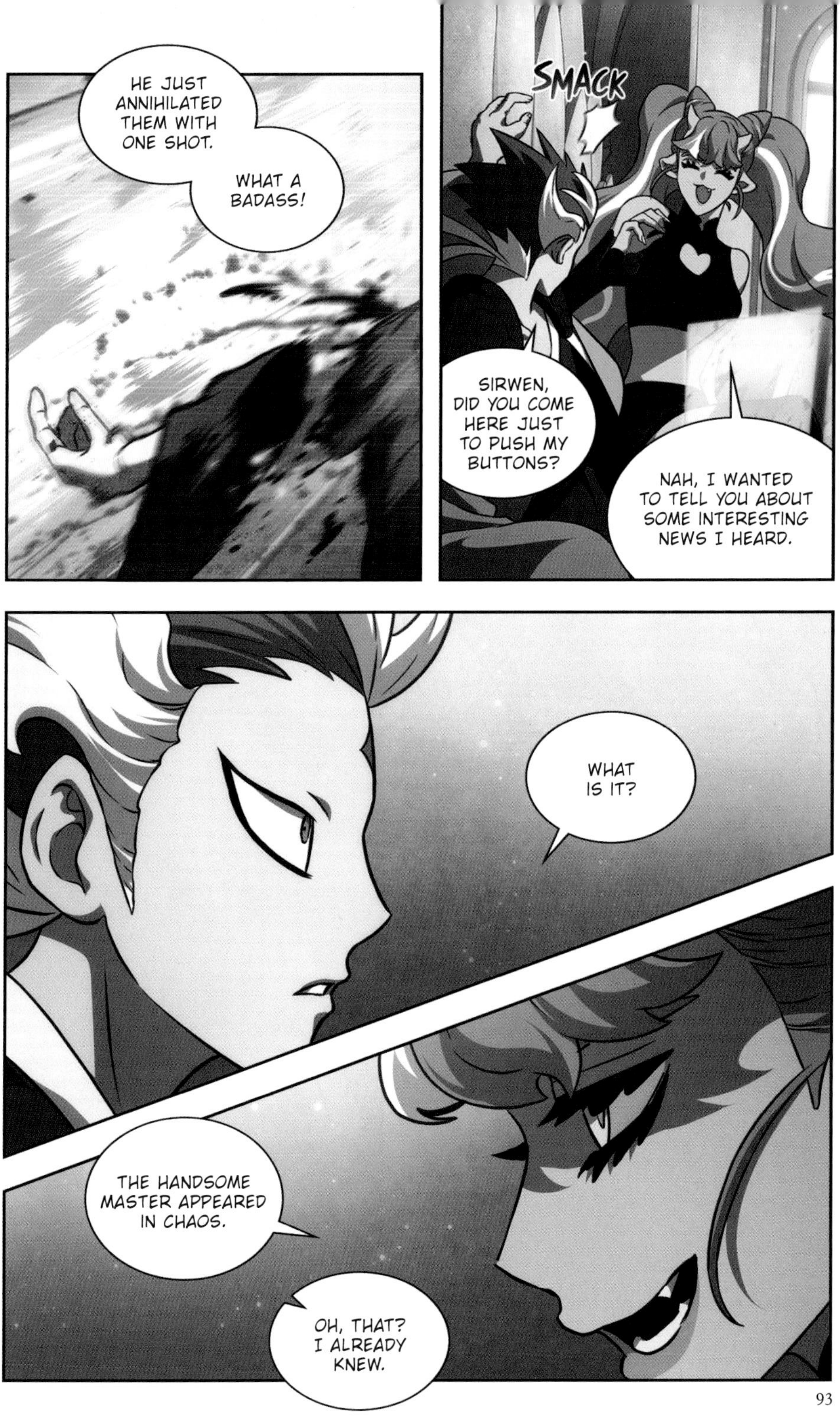
HE JUST ANNIHILATED THEM WITH ONE SHOT.
WHAT A BADASS!
SMACK
SIRWEN, DID YOU COME HERE JUST TO PUSH MY BUTTONS?
NAH, I WANTED TO TELL YOU ABOUT SOME INTERESTING NEWS I HEARD.
WHAT IS IT?
THE HANDSOME MASTER APPEARED IN CHAOS.
OH, THAT? I ALREADY KNEW.

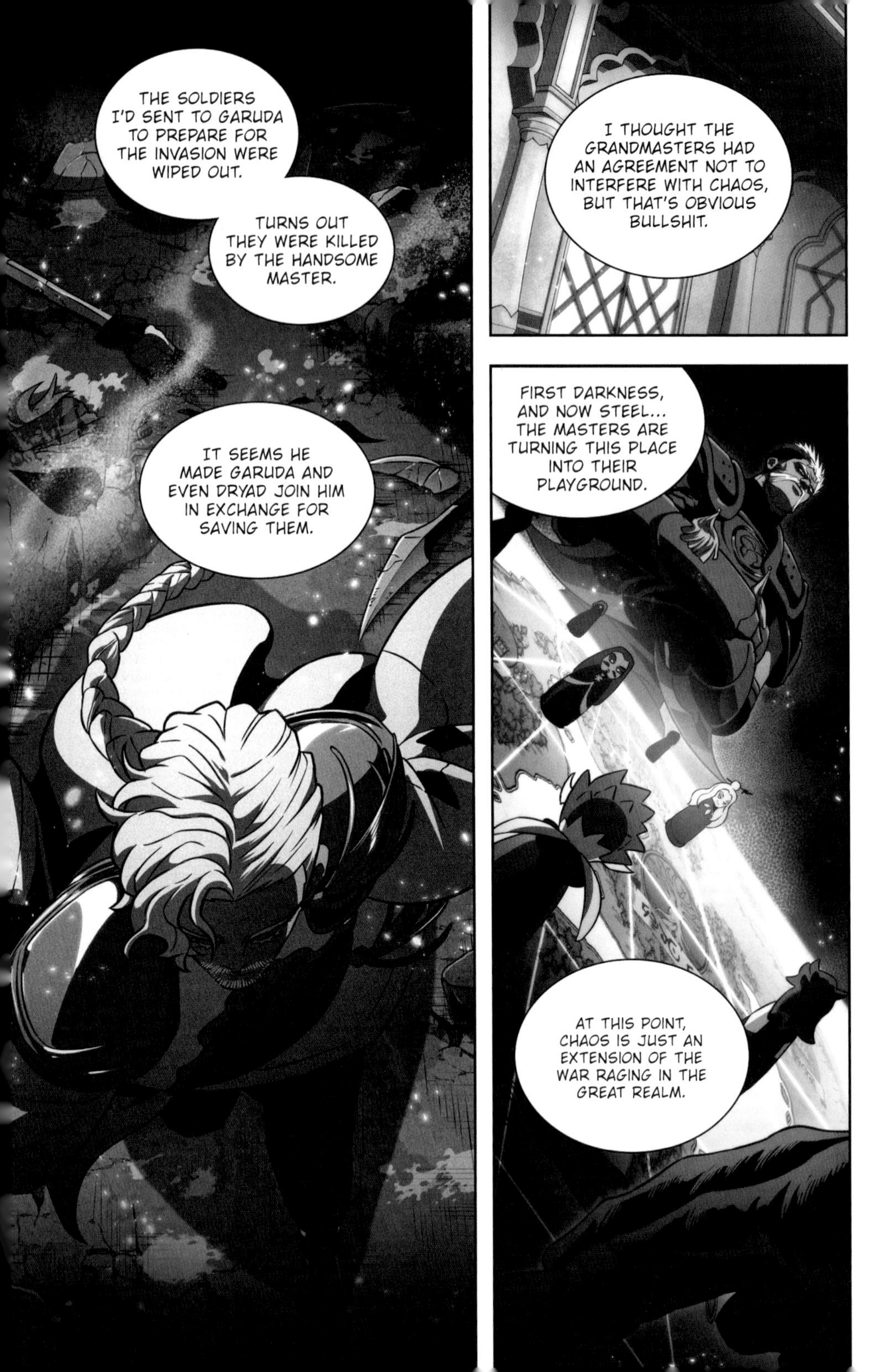
THE SOLDIERS I'D SENT TO GARUDA TO PREPARE FOR THE INVASION WERE WIPED OUT.
TURNS OUT THEY WERE KILLED BY THE HANDSOME MASTER.
IT SEEMS HE MADE GARUDA AND EVEN DRYAD JOIN HIM IN EXCHANGE FOR SAVING THEM.
I THOUGHT THE GRANDMASTERS HAD AN AGREEMENT NOT TO INTERFERE WITH CHAOS, BUT THAT'S OBVIOUS BULLSHIT.
FIRST DARKNESS, AND NOW STEEL... THE MASTERS ARE TURNING THIS PLACE INTO THEIR PLAYGROUND.
AT THIS POINT, CHAOS IS JUST AN EXTENSION OF THE WAR RAGING IN THE GREAT REALM.

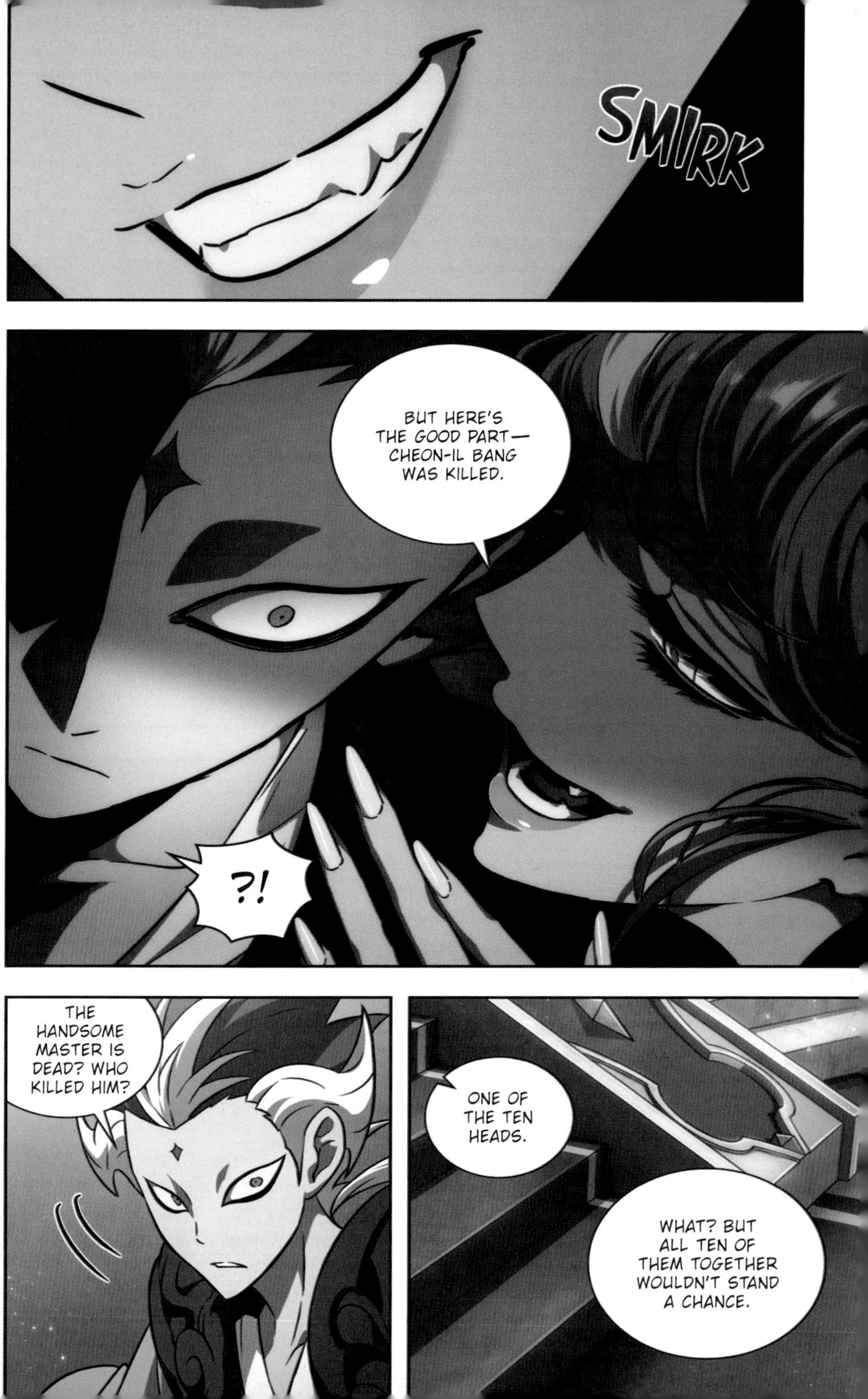
SMIRK
BUT HERE'S THE GOOD PART— CHEON-IL BANG WAS KILLED.
?!
THE HANDSOME MASTER IS DEAD? WHO KILLED HIM?
ONE OF THE TEN HEADS.
WHAT? BUT ALL TEN OF THEM TOGETHER WOULDN'T STAND A CHANCE.

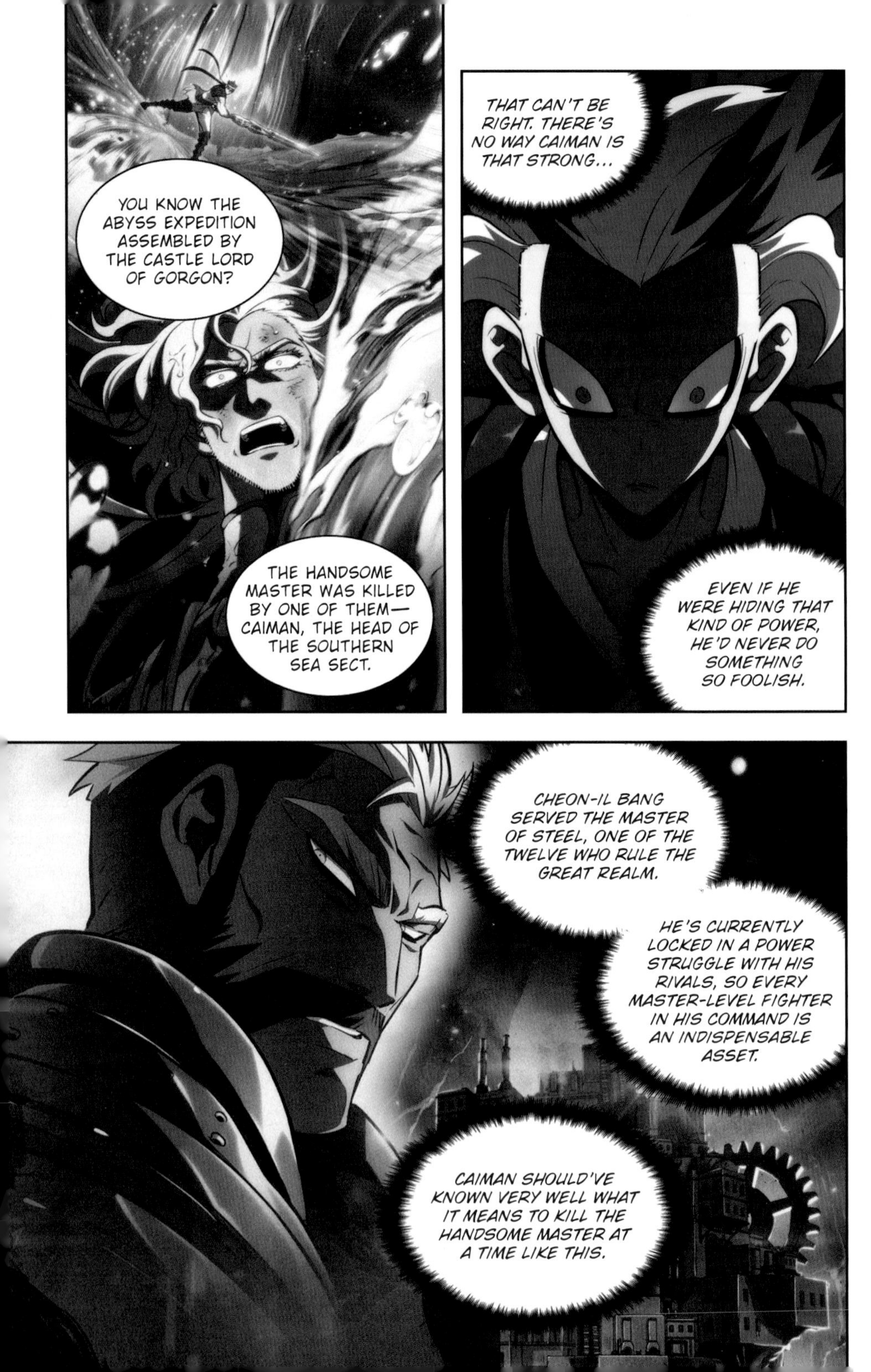
YOU KNOW THE ABYSS EXPEDITION ASSEMBLED BY THE CASTLE LORD OF GORGON?
THE HANDSOME MASTER WAS KILLED BY ONE OF THEM— CAIMAN, THE HEAD OF THE SOUTHERN SEA SECT.
THAT CAN'T BE RIGHT. THERE'S NO WAY CAIMAN IS THAT STRONG...
EVEN IF HE WERE HIDING THAT KIND OF POWER, HE'D NEVER DO SOMETHING SO FOOLISH.
CHEON-IL BANG SERVED THE MASTER OF STEEL, ONE OF THE TWELVE WHO RULE THE GREAT REALM.
HE'S CURRENTLY LOCKED IN A POWER STRUGGLE WITH HIS RIVALS, SO EVERY MASTER-LEVEL FIGHTER IN HIS COMMAND IS AN INDISPENSABLE ASSET.
CAIMAN SHOULD'VE KNOWN VERY WELL WHAT IT MEANS TO KILL THE HANDSOME MASTER AT A TIME LIKE THIS.

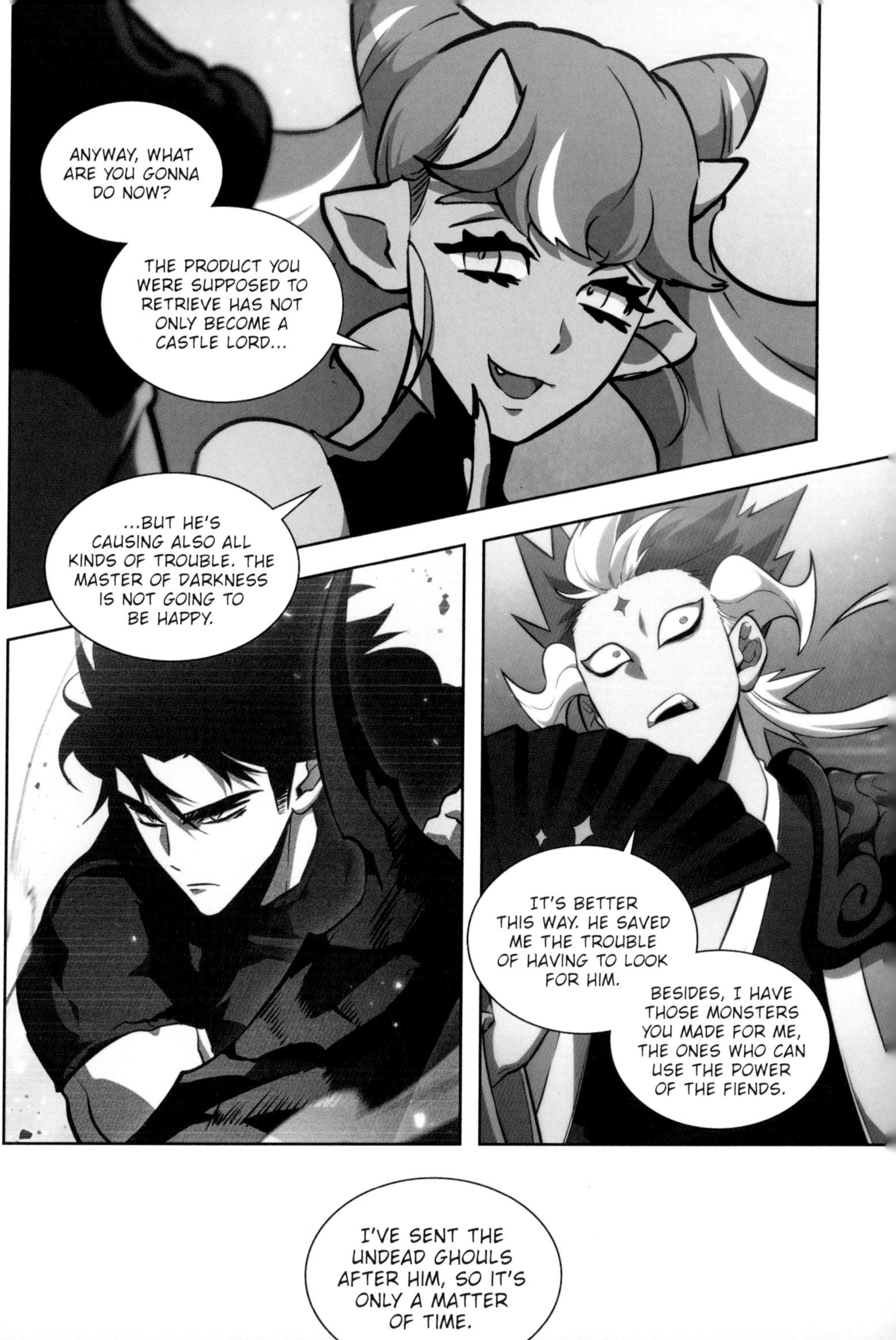
ANYWAY, WHAT ARE YOU GONNA DO NOW?
THE PRODUCT YOU WERE SUPPOSED TO RETRIEVE HAS NOT ONLY BECOME A CASTLE LORD...
...BUT HE'S CAUSING ALSO ALL KINDS OF TROUBLE. THE MASTER OF DARKNESS IS NOT GOING TO BE HAPPY.
IT'S BETTER THIS WAY. HE SAVED ME THE TROUBLE OF HAVING TO LOOK FOR HIM.
BESIDES, I HAVE THOSE MONSTERS YOU MADE FOR ME, THE ONES WHO CAN USE THE POWER OF THE FIENDS.
I'VE SENT THE UNDEAD GHOULS AFTER HIM, SO IT'S ONLY A MATTER OF TIME.

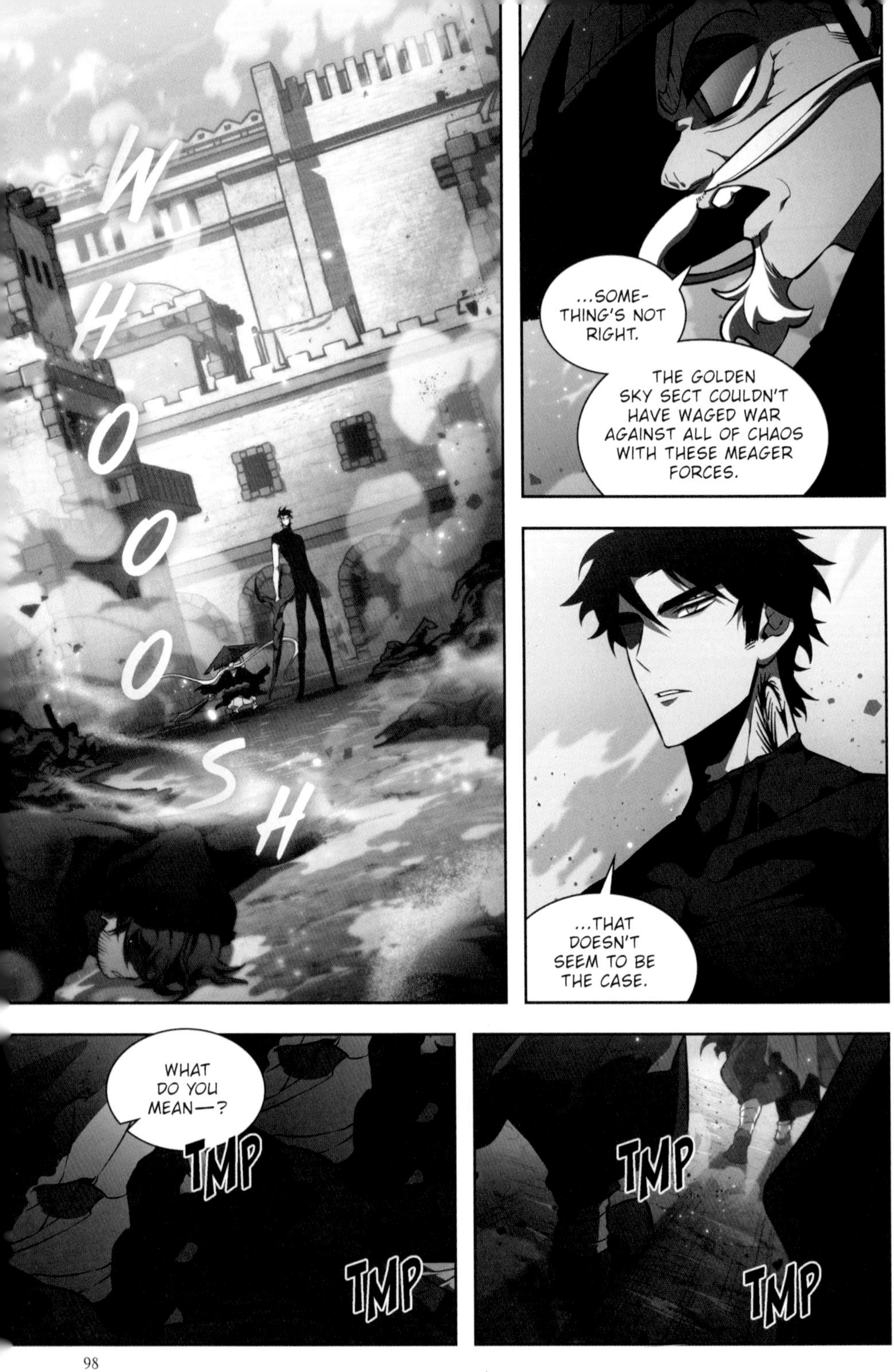
WHOOOOSH
...SOME-THING'S NOT RIGHT.
THE GOLDEN SKY SECT COULDN'T HAVE WAGED WAR AGAINST ALL OF CHAOS WITH THESE MEAGER FORCES.
...THAT DOESN'T SEEM TO BE THE CASE.
WHAT DO YOU MEAN—?
TMP
TMP
TMP
TMP

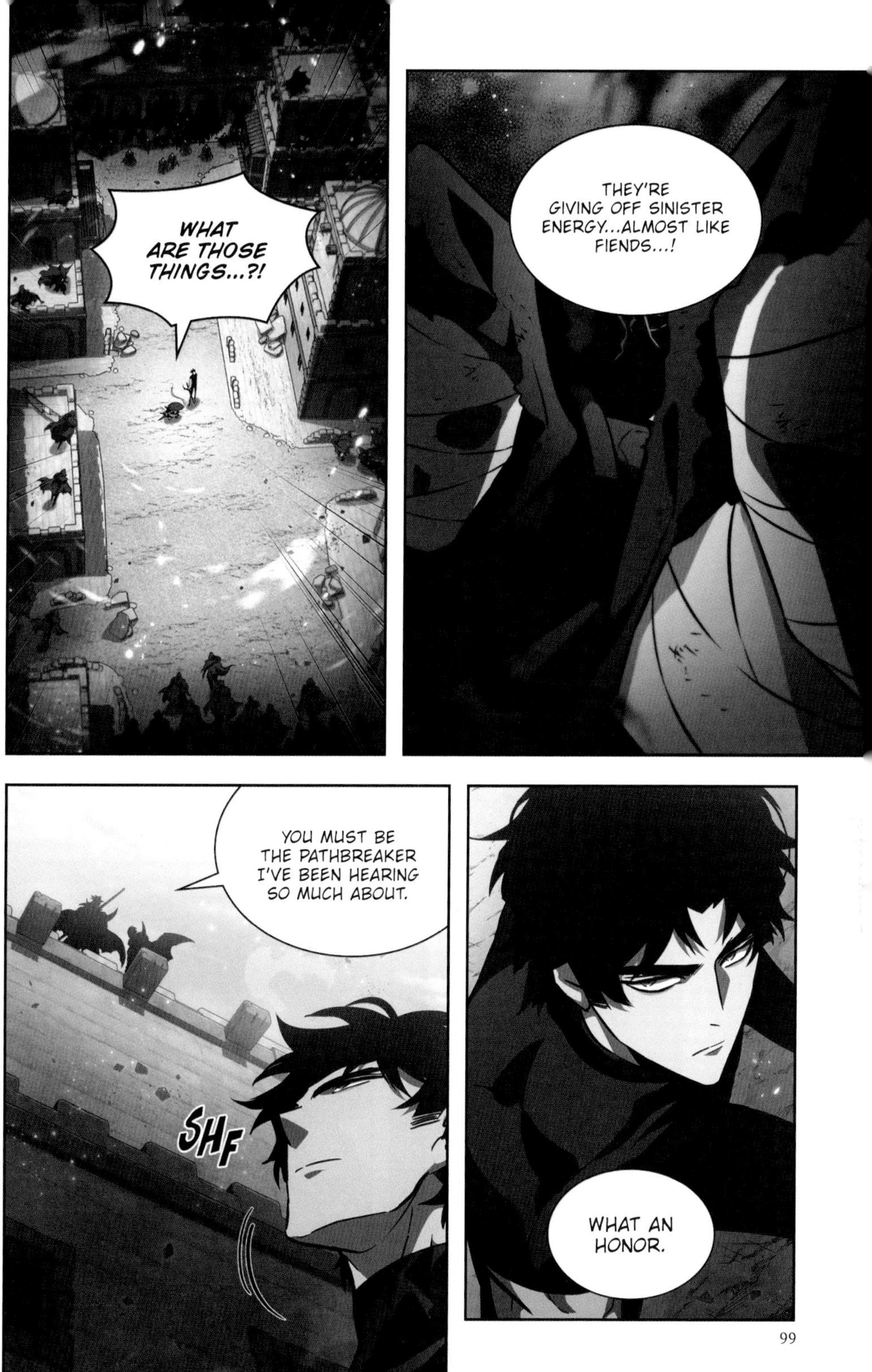
WHAT ARE THOSE THINGS...?!
THEY'RE GIVING OFF SINISTER ENERGY...ALMOST LIKE FIENDS...!
YOU MUST BE THE PATHBREAKER I'VE BEEN HEARING SO MUCH ABOUT.
SHF
WHAT AN HONOR.

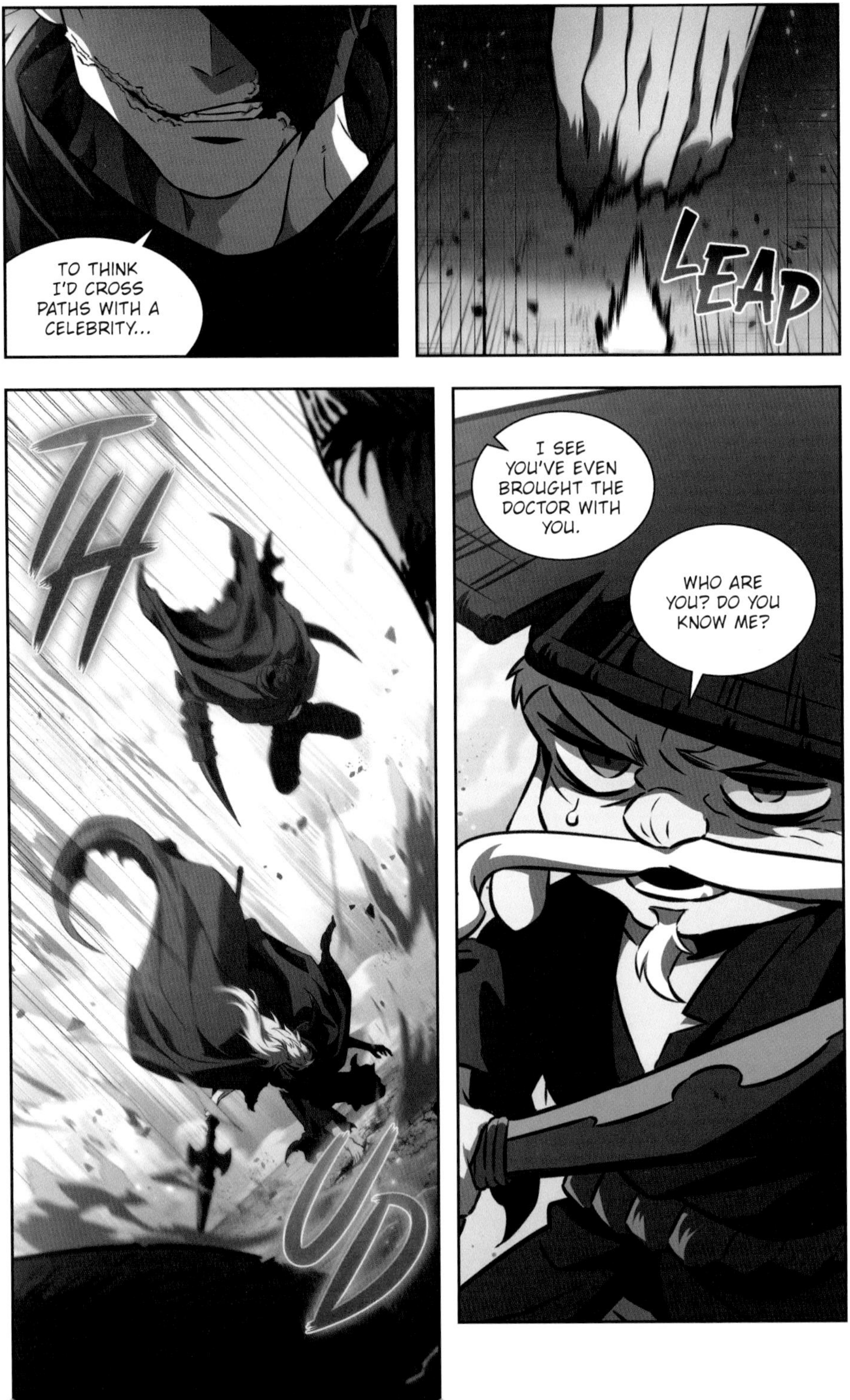
TO THINK I'D CROSS PATHS WITH A CELEBRITY...
LEAP
THUD
I SEE YOU'VE EVEN BROUGHT THE DOCTOR WITH YOU.
WHO ARE YOU? DO YOU KNOW ME?

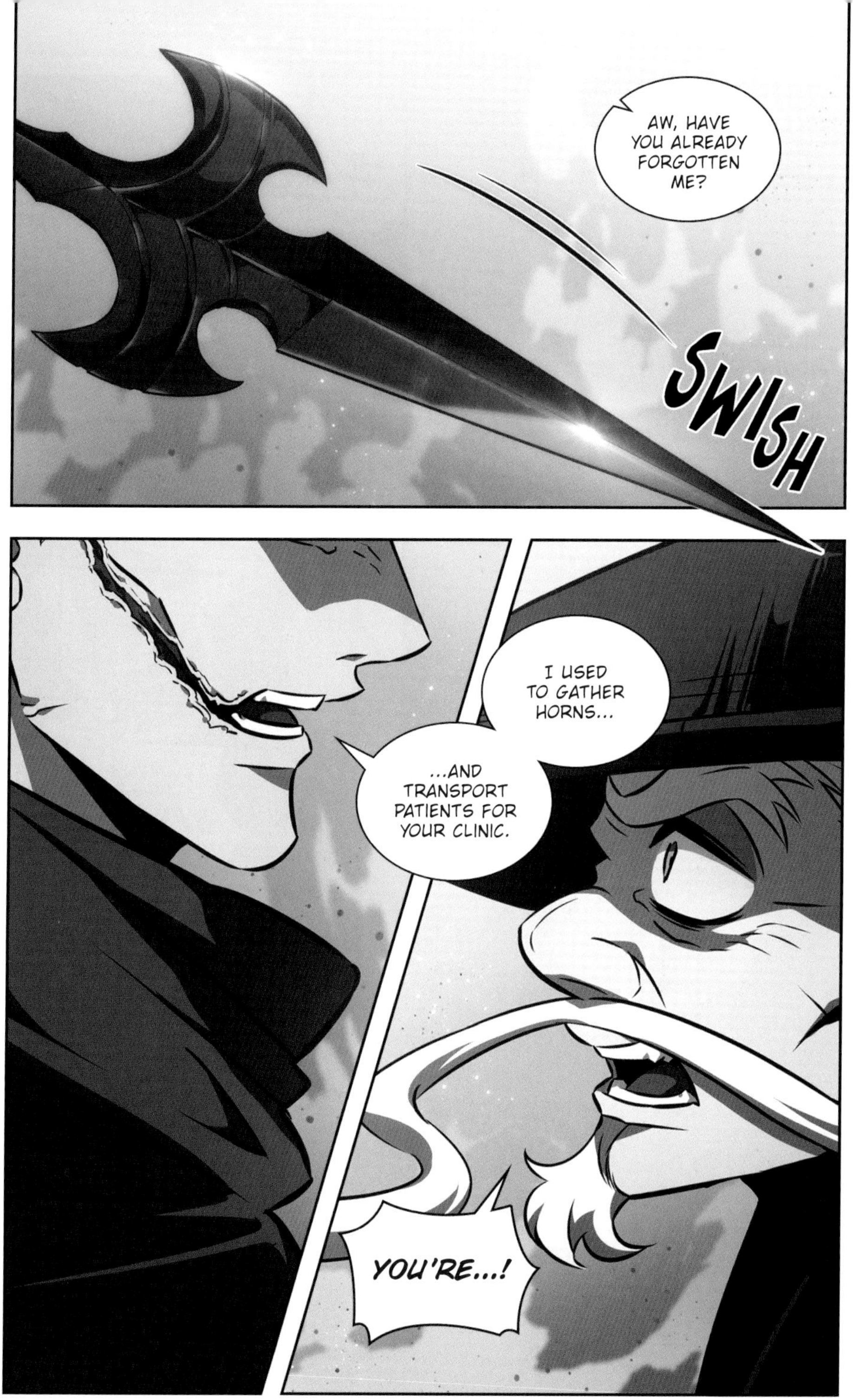
AW, HAVE YOU ALREADY FORGOTTEN ME?
SWISH
I USED TO GATHER HORNS...
...AND TRANSPORT PATIENTS FOR YOUR CLINIC.
YOU'RE...!

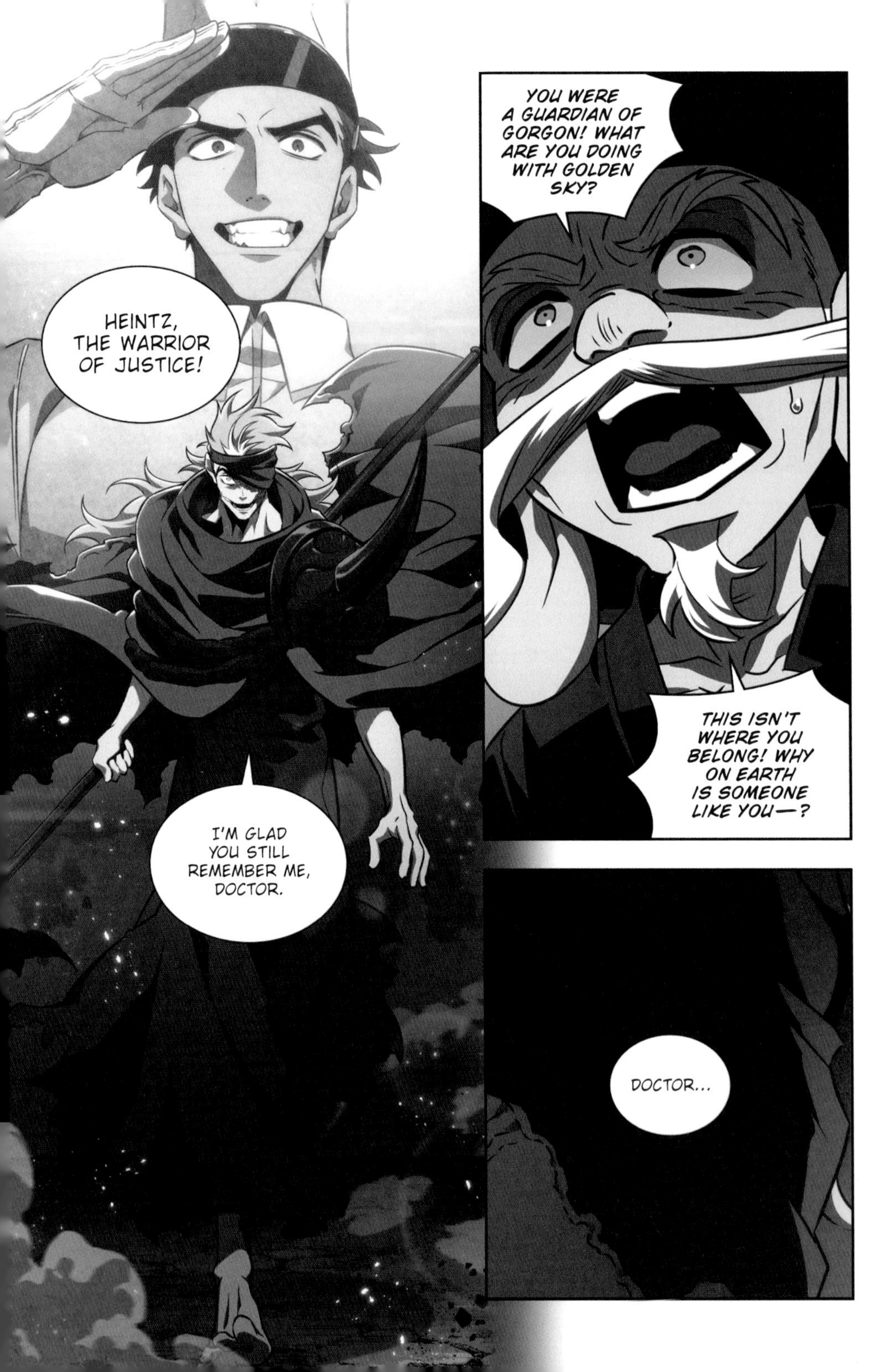
HEINTZ, THE WARRIOR OF JUSTICE!
I'M GLAD YOU STILL REMEMBER ME, DOCTOR.
YOU WERE A GUARDIAN OF GORGON! WHAT ARE YOU DOING WITH GOLDEN SKY?
THIS ISN'T WHERE YOU BELONG! WHY ON EARTH IS SOMEONE LIKE YOU—?
DOCTOR...

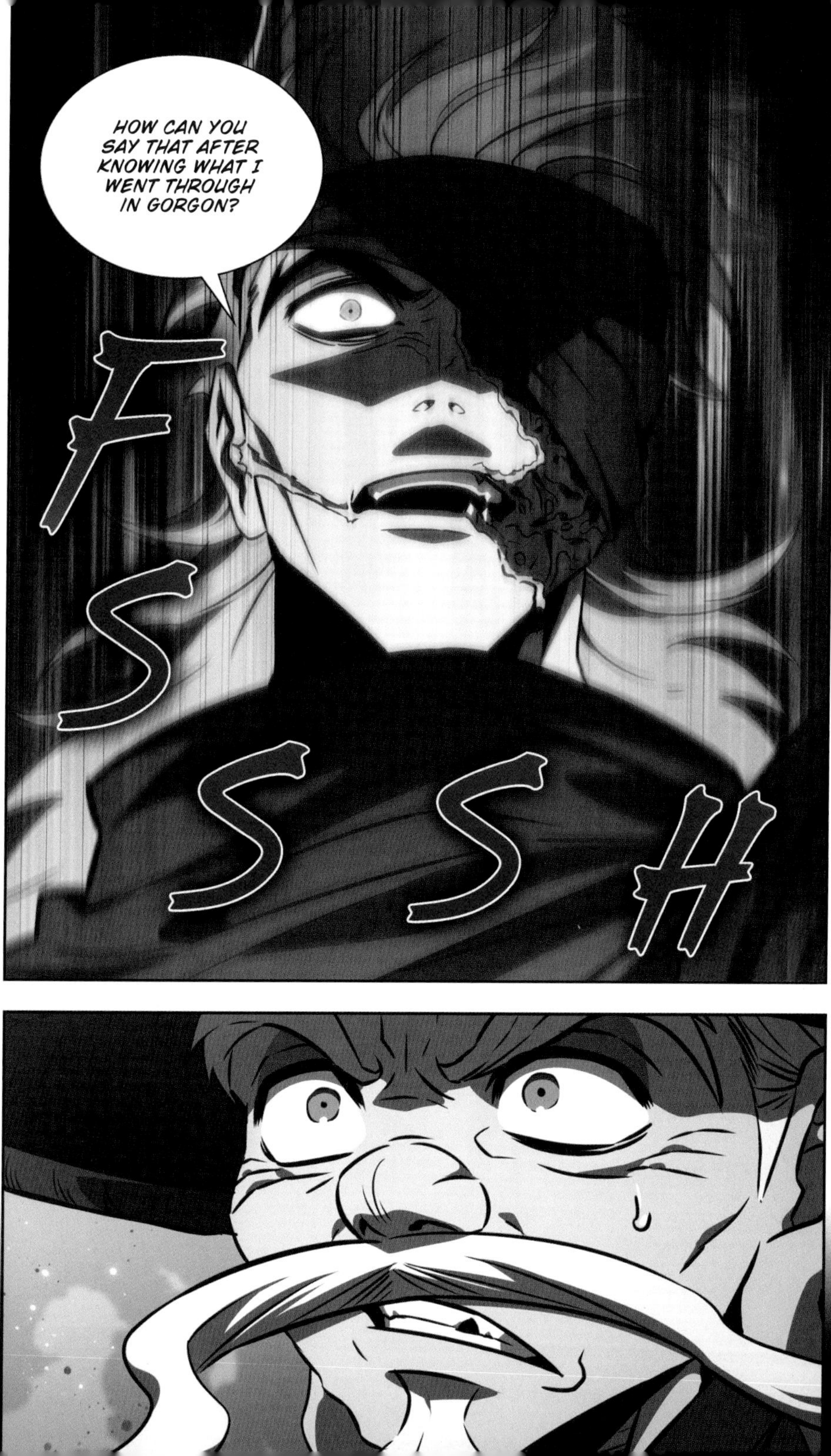
HOW CAN YOU SAY THAT AFTER KNOWING WHAT I WENT THROUGH IN GORGON?
FSSSH

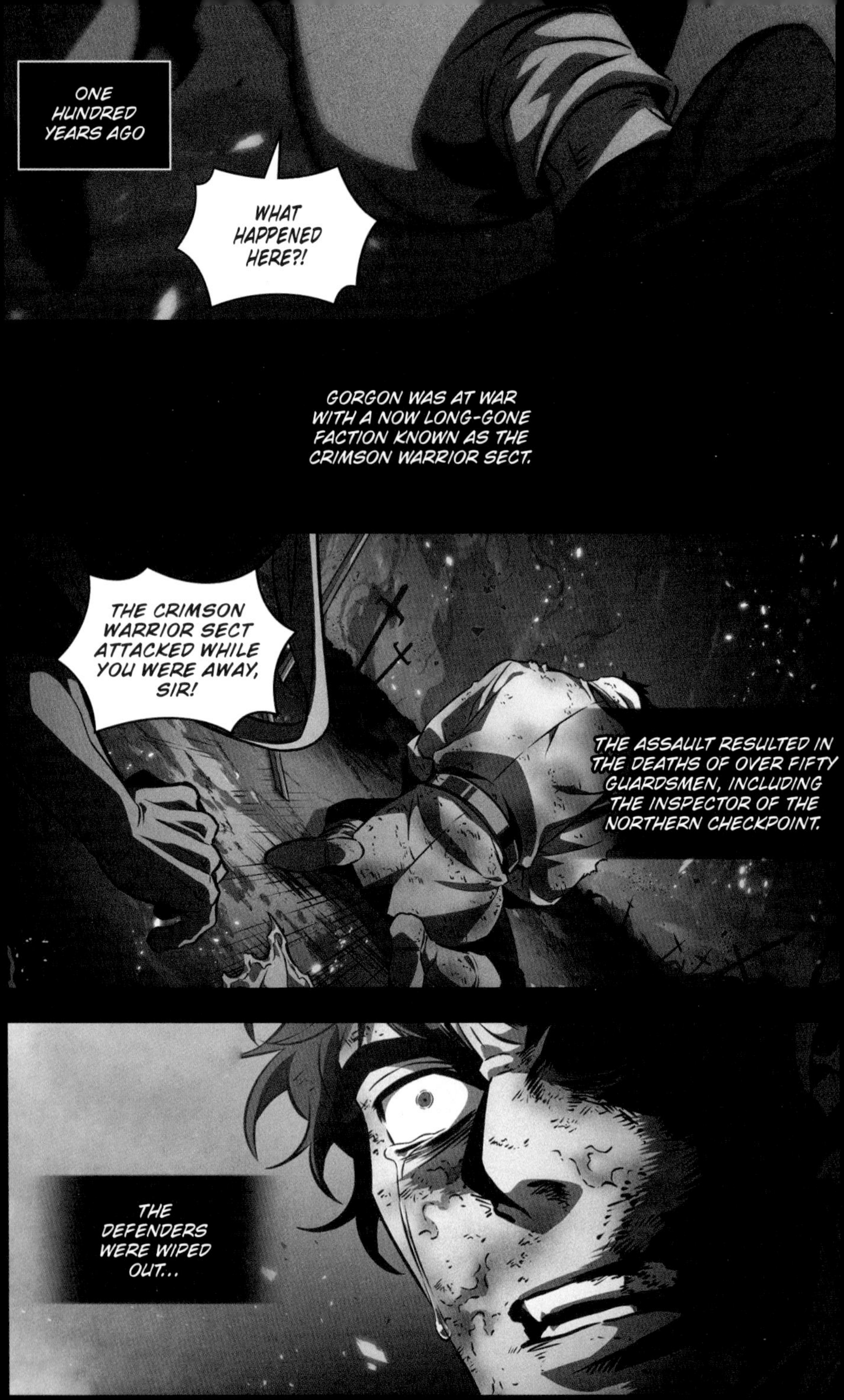

ONE HUNDRED YEARS AGO
WHAT HAPPENED HERE?!
GORGON WAS AT WAR WITH A NOW LONG-GONE FACTION KNOWN AS THE CRIMSON WARRIOR SECT.
THE CRIMSON WARRIOR SECT ATTACKED WHILE YOU WERE AWAY, SIR!
THE ASSAULT RESULTED IN THE DEATHS OF OVER FIFTY GUARDSMEN, INCLUDING THE INSPECTOR OF THE NORTHERN CHECKPOINT.
THE DEFENDERS WERE WIPED OUT...

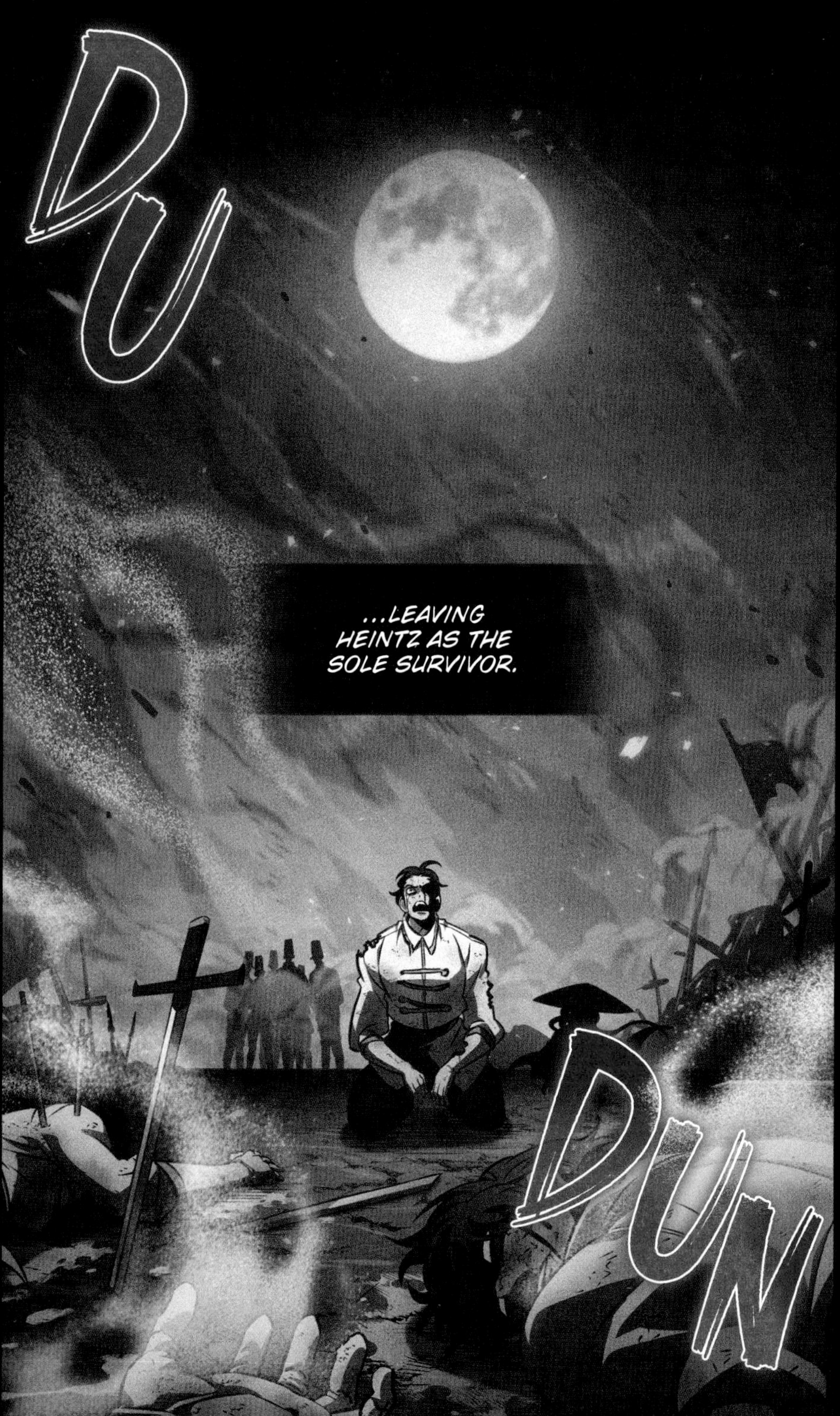
DU
...LEAVING HEINTZ AS THE SOLE SURVIVOR.
DUN

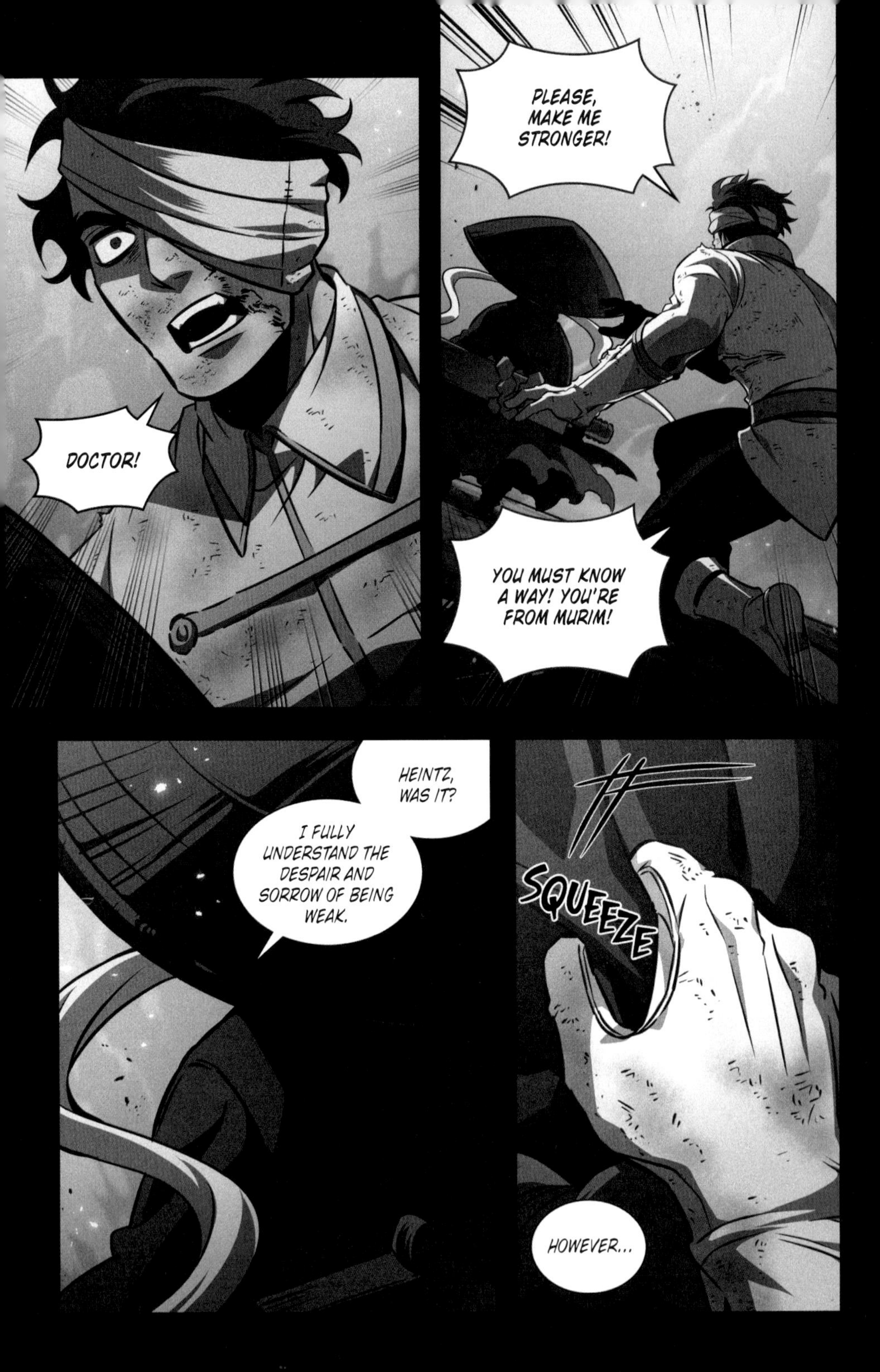
DOCTOR!
PLEASE, MAKE ME STRONGER!
YOU MUST KNOW A WAY! YOU'RE FROM MURIM!
HEINTZ, WAS IT?
I FULLY UNDERSTAND THE DESPAIR AND SORROW OF BEING WEAK.
SQUEEZE
HOWEVER...

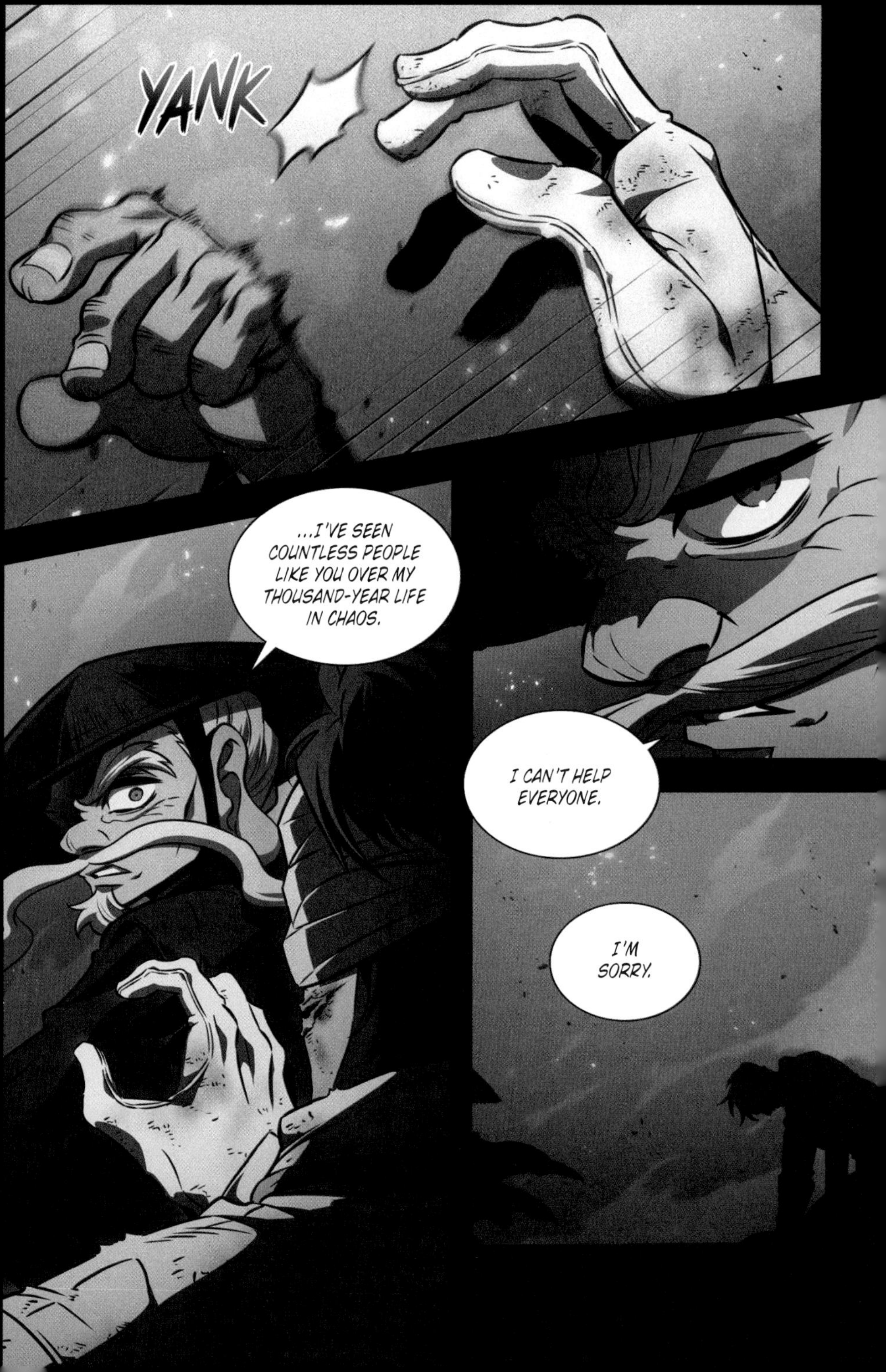
YANK
...I'VE SEEN COUNTLESS PEOPLE LIKE YOU OVER MY THOUSAND-YEAR LIFE IN CHAOS.
I CAN'T HELP EVERYONE.
I'M SORRY.

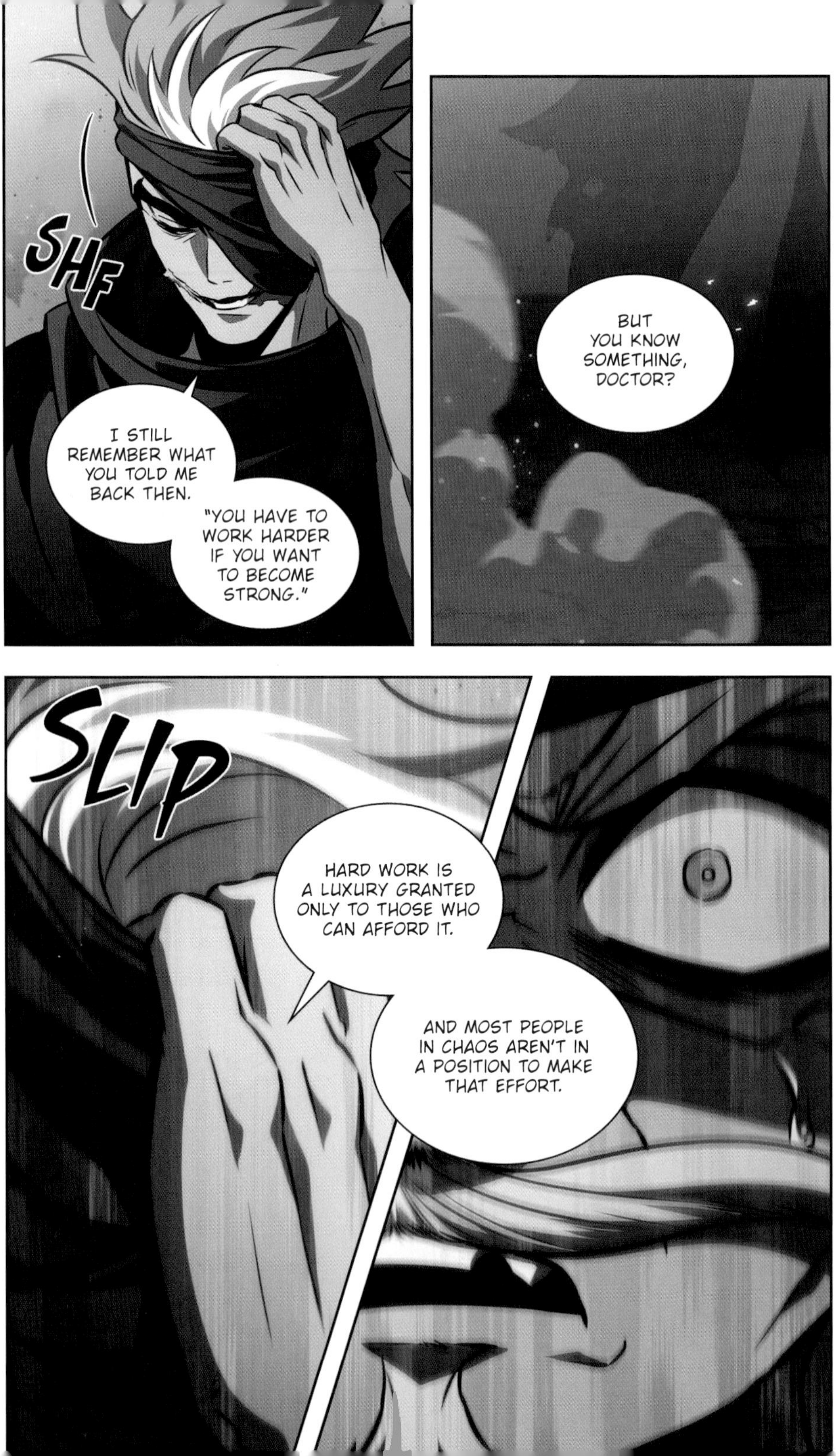
SHF
I STILL REMEMBER WHAT YOU TOLD ME BACK THEN.
"YOU HAVE TO WORK HARDER IF YOU WANT TO BECOME STRONG."
BUT YOU KNOW SOMETHING, DOCTOR?
SLIP
HARD WORK IS A LUXURY GRANTED ONLY TO THOSE WHO CAN AFFORD IT.
AND MOST PEOPLE IN CHAOS AREN'T IN A POSITION TO MAKE THAT EFFORT.

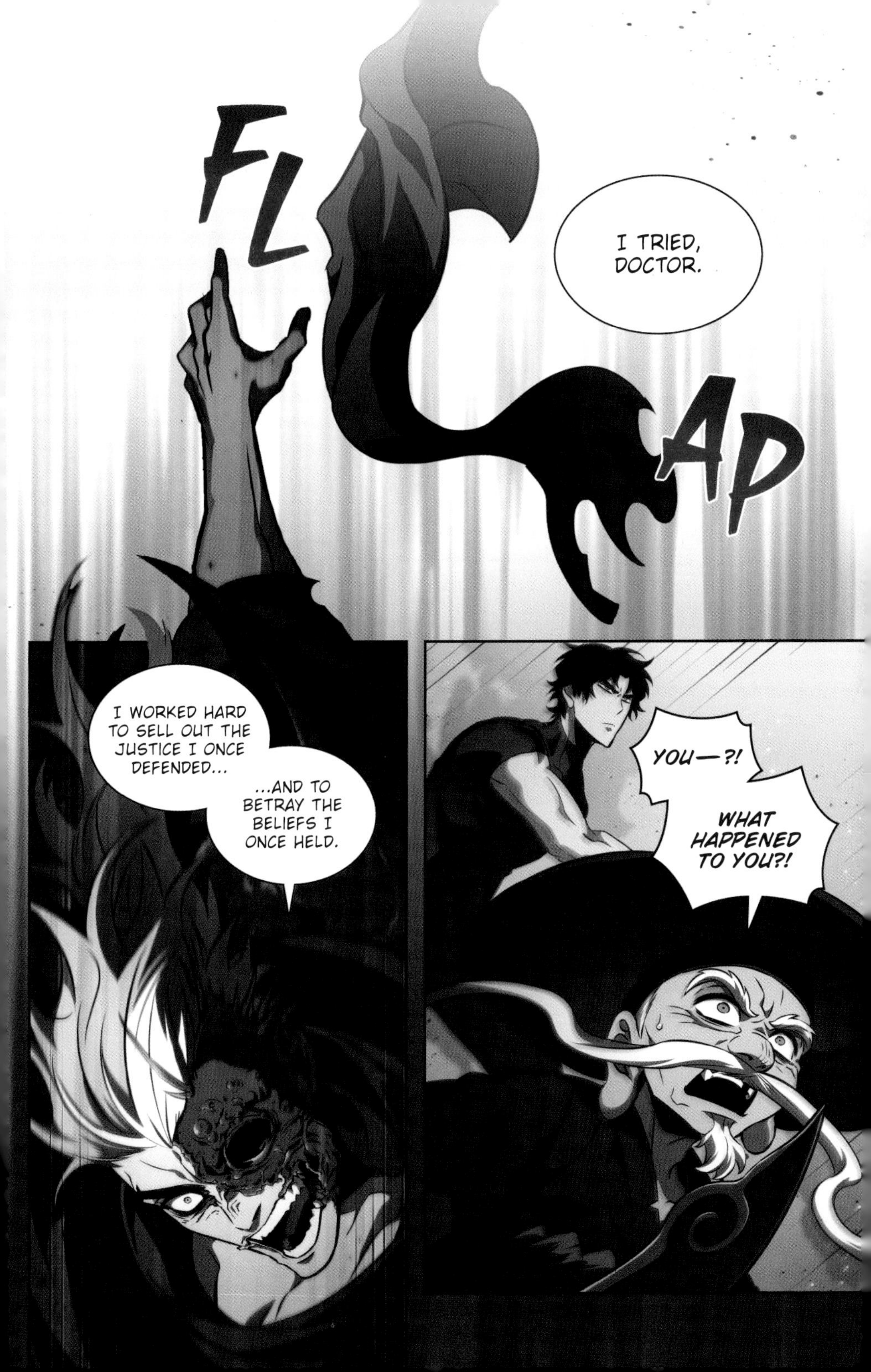
FL
AP
I TRIED, DOCTOR.
I WORKED HARD TO SELL OUT THE JUSTICE I ONCE DEFENDED...
...AND TO BETRAY THE BELIEFS I ONCE HELD.
YOU—?!
WHAT HAPPENED TO YOU?!

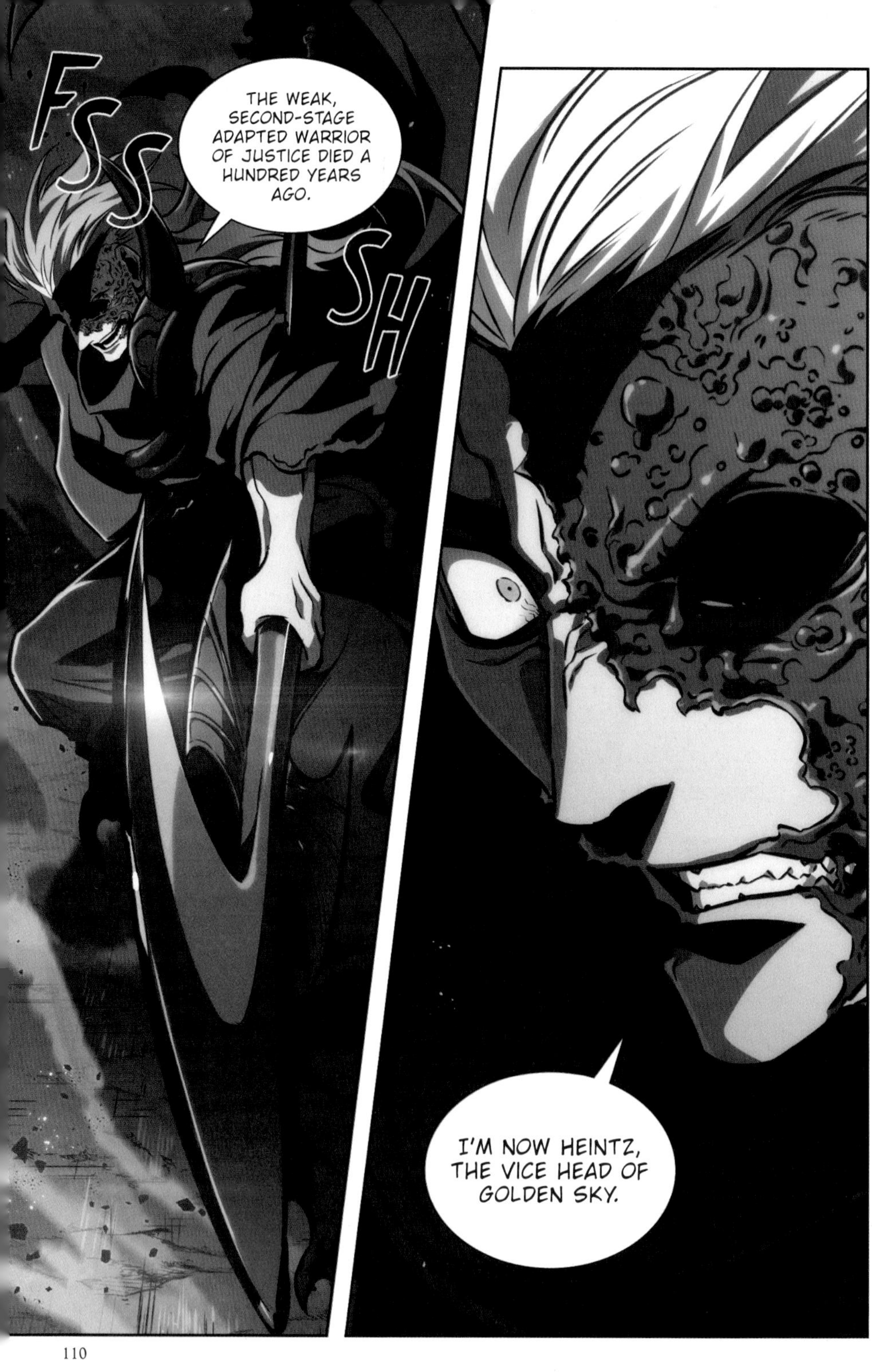
FSSSH
THE WEAK, SECOND-STAGE ADAPTED WARRIOR OF JUSTICE DIED A HUNDRED YEARS AGO.
I'M NOW HEINTZ, THE VICE HEAD OF GOLDEN SKY.

The World After the Fall

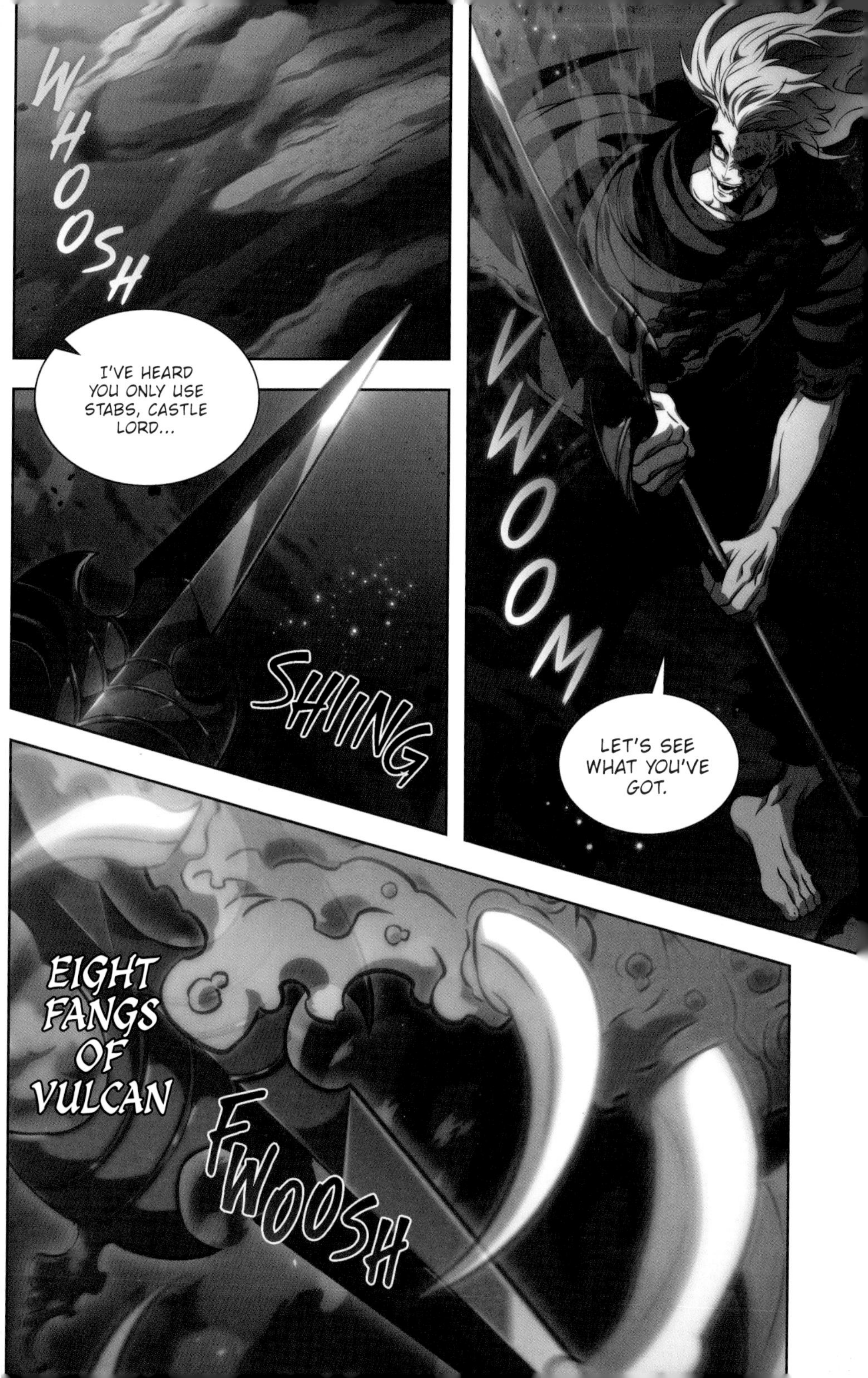
WHOOSH
I'VE HEARD YOU ONLY USE STABS, CASTLE LORD...
SHING
VWOOOM
LET'S SEE WHAT YOU'VE GOT.
EIGHT FANGS OF VULCAN
FWOOSH

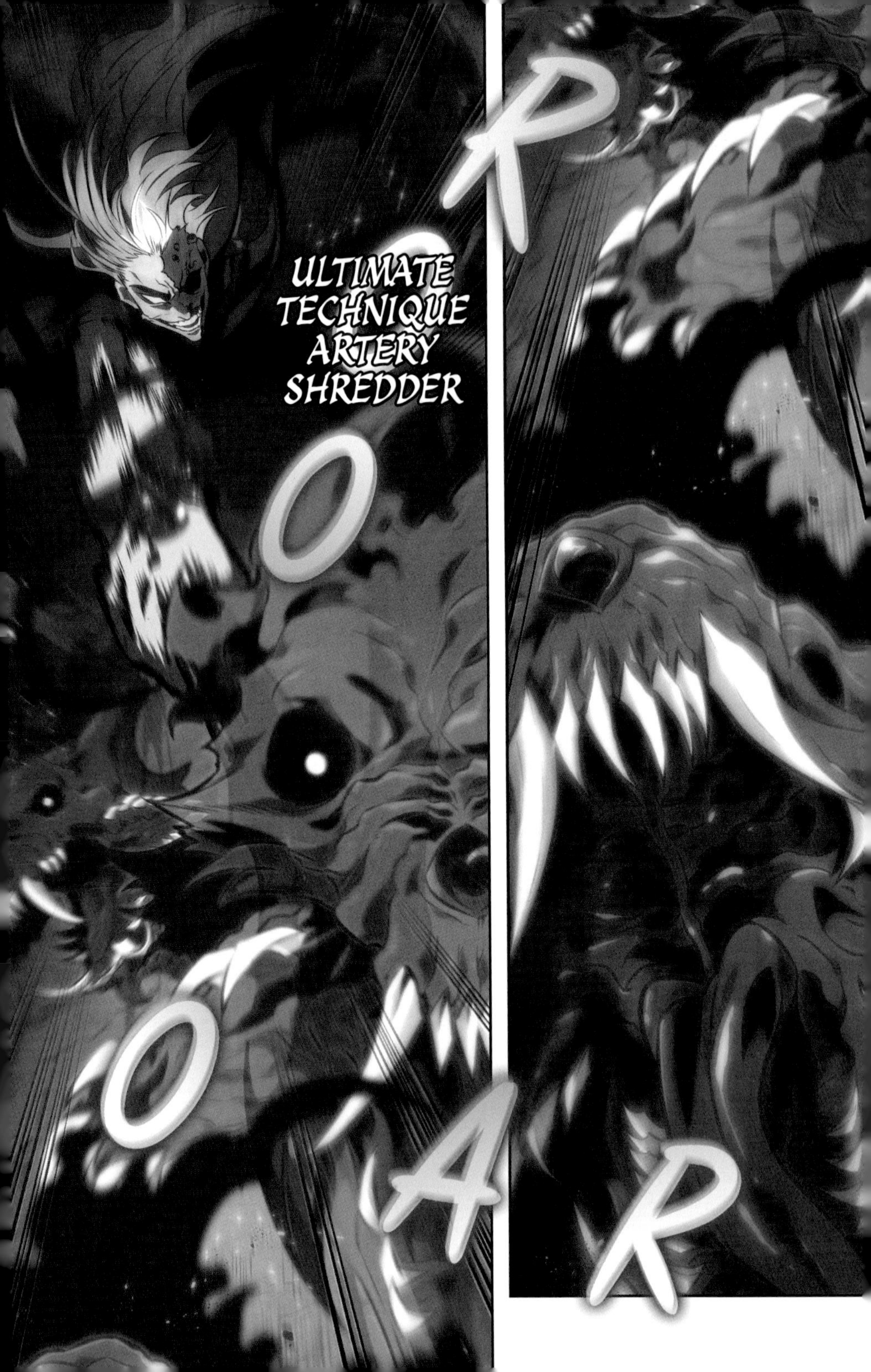
ULTIMATE TECHNIQUE ARTERY SHREDDER
ROOAR

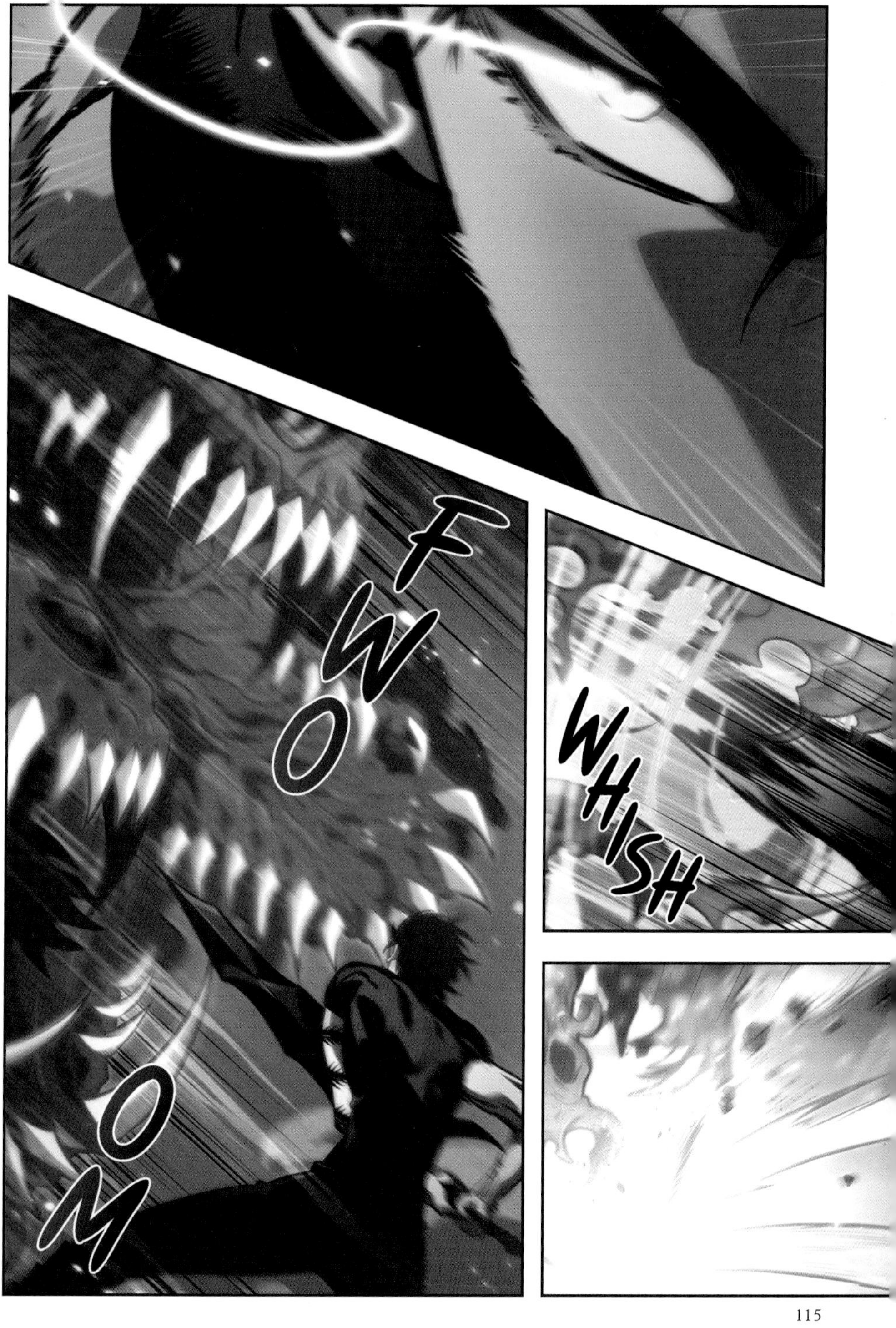
FWOOM
WHISH

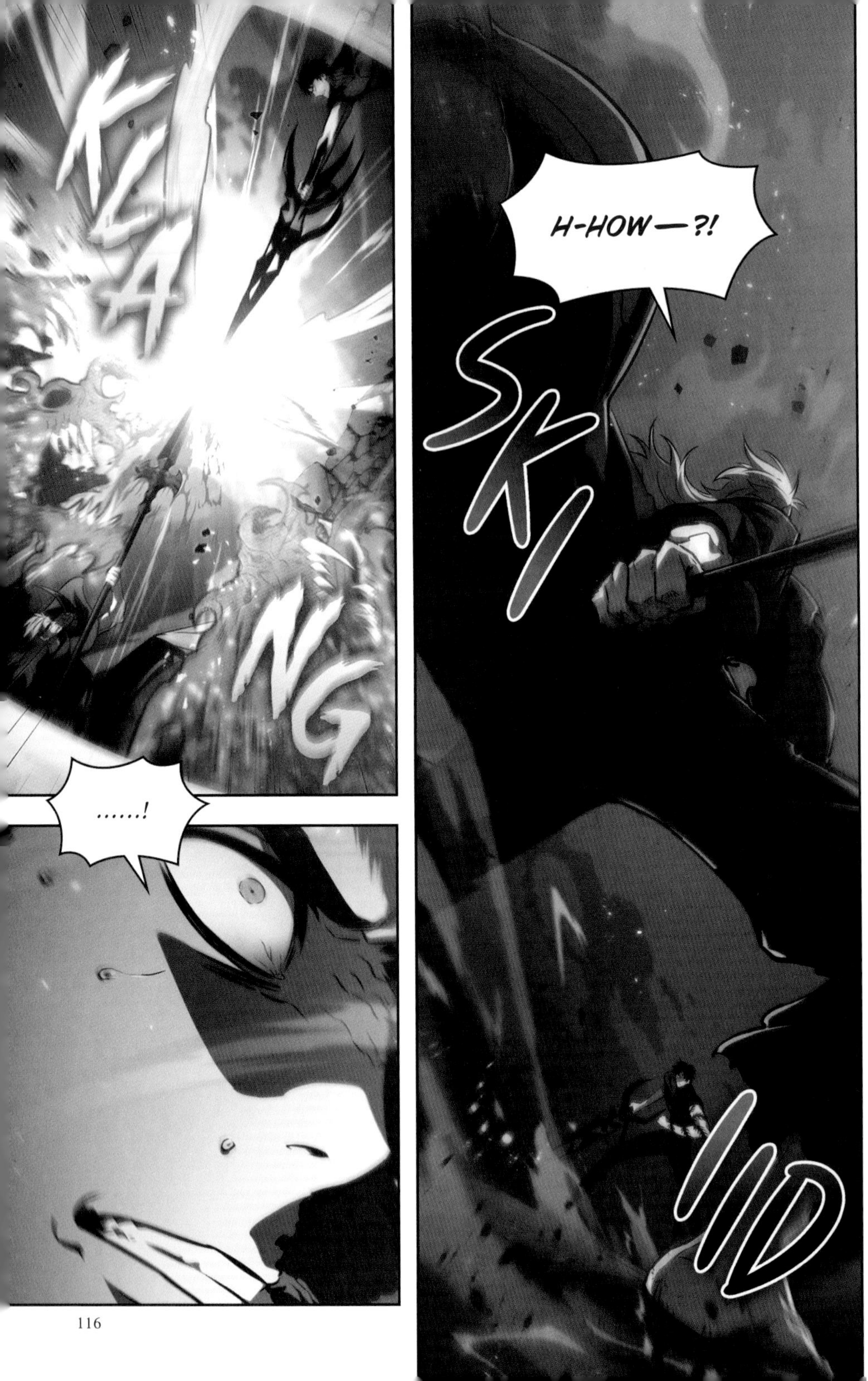
KLANG
......!
H-HOW—?!
SKIIID

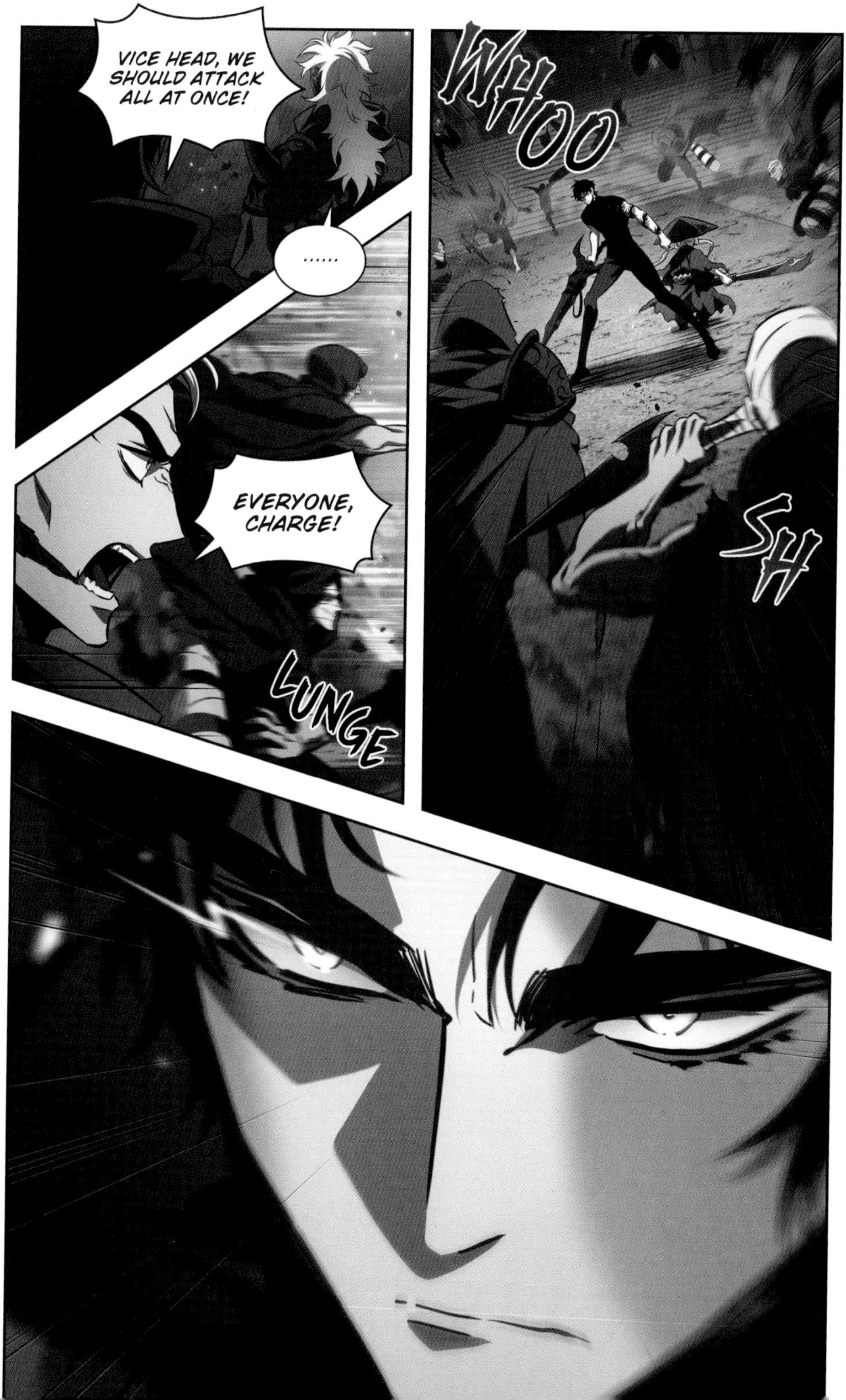
VICE HEAD, WE SHOULD ATTACK ALL AT ONCE!
......
EVERYONE, CHARGE!
LUNGE
WHOO
SH

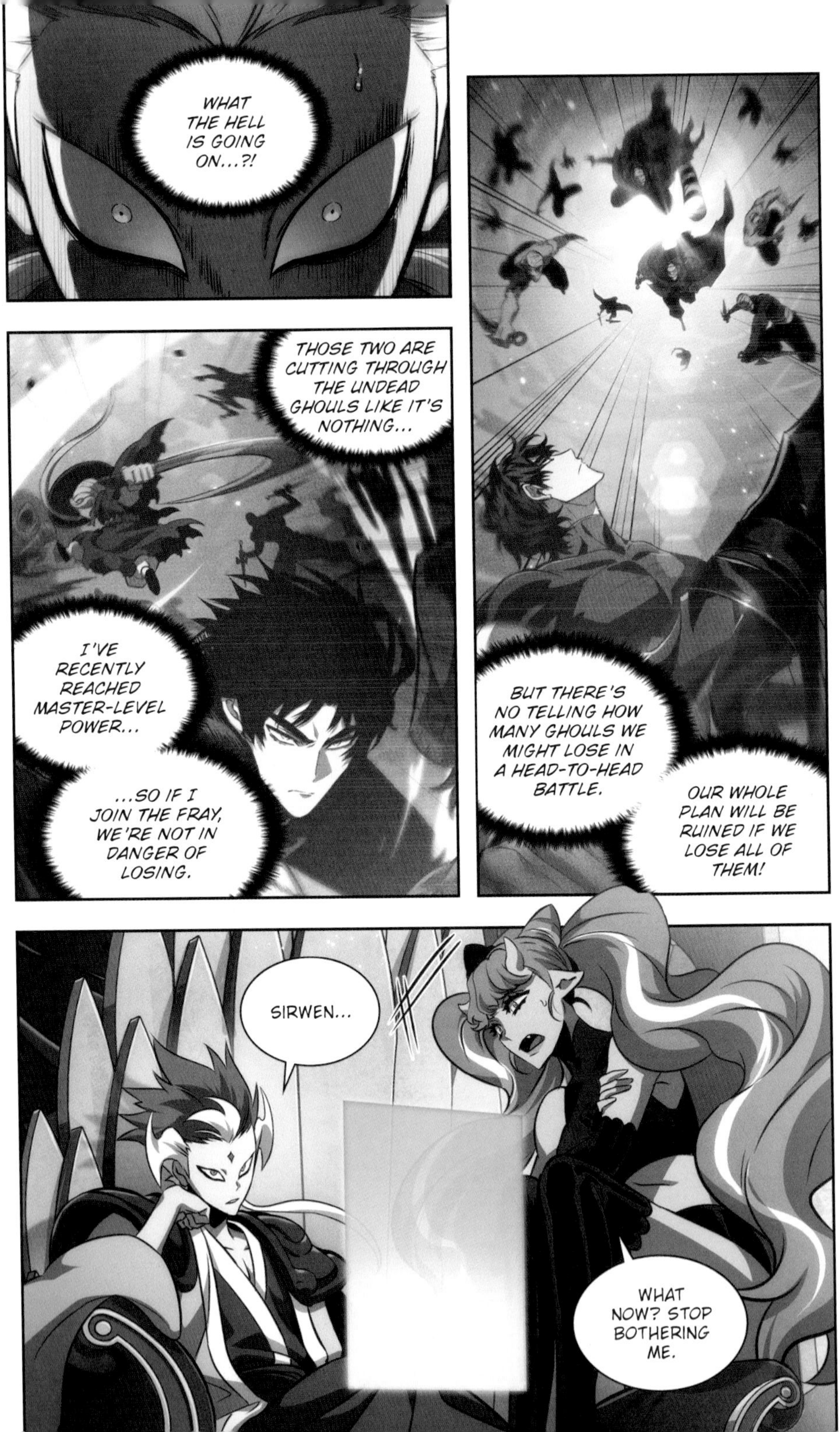
WHAT THE HELL IS GOING ON...?!
THOSE TWO ARE CUTTING THROUGH THE UNDEAD GHOULS LIKE IT'S NOTHING...
I'VE RECENTLY REACHED MASTER-LEVEL POWER...
...SO IF I JOIN THE FRAY, WE'RE NOT IN DANGER OF LOSING.
BUT THERE'S NO TELLING HOW MANY GHOULS WE MIGHT LOSE IN A HEAD-TO-HEAD BATTLE.
OUR WHOLE PLAN WILL BE RUINED IF WE LOSE ALL OF THEM!
SIRWEN...
WHAT NOW? STOP BOTHERING ME.

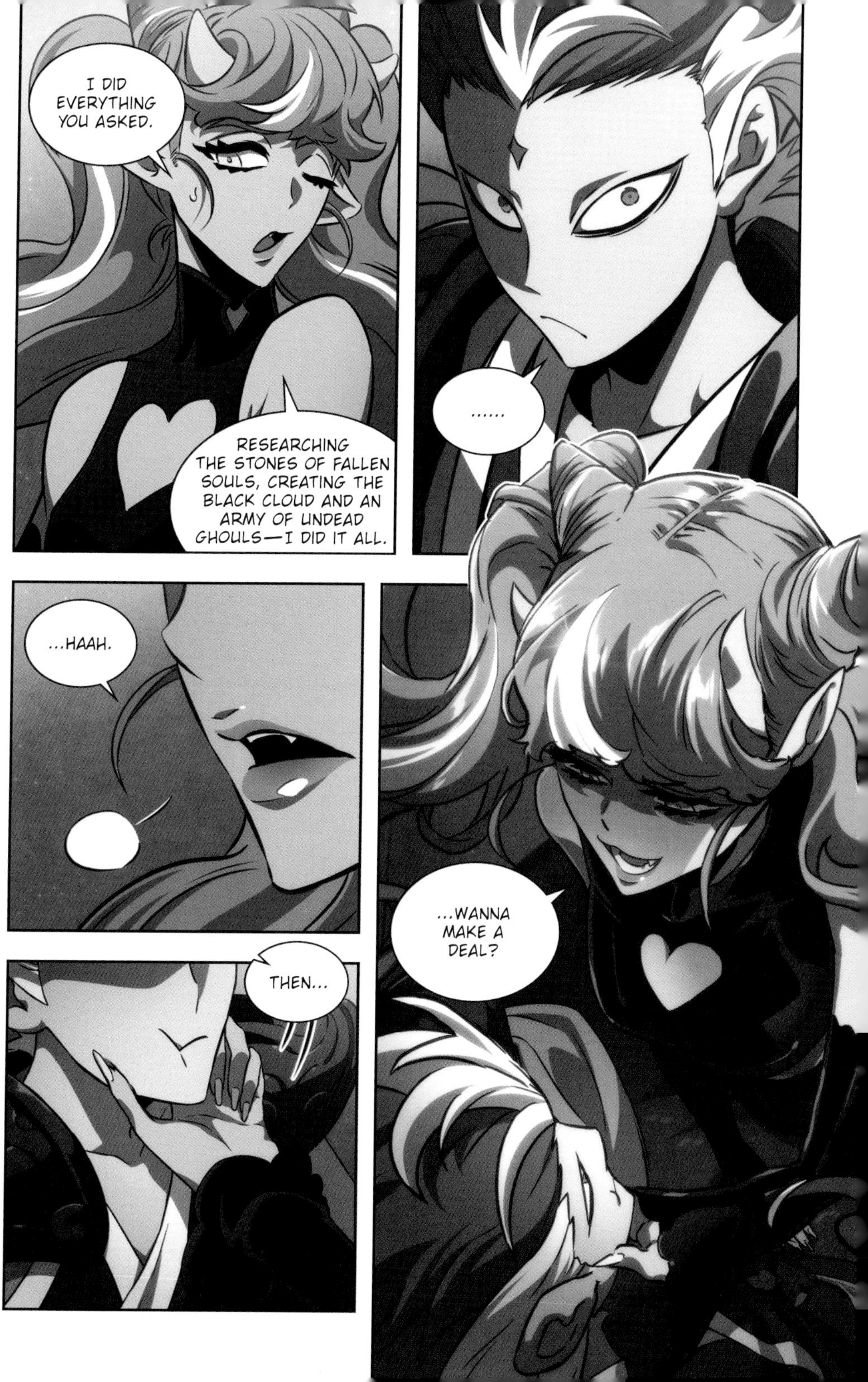
I DID EVERYTHING YOU ASKED.
RESEARCHING THE STONES OF FALLEN SOULS, CREATING THE BLACK CLOUD AND AN ARMY OF UNDEAD GHOULS—I DID IT ALL.
......
...HAAH.
THEN...
...WANNA MAKE A DEAL?

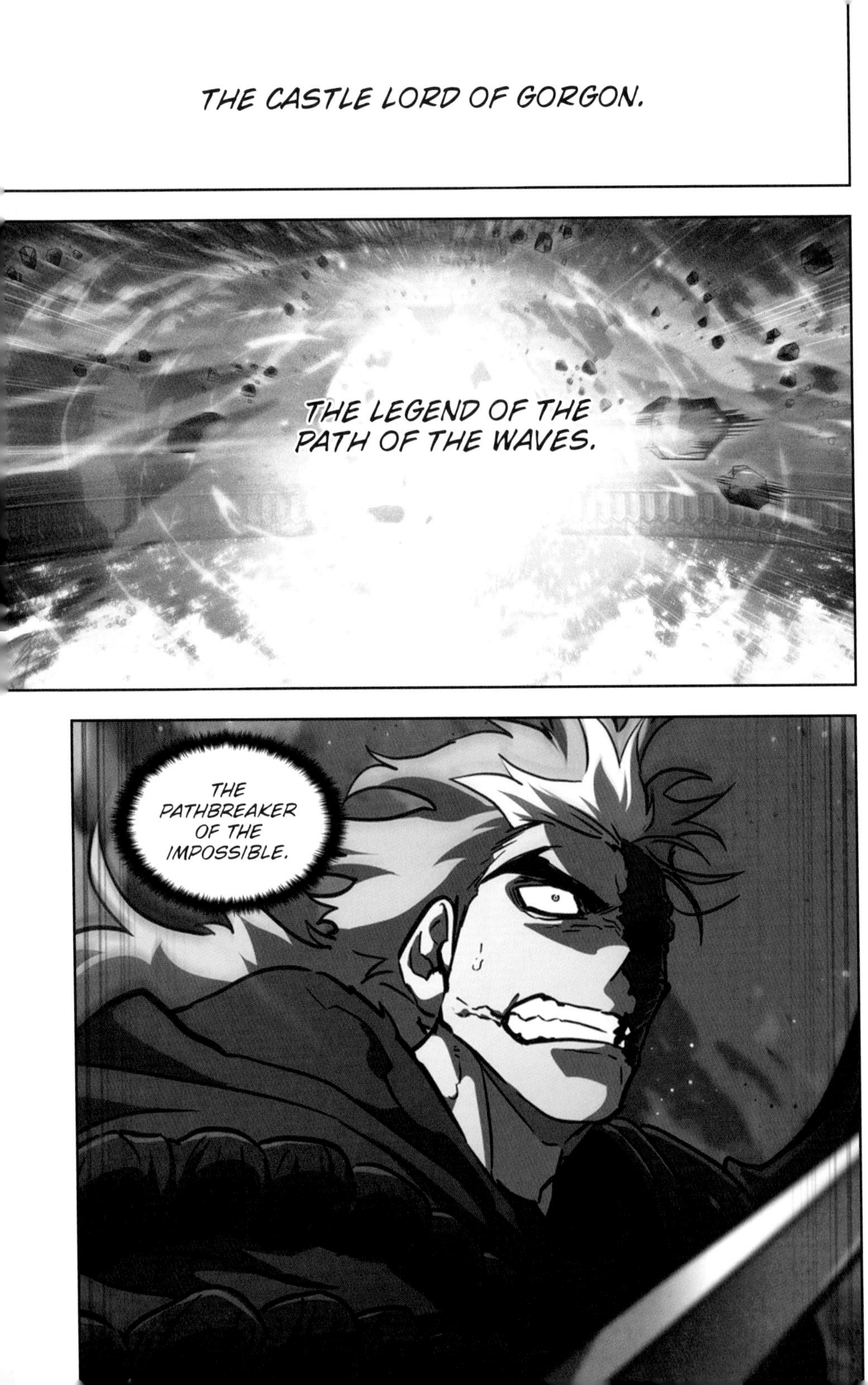
THE CASTLE LORD OF GORGON.
THE LEGEND OF THE PATH OF THE WAVES.
THE PATHBREAKER OF THE IMPOSSIBLE.

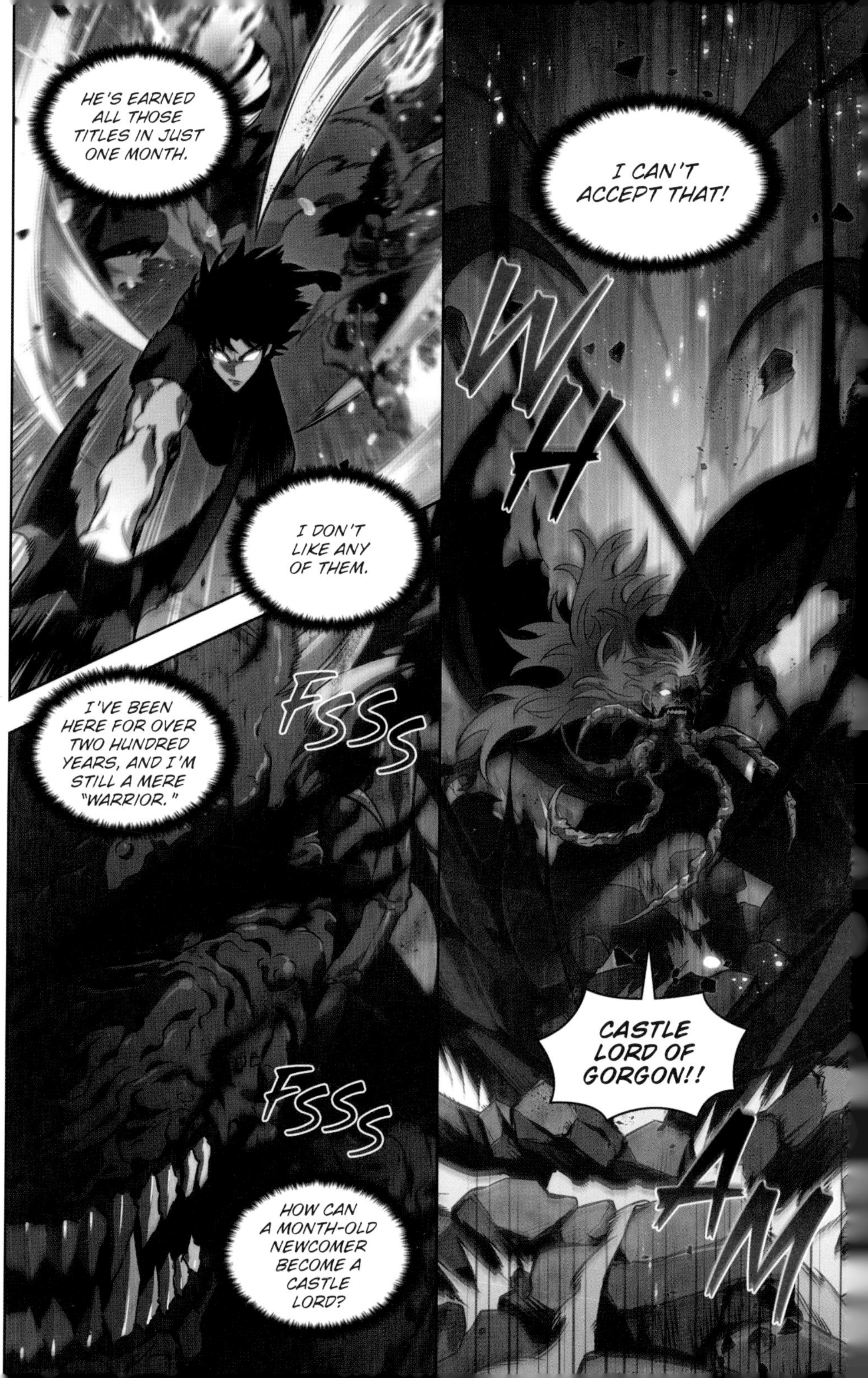
HE'S EARNED ALL THOSE TITLES IN JUST ONE MONTH.
I DON'T LIKE ANY OF THEM.
I'VE BEEN HERE FOR OVER TWO HUNDRED YEARS, AND I'M STILL A MERE "WARRIOR."
FSSS
FSSS
HOW CAN A MONTH-OLD NEWCOMER BECOME A CASTLE LORD?
I CAN'T ACCEPT THAT!
WH
CASTLE LORD OF GORGON!!
AM

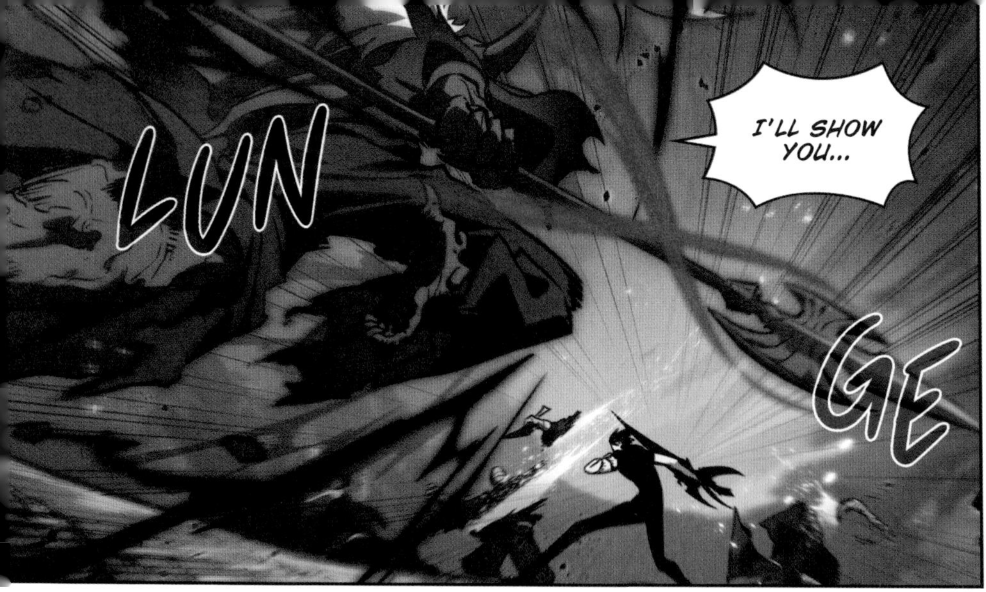
LUN
I'LL SHOW YOU...
GE

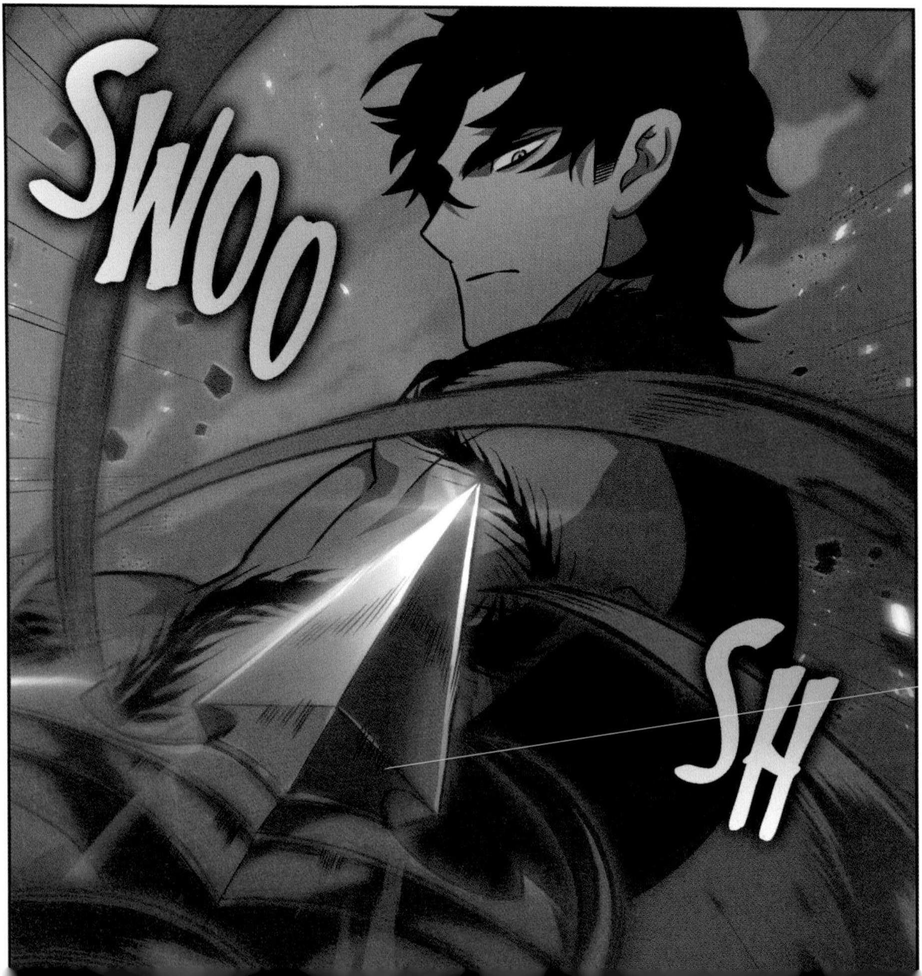
SWOO
SH

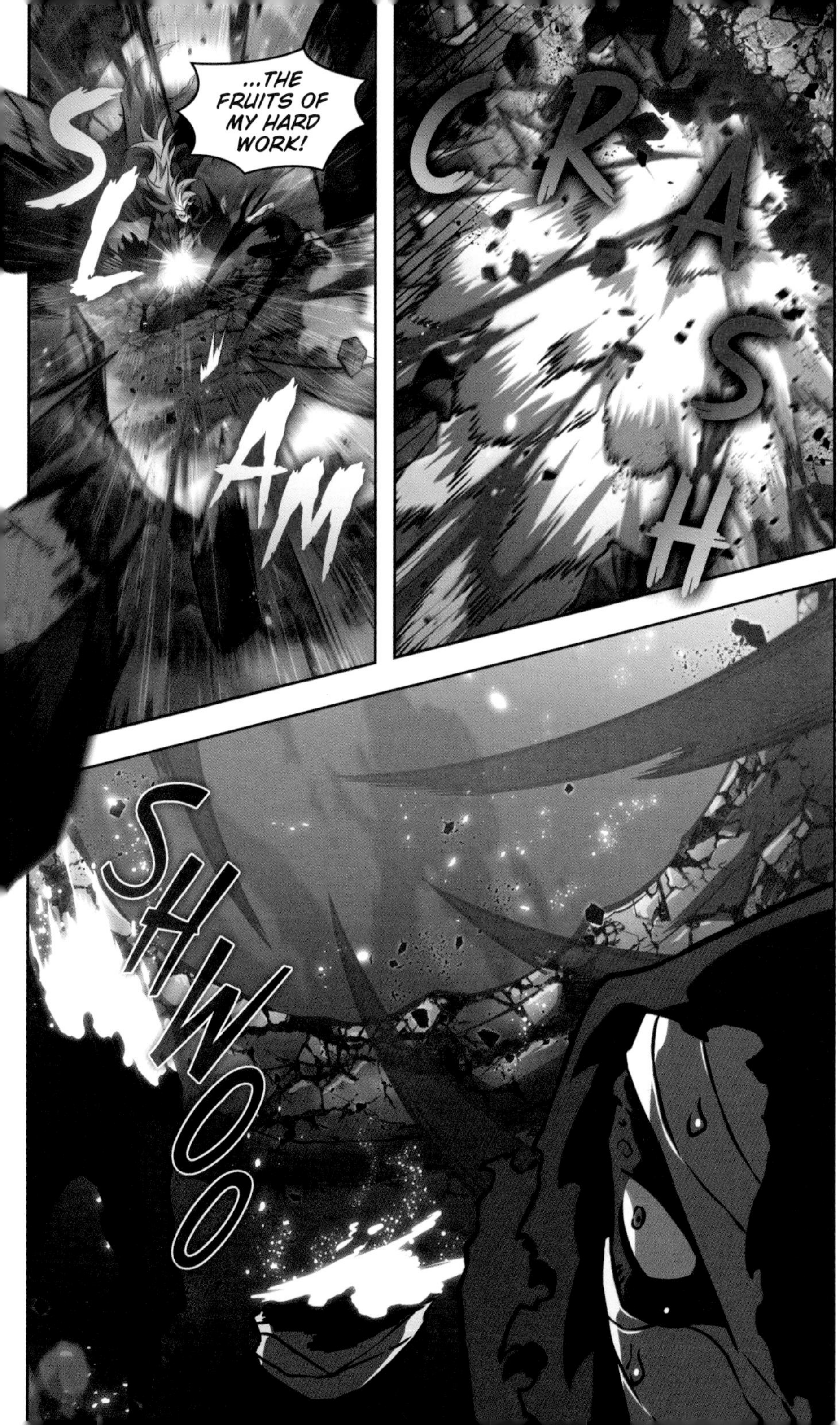

...THE FRUITS OF MY HARD WORK!
SLAM
CRASH
SHWOO

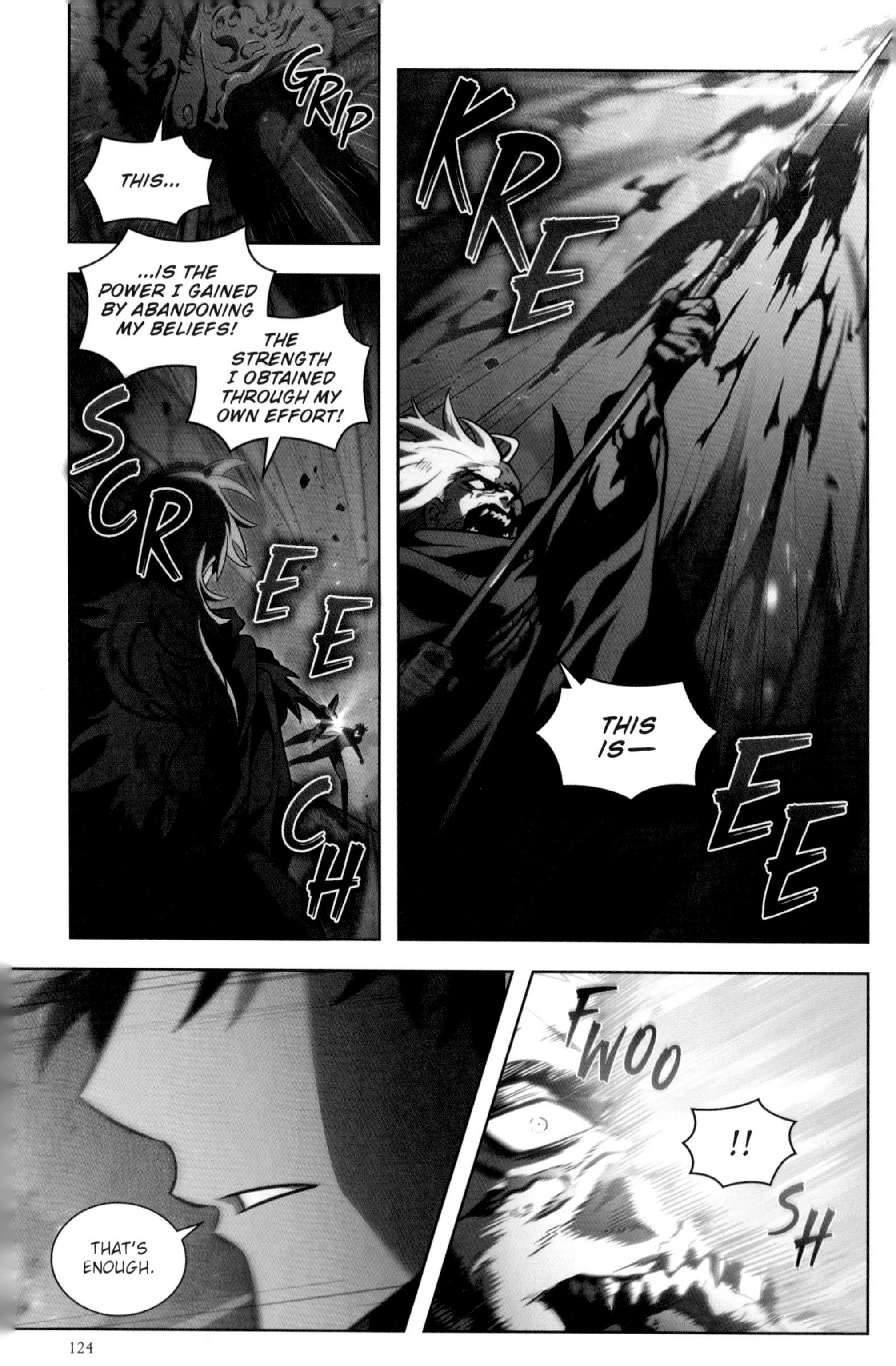
GRIP
THIS...
...IS THE POWER I GAINED BY ABANDONING MY BELIEFS!
THE STRENGTH I OBTAINED THROUGH MY OWN EFFORT!
SCREEECH
KREEEE
THIS IS—
THAT'S ENOUGH.
FWOOSH
!!

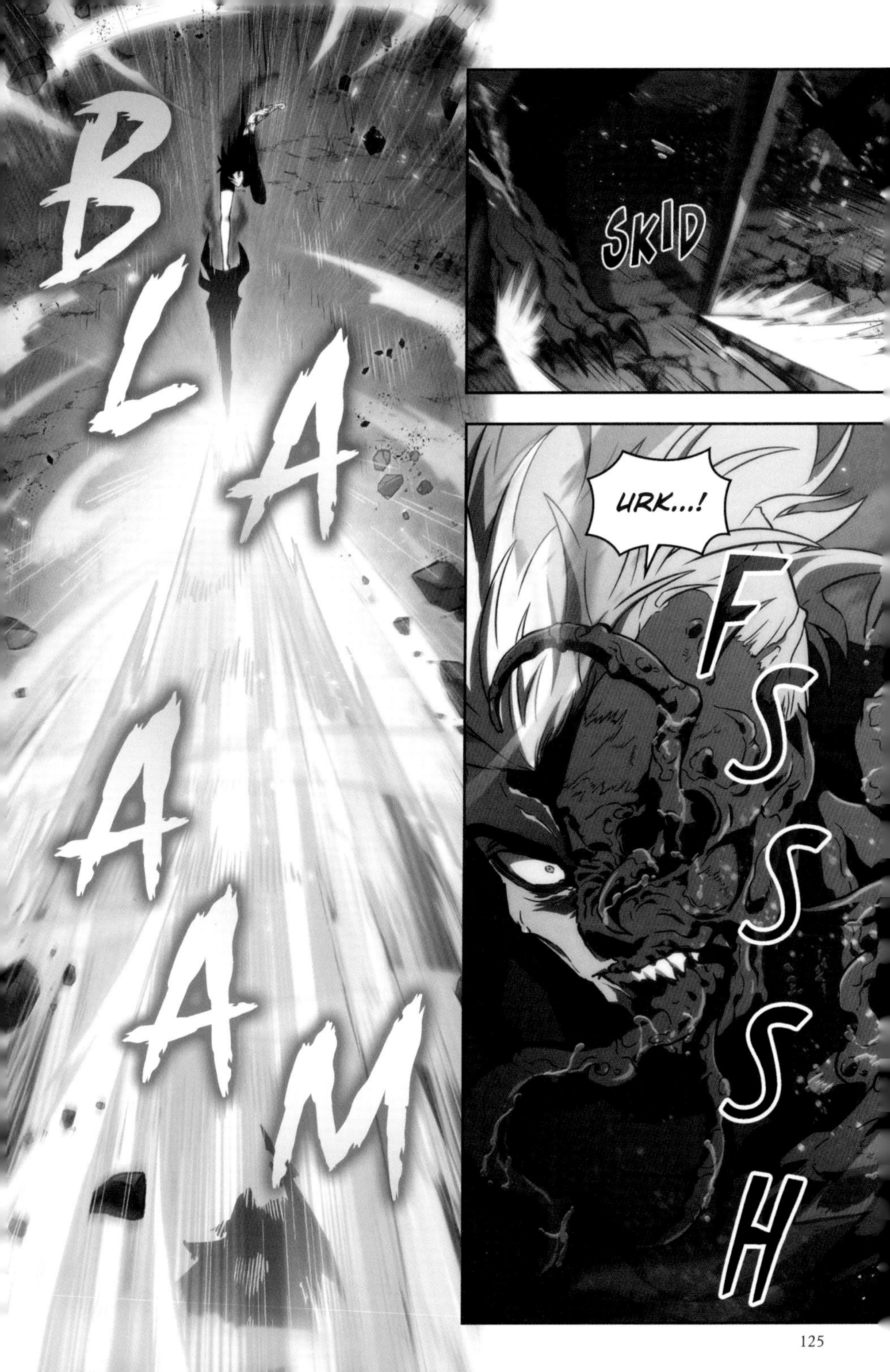
BLAAAAM
SKID
URK...!
FSSSH

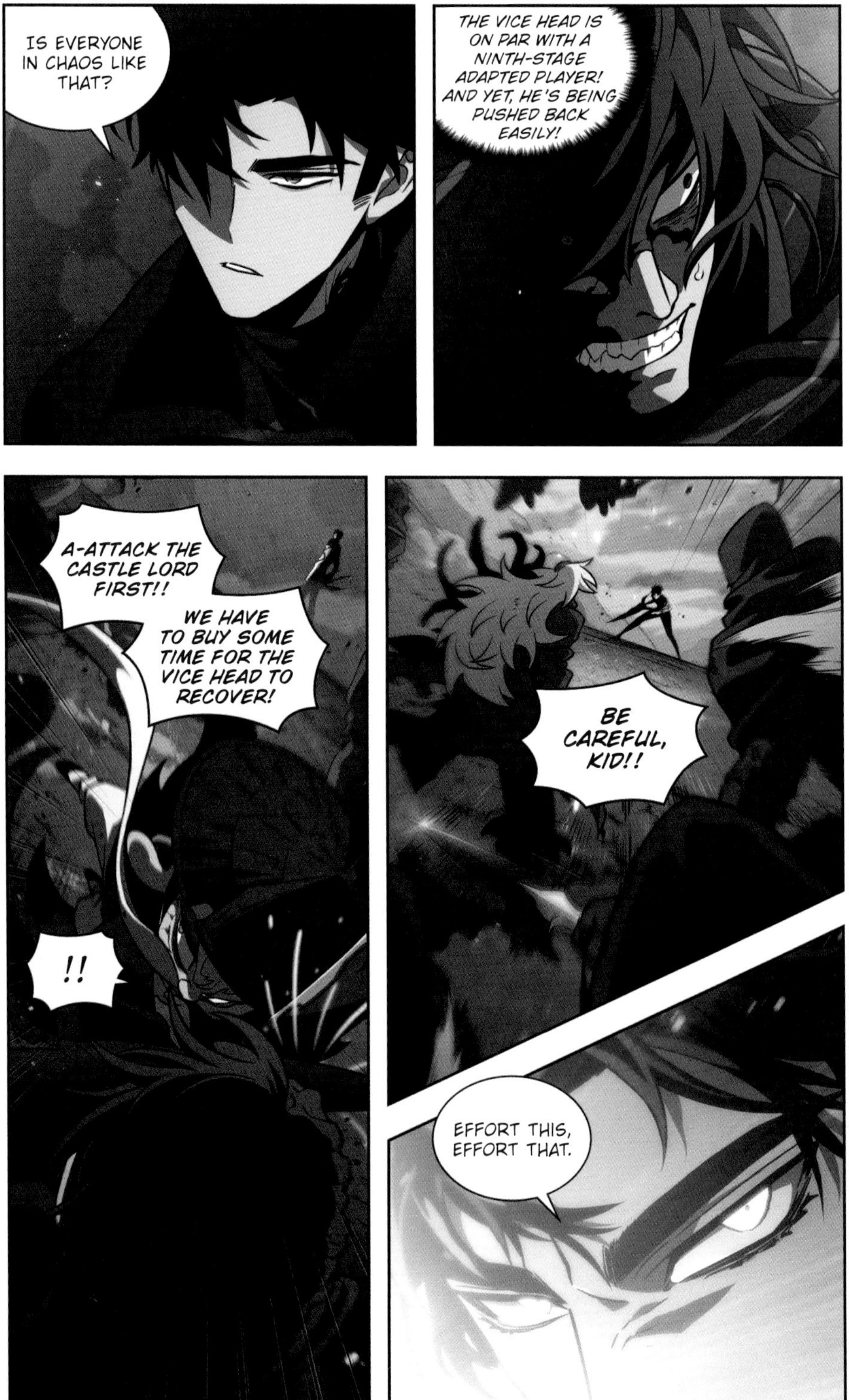
IS EVERYONE IN CHAOS LIKE THAT?
THE VICE HEAD IS ON PAR WITH A NINTH-STAGE ADAPTED PLAYER! AND YET, HE'S BEING PUSHED BACK EASILY!
A-ATTACK THE CASTLE LORD FIRST!!
WE HAVE TO BUY SOME TIME FOR THE VICE HEAD TO RECOVER!
!!
BE CAREFUL, KID!!
EFFORT THIS, EFFORT THAT.

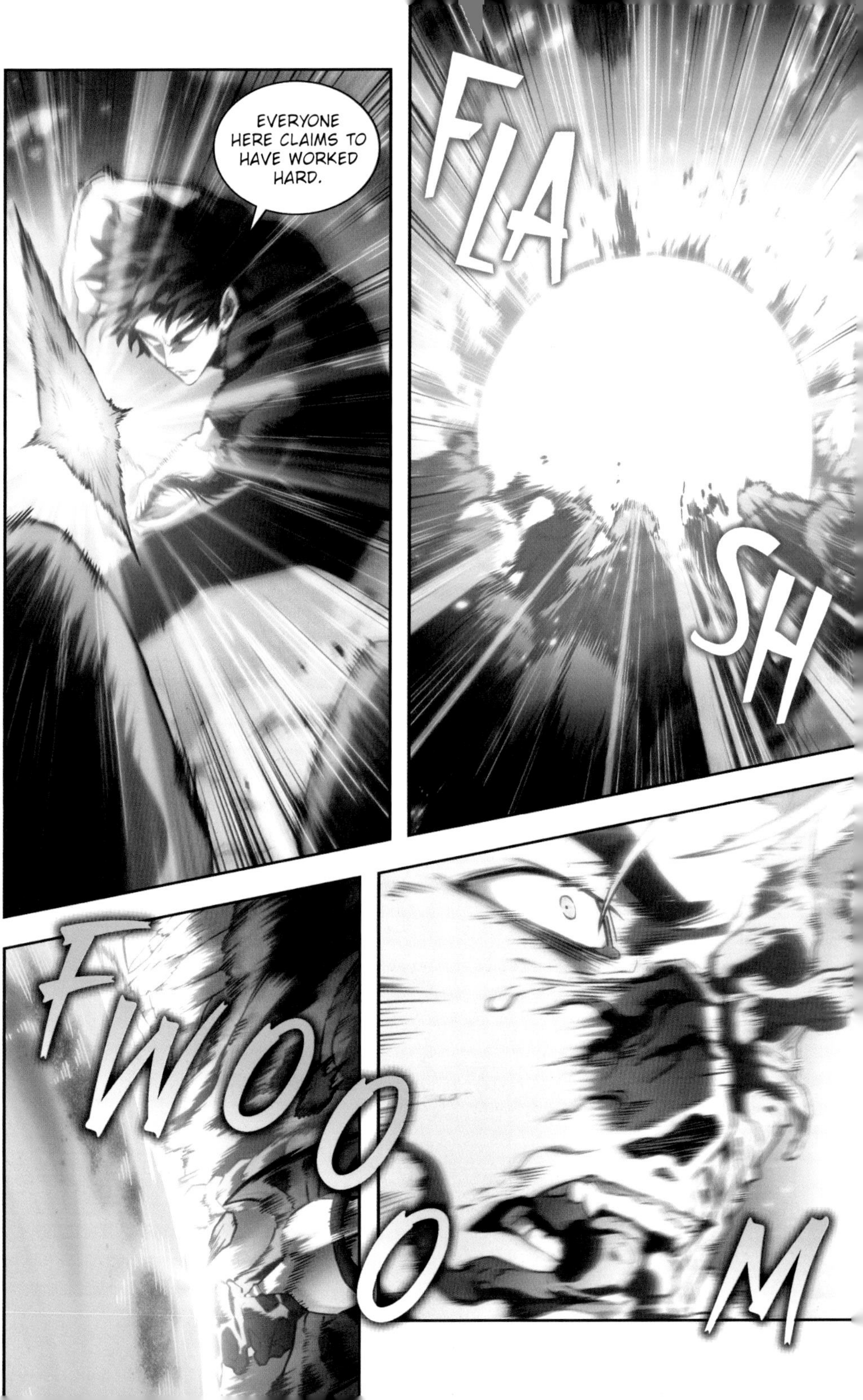
EVERYONE HERE CLAIMS TO HAVE WORKED HARD.
FLASH
FWOOOOM

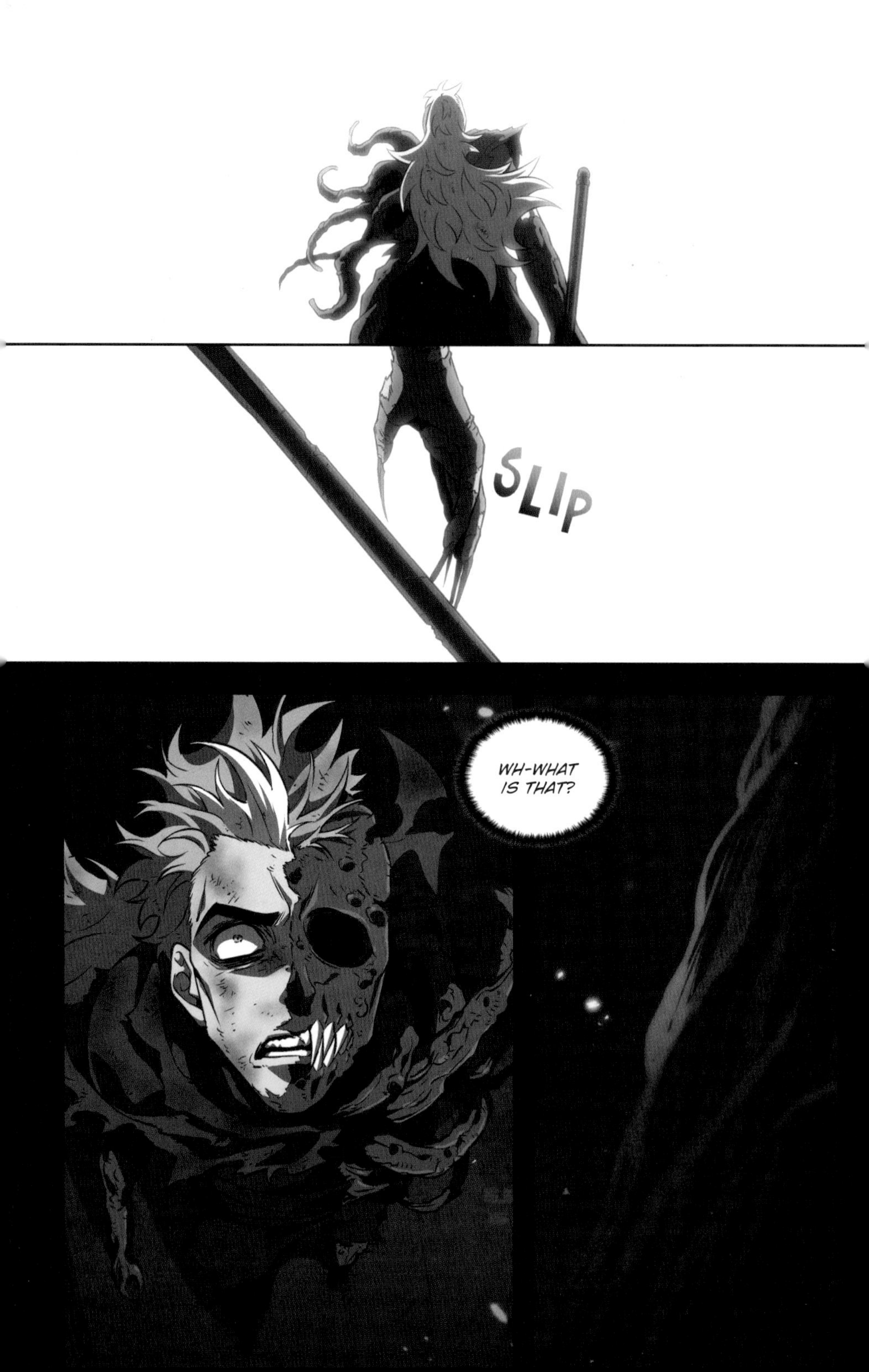
SLIP
WH-WHAT IS THAT?

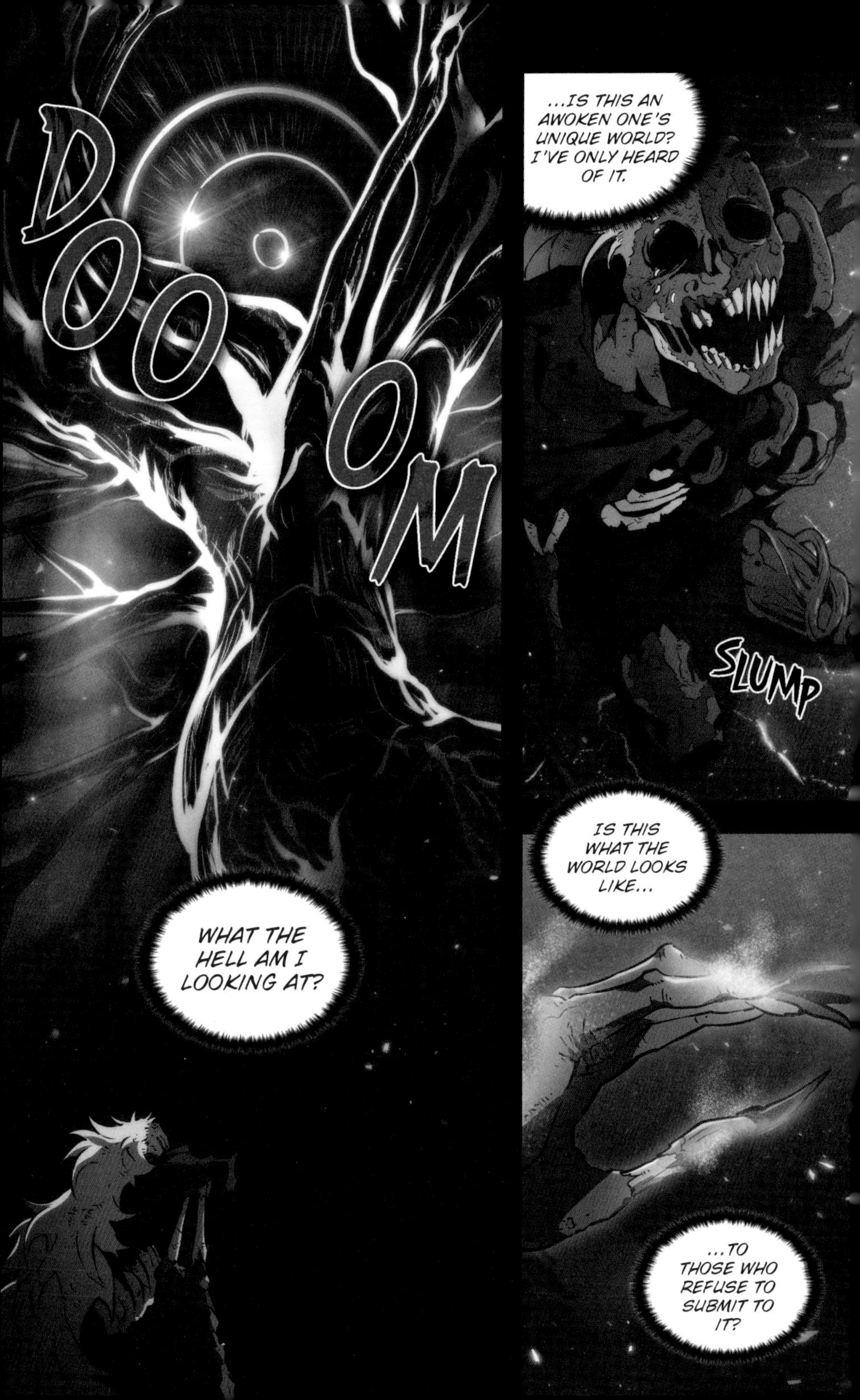
DOOOOOM
...IS THIS AN AWOKEN ONE'S UNIQUE WORLD? I'VE ONLY HEARD OF IT.
SLUMP
WHAT THE HELL AM I LOOKING AT?
IS THIS WHAT THE WORLD LOOKS LIKE...
...TO THOSE WHO REFUSE TO SUBMIT TO IT?

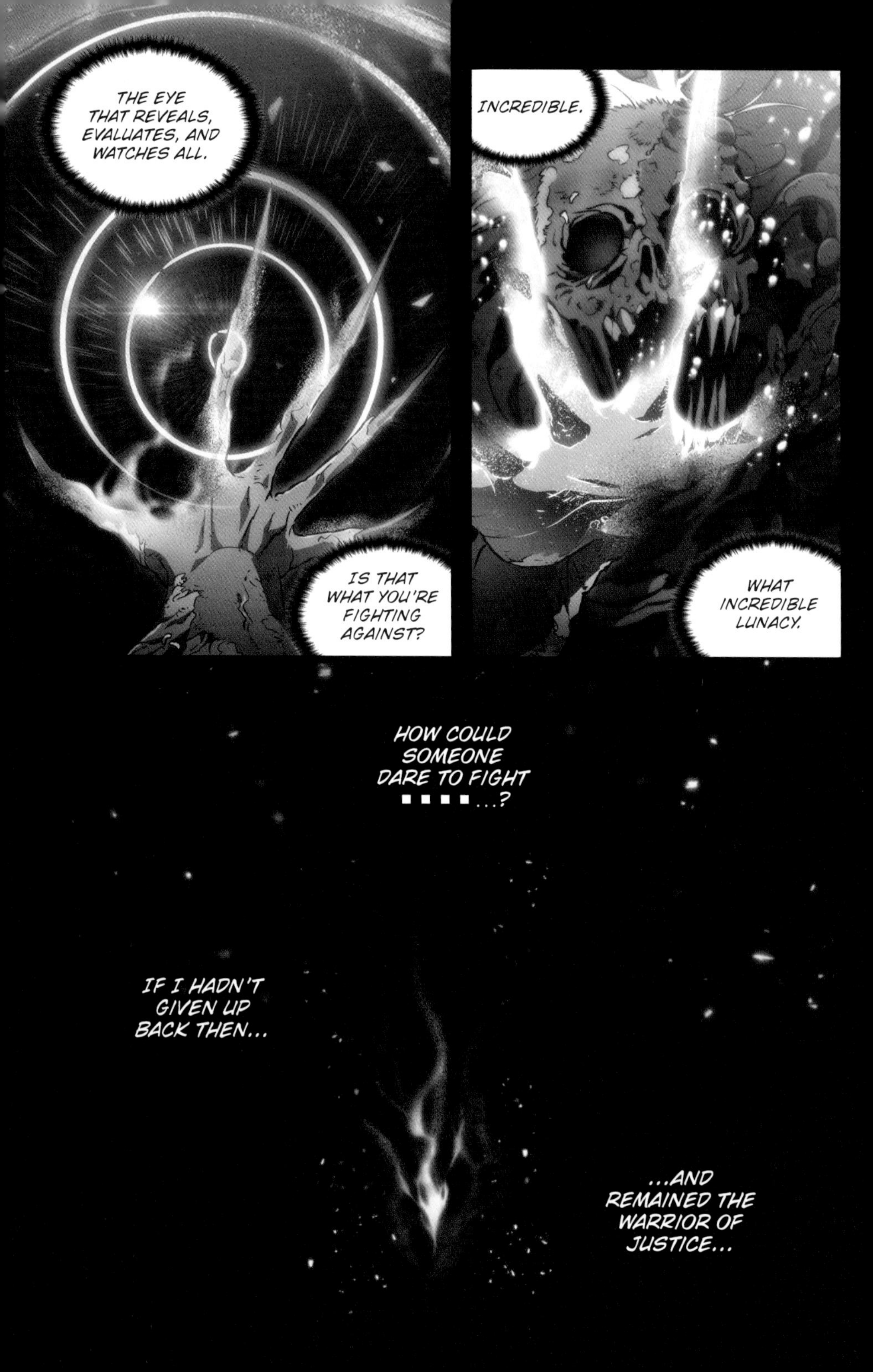
THE EYE THAT REVEALS, EVALUATES, AND WATCHES ALL.
IS THAT WHAT YOU'RE FIGHTING AGAINST?
INCREDIBLE.
WHAT INCREDIBLE LUNACY.
HOW COULD SOMEONE DARE TO FIGHT ■■■■...?
IF I HADN'T GIVEN UP BACK THEN...
...AND REMAINED THE WARRIOR OF JUSTICE...

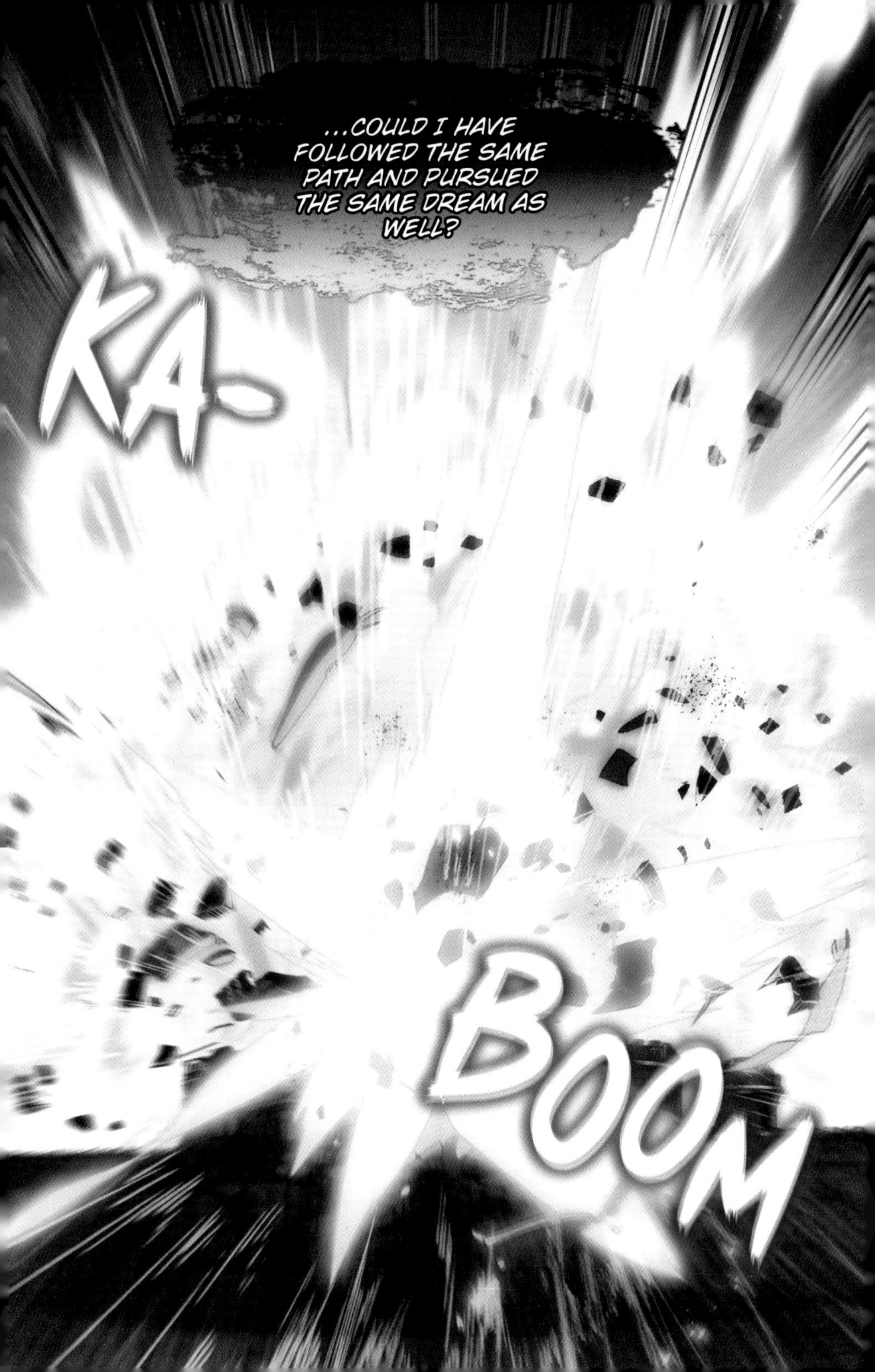
...COULD I HAVE FOLLOWED THE SAME PATH AND PURSUED THE SAME DREAM AS WELL?
KA-
BOOM

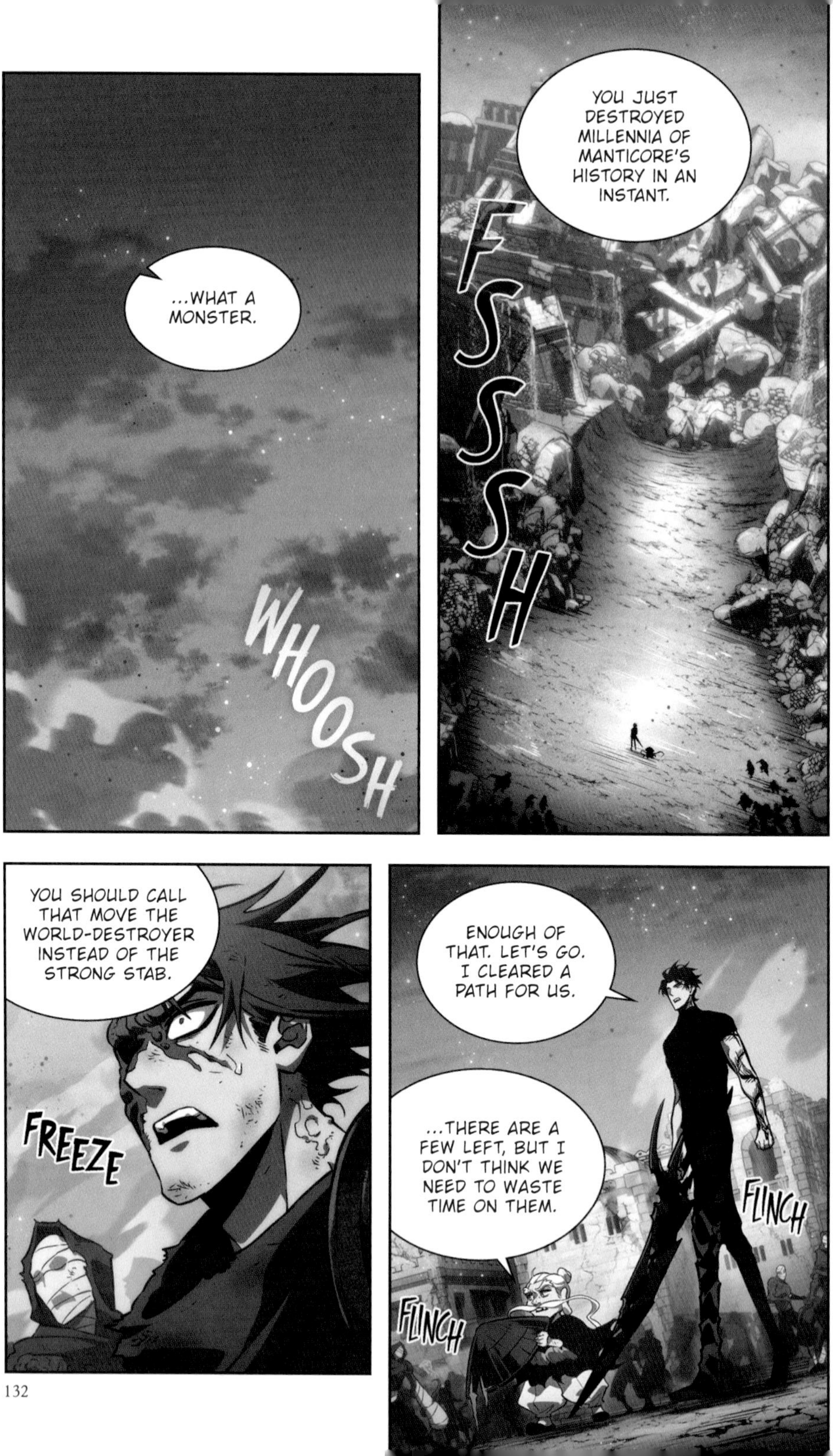
...WHAT A MONSTER.
WHOOSH
YOU JUST DESTROYED MILLENNIA OF MANTICORE'S HISTORY IN AN INSTANT.
FSSSH
YOU SHOULD CALL THAT MOVE THE WORLD-DESTROYER INSTEAD OF THE STRONG STAB.
FREEZE
ENOUGH OF THAT. LET'S GO. I CLEARED A PATH FOR US.
...THERE ARE A FEW LEFT, BUT I DON'T THINK WE NEED TO WASTE TIME ON THEM.
FLINCH
FLINCH

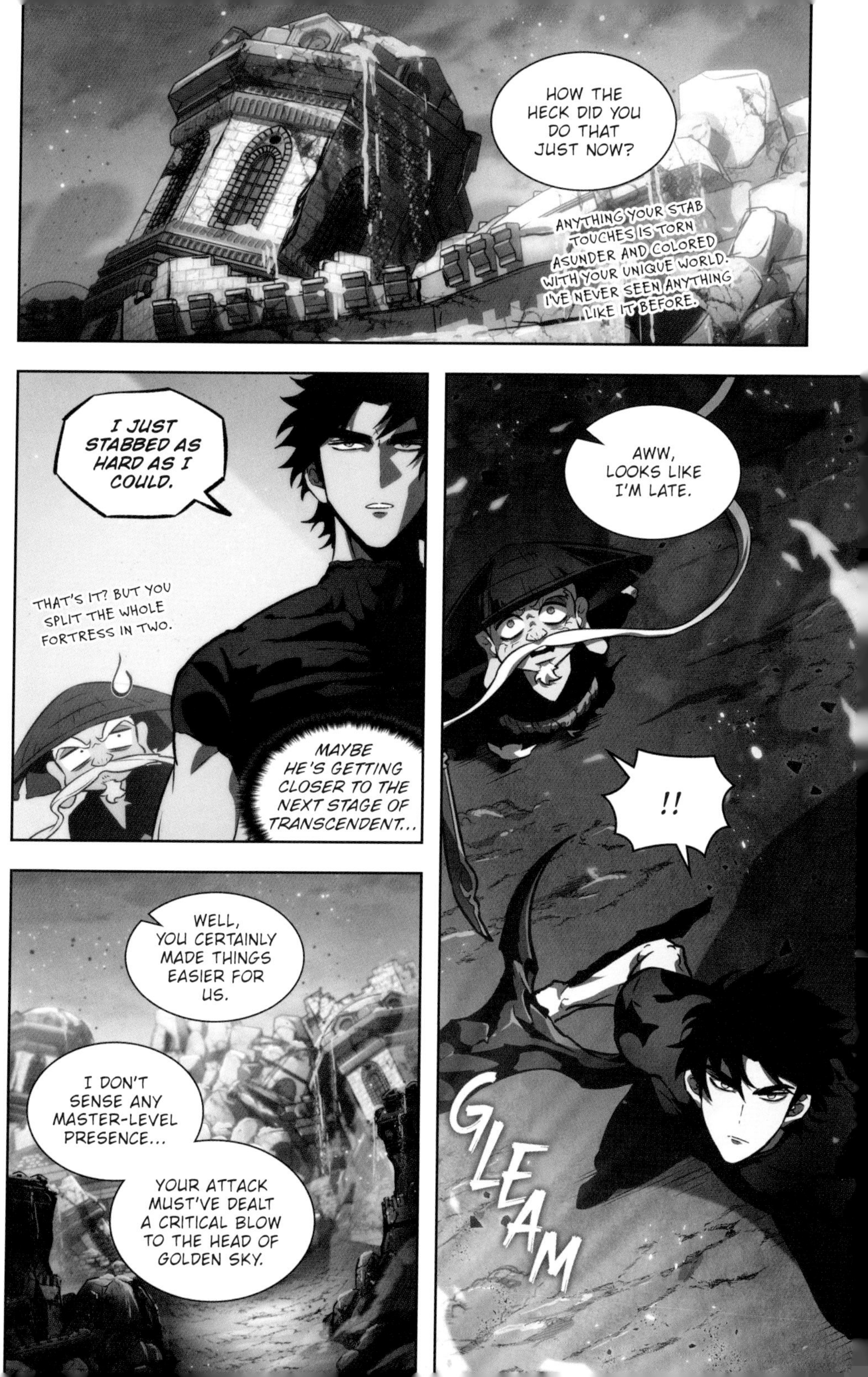
HOW THE HECK DID YOU DO THAT JUST NOW?
ANYTHING YOUR STAB TOUCHES IS TORN ASUNDER AND COLORED WITH YOUR UNIQUE WORLD. I'VE NEVER SEEN ANYTHING LIKE IT BEFORE.
I JUST STABBED AS HARD AS I COULD.
THAT'S IT? BUT YOU SPLIT THE WHOLE FORTRESS IN TWO.
MAYBE HE'S GETTING CLOSER TO THE NEXT STAGE OF TRANSCENDENT...
WELL, YOU CERTAINLY MADE THINGS EASIER FOR US.
I DON'T SENSE ANY MASTER-LEVEL PRESENCE...
YOUR ATTACK MUST'VE DEALT A CRITICAL BLOW TO THE HEAD OF GOLDEN SKY.
AWW, LOOKS LIKE I'M LATE.
!!
GLEAM

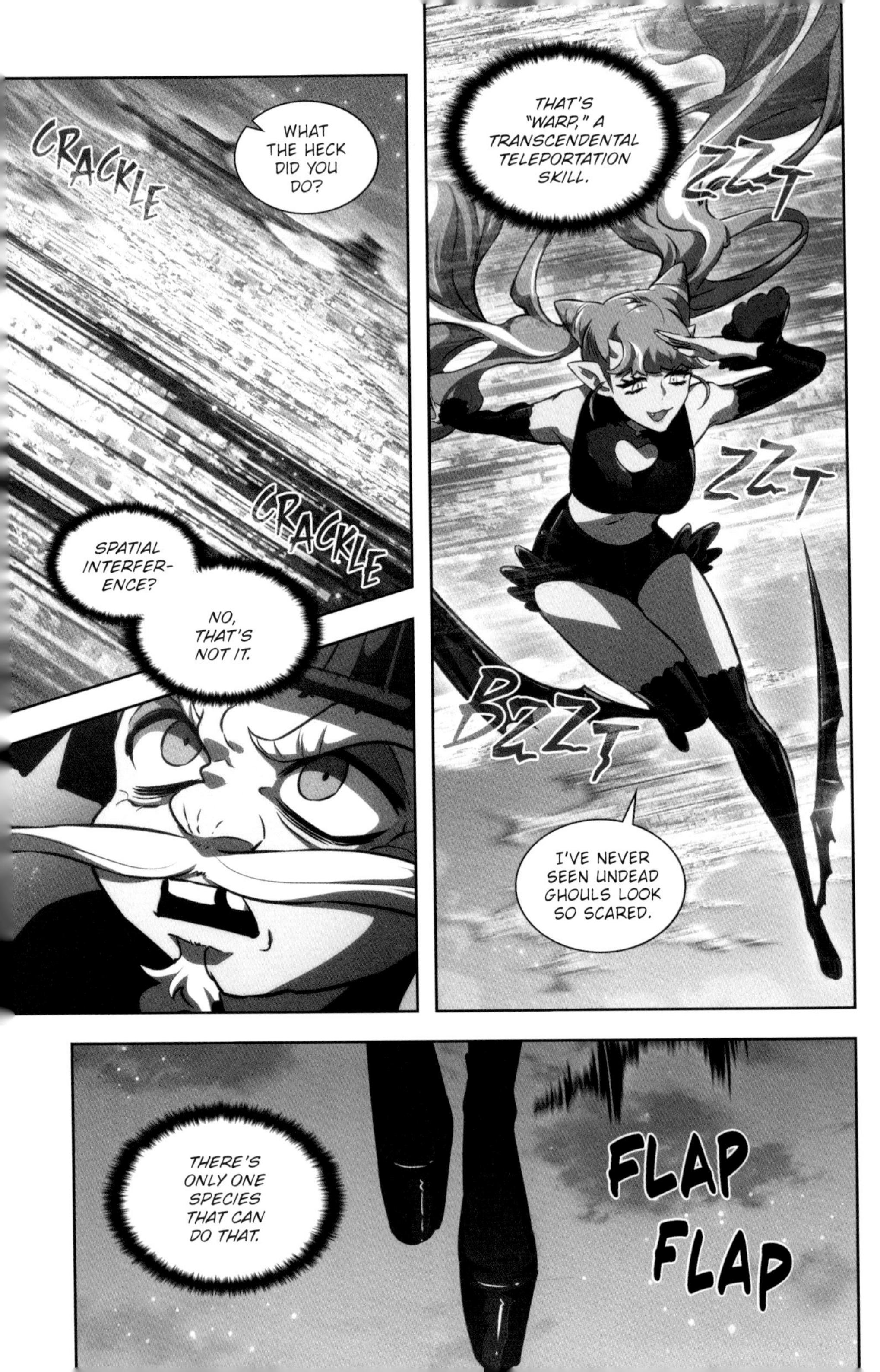
CRACKLE
WHAT THE HECK DID YOU DO?
CRACKLE
SPATIAL INTERFER-ENCE?
NO, THAT'S NOT IT.
THAT'S "WARP," A TRANSCENDENTAL TELEPORTATION SKILL.
ZZZT
ZZZT
BZZZT
I'VE NEVER SEEN UNDEAD GHOULS LOOK SO SCARED.
THERE'S ONLY ONE SPECIES THAT CAN DO THAT.
FLAP
FLAP

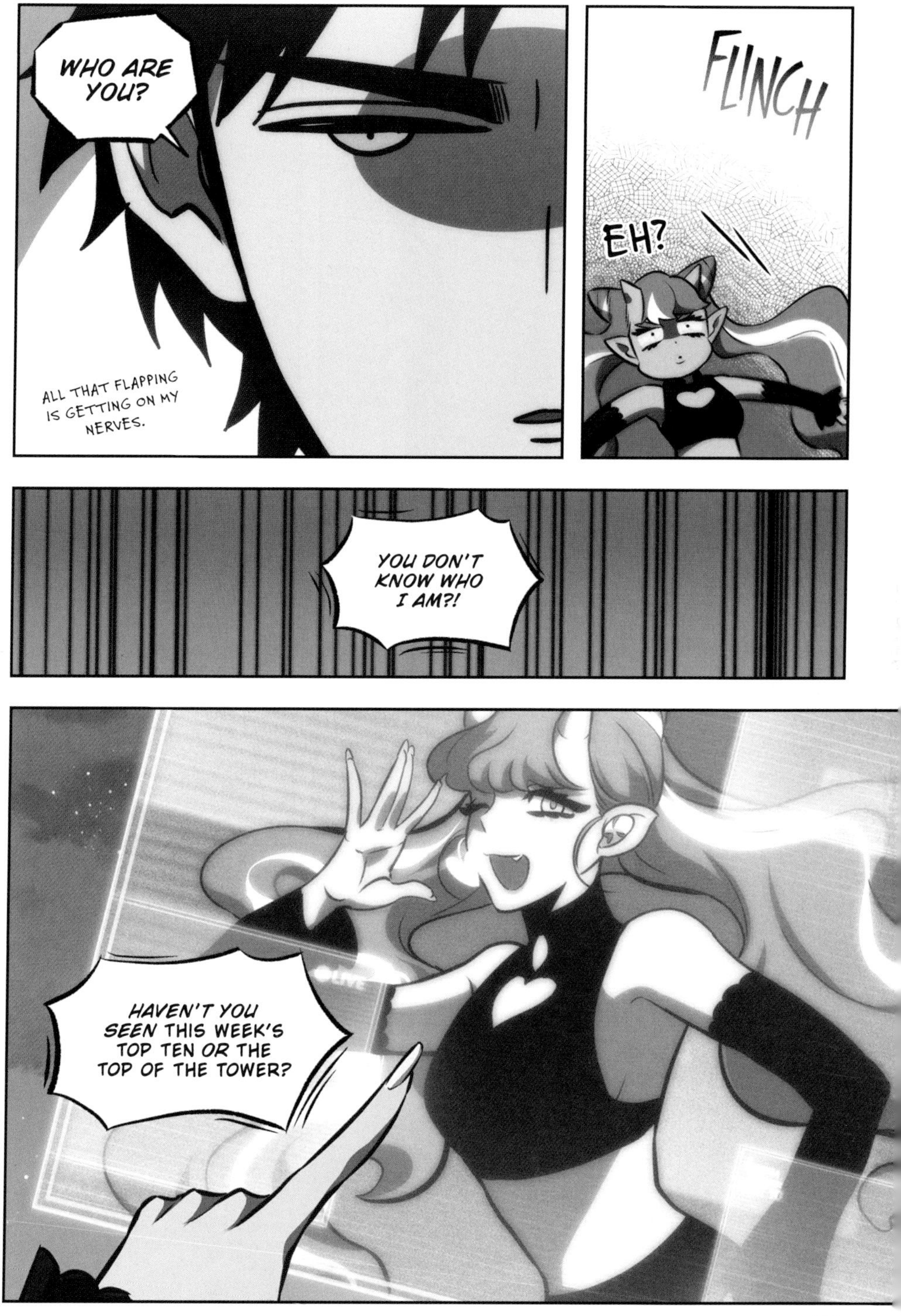
WHO ARE YOU?
ALL THAT FLAPPING IS GETTING ON MY NERVES.
FLINCH
EH?
YOU DON'T KNOW WHO I AM?!
HAVEN'T YOU SEEN THIS WEEK'S TOP TEN OR THE TOP OF THE TOWER?

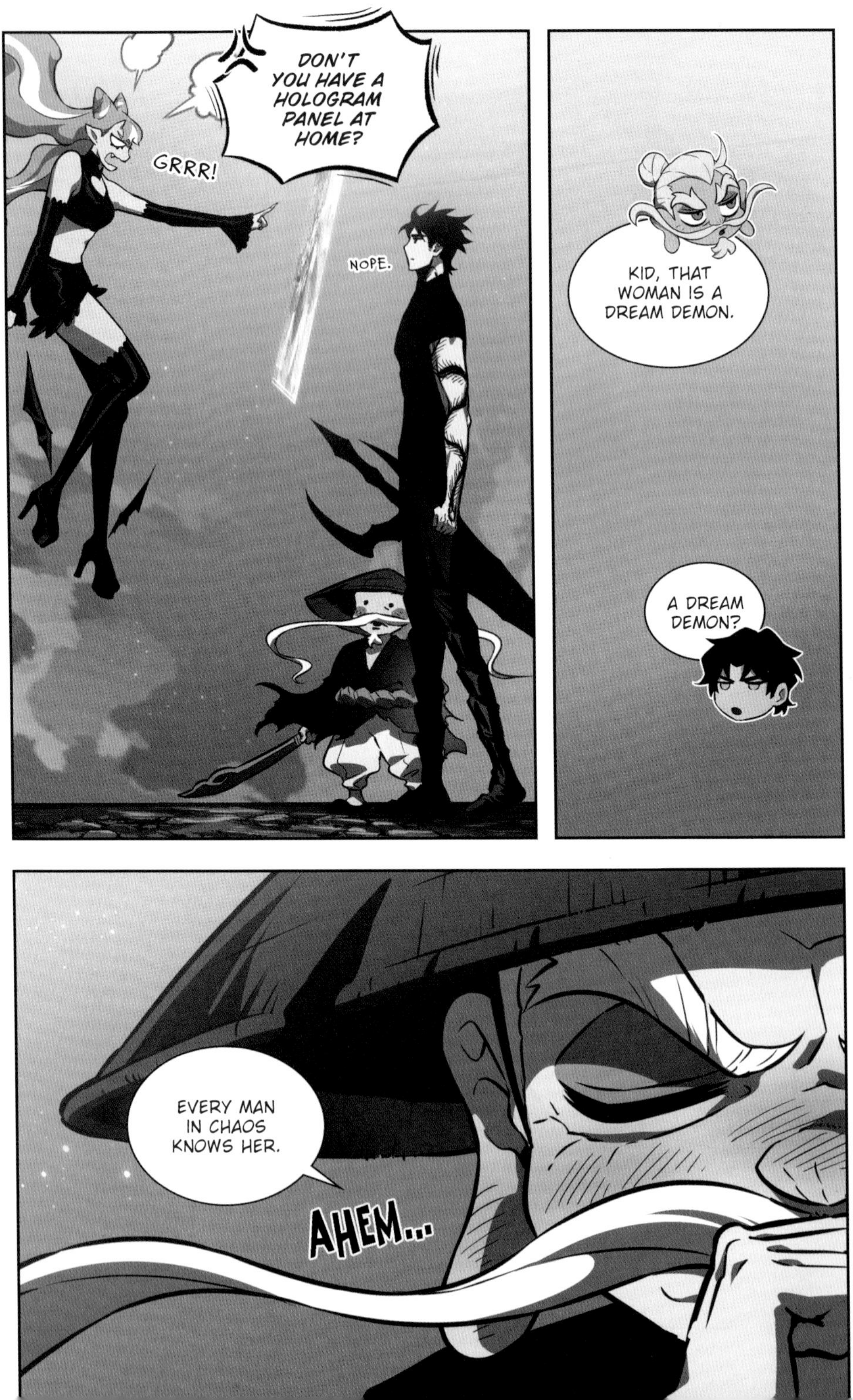
DON'T YOU HAVE A HOLOGRAM PANEL AT HOME?
GRRR!
NOPE.
KID, THAT WOMAN IS A DREAM DEMON.
A DREAM DEMON?
EVERY MAN IN CHAOS KNOWS HER.
AHEM...

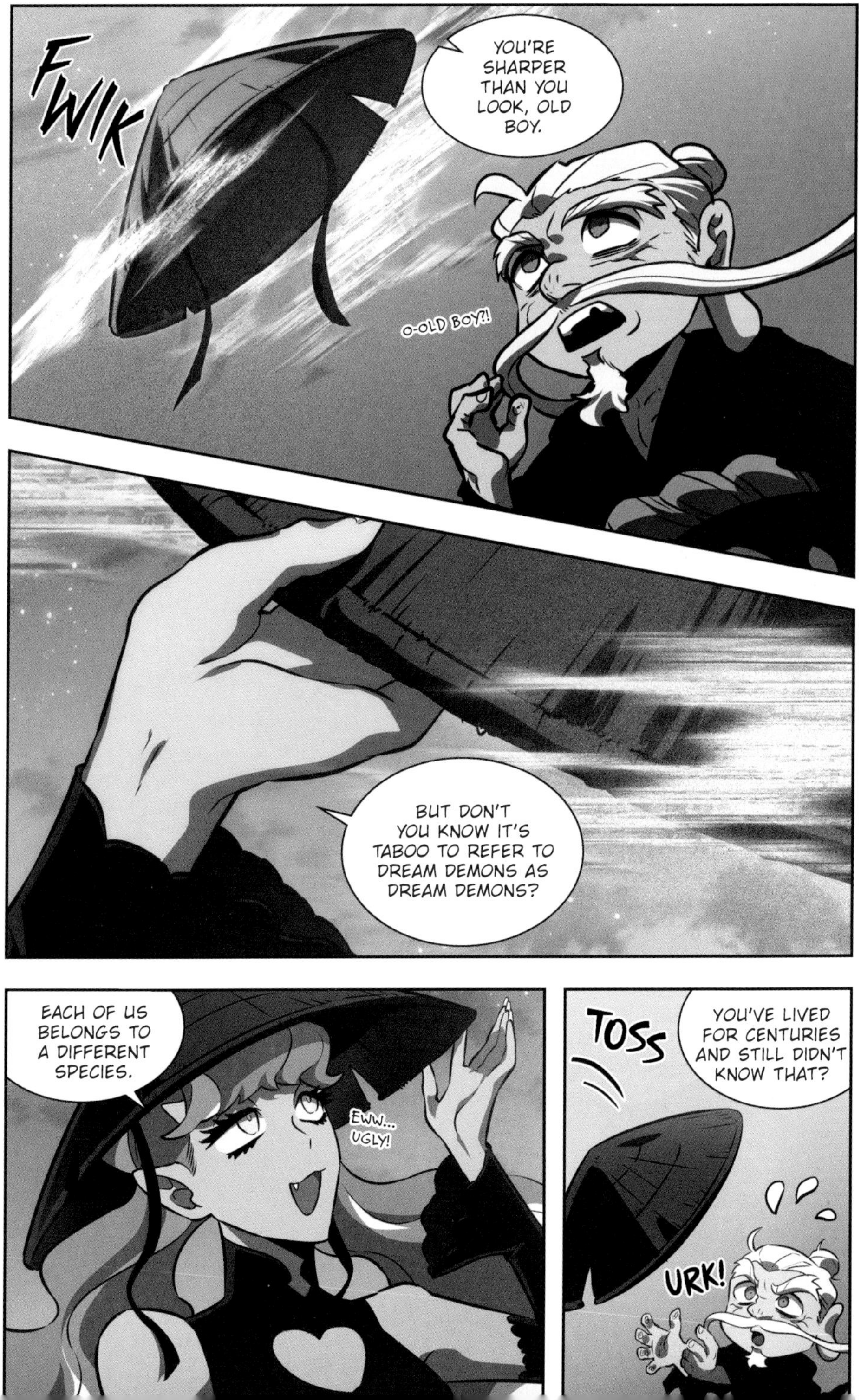
FWIK
YOU'RE SHARPER THAN YOU LOOK, OLD BOY.
O-OLD BOY?!
BUT DON'T YOU KNOW IT'S TABOO TO REFER TO DREAM DEMONS AS DREAM DEMONS?
EACH OF US BELONGS TO A DIFFERENT SPECIES.
EWW... UGLY!
TOSS
YOU'VE LIVED FOR CENTURIES AND STILL DIDN'T KNOW THAT?
URK!

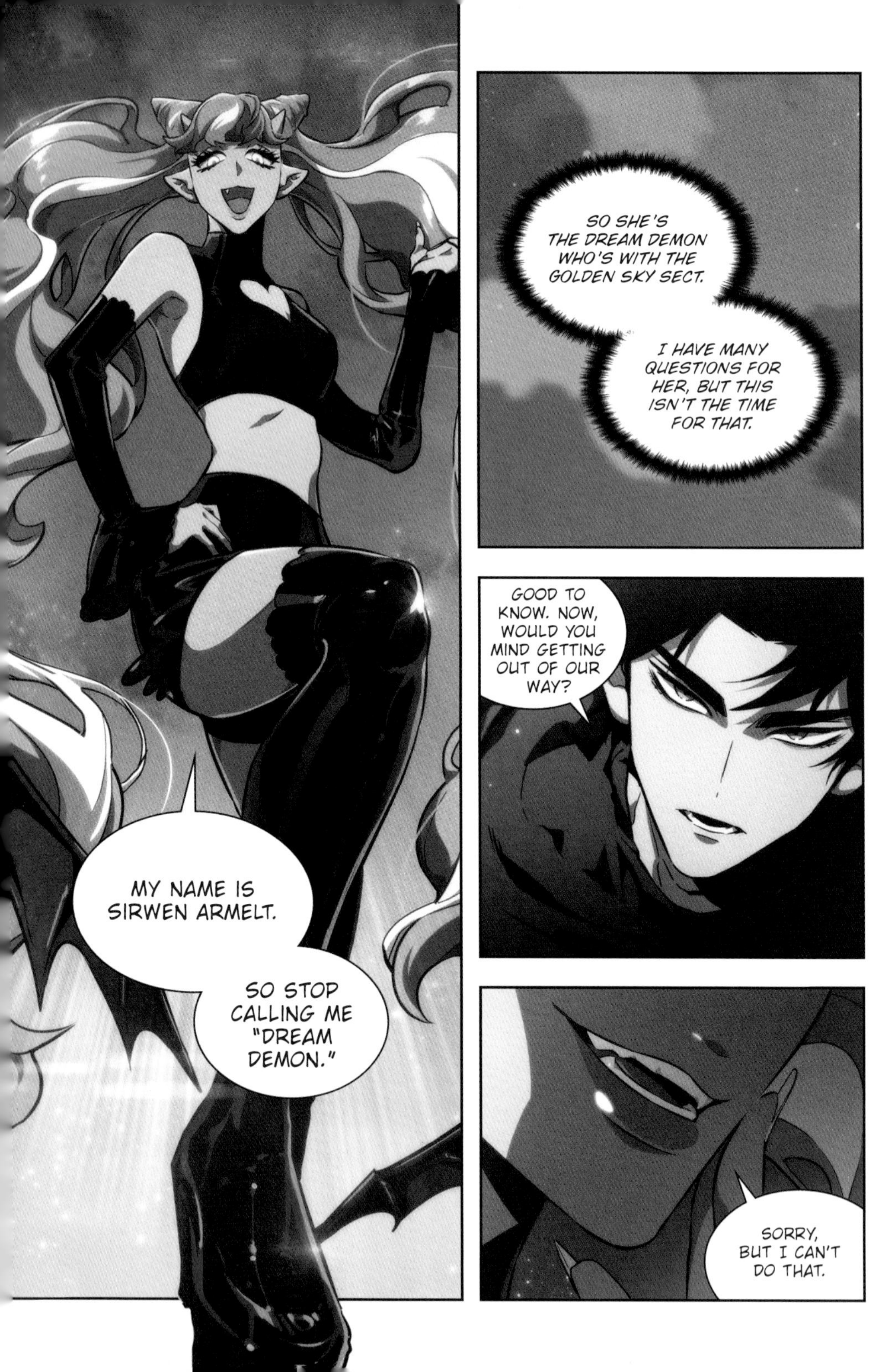
SO SHE'S THE DREAM DEMON WHO'S WITH THE GOLDEN SKY SECT.
I HAVE MANY QUESTIONS FOR HER, BUT THIS ISN'T THE TIME FOR THAT.
MY NAME IS SIRWEN ARMELT.
SO STOP CALLING ME "DREAM DEMON."
GOOD TO KNOW. NOW, WOULD YOU MIND GETTING OUT OF OUR WAY?
SORRY, BUT I CAN'T DO THAT.

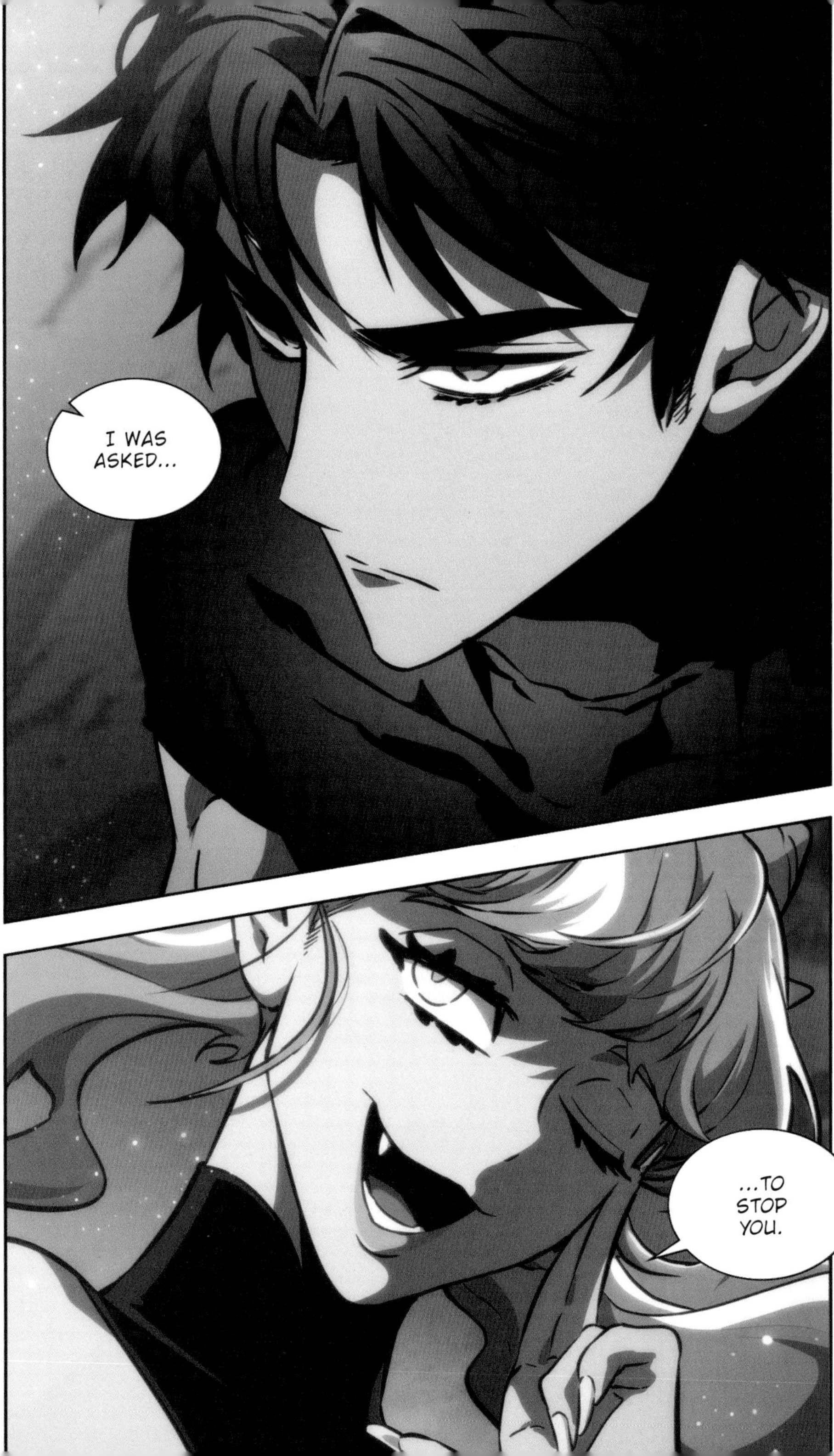
I WAS ASKED...
...TO STOP YOU.

The World After the Fall

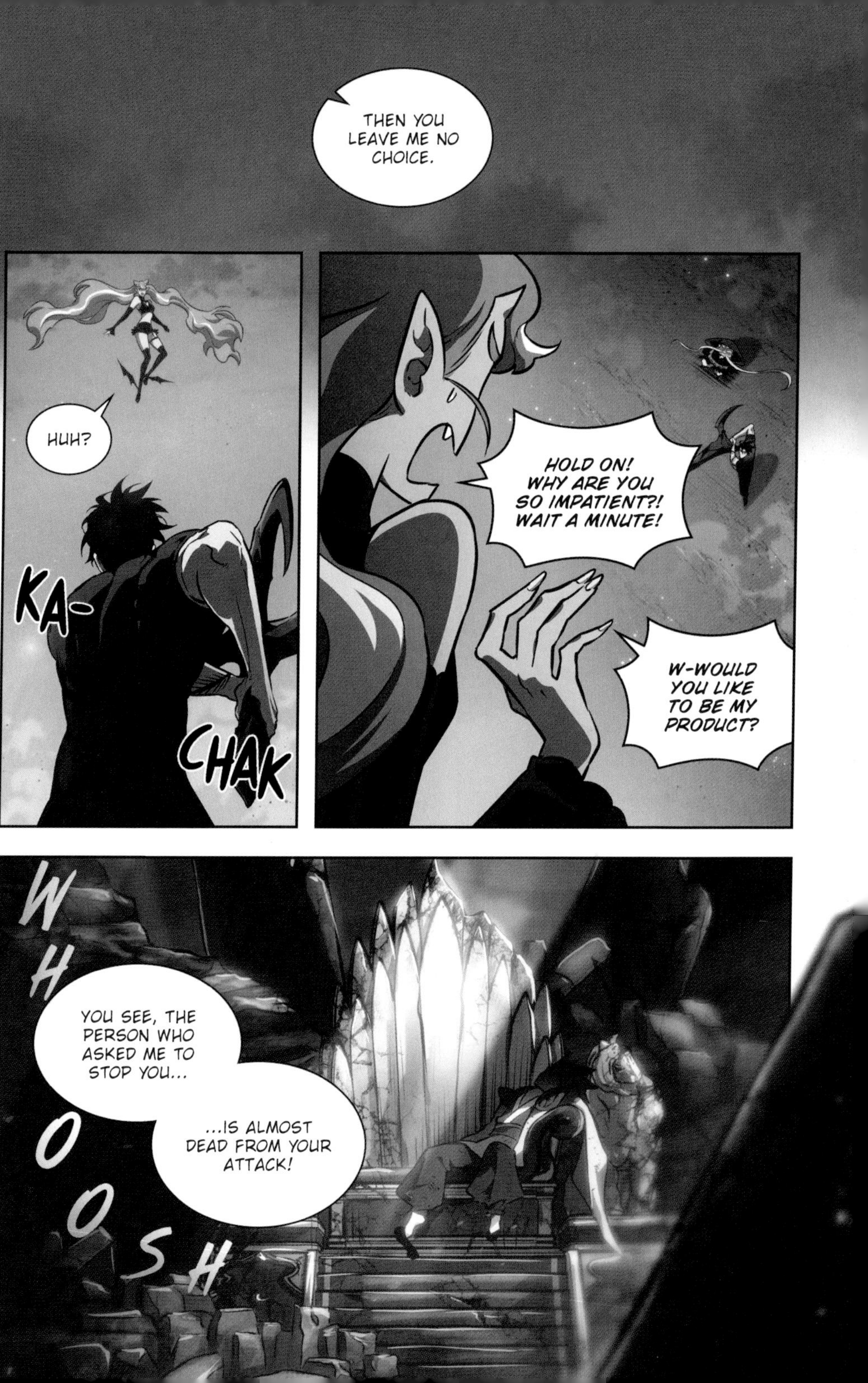
THEN YOU LEAVE ME NO CHOICE.
HUH?
KA-
CHAK
HOLD ON! WHY ARE YOU SO IMPATIENT?! WAIT A MINUTE!
W-WOULD YOU LIKE TO BE MY PRODUCT?
WHOOOSH
YOU SEE, THE PERSON WHO ASKED ME TO STOP YOU...
...IS ALMOST DEAD FROM YOUR ATTACK!

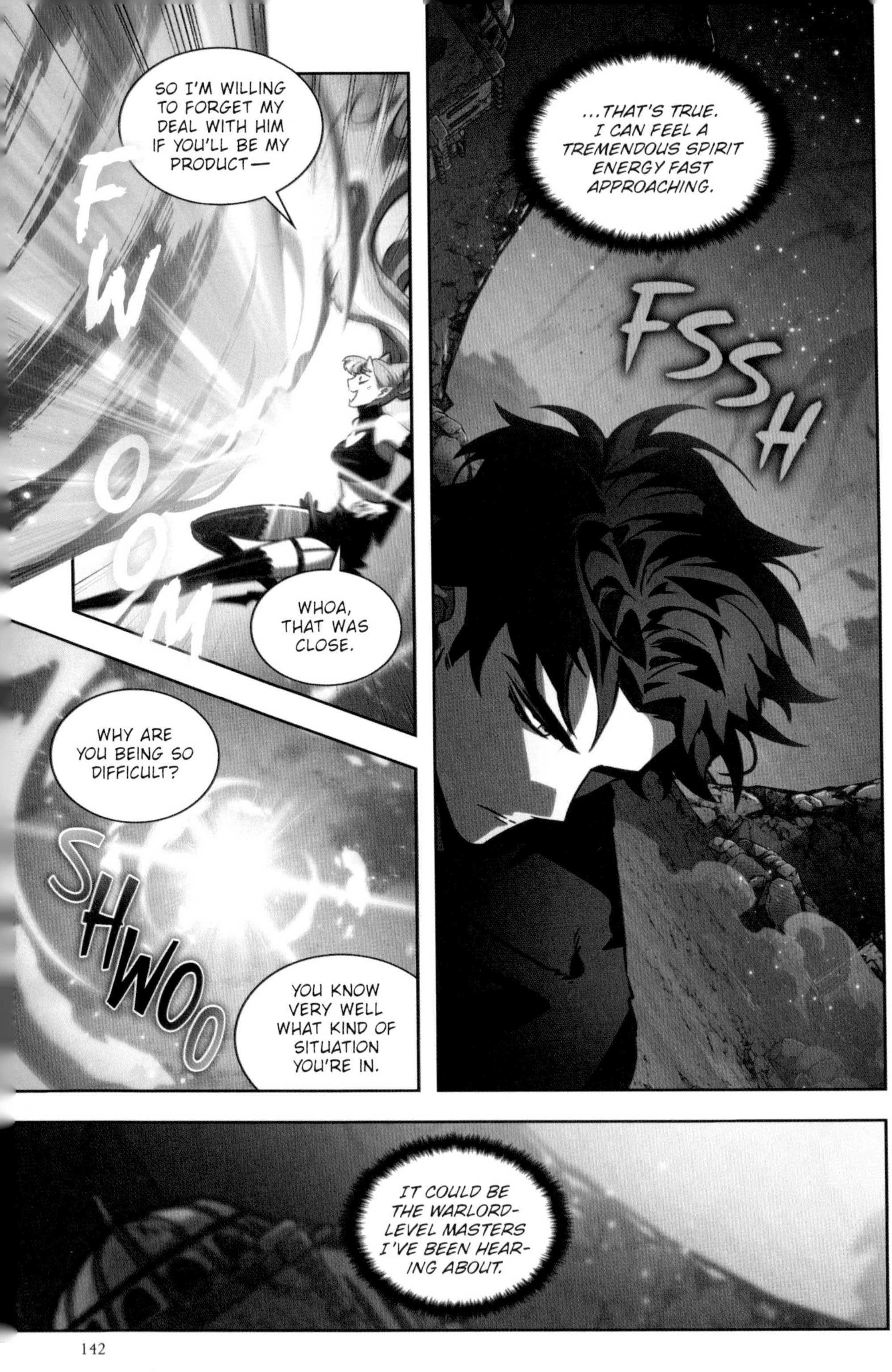
SO I'M WILLING TO FORGET MY DEAL WITH HIM IF YOU'LL BE MY PRODUCT—
FWOOOM
WHOA, THAT WAS CLOSE.
WHY ARE YOU BEING SO DIFFICULT?
SHWOO
YOU KNOW VERY WELL WHAT KIND OF SITUATION YOU'RE IN.
...THAT'S TRUE. I CAN FEEL A TREMENDOUS SPIRIT ENERGY FAST APPROACHING.
FSSH
IT COULD BE THE WARLORD-LEVEL MASTERS I'VE BEEN HEARING ABOUT.

THE MASTER OF DARKNESS IS LOOKING FOR YOU. YOU KNOW WHAT THAT MEANS, RIGHT?

BUT I CAN HIDE YOU FROM HIM!

AS LONG AS YOU'RE MINE, I'LL MAKE SURE NO ONE IN THE TWELVE ZONES CAN HARM YOU!

I REFUSE.

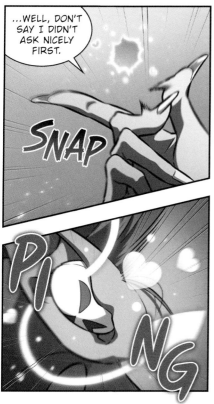

...WELL, DON'T SAY I DIDN'T ASK NICELY FIRST.

SNAP

PI NG

FWISH

FWISH

143

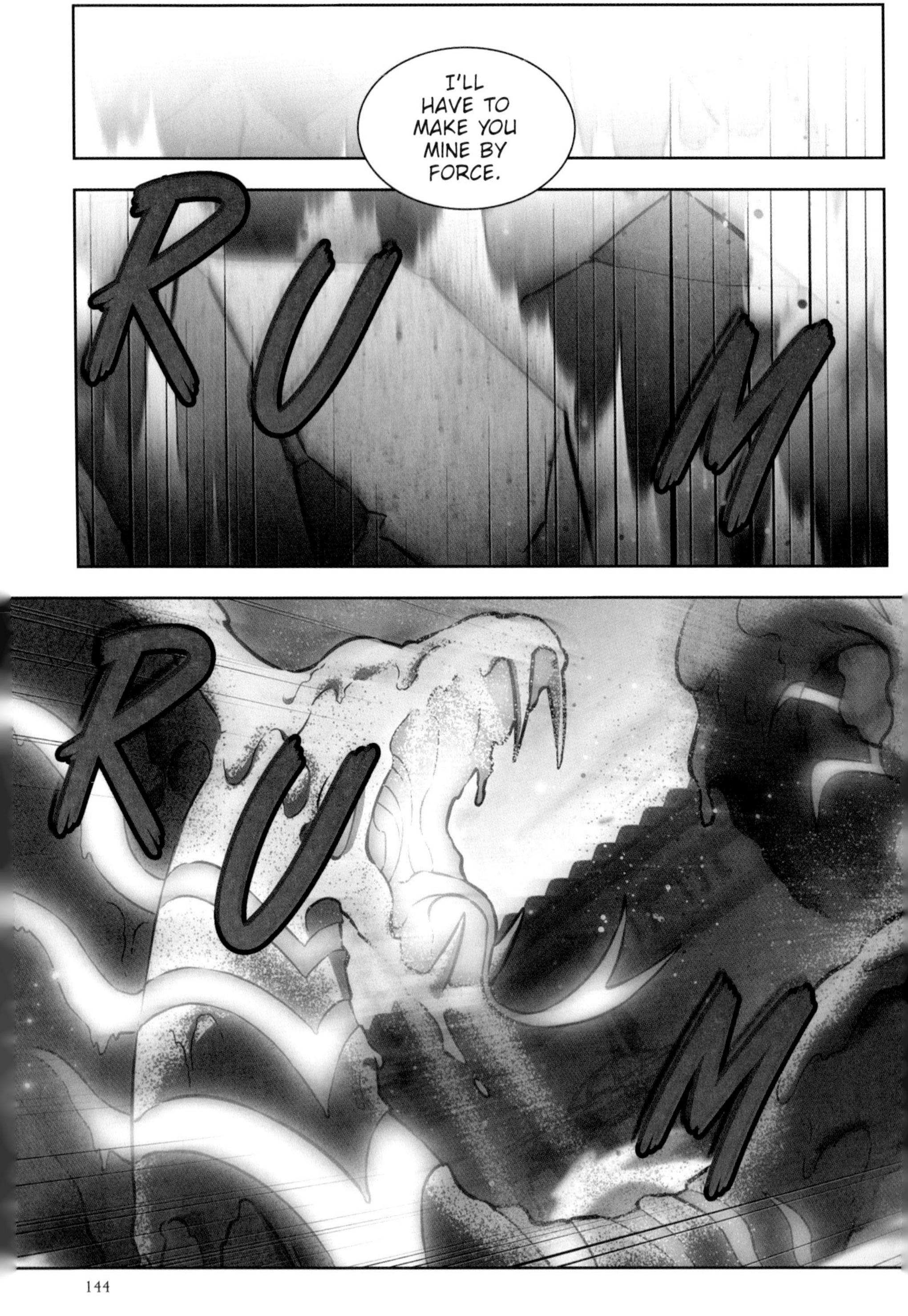
I'LL HAVE TO MAKE YOU MINE BY FORCE.
RUM
RUM

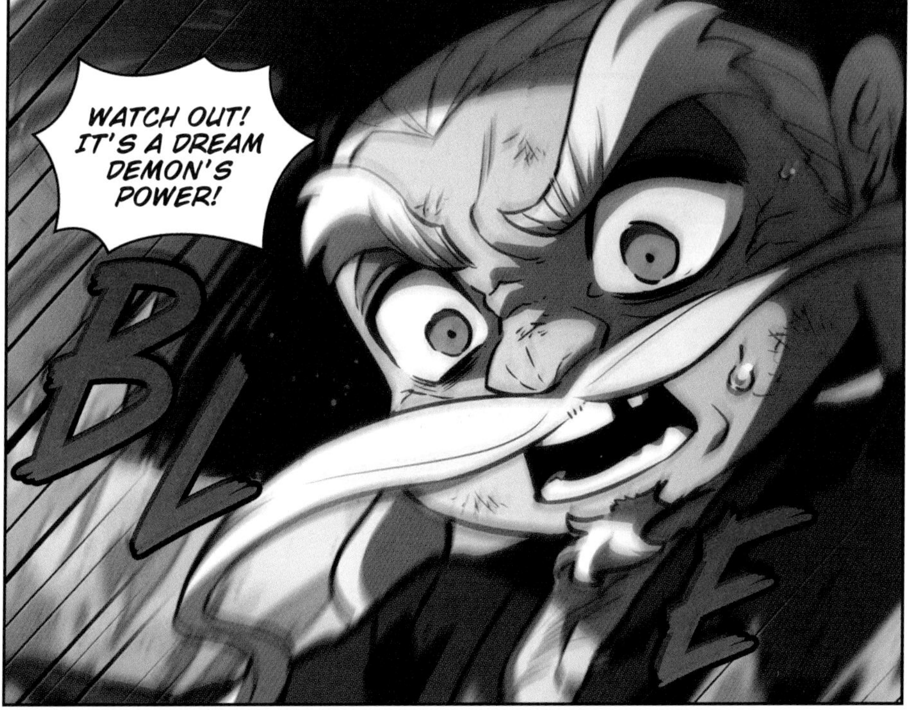
WATCH OUT! IT'S A DREAM DEMON'S POWER!
BLE

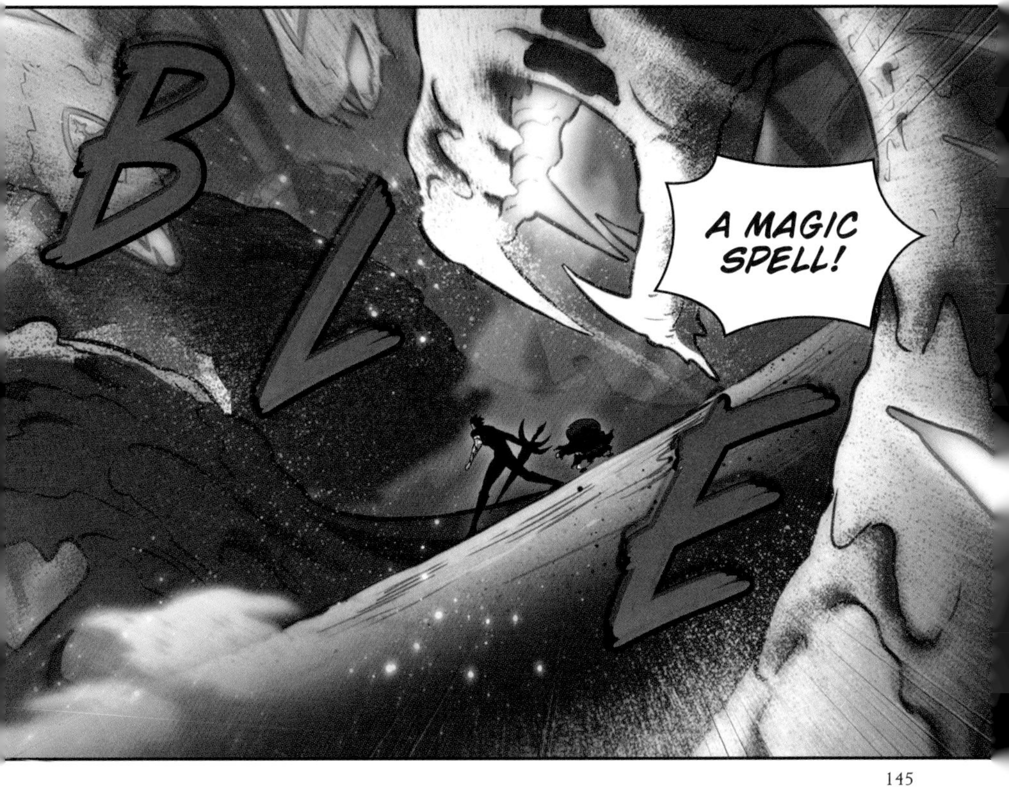
BLE
A MAGIC SPELL!

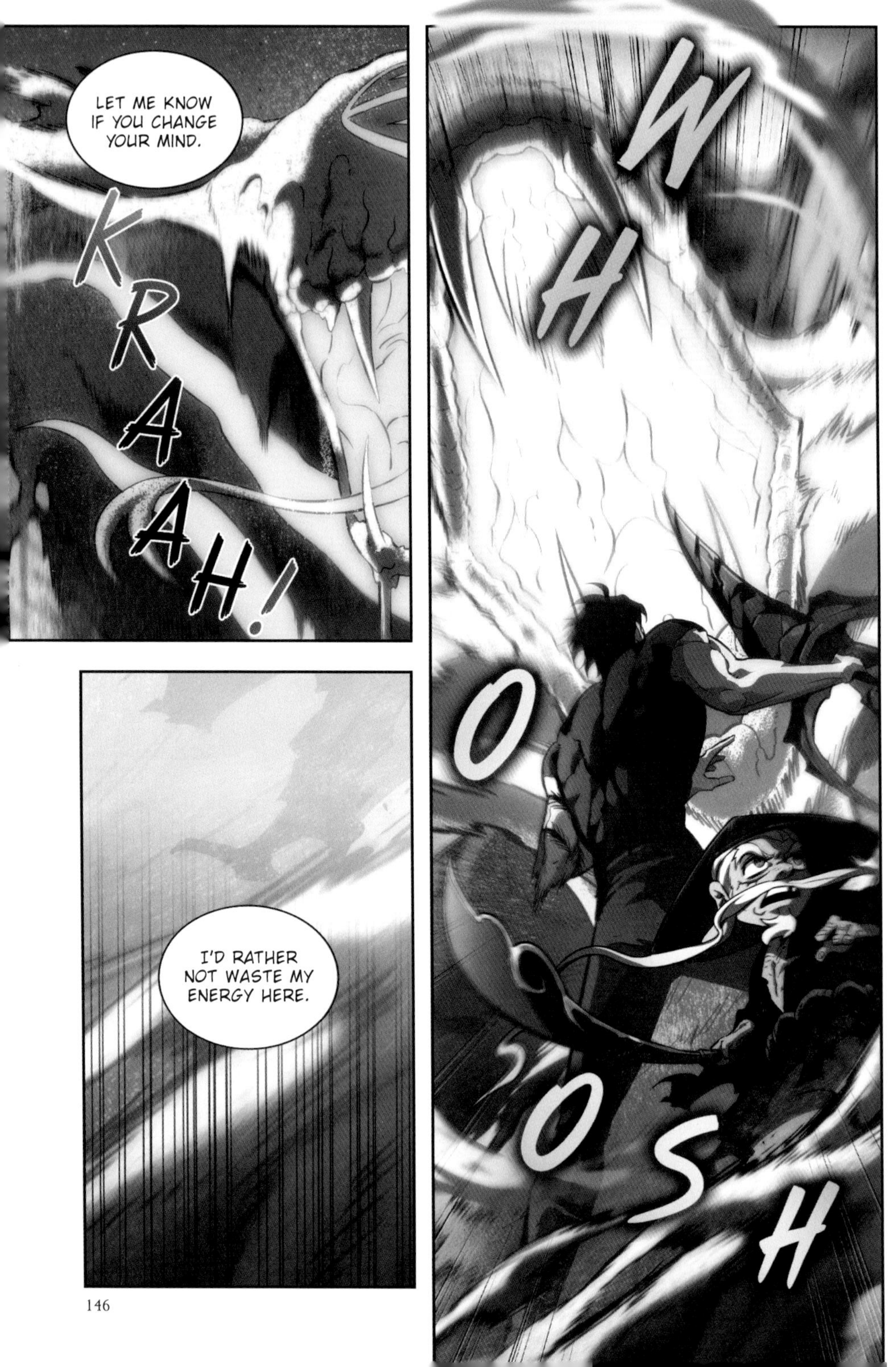
LET ME KNOW IF YOU CHANGE YOUR MIND.
KRAAAH!
I'D RATHER NOT WASTE MY ENERGY HERE.
WHOOOOSH

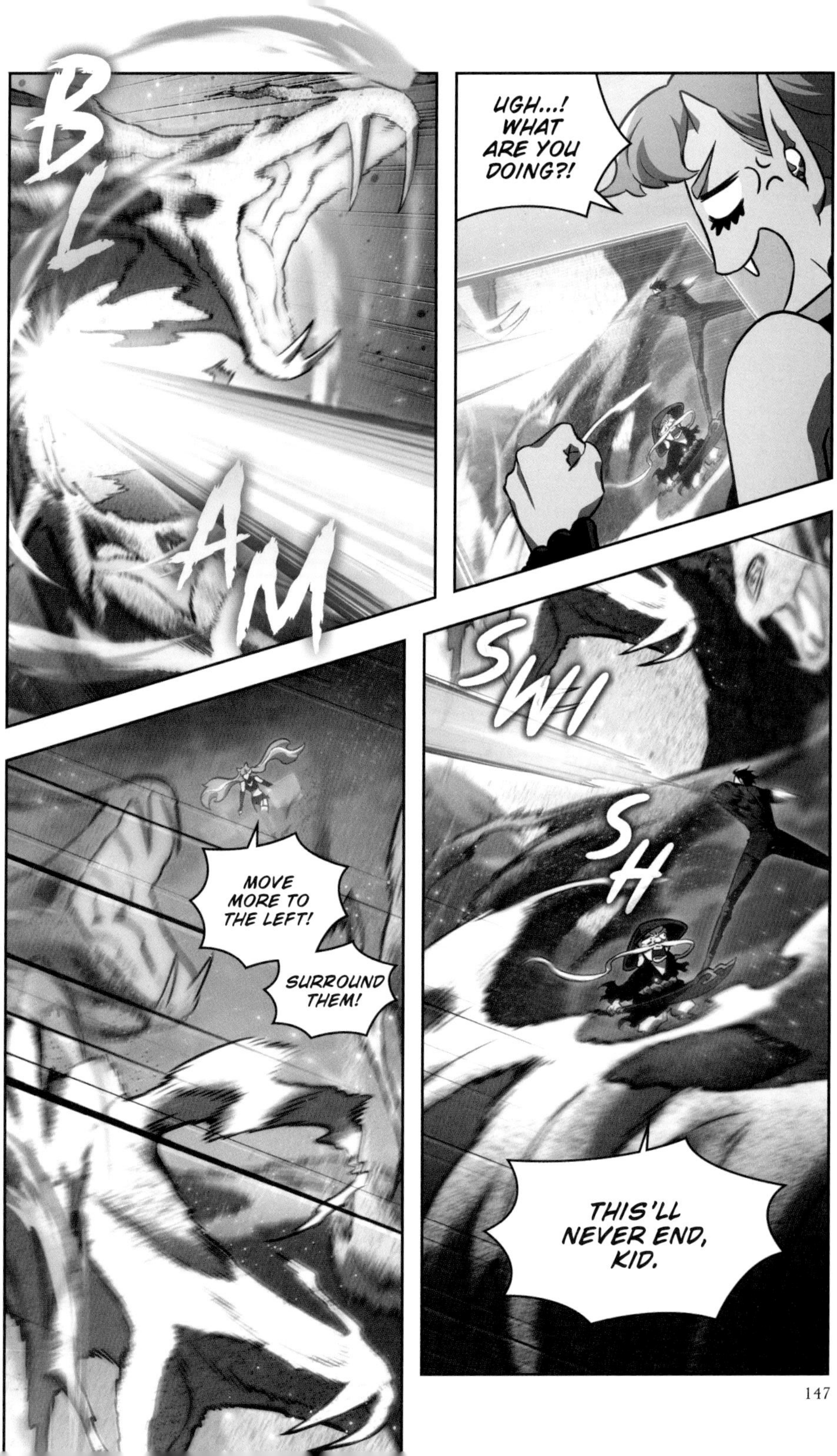
BLAM
UGH...! WHAT ARE YOU DOING?!
SWISH
MOVE MORE TO THE LEFT!
SURROUND THEM!
THIS'LL NEVER END, KID.

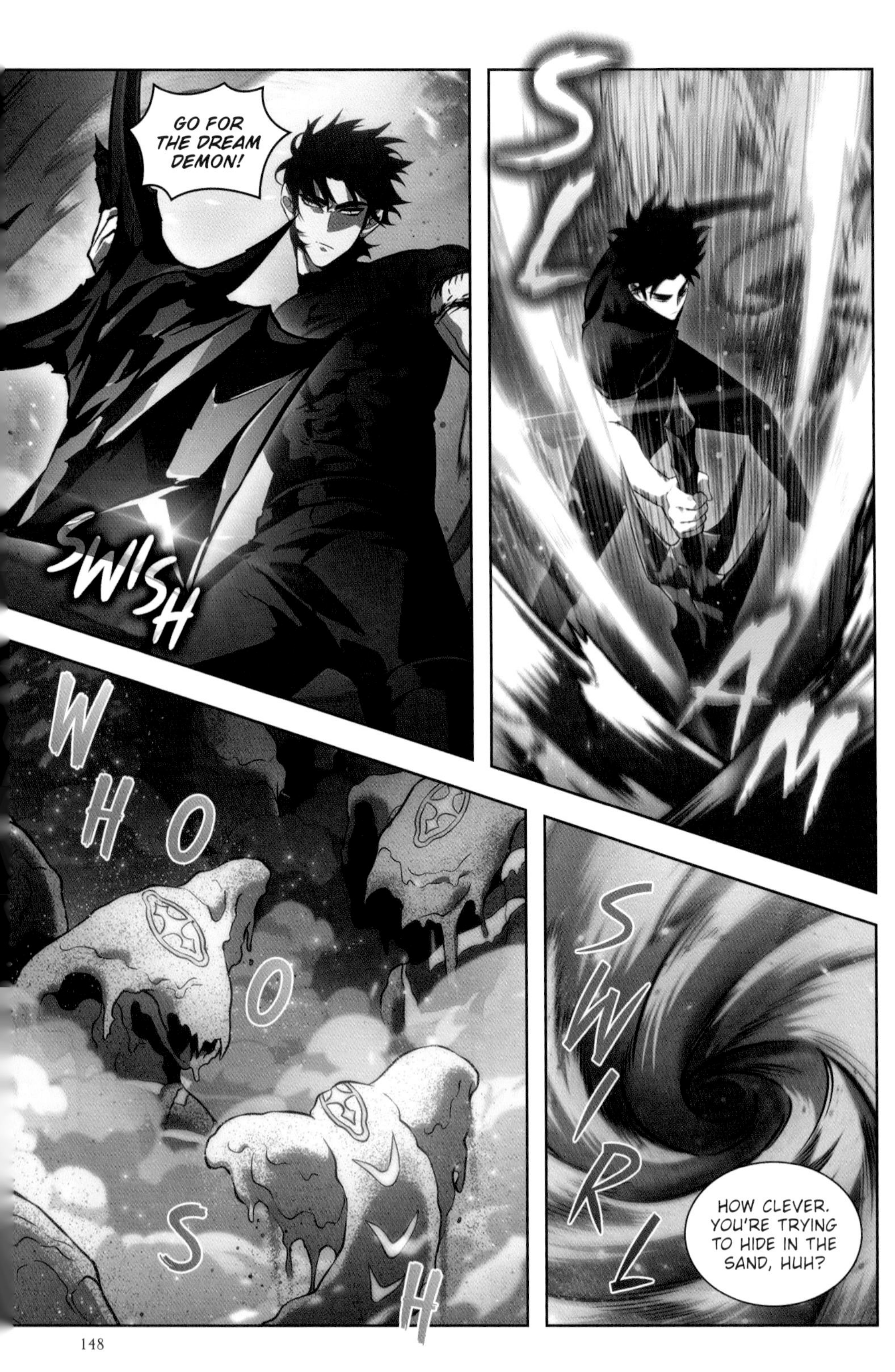
GO FOR THE DREAM DEMON!
SWISH
SLAM
WHOOSH
SWIRL
HOW CLEVER. YOU'RE TRYING TO HIDE IN THE SAND, HUH?

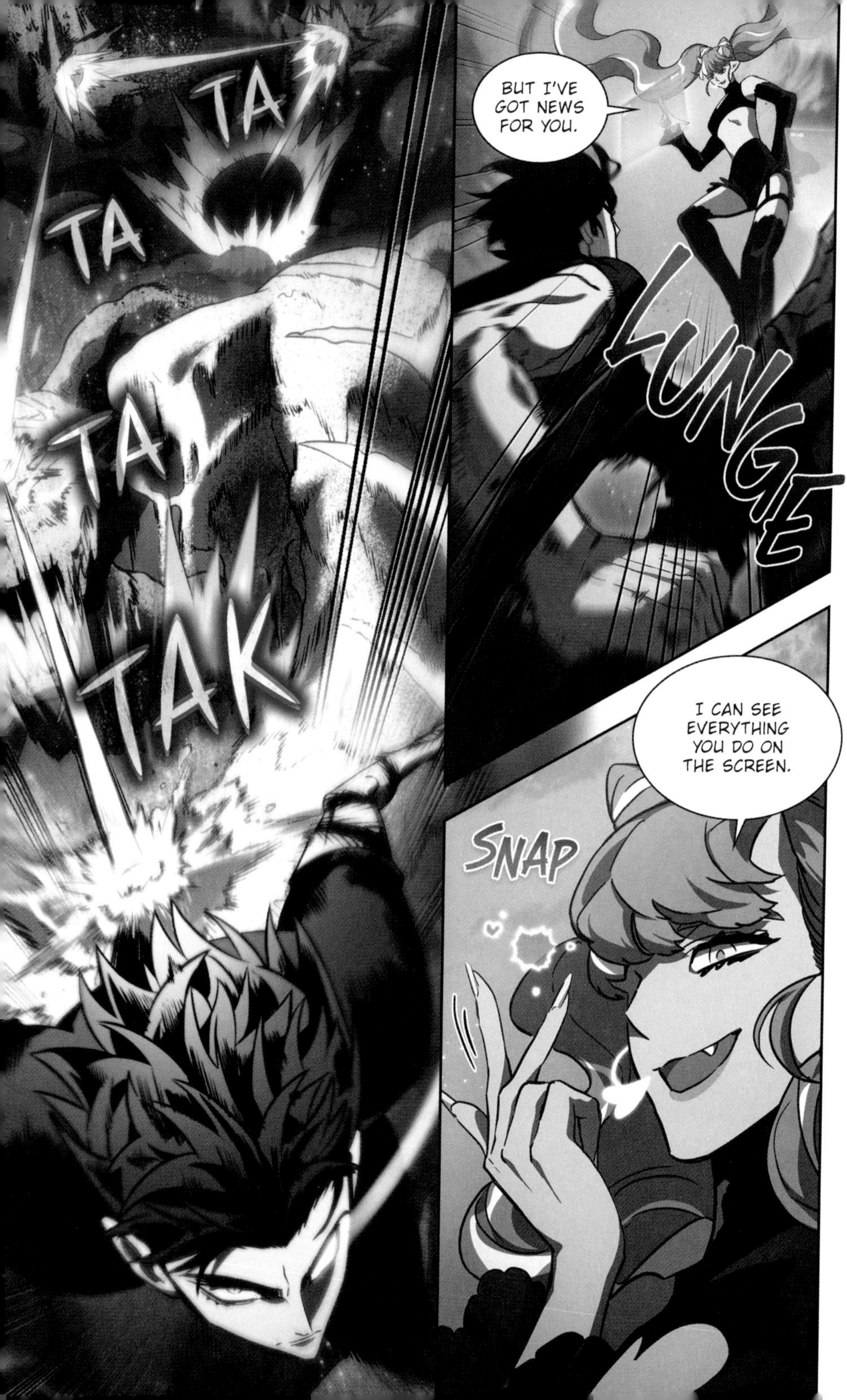
TA TA
TA
TA
TAK
BUT I'VE GOT NEWS FOR YOU.
LUNGE
I CAN SEE EVERYTHING YOU DO ON THE SCREEN.
SNAP

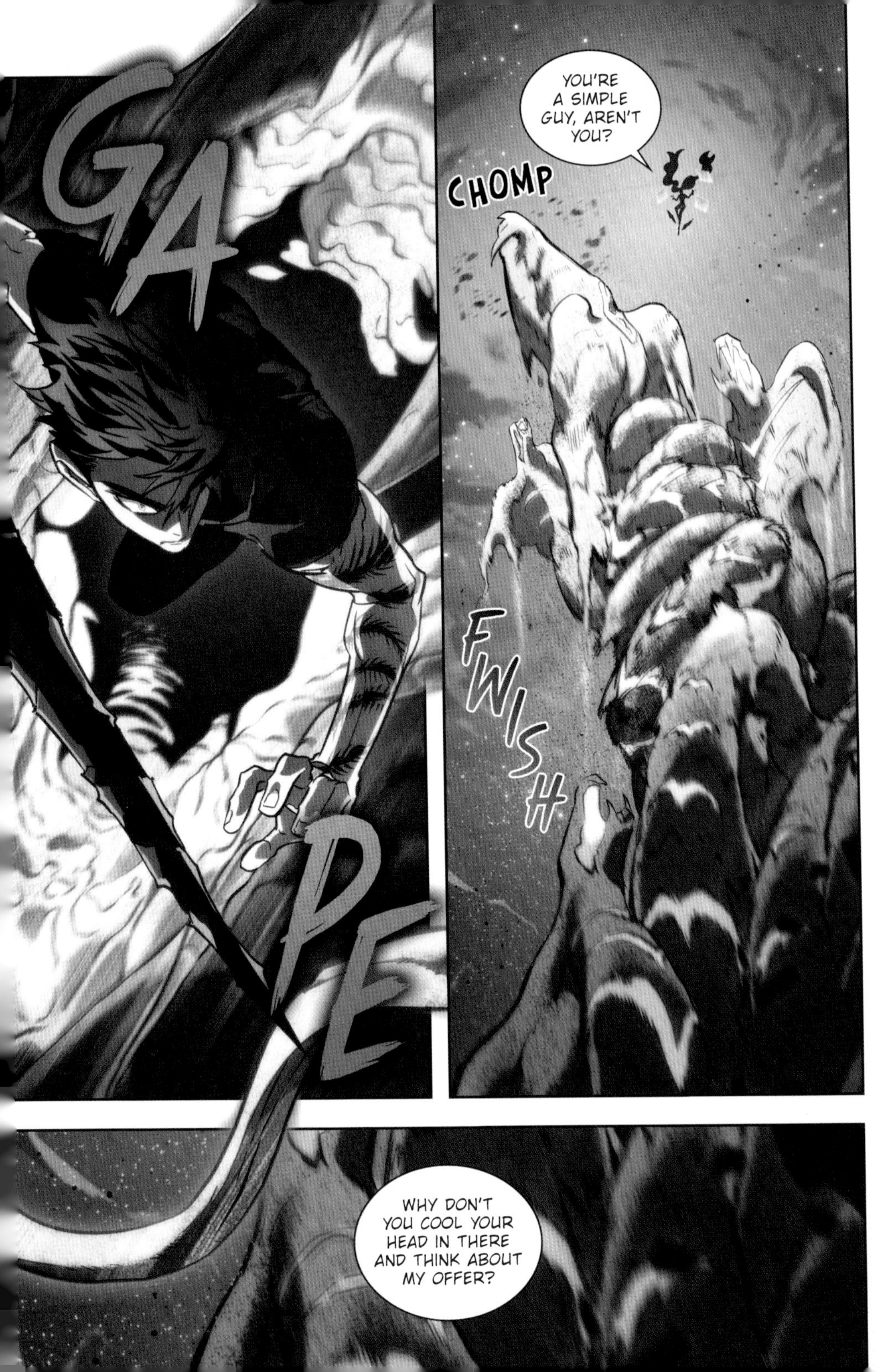
GA
PE
YOU'RE A SIMPLE GUY, AREN'T YOU?
CHOMP
FWISH
WHY DON'T YOU COOL YOUR HEAD IN THERE AND THINK ABOUT MY OFFER?

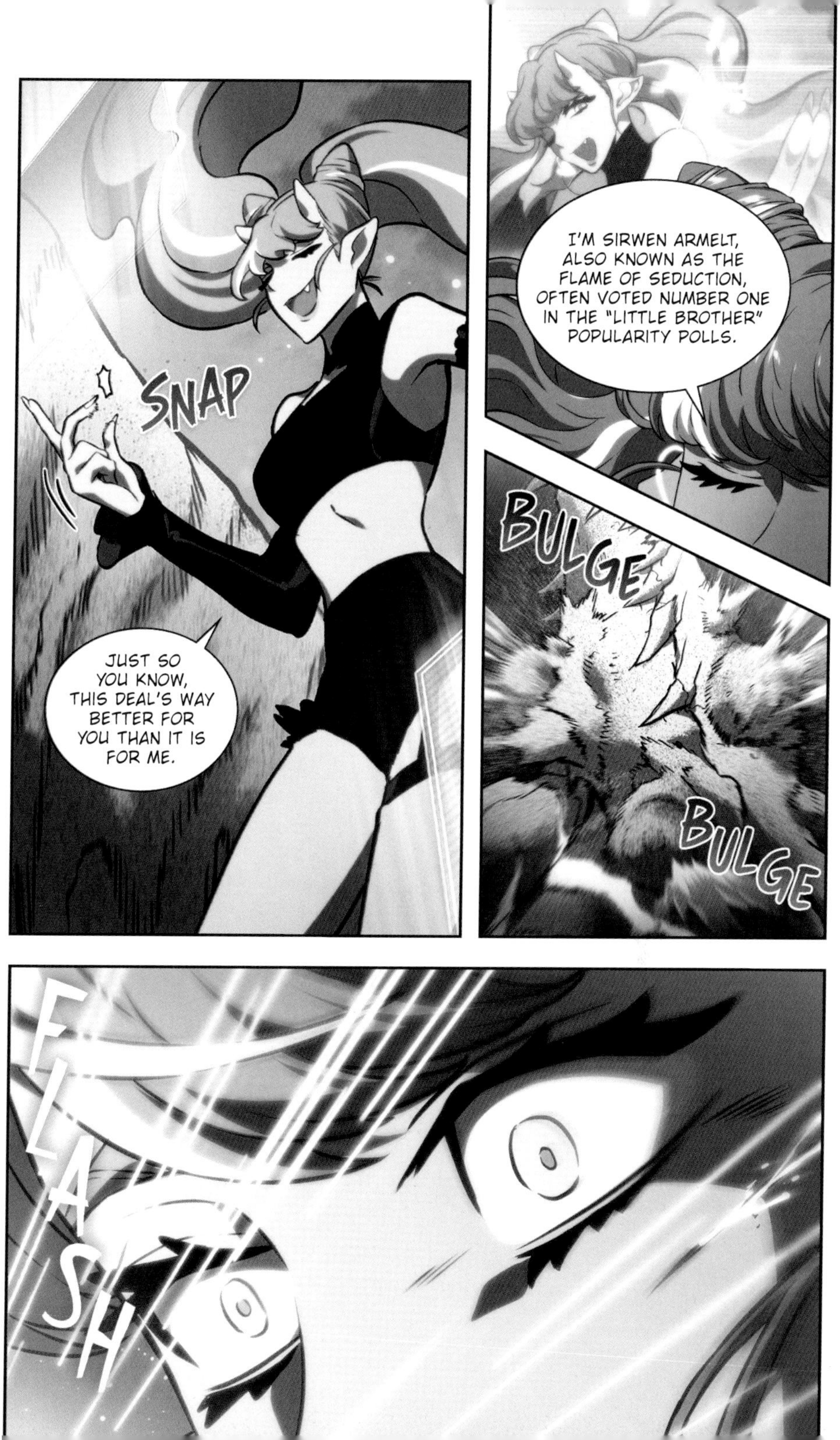
SNAP
JUST SO YOU KNOW, THIS DEAL'S WAY BETTER FOR YOU THAN IT IS FOR ME.
I'M SIRWEN ARMELT, ALSO KNOWN AS THE FLAME OF SEDUCTION, OFTEN VOTED NUMBER ONE IN THE "LITTLE BROTHER" POPULARITY POLLS.
BULGE
BULGE
FLASH

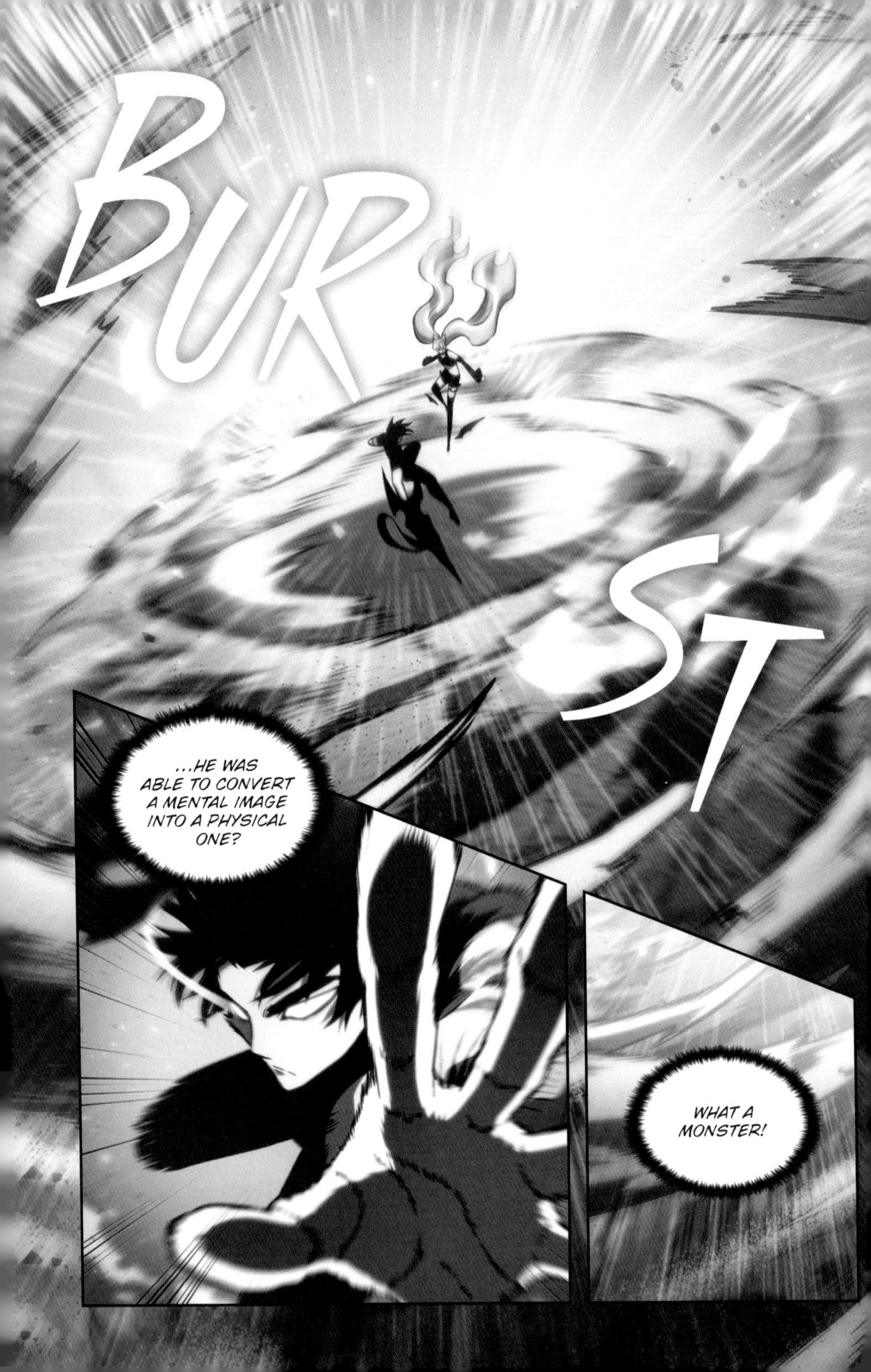
BURST
...HE WAS ABLE TO CONVERT A MENTAL IMAGE INTO A PHYSICAL ONE?
WHAT A MONSTER!

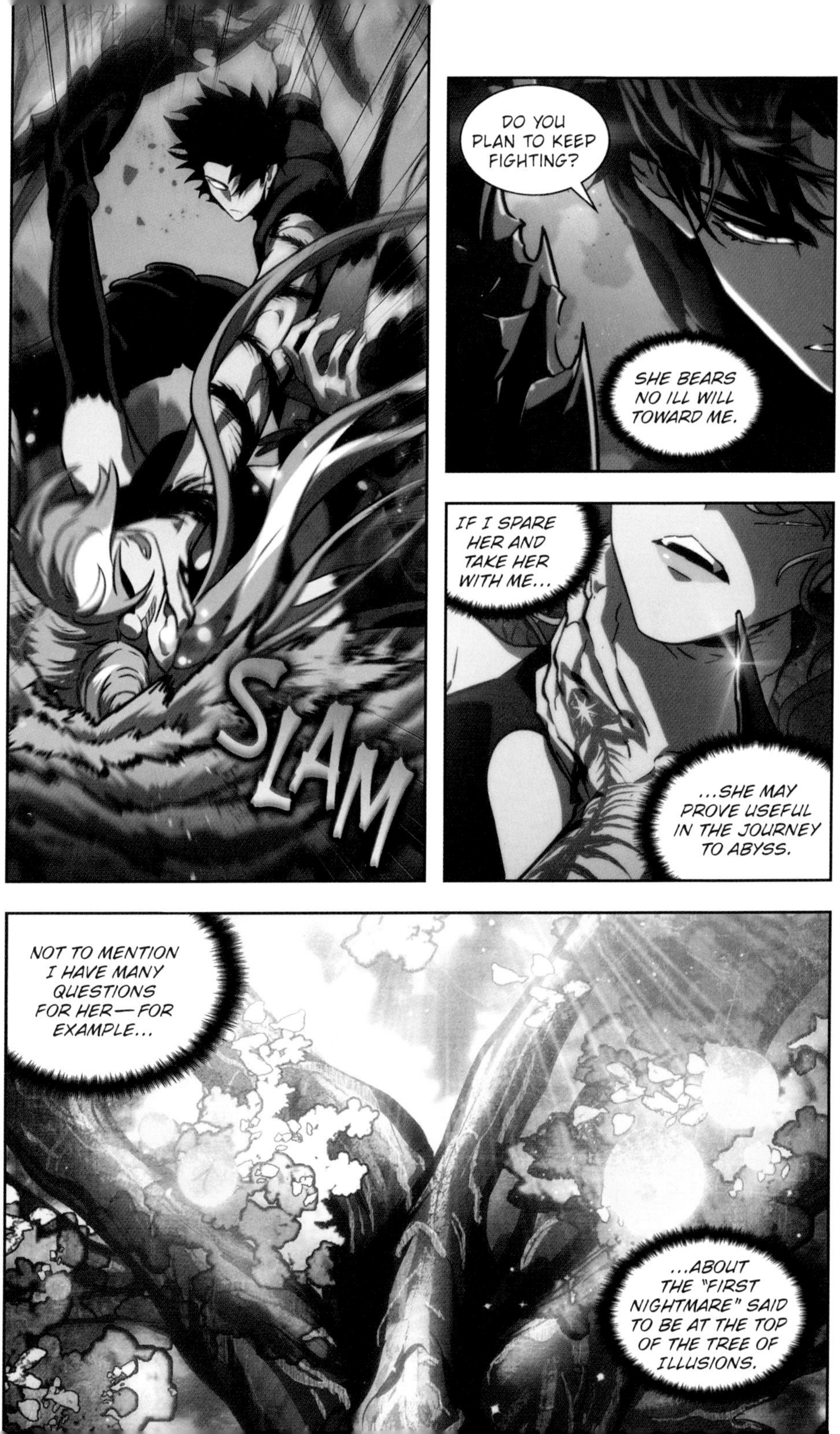
SLAM
DO YOU PLAN TO KEEP FIGHTING?
SHE BEARS NO ILL WILL TOWARD ME.
IF I SPARE HER AND TAKE HER WITH ME...
...SHE MAY PROVE USEFUL IN THE JOURNEY TO ABYSS.
NOT TO MENTION I HAVE MANY QUESTIONS FOR HER—FOR EXAMPLE...
...ABOUT THE "FIRST NIGHTMARE" SAID TO BE AT THE TOP OF THE TREE OF ILLUSIONS.

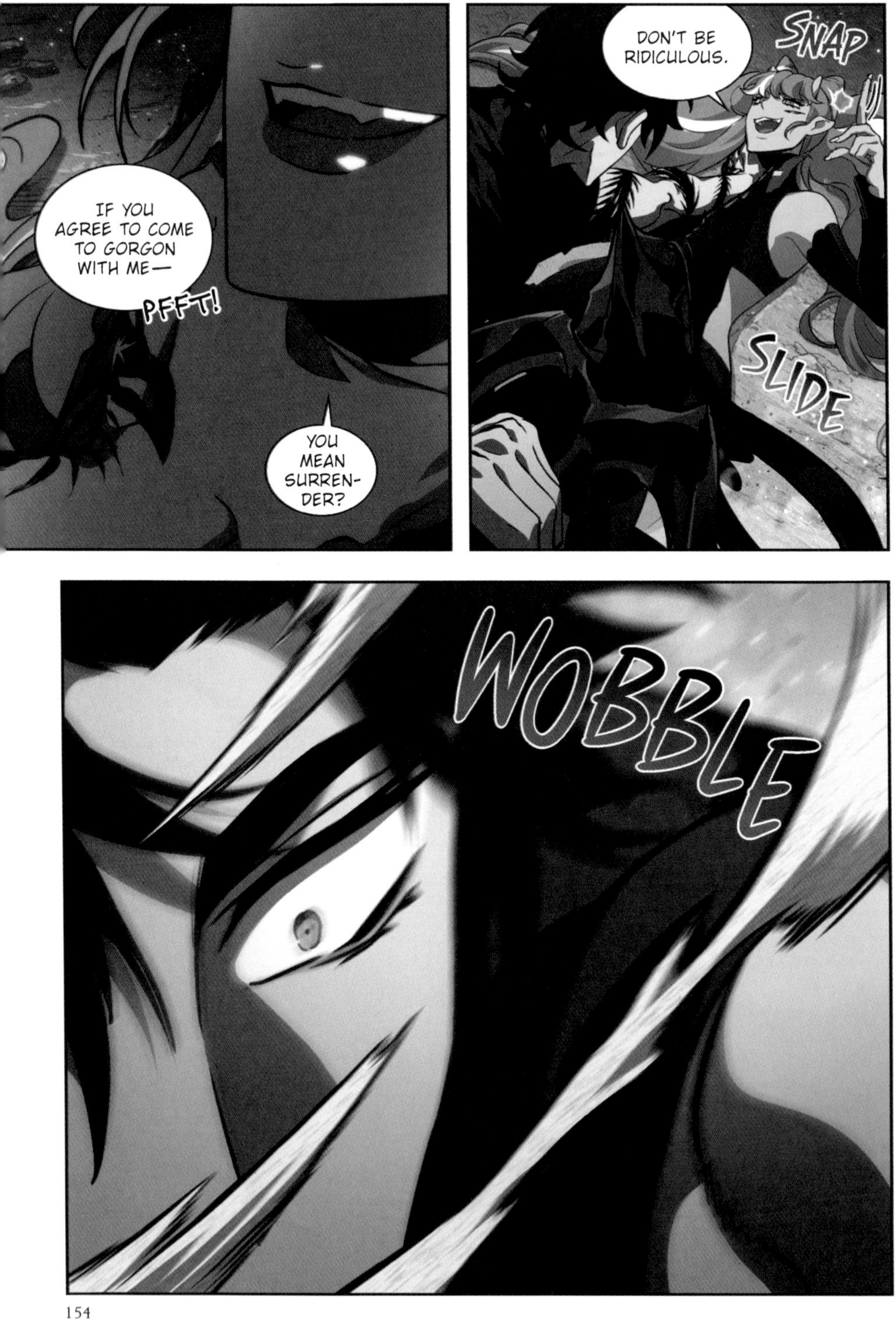
IF YOU AGREE TO COME TO GORGON WITH ME—
PFFT!
YOU MEAN SURREN-DER?
DON'T BE RIDICULOUS.
SNAP
SLIDE
WOBBLE

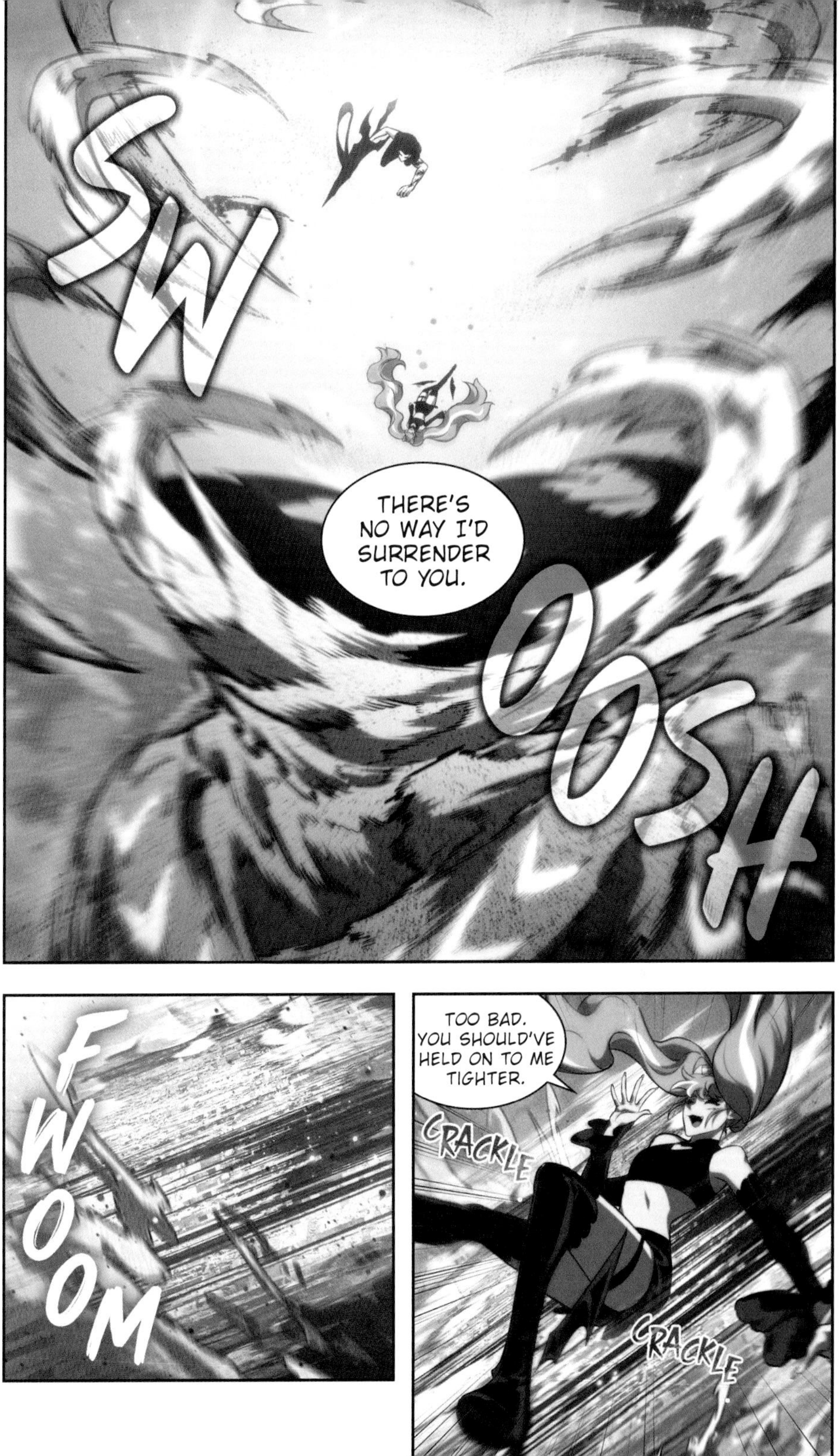

SW
THERE'S NO WAY I'D SURRENDER TO YOU.
OOSH
FWOOM
TOO BAD. YOU SHOULD'VE HELD ON TO ME TIGHTER.
CRACKLE
CRACKLE

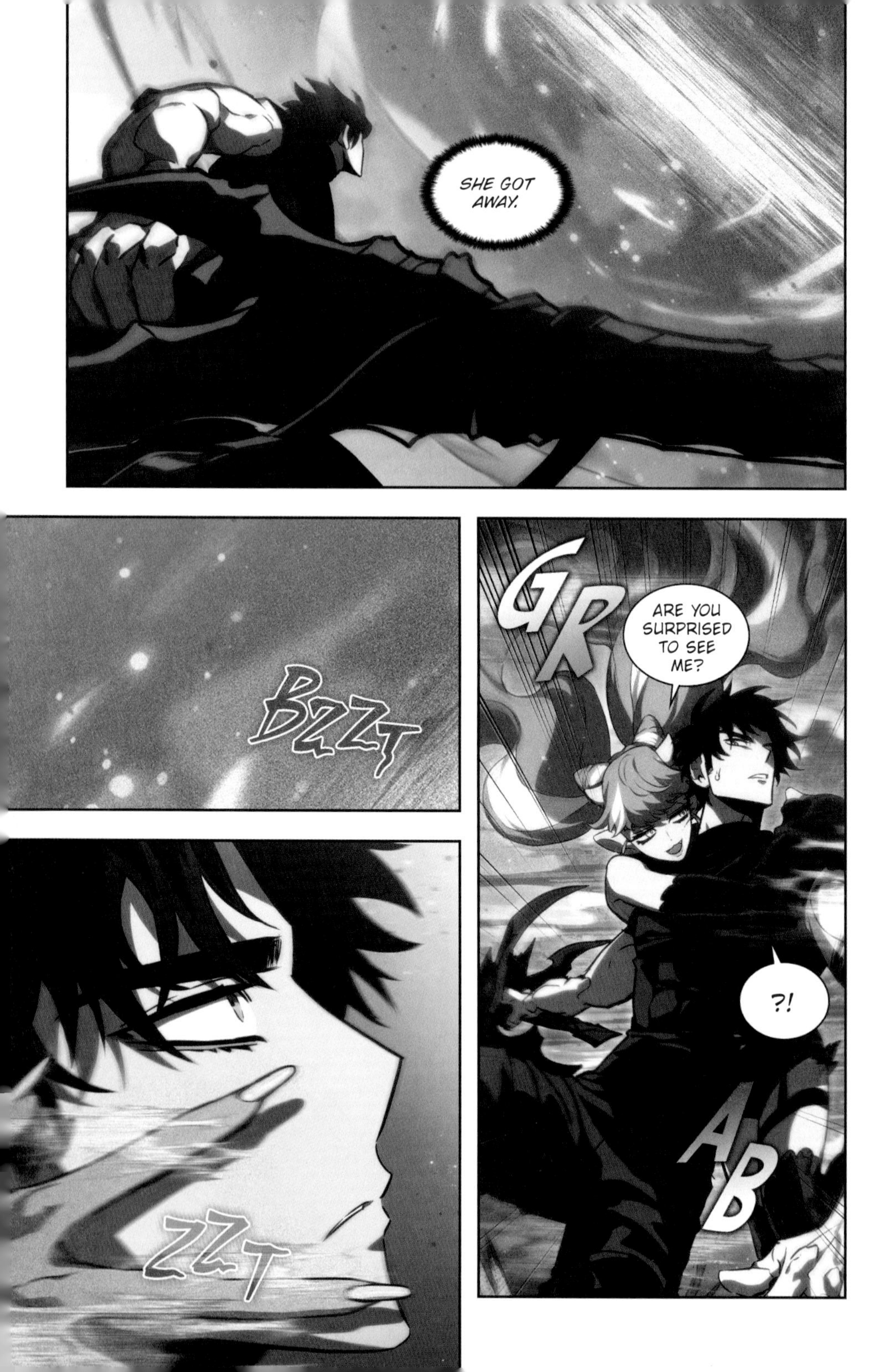
SHE GOT AWAY.
BZZT
ZZT
GR
ARE YOU SURPRISED TO SEE ME?
?!
AB

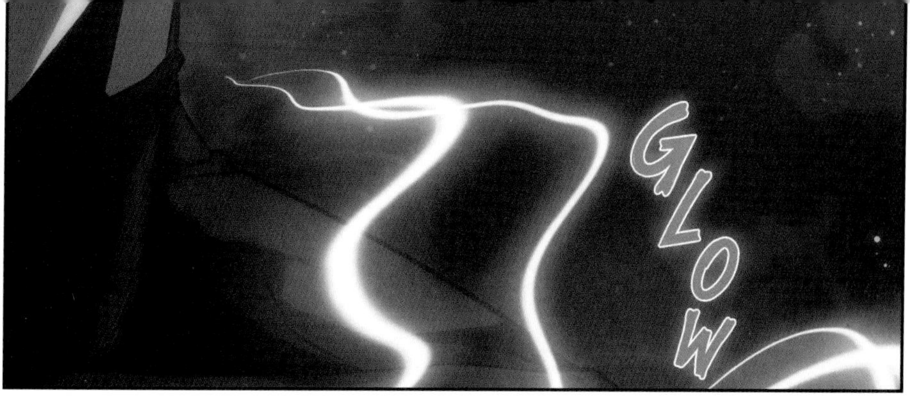
GLOW

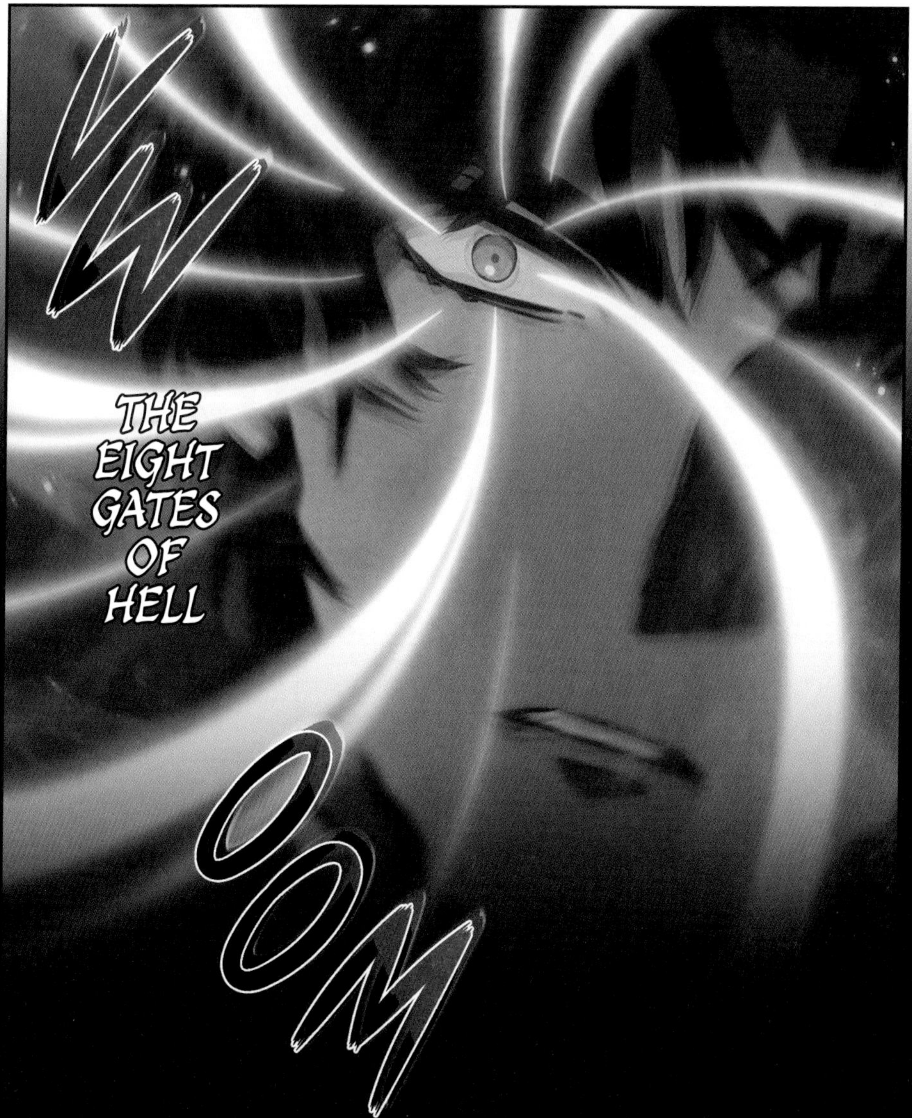
VVW
THE EIGHT GATES OF HELL
OOOM

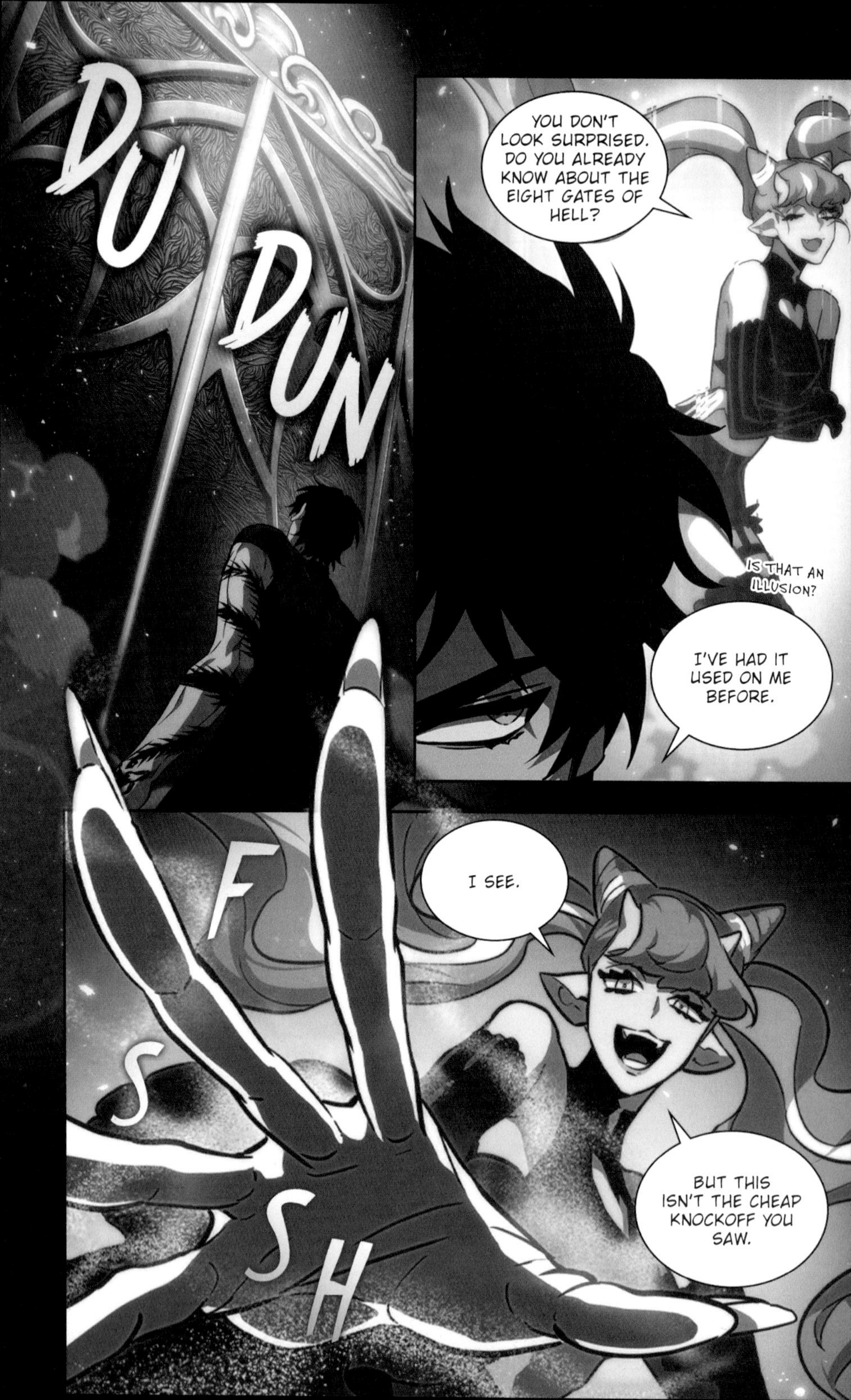
DU
DUN
YOU DON'T LOOK SURPRISED. DO YOU ALREADY KNOW ABOUT THE EIGHT GATES OF HELL?
IS THAT AN ILLUSION?
I'VE HAD IT USED ON ME BEFORE.
F
S
S
H
I SEE.
BUT THIS ISN'T THE CHEAP KNOCKOFF YOU SAW.

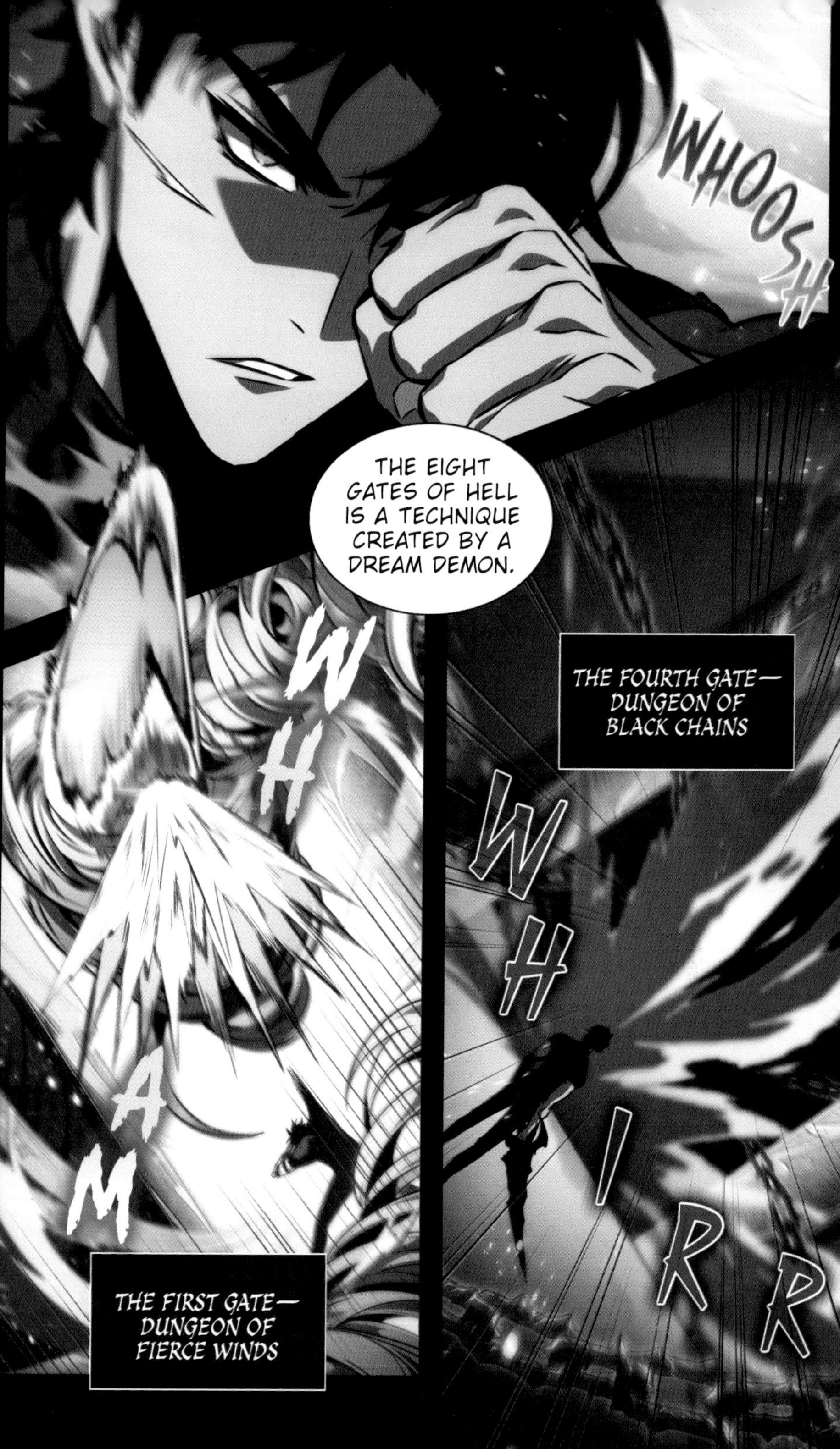
WHOOSH
THE EIGHT GATES OF HELL IS A TECHNIQUE CREATED BY A DREAM DEMON.
WHAAM
THE FIRST GATE— DUNGEON OF FIERCE WINDS
THE FOURTH GATE— DUNGEON OF BLACK CHAINS
WHIRR

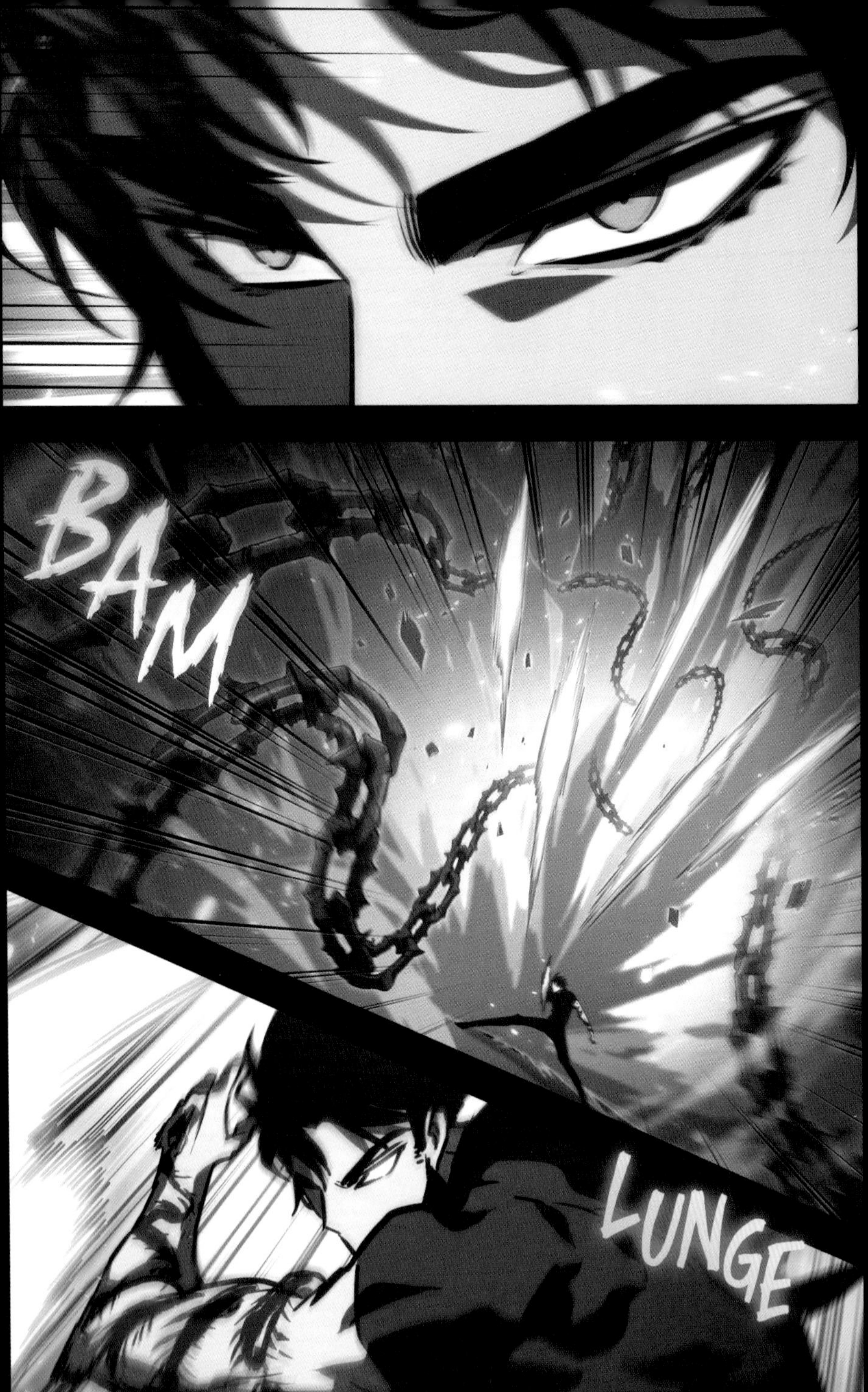
BAM
LUNGE

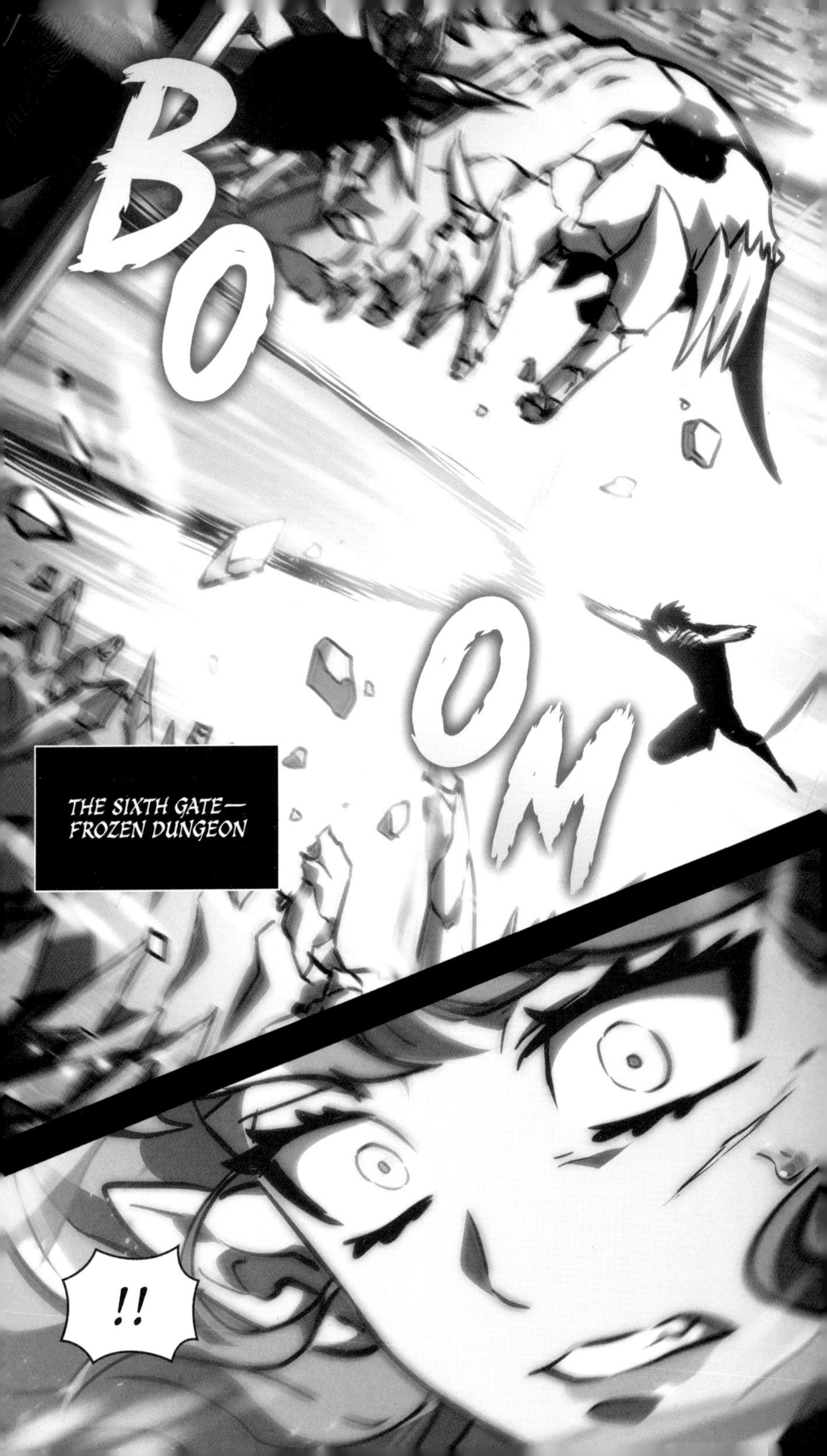
BOOM
THE SIXTH GATE—
FROZEN DUNGEON
!!

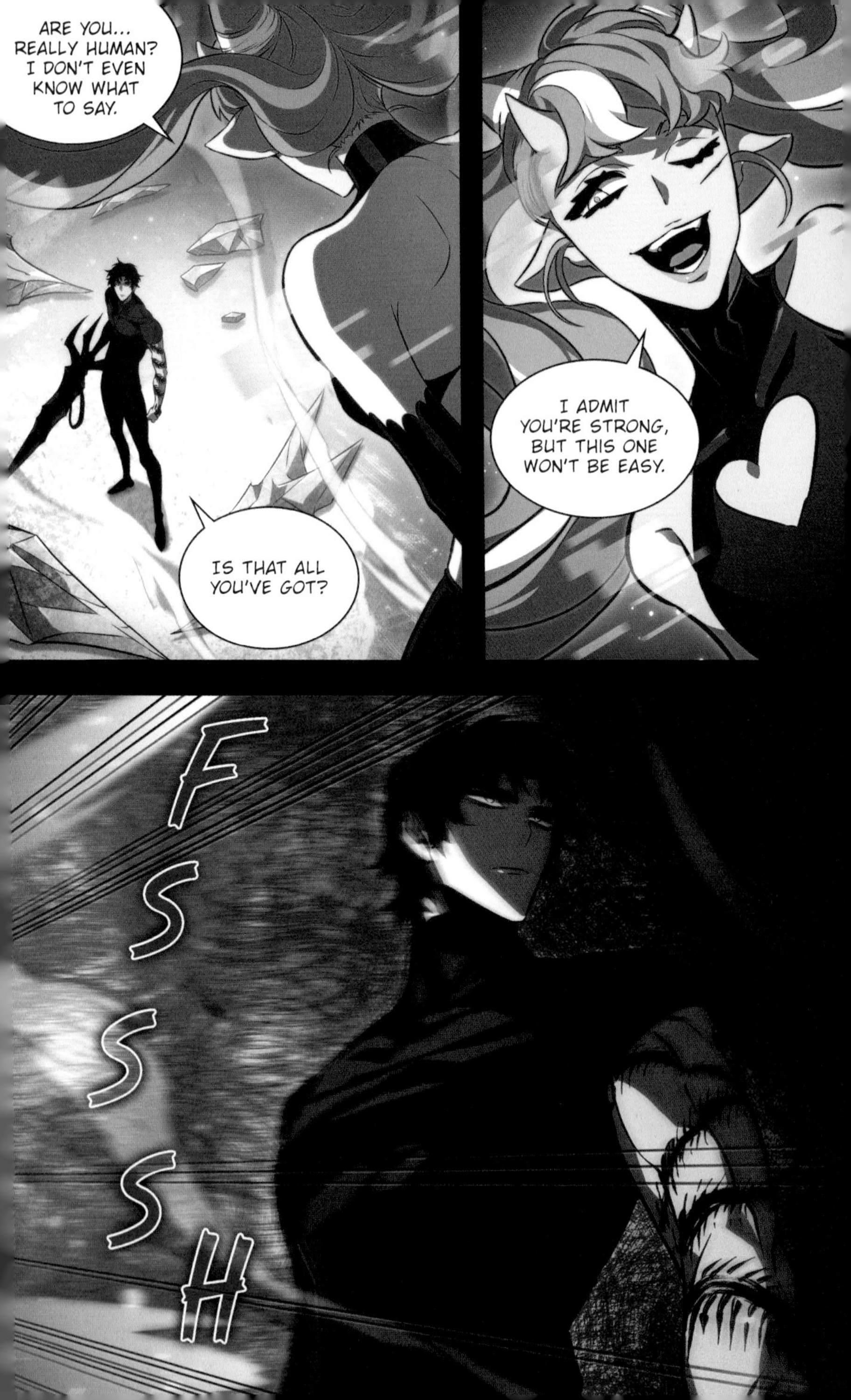
ARE YOU... REALLY HUMAN? I DON'T EVEN KNOW WHAT TO SAY.
IS THAT ALL YOU'VE GOT?
I ADMIT YOU'RE STRONG, BUT THIS ONE WON'T BE EASY.
FSSSH

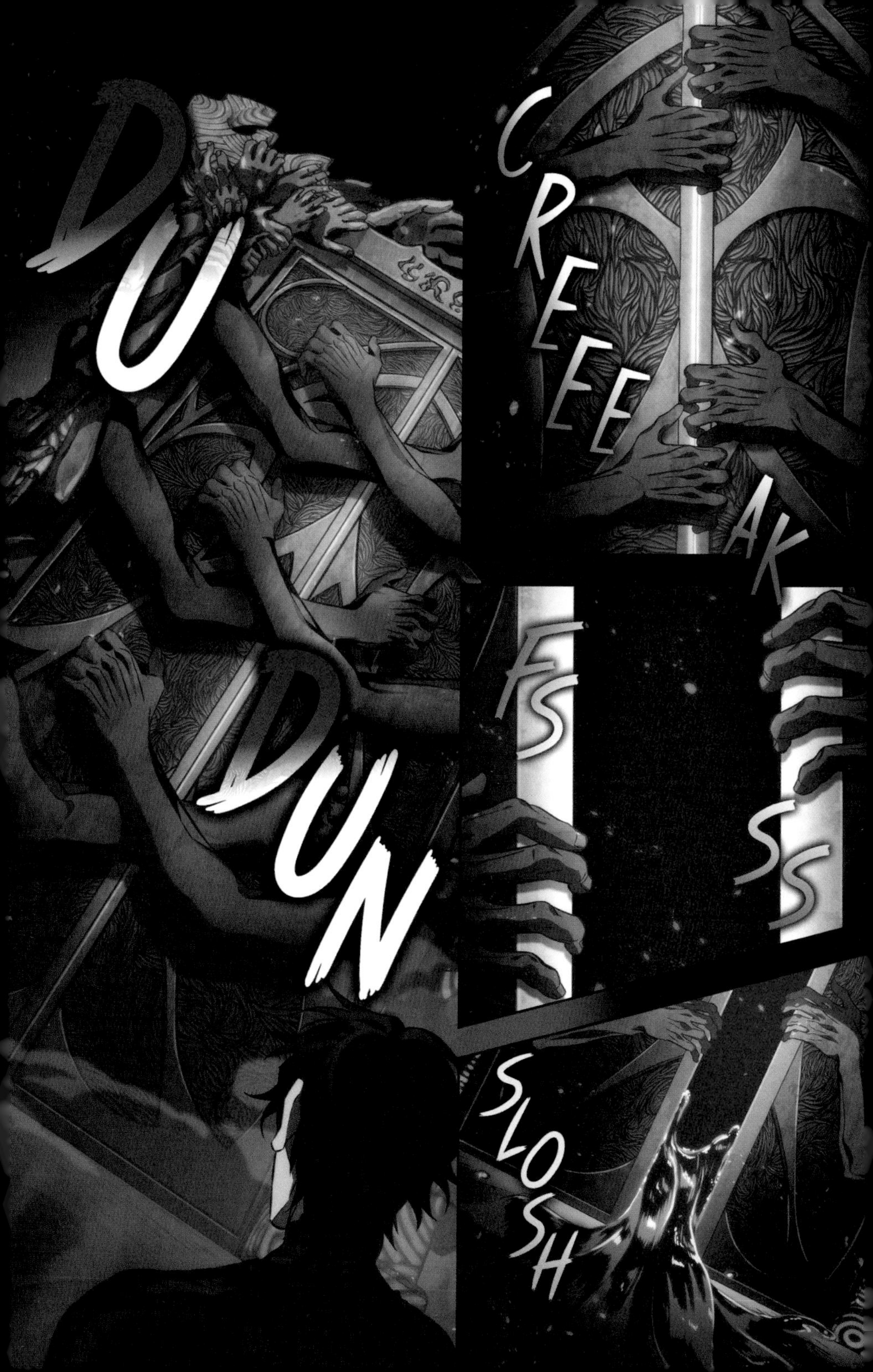
DU
DUN
CREEEAK
FS
SS
SLOSH

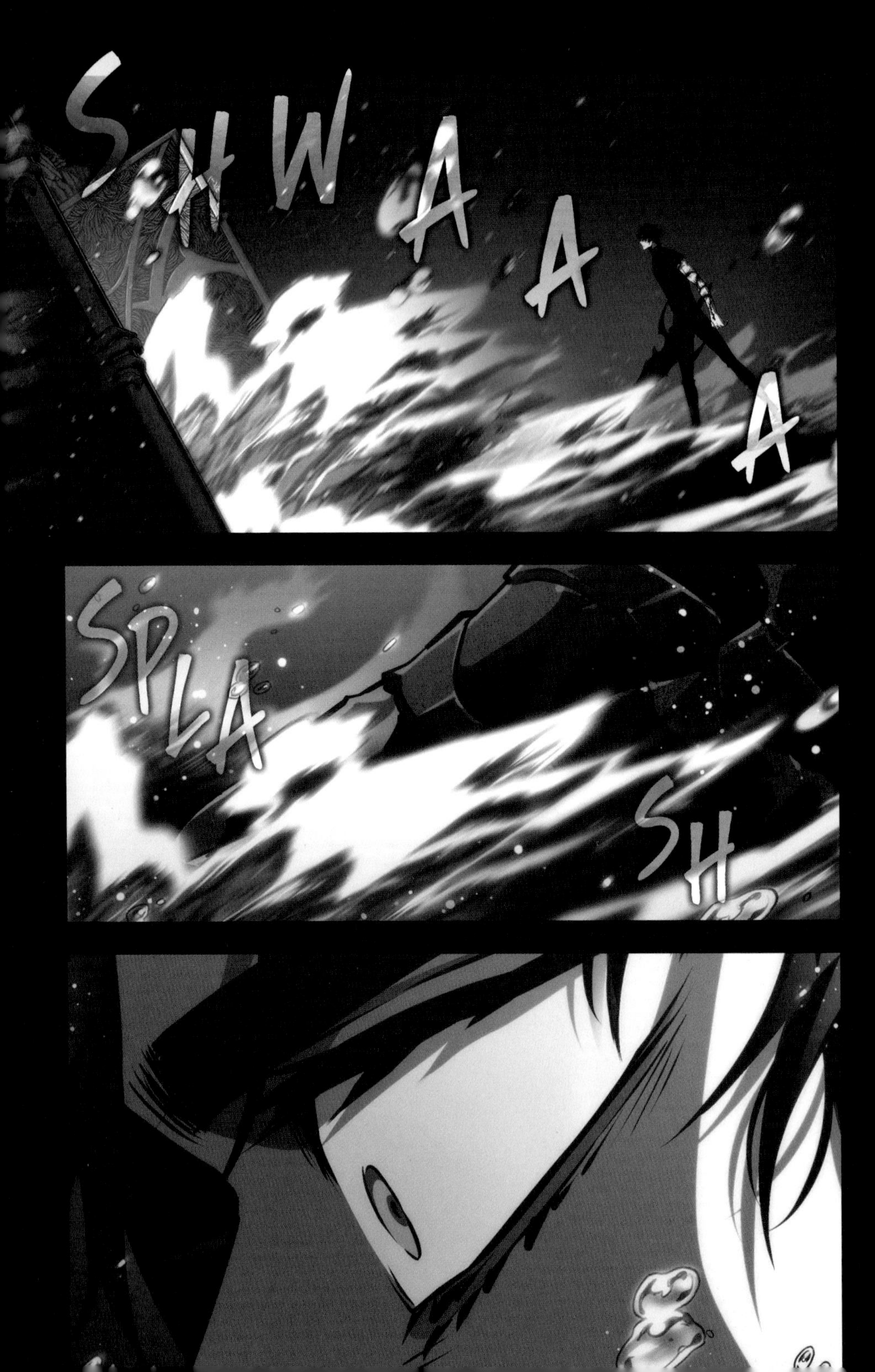
SHWAAAA
SPLA
SH

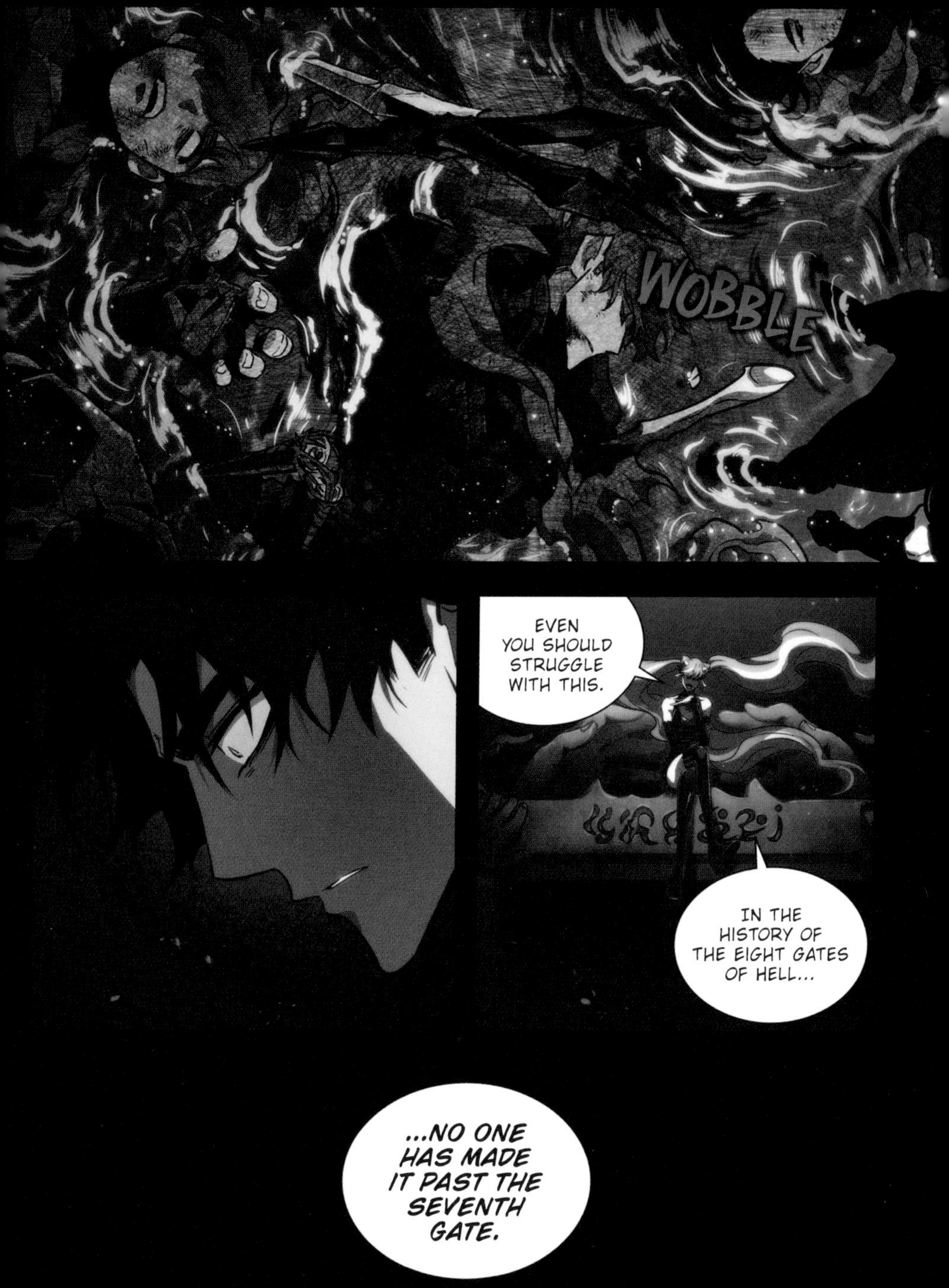
WOBBLE
EVEN YOU SHOULD STRUGGLE WITH THIS.
IN THE HISTORY OF THE EIGHT GATES OF HELL...
...NO ONE HAS MADE IT PAST THE SEVENTH GATE.

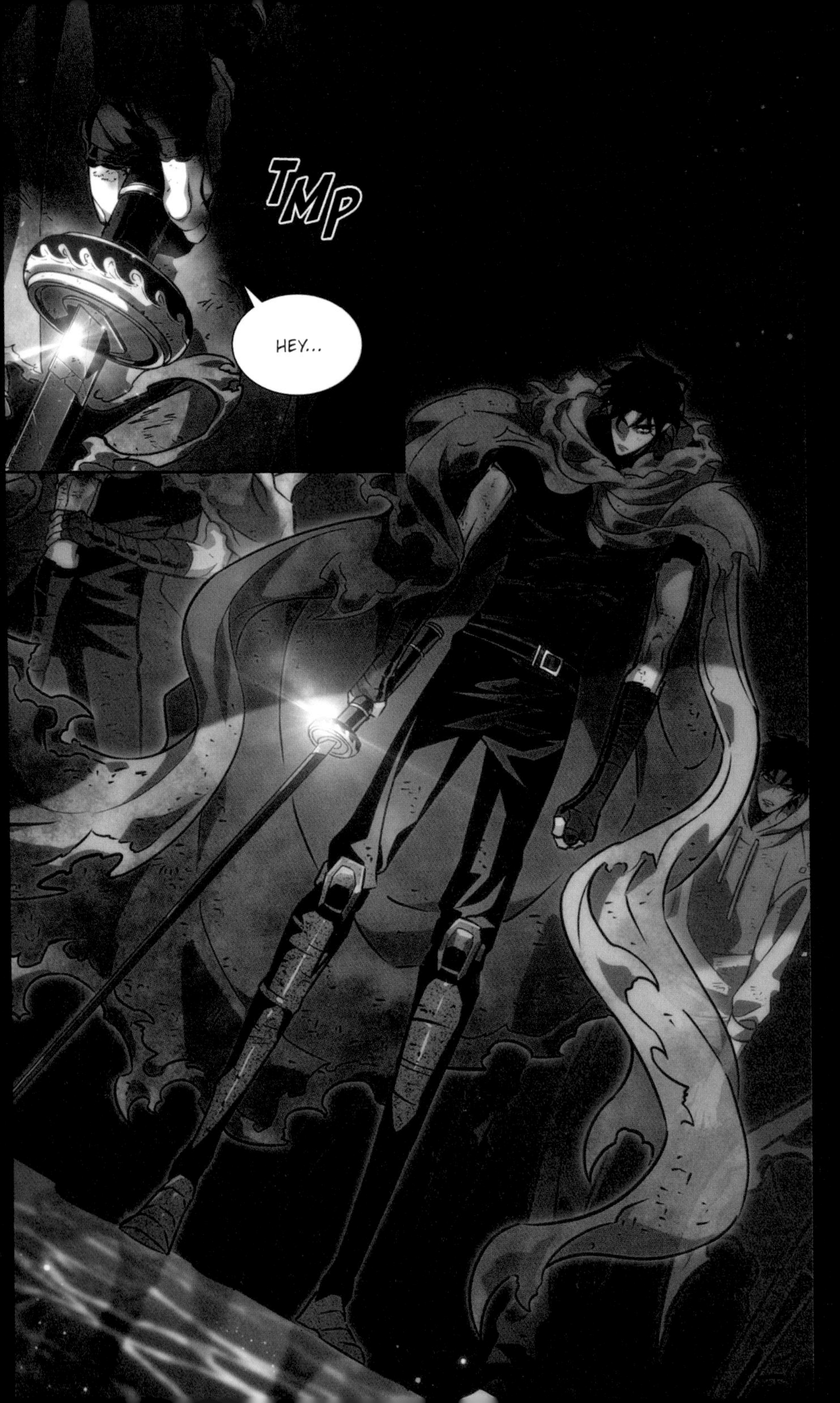
TMP
HEY...

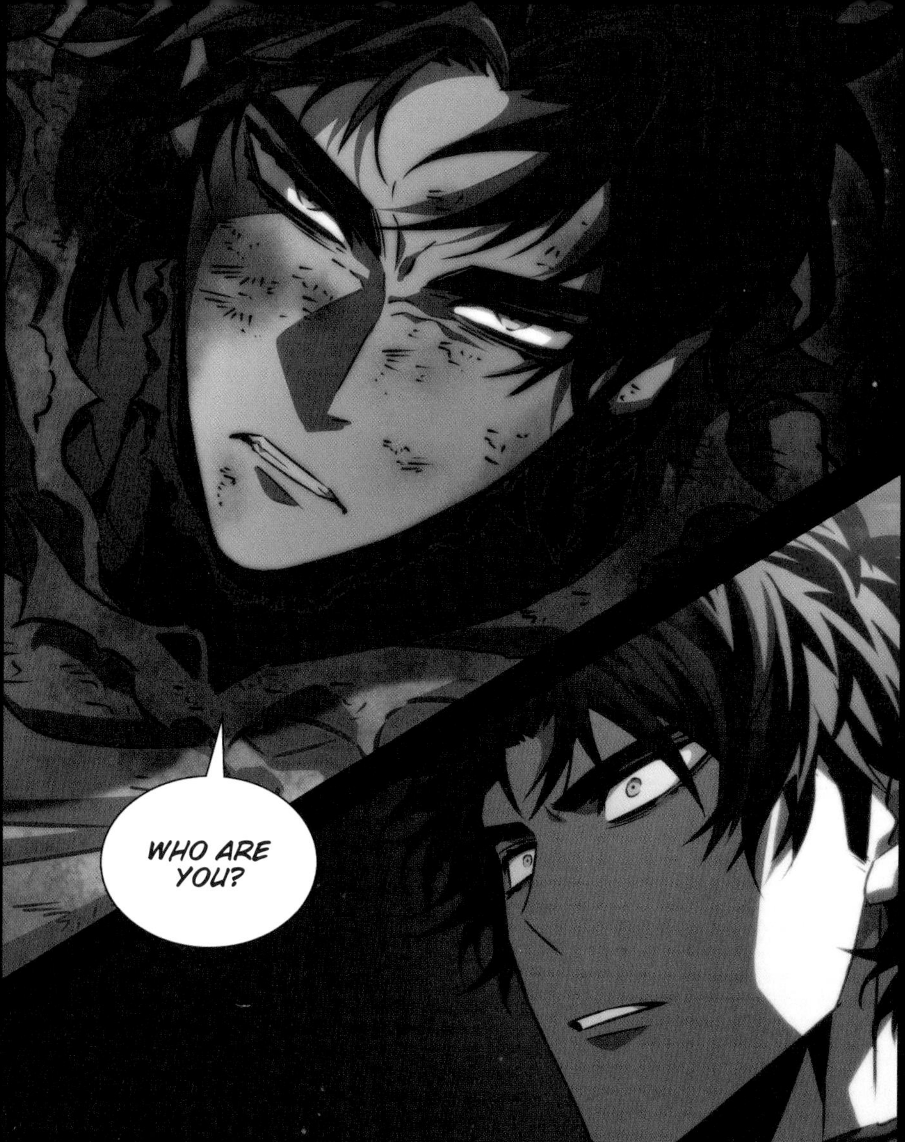
WHO ARE YOU?
THE SEVENTH GATE—DUNGEON OF THE SELF

The WORLD After the Fall

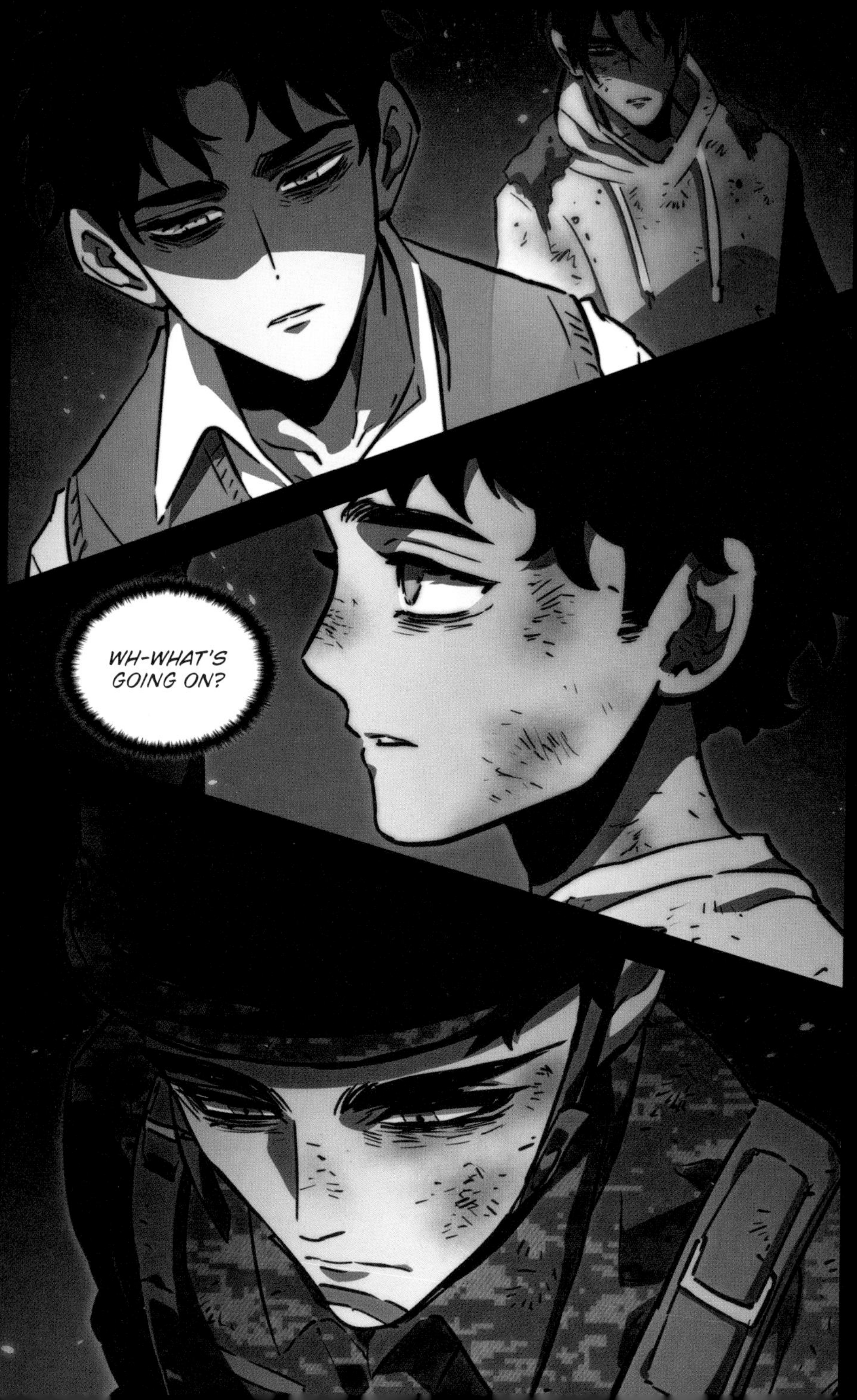
WH-WHAT'S GOING ON?

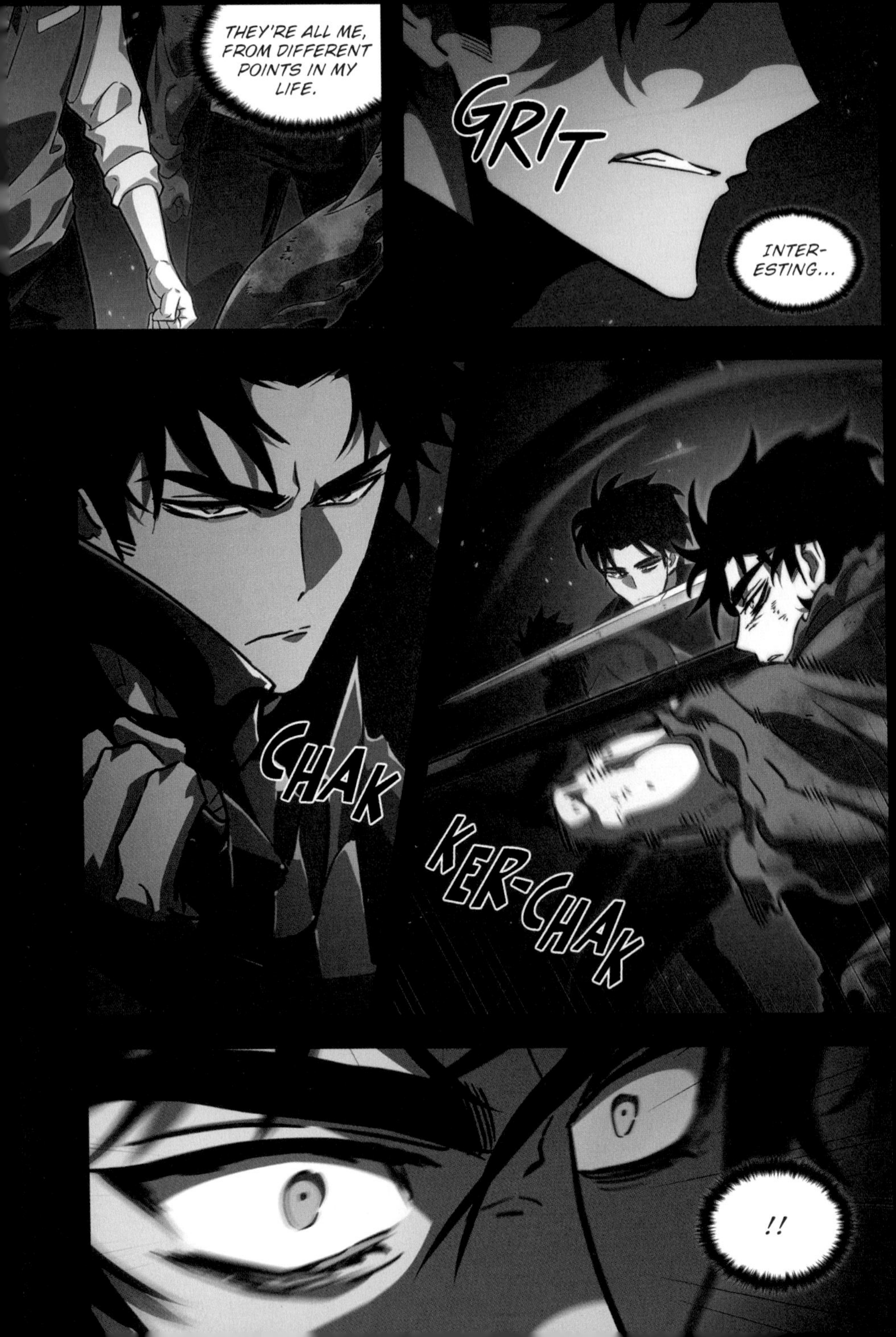
THEY'RE ALL ME, FROM DIFFERENT POINTS IN MY LIFE.
GRIT
INTER-ESTING...
CHAK
KER-CHAK
!!

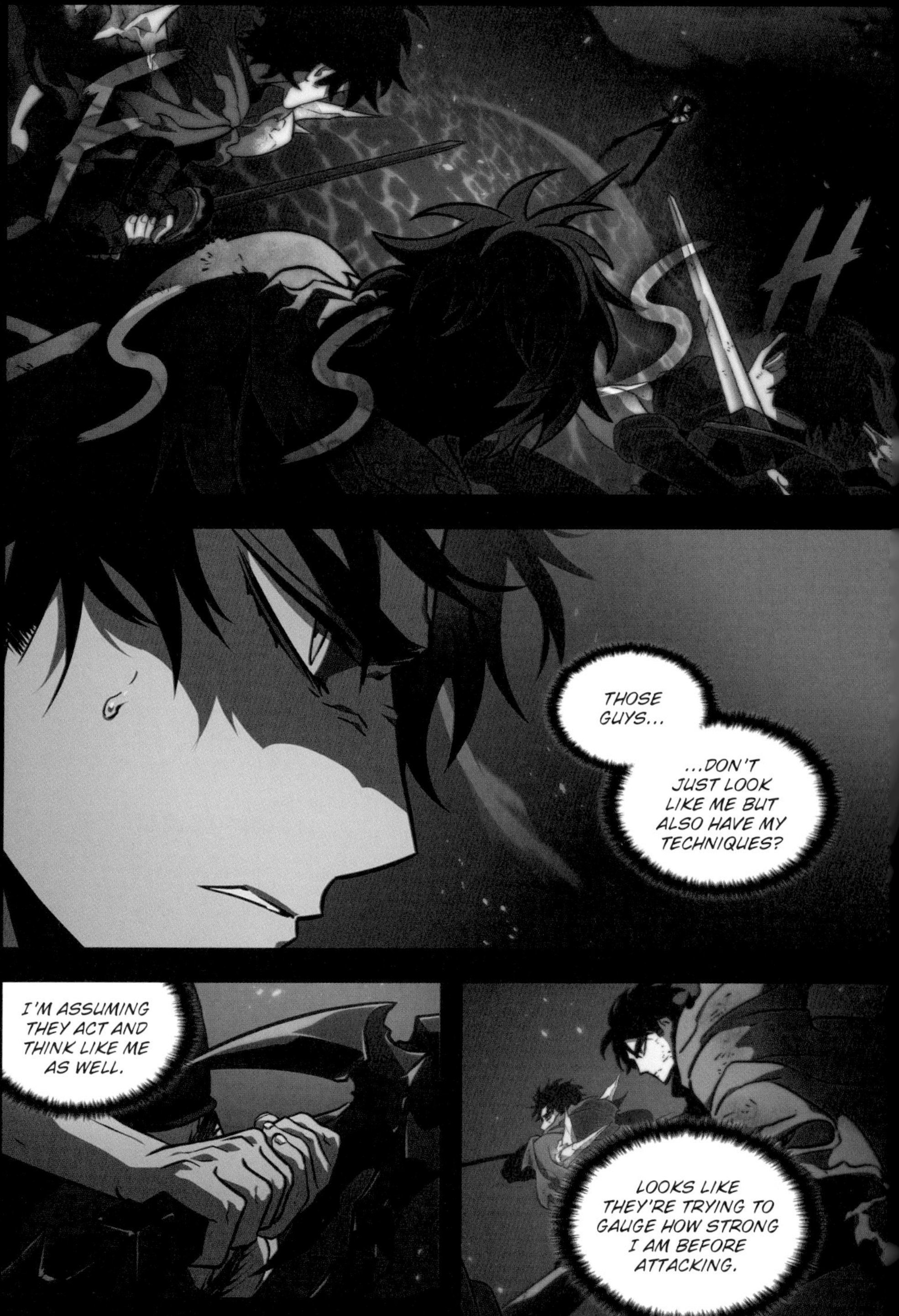
SSSH
THOSE GUYS...
...DON'T JUST LOOK LIKE ME BUT ALSO HAVE MY TECHNIQUES?
I'M ASSUMING THEY ACT AND THINK LIKE ME AS WELL.
LOOKS LIKE THEY'RE TRYING TO GAUGE HOW STRONG I AM BEFORE ATTACKING.

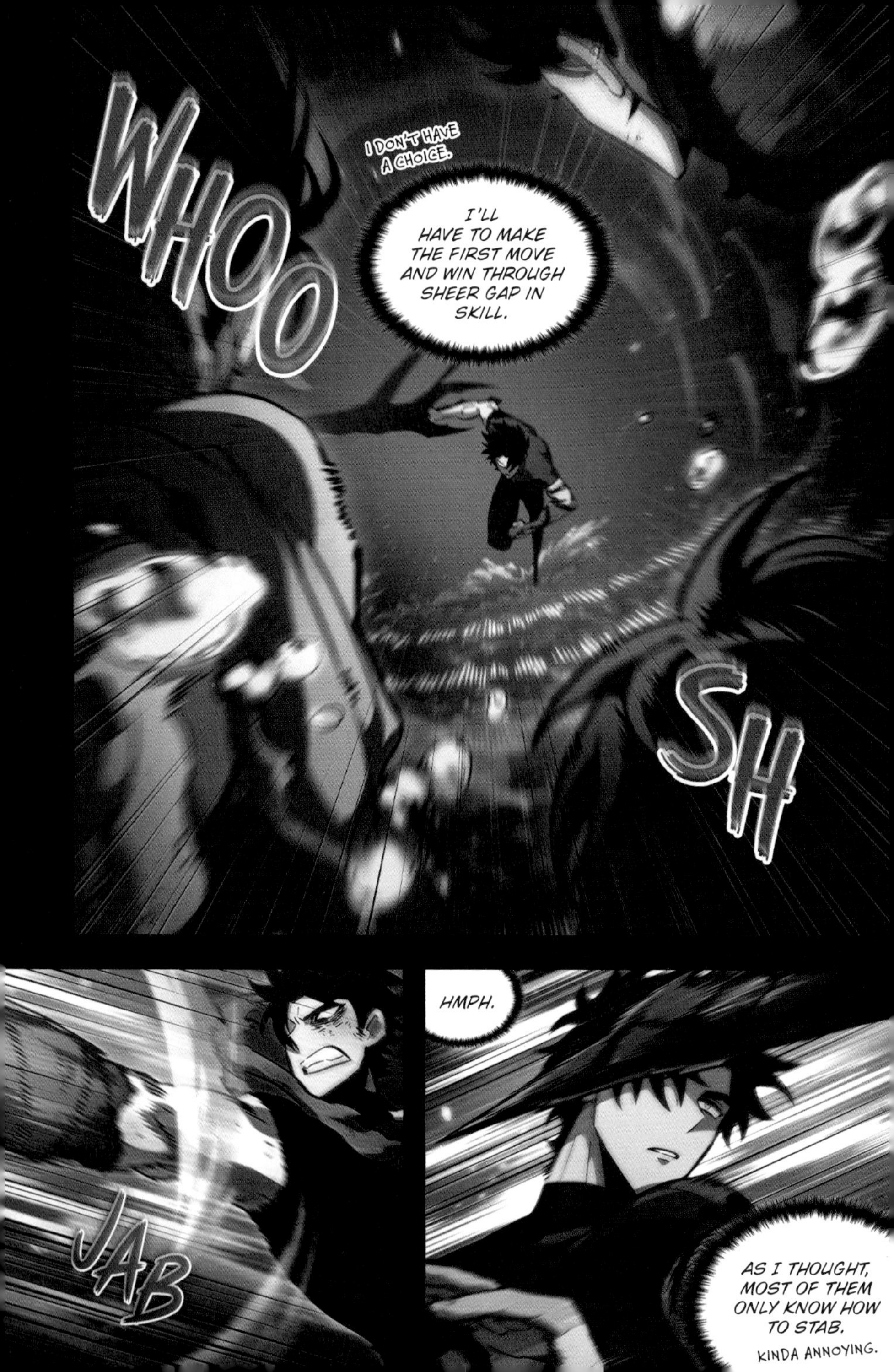
WHOOO
I DON'T HAVE A CHOICE.
I'LL HAVE TO MAKE THE FIRST MOVE AND WIN THROUGH SHEER GAP IN SKILL.
SH
JAB
HMPH.
AS I THOUGHT, MOST OF THEM ONLY KNOW HOW TO STAB.
KINDA ANNOYING.

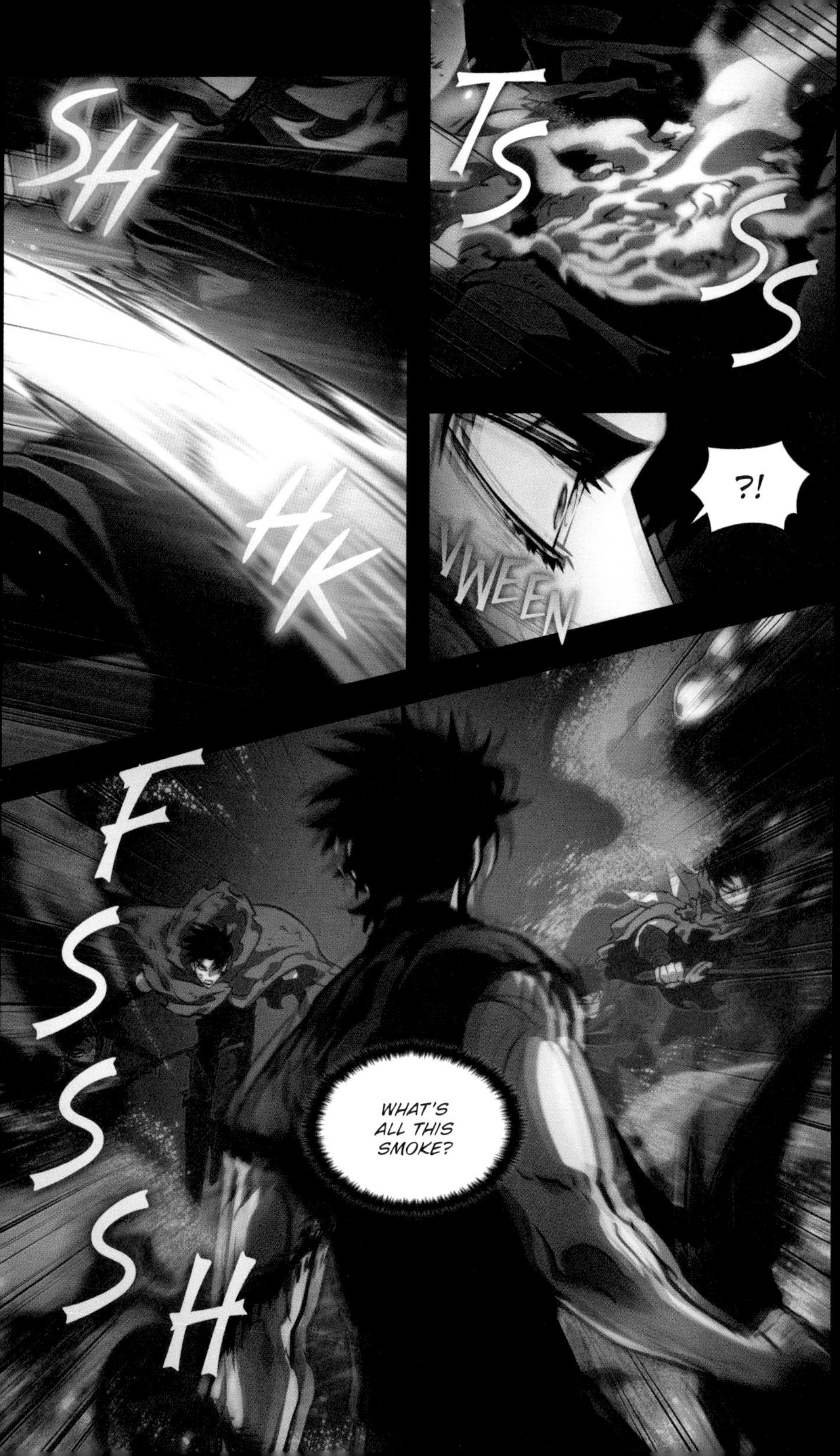
SHHK
TSSS
VWEEN
?!
FSSSH
WHAT'S ALL THIS SMOKE?

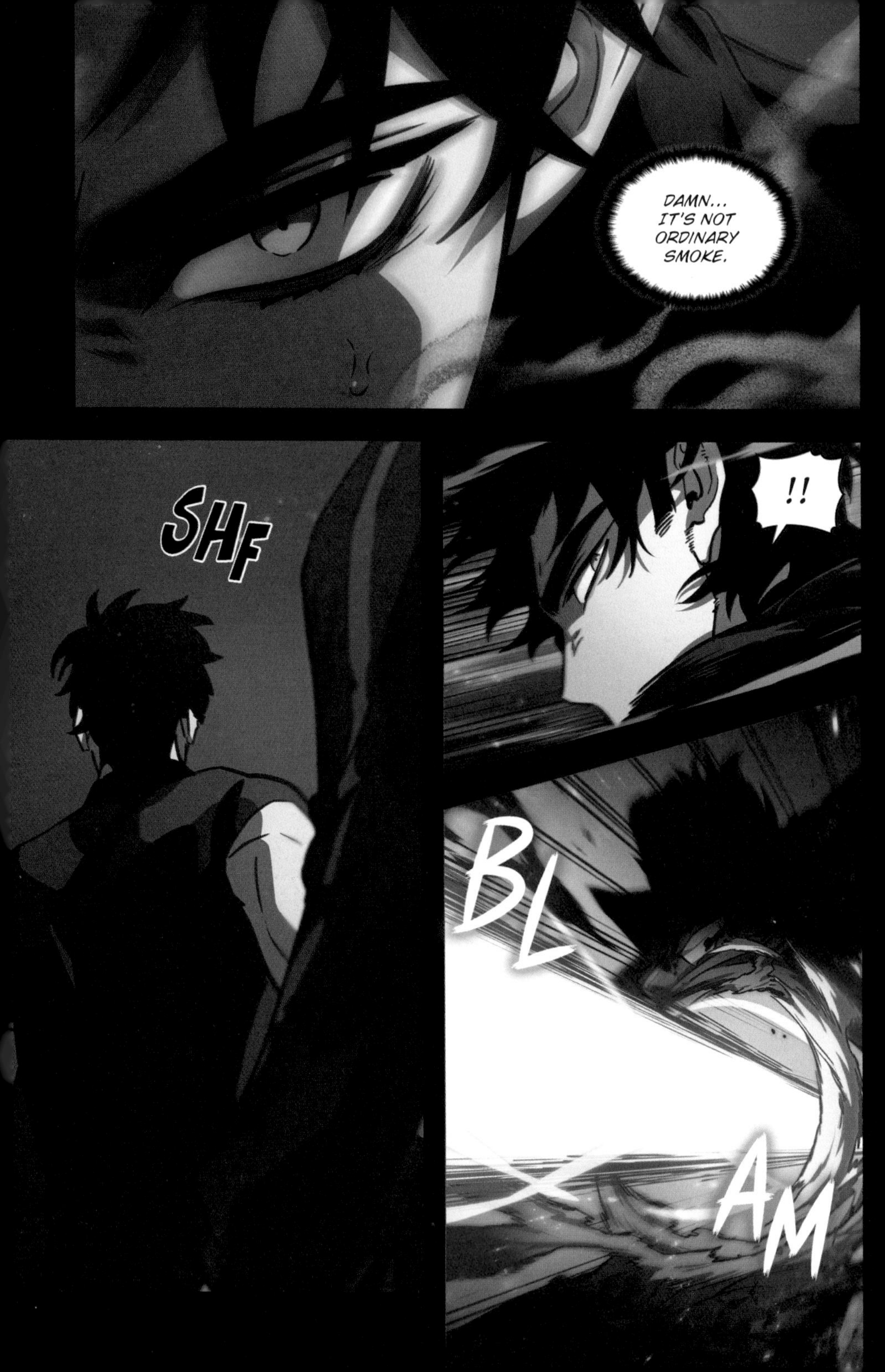
DAMN... IT'S NOT ORDINARY SMOKE.
SHF
!!
BLAM

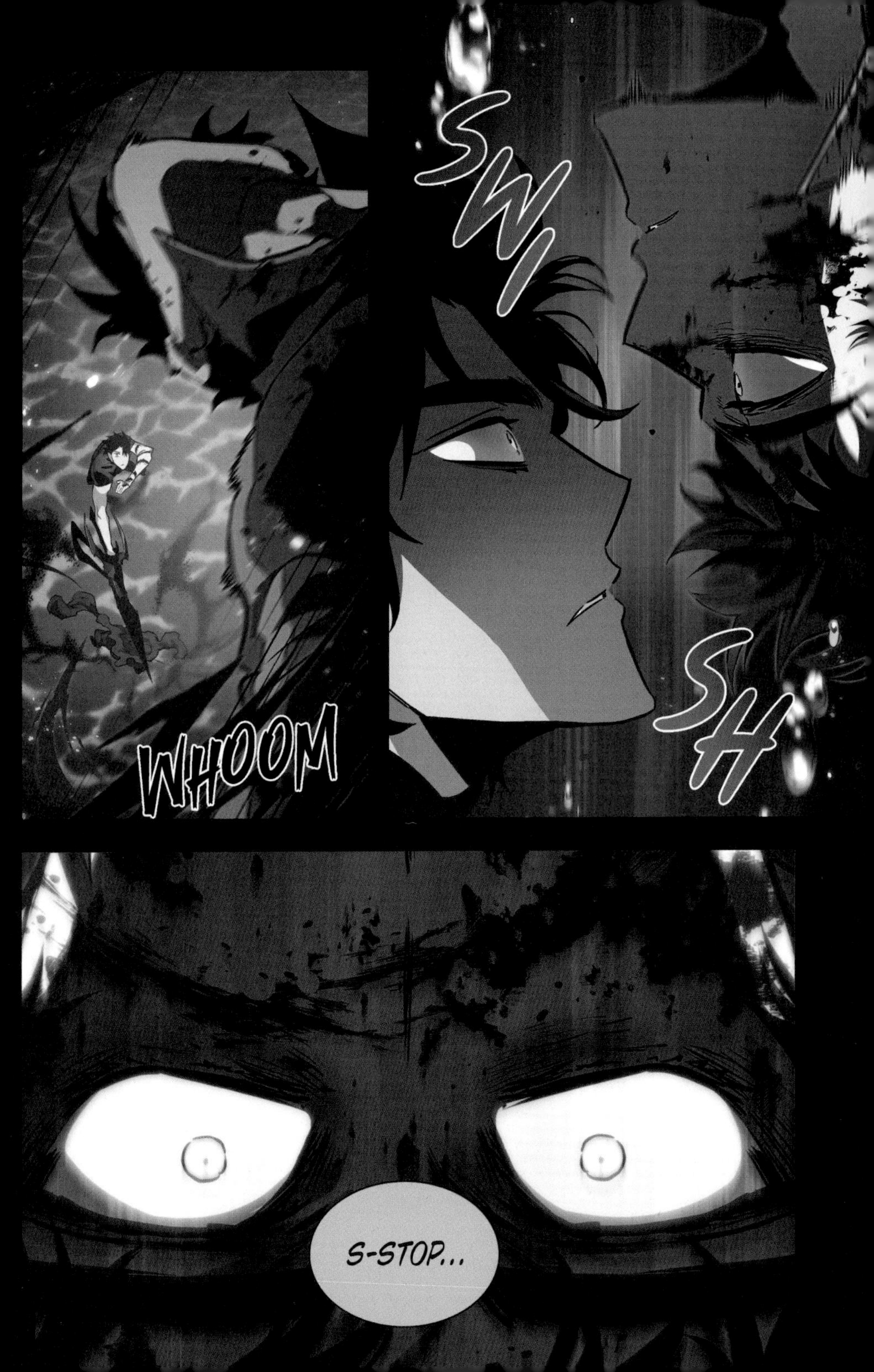
WHOOM
SWI
SH
S-STOP...

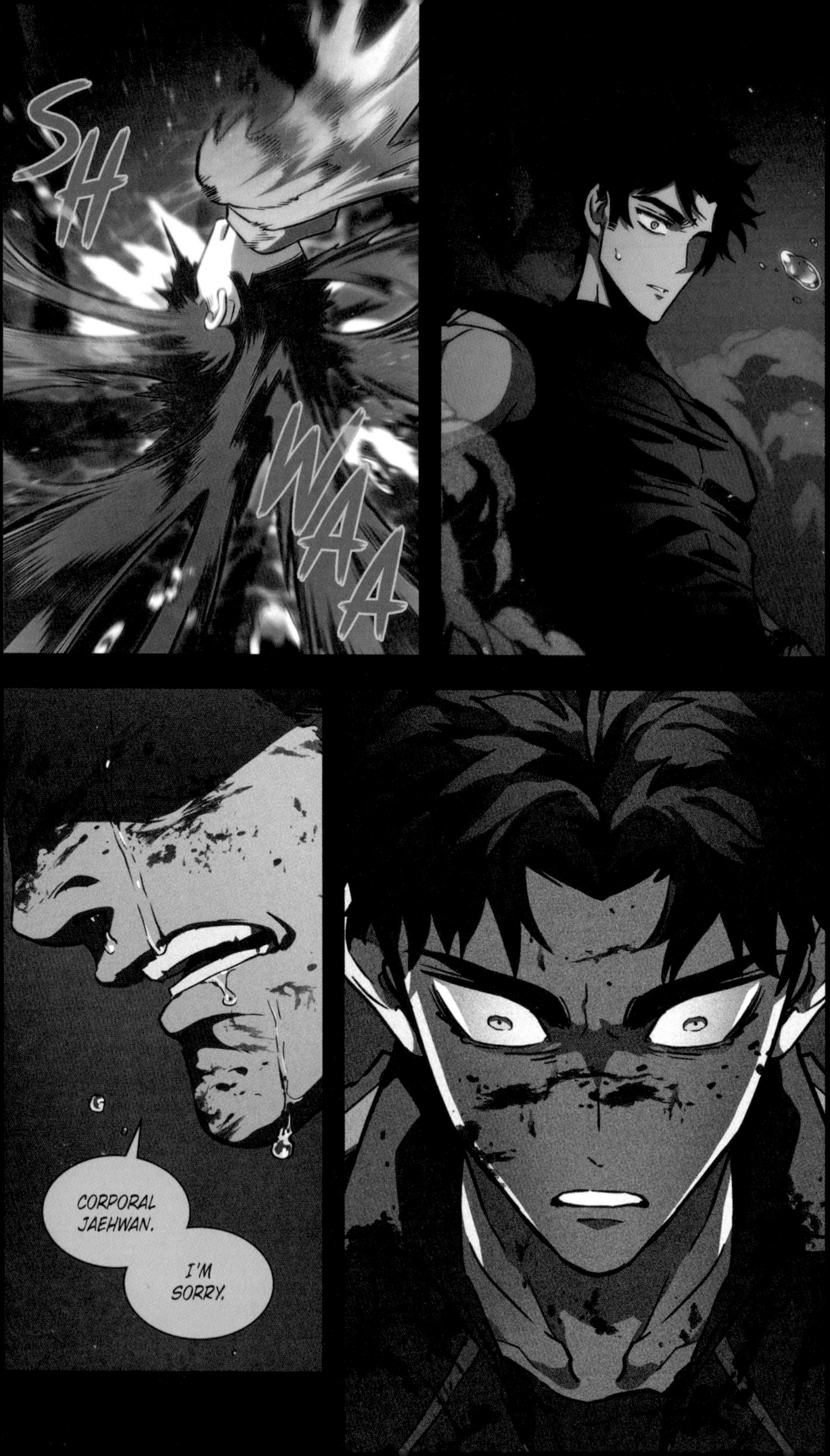
SHWAA
CORPORAL JAEHWAN.
I'M SORRY.

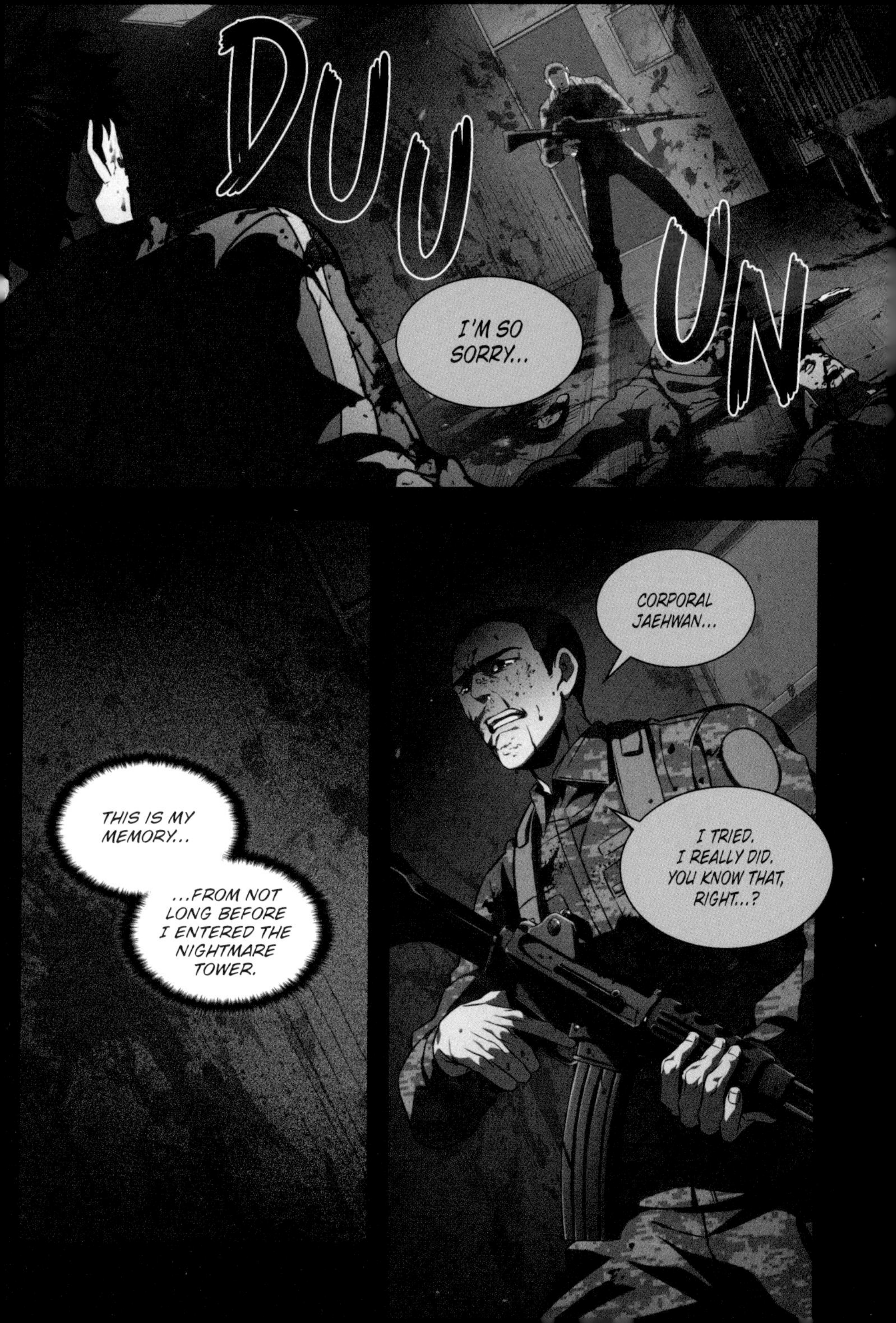
DUUUN
I'M SO SORRY...
CORPORAL JAEHWAN...
THIS IS MY MEMORY...
...FROM NOT LONG BEFORE I ENTERED THE NIGHTMARE TOWER.
I TRIED. I REALLY DID. YOU KNOW THAT, RIGHT...?

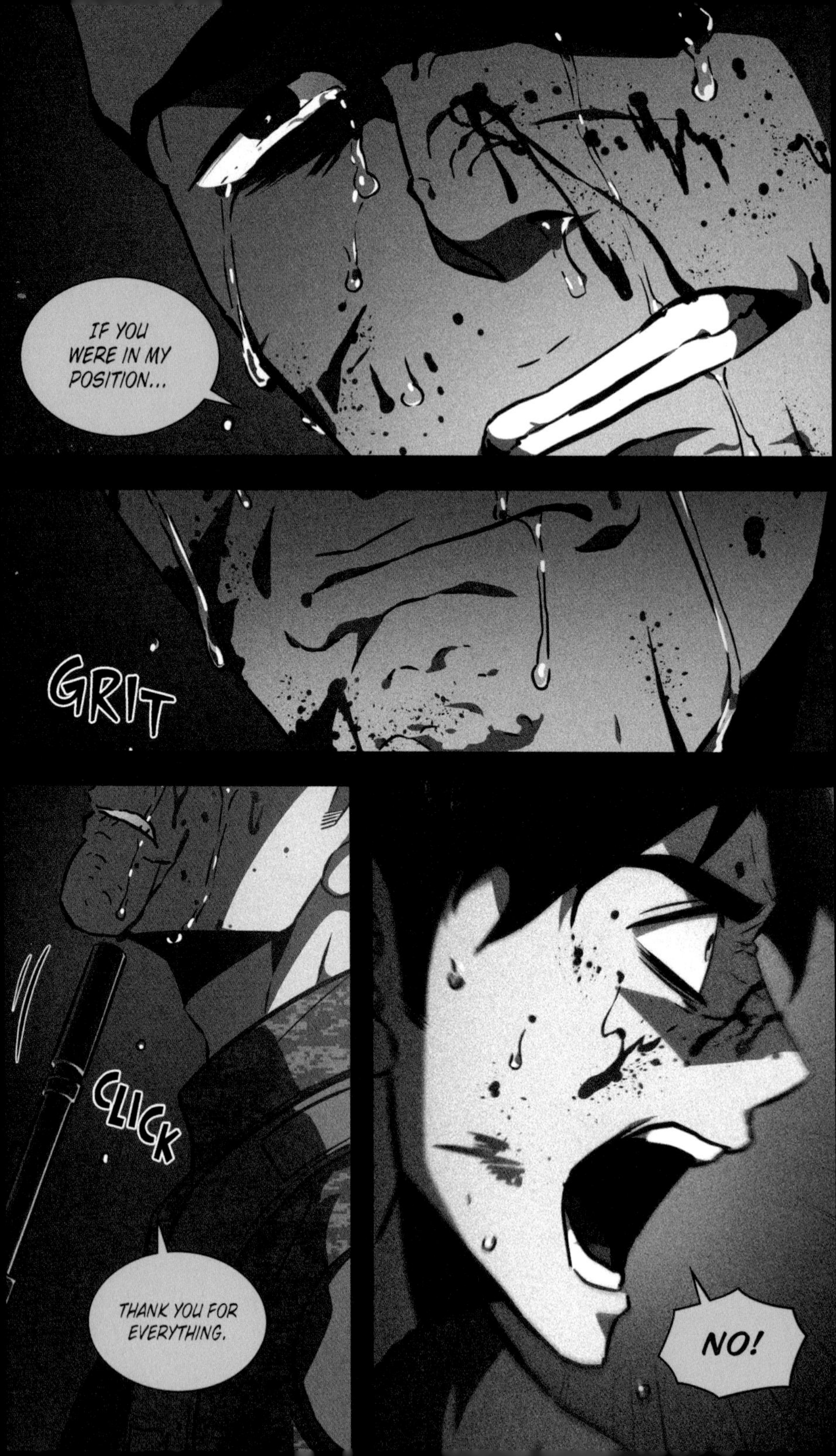
IF YOU WERE IN MY POSITION...
GRIT
CLICK
THANK YOU FOR EVERYTHING.
NO!

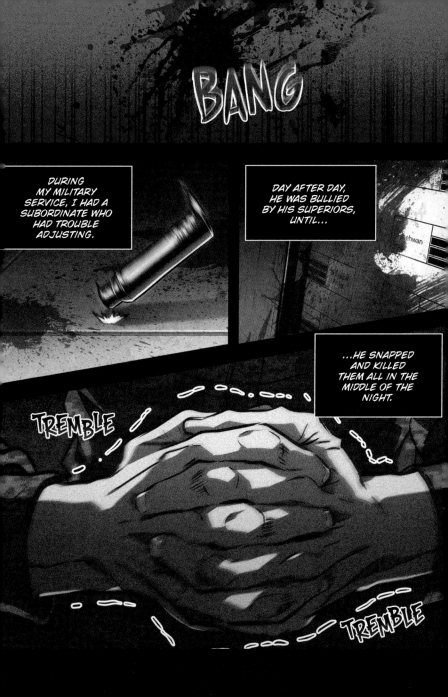

BANG

DURING MY MILITARY SERVICE, I HAD A SUBORDINATE WHO HAD TROUBLE ADJUSTING.

DAY AFTER DAY, HE WAS BULLIED BY HIS SUPERIORS, UNTIL...

...HE SNAPPED AND KILLED THEM ALL IN THE MIDDLE OF THE NIGHT.

TREMBLE

TREMBLE

I WAS THE ONLY SURVIVOR IN THE SQUAD.

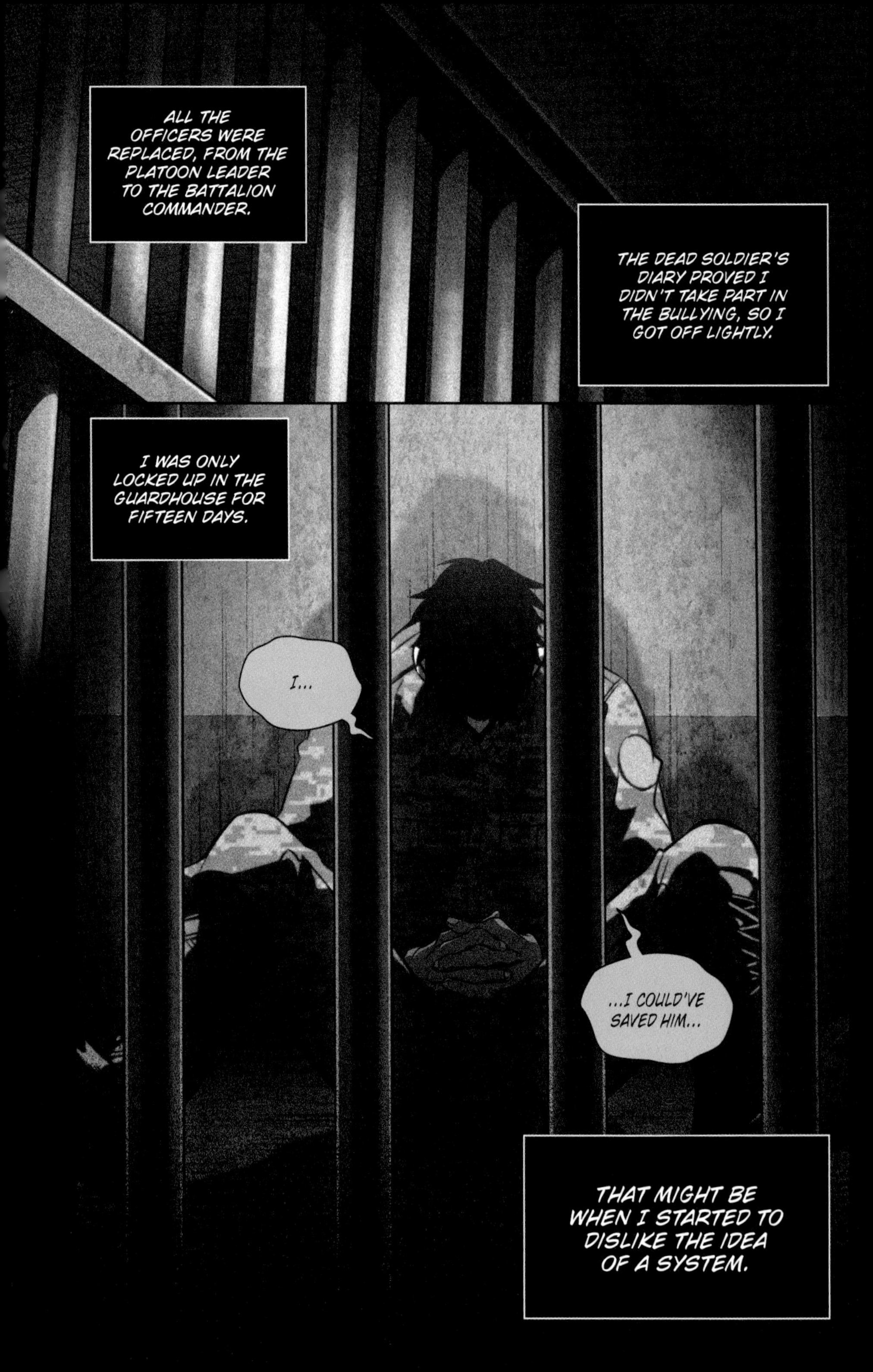
ALL THE OFFICERS WERE REPLACED, FROM THE PLATOON LEADER TO THE BATTALION COMMANDER.
THE DEAD SOLDIER'S DIARY PROVED I DIDN'T TAKE PART IN THE BULLYING, SO I GOT OFF LIGHTLY.
I WAS ONLY LOCKED UP IN THE GUARDHOUSE FOR FIFTEEN DAYS.
I...
...I COULD'VE SAVED HIM...
THAT MIGHT BE WHEN I STARTED TO DISLIKE THE IDEA OF A SYSTEM.

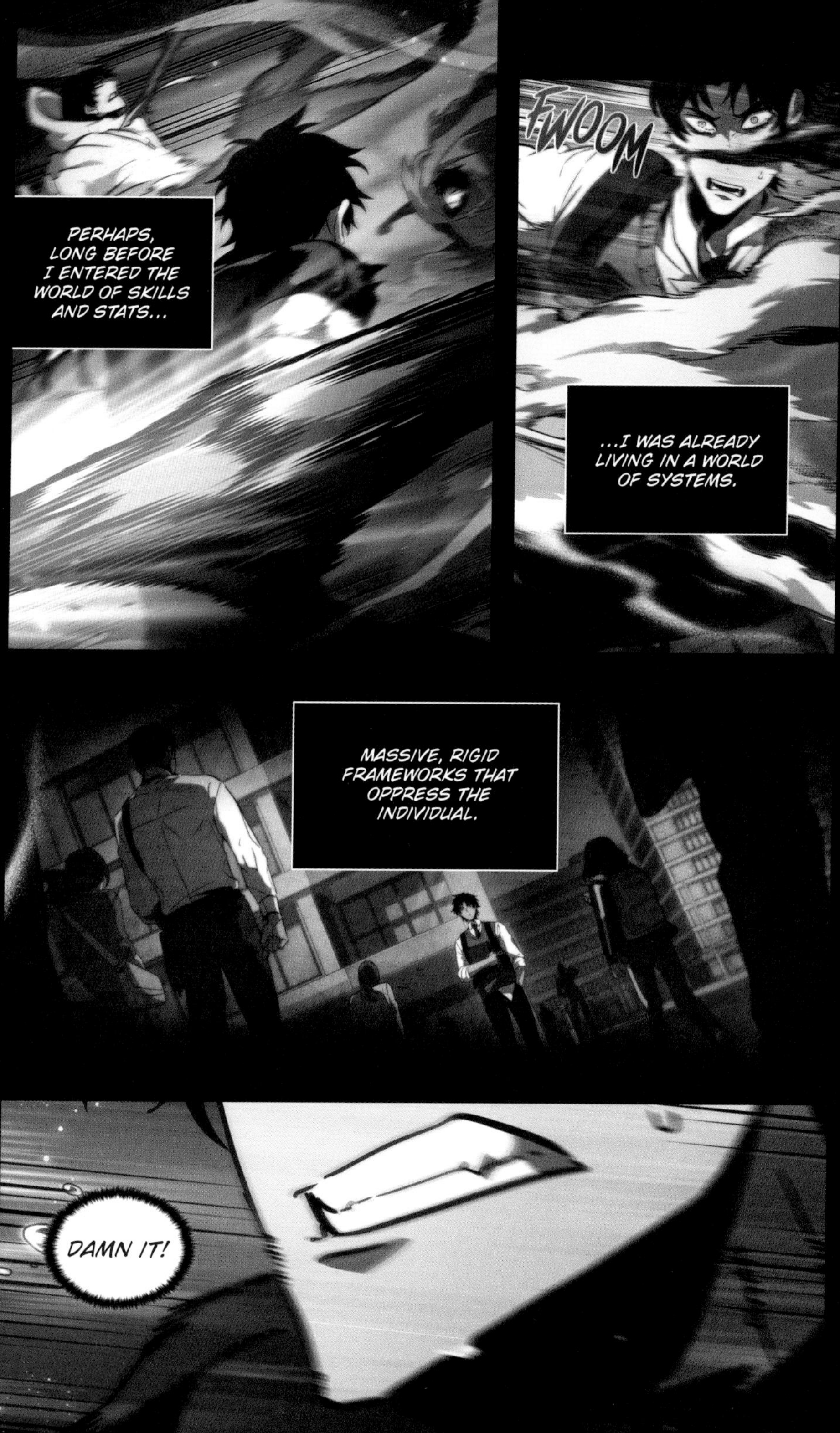
PERHAPS, LONG BEFORE I ENTERED THE WORLD OF SKILLS AND STATS...
FWOOM
...I WAS ALREADY LIVING IN A WORLD OF SYSTEMS.
MASSIVE, RIGID FRAMEWORKS THAT OPPRESS THE INDIVIDUAL.
DAMN IT!

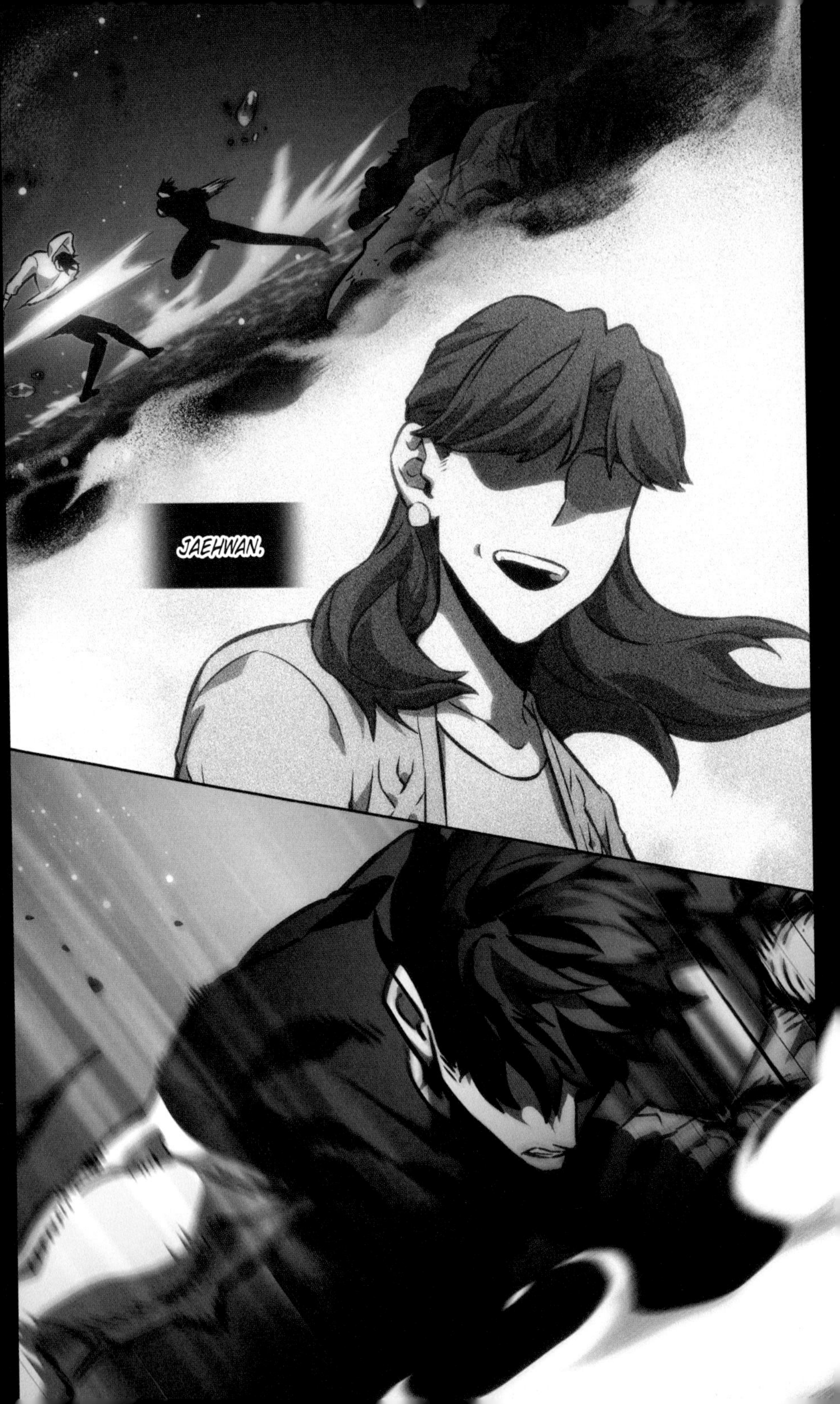
JAEHWAN.

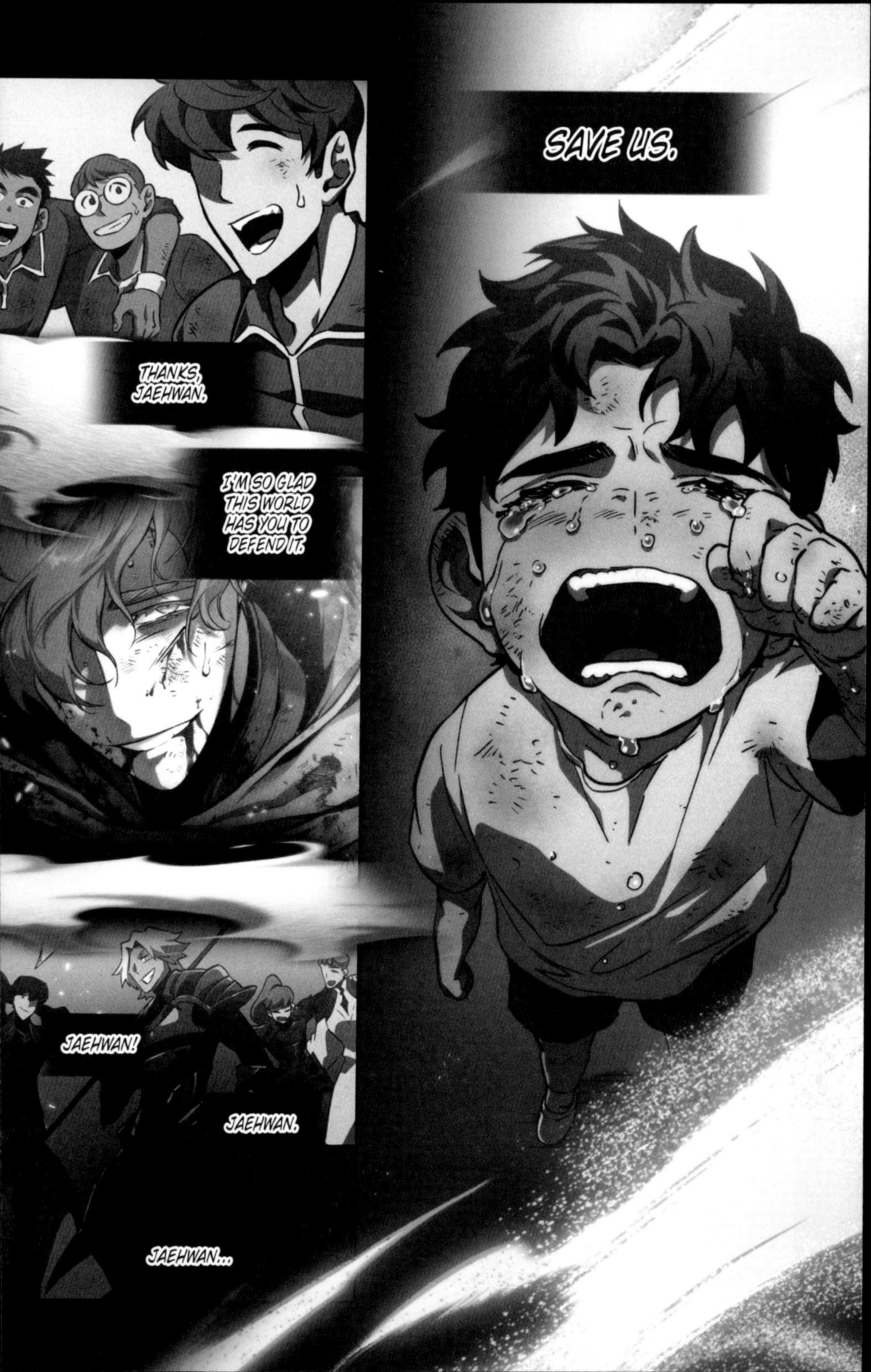
SAVE US.
THANKS, JAEHWAN.
I'M SO GLAD THIS WORLD HAS YOU TO DEFEND IT.
JAEHWAN!
JAEHWAN.
JAEHWAN...

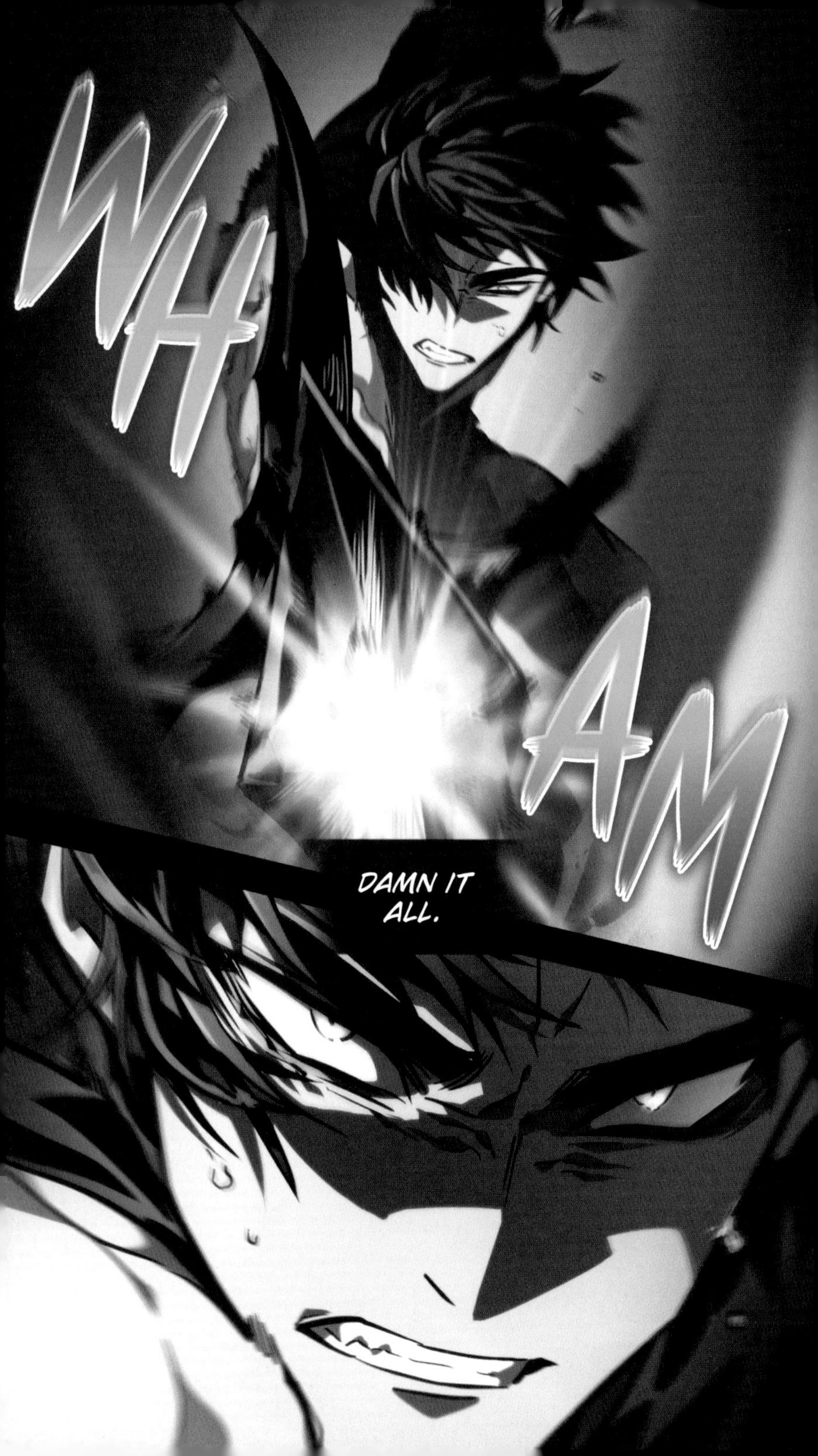
WHAM
DAMN IT ALL.

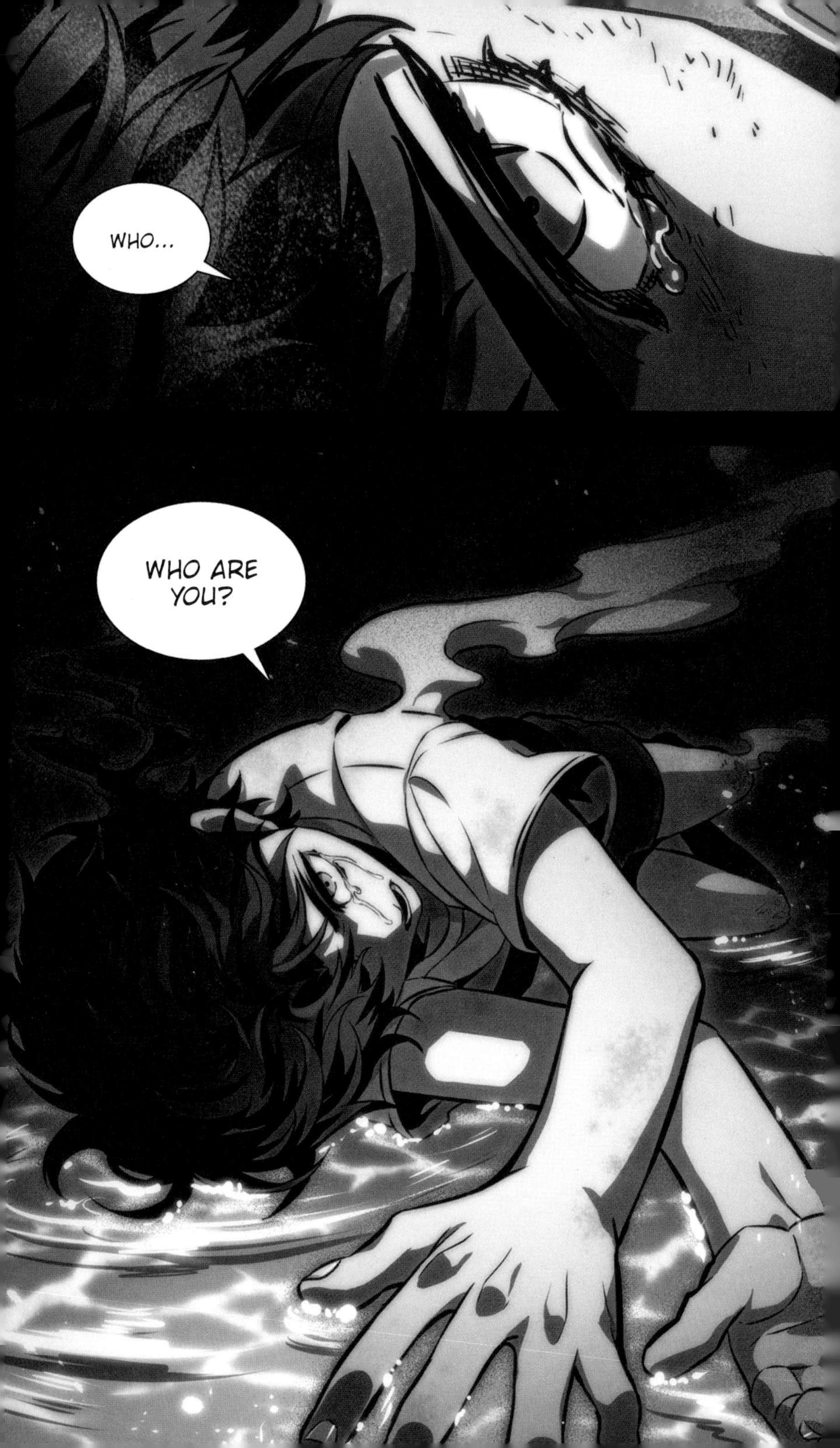
WHO...
WHO ARE YOU?

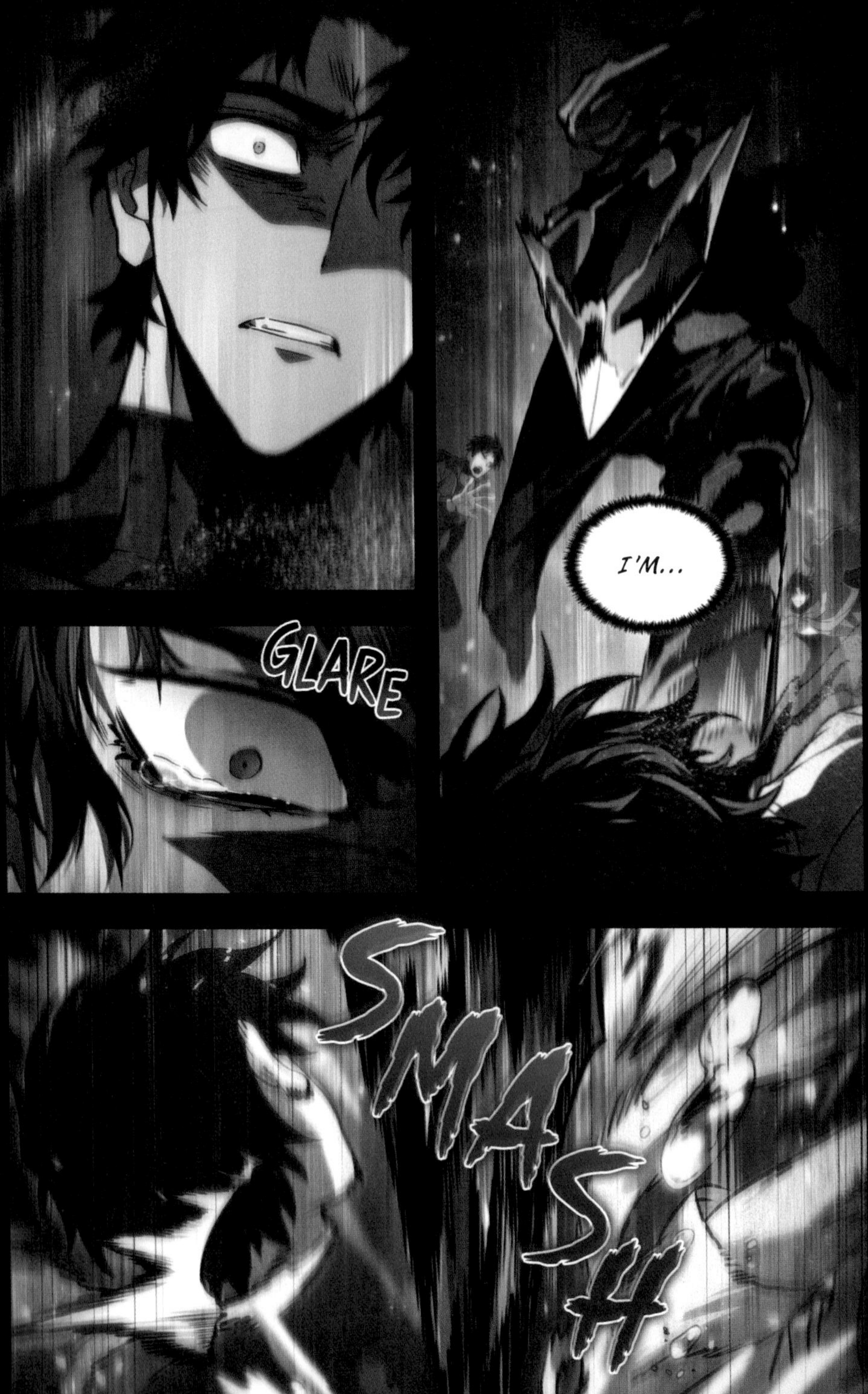
I'M...
GLARE
SMASH

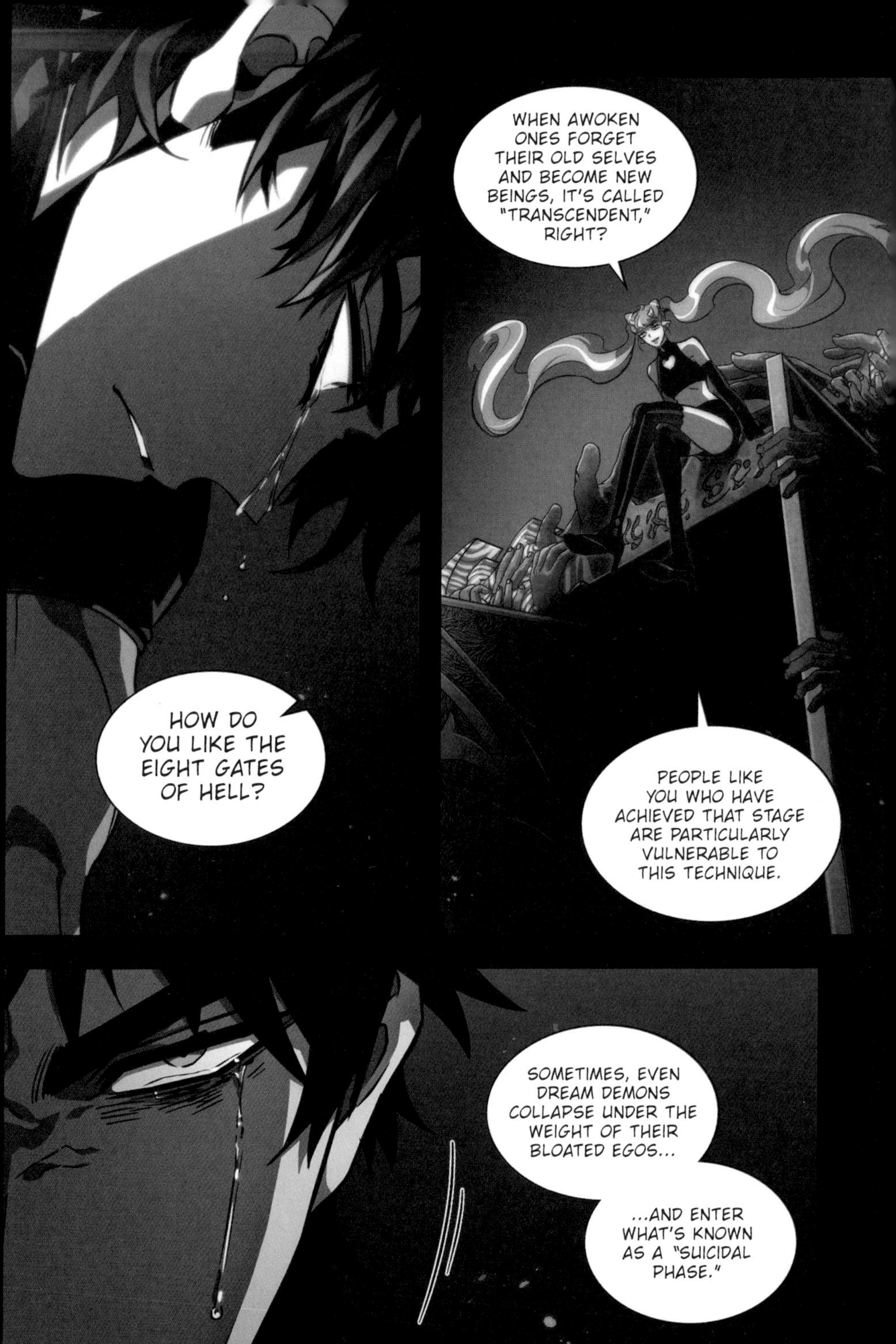
WHEN AWOKEN ONES FORGET THEIR OLD SELVES AND BECOME NEW BEINGS, IT'S CALLED "TRANSCENDENT," RIGHT?
HOW DO YOU LIKE THE EIGHT GATES OF HELL?
PEOPLE LIKE YOU WHO HAVE ACHIEVED THAT STAGE ARE PARTICULARLY VULNERABLE TO THIS TECHNIQUE.
SOMETIMES, EVEN DREAM DEMONS COLLAPSE UNDER THE WEIGHT OF THEIR BLOATED EGOS...
...AND ENTER WHAT'S KNOWN AS A "SUICIDAL PHASE."

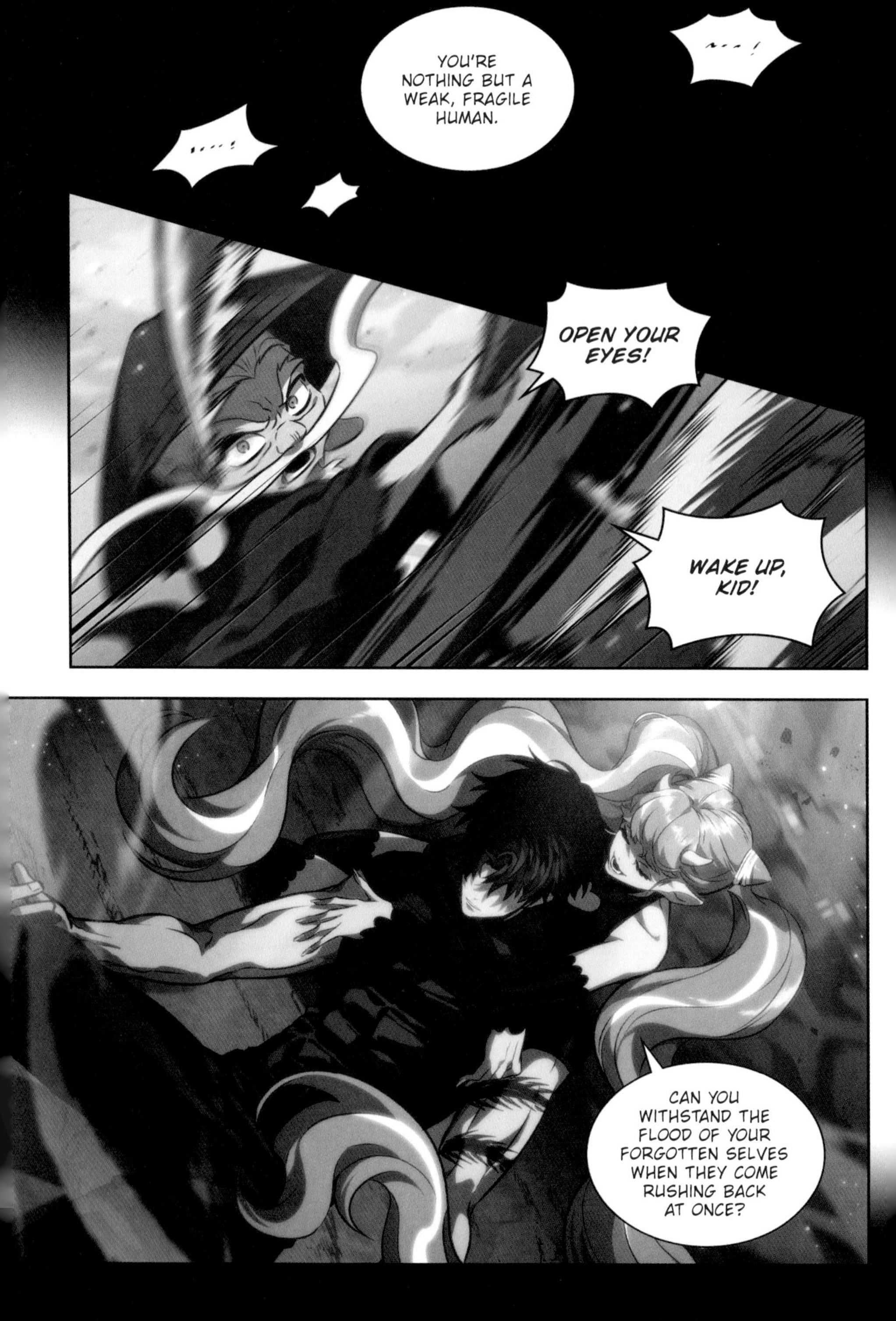
...!
YOU'RE NOTHING BUT A WEAK, FRAGILE HUMAN.
...!
OPEN YOUR EYES!
WAKE UP, KID!
CAN YOU WITHSTAND THE FLOOD OF YOUR FORGOTTEN SELVES WHEN THEY COME RUSHING BACK AT ONCE?

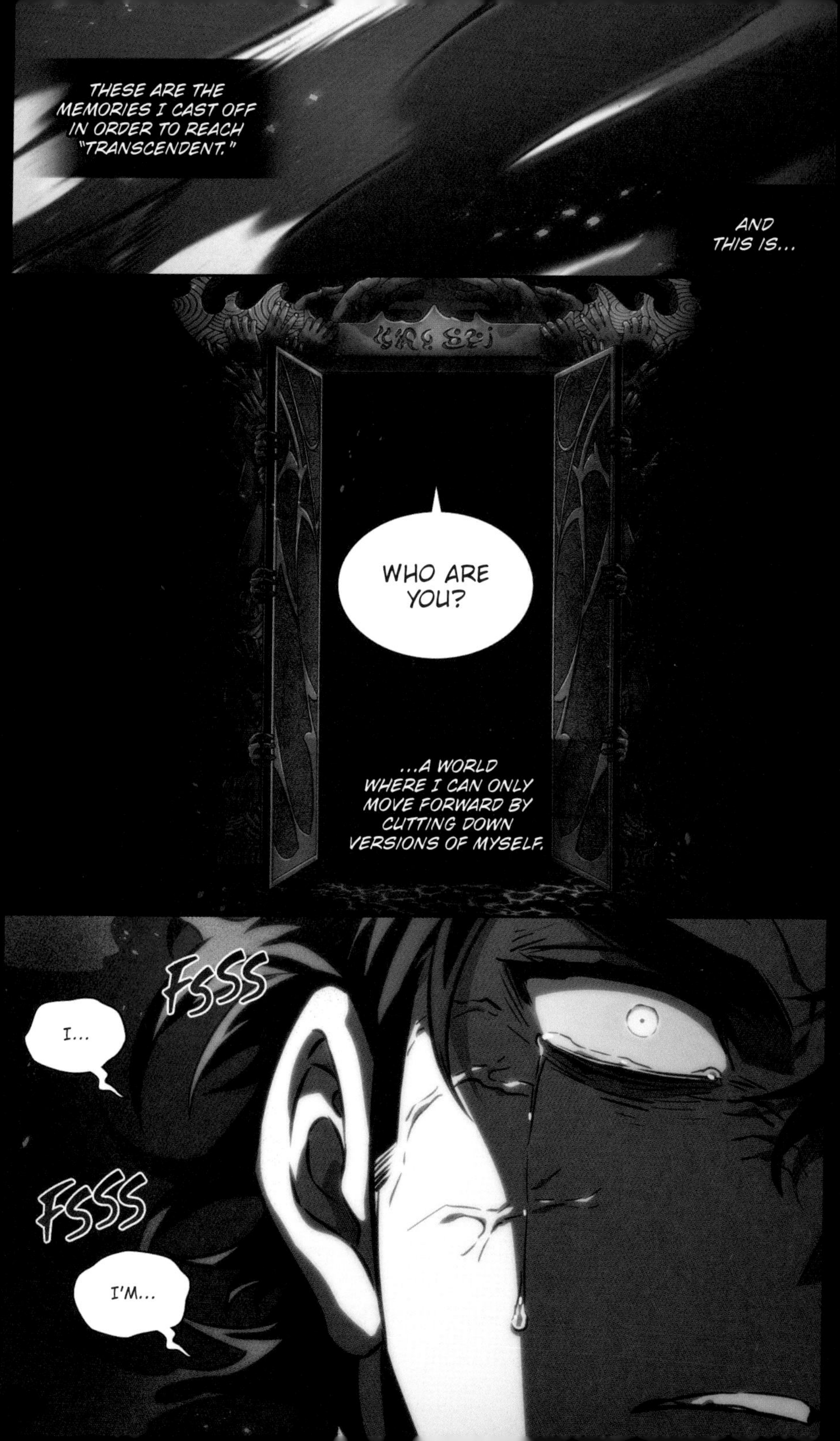
THESE ARE THE MEMORIES I CAST OFF IN ORDER TO REACH "TRANSCENDENT."
AND THIS IS...
WHO ARE YOU?
...A WORLD WHERE I CAN ONLY MOVE FORWARD BY CUTTING DOWN VERSIONS OF MYSELF.
FSSS
I...
FSSS
I'M...

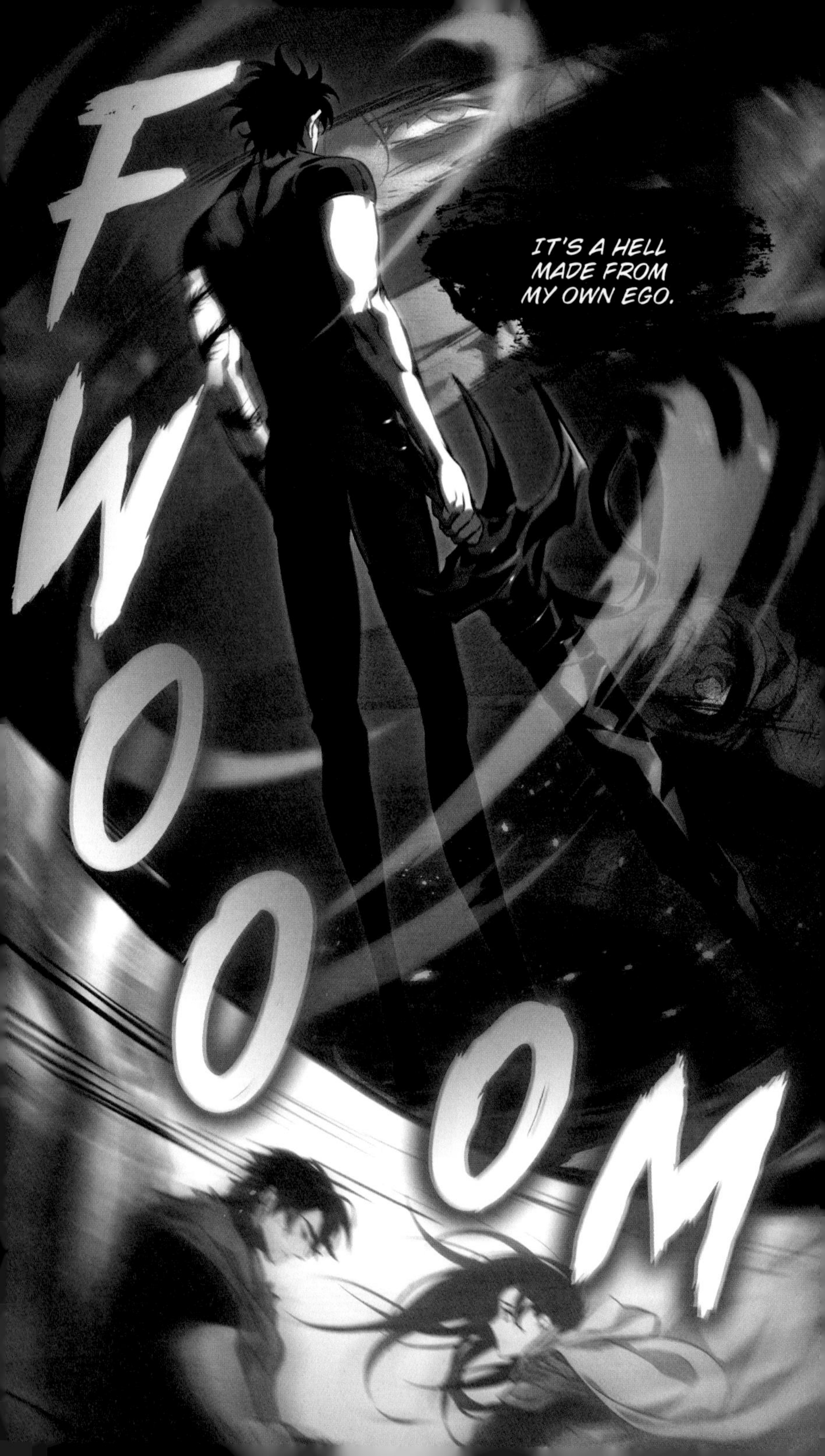
IT'S A HELL MADE FROM MY OWN EGO.
FWOOOOM

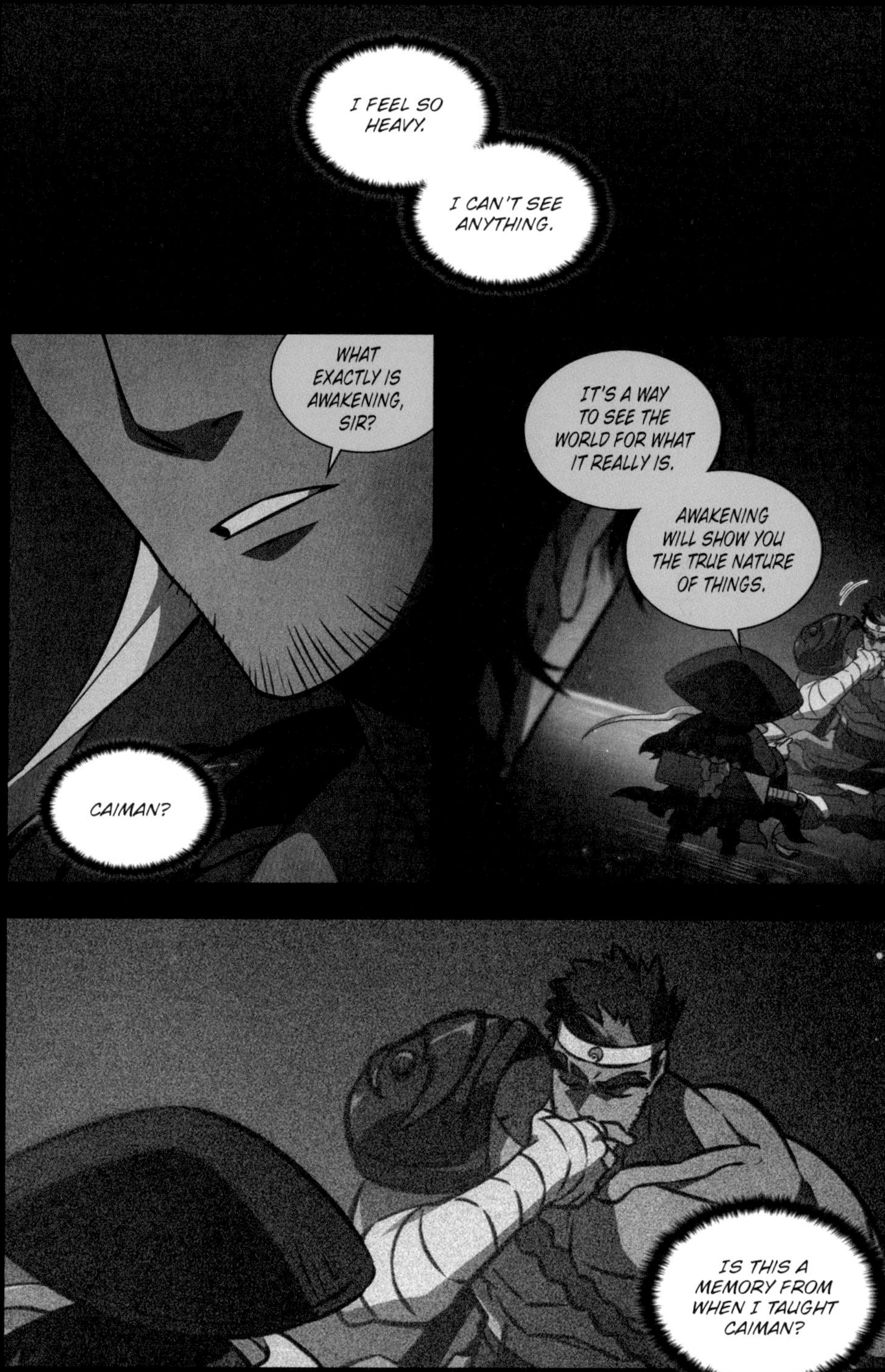
I FEEL SO HEAVY.
I CAN'T SEE ANYTHING.
WHAT EXACTLY IS AWAKENING, SIR?
CAIMAN?
IT'S A WAY TO SEE THE WORLD FOR WHAT IT REALLY IS.
AWAKENING WILL SHOW YOU THE TRUE NATURE OF THINGS.
IS THIS A MEMORY FROM WHEN I TAUGHT CAIMAN?

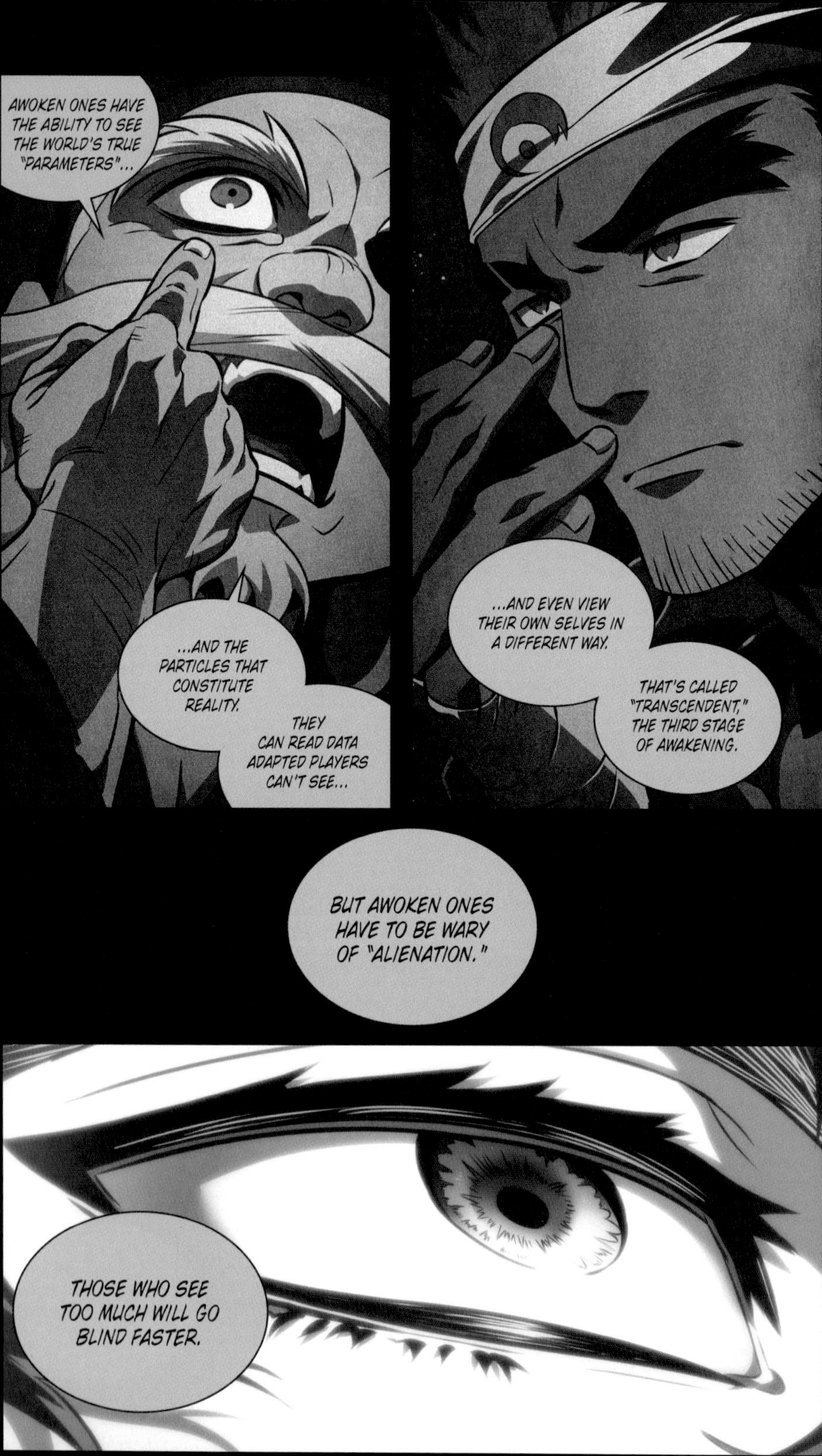
AWOKEN ONES HAVE THE ABILITY TO SEE THE WORLD'S TRUE "PARAMETERS"...
...AND THE PARTICLES THAT CONSTITUTE REALITY.
THEY CAN READ DATA ADAPTED PLAYERS CAN'T SEE...
...AND EVEN VIEW THEIR OWN SELVES IN A DIFFERENT WAY.
THAT'S CALLED "TRANSCENDENT," THE THIRD STAGE OF AWAKENING.
BUT AWOKEN ONES HAVE TO BE WARY OF "ALIENATION."
THOSE WHO SEE TOO MUCH WILL GO BLIND FASTER.

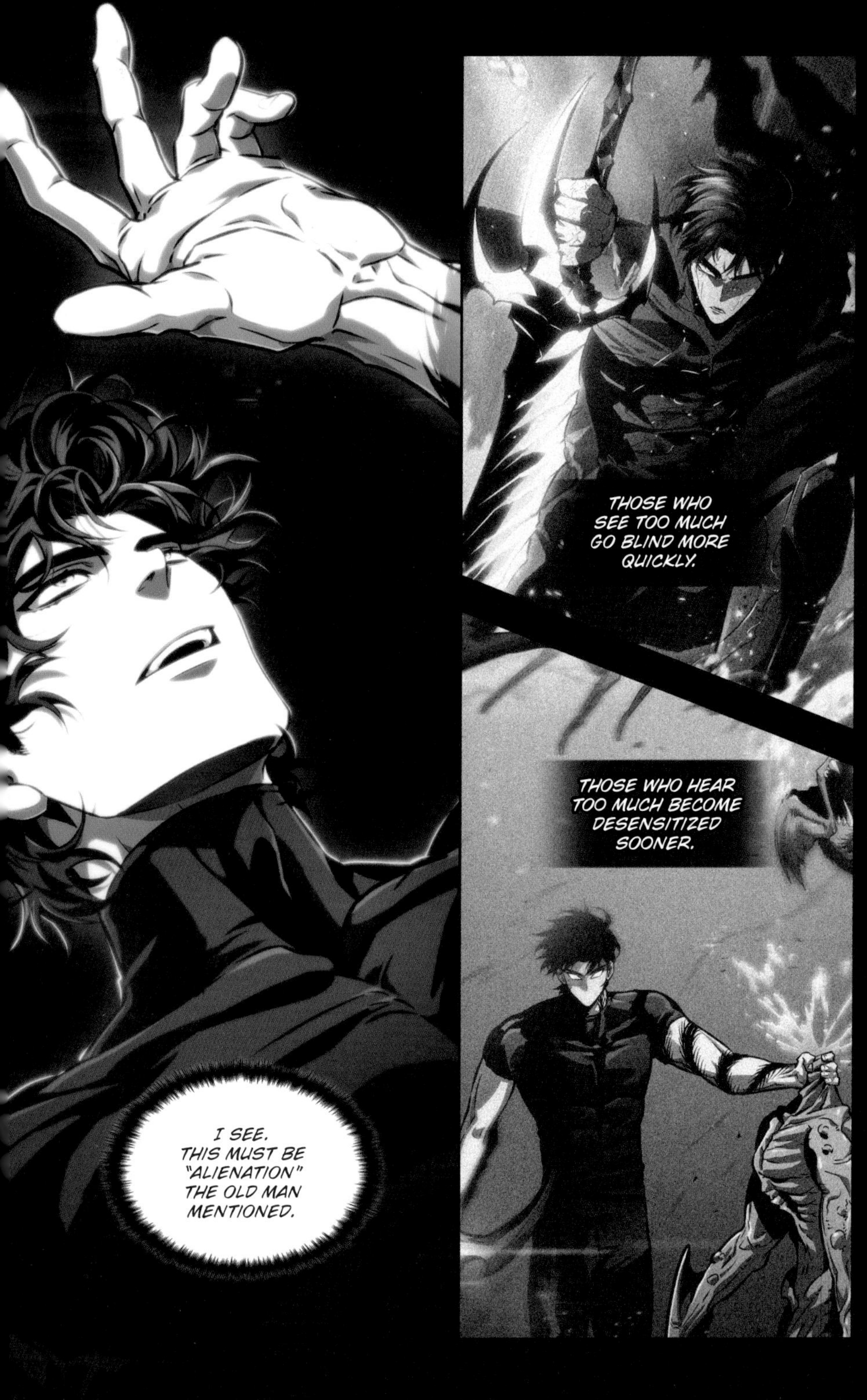
THOSE WHO SEE TOO MUCH GO BLIND MORE QUICKLY.
THOSE WHO HEAR TOO MUCH BECOME DESENSITIZED SOONER.
I SEE. THIS MUST BE "ALIENATION" THE OLD MAN MENTIONED.

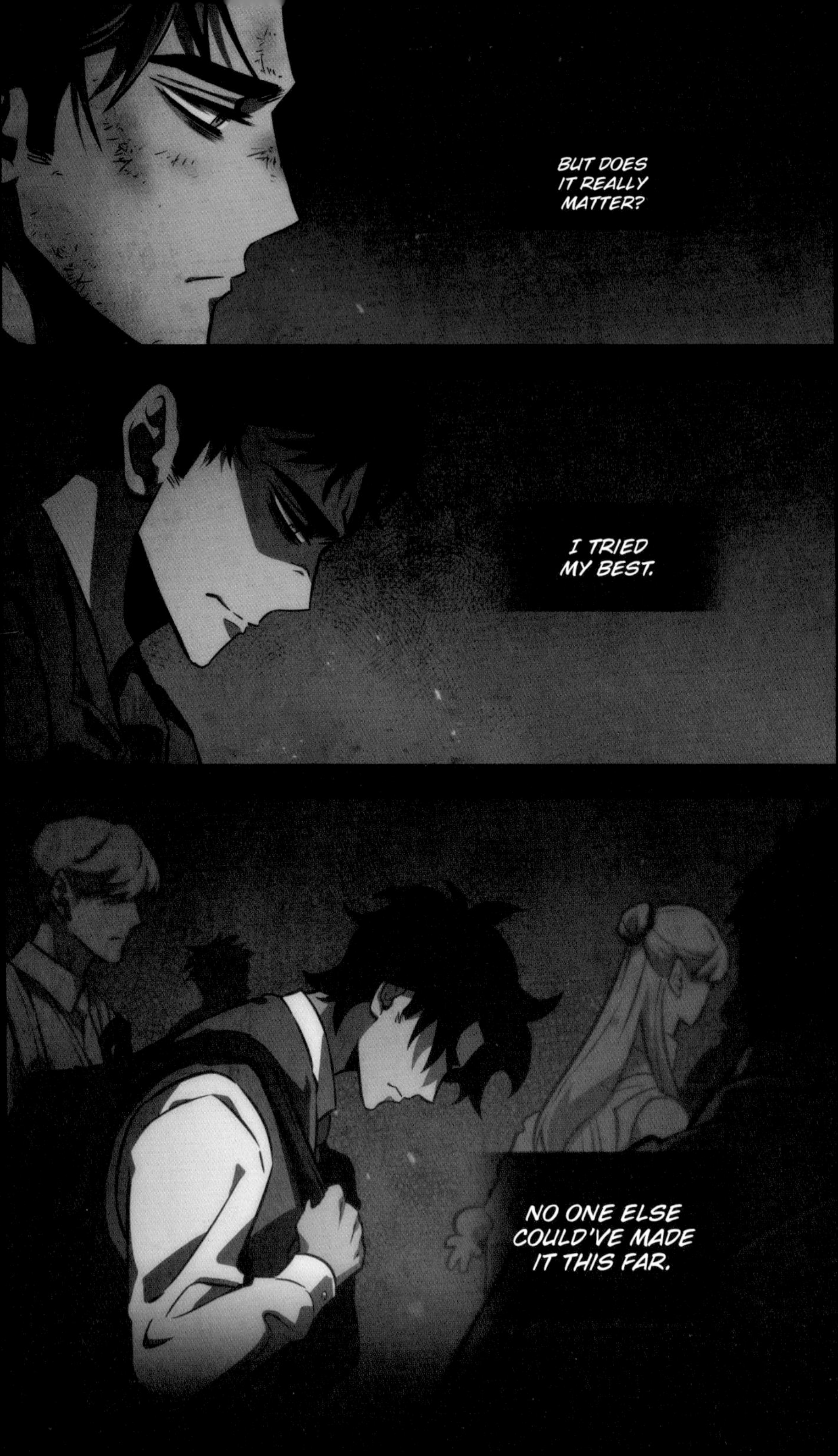
BUT DOES IT REALLY MATTER?
I TRIED MY BEST.
NO ONE ELSE COULD'VE MADE IT THIS FAR.

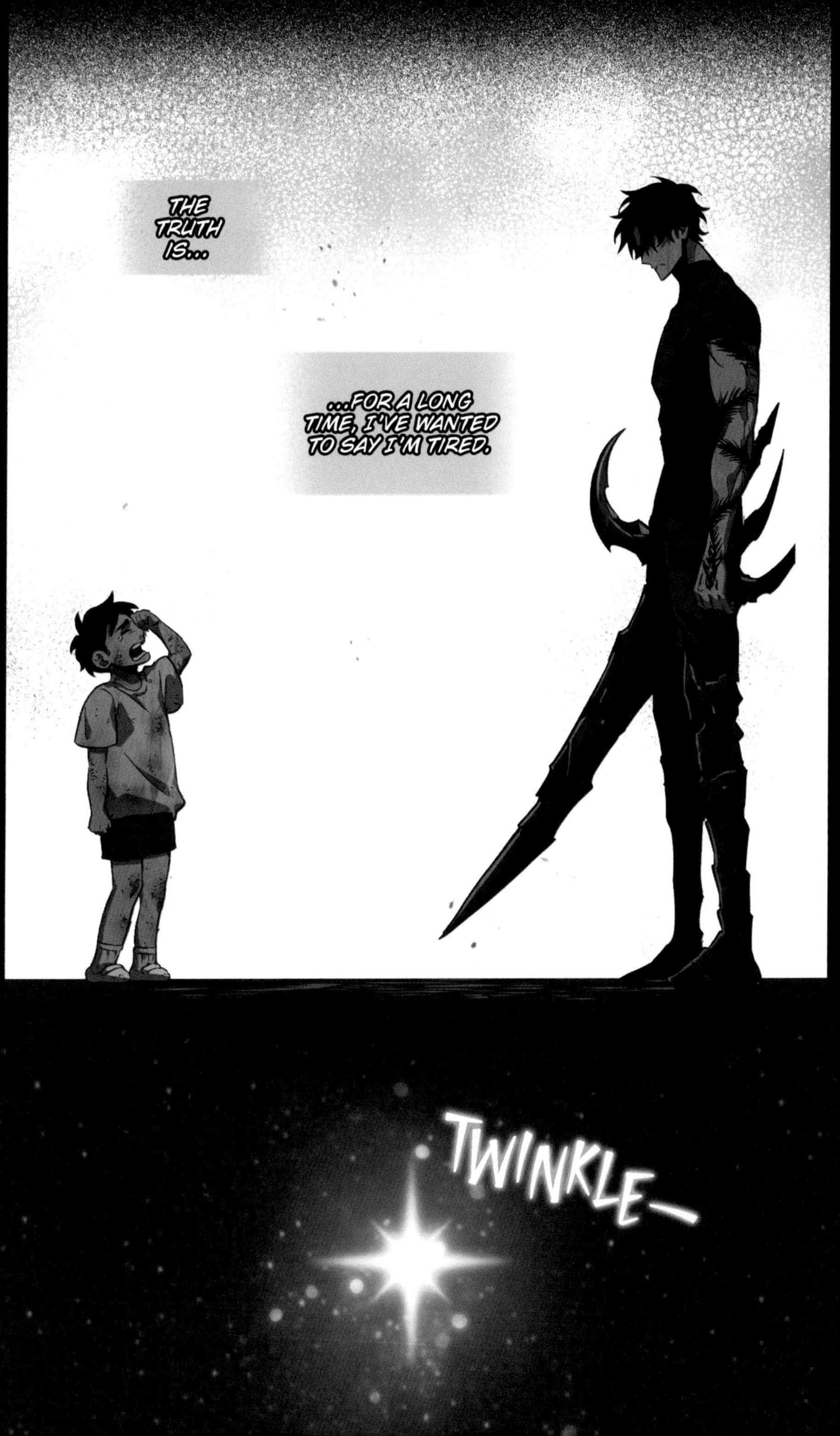
THE TRUTH IS...
...FOR A LONG TIME, I'VE WANTED TO SAY I'M TIRED.
TWINKLE—

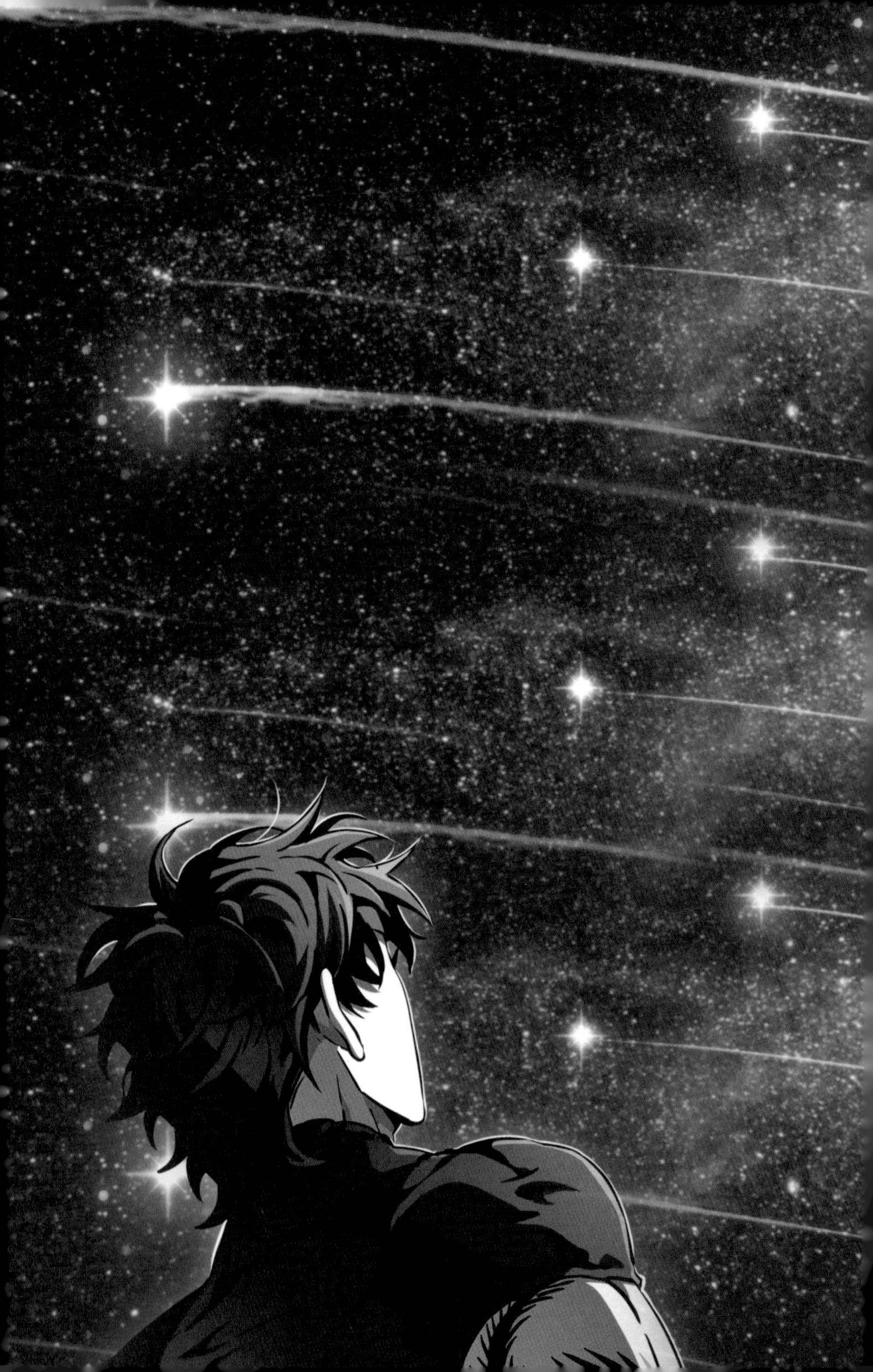

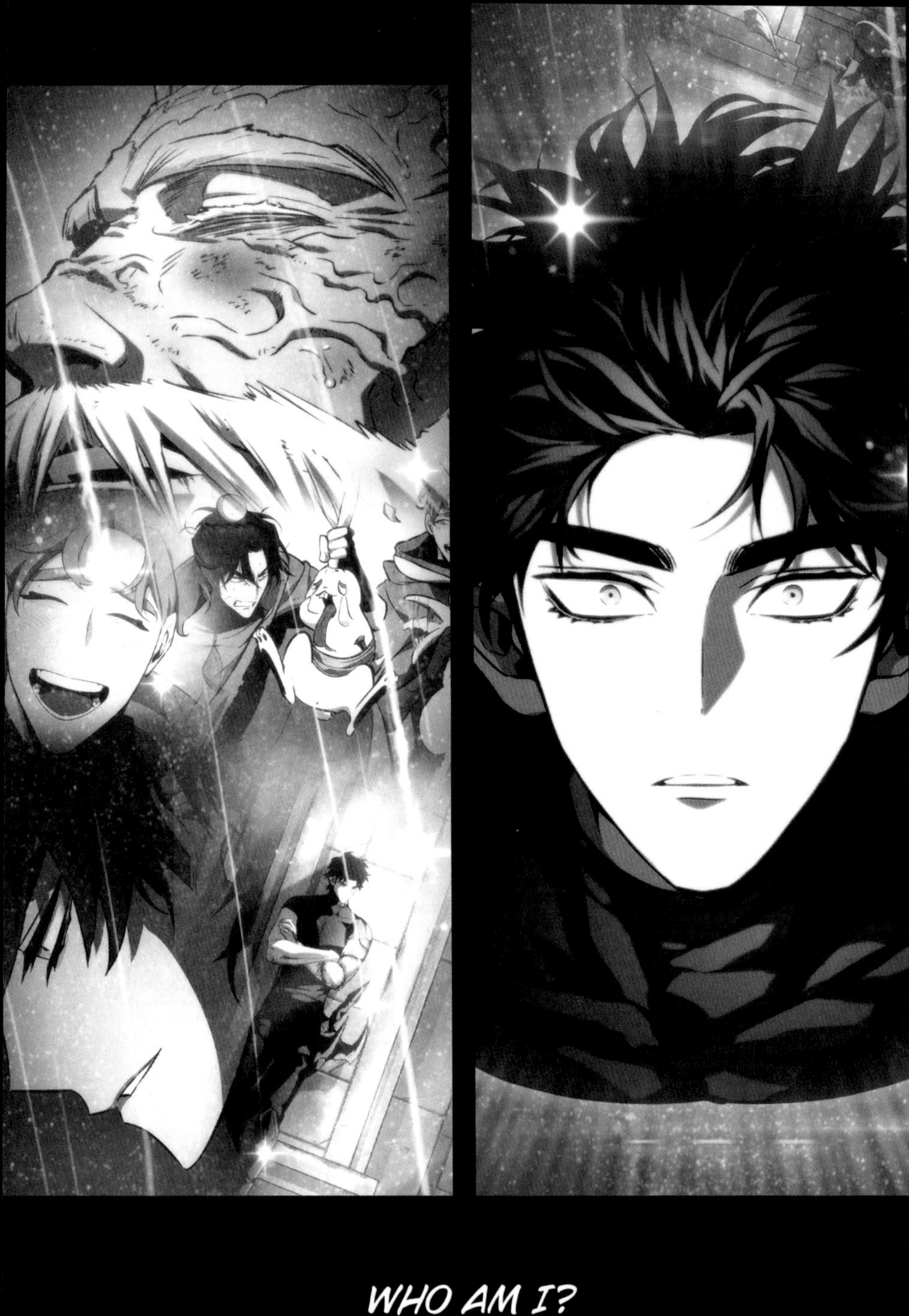
WHO AM I?

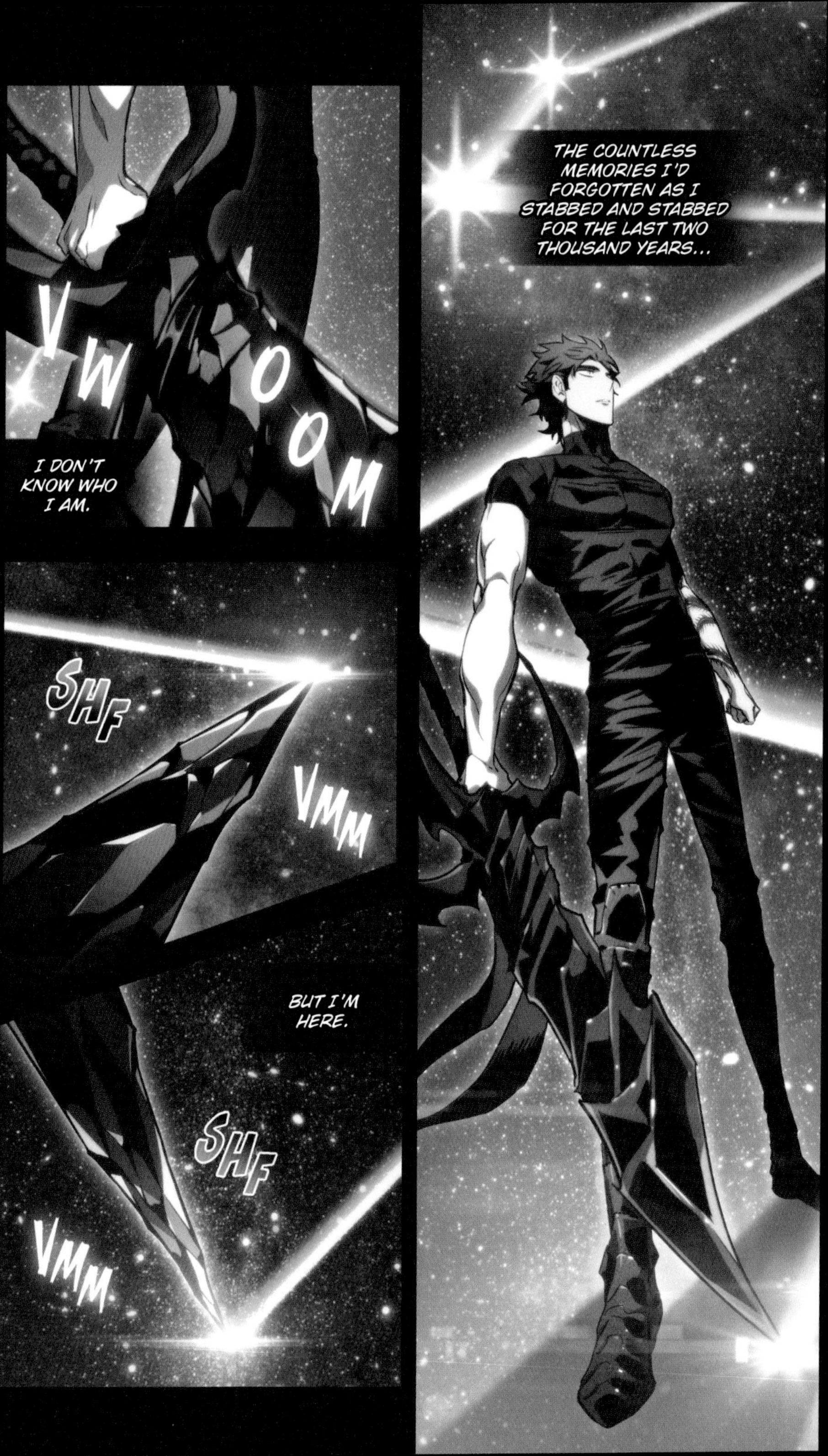
VWOOM
I DON'T KNOW WHO I AM.
SHF
VMM
BUT I'M HERE.
SHF
VMM
THE COUNTLESS MEMORIES I'D FORGOTTEN AS I STABBED AND STABBED FOR THE LAST TWO THOUSAND YEARS...

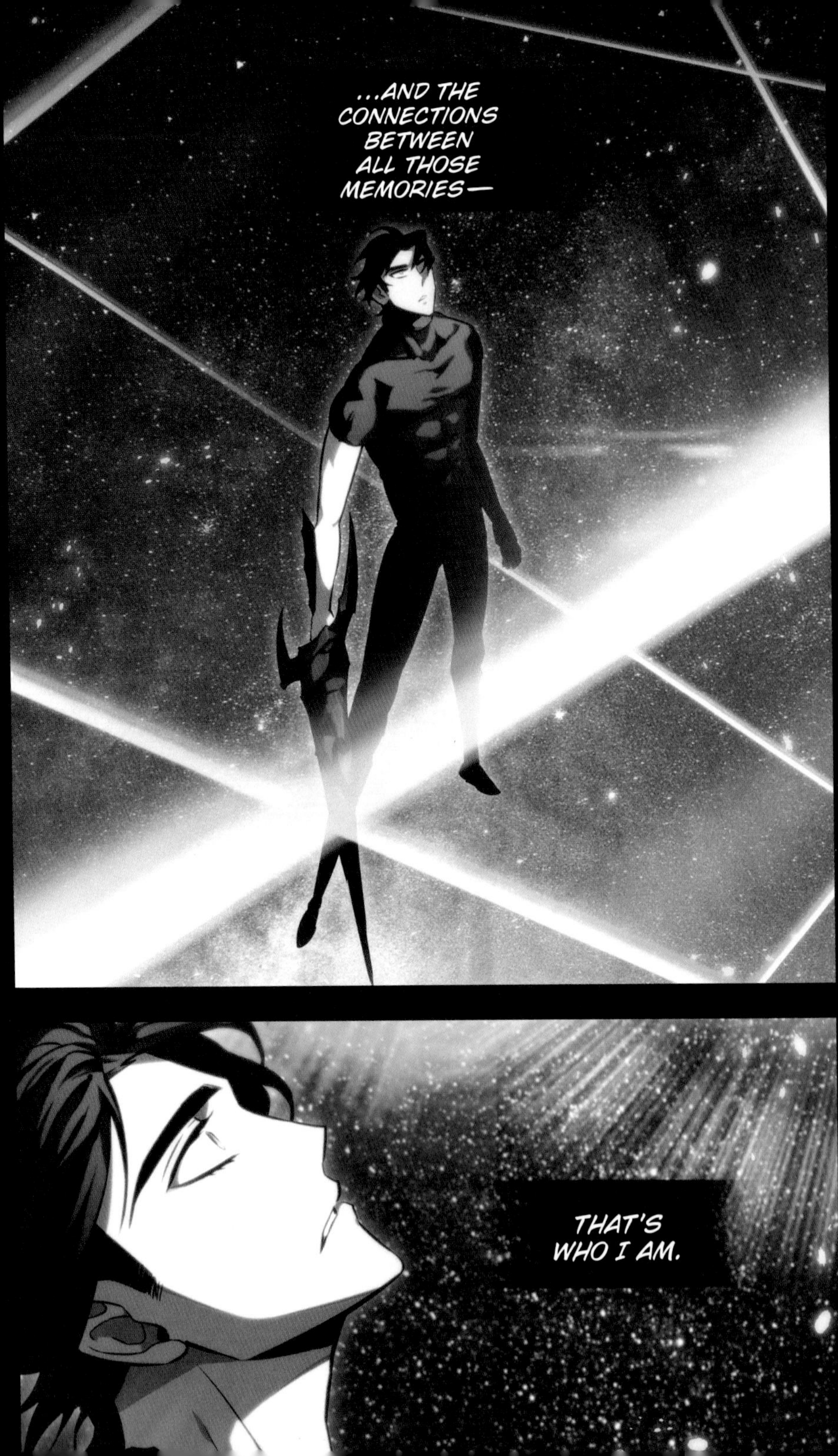
...AND THE CONNECTIONS BETWEEN ALL THOSE MEMORIES—
THAT'S WHO I AM.

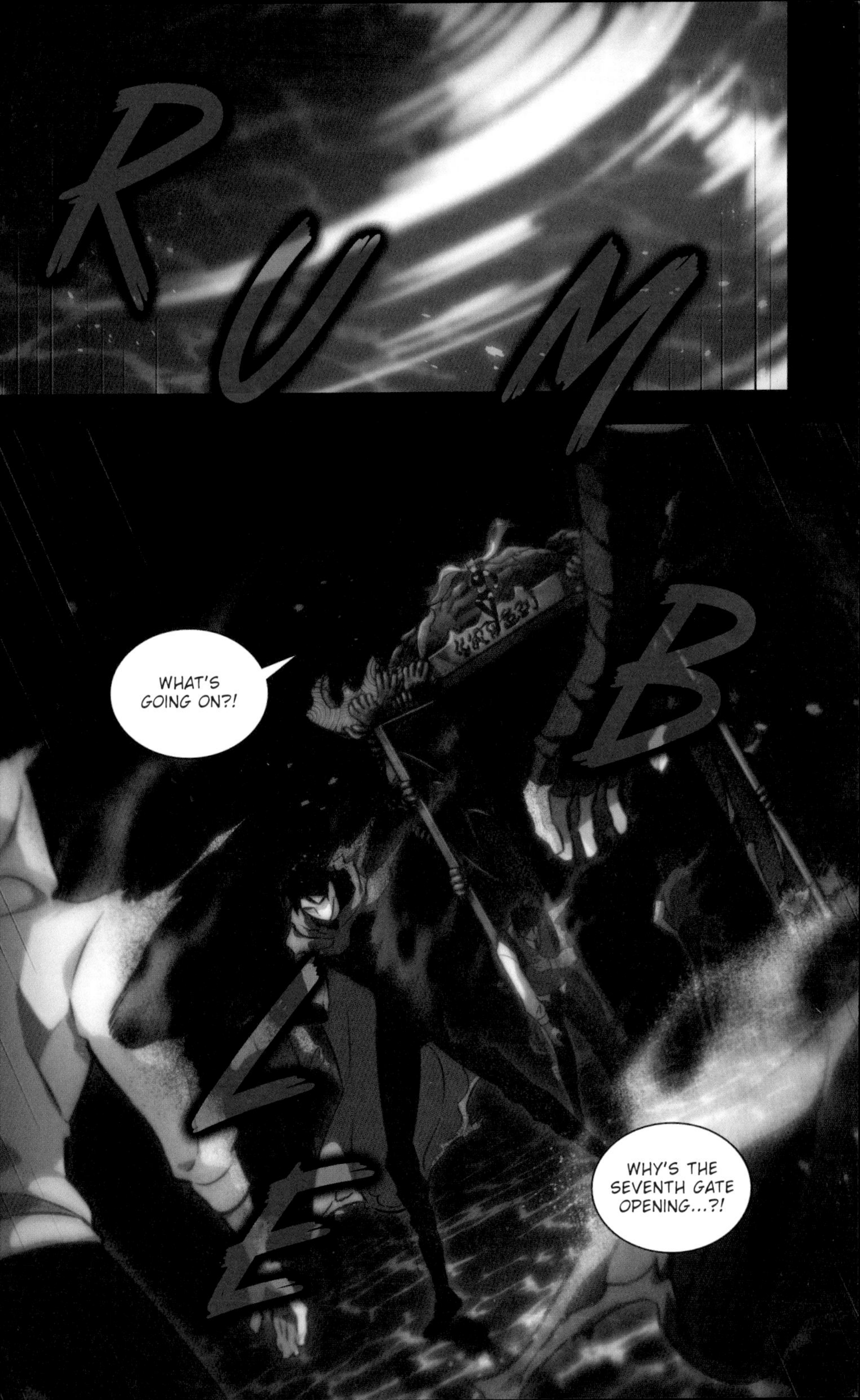
RUMBLE
WHAT'S GOING ON?!
WHY'S THE SEVENTH GATE OPENING...?!

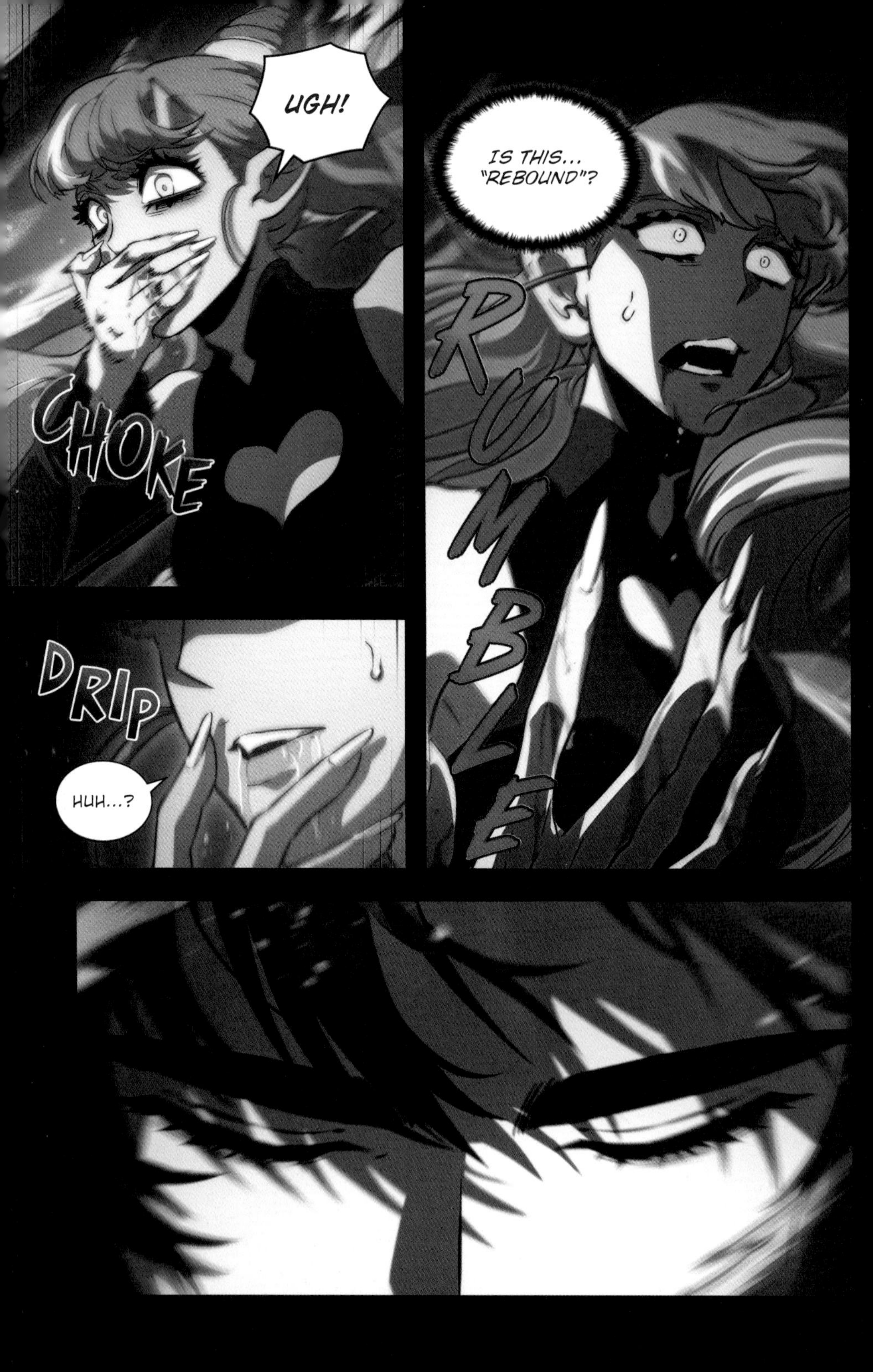
UGH!
CHOKE
IS THIS... "REBOUND"?
RUMBLE
DRIP
HUH...?

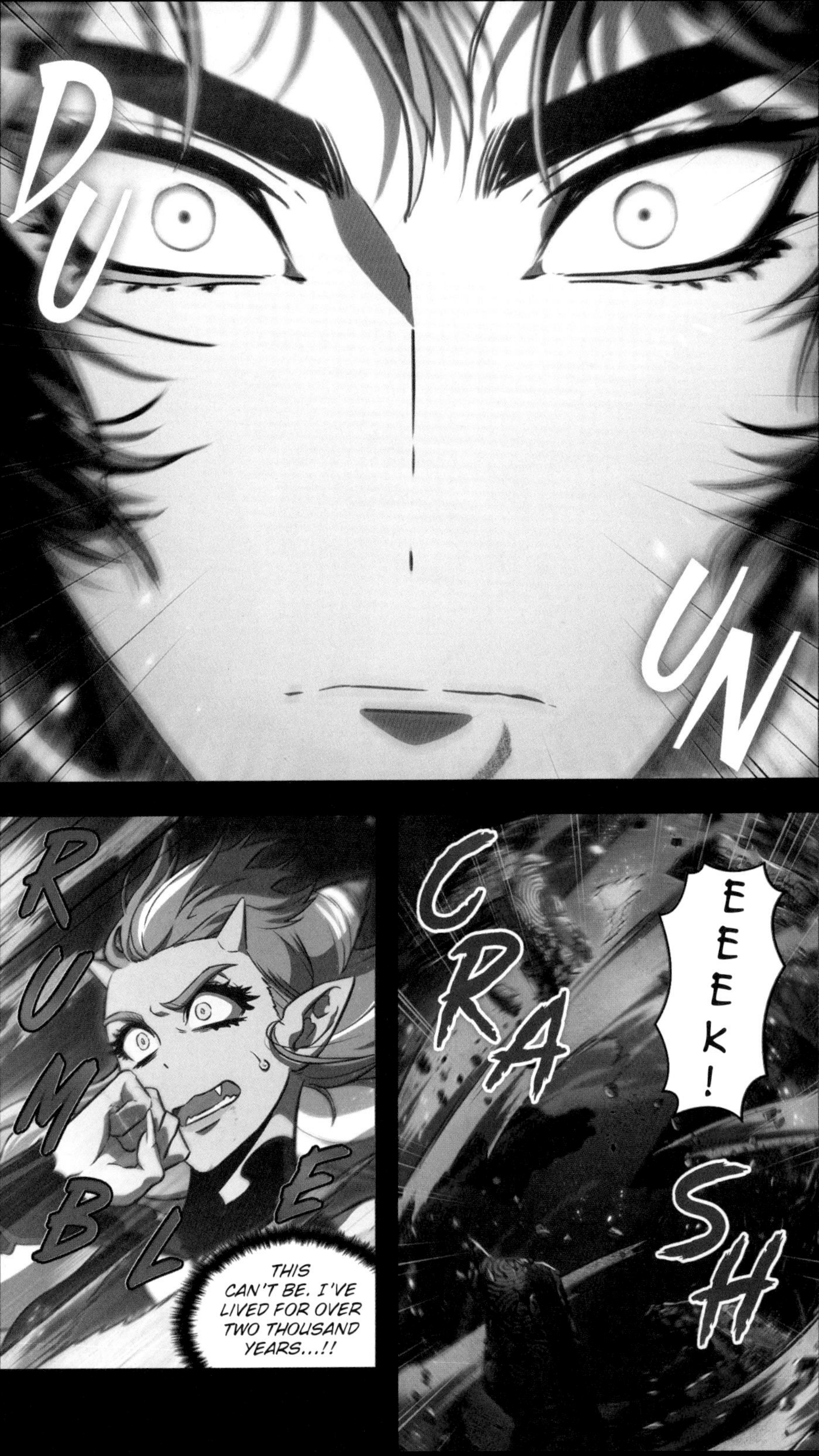
DU
UN
RUMBLE
THIS CAN'T BE. I'VE LIVED FOR OVER TWO THOUSAND YEARS...!!
CRASH
EEEEK!

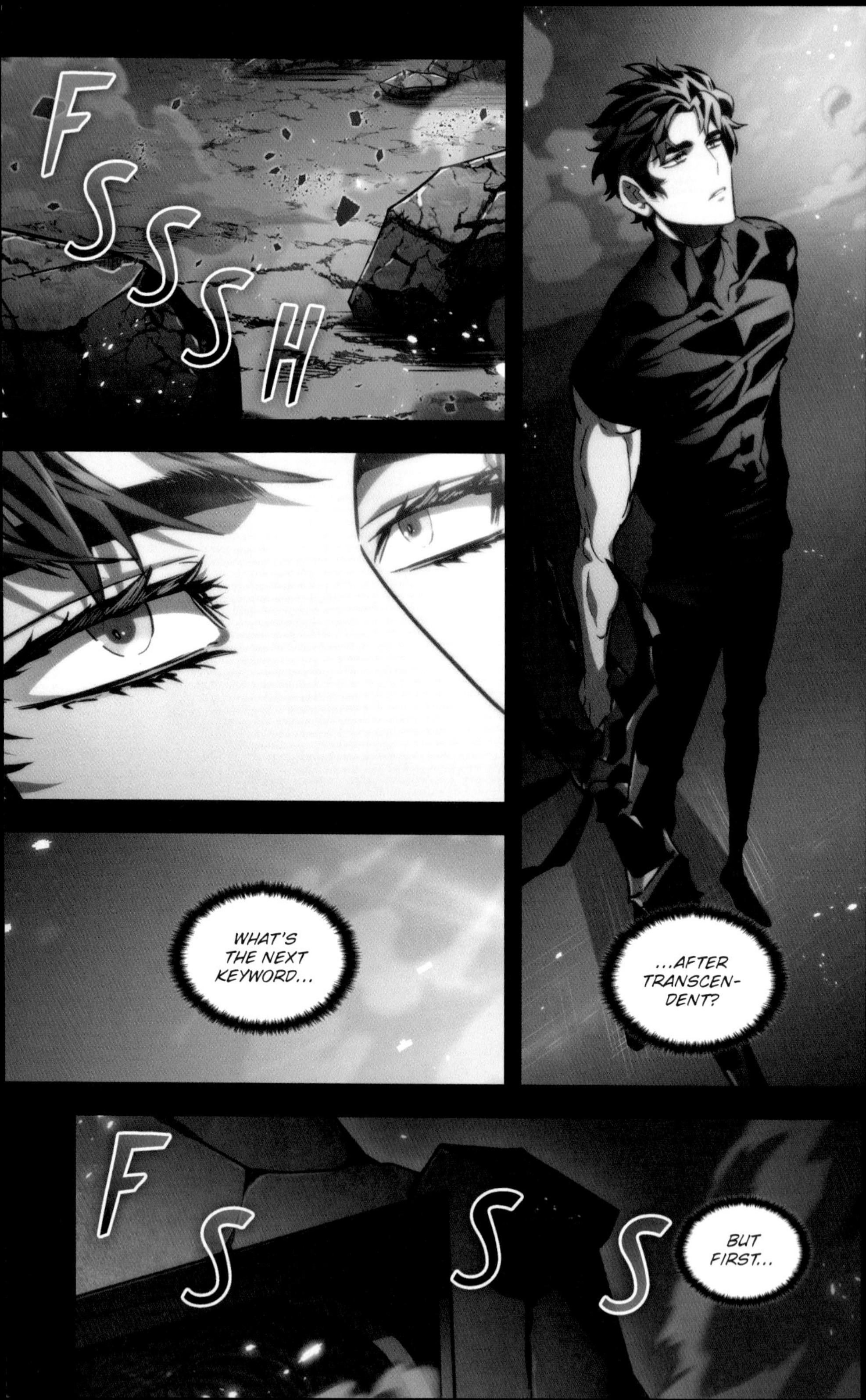
FSSSH
WHAT'S THE NEXT KEYWORD...
...AFTER TRANSCEN-DENT?
FSSS
BUT FIRST...

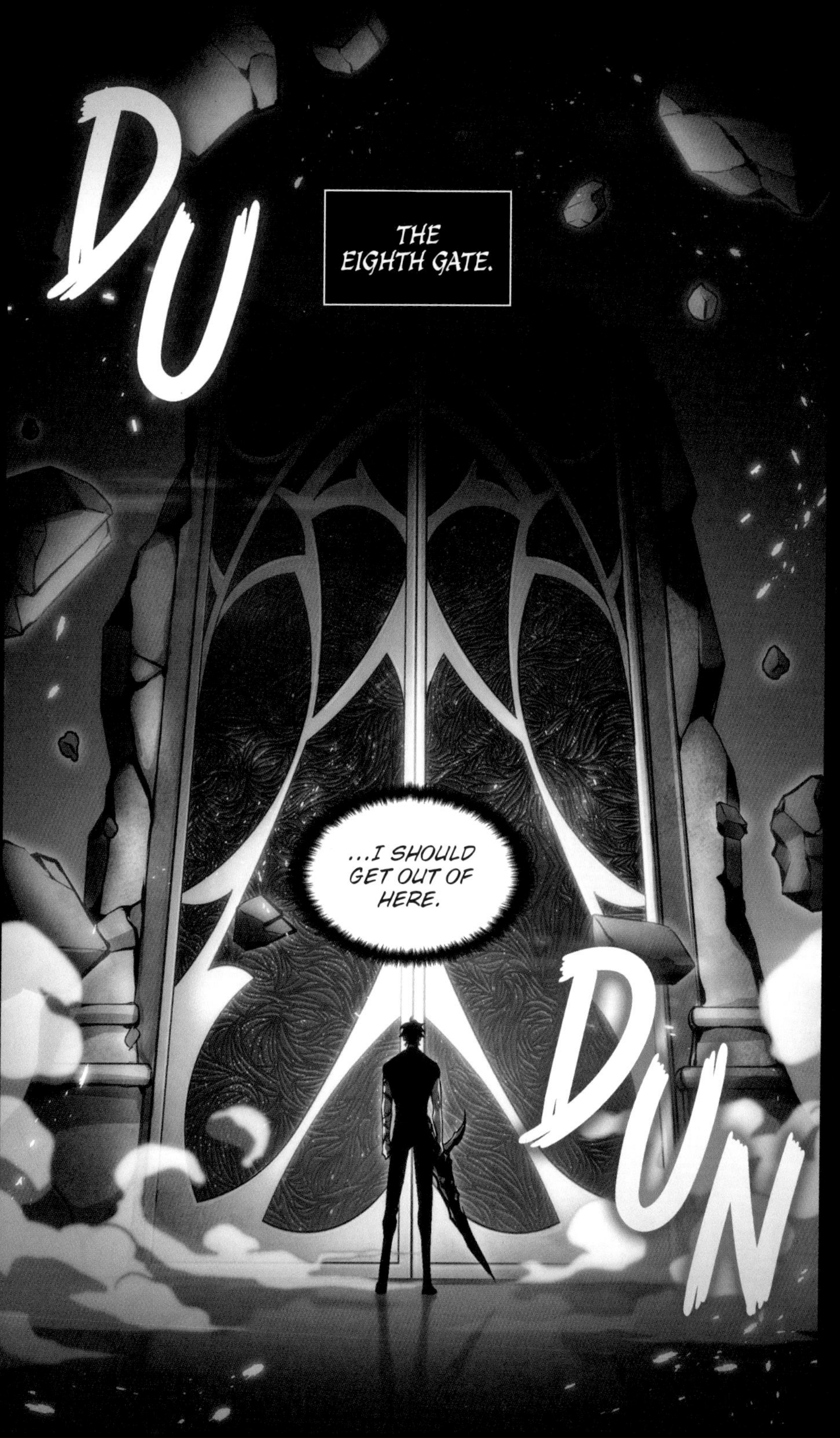
DU
THE EIGHTH GATE.
...I SHOULD GET OUT OF HERE.
DUDUN

The WORLD After the Fall

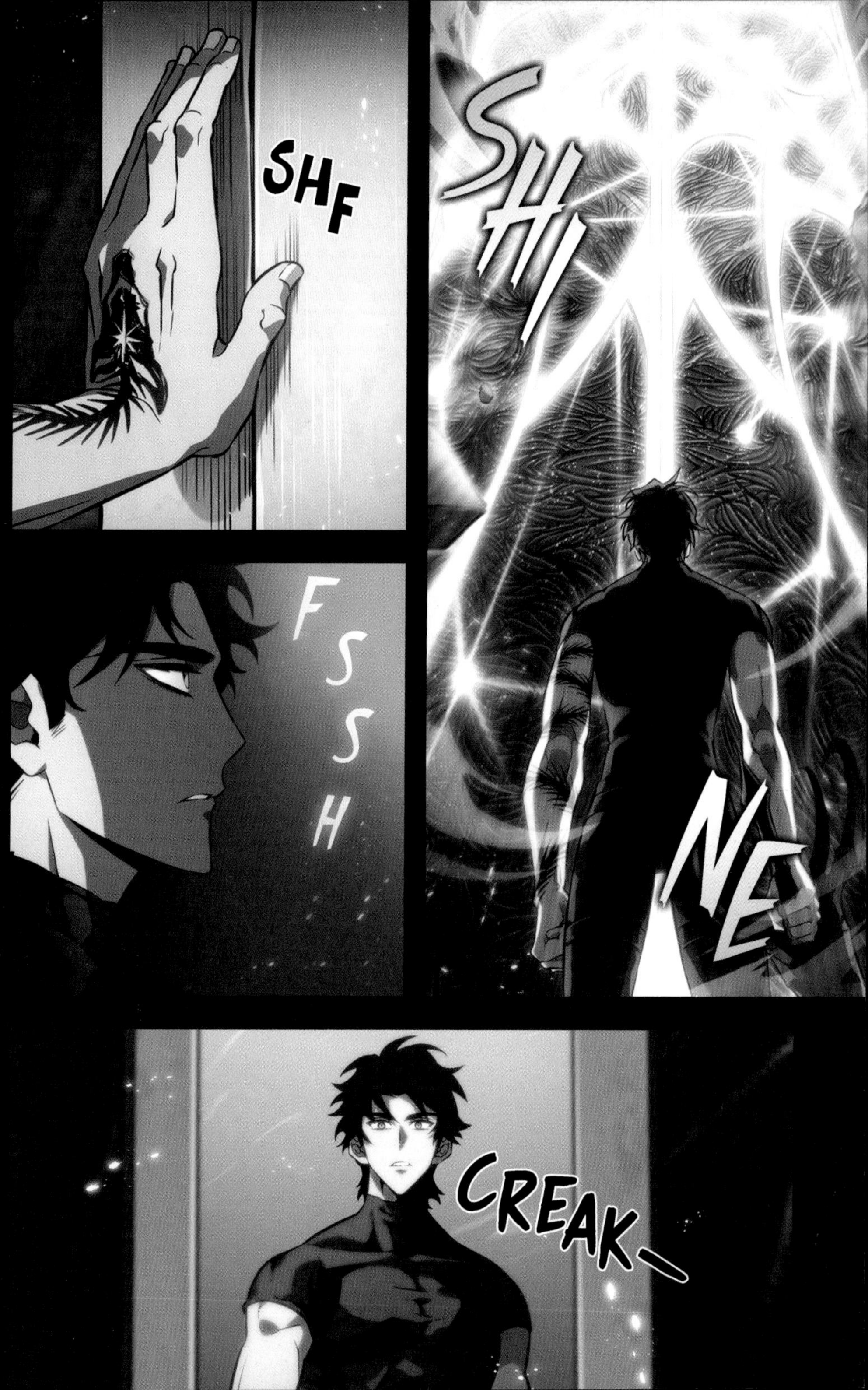
SHF
SHINE
FSSH
CREAK—

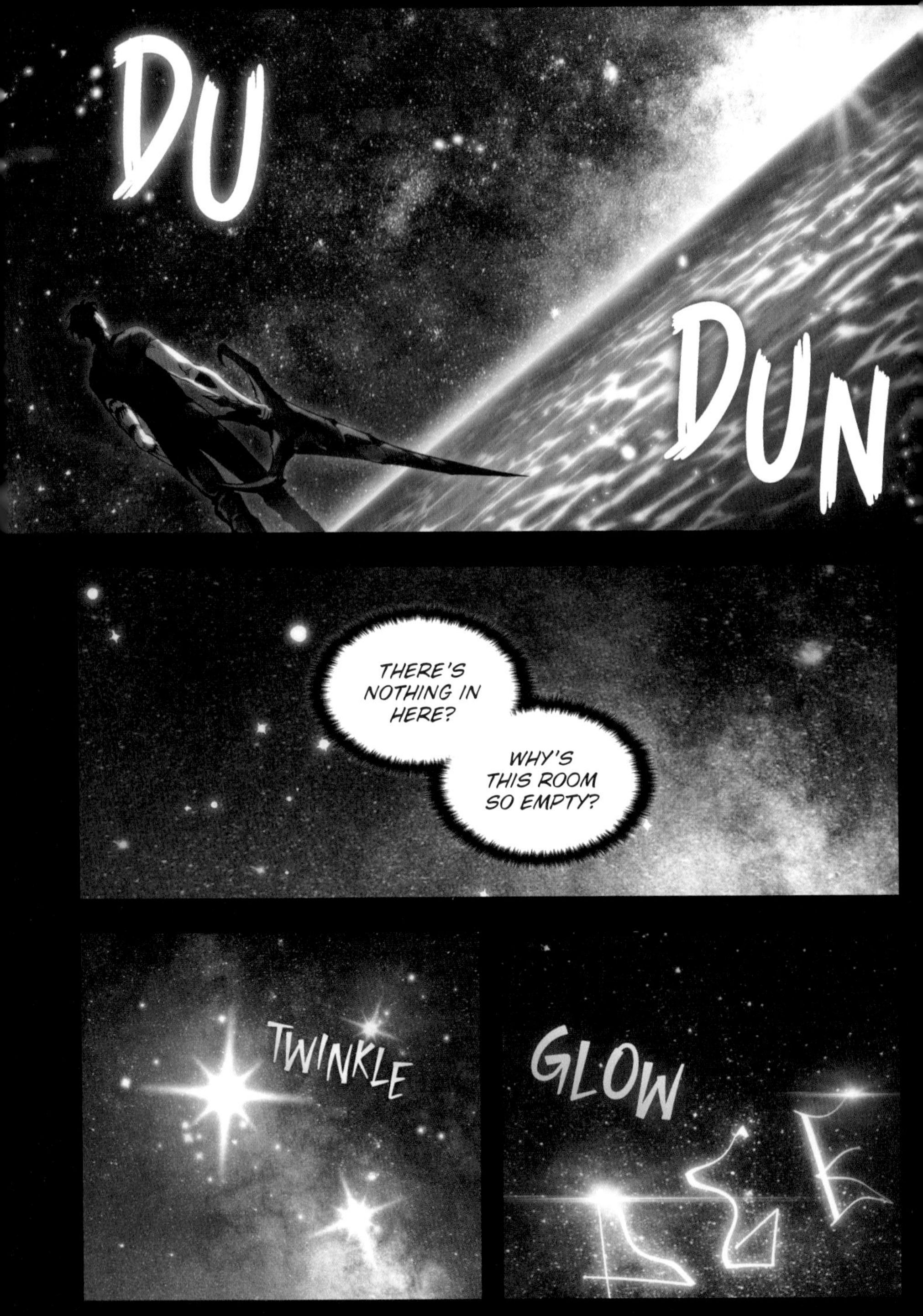
DU
DUN
THERE'S NOTHING IN HERE?
WHY'S THIS ROOM SO EMPTY?
TWINKLE
GLOW

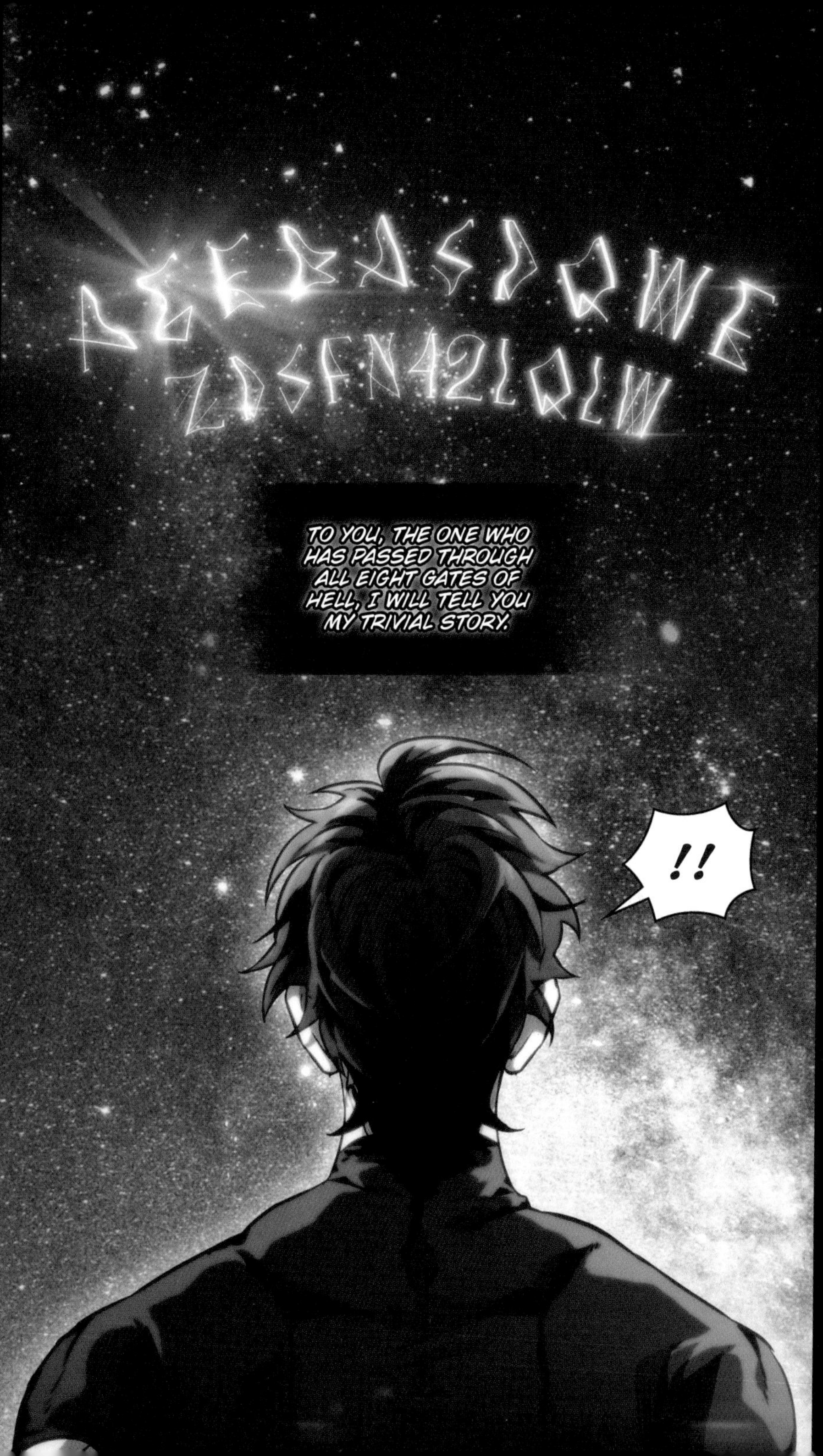
TO YOU, THE ONE WHO HAS PASSED THROUGH ALL EIGHT GATES OF HELL, I WILL TELL YOU MY TRIVIAL STORY.
!!

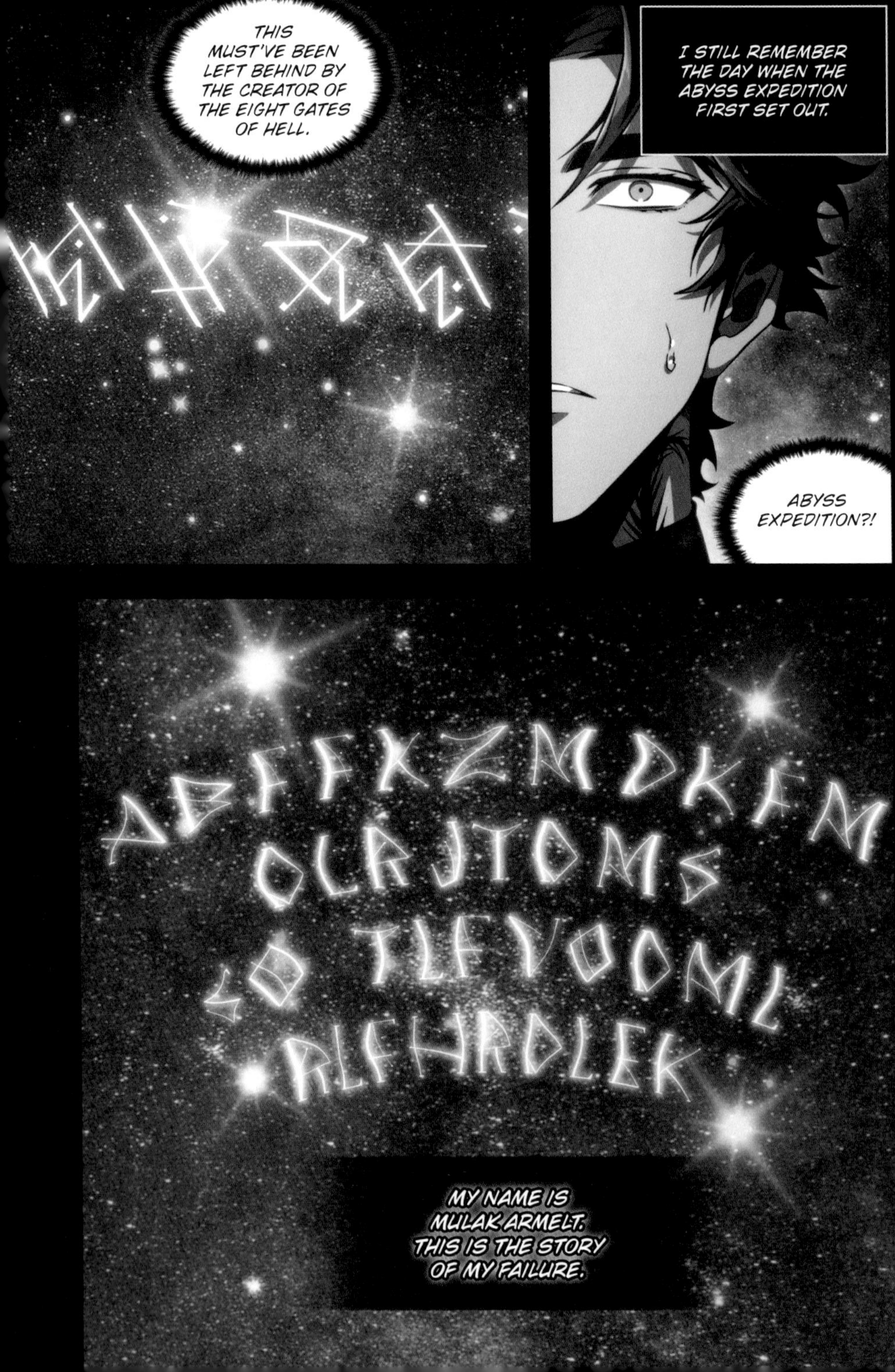

THIS MUST'VE BEEN LEFT BEHIND BY THE CREATOR OF THE EIGHT GATES OF HELL.
I STILL REMEMBER THE DAY WHEN THE ABYSS EXPEDITION FIRST SET OUT.
ABYSS EXPEDITION?!
MY NAME IS MULAK ARMELT. THIS IS THE STORY OF MY FAILURE.

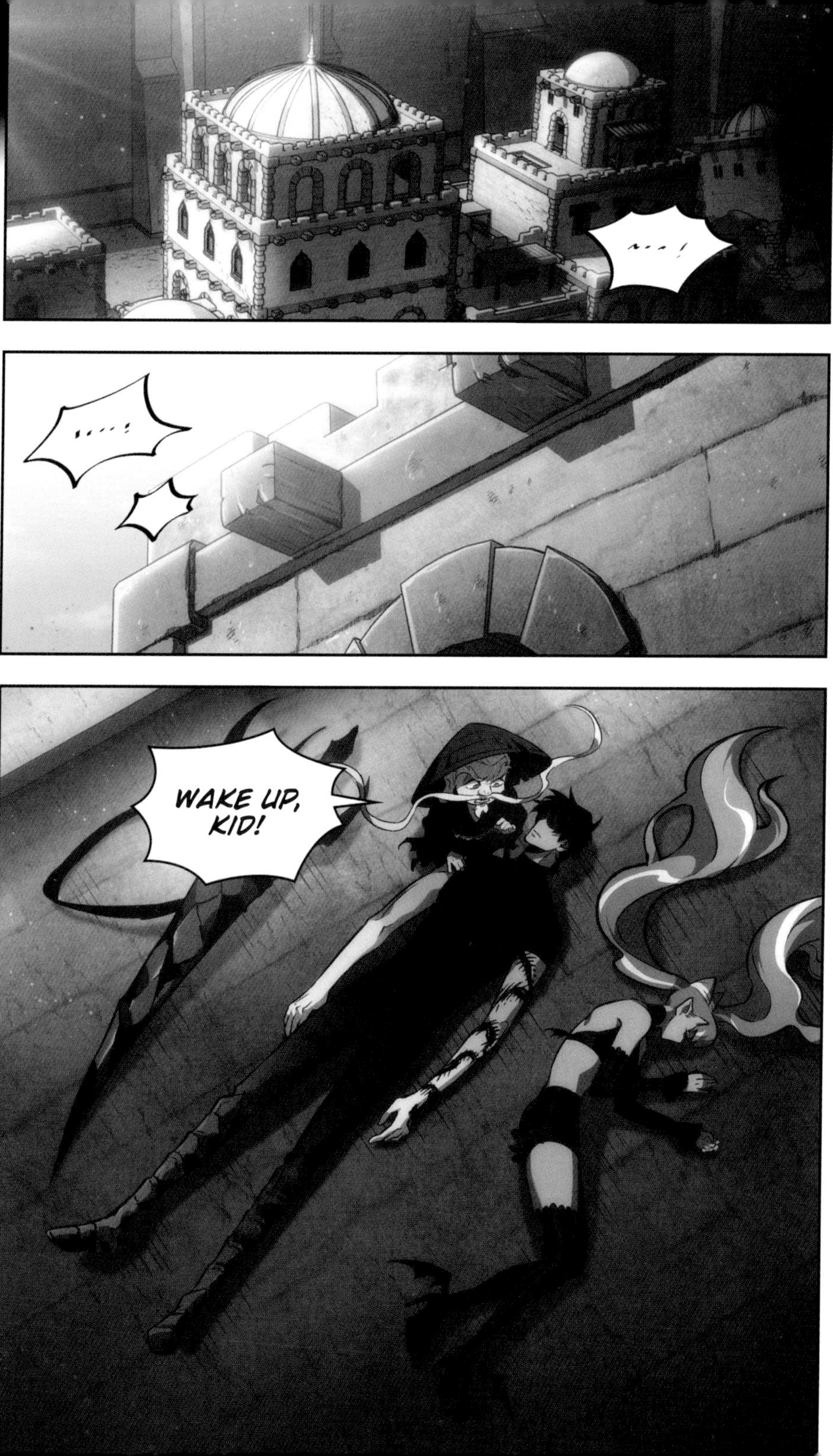
WAKE UP, KID!

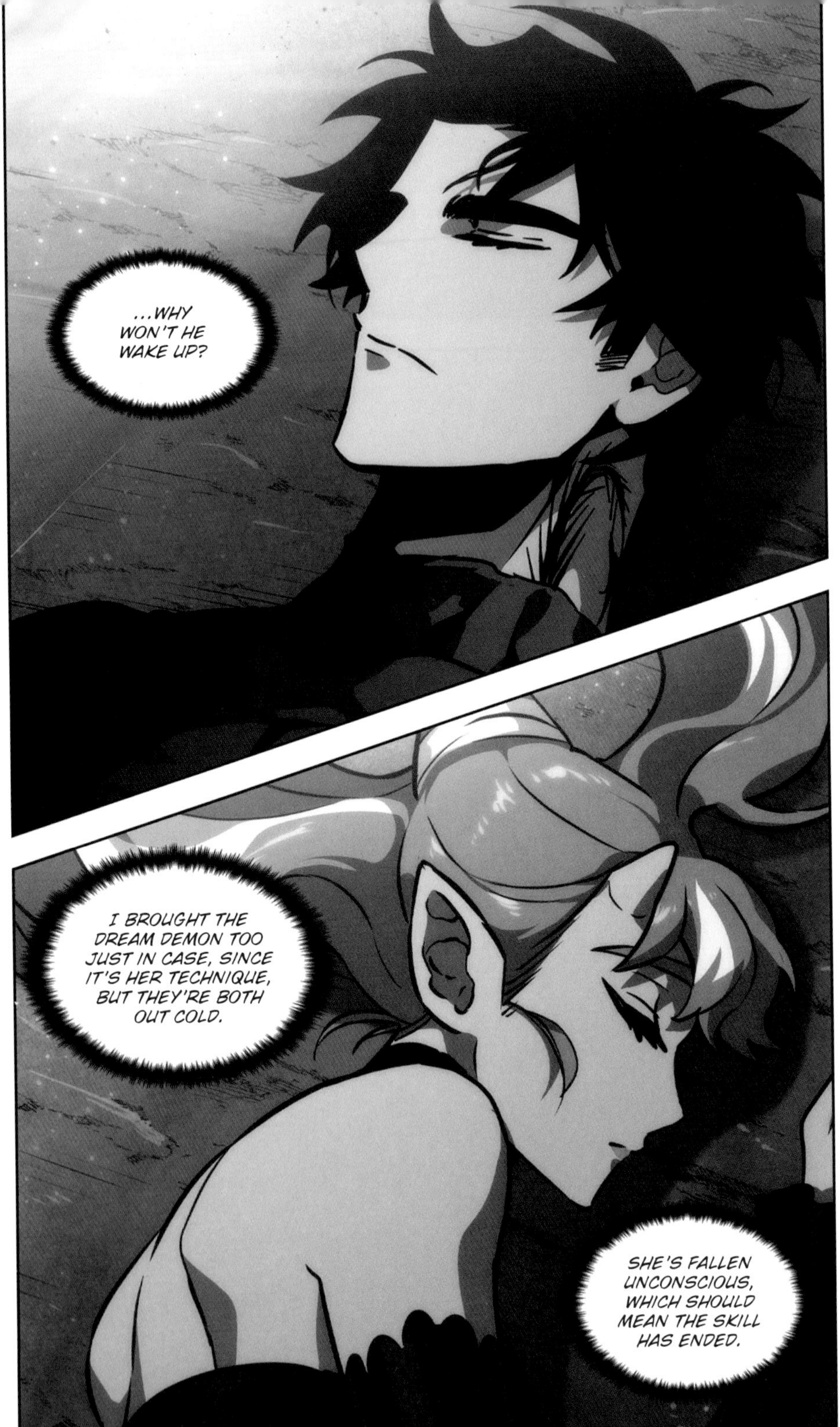
...WHY WON'T HE WAKE UP?
I BROUGHT THE DREAM DEMON TOO JUST IN CASE, SINCE IT'S HER TECHNIQUE, BUT THEY'RE BOTH OUT COLD.
SHE'S FALLEN UNCONSCIOUS, WHICH SHOULD MEAN THE SKILL HAS ENDED.

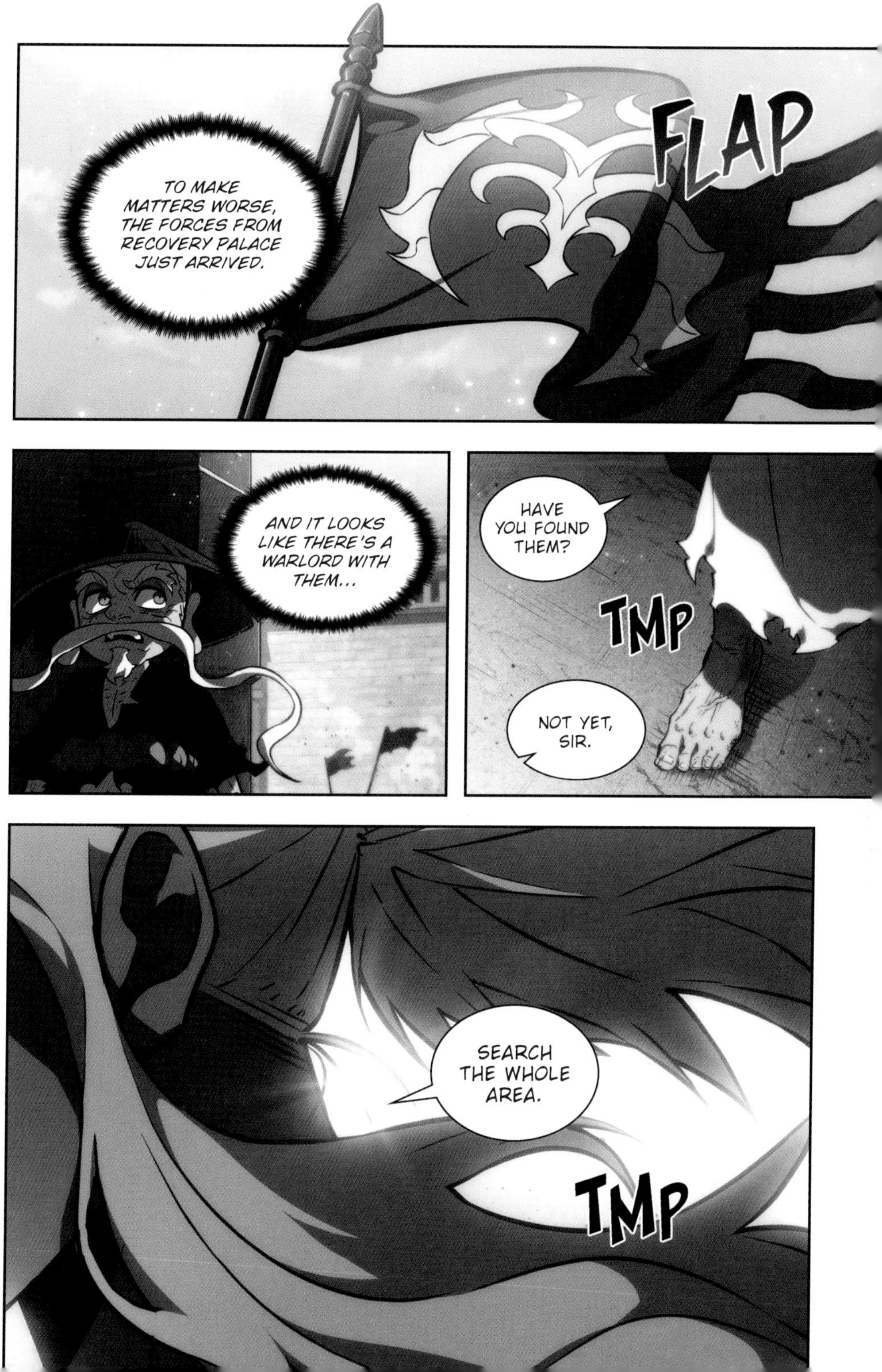
TO MAKE MATTERS WORSE, THE FORCES FROM RECOVERY PALACE JUST ARRIVED.
FLAP
AND IT LOOKS LIKE THERE'S A WARLORD WITH THEM...
HAVE YOU FOUND THEM?
TMP
NOT YET, SIR.
SEARCH THE WHOLE AREA.
TMP

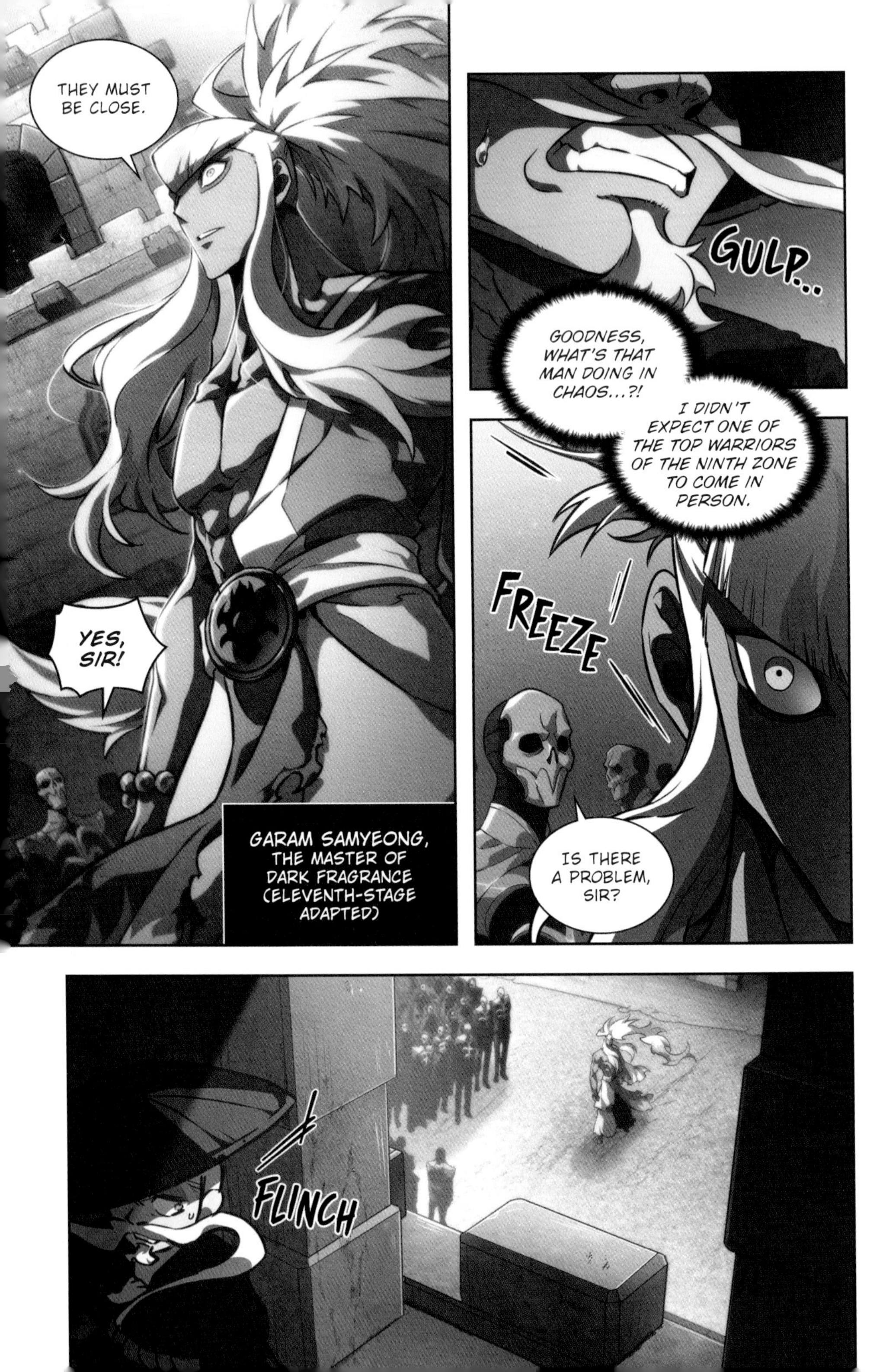
THEY MUST BE CLOSE.
YES, SIR!
GARAM SAMYEONG, THE MASTER OF DARK FRAGRANCE (ELEVENTH-STAGE ADAPTED)
GULP...
GOODNESS, WHAT'S THAT MAN DOING IN CHAOS...?!
I DIDN'T EXPECT ONE OF THE TOP WARRIORS OF THE NINTH ZONE TO COME IN PERSON.
FREEZE
IS THERE A PROBLEM, SIR?
FLINCH

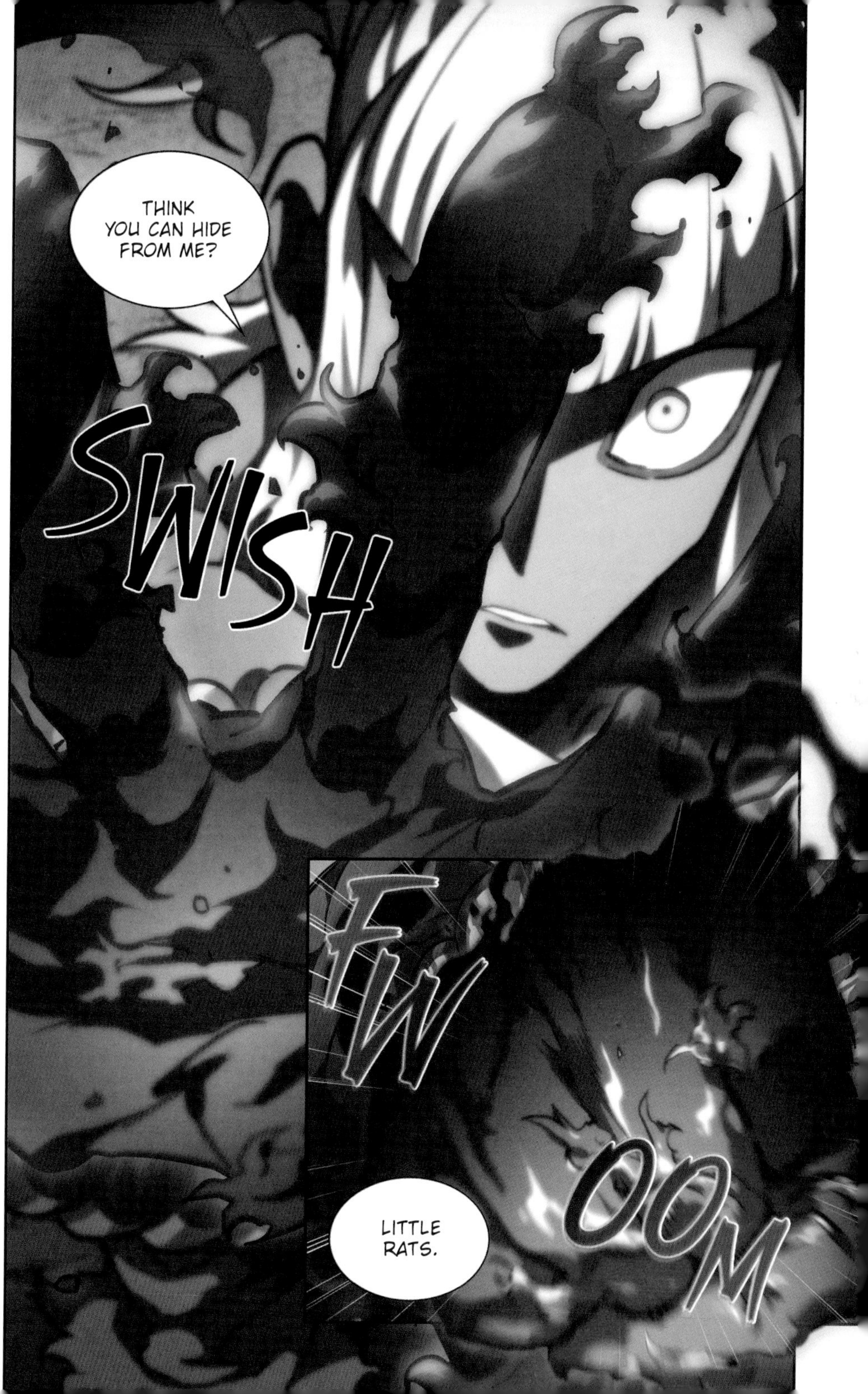
THINK YOU CAN HIDE FROM ME?
SWISH
FWOOM
LITTLE RATS.

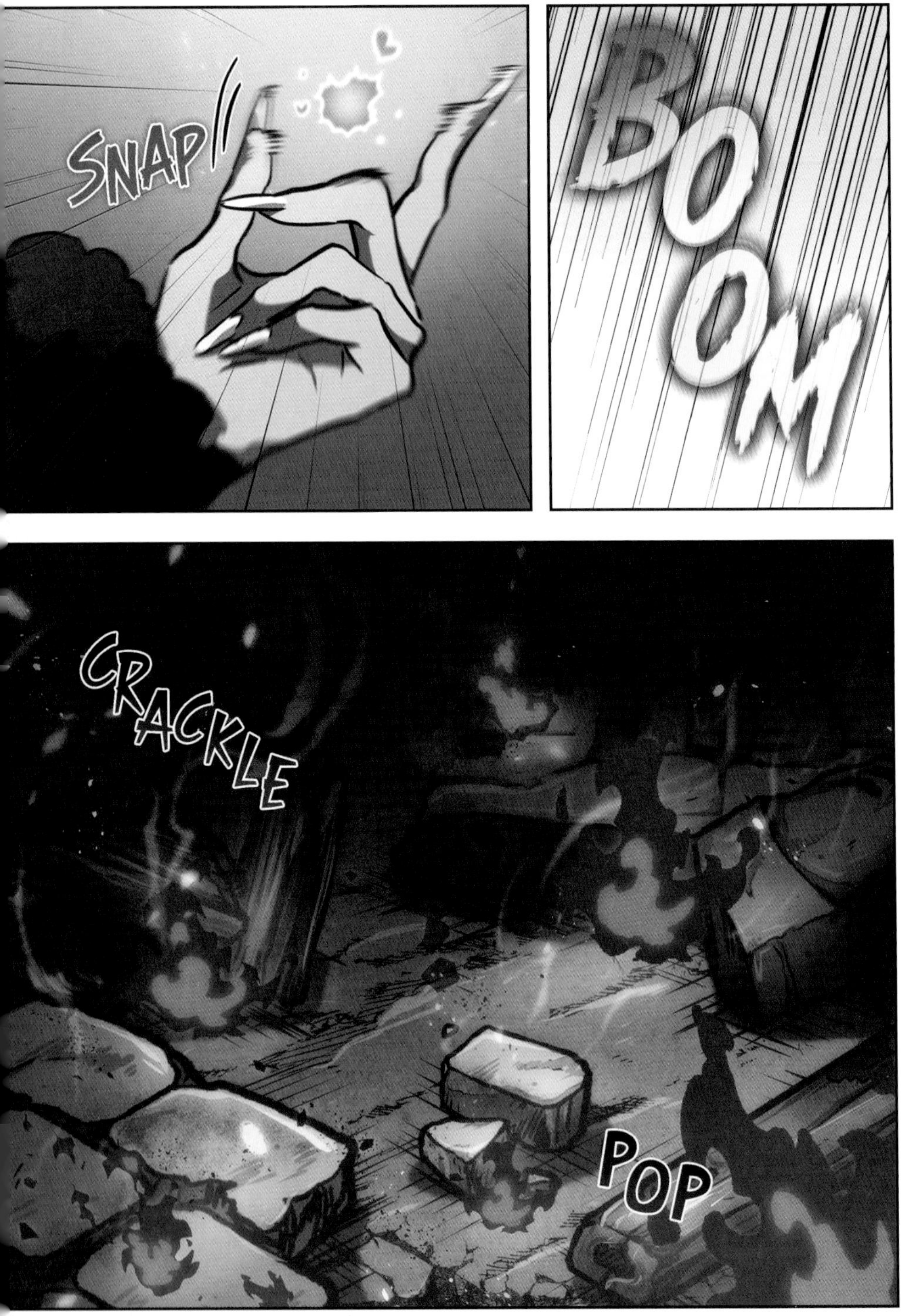
SNAP!!
BOOM
CRACKLE
POP

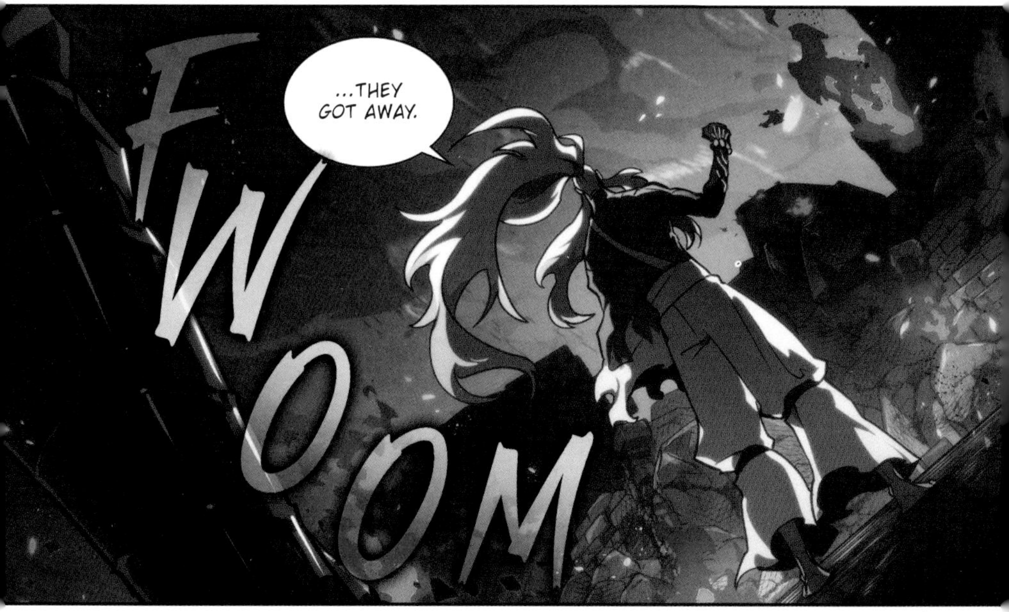
...THEY GOT AWAY.
FWOOOM

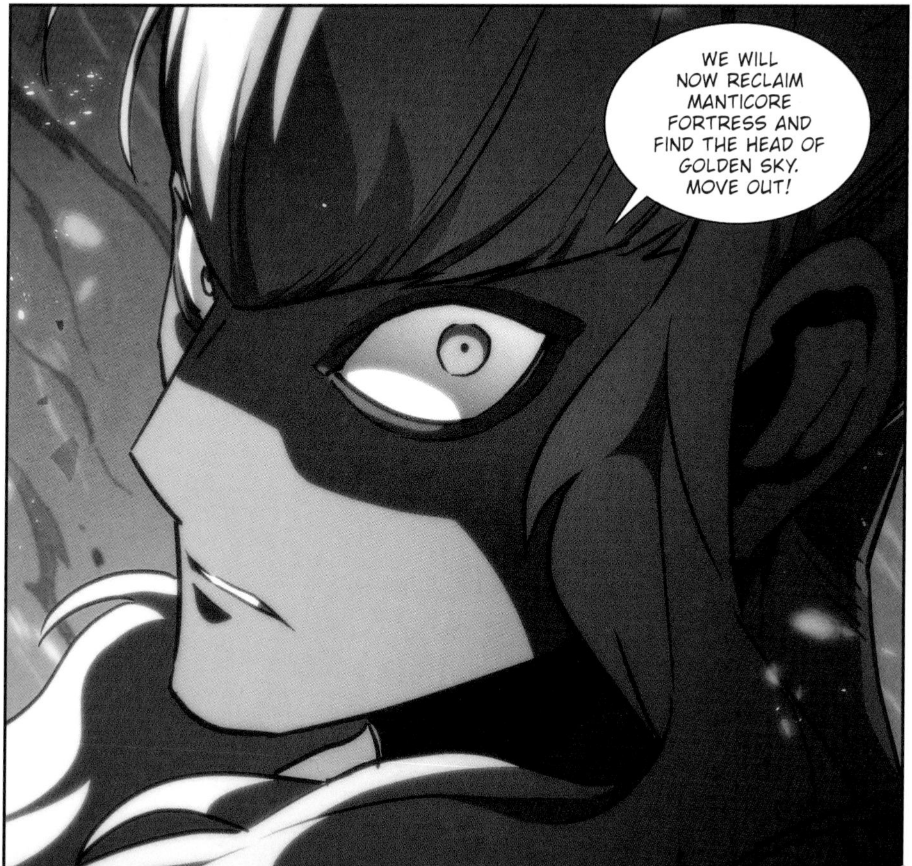
WE WILL NOW RECLAIM MANTICORE FORTRESS AND FIND THE HEAD OF GOLDEN SKY. MOVE OUT!

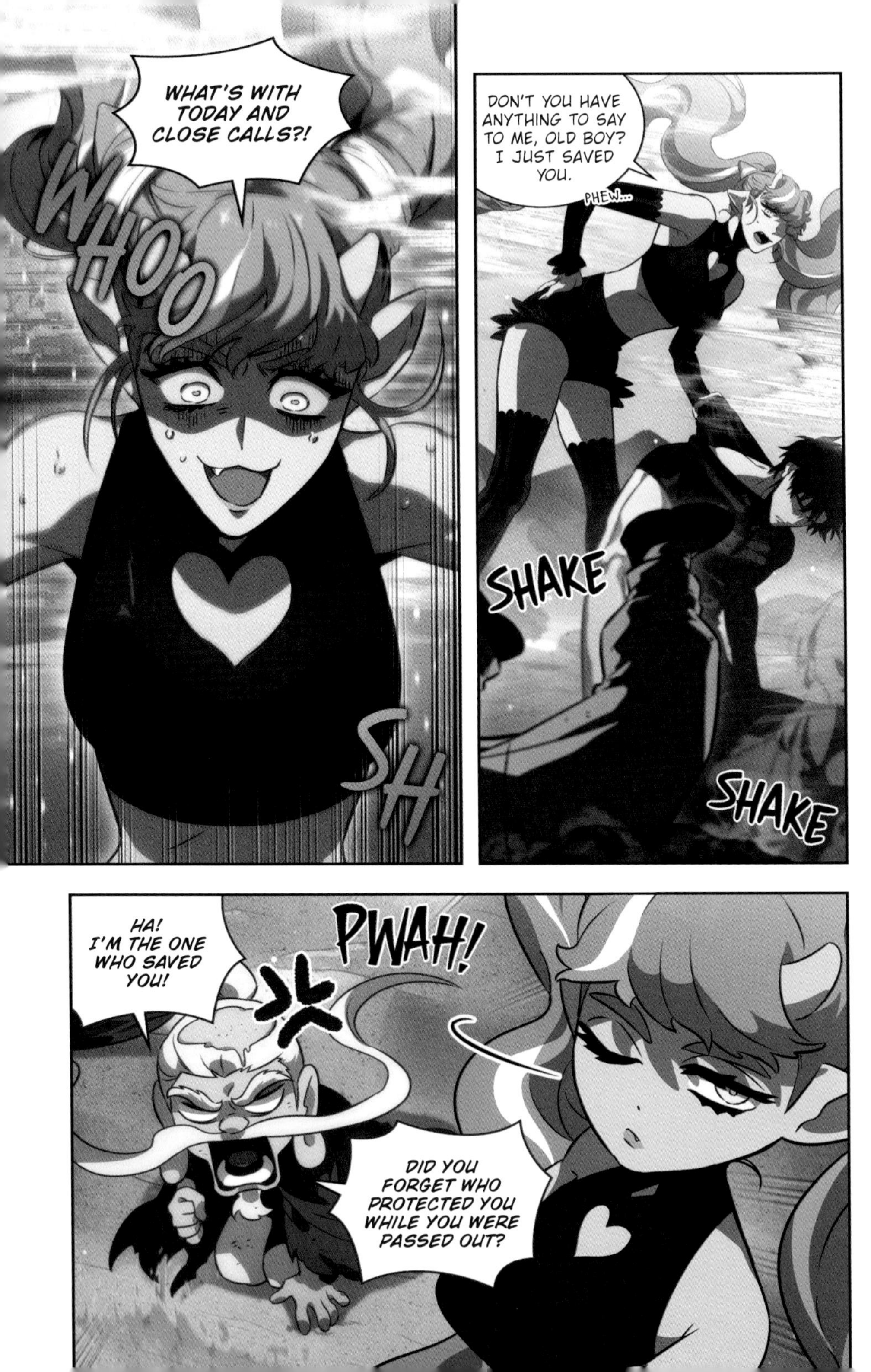

WHAT'S WITH TODAY AND CLOSE CALLS?!
WHOOOSH
DON'T YOU HAVE ANYTHING TO SAY TO ME, OLD BOY? I JUST SAVED YOU.
PHEW...
SHAKE
SHAKE
HA! I'M THE ONE WHO SAVED YOU!
PWAH!
DID YOU FORGET WHO PROTECTED YOU WHILE YOU WERE PASSED OUT?

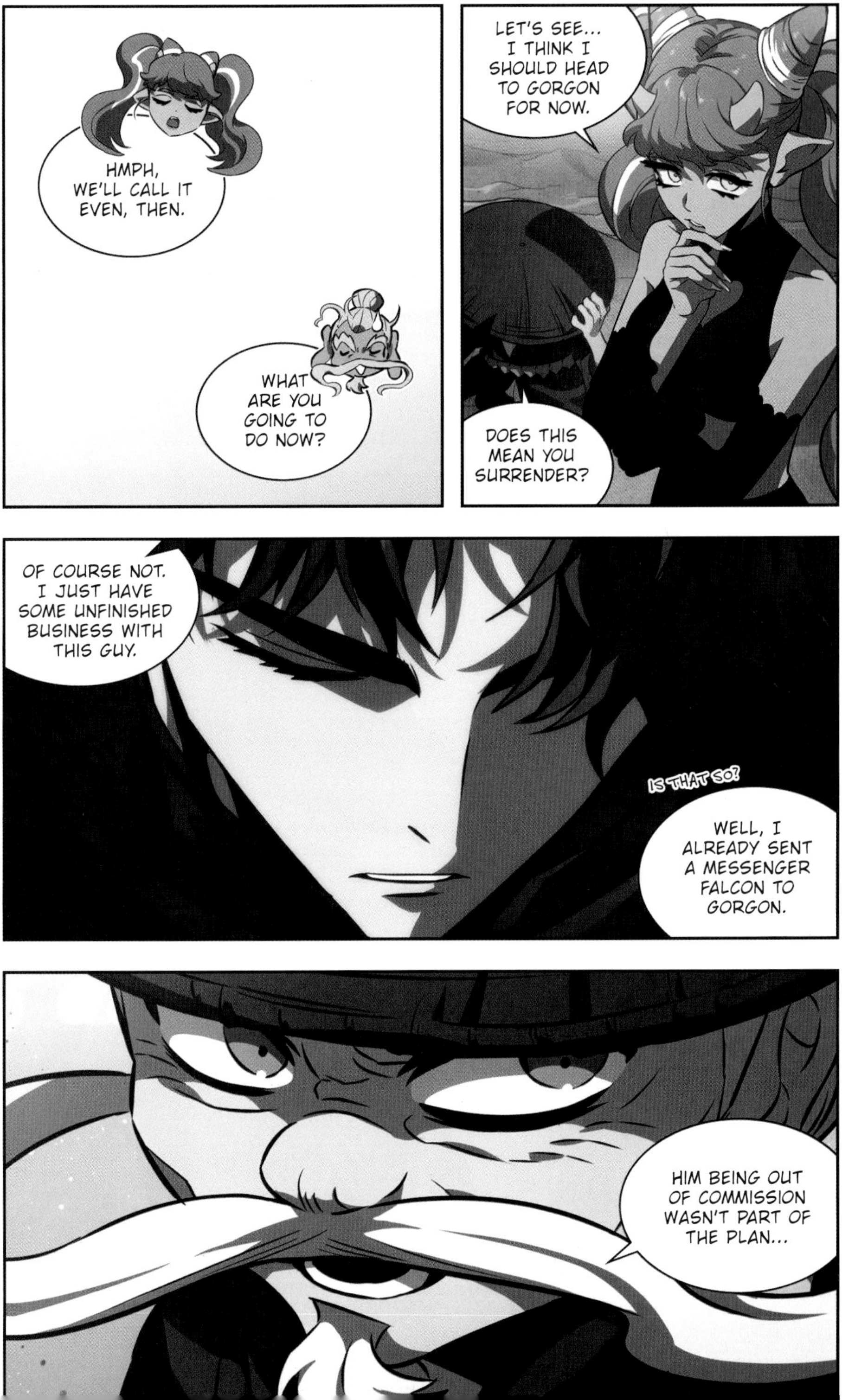
HMPH, WE'LL CALL IT EVEN, THEN.
WHAT ARE YOU GOING TO DO NOW?
LET'S SEE... I THINK I SHOULD HEAD TO GORGON FOR NOW.
DOES THIS MEAN YOU SURRENDER?
OF COURSE NOT. I JUST HAVE SOME UNFINISHED BUSINESS WITH THIS GUY.
IS THAT SO?
WELL, I ALREADY SENT A MESSENGER FALCON TO GORGON.
HIM BEING OUT OF COMMISSION WASN'T PART OF THE PLAN...

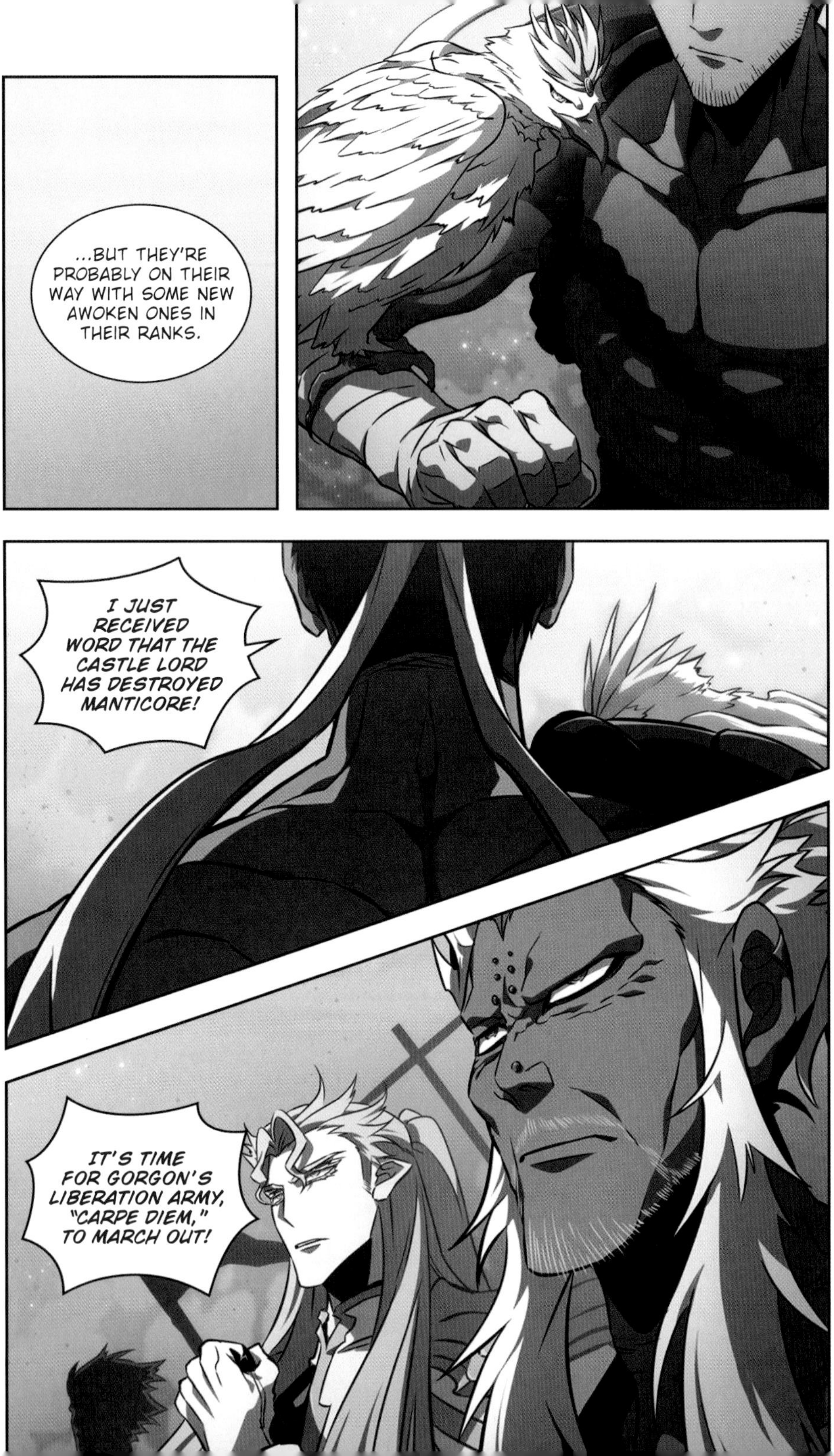
...BUT THEY'RE PROBABLY ON THEIR WAY WITH SOME NEW AWOKEN ONES IN THEIR RANKS.
I JUST RECEIVED WORD THAT THE CASTLE LORD HAS DESTROYED MANTICORE!
IT'S TIME FOR GORGON'S LIBERATION ARMY, "CARPE DIEM," TO MARCH OUT!

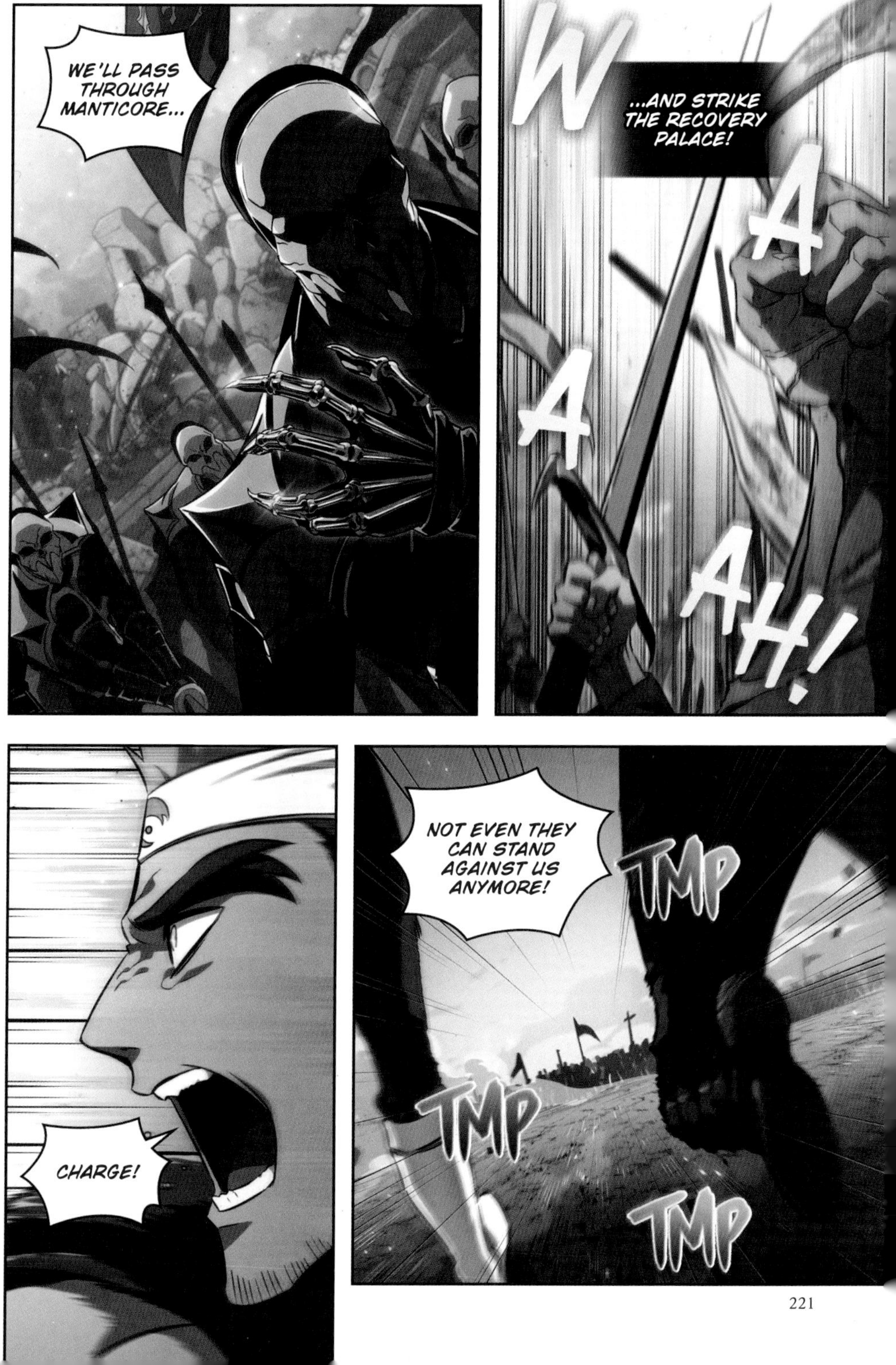
WE'LL PASS THROUGH MANTICORE...
W
...AND STRIKE THE RECOVERY PALACE!
A
A
AAH!
CHARGE!
NOT EVEN THEY CAN STAND AGAINST US ANYMORE!
TMP
TMP
TMP

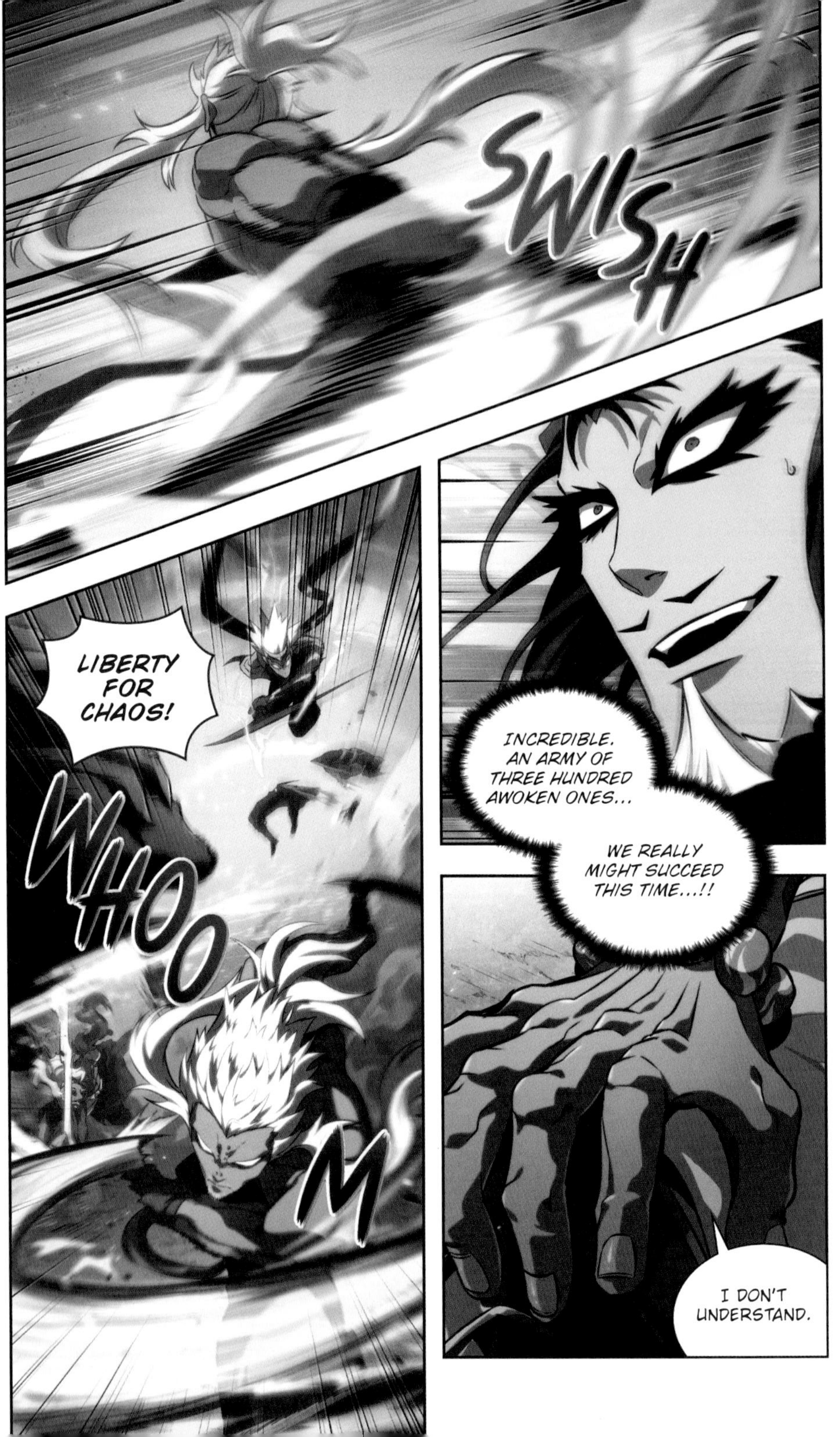
SWISH
INCREDIBLE. AN ARMY OF THREE HUNDRED AWOKEN ONES...
WE REALLY MIGHT SUCCEED THIS TIME...!!
LIBERTY FOR CHAOS!
WHOOOM
I DON'T UNDERSTAND.

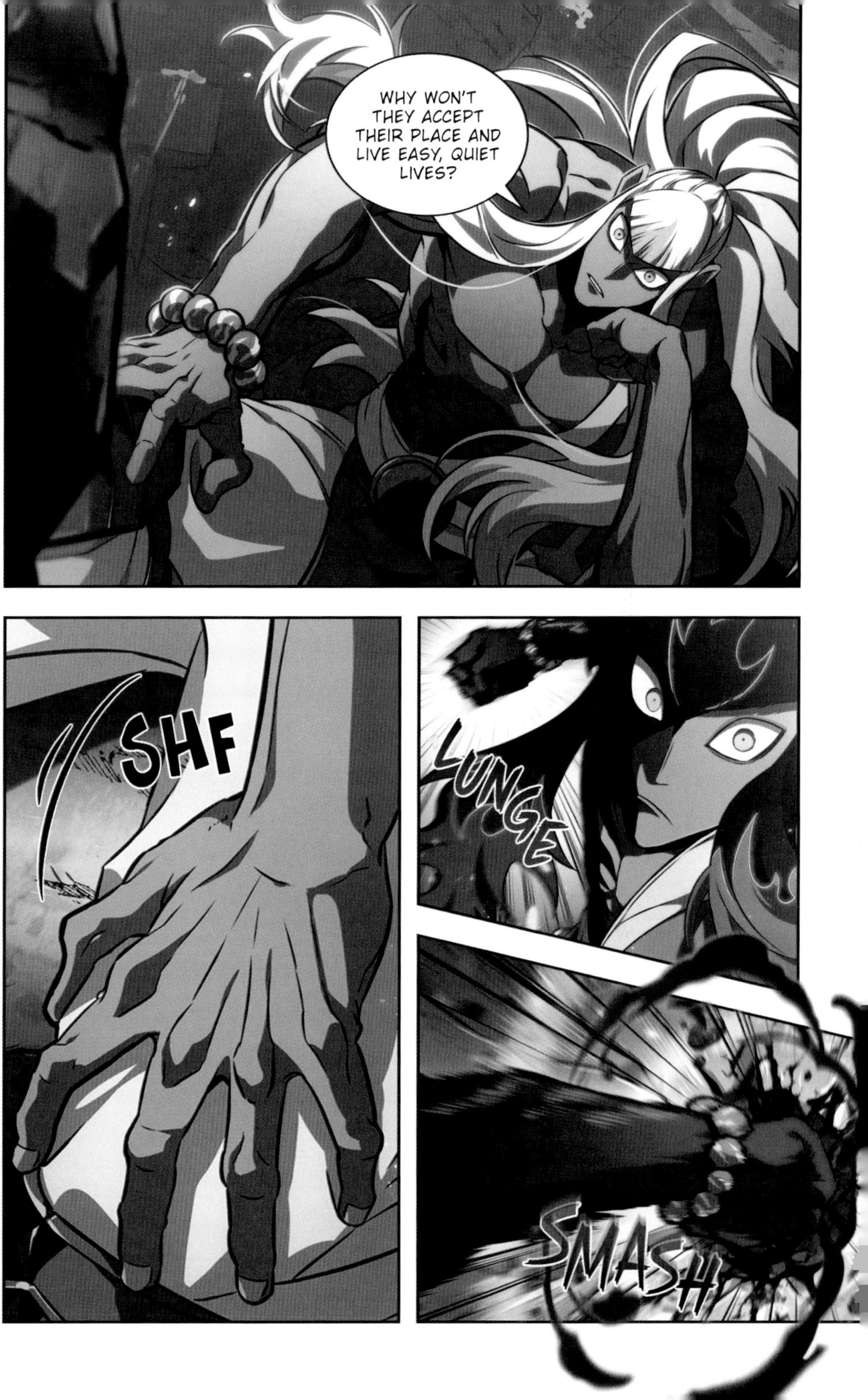
WHY WON'T THEY ACCEPT THEIR PLACE AND LIVE EASY, QUIET LIVES?
SHF
LUNGE
SMASH

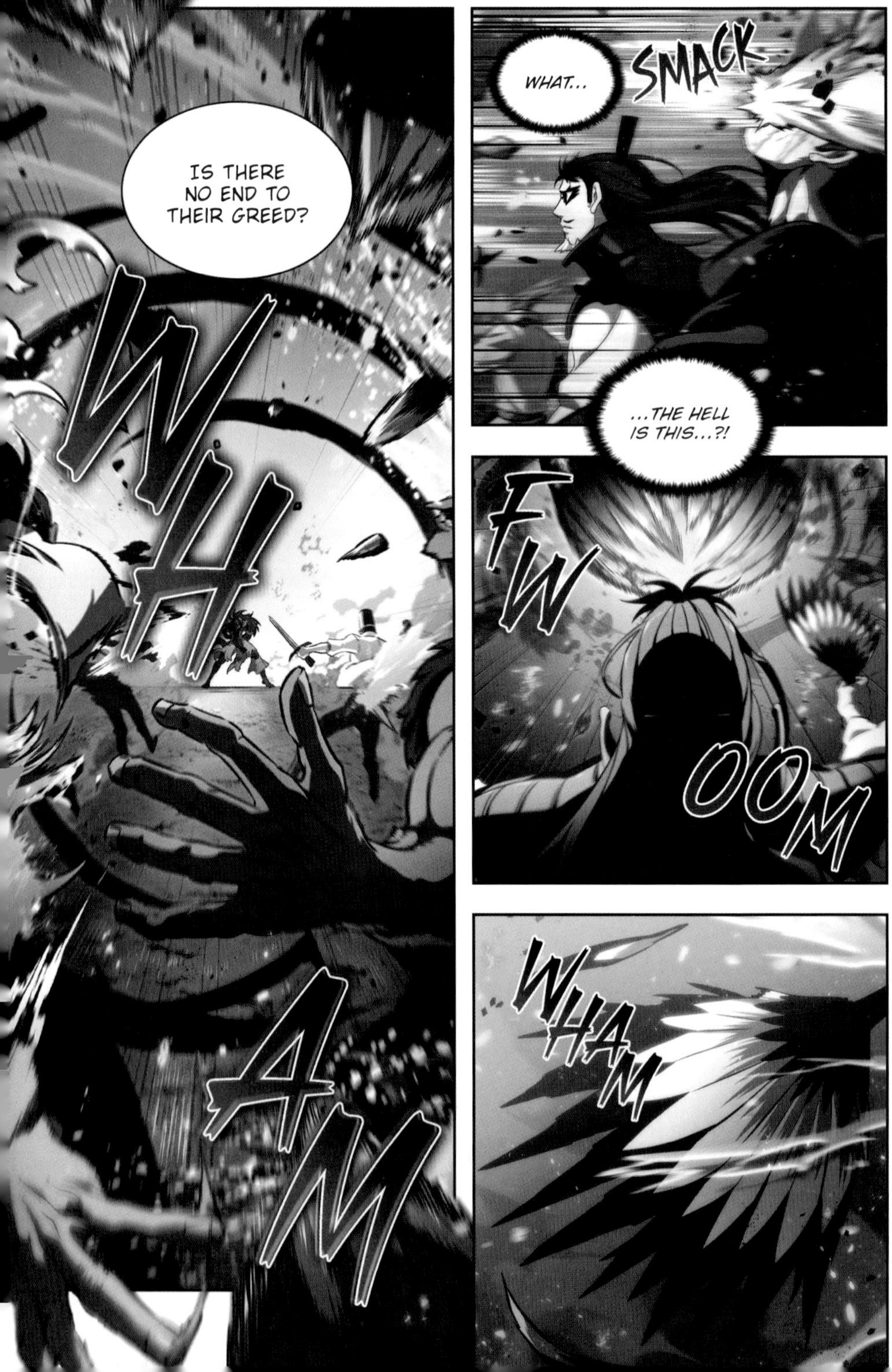

IS THERE NO END TO THEIR GREED?
WHAM
WHAT...
SMACK
...THE HELL IS THIS...?!
FWOOM
WHAM

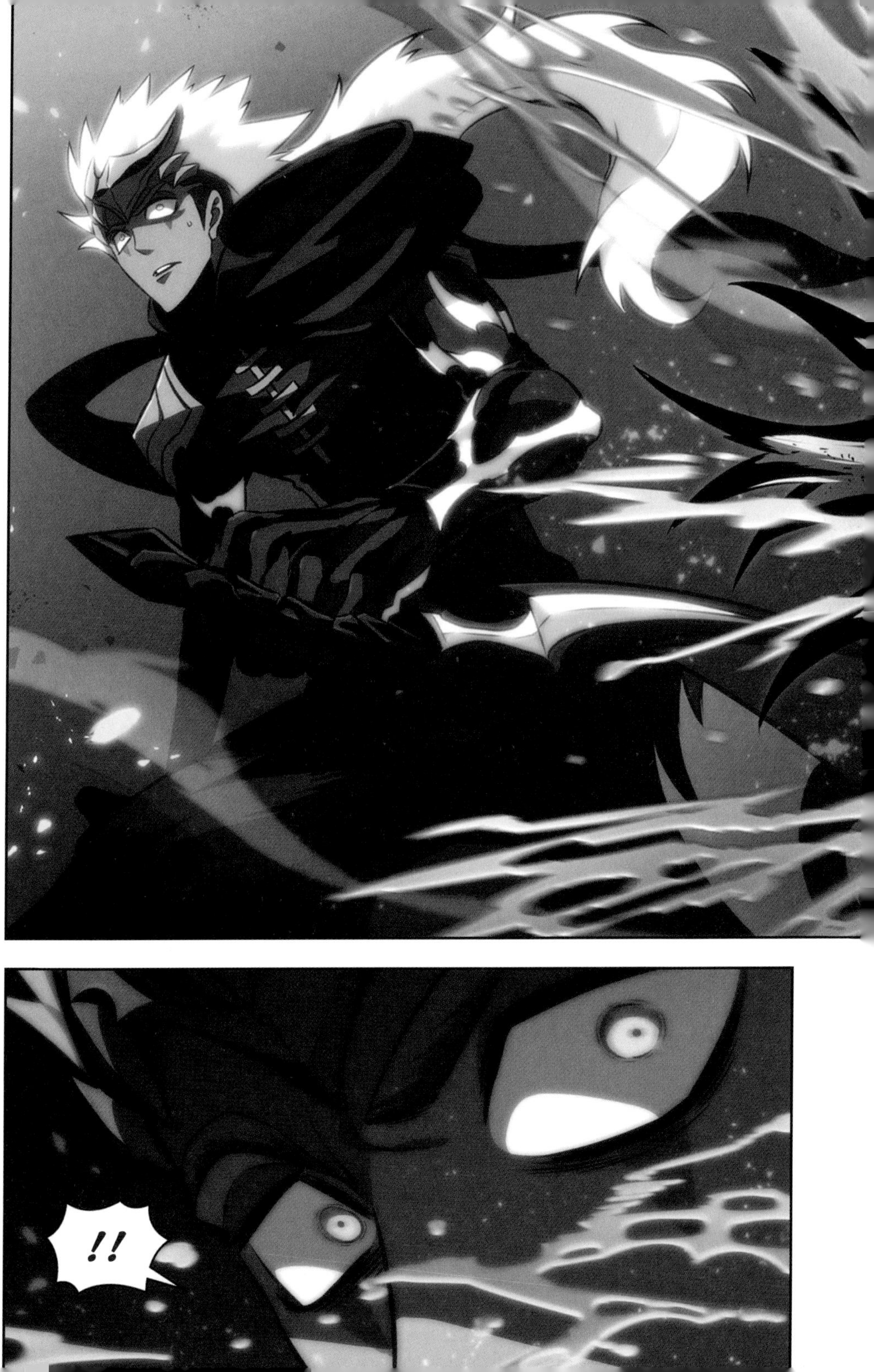
!!

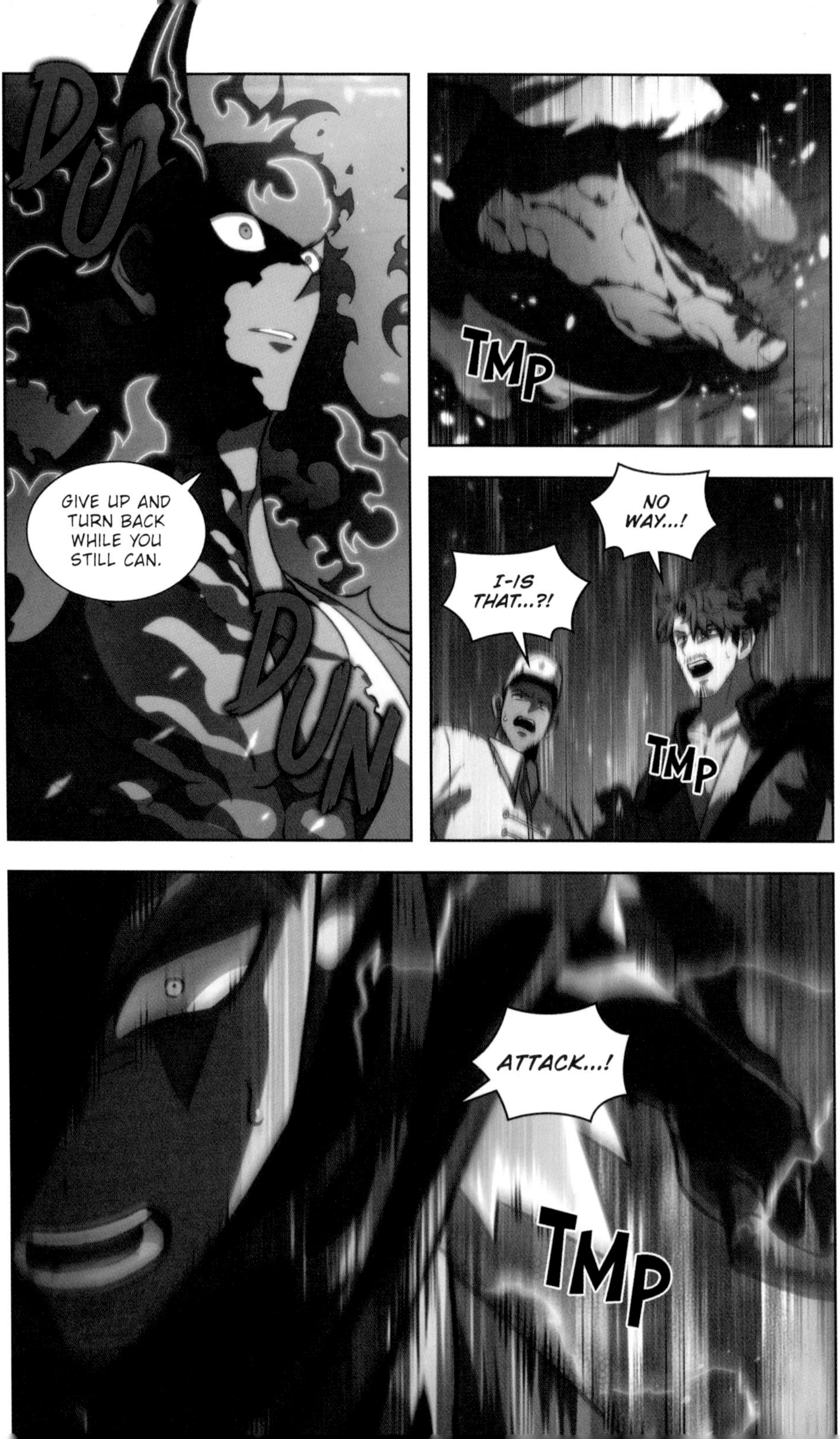
DU
GIVE UP AND TURN BACK WHILE YOU STILL CAN.
DUN
TMP
NO WAY...!
I-IS THAT...?!
TMP
ATTACK...!
TMP

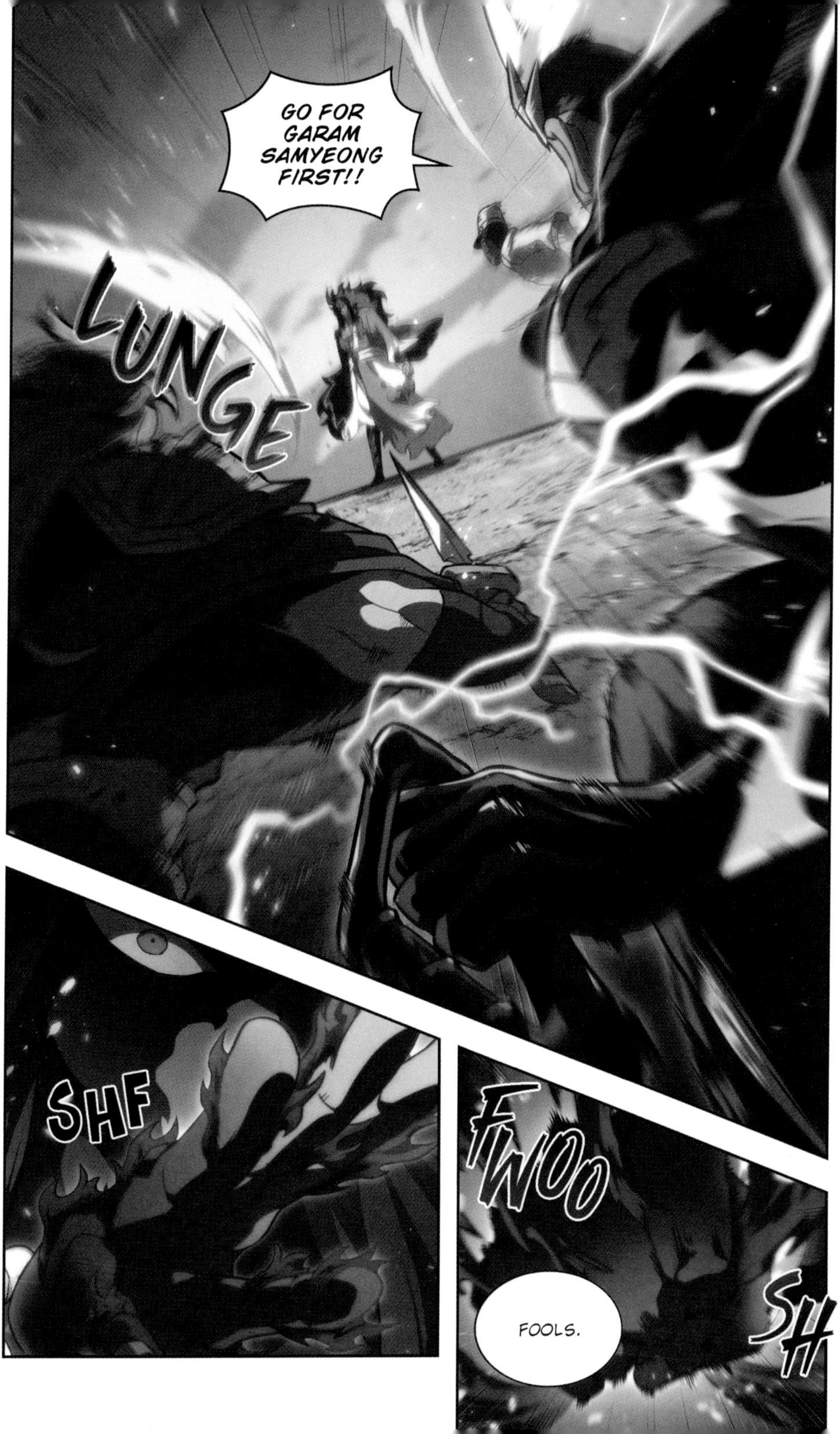
GO FOR GARAM SAMYEONG FIRST!!
LUNGE
SHF
FWOO
FOOLS.
SH

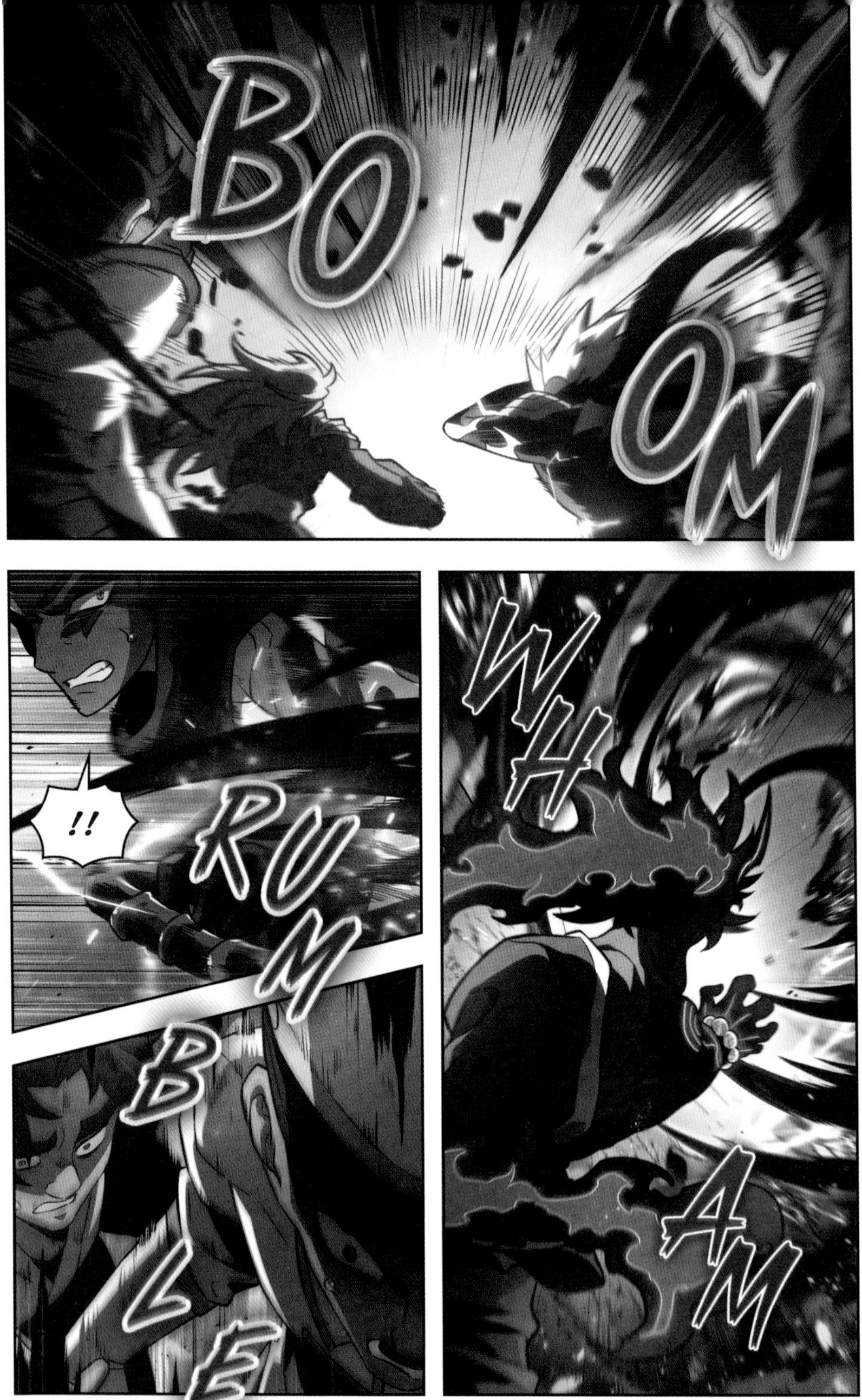
BOOM
!!
RUMBLE
WHAM

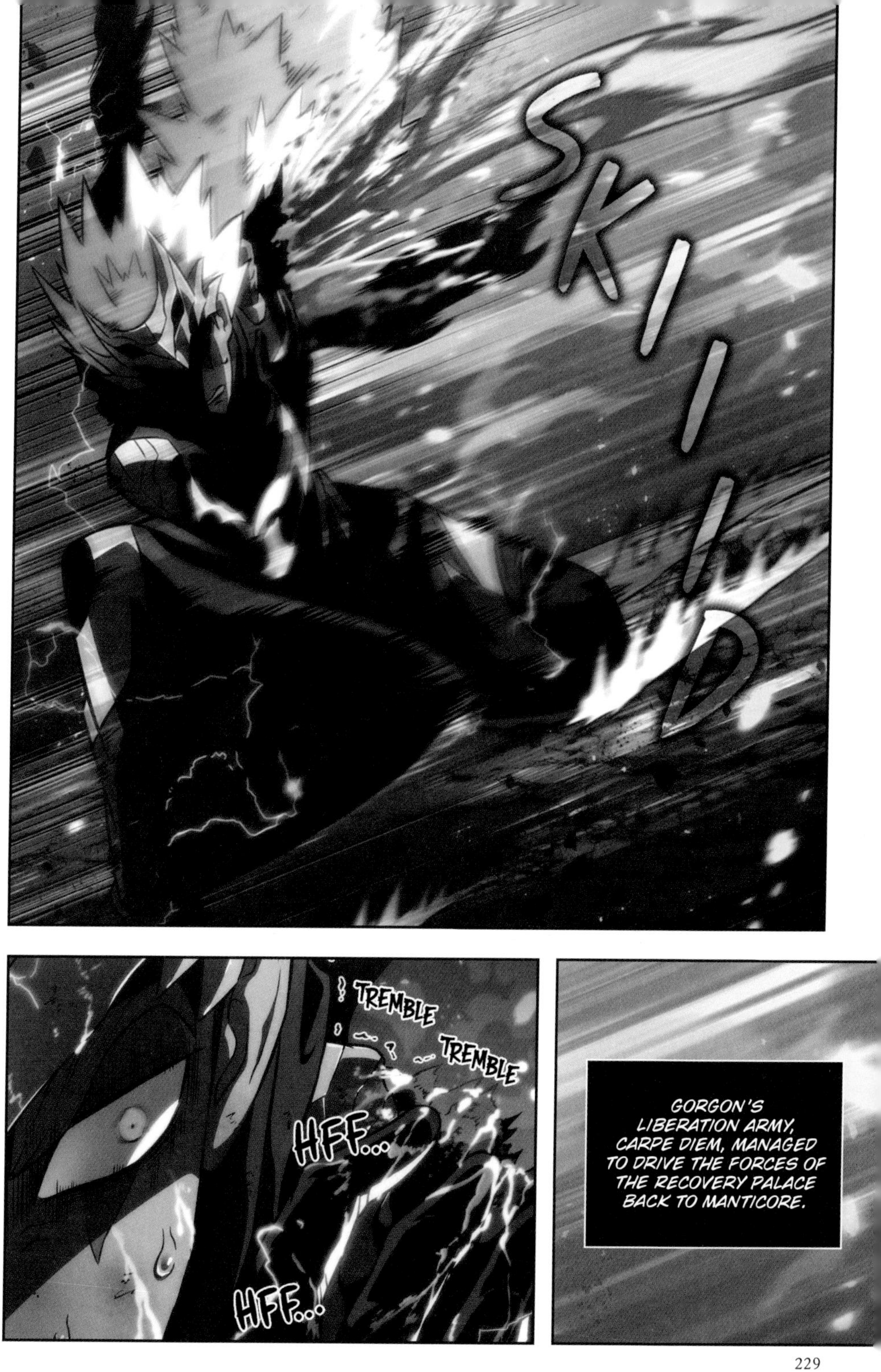
SKIIID
TREMBLE
TREMBLE
HFF...
HFF...
GORGON'S LIBERATION ARMY, CARPE DIEM, MANAGED TO DRIVE THE FORCES OF THE RECOVERY PALACE BACK TO MANTICORE.

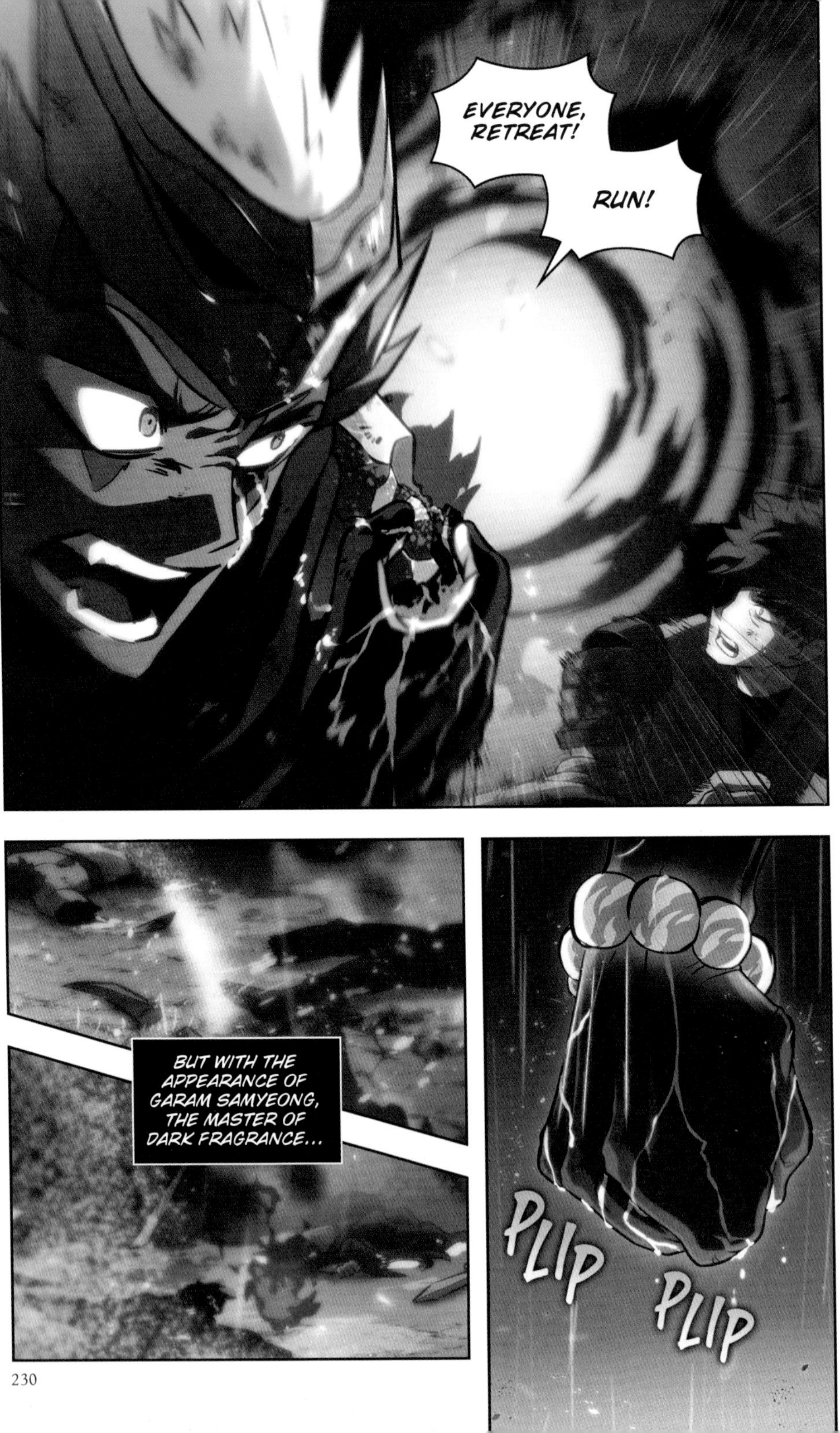
EVERYONE, RETREAT!
RUN!
BUT WITH THE APPEARANCE OF GARAM SAMYEONG, THE MASTER OF DARK FRAGRANCE...
PLIP
PLIP

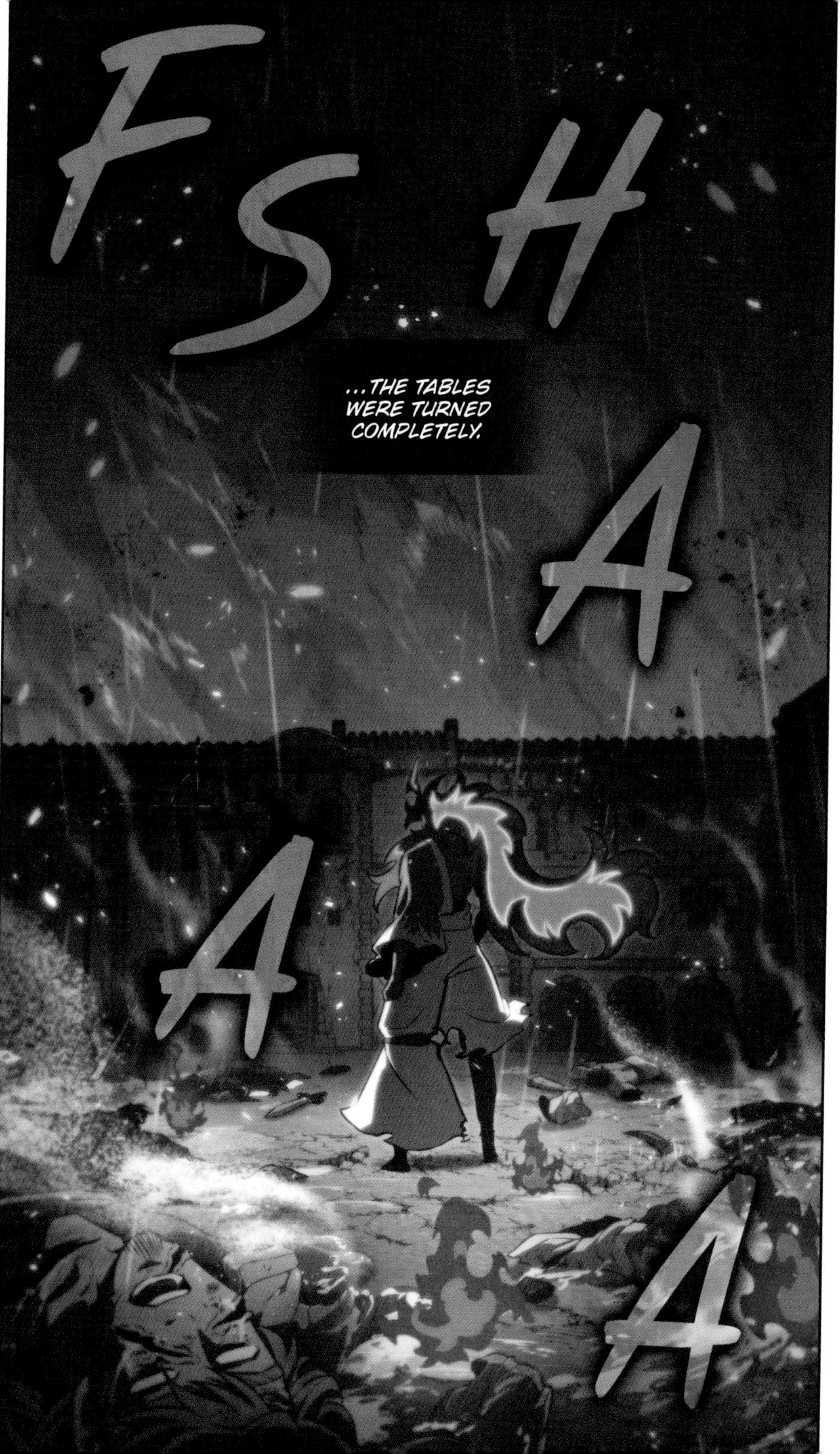
FSHAAA
...THE TABLES WERE TURNED COMPLETELY.

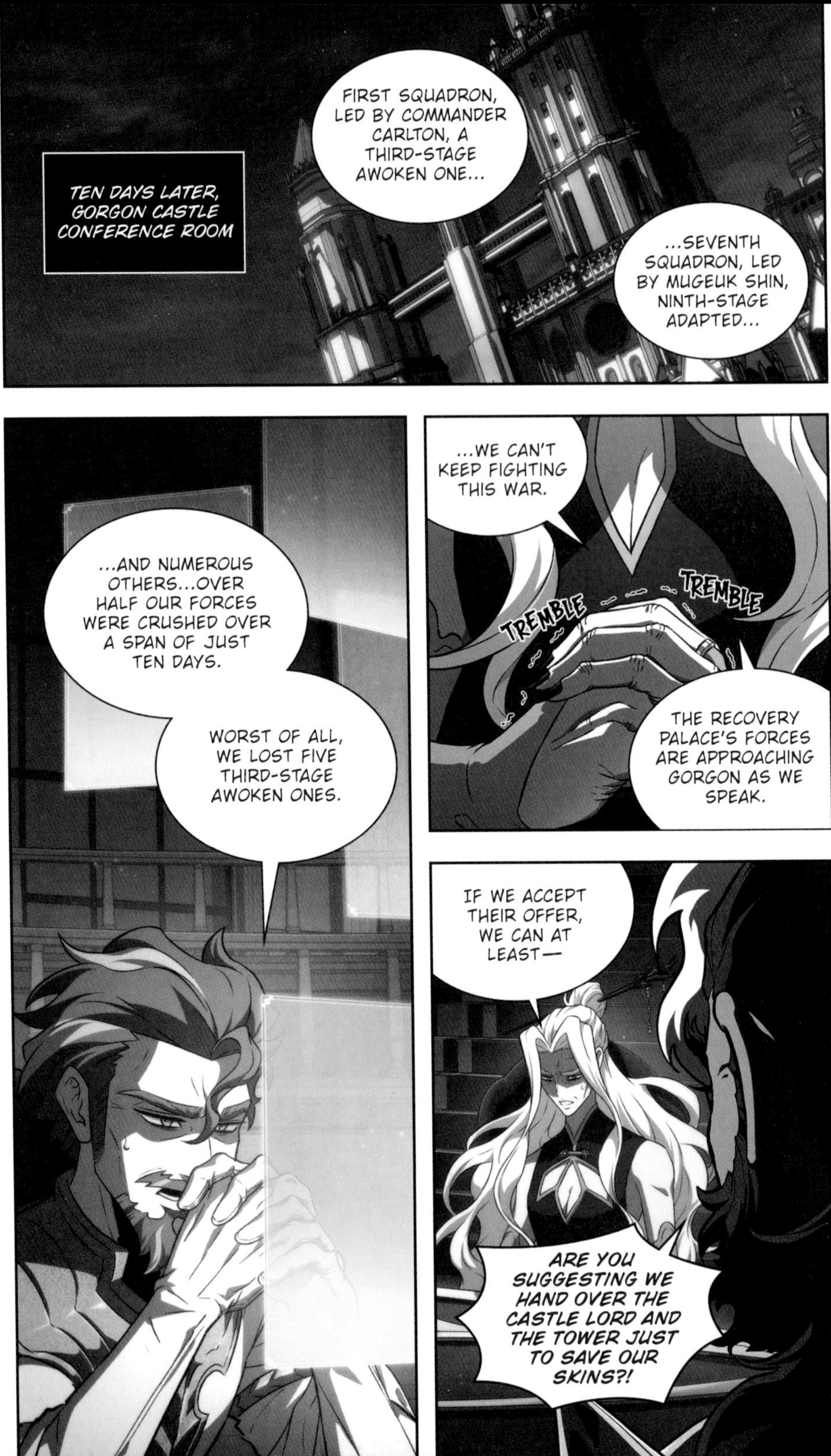
TEN DAYS LATER, GORGON CASTLE CONFERENCE ROOM
FIRST SQUADRON, LED BY COMMANDER CARLTON, A THIRD-STAGE AWOKEN ONE...
...SEVENTH SQUADRON, LED BY MUGEUK SHIN, NINTH-STAGE ADAPTED...
...AND NUMEROUS OTHERS...OVER HALF OUR FORCES WERE CRUSHED OVER A SPAN OF JUST TEN DAYS.
WORST OF ALL, WE LOST FIVE THIRD-STAGE AWOKEN ONES.
...WE CAN'T KEEP FIGHTING THIS WAR.
TREMBLE
TREMBLE
THE RECOVERY PALACE'S FORCES ARE APPROACHING GORGON AS WE SPEAK.
IF WE ACCEPT THEIR OFFER, WE CAN AT LEAST—
ARE YOU SUGGESTING WE HAND OVER THE CASTLE LORD AND THE TOWER JUST TO SAVE OUR SKINS?!

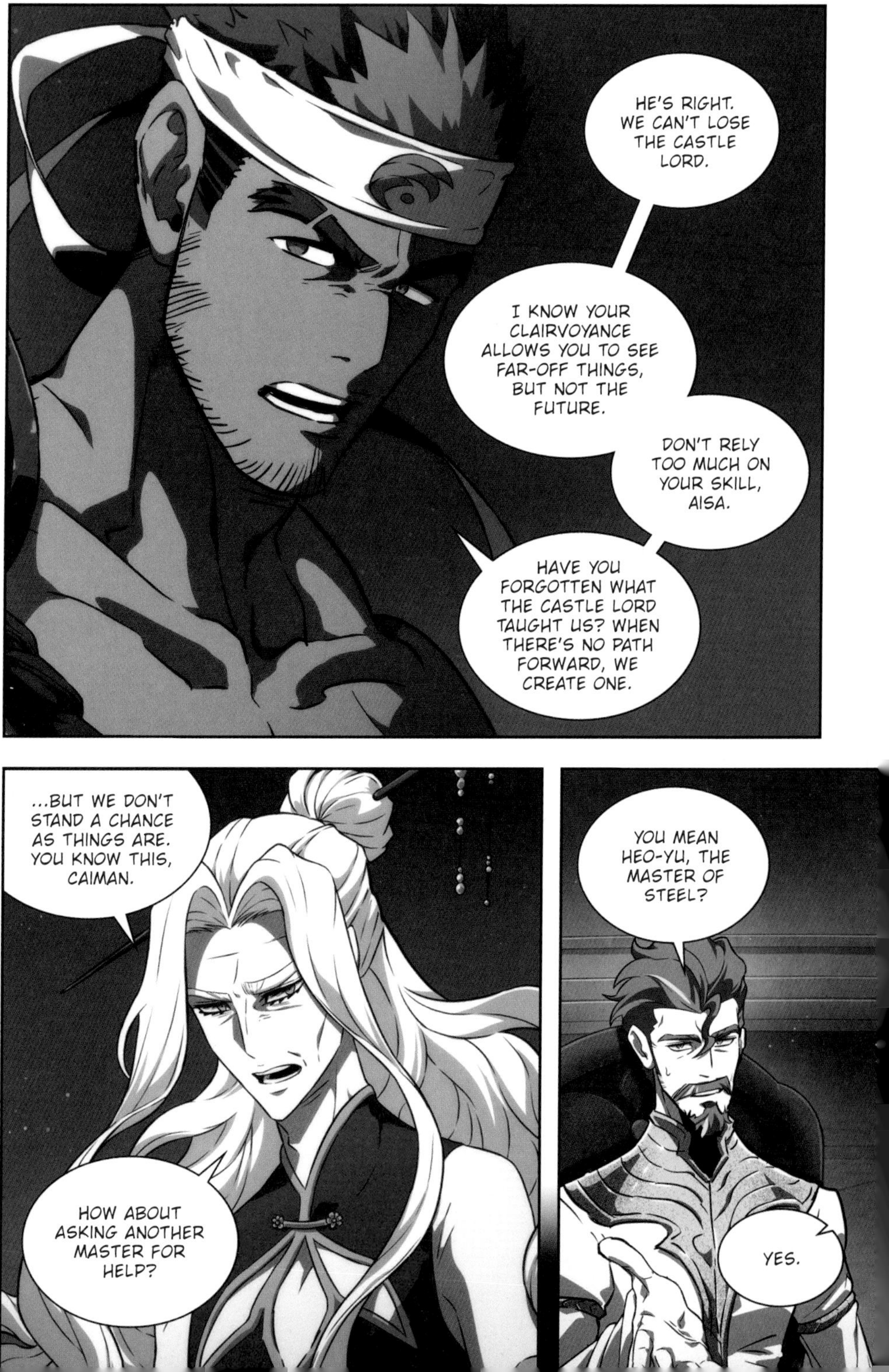
HE'S RIGHT. WE CAN'T LOSE THE CASTLE LORD.
I KNOW YOUR CLAIRVOYANCE ALLOWS YOU TO SEE FAR-OFF THINGS, BUT NOT THE FUTURE.
DON'T RELY TOO MUCH ON YOUR SKILL, AISA.
HAVE YOU FORGOTTEN WHAT THE CASTLE LORD TAUGHT US? WHEN THERE'S NO PATH FORWARD, WE CREATE ONE.
...BUT WE DON'T STAND A CHANCE AS THINGS ARE. YOU KNOW THIS, CAIMAN.
HOW ABOUT ASKING ANOTHER MASTER FOR HELP?
YOU MEAN HEO-YU, THE MASTER OF STEEL?
YES.

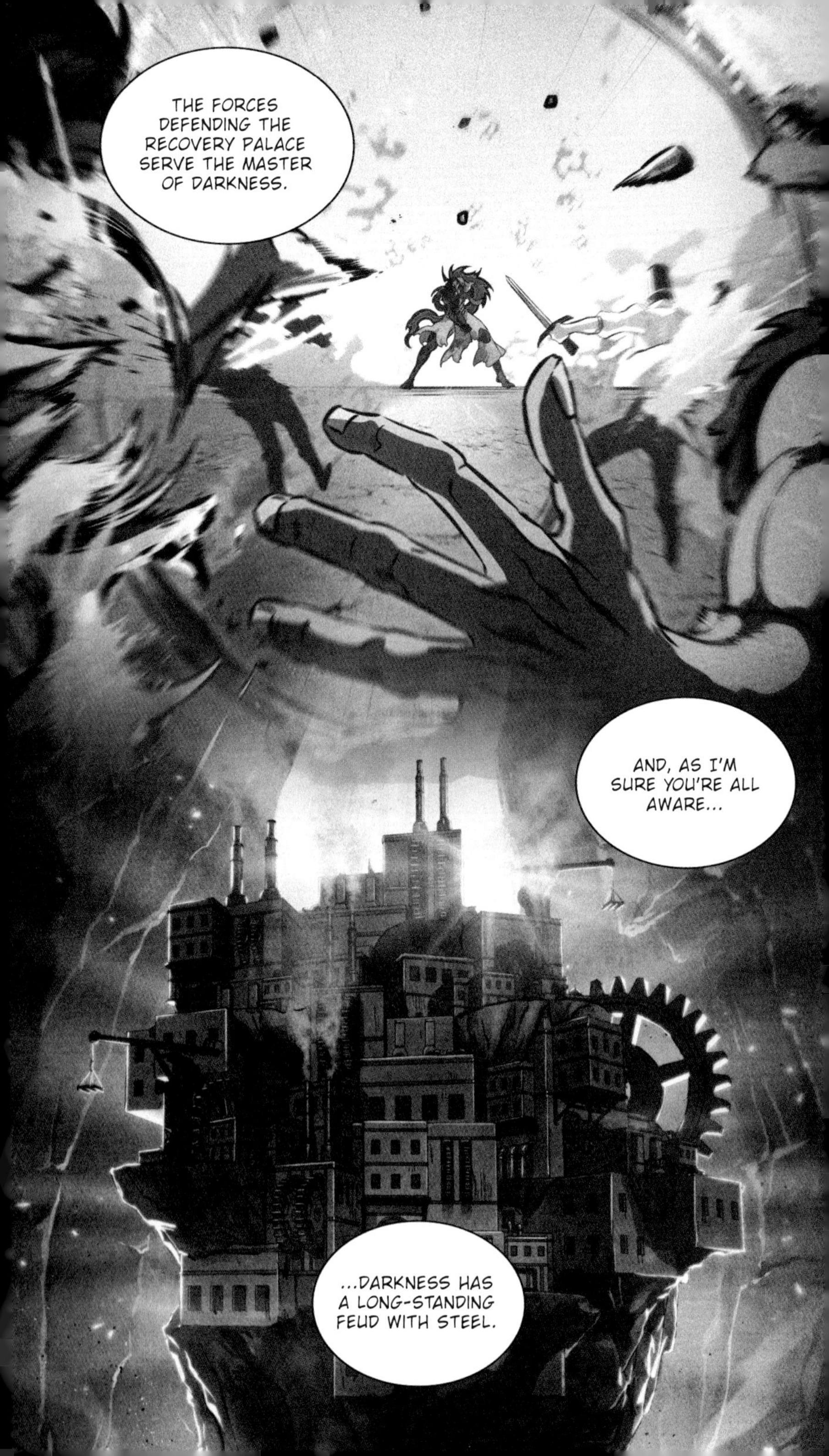
THE FORCES DEFENDING THE RECOVERY PALACE SERVE THE MASTER OF DARKNESS.
AND, AS I'M SURE YOU'RE ALL AWARE...
...DARKNESS HAS A LONG-STANDING FEUD WITH STEEL.

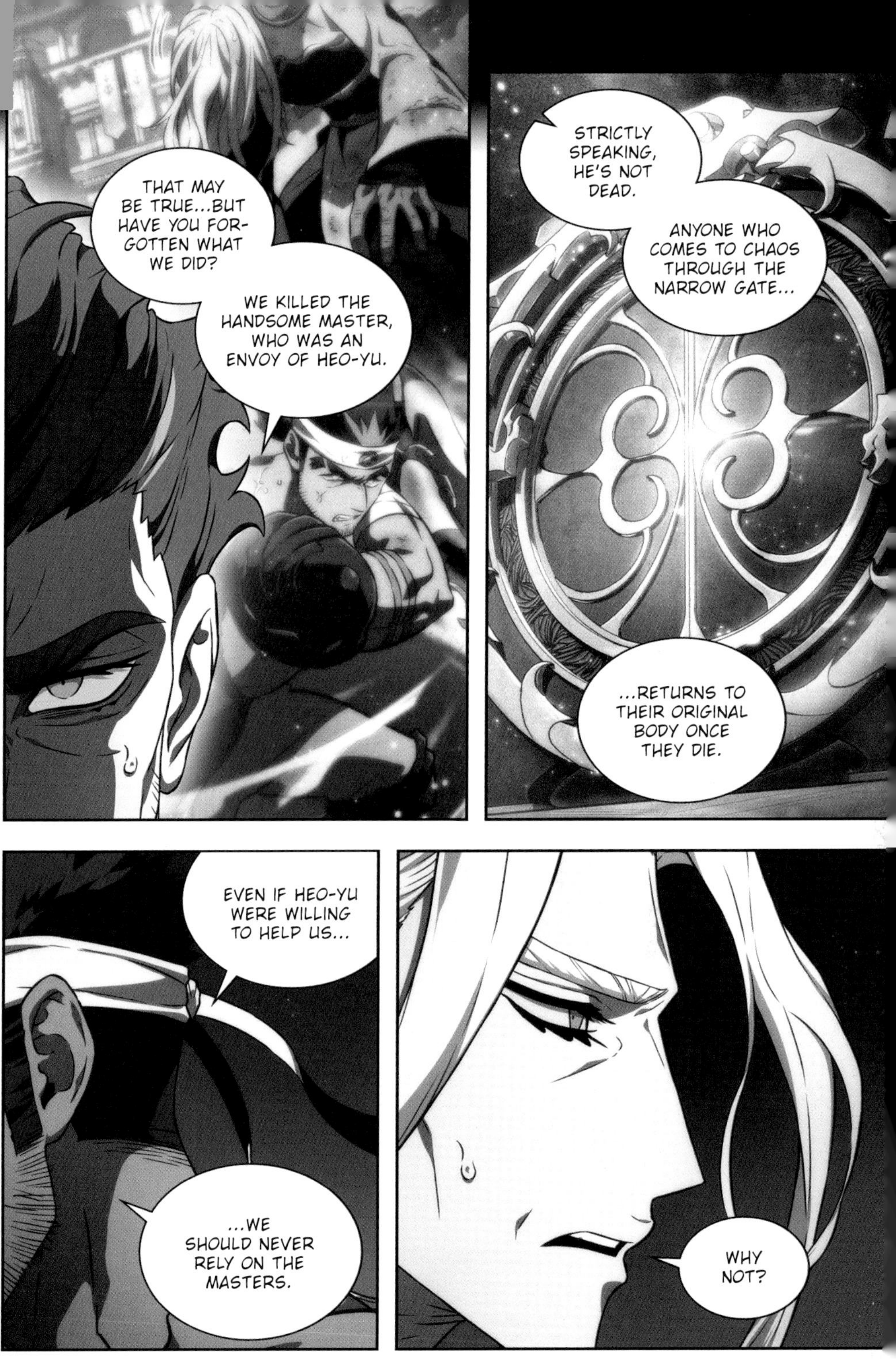
THAT MAY BE TRUE...BUT HAVE YOU FOR-GOTTEN WHAT WE DID?
WE KILLED THE HANDSOME MASTER, WHO WAS AN ENVOY OF HEO-YU.
STRICTLY SPEAKING, HE'S NOT DEAD.
ANYONE WHO COMES TO CHAOS THROUGH THE NARROW GATE...
...RETURNS TO THEIR ORIGINAL BODY ONCE THEY DIE.
EVEN IF HEO-YU WERE WILLING TO HELP US...
...WE SHOULD NEVER RELY ON THE MASTERS.
WHY NOT?

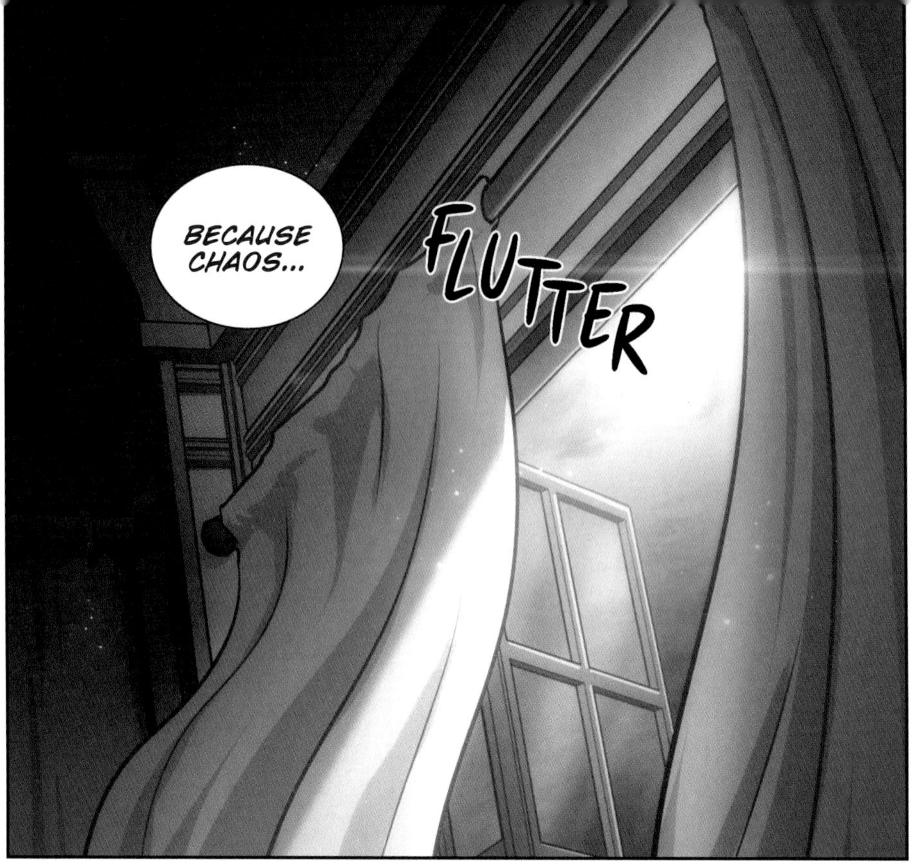
BECAUSE CHAOS...
FLUTTER

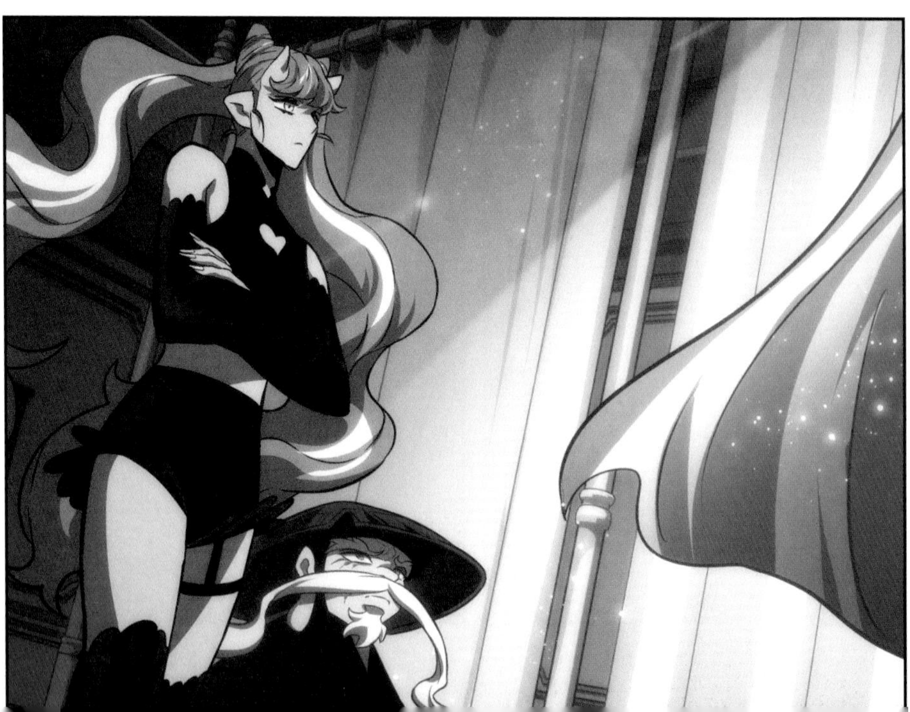

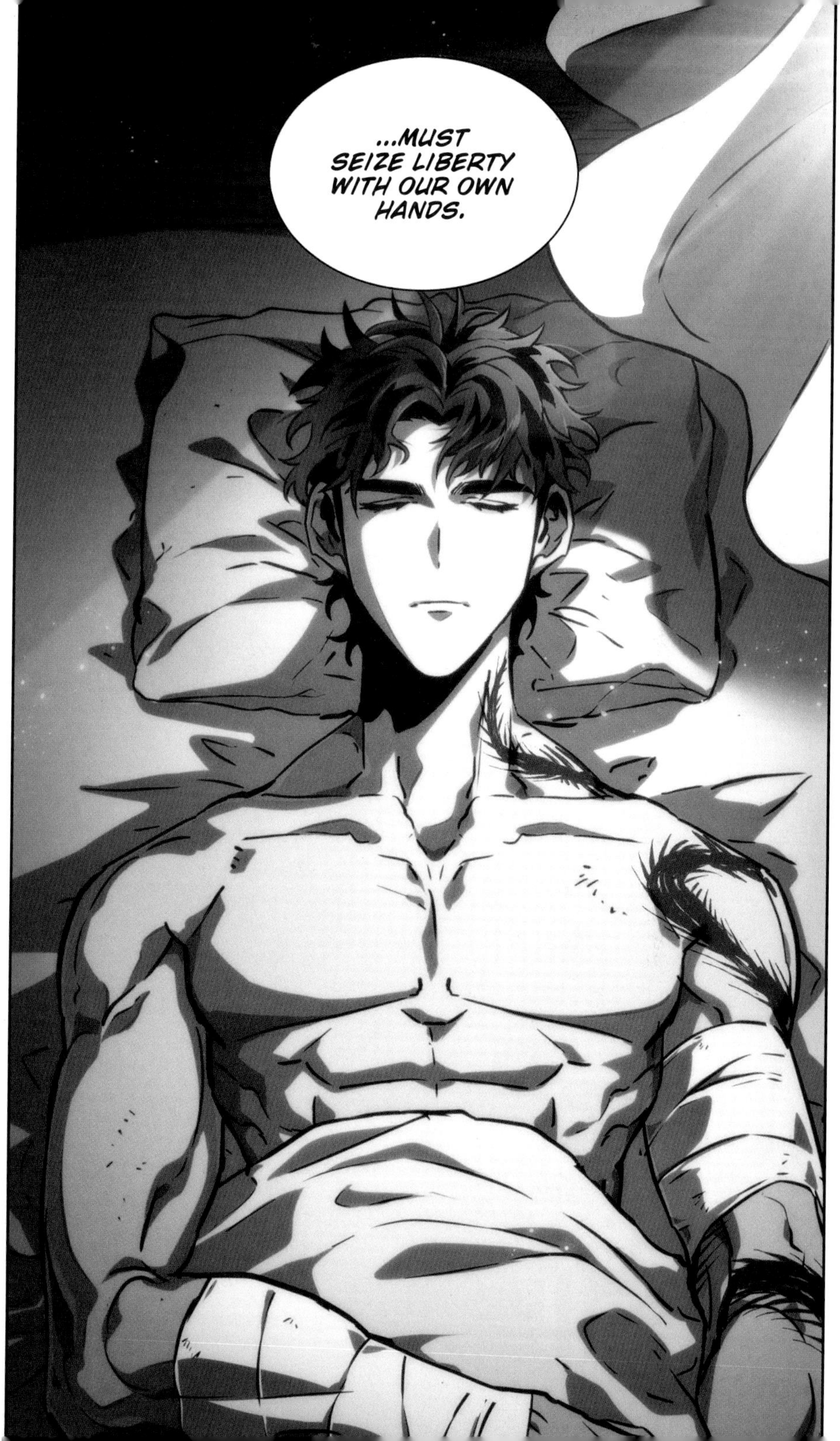
...MUST SEIZE LIBERTY WITH OUR OWN HANDS.

The World After the Fall

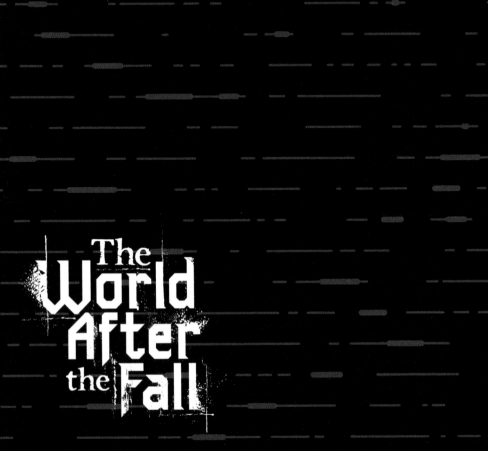

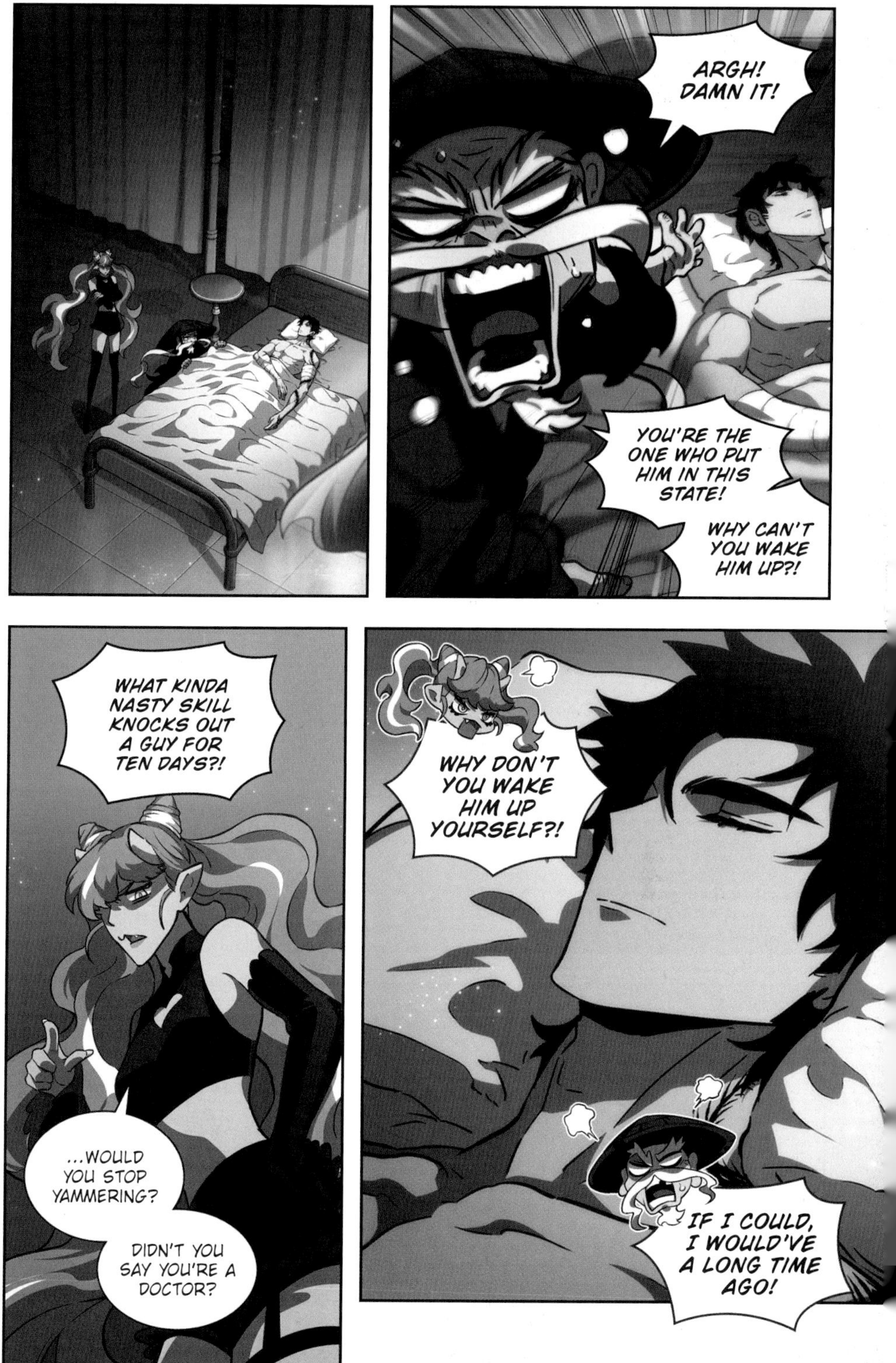
ARGH! DAMN IT!
YOU'RE THE ONE WHO PUT HIM IN THIS STATE!
WHY CAN'T YOU WAKE HIM UP?!
WHAT KINDA NASTY SKILL KNOCKS OUT A GUY FOR TEN DAYS?!
...WOULD YOU STOP YAMMERING?
DIDN'T YOU SAY YOU'RE A DOCTOR?
WHY DON'T YOU WAKE HIM UP YOURSELF?!
IF I COULD, I WOULD'VE A LONG TIME AGO!

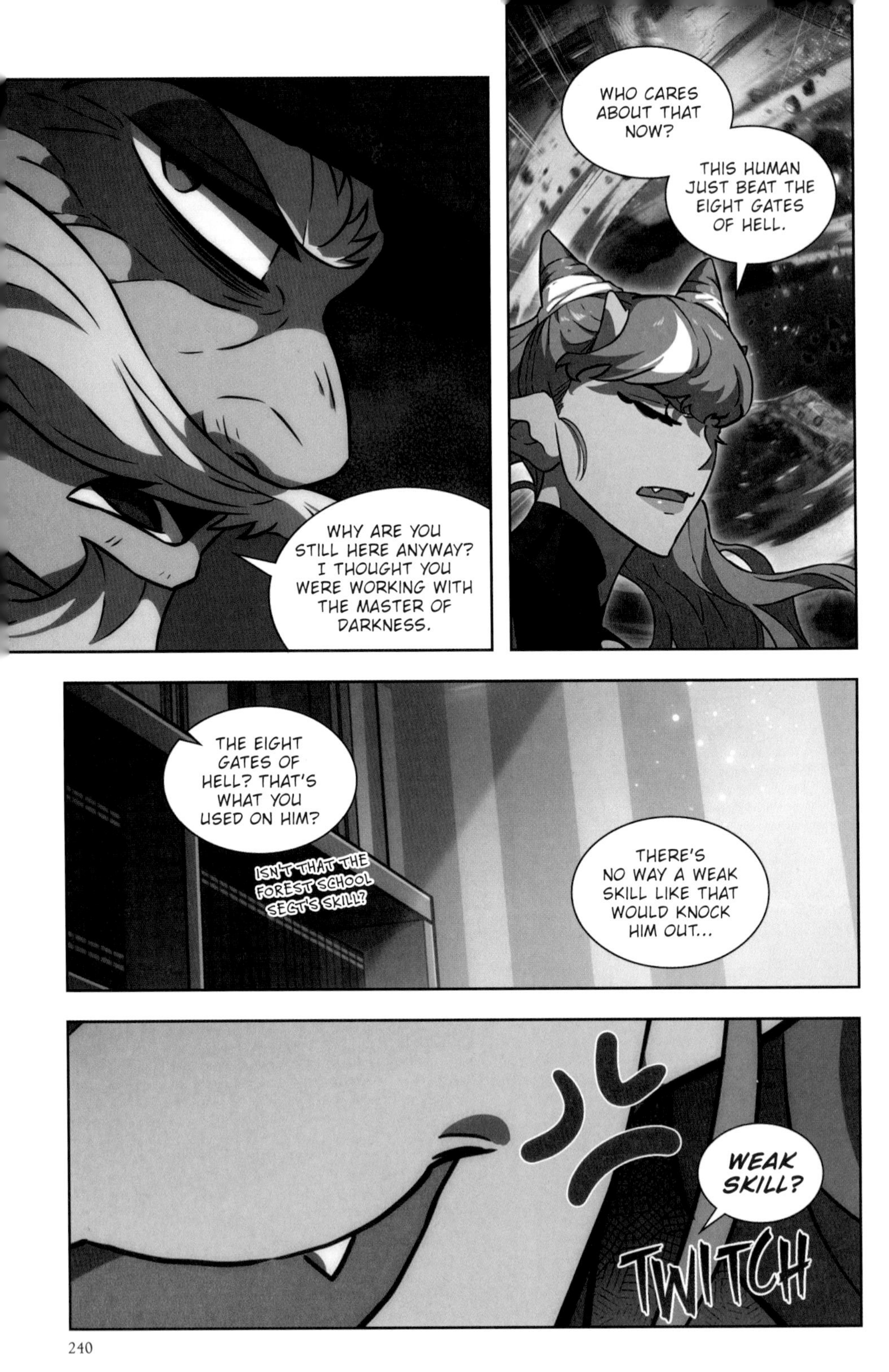
WHY ARE YOU STILL HERE ANYWAY? I THOUGHT YOU WERE WORKING WITH THE MASTER OF DARKNESS.
WHO CARES ABOUT THAT NOW?
THIS HUMAN JUST BEAT THE EIGHT GATES OF HELL.
THE EIGHT GATES OF HELL? THAT'S WHAT YOU USED ON HIM?
ISN'T THAT THE FOREST SCHOOL SECT'S SKILL?
THERE'S NO WAY A WEAK SKILL LIKE THAT WOULD KNOCK HIM OUT...
WEAK SKILL?
TWITCH

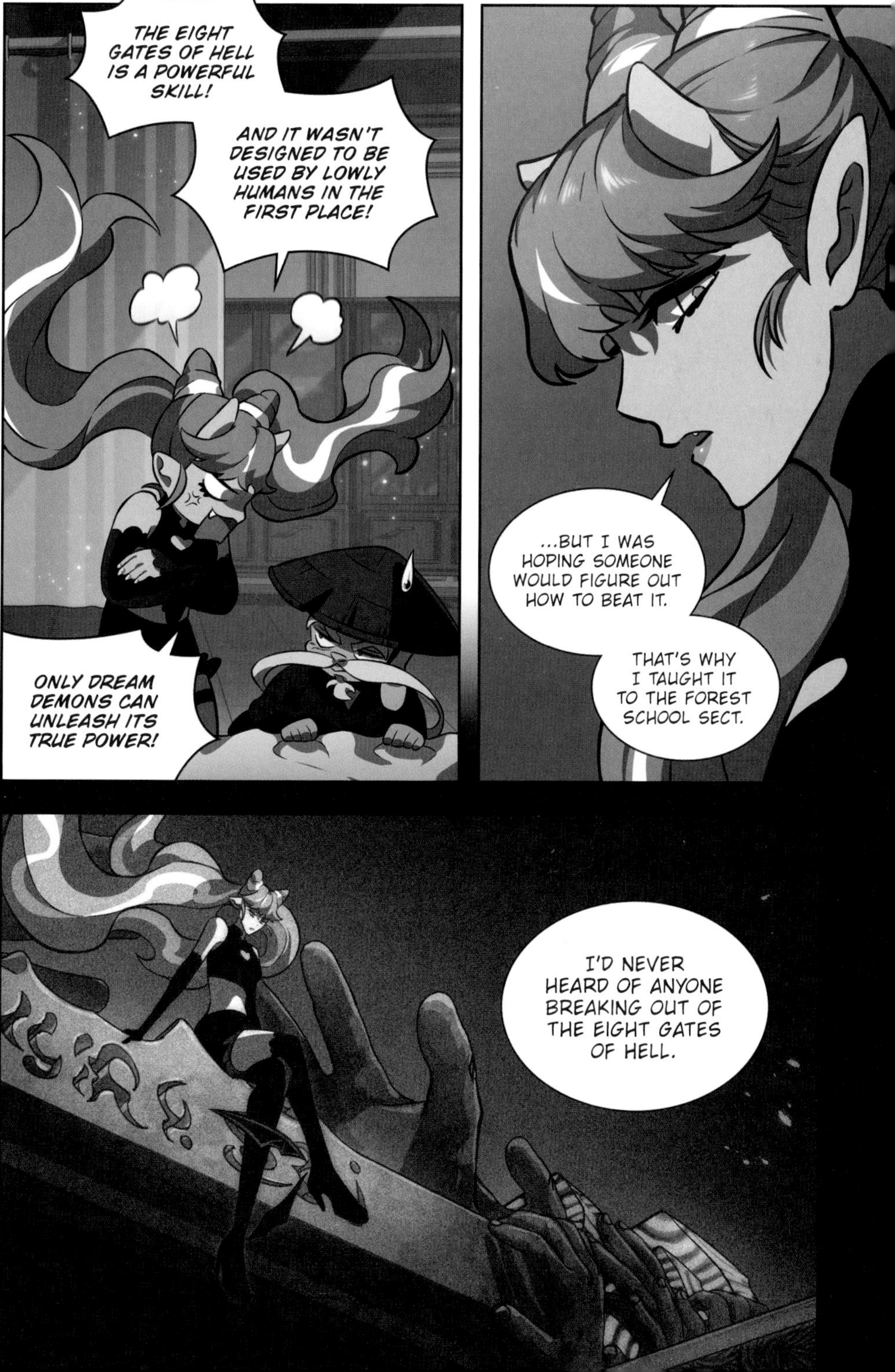
THE EIGHT GATES OF HELL IS A POWERFUL SKILL!
AND IT WASN'T DESIGNED TO BE USED BY LOWLY HUMANS IN THE FIRST PLACE!
ONLY DREAM DEMONS CAN UNLEASH ITS TRUE POWER!
...BUT I WAS HOPING SOMEONE WOULD FIGURE OUT HOW TO BEAT IT.
THAT'S WHY I TAUGHT IT TO THE FOREST SCHOOL SECT.
I'D NEVER HEARD OF ANYONE BREAKING OUT OF THE EIGHT GATES OF HELL.

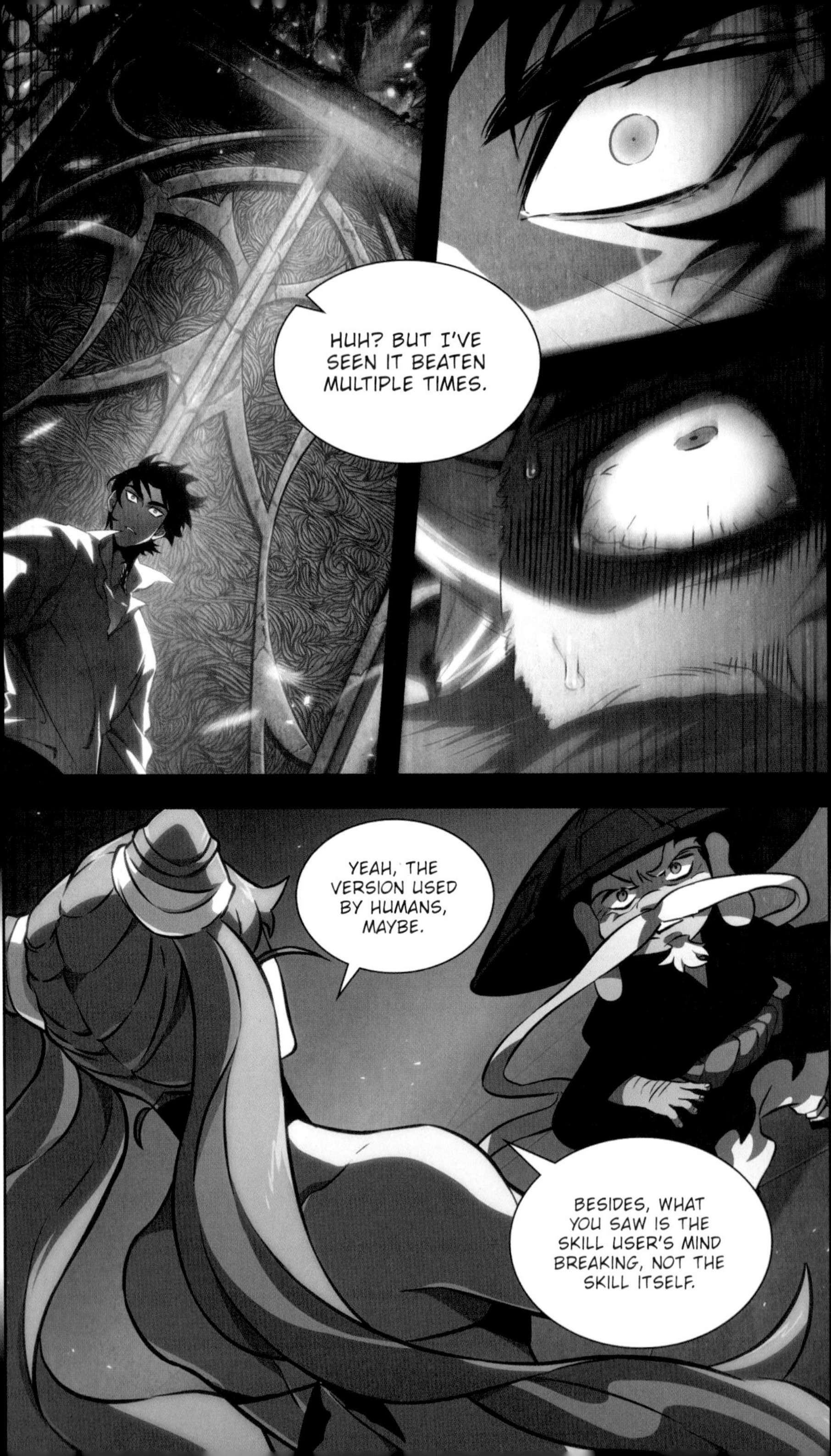
HUH? BUT I'VE SEEN IT BEATEN MULTIPLE TIMES.
YEAH, THE VERSION USED BY HUMANS, MAYBE.
BESIDES, WHAT YOU SAW IS THE SKILL USER'S MIND BREAKING, NOT THE SKILL ITSELF.

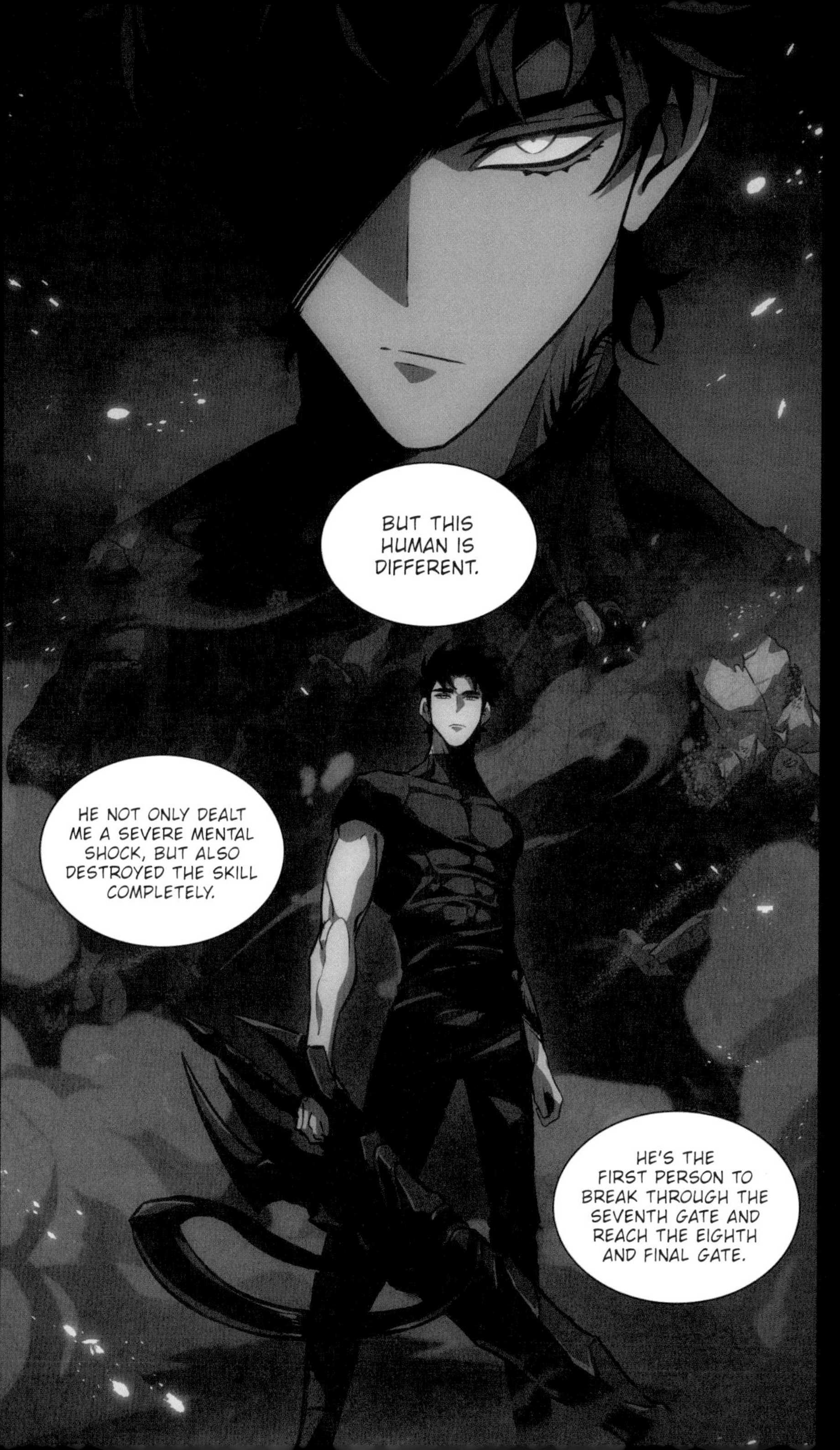
BUT THIS HUMAN IS DIFFERENT.
HE NOT ONLY DEALT ME A SEVERE MENTAL SHOCK, BUT ALSO DESTROYED THE SKILL COMPLETELY.
HE'S THE FIRST PERSON TO BREAK THROUGH THE SEVENTH GATE AND REACH THE EIGHTH AND FINAL GATE.

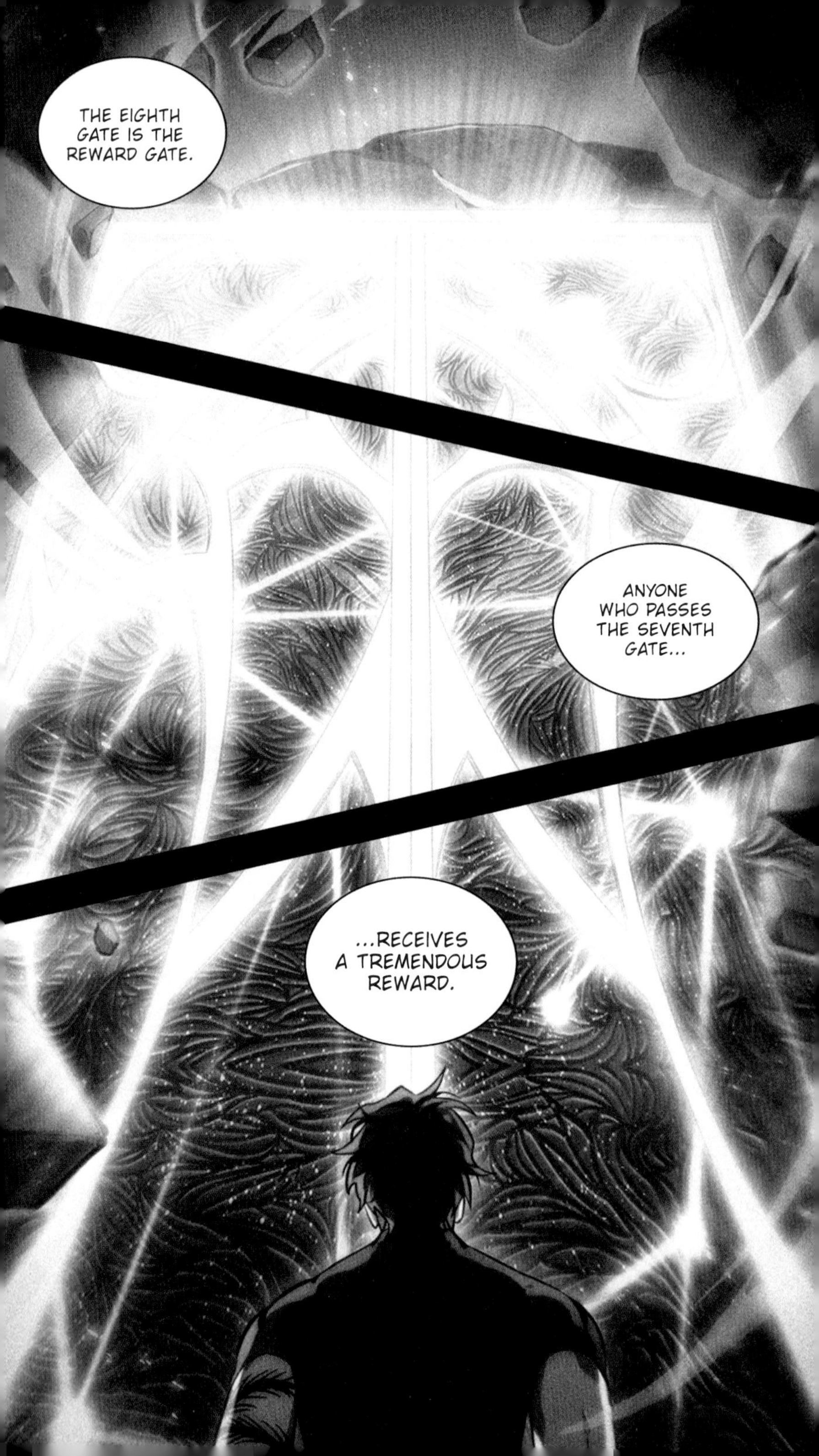
THE EIGHTH GATE IS THE REWARD GATE.
ANYONE WHO PASSES THE SEVENTH GATE...
...RECEIVES A TREMENDOUS REWARD.

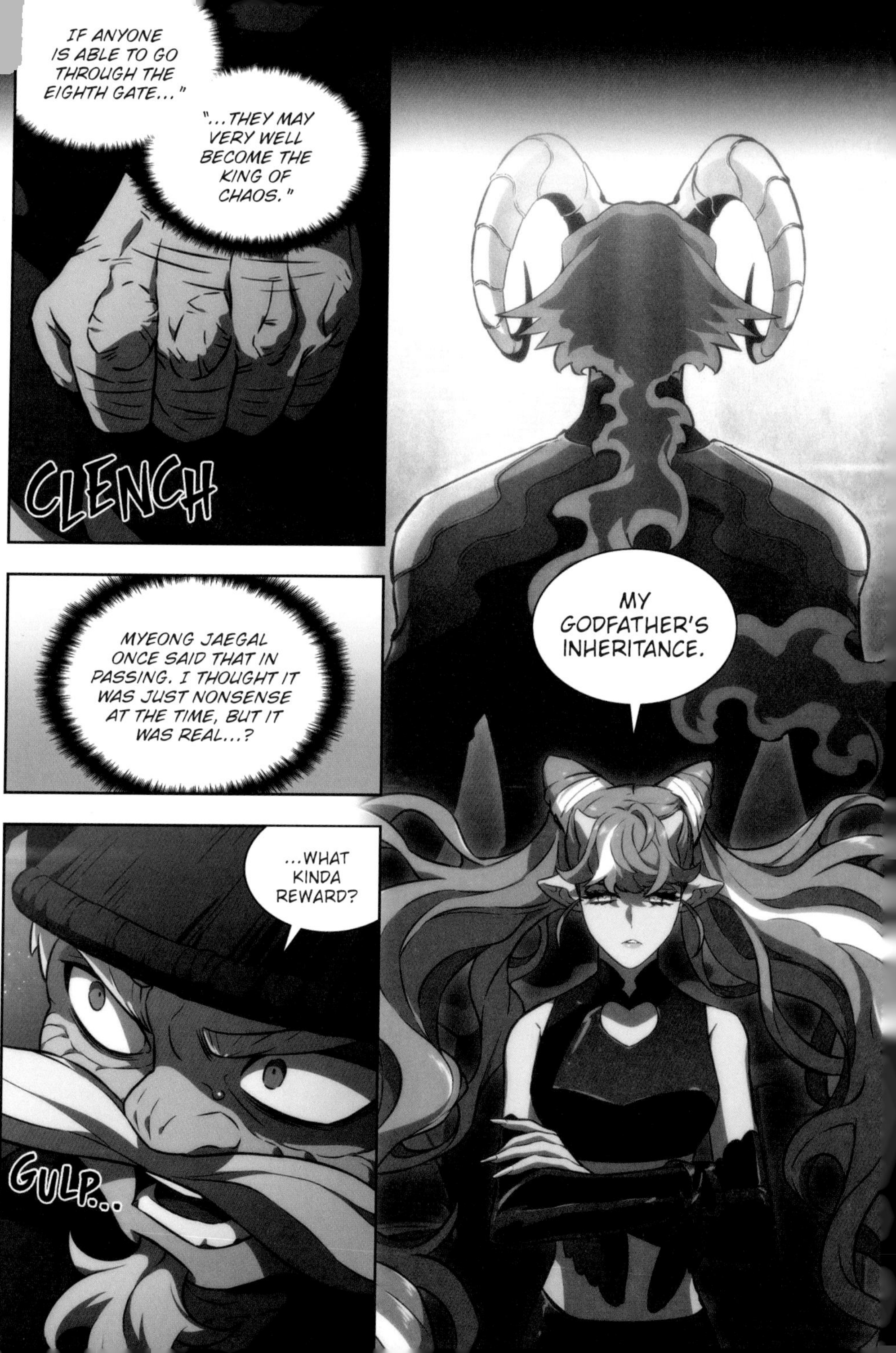
IF ANYONE IS ABLE TO GO THROUGH THE EIGHTH GATE..."
"...THEY MAY VERY WELL BECOME THE KING OF CHAOS."
CLENCH
MY GODFATHER'S INHERITANCE.
MYEONG JAEGAL ONCE SAID THAT IN PASSING. I THOUGHT IT WAS JUST NONSENSE AT THE TIME, BUT IT WAS REAL...?
...WHAT KINDA REWARD?
GULP...

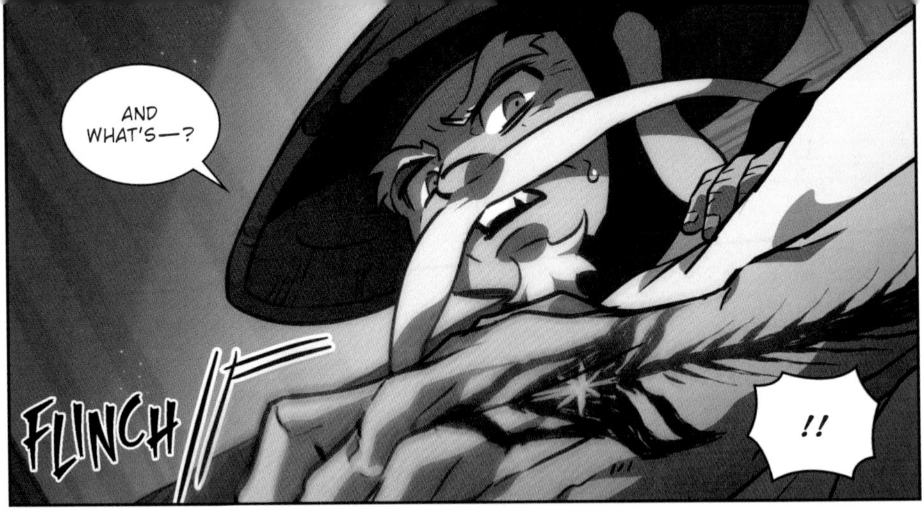
AND WHAT'S—?
FLINCH
!!

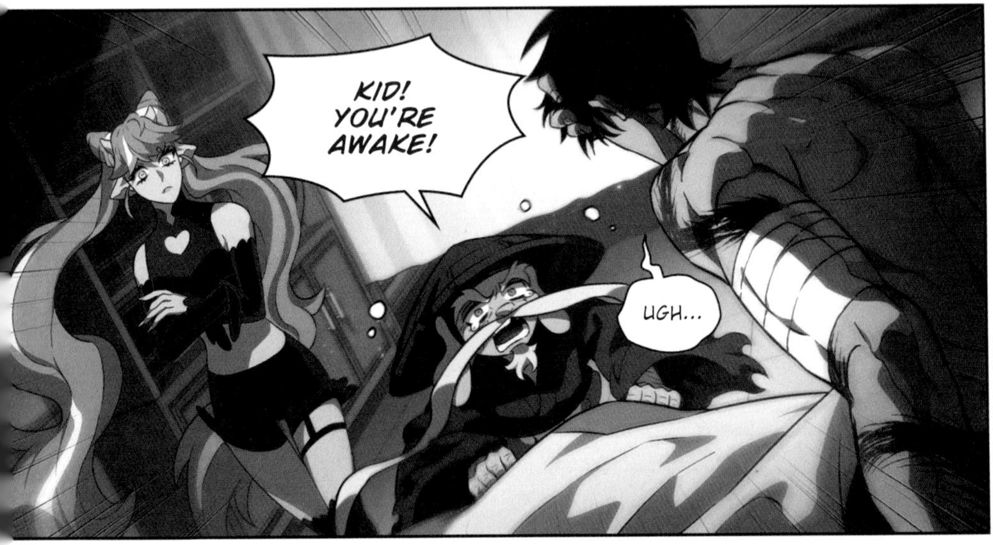
KID! YOU'RE AWAKE!
UGH...

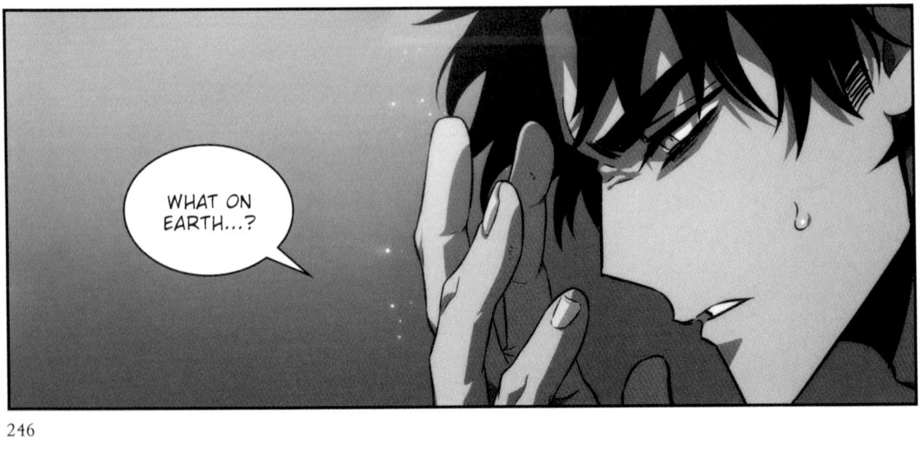
WHAT ON EARTH...?

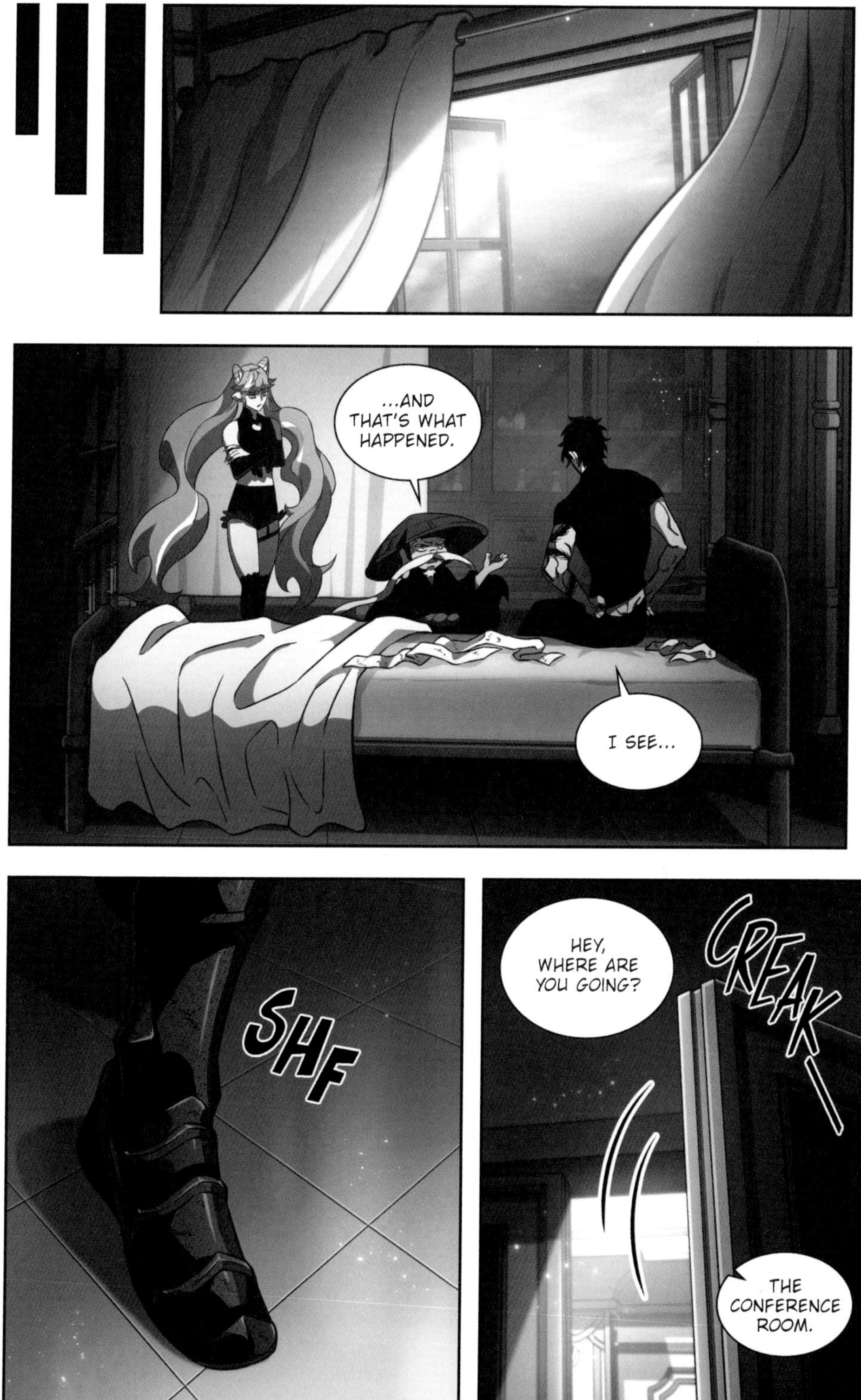
...AND THAT'S WHAT HAPPENED.
I SEE...
SHF
HEY, WHERE ARE YOU GOING?
CREAK
THE CONFERENCE ROOM.

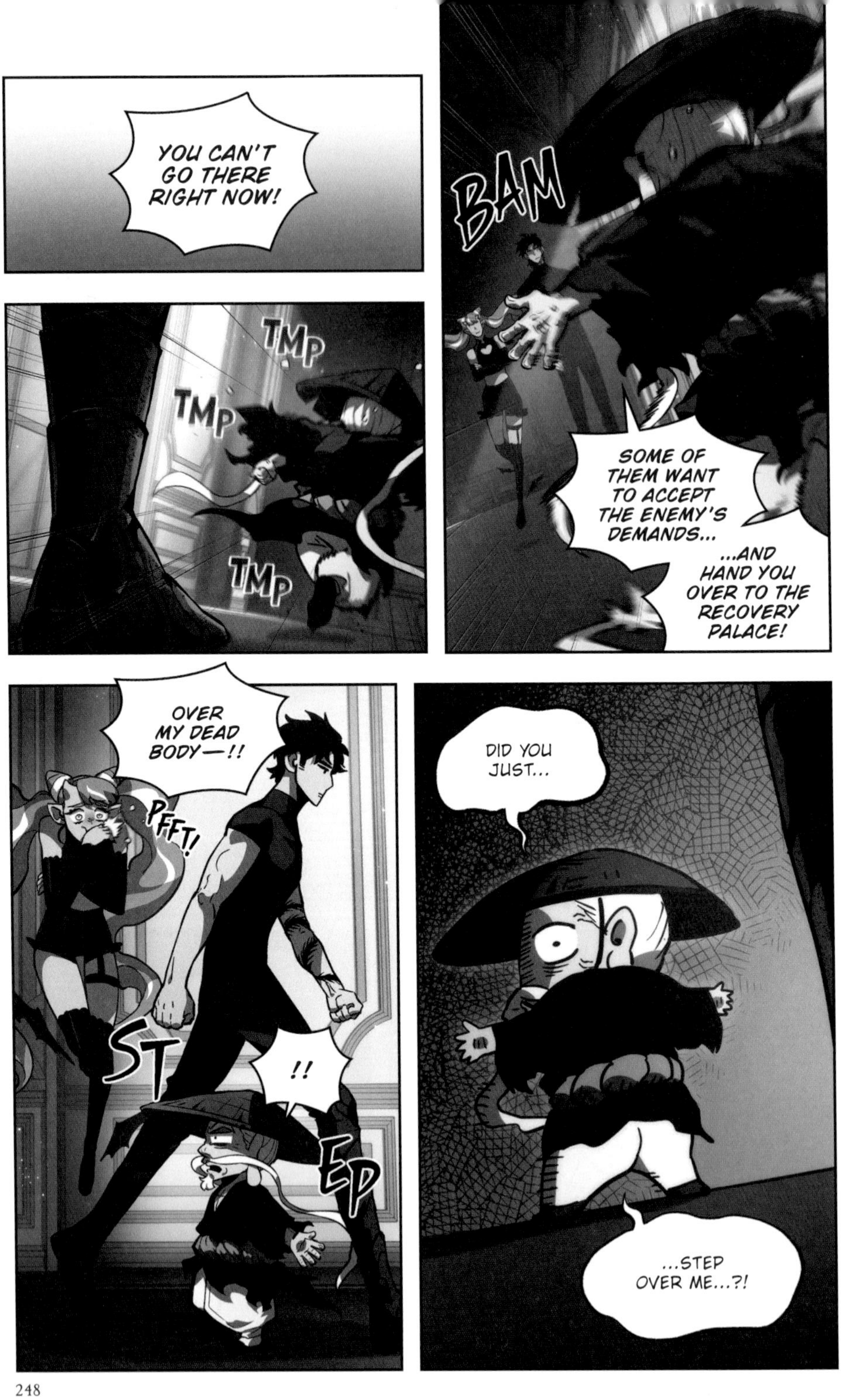

YOU CAN'T GO THERE RIGHT NOW!
TMP
TMP
TMP
BAM
SOME OF THEM WANT TO ACCEPT THE ENEMY'S DEMANDS...
...AND HAND YOU OVER TO THE RECOVERY PALACE!
OVER MY DEAD BODY—!!
PFFT!
ST
!!
EP
DID YOU JUST...
...STEP OVER ME...?!

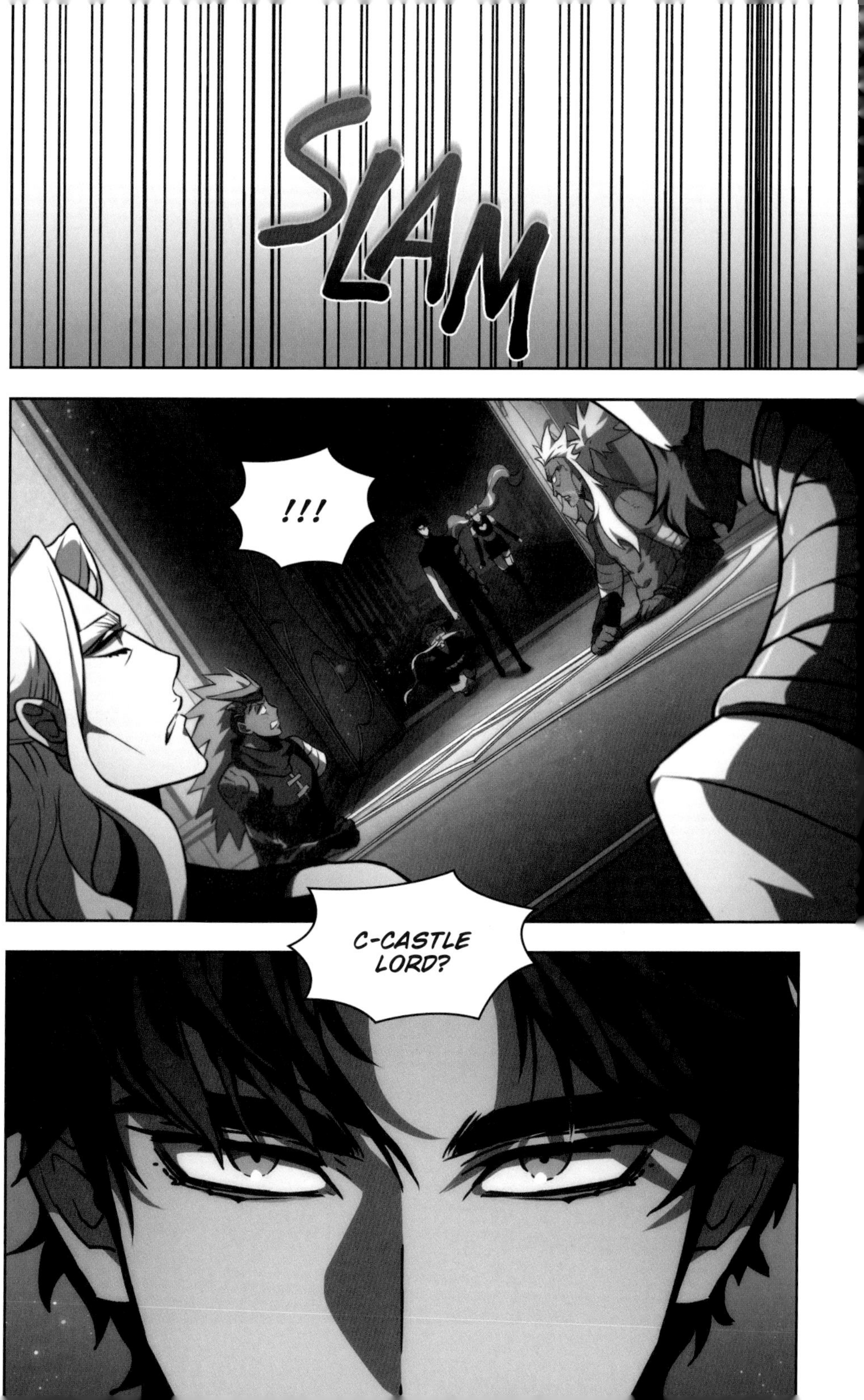
SLAM
!!!
C-CASTLE LORD?

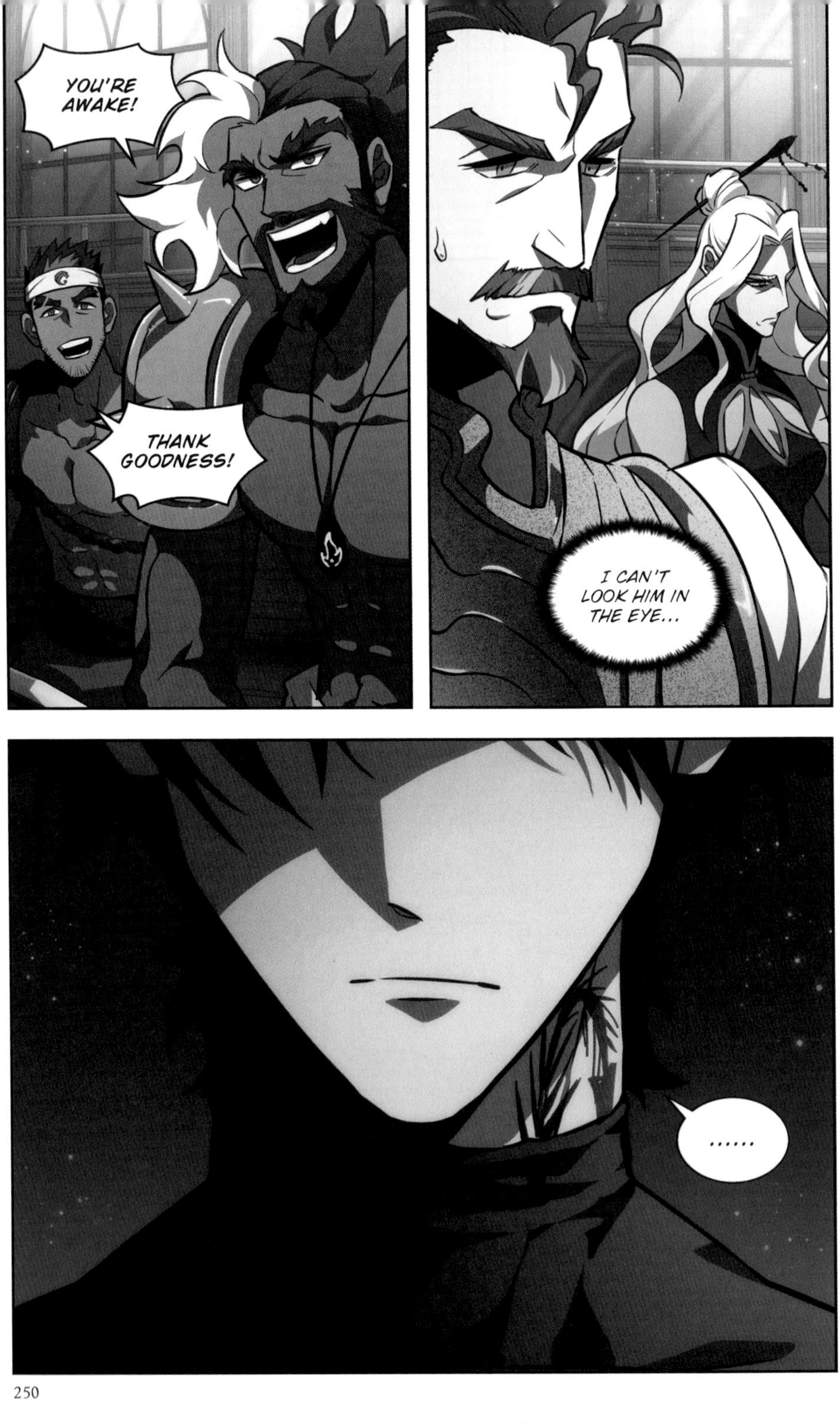
YOU'RE AWAKE!
THANK GOODNESS!
I CAN'T LOOK HIM IN THE EYE...
......

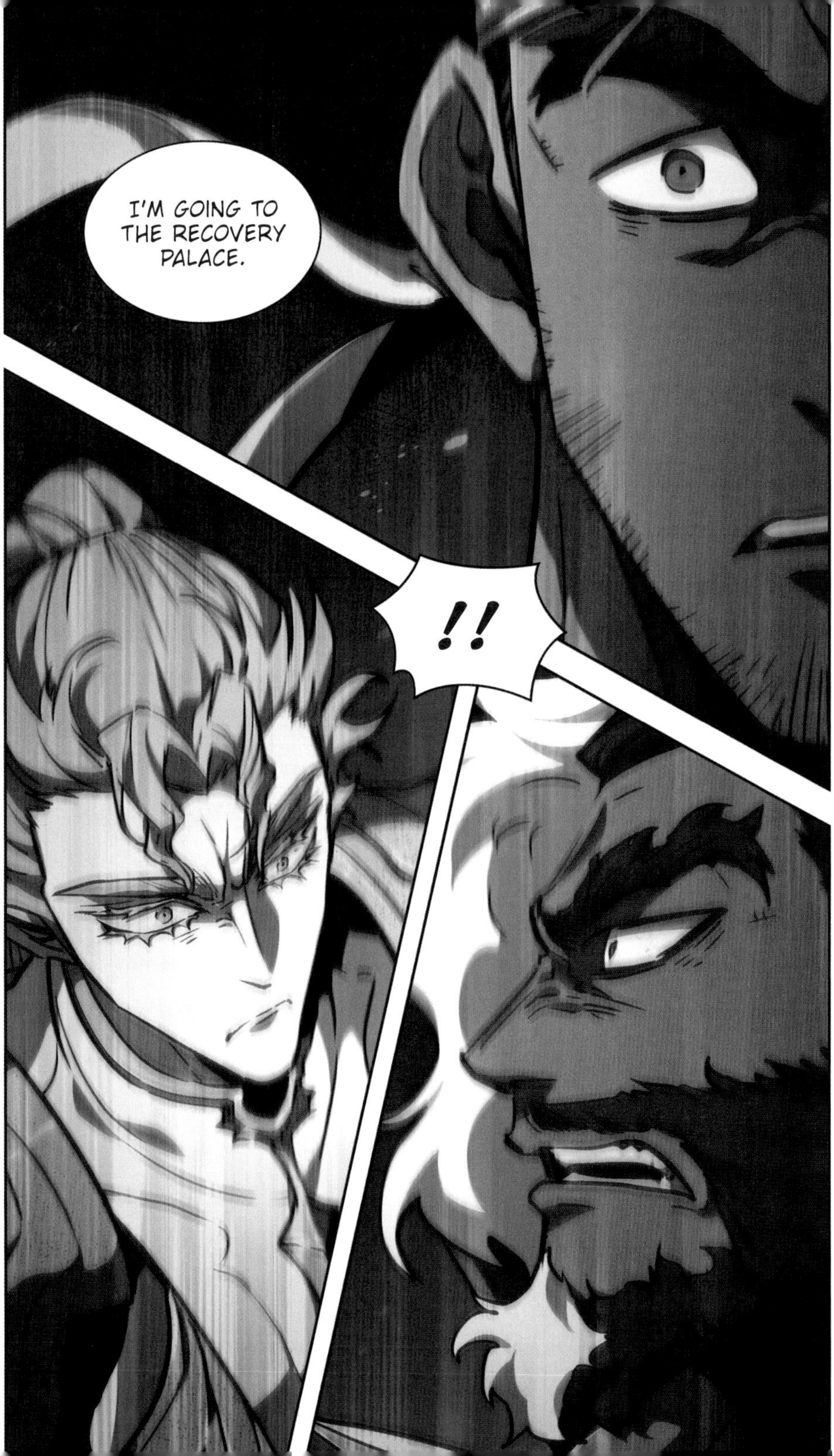
I'M GOING TO THE RECOVERY PALACE.
!!

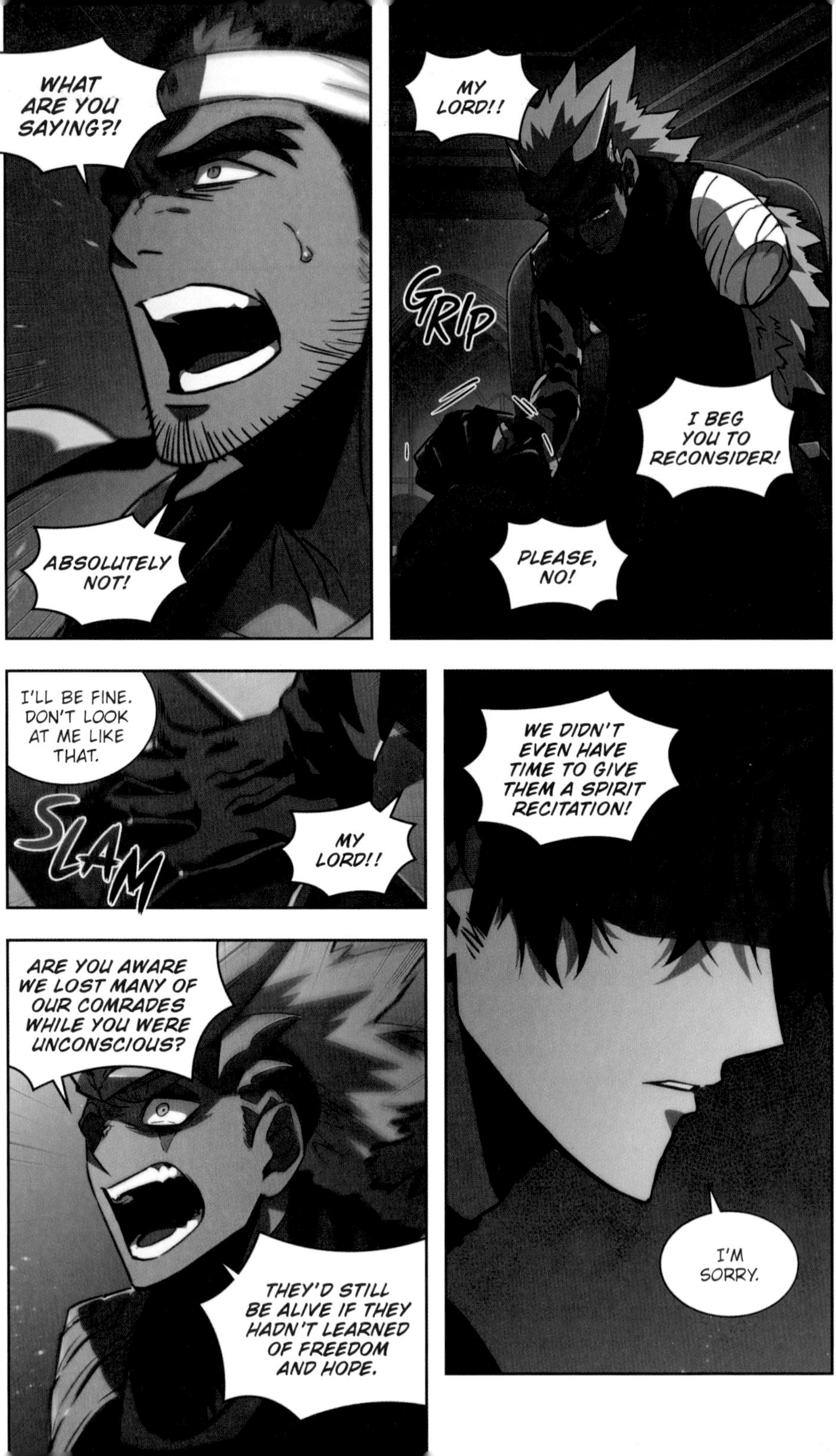
WHAT ARE YOU SAYING?!
ABSOLUTELY NOT!
MY LORD!!
GRIP
I BEG YOU TO RECONSIDER!
PLEASE, NO!
I'LL BE FINE. DON'T LOOK AT ME LIKE THAT.
SLAM
MY LORD!!
ARE YOU AWARE WE LOST MANY OF OUR COMRADES WHILE YOU WERE UNCONSCIOUS?
THEY'D STILL BE ALIVE IF THEY HADN'T LEARNED OF FREEDOM AND HOPE.
WE DIDN'T EVEN HAVE TIME TO GIVE THEM A SPIRIT RECITATION!
I'M SORRY.

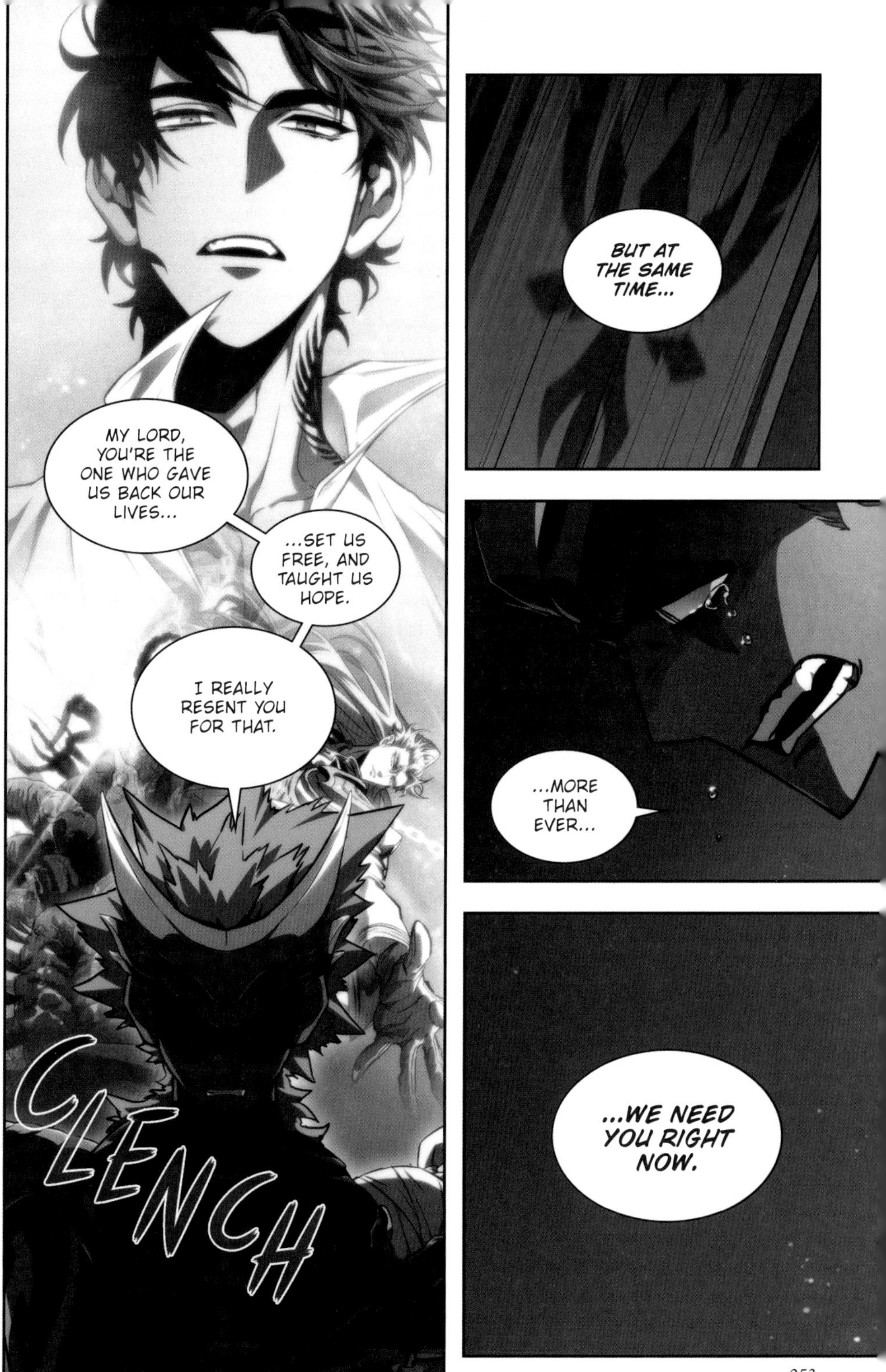
MY LORD, YOU'RE THE ONE WHO GAVE US BACK OUR LIVES...
...SET US FREE, AND TAUGHT US HOPE.
I REALLY RESENT YOU FOR THAT.
CLENCH
BUT AT THE SAME TIME...
...MORE THAN EVER...
...WE NEED YOU RIGHT NOW.

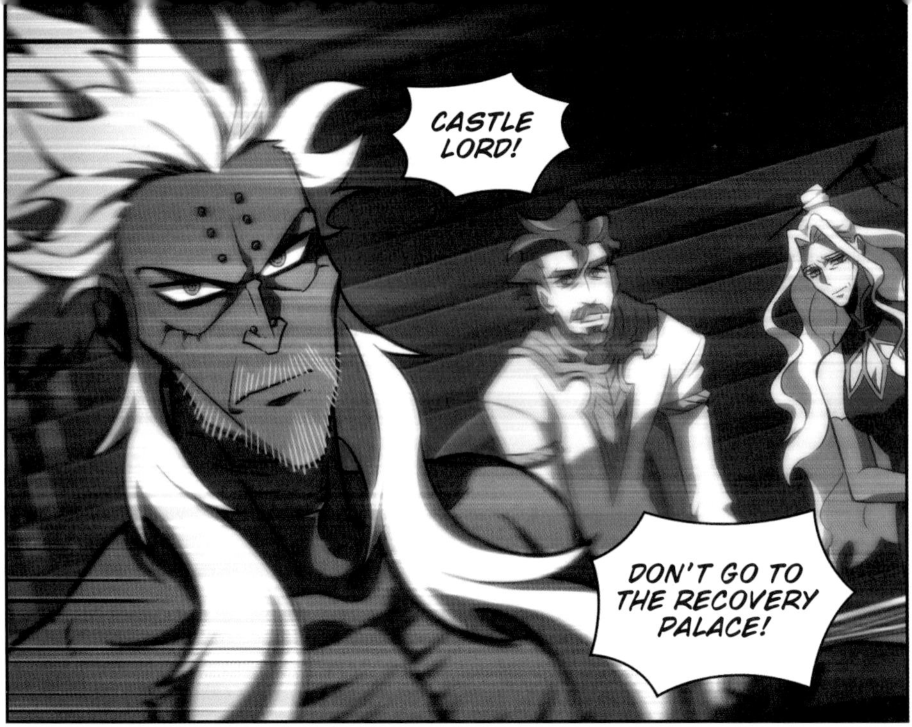
CASTLE LORD!
DON'T GO TO THE RECOVERY PALACE!

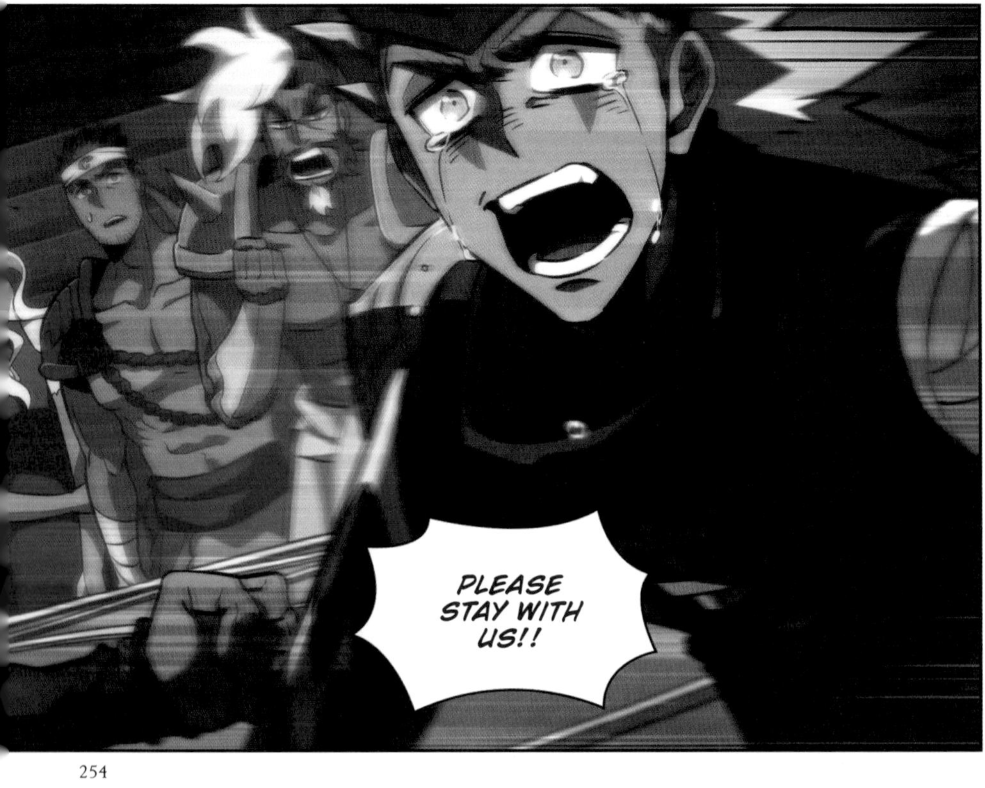
PLEASE STAY WITH US!!

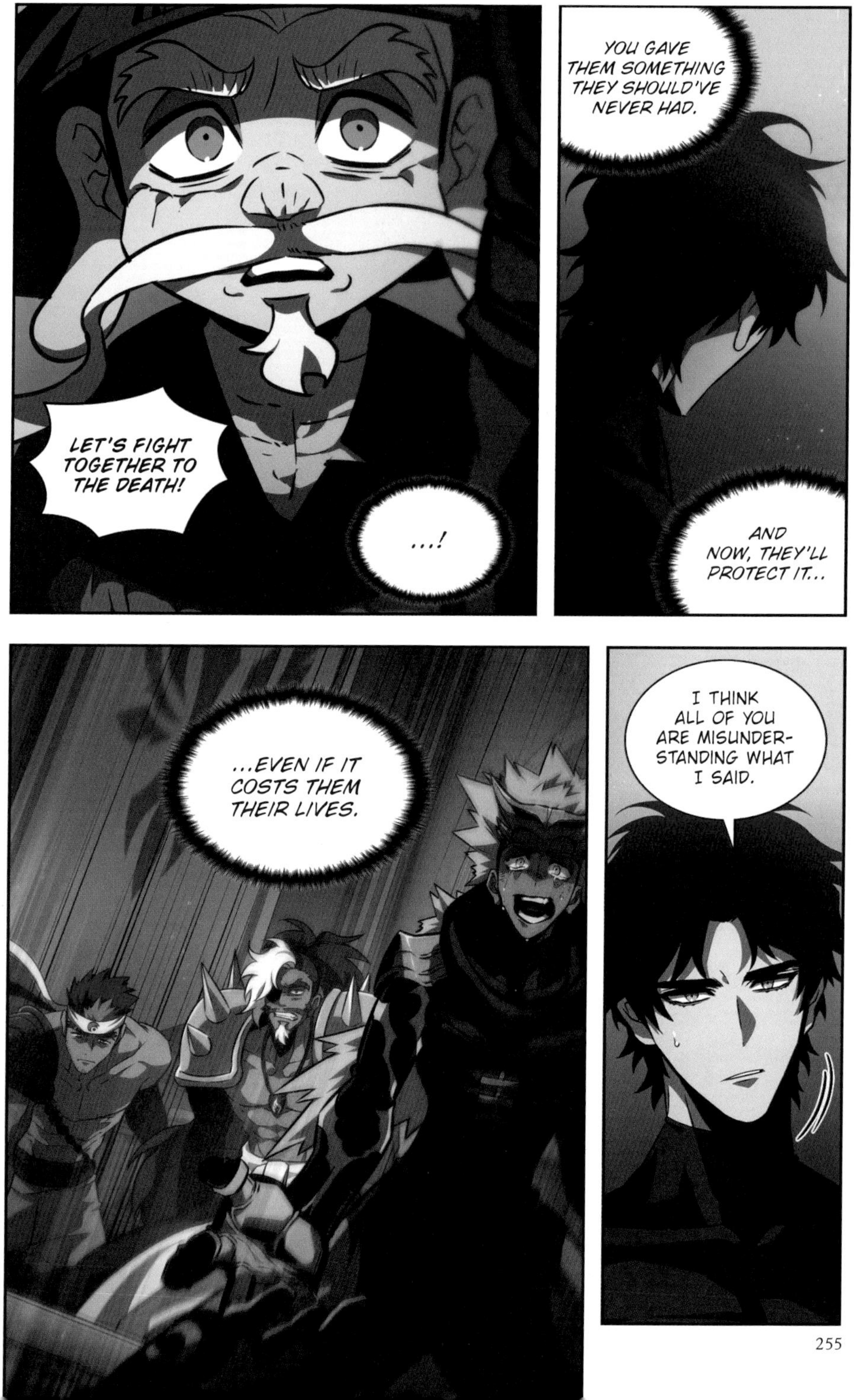
LET'S FIGHT TOGETHER TO THE DEATH!
...!
YOU GAVE THEM SOMETHING THEY SHOULD'VE NEVER HAD.
AND NOW, THEY'LL PROTECT IT...
...EVEN IF IT COSTS THEM THEIR LIVES.
I THINK ALL OF YOU ARE MISUNDER-STANDING WHAT I SAID.

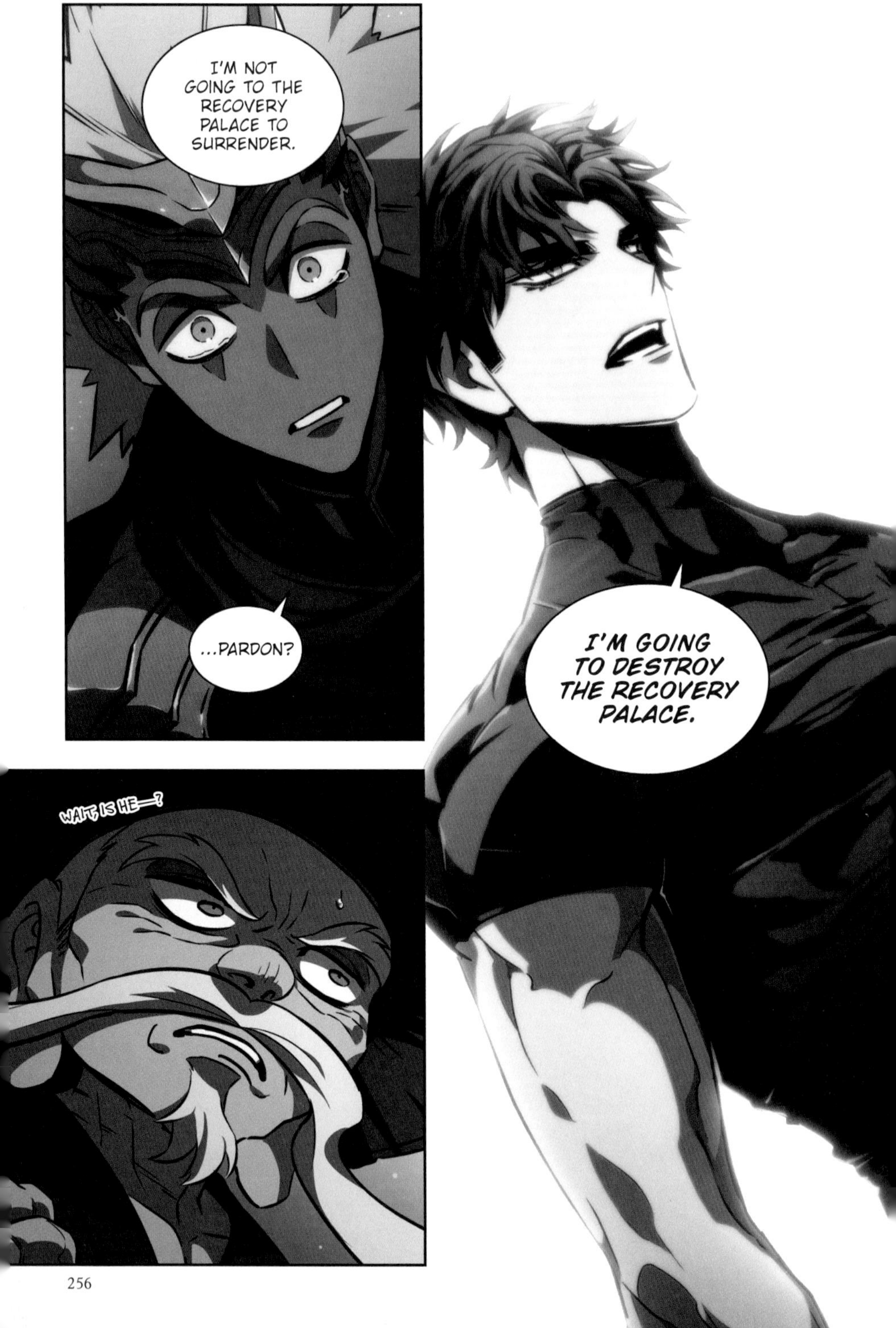
I'M NOT GOING TO THE RECOVERY PALACE TO SURRENDER.
...PARDON?
I'M GOING TO DESTROY THE RECOVERY PALACE.
WAIT, IS HE—?

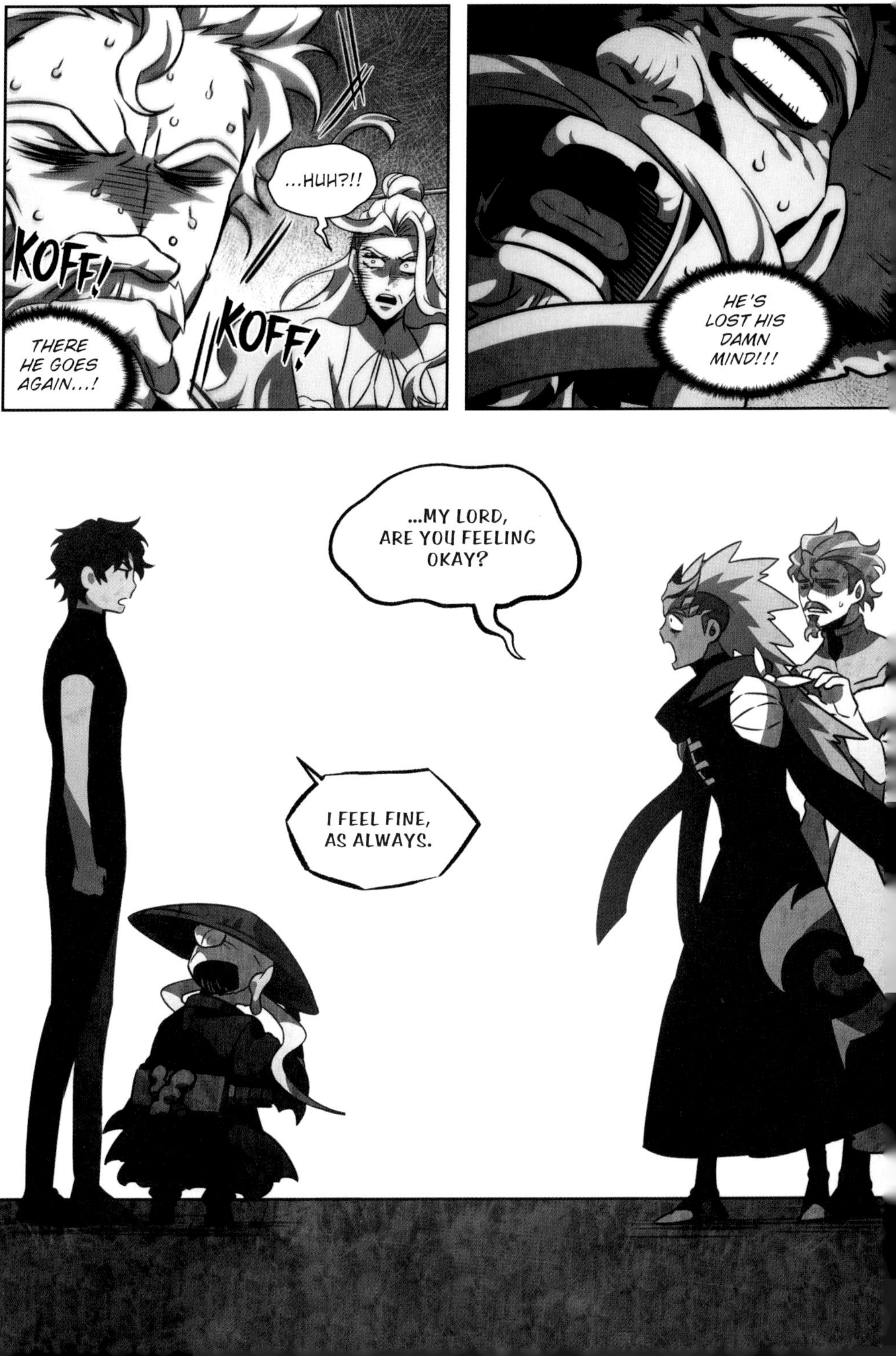
...HUH?!!
KOFF!
KOFF!
THERE HE GOES AGAIN...!
HE'S LOST HIS DAMN MIND!!!
...MY LORD, ARE YOU FEELING OKAY?
I FEEL FINE, AS ALWAYS.

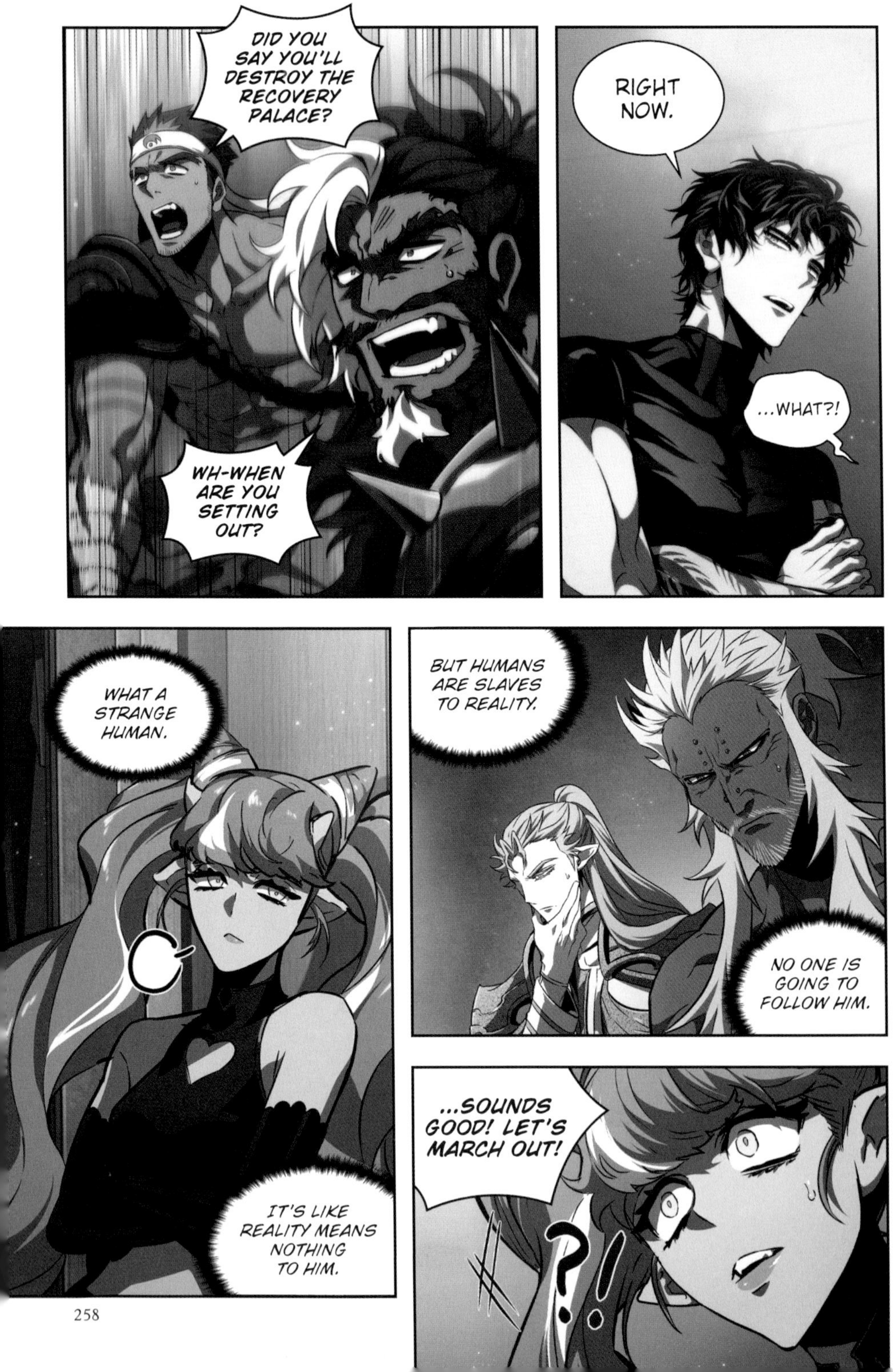
DID YOU SAY YOU'LL DESTROY THE RECOVERY PALACE?
WH-WHEN ARE YOU SETTING OUT?
RIGHT NOW.
...WHAT?!
WHAT A STRANGE HUMAN.
IT'S LIKE REALITY MEANS NOTHING TO HIM.
BUT HUMANS ARE SLAVES TO REALITY.
NO ONE IS GOING TO FOLLOW HIM.
...SOUNDS GOOD! LET'S MARCH OUT!
?!

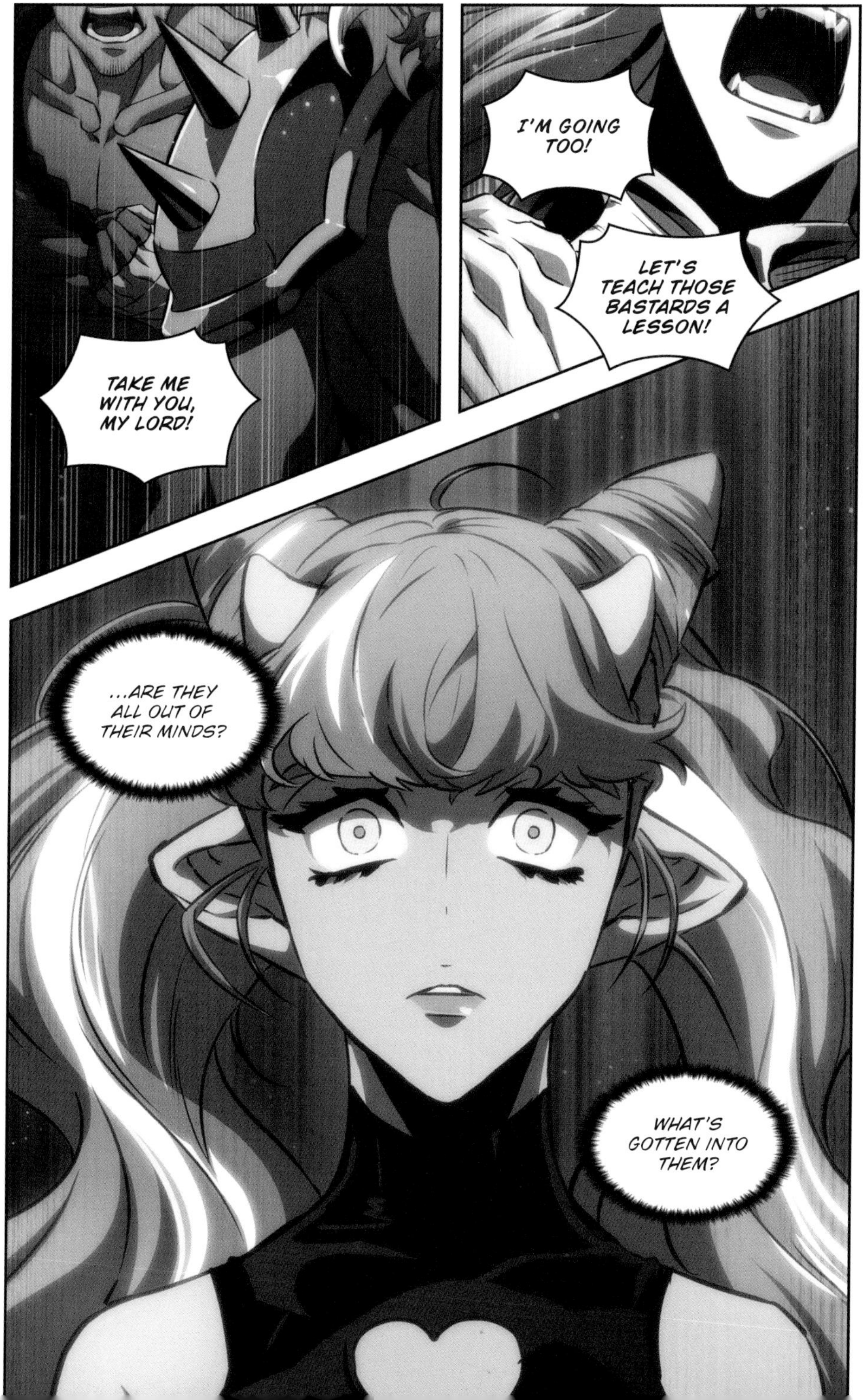
TAKE ME WITH YOU, MY LORD!
I'M GOING TOO!
LET'S TEACH THOSE BASTARDS A LESSON!
...ARE THEY ALL OUT OF THEIR MINDS?
WHAT'S GOTTEN INTO THEM?

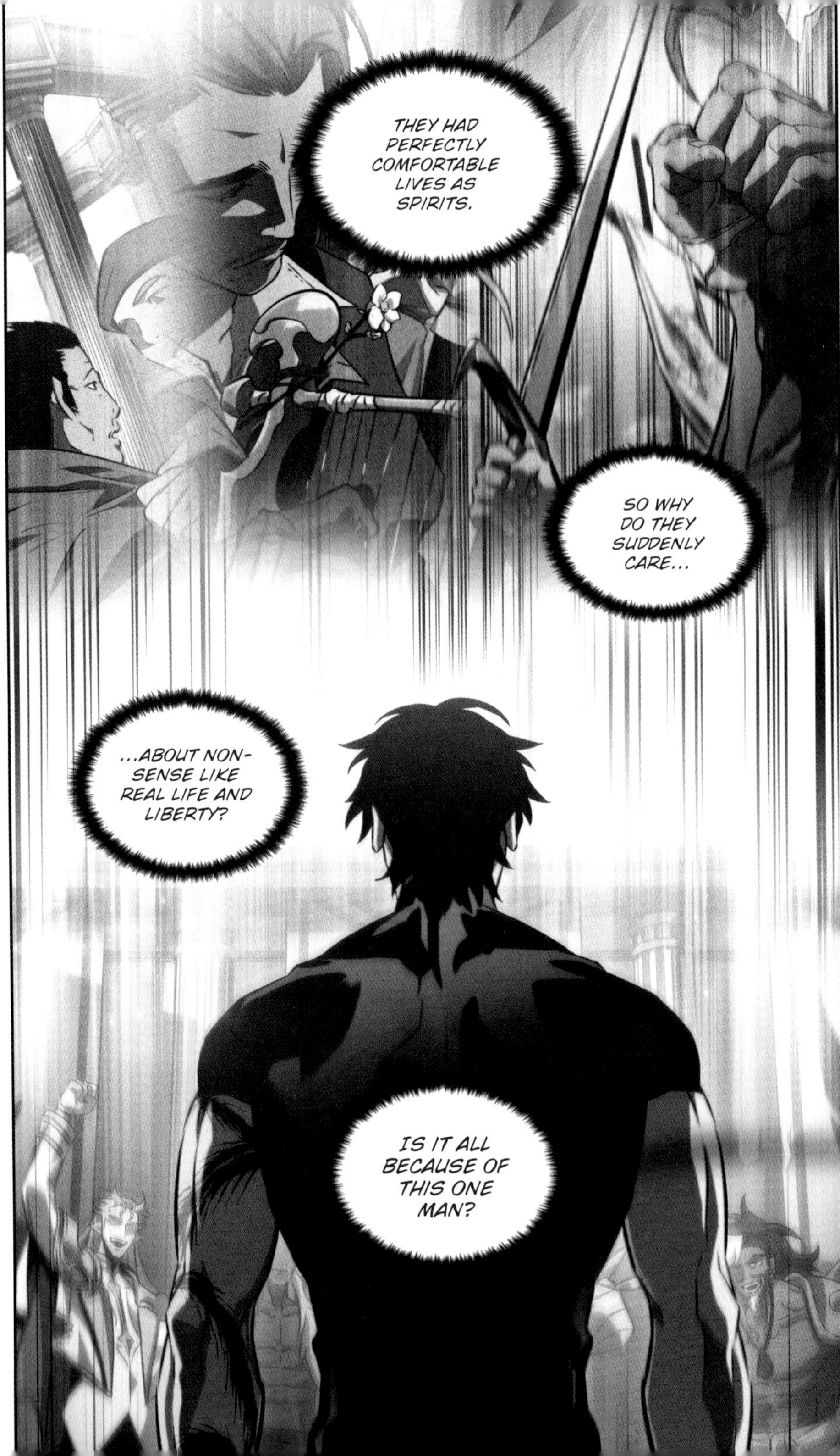
THEY HAD PERFECTLY COMFORTABLE LIVES AS SPIRITS.
SO WHY DO THEY SUDDENLY CARE...
...ABOUT NON-SENSE LIKE REAL LIFE AND LIBERTY?
IS IT ALL BECAUSE OF THIS ONE MAN?

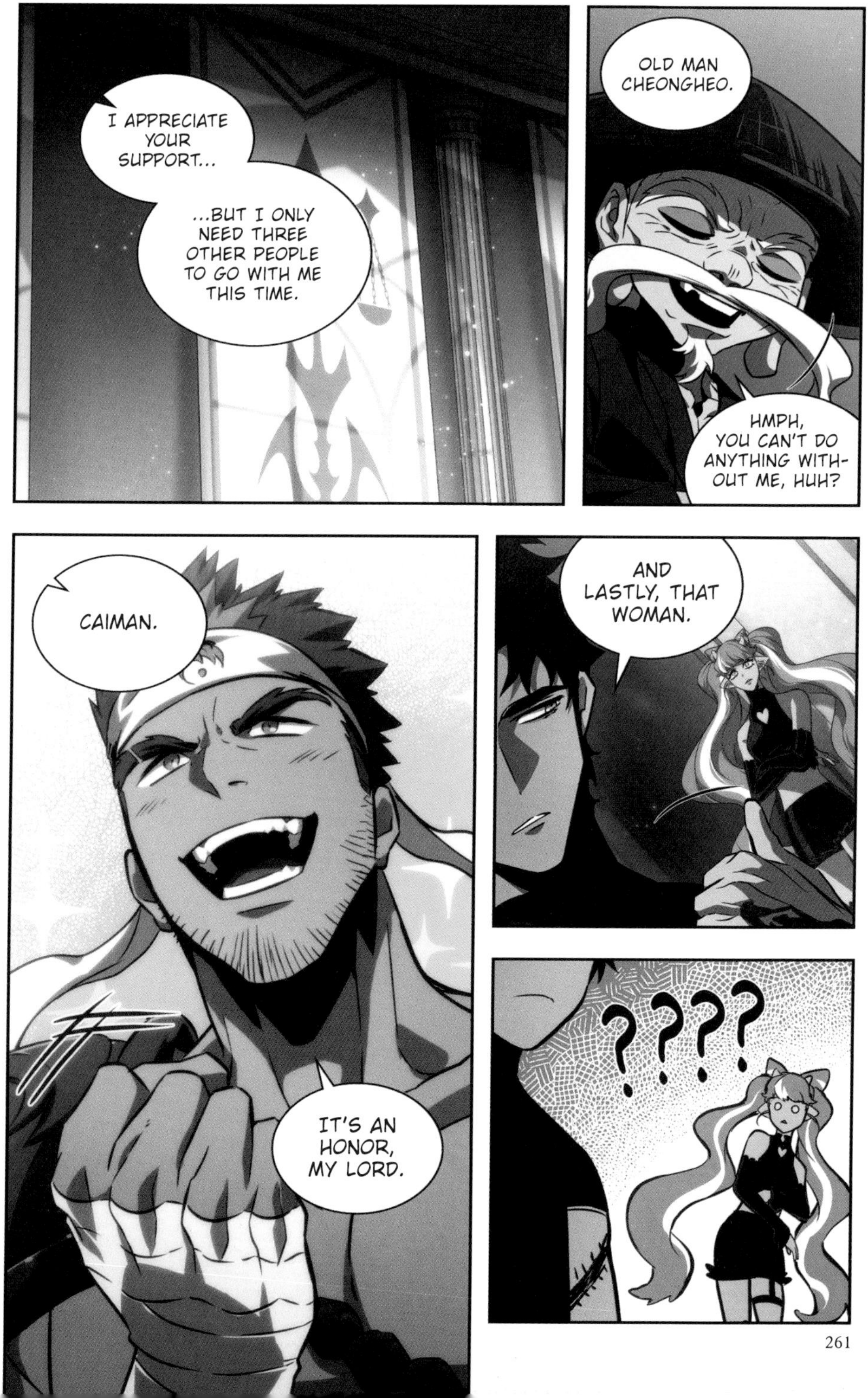
I APPRECIATE YOUR SUPPORT...
...BUT I ONLY NEED THREE OTHER PEOPLE TO GO WITH ME THIS TIME.
OLD MAN CHEONGHEO.
HMPH, YOU CAN'T DO ANYTHING WITH-OUT ME, HUH?
CAIMAN.
IT'S AN HONOR, MY LORD.
AND LASTLY, THAT WOMAN.
????

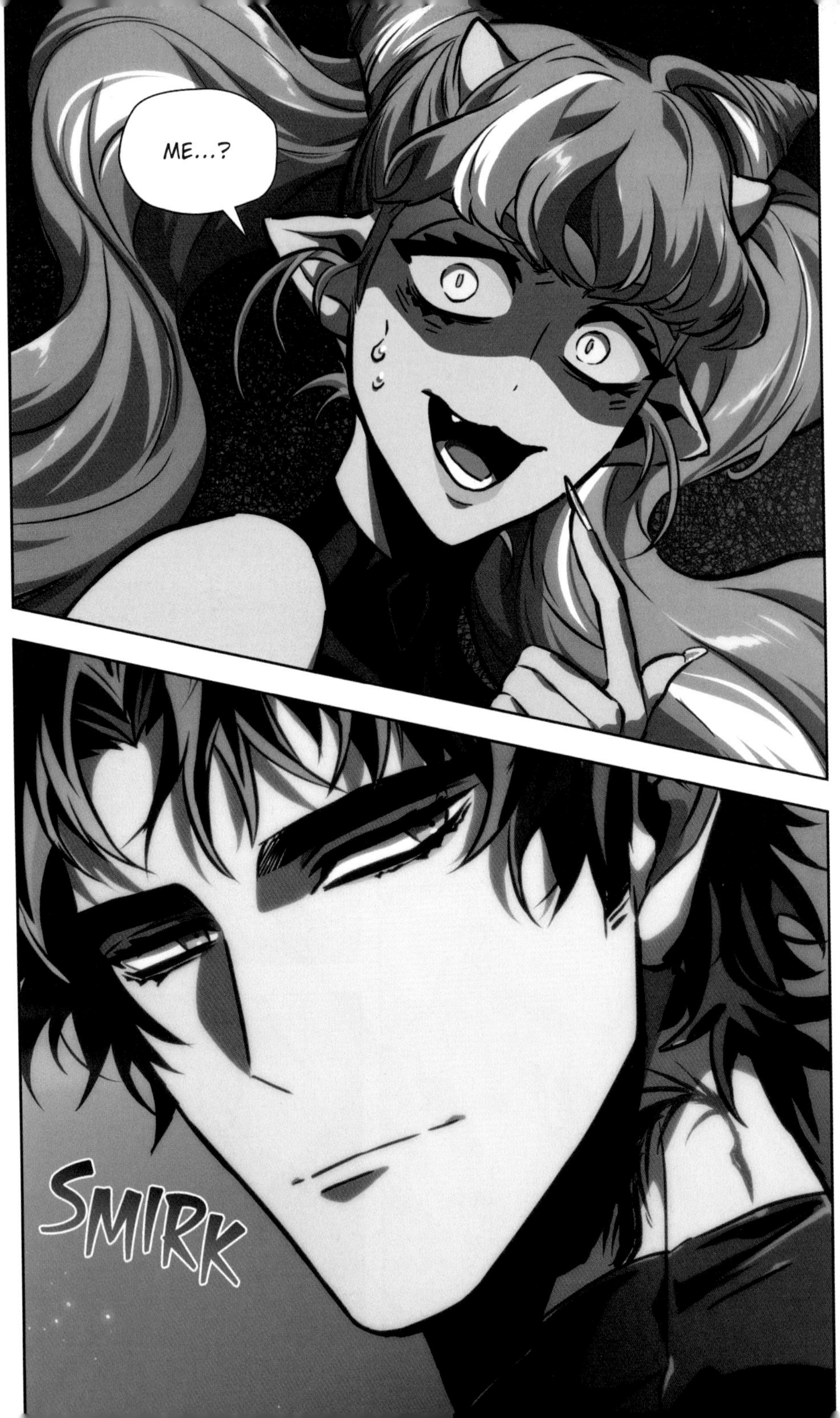
ME...?
SMIRK

The WORLD After the Fall

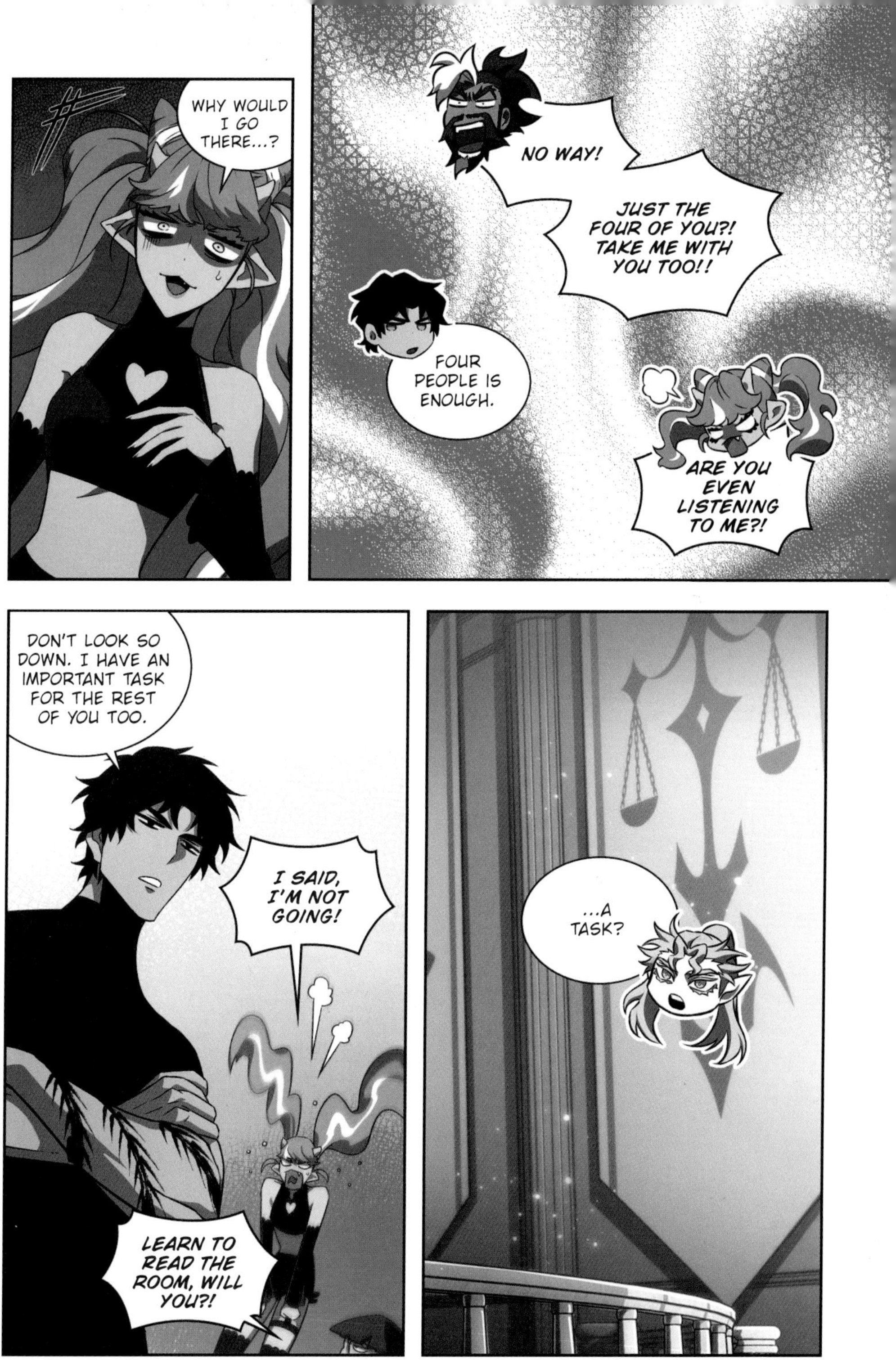
WHY WOULD I GO THERE...?
NO WAY!
JUST THE FOUR OF YOU?! TAKE ME WITH YOU TOO!!
FOUR PEOPLE IS ENOUGH.
ARE YOU EVEN LISTENING TO ME?!
DON'T LOOK SO DOWN. I HAVE AN IMPORTANT TASK FOR THE REST OF YOU TOO.
I SAID, I'M NOT GOING!
LEARN TO READ THE ROOM, WILL YOU?!
...A TASK?

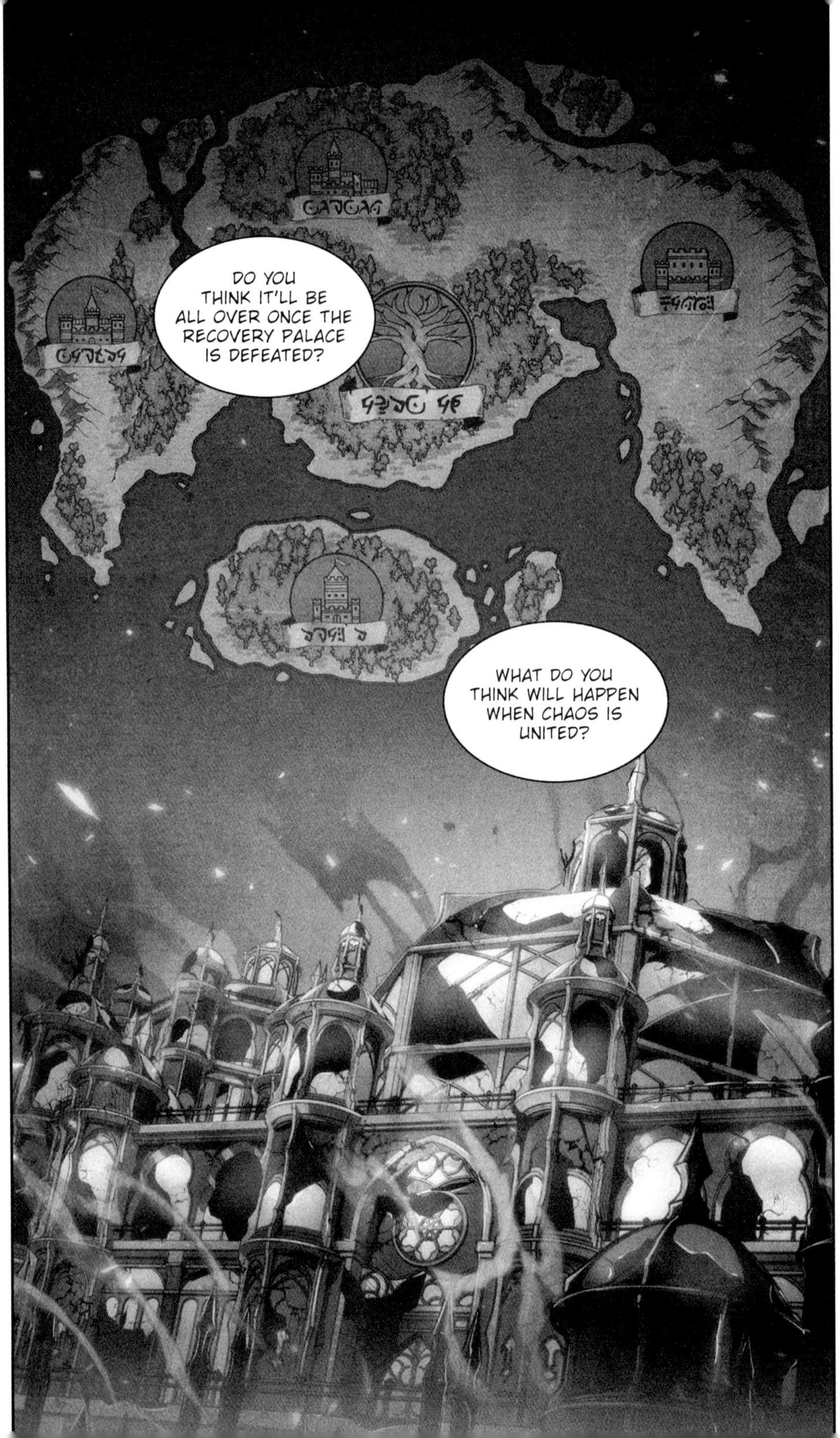
DO YOU THINK IT'LL BE ALL OVER ONCE THE RECOVERY PALACE IS DEFEATED?
WHAT DO YOU THINK WILL HAPPEN WHEN CHAOS IS UNITED?

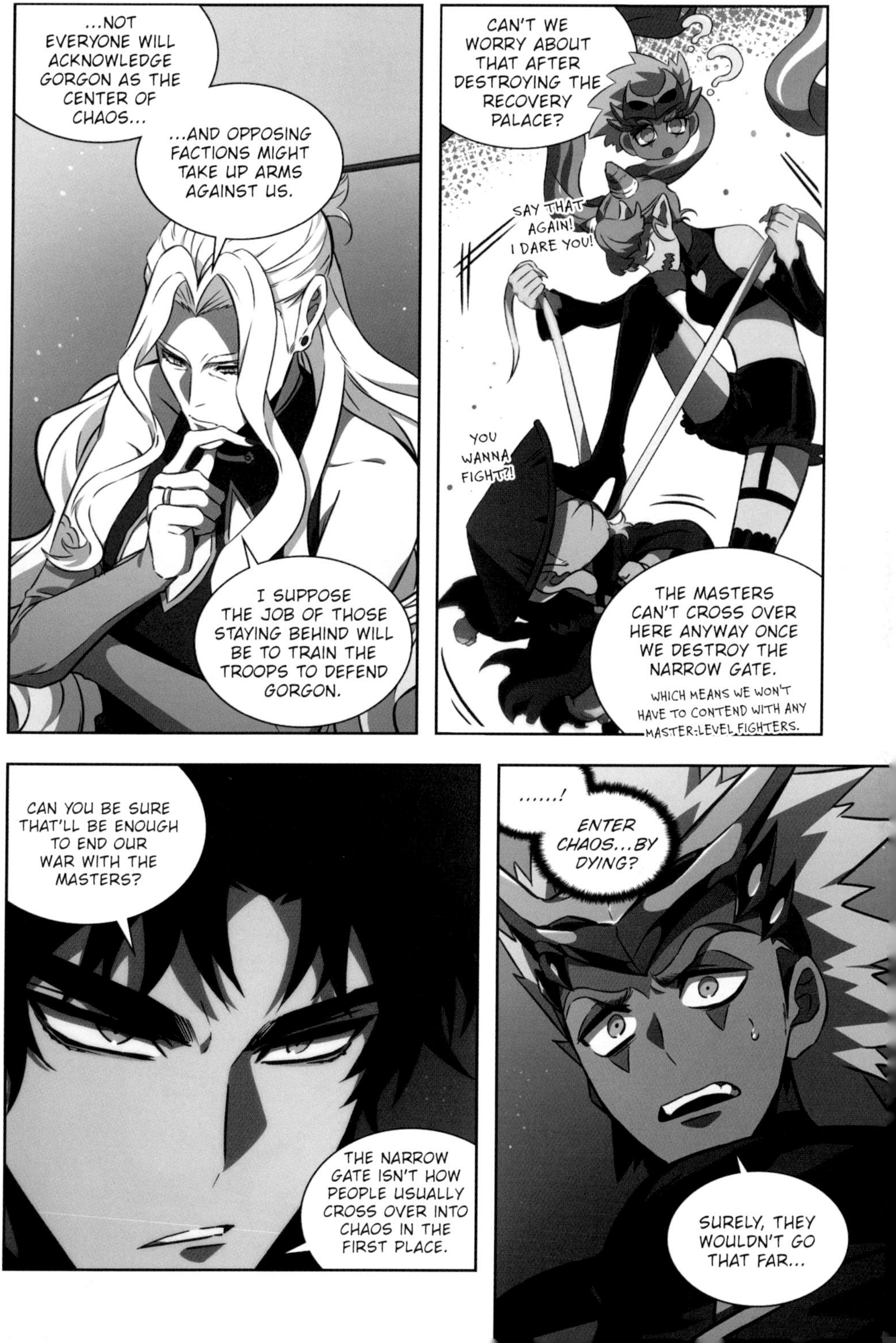
...NOT EVERYONE WILL ACKNOWLEDGE GORGON AS THE CENTER OF CHAOS...
...AND OPPOSING FACTIONS MIGHT TAKE UP ARMS AGAINST US.
I SUPPOSE THE JOB OF THOSE STAYING BEHIND WILL BE TO TRAIN THE TROOPS TO DEFEND GORGON.
CAN'T WE WORRY ABOUT THAT AFTER DESTROYING THE RECOVERY PALACE?
SAY THAT AGAIN! I DARE YOU!
YOU WANNA FIGHT?!
THE MASTERS CAN'T CROSS OVER HERE ANYWAY ONCE WE DESTROY THE NARROW GATE.
WHICH MEANS WE WON'T HAVE TO CONTEND WITH ANY MASTER-LEVEL FIGHTERS.
CAN YOU BE SURE THAT'LL BE ENOUGH TO END OUR WAR WITH THE MASTERS?
THE NARROW GATE ISN'T HOW PEOPLE USUALLY CROSS OVER INTO CHAOS IN THE FIRST PLACE.
......!
ENTER CHAOS...BY DYING?
SURELY, THEY WOULDN'T GO THAT FAR...

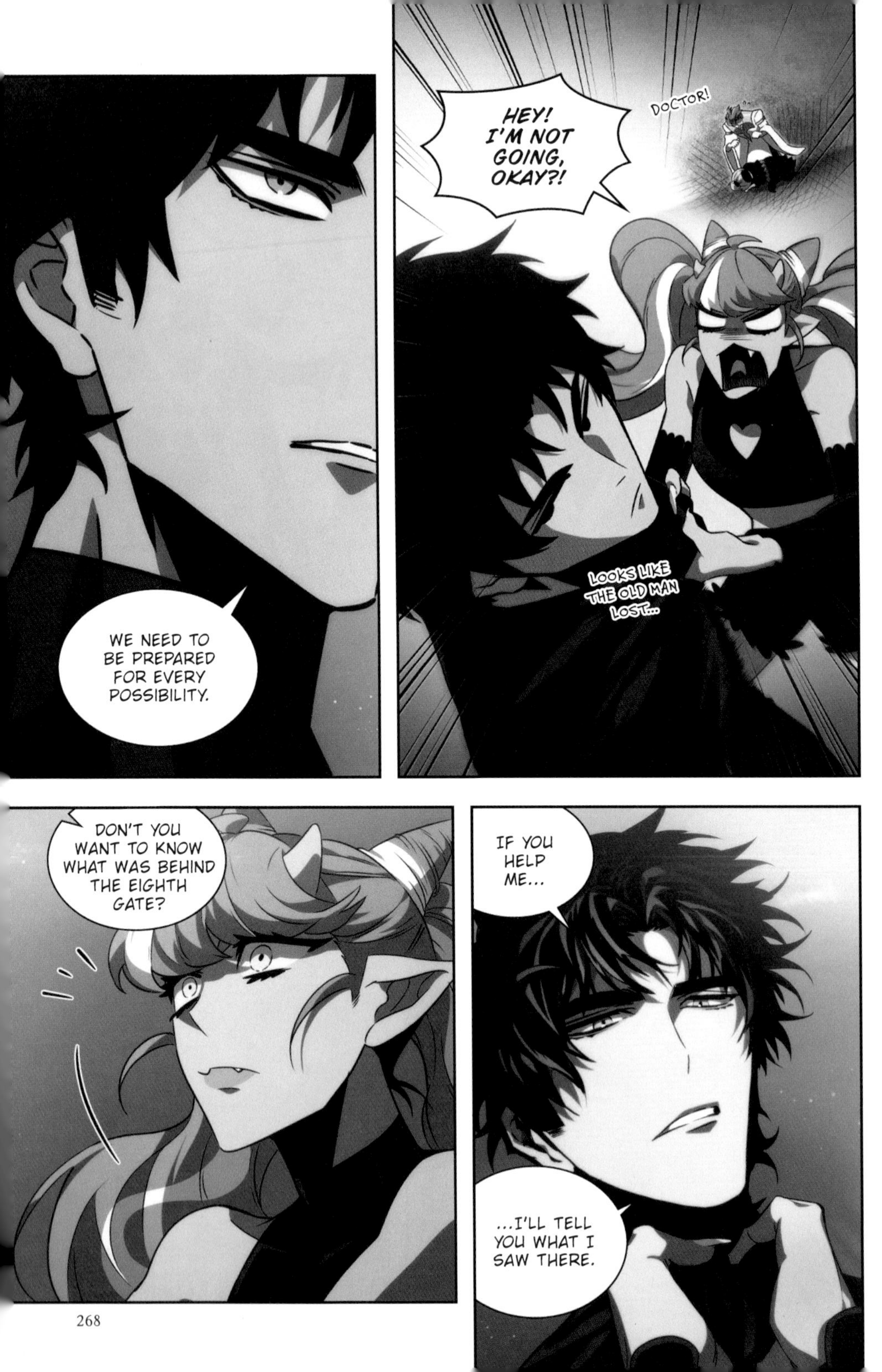
WE NEED TO BE PREPARED FOR EVERY POSSIBILITY.
HEY! I'M NOT GOING, OKAY?!
DOCTOR!
LOOKS LIKE THE OLD MAN LOST...
DON'T YOU WANT TO KNOW WHAT WAS BEHIND THE EIGHTH GATE?
IF YOU HELP ME...
...I'LL TELL YOU WHAT I SAW THERE.

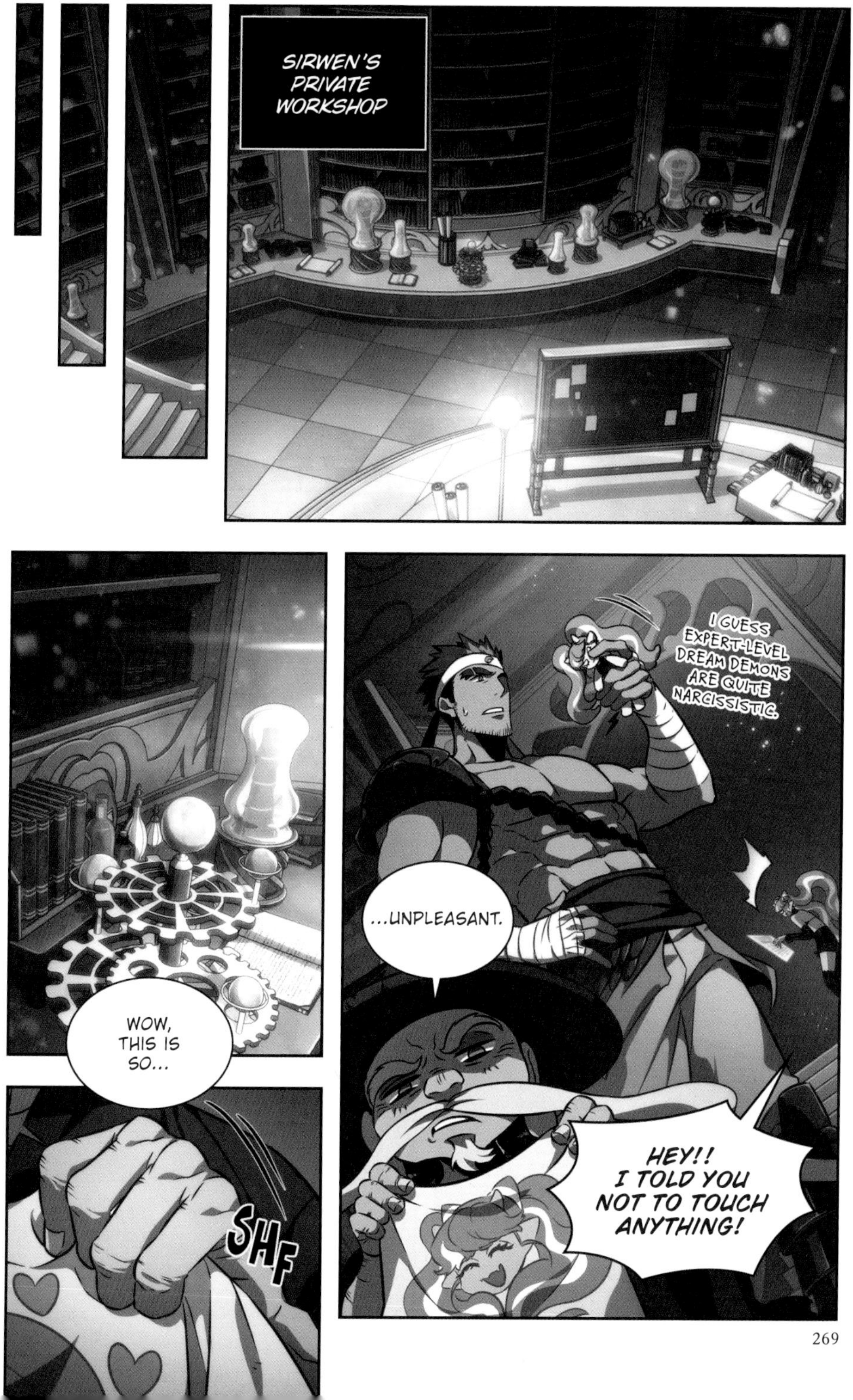
SIRWEN'S PRIVATE WORKSHOP
WOW, THIS IS SO...
...UNPLEASANT.
I GUESS EXPERT-LEVEL DREAM DEMONS ARE QUITE NARCISSISTIC.
SHF
HEY!! I TOLD YOU NOT TO TOUCH ANYTHING!

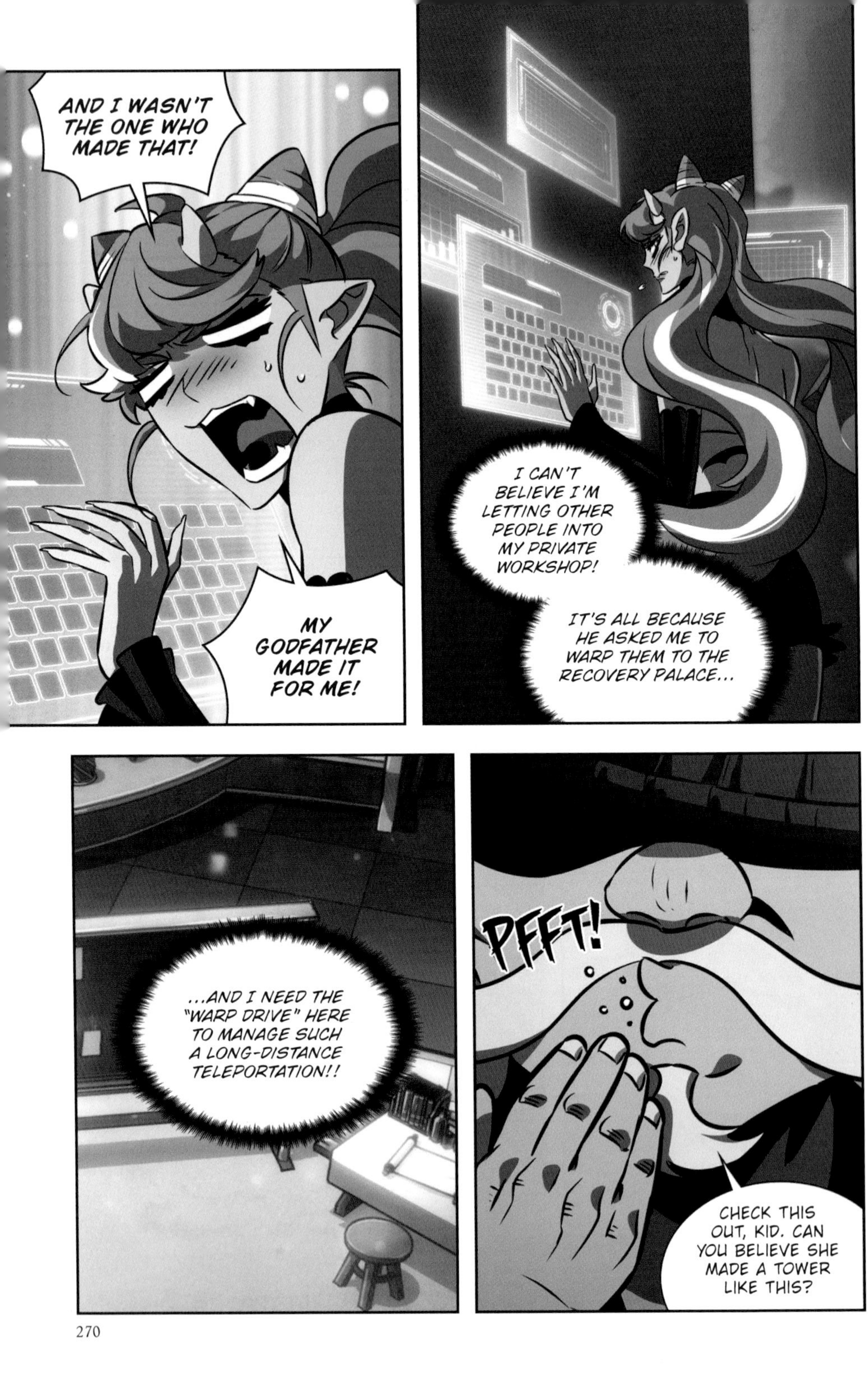
AND I WASN'T THE ONE WHO MADE THAT!
MY GODFATHER MADE IT FOR ME!
I CAN'T BELIEVE I'M LETTING OTHER PEOPLE INTO MY PRIVATE WORKSHOP!
IT'S ALL BECAUSE HE ASKED ME TO WARP THEM TO THE RECOVERY PALACE...
...AND I NEED THE "WARP DRIVE" HERE TO MANAGE SUCH A LONG-DISTANCE TELEPORTATION!!
PFFT!
CHECK THIS OUT, KID. CAN YOU BELIEVE SHE MADE A TOWER LIKE THIS?

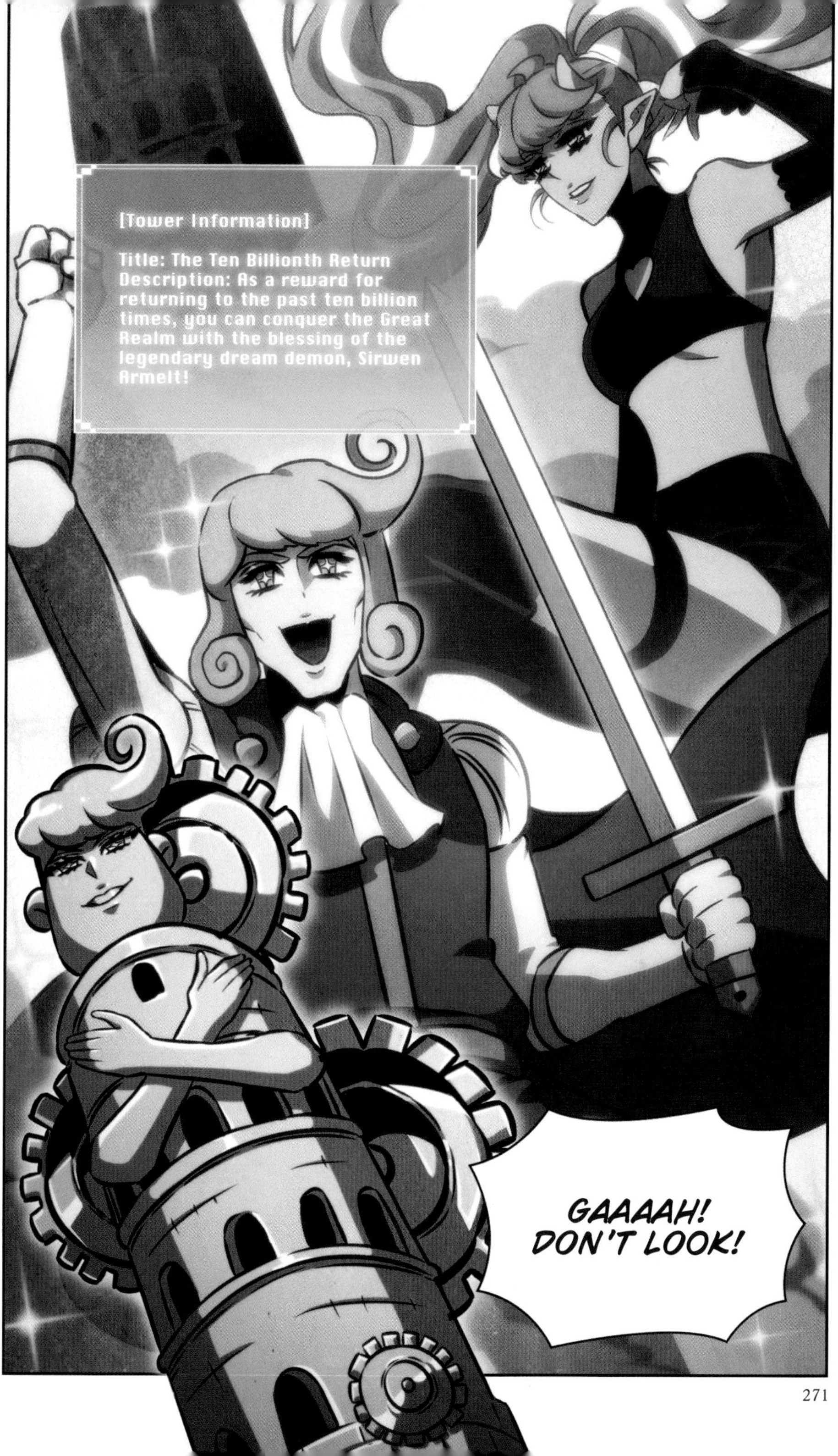
[Tower Information]
Title: The Ten Billionth Return
Description: As a reward for returning to the past ten billion times, you can conquer the Great Realm with the blessing of the legendary dream demon, Sirwen Armelt!
GAAAAH! DON'T LOOK!

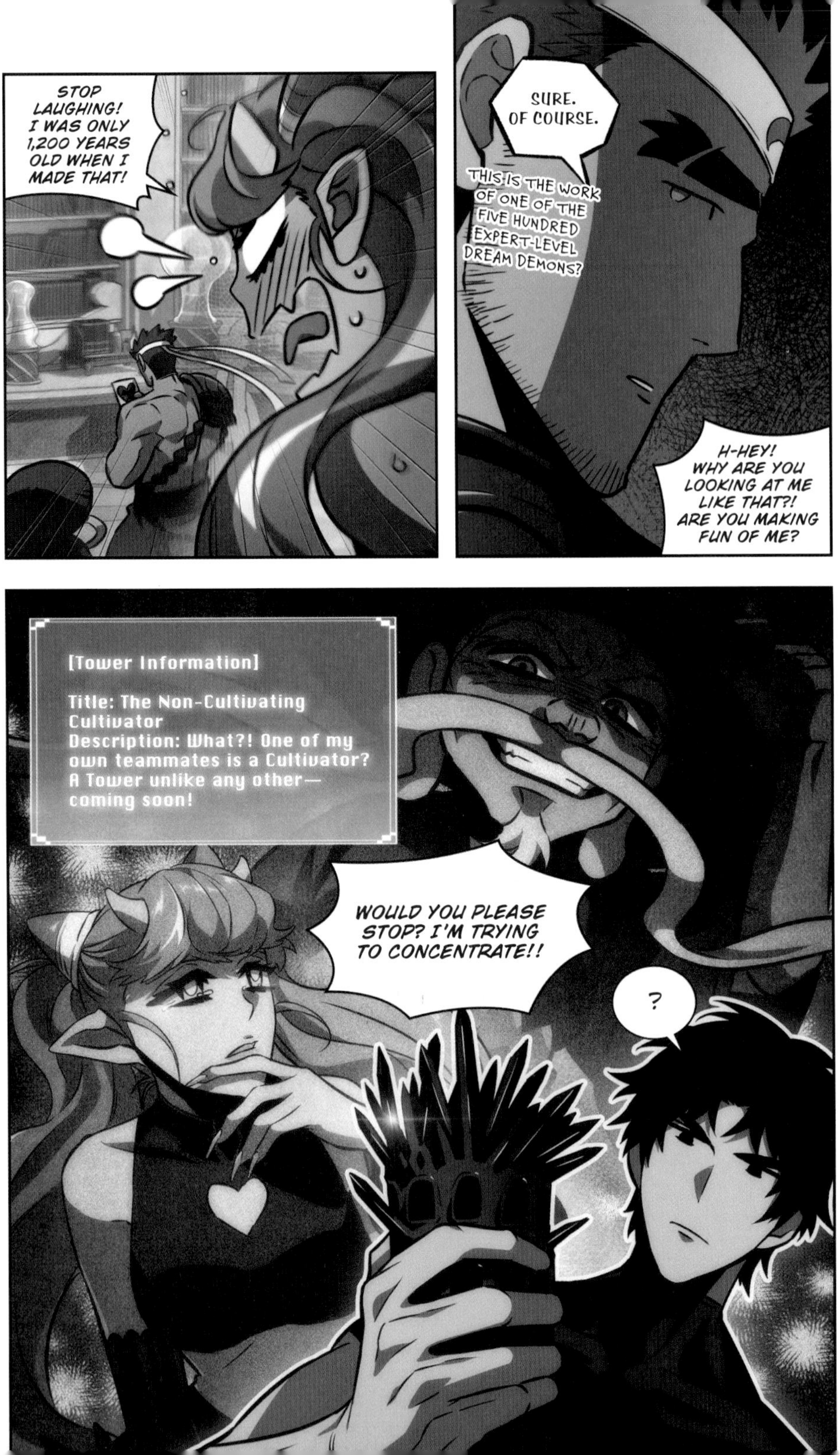
STOP LAUGHING! I WAS ONLY 1,200 YEARS OLD WHEN I MADE THAT!
SURE. OF COURSE.
THIS IS THE WORK OF ONE OF THE FIVE HUNDRED EXPERT-LEVEL DREAM DEMONS?
H-HEY! WHY ARE YOU LOOKING AT ME LIKE THAT?! ARE YOU MAKING FUN OF ME?
[Tower Information]
Title: The Non-Cultivating Cultivator
Description: What?! One of my own teammates is a Cultivator? A Tower unlike any other—coming soon!
WOULD YOU PLEASE STOP? I'M TRYING TO CONCENTRATE!!
?

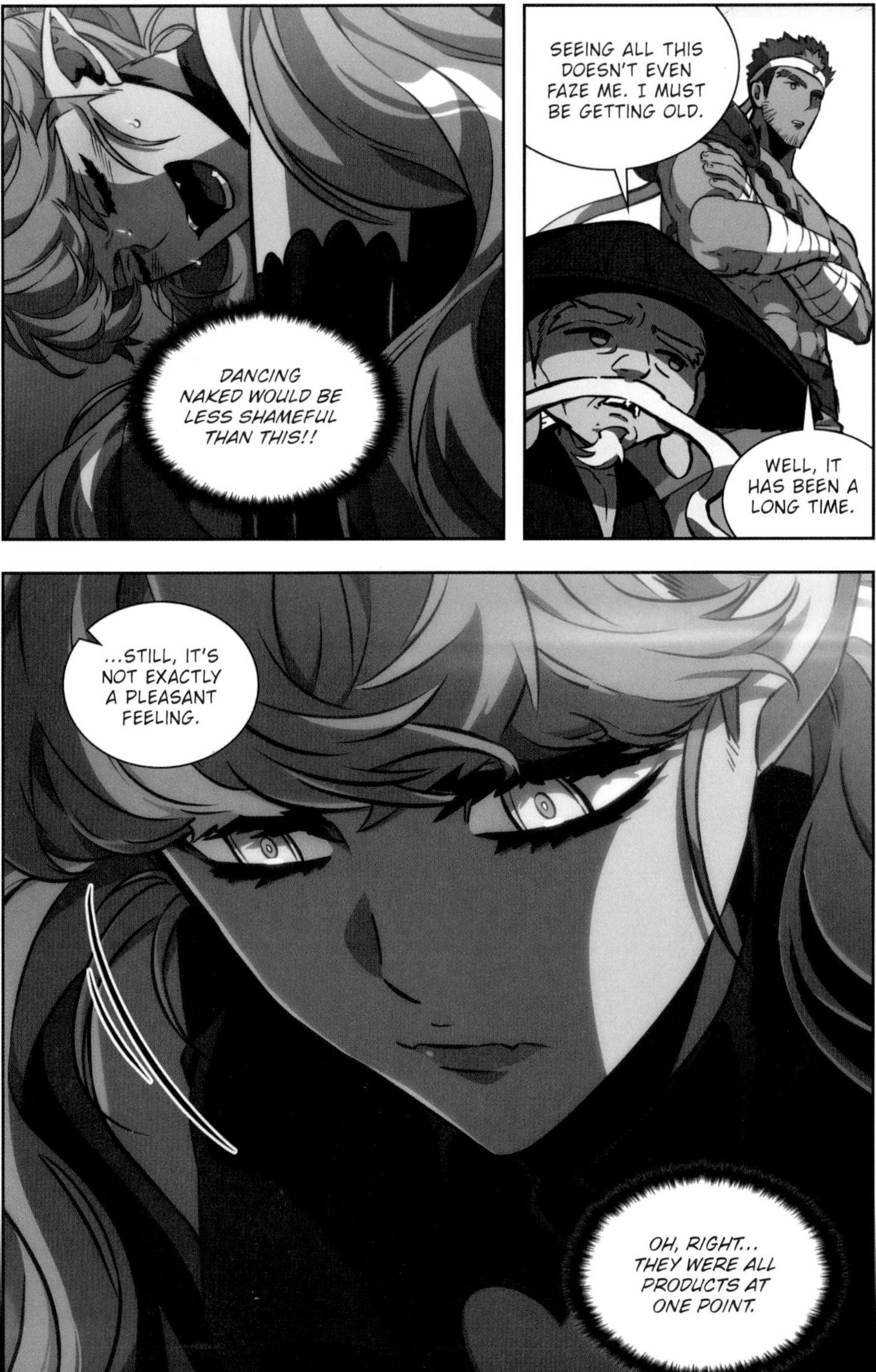
DANCING NAKED WOULD BE LESS SHAMEFUL THAN THIS!!
SEEING ALL THIS DOESN'T EVEN FAZE ME. I MUST BE GETTING OLD.
WELL, IT HAS BEEN A LONG TIME.
...STILL, IT'S NOT EXACTLY A PLEASANT FEELING.
OH, RIGHT... THEY WERE ALL PRODUCTS AT ONE POINT.

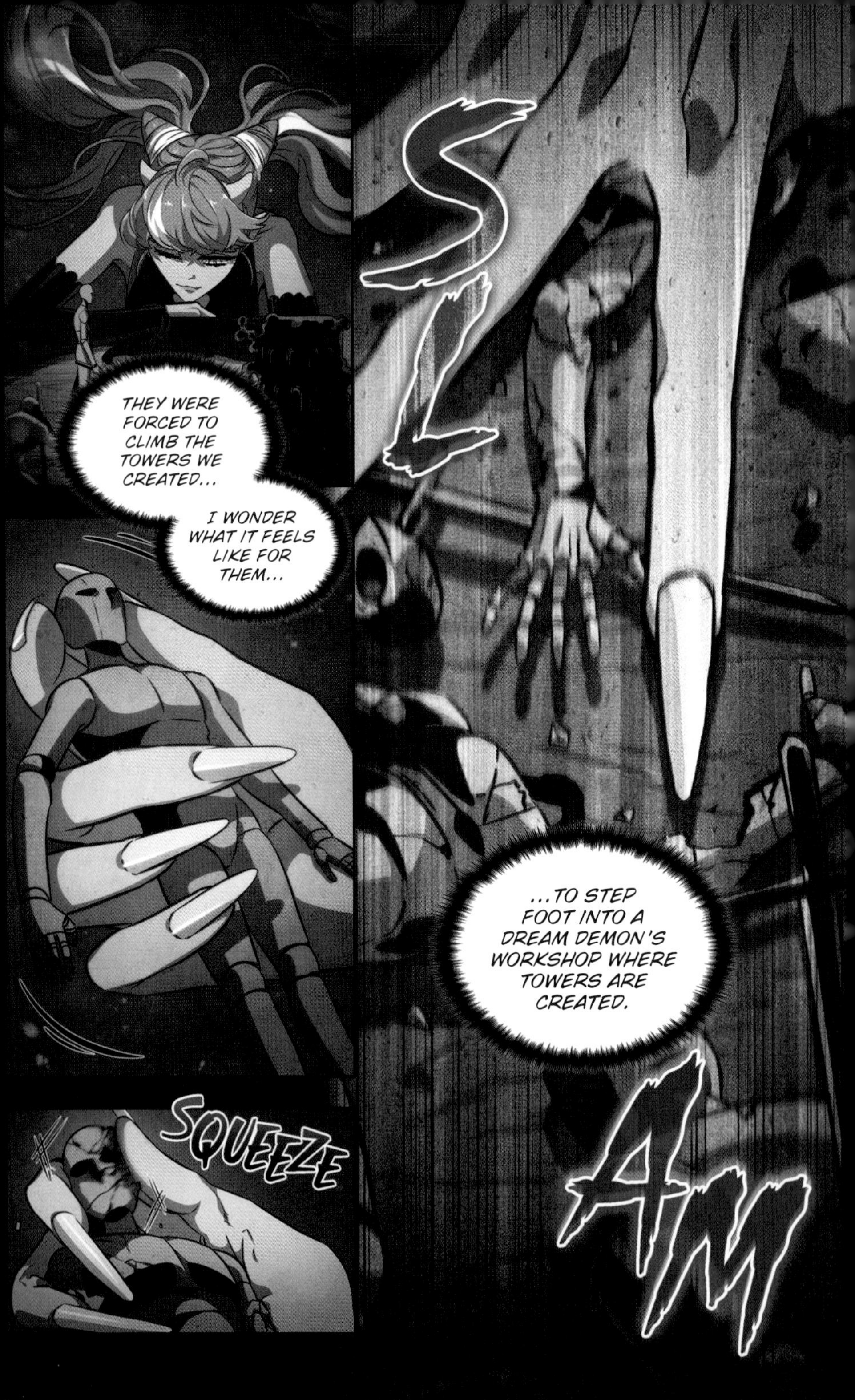

THEY WERE FORCED TO CLIMB THE TOWERS WE CREATED...
I WONDER WHAT IT FEELS LIKE FOR THEM...
SQUEEZE
SL
...TO STEP FOOT INTO A DREAM DEMON'S WORKSHOP WHERE TOWERS ARE CREATED.
AM

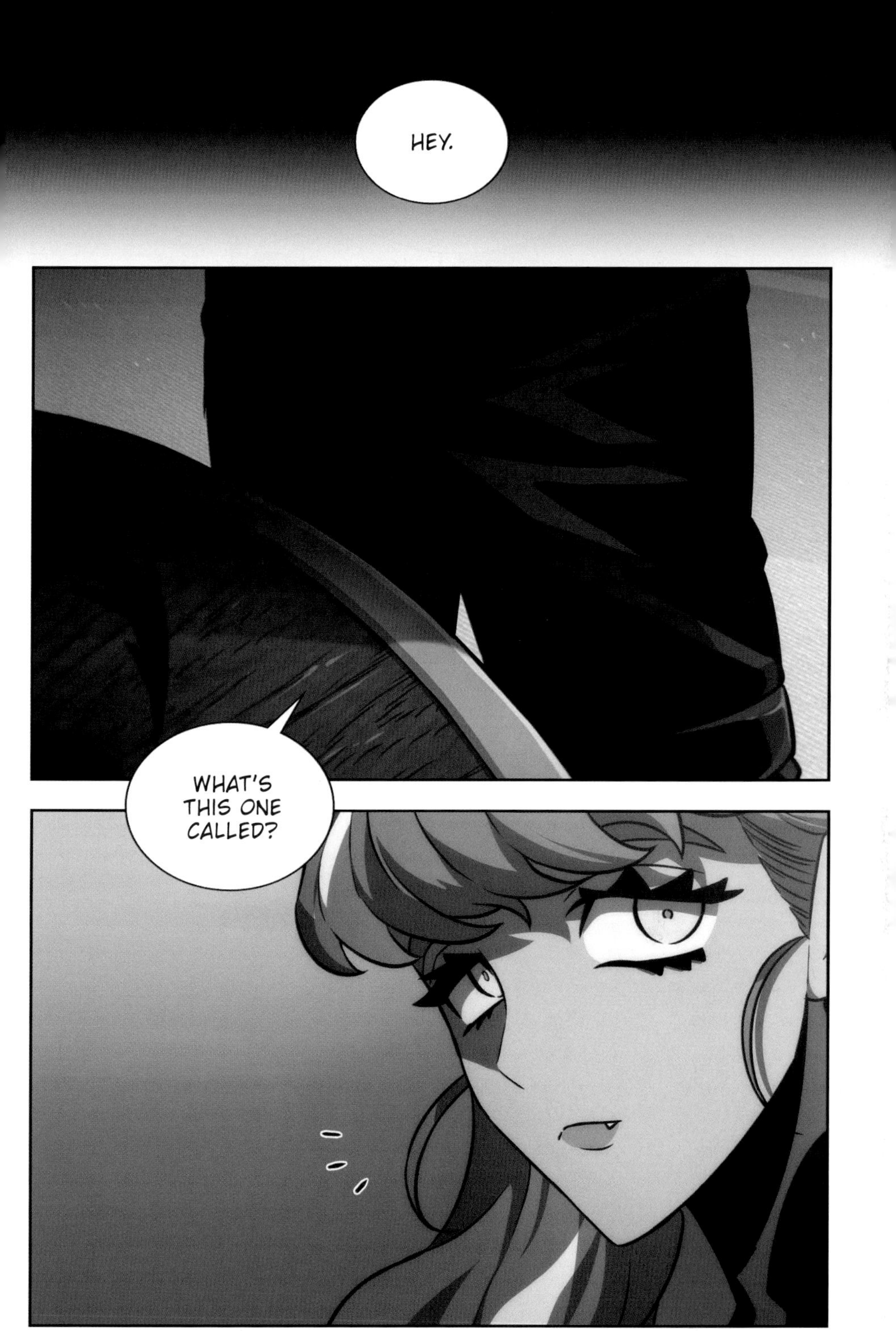
HEY.
WHAT'S THIS ONE CALLED?

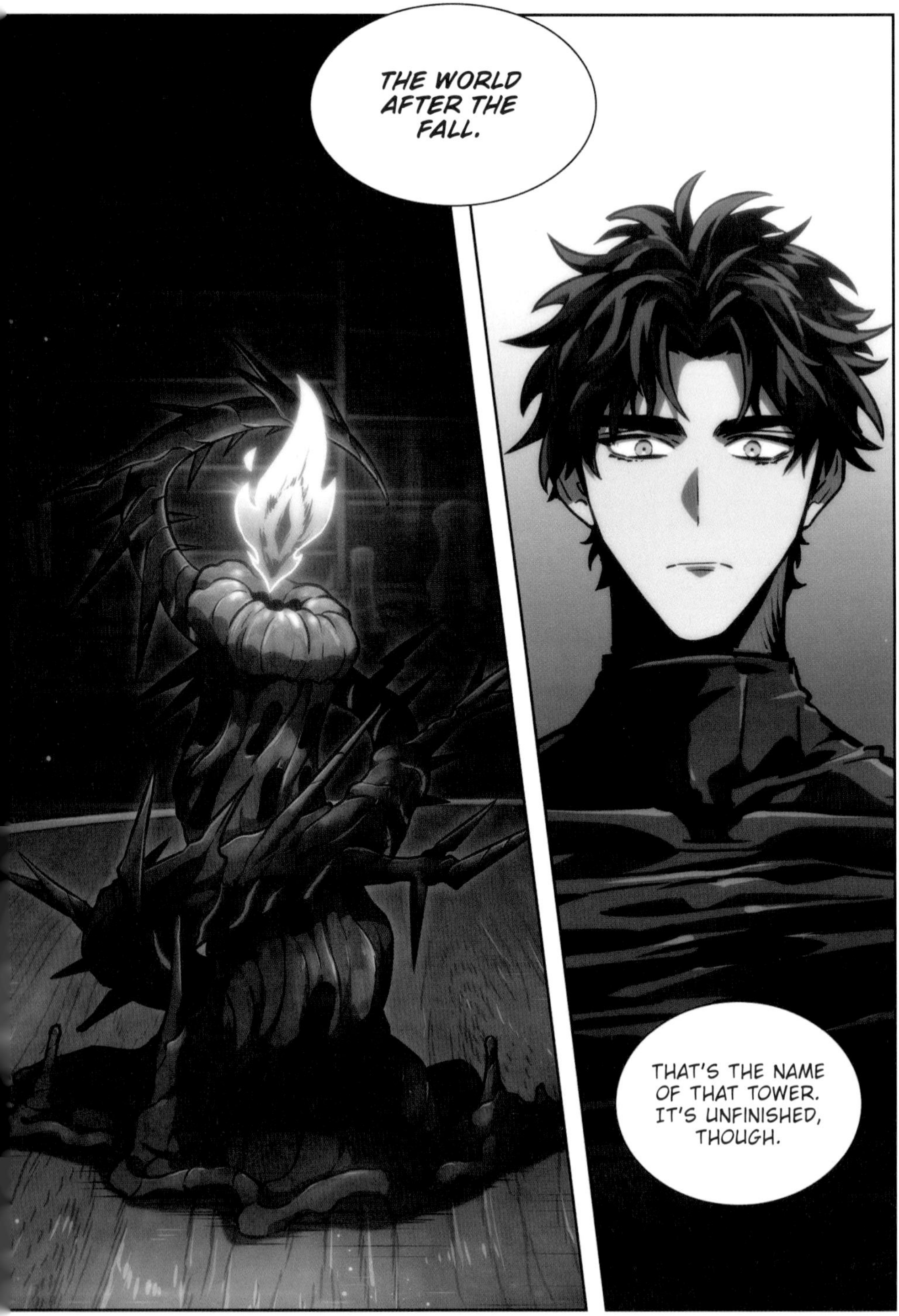
THE WORLD AFTER THE FALL.
THAT'S THE NAME OF THAT TOWER. IT'S UNFINISHED, THOUGH.

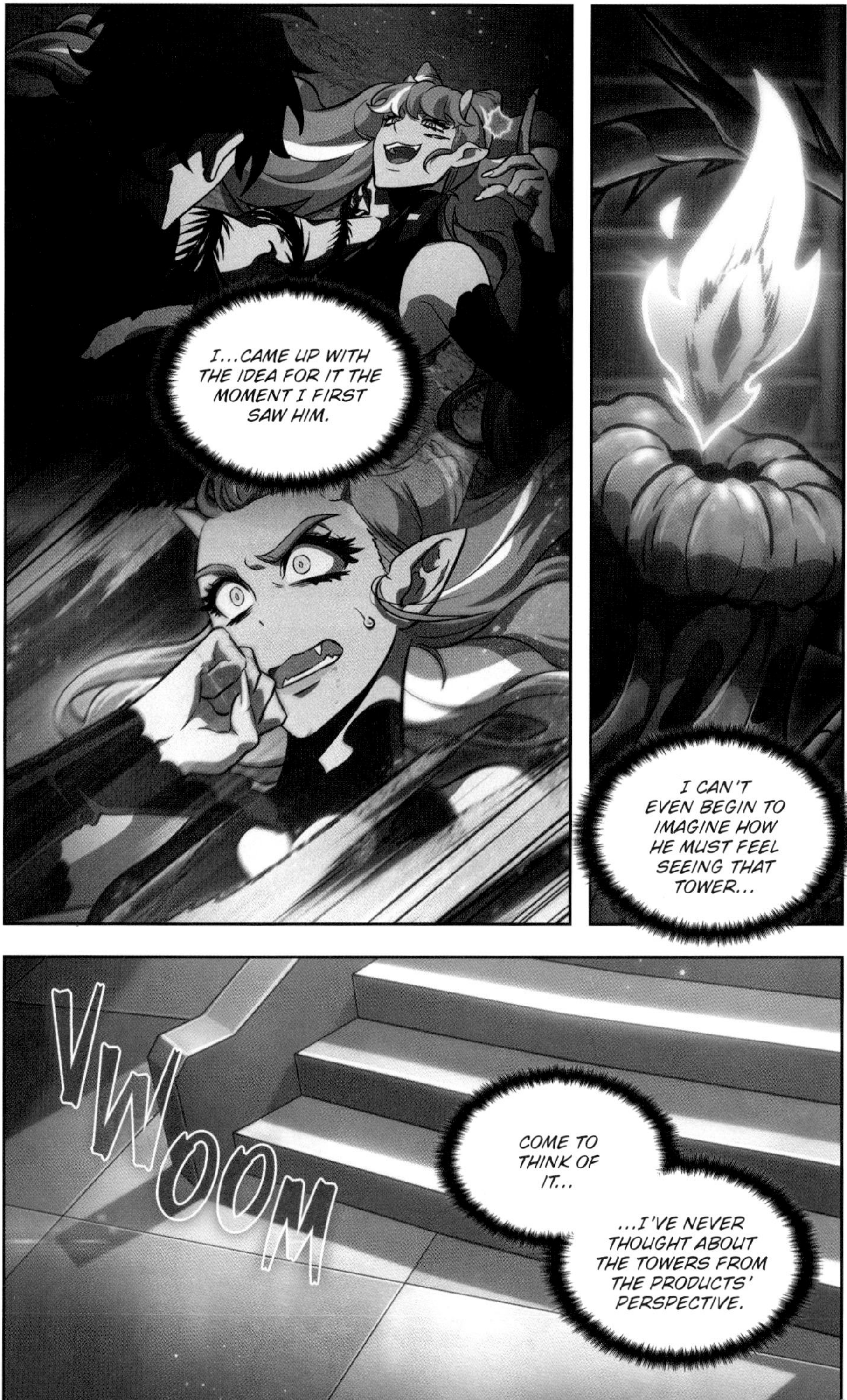
I...CAME UP WITH THE IDEA FOR IT THE MOMENT I FIRST SAW HIM.
I CAN'T EVEN BEGIN TO IMAGINE HOW HE MUST FEEL SEEING THAT TOWER...
VWOOM
COME TO THINK OF IT...
...I'VE NEVER THOUGHT ABOUT THE TOWERS FROM THE PRODUCTS' PERSPECTIVE.

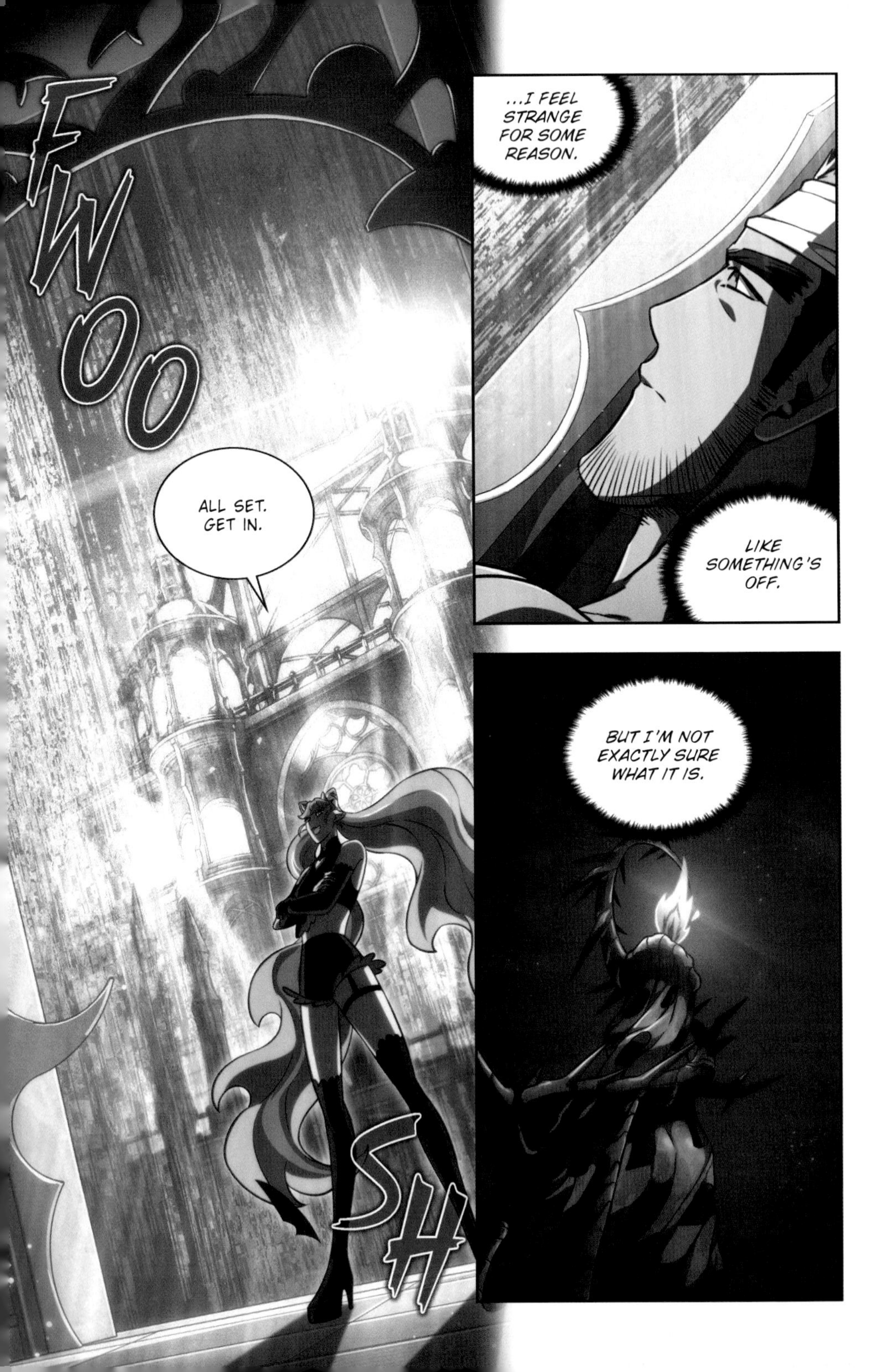
FWOOO
ALL SET. GET IN.
SH
...I FEEL STRANGE FOR SOME REASON.
LIKE SOMETHING'S OFF.
BUT I'M NOT EXACTLY SURE WHAT IT IS.

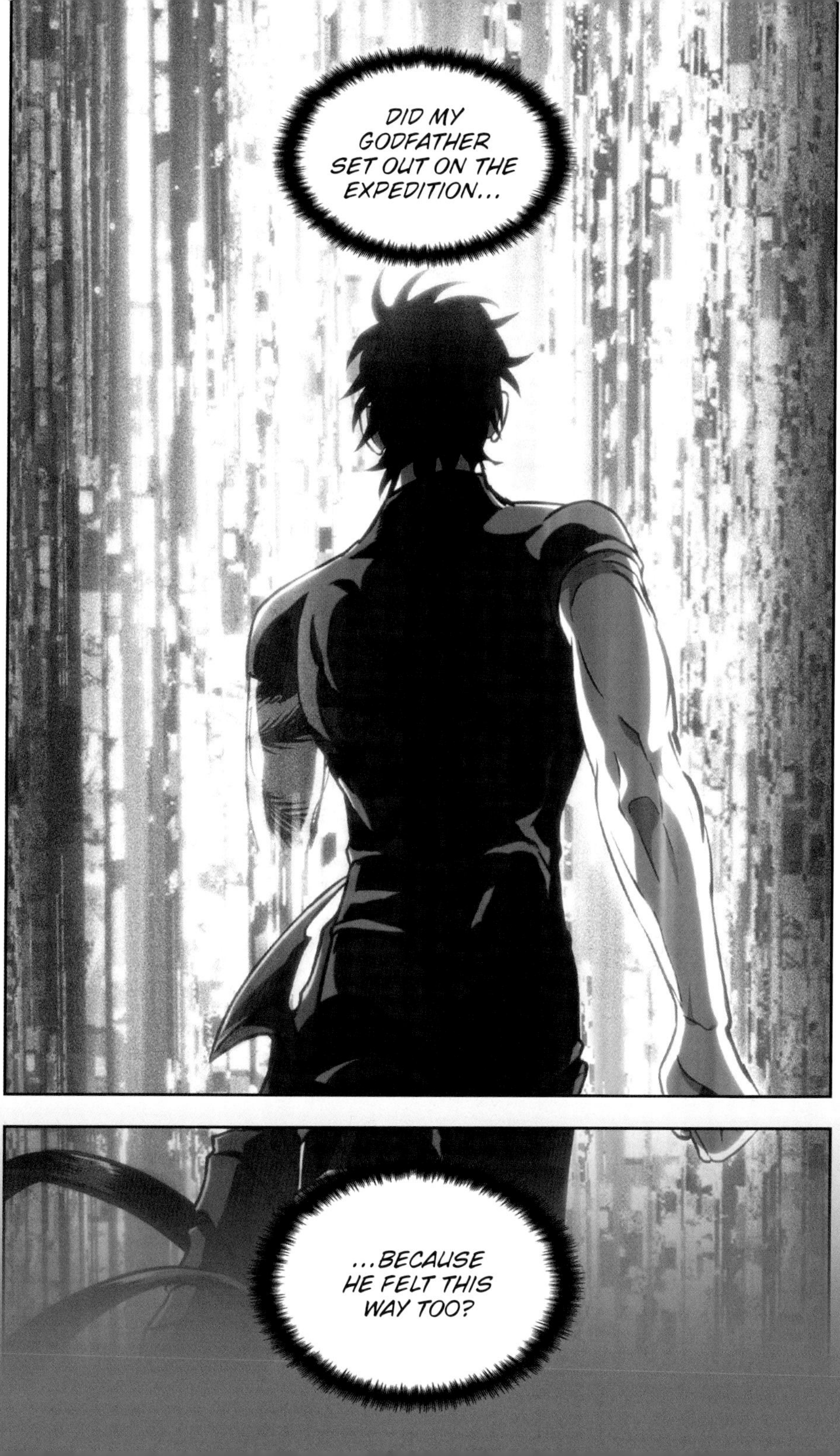
DID MY GODFATHER SET OUT ON THE EXPEDITION...
...BECAUSE HE FELT THIS WAY TOO?

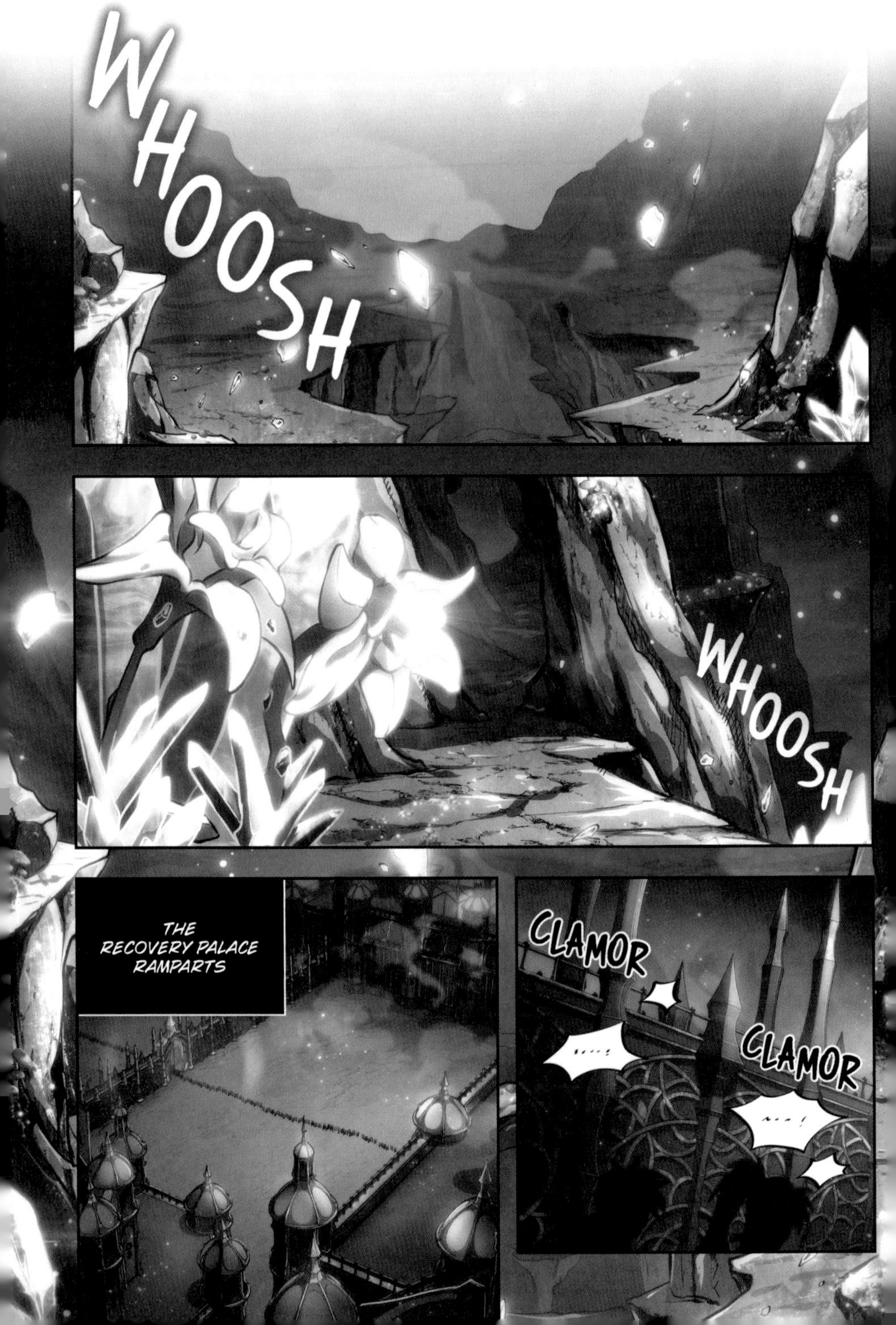
WHOOSH
WHOOSH
THE RECOVERY PALACE RAMPARTS
CLAMOR
CLAMOR

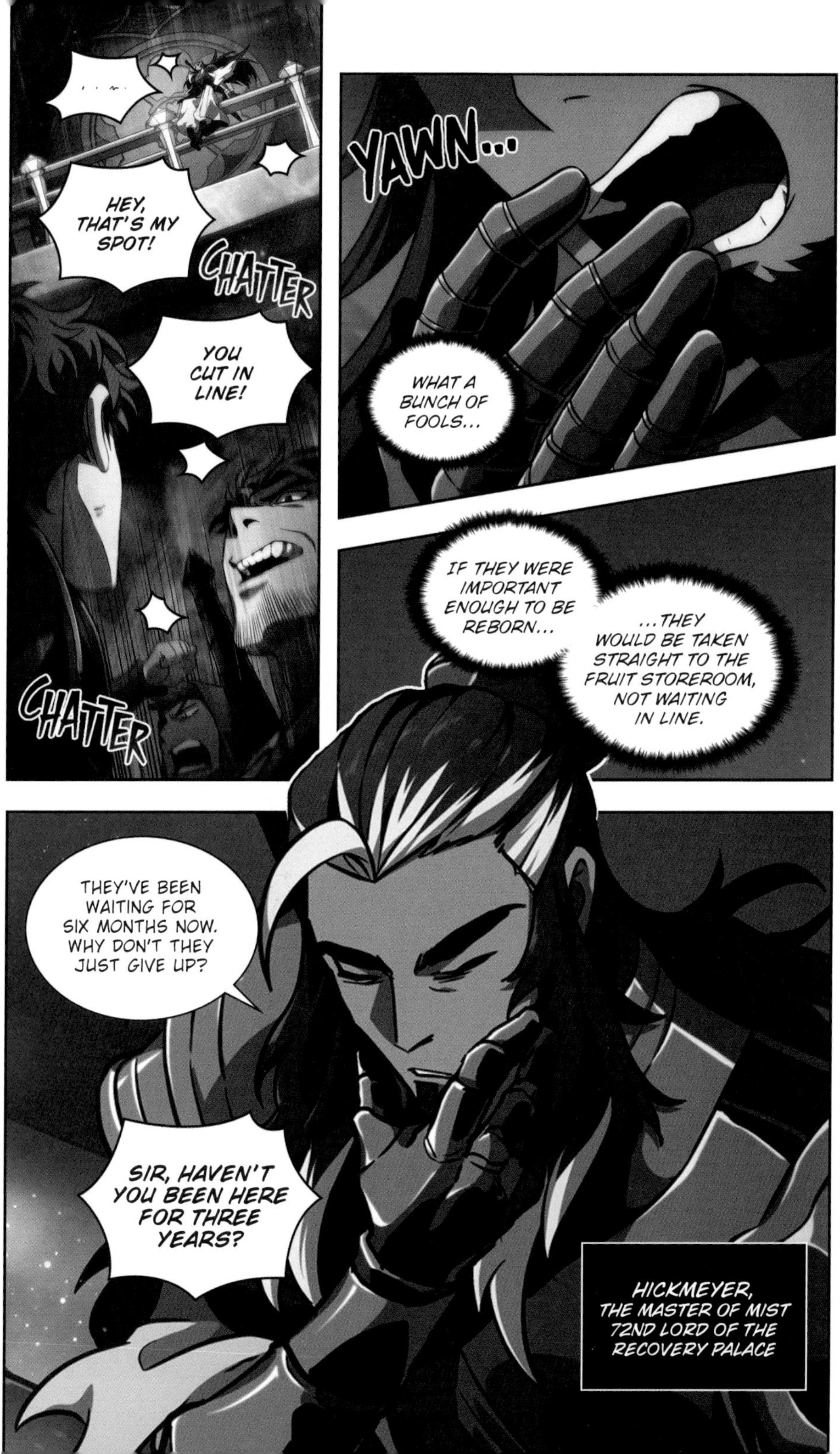
. . . ~ .
HEY, THAT'S MY SPOT!
CHATTER
YOU CUT IN LINE!
CHATTER
YAWN...
WHAT A BUNCH OF FOOLS...
IF THEY WERE IMPORTANT ENOUGH TO BE REBORN...
...THEY WOULD BE TAKEN STRAIGHT TO THE FRUIT STOREROOM, NOT WAITING IN LINE.
THEY'VE BEEN WAITING FOR SIX MONTHS NOW. WHY DON'T THEY JUST GIVE UP?
SIR, HAVEN'T YOU BEEN HERE FOR THREE YEARS?
HICKMEYER, THE MASTER OF MIST 72ND LORD OF THE RECOVERY PALACE

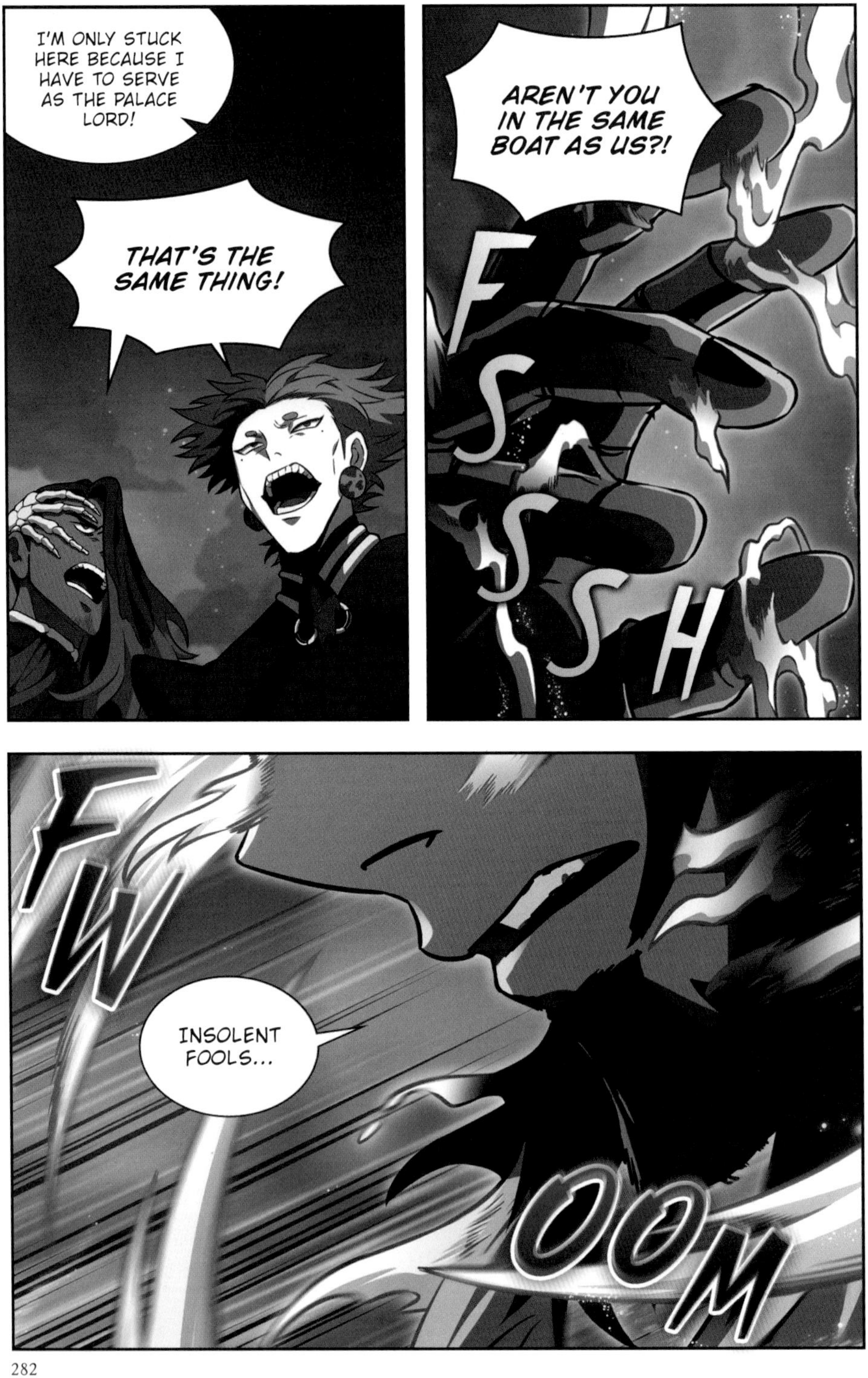
I'M ONLY STUCK HERE BECAUSE I HAVE TO SERVE AS THE PALACE LORD!
THAT'S THE SAME THING!
AREN'T YOU IN THE SAME BOAT AS US?!
FSSSH
FW
INSOLENT FOOLS...
OOOM

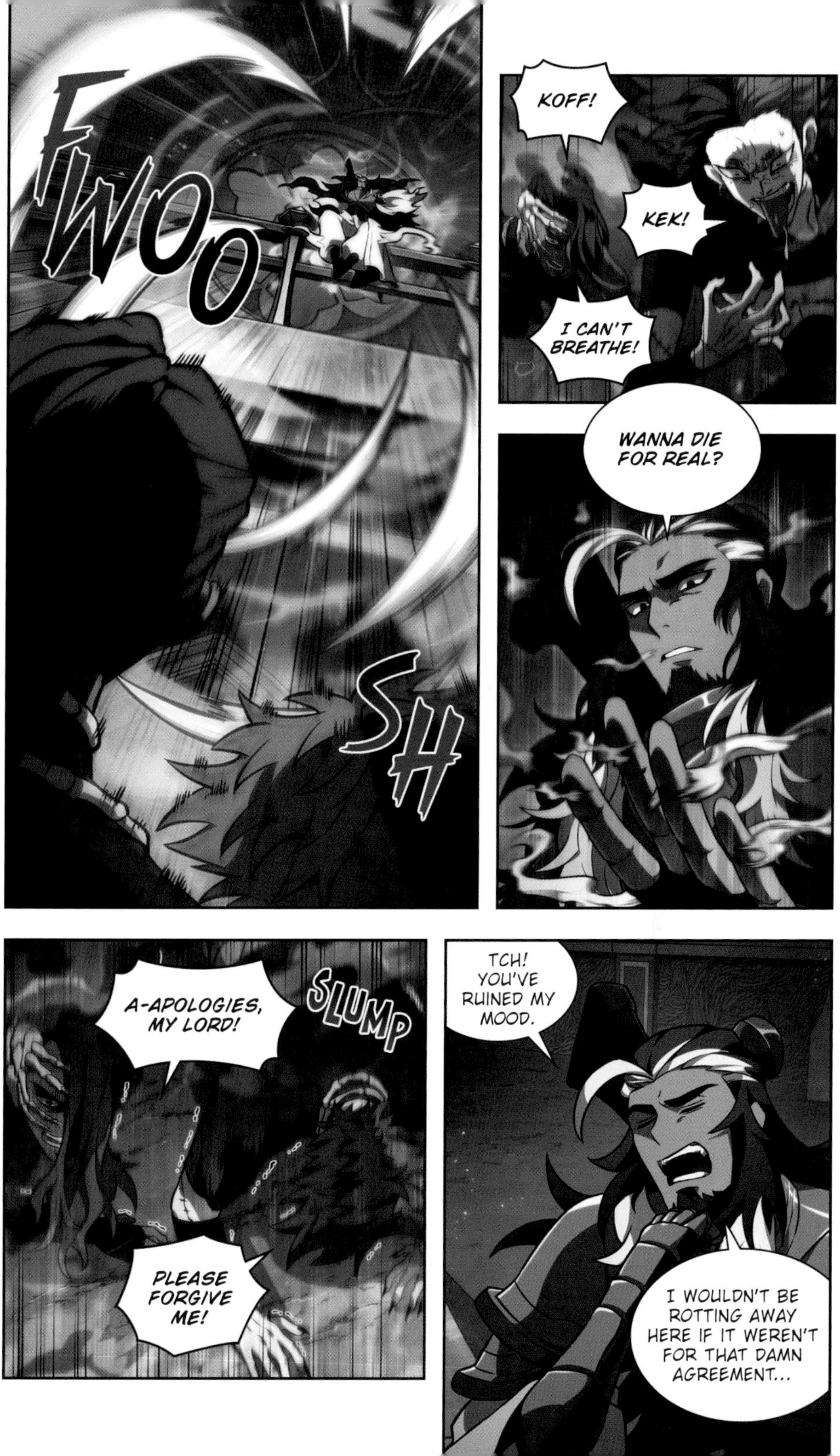
FWOOO
SH
KOFF!
KEK!
I CAN'T BREATHE!
WANNA DIE FOR REAL?
A-APOLOGIES, MY LORD!
SLUMP
PLEASE FORGIVE ME!
TCH! YOU'VE RUINED MY MOOD.
I WOULDN'T BE ROTTING AWAY HERE IF IT WEREN'T FOR THAT DAMN AGREEMENT...

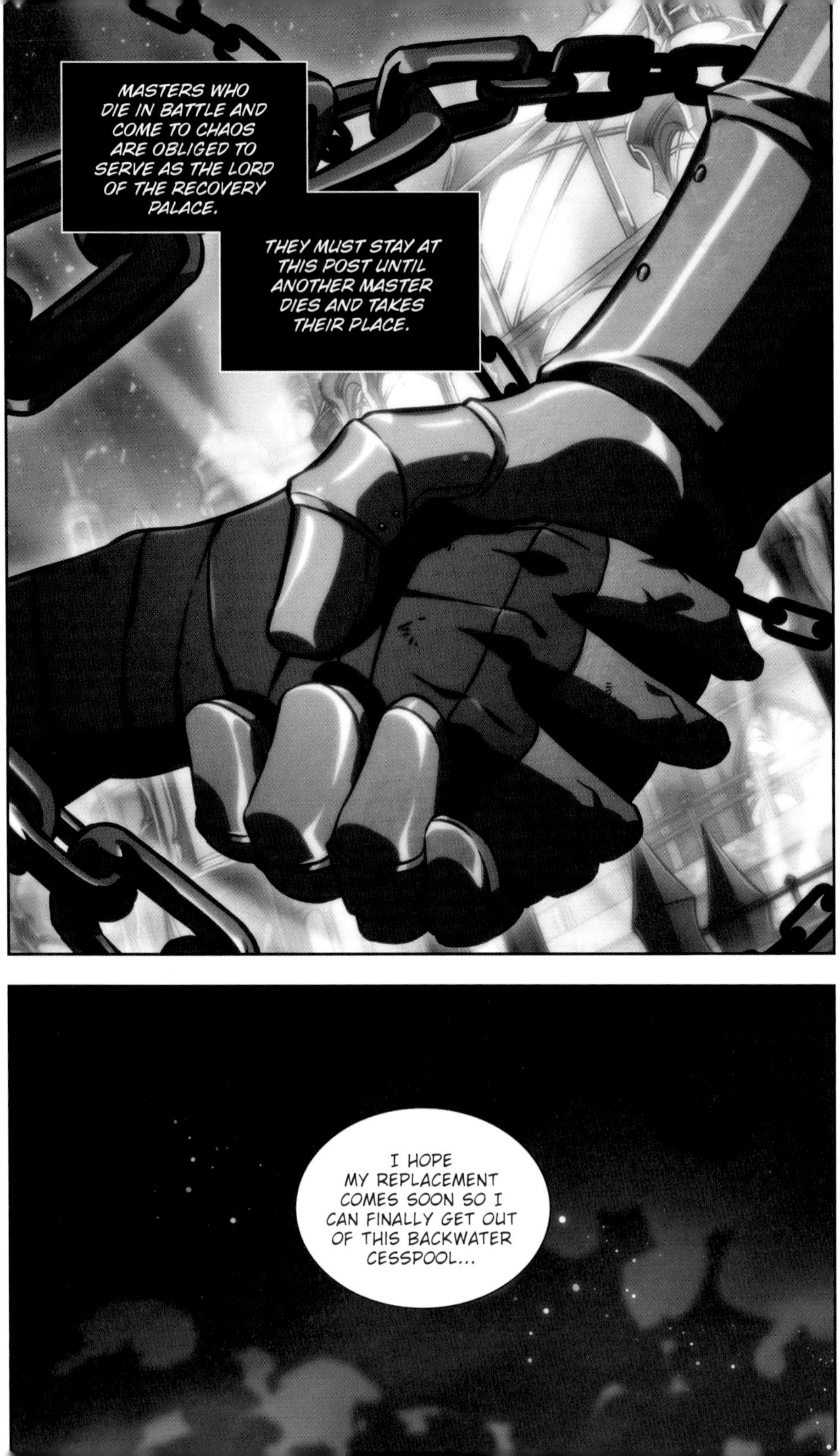
MASTERS WHO DIE IN BATTLE AND COME TO CHAOS ARE OBLIGED TO SERVE AS THE LORD OF THE RECOVERY PALACE.
THEY MUST STAY AT THIS POST UNTIL ANOTHER MASTER DIES AND TAKES THEIR PLACE.
I HOPE MY REPLACEMENT COMES SOON SO I CAN FINALLY GET OUT OF THIS BACKWATER CESSPOOL...

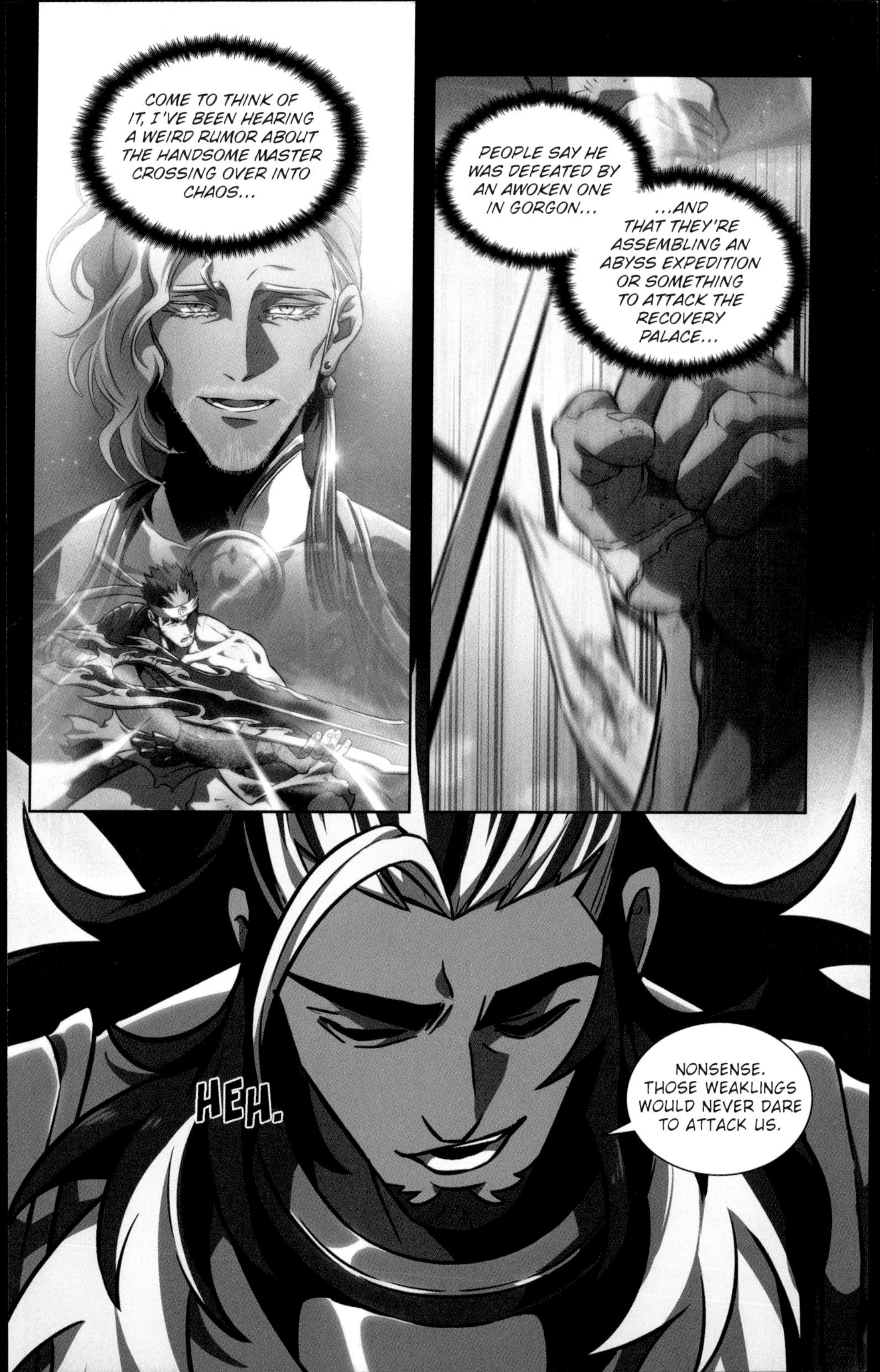
COME TO THINK OF IT, I'VE BEEN HEARING A WEIRD RUMOR ABOUT THE HANDSOME MASTER CROSSING OVER INTO CHAOS...
PEOPLE SAY HE WAS DEFEATED BY AN AWOKEN ONE IN GORGON...
...AND THAT THEY'RE ASSEMBLING AN ABYSS EXPEDITION OR SOMETHING TO ATTACK THE RECOVERY PALACE...
HEH.
NONSENSE. THOSE WEAKLINGS WOULD NEVER DARE TO ATTACK US.

ALTHOUGH, MASTERS FROM THE NINTH ZONE DID COME THROUGH THE NARROW GATE RECENTLY...

...SO MAYBE SOMETHING'S GOING ON AFTER ALL.

BUT I'M NOT ALLOWED TO LEAVE THIS PLACE AS THE PALACE LORD...

...SO I CAN'T EVEN CHECK FOR MYSELF...

CRACK—

CRACK—

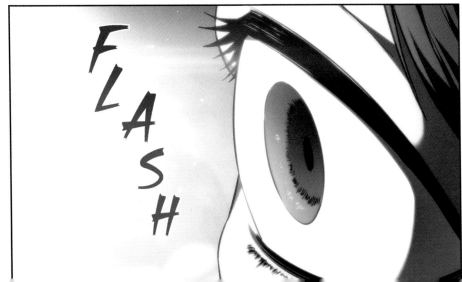

FLASH

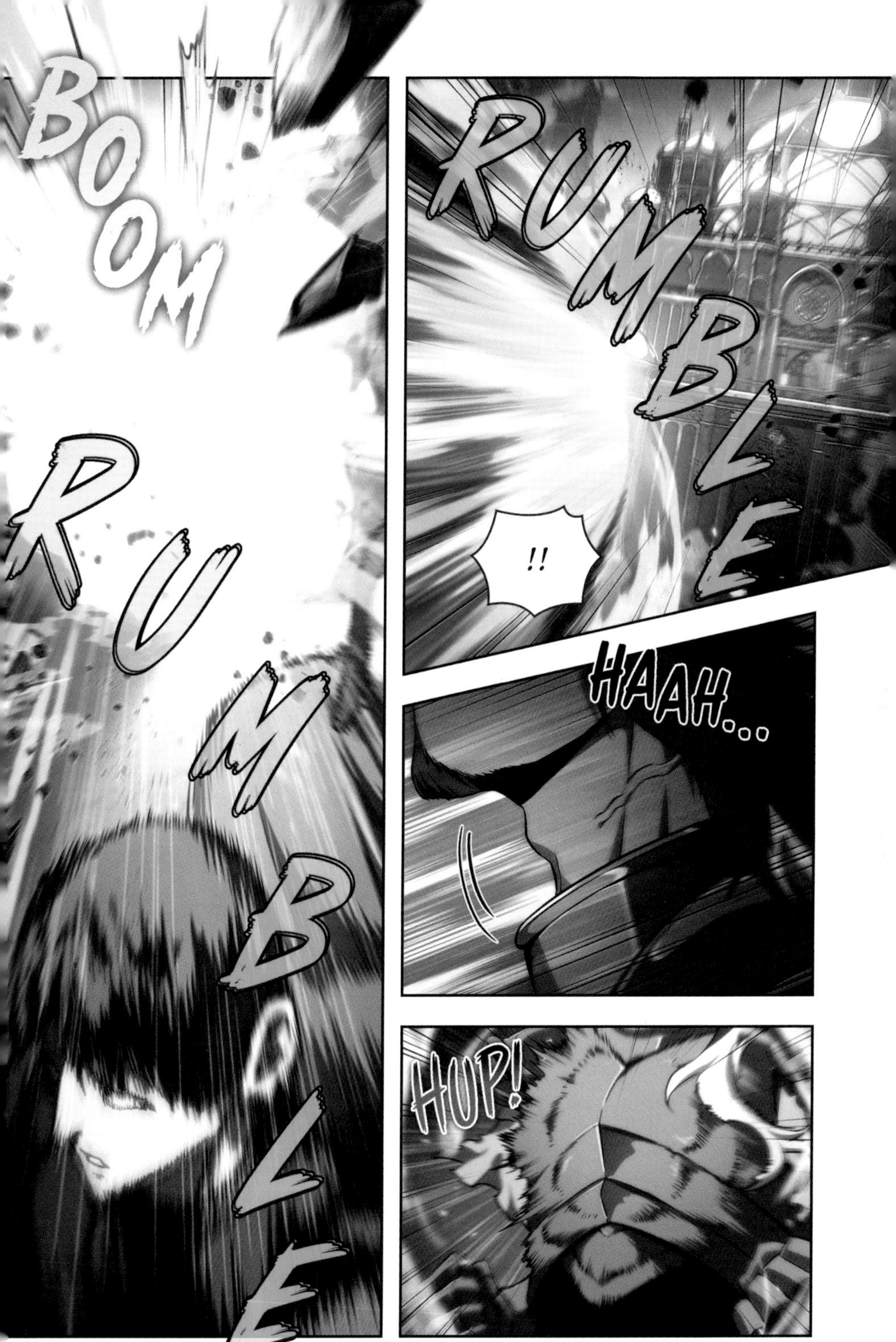
BOOM
RUMBLE
RUMBLE
!!
HAAH...
HUP!

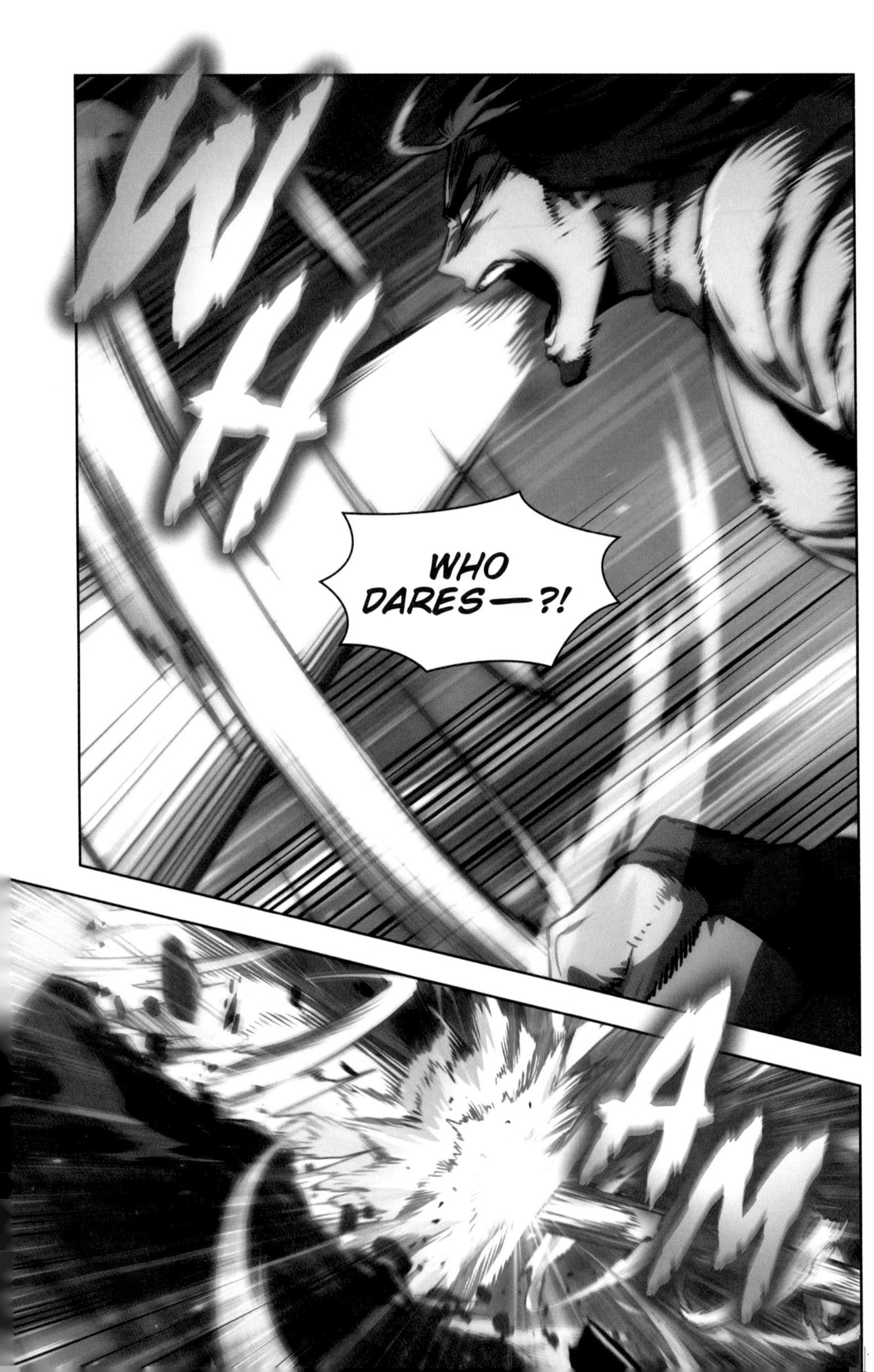
WHO DARES—?!

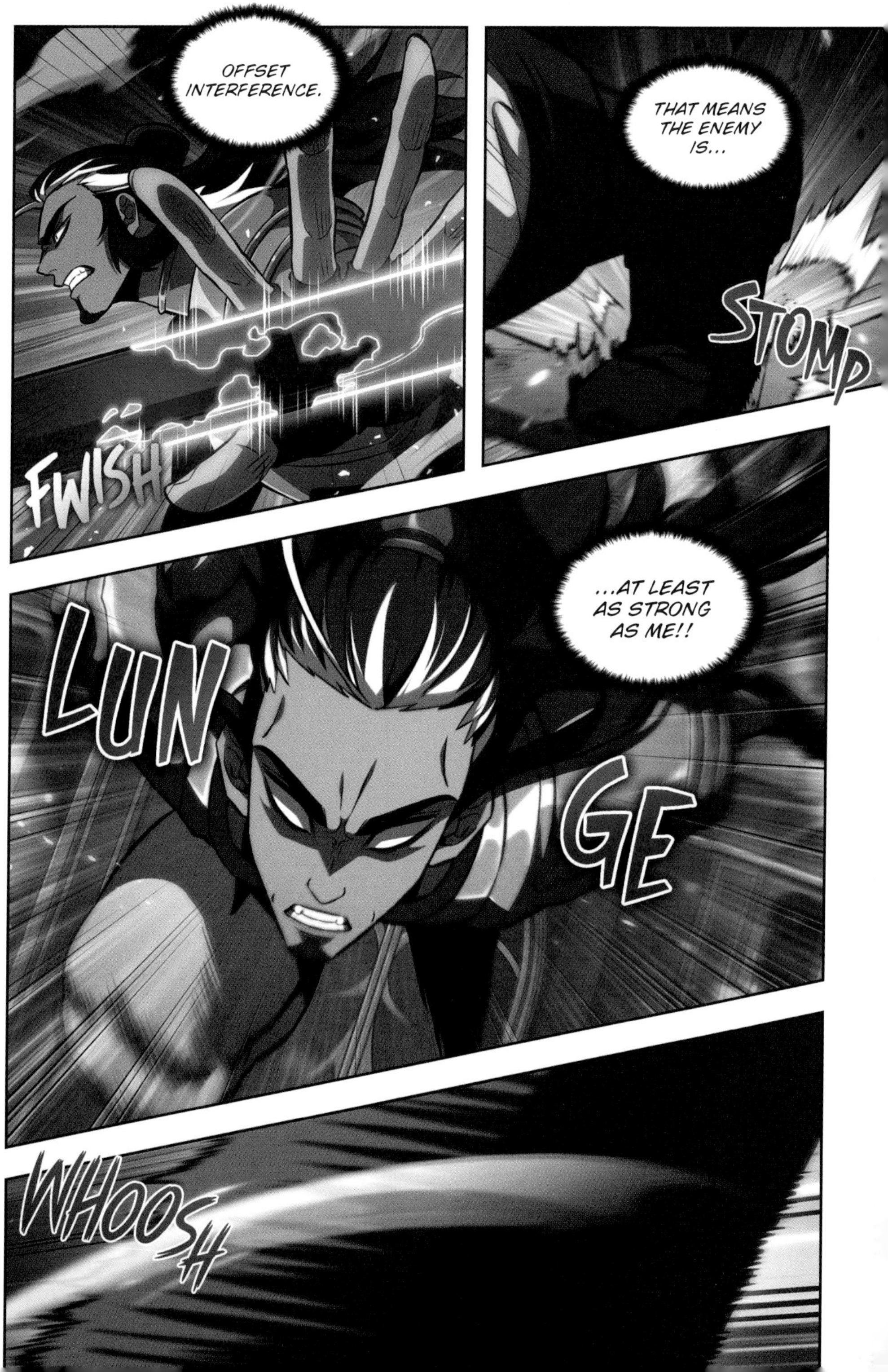
OFFSET INTERFERENCE.
FWISH
THAT MEANS THE ENEMY IS...
STOMP
...AT LEAST AS STRONG AS ME!!
LUNGE
WHOOSH

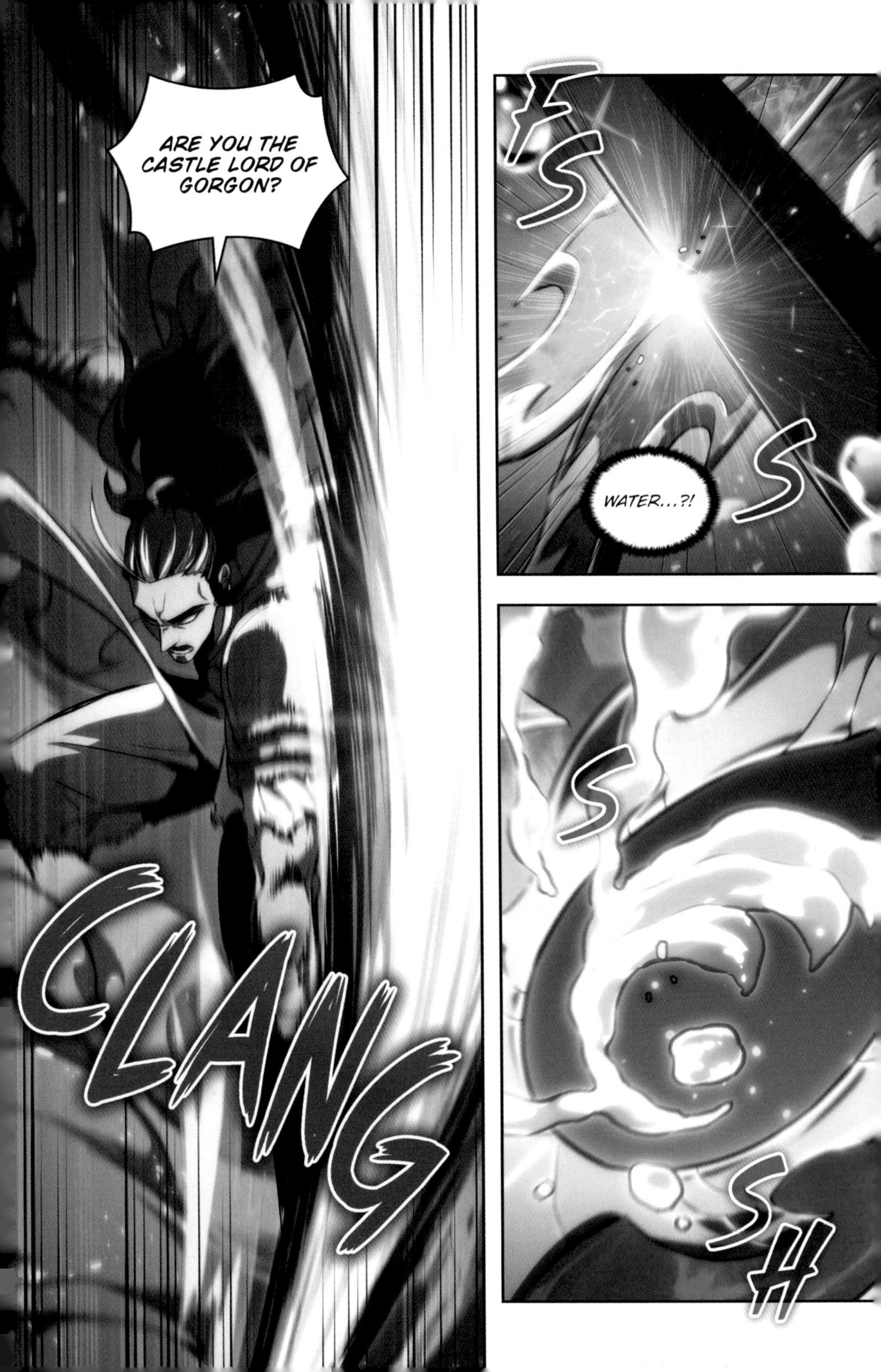
ARE YOU THE CASTLE LORD OF GORGON?
CLANG
FSSS
WATER...?!
SSH

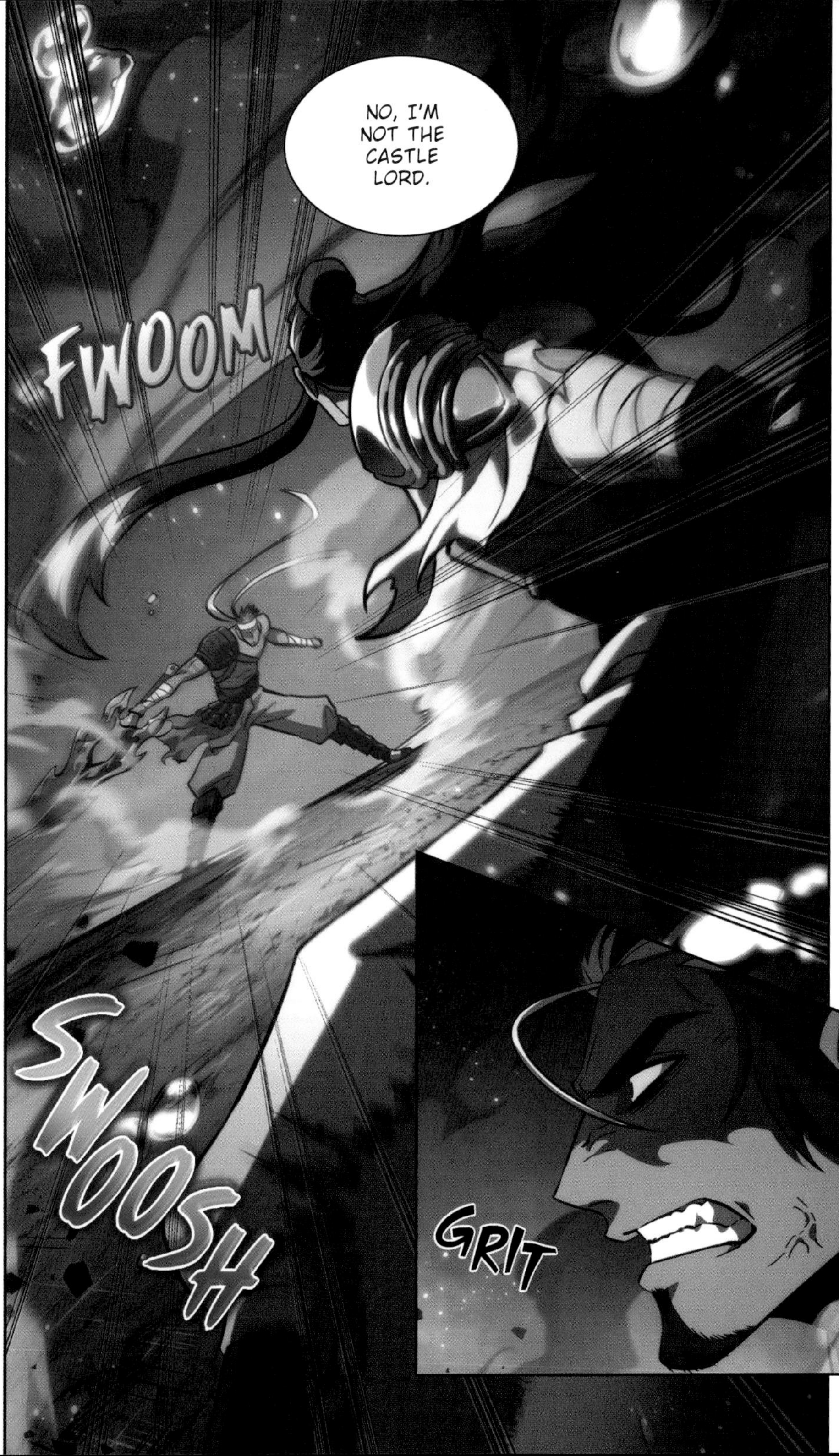
NO, I'M NOT THE CASTLE LORD.
FWOOM
SWOOSH
GRIT

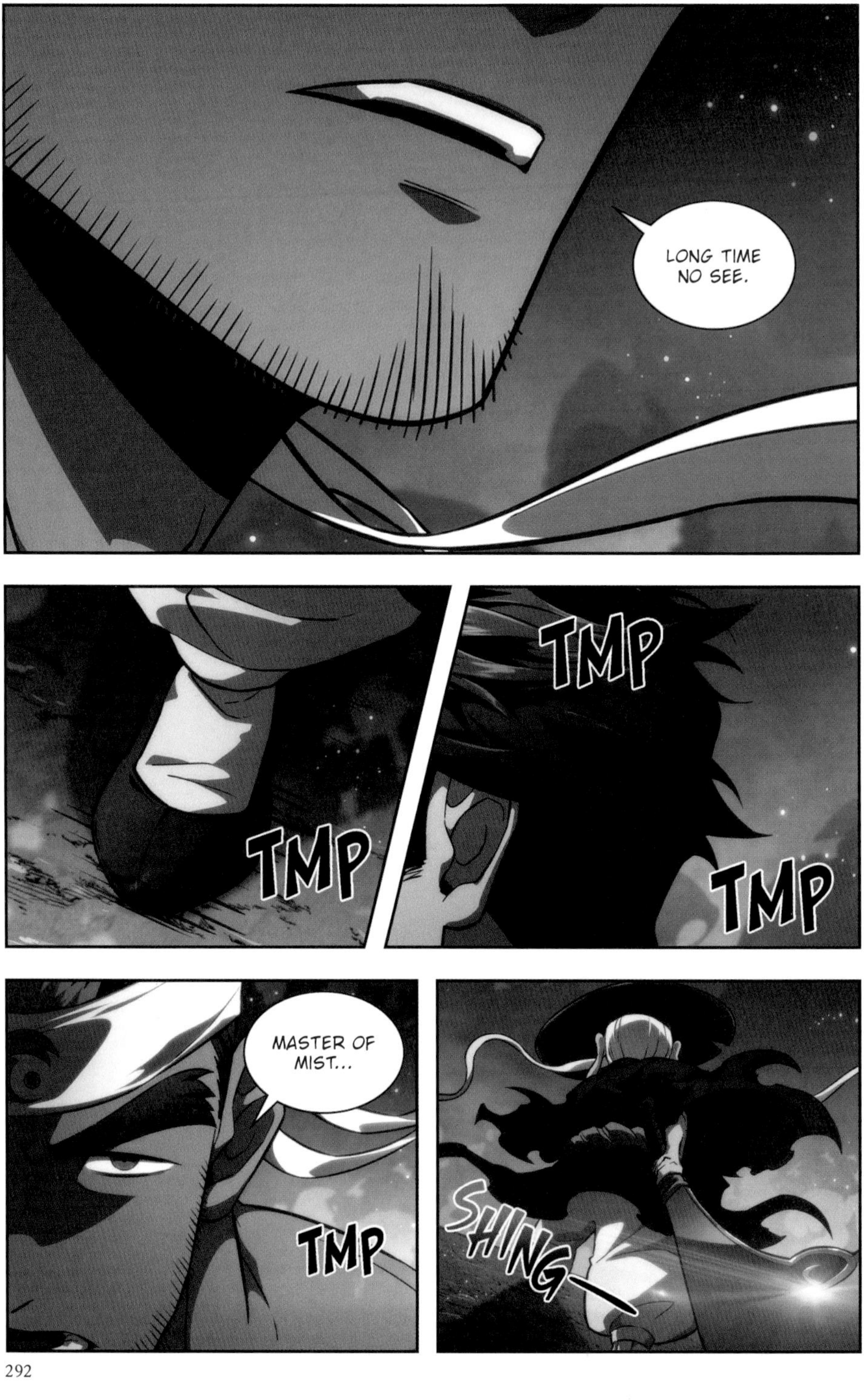
LONG TIME NO SEE.
TMP
TMP
TMP
MASTER OF MIST...
TMP
SHING—

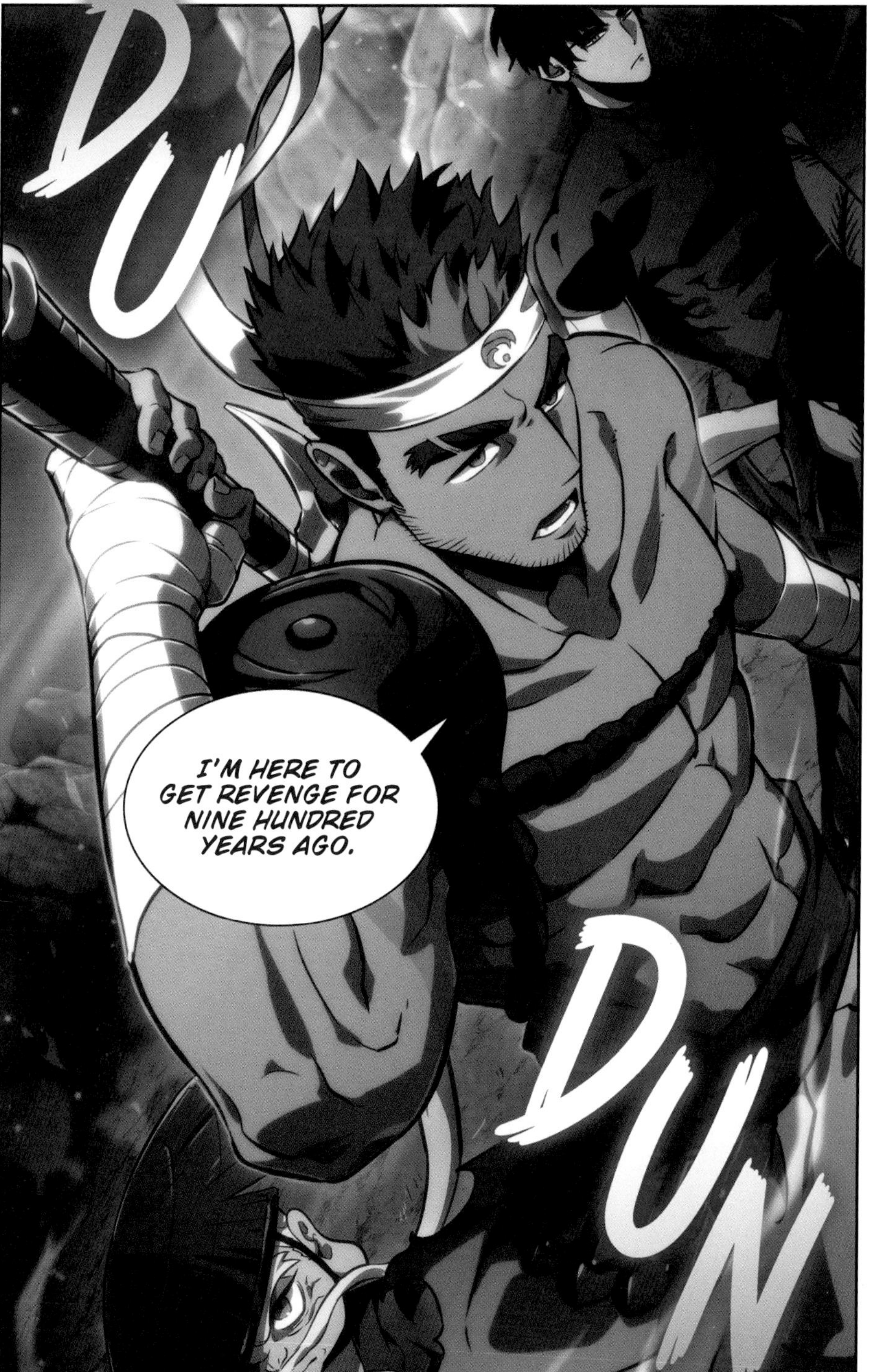
DU
I'M HERE TO GET REVENGE FOR NINE HUNDRED YEARS AGO.
DUN
TO BE CONTINUED IN VOLUME 7...

The World After the Fall

6

Undead Gamja(3B2S STUDIO)
Original story by singNsong ⅄ Adapted by S-Cynan

Translation: WEBTOON   Lettering: PHIL CHRISTIE

The World After the Fall, Volume 6
© Undead Gamja(3B2S STUDIO), S-Cynan, singNsong 2022 / REDICE STUDIO
All rights reserved.
English edition published by arrangement with REDICE STUDIO
through RIVERSE Inc.

English translation © 2022 WEBTOON
English edition © 2024 Ize Press

Ize Press
150 West 30th Street, 19th Floor
New York, NY 10001

Visit us at izepress.com ⅄ facebook.com/izepress
twitter.com/izepress ⅄ instagram.com/izepress

First Ize Press Edition: May 2024
Edited by Ize Press Editorial: Stephen Kim, JuYoun Lee
Designed by Ize Press Design: Lilliana Checo, Wendy Chan

Library of Congress Control Number: 2022942912

ISBN: 979-8-4009-0158-4 (paperback)

10 9 8 7 6 5 4 3 2 1

TPA

Printed in South Korea